LITERARY OPINION
IN AMERICA

VOLUME I

LITERARY OPINION
IN AMERICA

Essays Illustrating the Status, Methods,
and Problems of Criticism in the
United States in the Twentieth Century

EDITED BY
MORTON DAUWEN ZABEL

THIRD EDITION, REVISED

VOLUME I

HARPER TORCHBOOKS THE UNIVERSITY LIBRARY

HARPER & ROW, PUBLISHERS, NEW YORK AND EVANSTON

CONTENTS

VOLUME I

v

VOLUME II

PART IV. THE WRITER AND CRITIC IN AMERICA

Part V.   Modern Criticism: Its Problems,
                Methods, and Prospects

FOREWORD TO THE
TORCHBOOK EDITION: 1962

THE present edition of *Literary Opinion in America* is the third to appear. The first edition was published twenty-five years ago in 1937, contained fifty-three essays by thirty-two critics, and covered the two decades from 1917 to 1937. The second edition, appearing in 1951, was a fully revised, reorganized, and expanded version of the first. Its seventy-seven essays by fifty-four critics began in 1890 with the critics who then foreshadowed the developments in modern American criticism—Henry James, W. D. Howells, James G. Huneker, John Jay Chapman—and came down to the mid-point of the Twentieth Century. The present third edition is a reissue of the second, again covers the sixty years from 1890 to 1950, and carries over the content of the 1951 book with the exception of one essay which has been supplanted by a more recent study of the same writer, Sherwood Anderson, and with the addition of one supplementary essay on a writer not discussed in the previous editions, Scott Fitzgerald. This edition of 1962 thus reproduces the scope, historical range, and subject matter of the second, but with supplementary bibliographies to show the activities in American criticism of the past twelve years.

It was noted in the Foreword to the 1951 edition that when this collection originally appeared in 1937 it was one of the first exhibitions of what was then called the "new criticism." Even in 1937, however, the book did not confine itself to the activities that fell under that term. Most of the earlier critics included in both 1937 and 1951 were in their day "new." They represented as early as the 1890's a break with the critical standards or methods of the Nineteenth Century, with (in most cases) academic or conservative opinion, with the "genteel tradition" in literature, and with Victorian and European as well as American convention. They applied themselves to two general purposes: to defining or recovering the roots and origins of a native American literature and making them available to a new age of writing and innovation; and to bringing American literature into an intelligent relationship with the experimental or original developments in Europe. These two objectives became more fully evident in the 1951 edition when Howells,

Chapman, Mencken, Randolph Bourne, and Van Wyck Brooks represented the first, and Henry James, Huneker, Santayana, Spingarn, T. S. Eliot, Ezra Pound, and Edmund Wilson the second. The basis for a new age of American criticism was laid by these men, and the aims they defined and the standards they advocated have remained essential to the record of criticism in the United States down to the present day. Whatever the advances in critical technique, method, and insight that have appeared in more recent decades, their work and purposes are still traceable in the activities of their followers; and whatever gains American criticism can boast during the past half-century refer directly to their innovations and discoveries.

The term "new criticism," widely adopted during the decades of the 1920's, '30's, and '40's, has now receded and has even in some quarters become an epithet of reproach or embarrassment. But it was a term that once had its serious meaning, as much in the earlier years when James, Huneker, and Spingarn were its exponents as in the later decades when Eliot, Pound, Wilson, Kenneth Burke, Allen Tate, R. P. Blackmur, Yvor Winters, and John Crowe Ransom formed an advance guard for a later generation, and when a new series of magazines—*The Seven Arts, The Dial,* the early *New Republic, The Freeman,* later the *Partisan Review, The Southern Review,* and *The Kenyon Review*—were its leading journals. Spingarn's book on *The New Criticism* in 1911 was written as a manifesto for American critics of the years before 1914 as intentionally as Van Wyck Brooks's *America's Coming-of-Age* was in 1915, Mencken's *Book of Prefaces* in 1917, Eliot's "Tradition and the Individual Talent" in 1917 or *The Sacred Wood* in 1920, Pound's *Instigations* in 1920 or his *Make It New* in 1934, or Ransom's *The New Criticism* as late as 1941. The period of the earlier men as of the later was a time of programs, manifestoes, and reforms; and in the years between 1910 and 1930 "newness" was a recurring challenge or standard. The "new criticism" was accompanied by a "new poetry," "new novel," "new drama," not to mention a "new music," "new psychology," "new morality," and various other programs of novelty and experiment. America, boasting the second "renaissance" in its literary and cultural history, was going through what France had experienced in the time of the aesthetes, symbolists, and new realists of the later Nineteenth Century, and England, in its more derivative way, during the decades of the 1880's and '90's. From the vantage point of 1960 it is possible to look back on a large share of this activity with detachment or objectivity and to discount a good deal of what was then urgent, vital, and challenging. But this is the fate of most activities in novelty or discovery. A large part of the novelty has now receded into acceptance, convention, or even an outdated immaturity; but it has not lapsed into inconsequence. The new criticism of the earlier decades, as much as the new poetry and the new fiction, stimulated and invigorated the writing of America, as well as its general cultural intelligence and education, as no activity had done since the period between 1840 and 1860. The writing of the past twenty years that counts as serious, vital, or original is still drawing on the energy that was generated in the preceding three or four decades. And since such movements or revivals do not usually recur in any given age or century of literary history, it is likely that American writing and criticism will continue to derive from it for a considerable time to come.

The decade of the 1950's has unquestionably drawn on that energy in its writing and criticism, though it must be admitted that the past twelve years, perhaps the past twenty, show comparatively little of the innovation or originality of the preceding decades. On rereading, as objectively as possible, the essays included in the 1951 edition of this book and now carried over in the present edition, one is struck by the fact that most of them would be retained if the book were being edited totally anew in 1962. Many of the critics represented are still active; most of them are continuing in the lines of argument or analysis they established in their earlier work; a number of those still living have given up their critical activity. A new generation of critics has followed them, and some of these are writers of vigorous purpose, dissent, or personal method whose work could easily form a new collection. But it is noticeable that since 1945 few if any new critical programs or objectives have appeared in American criticism. The Existential activity in post-war France had some adherents in the United States for a time; certain advances can be traced in analysis and technical innovation; the psychological, social, and political study of literature has been carried to further lengths. But compared with the programs of James, Howells, Bourne, Spingarn, and Van Wyck Brooks in the years between 1890 and 1920, with the innovations of Pound, Eliot, Wilson, Burke, and their followers between 1915 and 1930, or with the social, political, and psychological experiments of the 1930's, the recent period has been one of continuation, reassessment, consolidation, and even sober-minded correction, rather than of novelty and original discovery. If original talents have appeared, they have usually followed the lines laid down for them by their pioneers of thirty and forty years ago.

In some quarters there has even appeared, among certain writers who were once in the advance guard of the new criticism, a serious doubt about the lengths to which criticism has been carried, especially in the academic or university field or in the critical quarterlies, and about the possible damage this activity has done to creative writing and talent. This is a normal and inevitable line of reaction. The past, in criticism as well as in other kinds of human activity, is bound to be reacted against, objected to, and found fault with, but it cannot be repudiated or dismissed. The critical habit and intelligence have become a part of our century. The Socratic principle that the unexamined life is not worth living has become translated into the idea that the unexamined book is an unread book. If this view has been discouraging to some creative writers, it has not seriously impaired the best of them. The critical mind is as active today in serious poetry, fiction, and drama as it is in criticism itself. No special insight into the nature and crises of our time is needed to see why this condition is inevitable, and why any retreat to sentimentality, self-assurance, or complacency has taken on the appearance of a danger or an abdication of responsibility. What is true in politics, social thinking, and morality is fully as urgent in literature. The spate of popular and vulgar writing, of cheap editions, of "made-up" or commissioned books, is greater than ever; and if this means an accessibility to writing by the general reader on a greater scale than before, it also means a levelling of quality, an indiscriminate kind of reading, a mechanical or mass-produced order of culture, that probably stands in greater need than formerly of intelligent guidance, teaching, and instruction. In any case, criticism, whatever its excesses, abuses, or prejudices, is impossible to dismiss or get rid of; and it remains a major problem of our time to make the best of it instead of the worst, to apply it intelligently and without fanaticism or personal extravagance, and to keep it subjected to the test of the literary text and thus to the quality of the experience and intelligence that literature at its best embodies. This is the only way in which criticism can be rescued from pedantry and self-conceit and become a living part of the art to which it is dedicated.

An effort was made, in the introduction to this volume, here retained, to trace the stages by which American criticism came into its contemporary gains and status. To look back over seventy years to the time when Henry James and a few of his contemporaries were isolated figures in their effort to define standards, elucidate values and quality, and bring American writing into a vital relationship with the literature of Europe, is to realize how far criticism has advanced in these purposes, and how they have become an indispensable equipment for the practising critic today. America had had her pioneers in these lines in the Nineteenth Century. Poe, Lowell, Emerson, and presently Howells and the realists or aesthetes at the end of the century, had all served their turn in bringing the critical activity of their countrymen forward, by clearly defined stages, from its apprenticeship to English models or its provincial prejudices into an understanding of what a responsible criticism involves in the way of taste, discrimination, alertness, a superiority to conformity or discretion, an independence of coteries and vested interests, a sense of the critical craft and its principles. But these stages were slow in declaring themselves, partly because the literary intelligence of the time lagged by comparison with the historical and the political, and partly because none of these men, however much they may be granted an eloquence or zeal in their cause, achieved the stature of fully equipped and philosophically instructed critics. None of them approached the status of the "great critic," that is, of men who establish themselves in relation to the whole body of literature and who apply that perspective and judgment to their time. They were too involved in the distraction of their contemporary American situation, in their conflict with the literary sects and sentimental prejudices around them, in their functions as polemicists and propagandists for American culture, in moral and ethical arguments which claimed precedence over the aesthetic and philosophic.

It is true that this was a general liability for the critic of the Nineteenth Century, as much in England and other parts of Europe as in America. Only a few "critics by vocation"—Coleridge, Arnold, Sainte-Beuve, Schlegel, De Sanctis, Brandes—rose to the full stature of their profession. It is also true that there were special reasons in the America of that era for lag and reluctance. A native literature was consciously in the making; the American imagination was struggling to discover and express, rather than to judge and evaluate, itself. Against it were set all the forces of caution, discretion, moral hostility, and suspicion of aesthetic principles and values that were a prevalent embarrassment of the time. The critic as much as the poet or novelist needs a certain favorable environment for his work, an atmosphere of response, receptivity, and sympathy for his effort. We can recognize the eloquence and vision of Poe, Emerson, and Whitman in their manifestoes and polemical statements, but what they offered in their specifically critical performances and judgments is less impressive. To compare, for instance, the work of the classic American historians—Prescott, Bancroft, Motley, Parkman, Adams—with that of these literary leaders is to be impressed by the greater capacity and craftsmanship of the former. They stood, both as historical technicians and as men of genuine historical perception, in the front rank of their age while their literary contemporaries were still comparative amateurs, apprentices, éclaireurs and pathfinders.

There doubtless existed at that time, and for another half century, the feeling or presentiment that America was not yet ready for her "age of criticism"; that there was, in fact, a radical incompatibility between the American experience or the tasks it confronted in declaring its nationhood, establishing its character, finding its true voice in literature, achieving its maturity, and the demands of the critical function and intelligence. The feeling is as evident in Emerson's rallying manifestoes as it is in Poe's accusations against his literary contemporaries, and it continues to be implicit in the criticism of Howells, Gates, Brownell, and More for another generation. But that the sensation was not inescapable or inevitable becomes apparent as early as 1867 in one writer of strong and confident vocation who today sounds much more prophetic of future developments than the other men of his time. Henry

James was only twenty-four years old when he wrote one of the most important of his early letters to his friend Thomas Sergeant Perry, declaring that it had already become his "vague desire" to do for the native literature *"something* of what Sainte-Beuve and the best French critics have done for theirs": of devoting himself to the "constant exchange and comparison," the "wear and tear of living and talking and observing," by which "works of art shape themselves into completeness."

> When I say [he continued] that I should like to do as Sainte-Beuve has done, I don't mean that I should like to imitate him, or reproduce him in English: but only that I should like to acquire something of his intelligence and patience and vigour. One feels—I feel at least, that he is a man of the past, of a dead generation; and that we young Americans are (without cant) men of the future. I feel that my only chance for success as a critic is to let all the breezes of the west blow through me at their will. We are Americans born—*il faut en prendre son parti.* I look upon it as a great blessing; and I think that to be an American is an excellent preparation for culture. We have exquisite qualities as a race, and it seems to me that we are ahead of the European races in the fact that more than either of them we can deal freely with forms of civilization not our own, can pick and choose and assimilate and in short (aesthetically &c) claim our property wherever we find it. To have no national stamp has hitherto been a regret and a drawback, but I think it not unlikely that American writers may yet indicate that a vast intellectual fusion and synthesis of the various National tendencies of the world is the condition of more important achievements than any we have yet seen. We must of course have something of our own—something distinctive and homogeneous—and I take it that we shall find it in our moral consciousness, our unprecedented spiritual lightness and vigour. In this sense at least we shall have a national *cachet.*—I expect nothing great during your lifetime or mine perhaps: but my instincts quite agree with yours in looking to see something original and beautiful disengage itself from our ceaseless fermentation and turmoil.

There is evident here the echo of Poe's ambition, of "The American Scholar" and Whitman's prefaces and *Democratic Vistas,* but it is brought into combination with a systematic and comprehensive critical purpose beyond theirs. James himself did not carry out that purpose during the fifty years of his literary career that remained to him. He went to Europe and remained there, and his writings on American literature form a comparatively small part of his future critical production. But his program was to persist as an ambition for the American critic in the decades that lay ahead, however slowly it emerged and declared itself among his followers. The ambition was to meet many delays and obstacles before it emerged in the revivalists of 1910 and the years following, but when it did emerge it took, in effect, the direction that James had indicated.

Looking back from the vantage point of the 1960's we can see today the logical stages of the process. There came first, in the wake of the age of Emerson and Whitman and the decline of their influence, the tentative aesthetic protests of the 1890's which found their leading champion in Huneker. Following them, the first stirring of a new principle of realism in criticism took Howells as its exponent and another continental impulse than the aesthetic as its impetus—the impulse of social morality and naturalism. Presently, as early as 1904, More (with Babbitt soon following) announced his intention of launching a comprehensive critical lifework as a "servant of the critical spirit" whose necessity was defined as a fusion of the "moral" and the "aesthetic" insight. This soon developed into reaction and conservative "humanism," and presently found itself challenged by Spingarn's proclamation on behalf of a "new," "creative," and "expressionist" criticism in 1911. By these stages there was released the challenge of a "coming-of-age" for American writers—the critical rebellion led by Bourne, Brooks, Mencken, and Mumford between 1914 and 1920. But as if to rescue that ambition from provincialism there appeared almost simultaneously a counter-movement on behalf of a historical and formal aesthetics, again European in inspiration and international in reference, as instigated by the early work of Pound and Eliot.

By this time, around 1920, the elements of a new age of criticism and literature were recreated. The aesthetic, the moral, the realistic, the social, the formal, the analytical, all strove to achieve their status and justification as valid factors in an active—and actively American—expression in the arts. The decade of the 1920's was their ground and moment of contention. It was then that a new creative spirit in poetry, drama, fiction, and the other arts came into a working collaboration with critical discovery and evaluation, on a scale more impressive and practical than had been achieved in the Nineteenth Century. It was then that the new schools of criticism, whatever their differences or hostilities, and facing the still formidable forces of academic reaction and didactic moralism, joined or stimulated each other in the work of assessment, the renovation of principle and practise, the enquiry into sources and values, the "recovery of a usable past," the derivation of technique and method from every possible aid to elucidation: the historical, the sociological, the political, the psychological, the anthropological, the formalistic, and the aesthetic. The classical masters of criticism were revived, reexamined, and adapted to modern uses. The Aristotelian, Scholastic, and Renaissance programs of analysis were scanned and rehabilitated. Freud, Jung, Frazer, and presently Marx were canvassed for their possible bearings on aesthetic content and interpretation. If criticism, as one critic was presently to describe it, established its doctrinal divergences "at the poles," it also became conscious of an implicit community of purpose and action; and the prevailing critical spirit among original writers encouraged it in the effort.

xviii   *FOREWORD TO TORCHBOOK EDITION*

The decade of the 1930's set the political and social principles against the aesthetic and the traditional; but when the 1940's arrived with their demonstration of what doctrinal extremism or fanaticism can produce in the way of human and political crisis, the balance was redressed in favor of the values of tradition and art. By this time the mere technical resources of criticism had advanced to formidable proportions. The verbal, the stylistic, the linguistic, the semantic, and the conceptual modes of dissection or analysis had come into full operation. The notion of "using all there is to use" became a prevailing tactic in the critical performance. Literary education in schools, seminars, and conferences joined in the activity, and produced an astonishing era of academic reforms and critical precocity. The decade of the 1950's, inheriting the discoveries and innovations of sixty years, was even more than its predecessors in the position of being able to consider itself the legatee of what one American writer, Lionel Trilling, already quoted here in 1951, called "one of the most aggressive, hardest-working, and portentous critical movements the history of literature has known"; or, more than that, of boasting of a hereditary priesthood of what Whitman called "a majestic office, perhaps an art, perhaps even a church."

It is to be expected that when criticism or any other activity—political, religious, psychological, aesthetic—achieves a status as aggressive or formidable as this, as encouraging to doctrine or dogmatism, it will call for dissent and skepticism, will invite protest and reaction; and criticism in our time has gained and even encouraged its skeptics and deflaters. The leading questions have been repeatedly sounded: Has this become an age of criticism at the cost of losing its creative confidence, its imaginative energy and resource? Has criticism advanced to a point of excess, perversity, and self-defeating ingenuity? Has "a brilliant period in literary criticism in both Britain and America . . . come to seem, in retrospect, too brilliant?" Questions like these are usually expected from sentimentalists and defenders of "enjoyment," from academic die-hards and exponents of the "historical approach," from the temperamentally uncritical or anti-critical, and of course by tradition from writers or artists themselves, whose tolerance of the critic is understandably limited. It is not enough to answer that ours is a pre-eminently critical age as much in its practical conditions as in its literary and intellectual ones; that without a constant exercise of the critical intelligence life would be even harder to cope with and modern confusion more difficult to survive than they already are; that without its critical animus contemporary literature would hardly, in large part, exist; and that without its origins in critical and moral insight a great share of the most valuable modern creation would not have come into being at all. The practical question remains one of the almost unprecedented lengths to which the critical function has been carried in our time; of the degree to which analytical and diagnostic techniques have outpaced mature insight and understanding; of the extent to which criticism has lost its contact with the vital experience—thought, imagination, emotion, vision—in which art of any valid kind originates; and of the risk the critic runs when his ingenuity or intellectual ambition exceeds his sympathy and *rapport* with the object to which he applies them. These doubts usually win the retort of being anti-intellectual; and of course they are encouraged by the effect of self-cancellation which a large part of contemporary critical writing conveys. The "criticism of criticism of criticism" has exceeded even the parody to which Mencken and his friends treated it forty years ago. But sometimes the doubt appears in quarters that demand a more attentive hearing.

It appears, in fact, most seriously among practising critics themselves, one of whose inescapable duties seems to be the examination of conscience. It was raised forty years ago by the pioneers, Brooks, Mencken, and Spingarn, who may have taken their cue from Henry James's doubts of 1891 ("the deluge of doctrine suspended in the void," etc.). It was sounded as a warning by Ezra Pound at recurring points in his career ("pay no attention to anyone who has not himself done a respectable piece of work"). The instigators of the 1920's, I. A. Richards and his associates, had their crises of uncertainty, in some cases leading to a resignation from critical writing and a turning to more practical forms of literary and semantic work. The question has been redefined as recently as 1948 by R. P. Blackmur in "A Burden for Critics" and as lately as 1951 by Allen Tate in "Is Literary Criticism Possible?" ("Literary criticism, like the Kingdom of God on earth, is perpetually necessary and, in the very nature of its middle position between imagination and philosophy, perpetually impossible. . . . It is of the nature of man and of criticism to occupy the intolerable position. Like man's, the intolerable position of criticism has its own glory. It is the only position that it is ever likely to have.") More recently still, it has been re-examined by T. S. Eliot.

If anyone is to be counted an instigator of criticism in our time it is the Eliot who wrote some of its charter essays in "The Function of Criticism," "The Perfect Critic," "Imperfect Critics," "Tradition and the Individual Talent"; who was one of the first to argue that for critics as much as for artists there needs to exist "an unconscious community," an "endeavor," if they are to "justify [their] existence," to discipline personal prejudice and cranks "in the common pursuit of true judgment"; who said that "the purely 'technical' critic—the critic, that is, who writes to expound some novelty or impart some lesson to practitioners of an art—can be called a critic only in a narrow sense"; and who pointed out that the "two directions of sensibility," the creative and the critical, "are complementary; and as sensibility is rare, unpopular, and desirable, it is to be expected that the critic and the creative artist should frequently be the same person." It became one of his leading purposes to warn against specialization, technicality, moralistic dogma, practical "use" and function. He repeatedly emphasized the risks of considering criticism as primarily philosophic in method, "autonomous," "autotelic," those recurrent vexations in the critical arguments of our time—in 1920: "One must be firmly distrustful of accepting Aristotle in a canonical spirit; this is to lose the whole living force of him"; in 1927: "when a writer is skillful in destructive criticism, the public is satisfied with that. If he has no constructive philosophy, it is not demanded; if he has, it is overlooked"; in 1935: "The 'greatness' of literature cannot be determined solely by literary standards; though we must remember that whether it is literature or not can be determined only by literary standards." In 1956 he returned to the problem in his lecture on "The Frontiers of Criticism" (now included in *On Poetry and Poets*) with the opening announcement of his thesis: "that there are limits, exceeding which in one direction literary criticism ceases to be literary, and exceeding which in another it ceases to be criticism." The excess in one direction is that of impressionism, "appreciation," subjectivity, the seduction of "experience" and of immersion in the life which literature creates; in the other, that of historical source-tracing, social and moral relevance, "explanation," psychological and personal exegesis, explication of "origins." Taking as his examples of the extremes, he singled out two books (not "bad books" but books which have had "a rather bad influence"): Joyce's *Finnegans Wake* and Lowes's *Road to Xanadu,* both "monumental" but having as their only obvious common characteristic the fact "that we may say of each: one book like this is enough." Viewing the virtuosities of interpretation, exegesis, and analysis which books of this kind (including his own verse) have elicited in our time, he gave it as his opinion that "if in literary criticism, we place all the emphasis upon *understanding,* we are in danger of slipping from understanding to mere explanation . . . of pursuing criticism as if it was a science, which it can never be"; but that if, "on the other hand, we overemphasize *enjoyment,* we will tend to fall into the subjective and impressionistic, and our enjoyment will profit us no more than mere amusement and pastime."

The difference, then, between the literary critic, and the critic who has passed beyond the frontier of literary criticism, is not that the literary critic is "purely" literary, or that he has no other interests. A critic who was interested in nothing but "literature" would have very little to say to us, for his literature would be a pure abstraction. Poets have other interests beside poetry —otherwise their poetry would be very empty: they are poets because their dominant interest has been in turning their experience and their thought (and to experience and to think means to have interests beyond poetry)—in turning their experience and their thinking into poetry. The critic accordingly is a *literary* critic if his primary interest, in writing criticism, is to help his readers to *understand and enjoy*. But he must have other interests, just as much as the poet himself; for the literary critic is not merely a technical expert, who has learned the rules to be observed by the writers he criticizes: the critic must be the whole man, a man with convictions and principles, and of knowledge and experience of life.

The issues which these passages deal with have certainly been put more abstrusely, technically, or dogmatically in our time; but they remain basic to the critic's work as much today as when the contemporary movement in criticism first emerged half a century ago, and it is only fitting that we turn for our reconsideration of them to one of the men who were among the first to formulate them and to give them the axiomatic statement that has directed and informed the critical intelligence of the age. It is easy enough to complain that this intelligence has become exorbitant and oppressive in recent decades; that it has encouraged every possible variety of self-conceit, smugness, and virtuosity; and that it has run the danger of overreaching its legitimate boundaries and limits. But the intelligence still exists. It has become a radical feature of contemporary reading and knowledge, of the best we have in both literary creation and criticism; and to discount it is to deny a fact of modern life and education wherever these show themselves, among so much that is debased, vulgarized, or corrupted, in the forms and activities that can be called civilized. To compare criticism today with what it was in the first decade of this century is to be convinced of what is elsewhere so dubious: a progress and an enhancement of values. These being to all but confirmed skeptics or pessimists a necessary objective in the desperations of the age, they remain gains to be respected instead of ridiculed, fostered rather than discouraged. They cannot, in any case, be ignored, and the critic who has respected his vocation in the years since 1945 remains one of the men of our time whose duty it is to see that they will not be.

M. D. Z.

May 1962

FOREWORD

THIS book, the second and revised edition of a volume of the same title that
first appeared in 1937, offers a selection of seventy-seven essays by some fifty
American critics of the past fifty years. The contents of the first edition were
dated from 1918 to 1937. They have now been amplified both in range and
in quantity, in order to show the full scope and development of American
criticism in the first half of the Twentieth Century.

Essays that appeared in the first edition—which means the greater part of
them—have been retained whenever they represent the characteristic work
of their writers, or when they deal with subjects that have retained their
value in illustrating the representative talents and literary issues of the
past thirty years. These have now been prefaced by a group of essays by
critics—Henry James, William Dean Howells, John Jay Chapman, James
Gibbons Huneker, Randolph Bourne—who defined the prospects and problems of American literature in the earlier years of the century. There has also
been added a considerable number of essays by younger men who show
developments in criticism since 1937, as well as new essays by critics who
appeared in the 1937 edition. The papers now collected range in date from
1889 to 1950—a period of sixty years. An effort has been made to show, by
selection and within necessary limits of space, the conditions under which
critics have worked in the United States, the problems they have met, the
methods and standards they have defined, during a time of exceptional activity, dispute, and decision in American literature.

When the 1937 edition of *Literary Opinion in America* appeared it was
one of the first exhibitions of what has come to be known during the past
fifteen years as "the new criticism." That was not, however, its sole intention.
The "new" criticism of the past two decades issued from earlier activities
which were also "new" in their day. The work of T. S. Eliot, Edmund Wilson,
Yvor Winters, Allen Tate, and the critics of the 1920's was thus rated a
quarter-century ago; so were the writings and manifestoes of Randolph
Bourne, Van Wyck Brooks, J. E. Spingarn, Ezra Pound, H. L. Mencken, and
the men who argued for the "coming-of-age" of American literature between

1910 and 1920; so also were the cultural or aesthetic programs put forward by George Santayana, Paul Elmer More, Irving Babbitt, William Crary Brownell, Lewis Gates, and John Jay Chapman before 1910; so again was the work of the pioneers of contemporary criticism—Henry James, William Dean Howells, James Gibbons Huneker—as early as the 1880's and 1890's. These successive generations of critics all came on the literary scene as in some sense new. Their work was concerned with a renovation of values, the definition of criteria, the appraisal of original talents, and also with a problem that became between 1890 and 1910 freshly urgent in the native literature—the special character such values, criteria, and talents assume when they appear or demand attention in America.

Emphasis in the present volume has again been divided among these concerns and kinds of criticism. While a considerable part of the contents still shows the stress on formal, stylistic, and moral qualities in contemporary writing that has become paramount in our latest "new criticism," another and important part of it deals with the specific situation and problems of writing in America, with the conditions that have shaped characteristic American talents, with European writers who have come to dominate or influence the modern imagination, or with the American writer in his relation to a larger and international cultural development which, after his reassertion of his local and native bearings, he has from the time of Henry James down to the present day discovered himself to share. Thus the essays in this book which show a preoccupation with specifically or exclusively aesthetic issues are necessarily balanced—if only to show the varieties of modern American criticism with any degree of faithfulness—by discussions of what his age, his society, his traditions, his distraction by rival claims and responsibilities, have meant to the American writer since, following the earlier claims of Poe, Cooper, Emerson, Hawthorne, Melville, and Whitman, he has reëmerged in his conscious American character.

A book of American criticism must inevitably be a book about American literature, even if both the criticism and the literature hope to become valid as something more than American. The nationalism of our criticism and our literature has been a primary issue throughout the period here represented. But a serious criticism, like a serious literature, looks beyond nationalism. If it was the concern of James, Howells, Huneker, Bourne, Mencken, Babbitt, and Van Wyck Brooks to define the issue of "Americanism" in criticism and art, they also took it as their duty—like most of their serious followers—to redress this emphasis by rescuing American writing from provincialism and a suspicious estrangement from the larger claims and responsibilities of art. Thus, while the writers discussed by critics in this book are representatively American, ranging from Melville and James to Eliot, Pound, Crane, Hemingway, Faulkner, Cummings, and other talents of the present moment, they are also the modern talents—Yeats, Mann, Joyce, Valéry, Sartre—who show the force and meaning of modern literature to be unconfined by local or national loyalties. And these topics have been supplemented by discussions of ideas or influences—social, psychological, religious, experimental, Freudian, Marxist—which have worked in contemporary thought and writing regardless of locality or nation. The critics here included are all American by birth or residence. Their subjects are both American and international. Those who discuss the larger issues of modern art and thought—aesthetic, moral, social; Marxist, Humanist, Freudian, Existentialist—show particularly that the work of men like James, Santayana, Eliot, Pound, and Wilson has not gone for nothing; that the American critic or artist, whatever his local attachments and loyalties, today knows himself to be a member of a larger community where creation and craftsmanship are neither eased nor simplified in the interests of a privileged nationalism.

The editor's problem of representing these developments fairly has been much greater than it was in 1937. For one thing, critical activity in America has enormously increased. The 1937 edition was already much more difficult to assemble from the large body of available material than a 1927 or a 1917 edition would have been. This 1951 edition has had to cope with a correspondingly greater mass of critical writing that has appeared in books and journals in the past thirteen years. Full justice has not, inevitably, been arrived at. The appendices to the book will show the range and variety of publications in criticism that no single volume could hope to contain, and it is their purpose to suggest further reading in critics for whom space could not be found. The reader is referred to those bibliographies if he wishes to carry out a more complete program of study.

It will immediately be apparent that there is as little community of method and belief among the critics in this book as among the talents they discuss. But perhaps they have at least found some common ground of seriousness or workmanship in their efforts to discover the quality and significance of their subjects, either in terms of the conditions under which writers have worked or through their integrity and originality as craftsmen.

Four divisions may be made among the essays. One portion of them describes the situation and prospects of American literature in the earlier years of this century. Another states, from contrasting positions, principles of critical intelligence and responsibility, in reference both to past traditions and to present or impending creative problems. A third is made up of demonstrations in critical technique, analyses of literary form and style—these having been allowed a greater share of the pages in order to avoid the emphasis on abstract theory which often prevents the critic or his reader from understanding how the ideal qualities of art actually get into the work of fiction, drama, or poetry. Lastly, the final section of the book is given over to the particular problems the American writer and critic face today, and to certain issues of wider scope which the world situation of recent years has emphasized.

This book is not a collaborative project. Its entries support neither a common point of view nor the beliefs and prejudices of the editor. It finds whatever unity it possesses chiefly in a general recognition among its contributors of what literary quality and sincerity are, and in an approach to these from recognized requirements of sympathy, sensitiveness, and taste. These standards have been strongly challenged during the past two or three decades by the demands laid on literature by political, propagandist, and public interests. Conversely, the period has seen the reappearance of aesthetic, formalist, and autonomous "approaches" to literature. But critical activity in the United States has not, as in some modern countries, lost its right to difference, freedom, and disputation. The debate among schools and principles may still be trusted to correct the excesses of specialized and limiting attitudes, even where it has also stressed the importance of responsibility of judgment and belief in artists and critics. That debate is present in these pages. The tracing of its progress during fifty years is one of the most serious opportunities such a book as this has to offer.

The essays have been chosen from American books and magazines, and in selecting material from the latter it has been the intention to show the importance of independent and experimental journals in the United States during the past few decades. While their work has often been short-lived in the item, it has been continuous in effect. Between 1912 and the present day they have formed a channel of expression and opinion not previously available in America on a like scale. Their styles and personalities have been of all kinds. Some have lived out their short careers as purely personal or group organs. But they have had the advantage of their independence from commercial influence. Some of these periodicals—*The Seven Arts, The Dial, Poetry, The Little Review, The Hound and Horn, The Symposium, The Southern Review, Partisan Review, The Kenyon Review, The Sewanee Review, Accent, The Western Review, The Hudson Review*—had no predecessors in the particular work they have done for American literature. It has been an aim of this book to show the results of their work, to print specimens of the best of it, and to show how they have refreshed and stimulated critical thinking at a time when commercial exploitation and the confusions of politics and parties have tended to cancel the gains in critical awareness gradually achieved since men like Henry James and Howells were active.

There are two kinds of anthology which escape the more obvious forms of critical rebuke. One offers an impersonal survey of a field or period, as objective as scholarship and common acceptance can make it. The other develops an editorial argument, a "criticism by selection," from a specific or emphatically personal position. The present collection claims neither of these advantages, though it has taken hints from both of them. It covers a period still too recent and unresolved in its decisions to allow for historical detachment or impersonal agreement. And it has not been the purpose of the editor to illustrate a special or personal thesis. Such specialization has been the merit—and the limitation—of a number of recent collections of American criticism illustrating the Impressionist, the Humanist, or the Communist arguments. Their value lies in their singleness and certainty of purpose. Their handicap usually appears when they show what the reader need have no hope of finding, for the narrower an argument or doctrine becomes, the more likely it is that what will be missing is criticism itself, and the free intelligence. Such books often end by convincing us that while (as one distinguished modern critic has said) "the 'greatness' of literature cannot be determined solely by literary standards, we must remember that whether it is literature or not can be determined only by literary standards."

In choosing and arranging these essays, it has been hoped to show what such standards count for in America today, how they emerge from the past or develop in the present, and how the recognition of them comes through the responsibility of criticism as a craft—a craft open to suggestion from many different quarters, social, scientific, psychological, moral, political, but as far as possible unconfused by such influences. One of the first claims of the modern critic to seriousness comes from his awareness of what these appeals are, what they rise from in the social and moral adjustments of the age, what legitimate role they may play in aesthetic evaluation, and what part they may claim in deciding the values of literature *after* its existence and quality as literature are determined. Some of the present essays are on writers rather than on writing. Some deal with external ideas or conditions that have shaped contemporary talents. A few are written from obvious doctrinal positions. These are a necessary part of the history the book records, the scene it observes, the latitude it respects. They show the role played by literary criticism in what James, Howells, Bourne, and Van Wyck Brooks early defined as a general critical movement in our national life. It is chiefly through their intelligent sense of that tendency that the serious critics of the United States at any time, but especially in the last thirty years, have done their most effective work.

Two activities often considered hostile to an active critical tradition in America have been slighted, though intentionally. One is popular bookreviewing; the other is academic scholarship. The services of both, at their best, are not denied. Their omission has deprived the book of several distinguished and influential names. But each is provided for elsewhere too generously to require representation here. The absence of historical and philosophic scholarship is doubtless regrettable. The genuine part of it, in any age or country, is an achievement without which the labor of critics is easily misspent. But it is often by nature unconcerned with the existing conditions of an original literature, and its formulations or findings are seldom tested by the active problems and practices of writers. The absence of popular journalism is less a privation. A number of literary journalists have done useful propaganda for modern books and writers. A few, Huneker and Mencken first among them, prepared the day for remarkable gains in original writing. But generally this activity has little to do with criticism. It is an adjunct of the book trade, of literary promotion, or of nationalist interests that soon prove inimical to serious literary purpose. The work of the responsible critic is something else. It must take a stand, in Henry James's words, for "Criticism, for Discrimination, for Appreciation on other than infantile lines—as against the so almost universal Anglo-Saxon absence of these things; which tends, in our general trade, it seems to me, to break the heart."

Literary criticism in the United States has not, even in our advanced day, wholly outgrown the fear of a chronic immaturity which Poe and Lowell felt in theirs. (There is no cause to feel on this score a special affliction in American culture. Coleridge, Hazlitt, Arnold, I. A. Richards, and F. R. Leavis have felt a like distress in their country during the past century and a half.) But it will be agreed that if there has been a conscious effort toward serious critical standards in the United States, it has been made during the past fifty years, and that what the critic of literature has achieved in that time has been prompted by a wider scrutiny and conscience in the fields of social, political, and moral thought. Such conscience has grown at a time when writing itself has enjoyed a phenomenal revival, a huge public enthusiasm, a popular following outdistancing anything of its kind in our earlier history. These two tendencies may seem to operate at odds. Actually they do not, or at least not entirely. The fervor of the one stimulates the skepticism of the other. While writers produce something to think about, dissect, and evaluate, critics, freed from the provincial habits and complacency of less disturbed periods, may sharpen their wits and tools on the material thus supplied them. Political argument, no less than aesthetic and moral, has played its part in this zest. Rivalry and contention have spurred argument. But the age has been too serious in its problems and ominous in its evils to permit these to remain a game of cliques and factions.

The impulse of honest critics toward a community of responsibility and function is urgent as never before. A community of this kind is apparent today even where immediate aims and methods are least agreed. The threat of authoritarian tyranny touches the literary life as much as the political, and critics have been compelled to reassess their rights as liberals, disputants, and free agents in the common cause of the freedom of art and of the mind. America is still a place in which those rights exist, and where their perpetuity is arguable. The critic remains, perhaps, their chief custodian. The writers who here defend them have been included less for their eloquence on behalf of moral or human truths than because they show some signs of realizing the force of these truths in terms of the one valid evidence permitted the critic— that of the literary craft and of the insight and intelligence it embodies.

Omissions always irk an anthologist, however space limits impose them and even when he has no ambition toward impartiality. The reader is therefore referred again to the appendices where critics and essays are listed which might have been included had this book been two or three times its size. Difficulties of copyright or permission have sometimes proved prohibitive. Essays showing on a fuller scale the different controversies that have engaged critics, as well as the specialized programs of various critical schools, appear especially in Appendix II ("Collections of Contemporary American Criticism") and Appendix III ("American Magazines Publishing Criticism"). These, like Appendix I ("Books of Recent American Criticism") are selective, but their range is wide and their suggestions for further investigation unlimited. Appendix V ("A Supplementary List of Essays in Criticism: 1900– 1950") has been designed as a guide to a more complete program of critical reading, both in critics whose work could not be represented in the book and in those who have been included. Appendix IV ("Notes on Contributors") gives bibliographies of the published works of the latter.

The reader or student will, in fact, find this book profitable to the degree in which it encourages him to become a critic himself, to disagree with the critics who speak here, to compare their findings, and to decide how far the effort at reading and writing seriously that has brought them into the sar e company can be achieved, perhaps improved upon, by studying the problems of modern literature.

M. D. Z.

January, 1951

ACKNOWLEDGMENTS

THE EDITOR acknowledges with gratitude the courtesy of the contributors to this volume whose permission to have their work included has made the collection possible. Full bibliographical details as to the serial and book publication of the essays are given at the end of each entry. In several cases the critics have written new essays or made extensive revisions of earlier ones. For this special thanks are due to Miss Marianne Moore, Horace Gregory, Philip Blair Rice, the late Theodore Spencer, William Troy, and Stark Young for essays carried over from the first edition, and to Cleanth Brooks, Randall Jarrell, Alfred Kazin, and Delmore Schwartz for essays which now appear in this second edition. The editor is also indebted to T. S. Eliot for permission to include two essays, "Poetry and Propaganda" and "Experiment in Criticism," which have not been included in his books of prose and which are reprinted here from *The Bookman* and from the 1937 edition of this book, as likewise for his permission to include the essay "From Poe to Valéry," which has thus far been published only in private form by Harcourt, Brace and Company of New York in 1948. Thanks are also due to the Librarian of Congress for the appearance of this last-named essay here, it having originally been given as a lecture at the Library of Congress in 1948.

For permission to use material from copyrighted volumes, acknowledgment is made to the following publishers:

Arrow Editions, New York, and Miss Florence Codman for "Notes on E. E. Cummings' Language" and "The Critic's Job of Work" from *The Double Agent: Essays in Craft and Elucidation,* by R. P. Blackmur, copyright 1935 by Richard P. Blackmur.

E. P. Dutton & Co. of New York for "The Critical Movement in America" from *Sketches in Criticism,* by Van Wyck Brooks, copyright 1932 by E. P. Dutton & Co.

Harcourt, Brace and Company, Inc. for "Thomas Mann and André Gide" and "Psychology and Form" from *Counter-Statement,* by Kenneth Burke, copyright 1931 by Harcourt, Brace and Company, Inc.; for "The American Critic" from *Creative Criticism and Other Essays* by J. E. Spingarn, copyright

1931 by J. E. Spingarn; for "Tradition and the Individual Talent" from *Selected Essays: 1917–1932,* by T. S. Eliot, copyright 1932 by Harcourt, Brace and Company, Inc.; for "Religion and Literature" from *Essays Ancient and Modern,* by T. S. Eliot, copyright 1933, 1936 by Harcourt, Brace and Company, Inc., now also included in *Selected Essays,* by T. S. Eliot, copyright 1950; and for "From Poe to Valéry," copyright 1948 by T. S. Eliot.

Harper & Brothers for selections from *Criticism and Fiction,* by William Dean Howells, copyright 1891 by Harper & Brothers, and for "Criticism" from *Essays in London and Elsewhere,* by Henry James, copyright 1893 by Harper and Bros.

Houghton Mifflin Company for "The Critic and American Life" from *On Being Creative and Other Essays,* by Irving Babbitt, copyright 1932 by Houghton Mifflin Company.

B. W. Huebsch of the Viking Press, New York, for "Our Cultural Humility" from *The History of a Literary Radical and Other Essays,* by Randolph Bourne, copyright 1920 by B. W. Huebsch, Inc.

Alfred A. Knopf, Inc., for "The American Novel" from *Prejudices: Fourth Series,* by H. L. Mencken, copyright 1924 by Alfred A. Knopf, Inc., and for "Attempts at an Integration" from *The Armed Vision,* by Stanley Edgar Hyman, copyright 1948 by Alfred A. Knopf, Inc.

Moffat, Yard and Company of New York for "The Aesthetic" from *Learning and Other Essays,* by John Jay Chapman, copyright 1910 by Moffat, Yard and Co.

New Directions for "How to Read: Part II" from *Polite Essays,* by Ezra Pound, copyright 1938 by Ezra Pound.

Oxford University Press for "T. S. Eliot: The *Four Quartets*" from *The Achievement of T. S. Eliot,* by F. O. Matthiessen, second edition, copyright 1947 by Oxford University Press; and for "Marxism and Literature" from *The Triple Thinkers,* by Edmund Wilson, revised and enlarged edition, copyright 1938, 1948 by Edmund Wilson.

Princeton University Press for "How to Read 'Lycidas'" from *On Being Human,* by Paul Elmer More, copyright 1936 by Princeton University Press; and for "Criticism as Pure Speculation" by John Crowe Ransom from *The Intent of the Critic,* edited by Donald A. Stauffer, copyright 1941 by Princeton University Press.

Paul Reynolds and Son, agents of the estate of Henry James, for permission to reprint "The Question of the Opportunities" and "The Great Form" by Henry James.

Charles Scribner's Sons for "The Great American Novel" from *Unicorns,* by J. G. Huneker, copyright 1917 by Charles Scribner's Sons; for "James Joyce" and "T. S. Eliot" from *Axel's Castle: A Study in the Imaginative Literature of 1870–1930,* by Edmund Wilson, copyright 1931 by Charles Scribner's

Sons; for "Penitent Art" from *Obiter Scripta,* by George Santayana, copyright 1936 by Charles Scribner's Sons, and "Tragic Philosophy" from *The Works of George Santayana,* Triton Edition, Volume II, copyright 1936 by Charles Scribner's Sons; for "Hart Crane" and "Ezra Pound" from *Reactionary Essays on Poetry and Ideas,* by Allen Tate, copyright 1936 by Charles Scribner's Sons; and for "Hemingway" by Robert Penn Warren which appears as a preface to a new edition of *A Farewell to Arms* by Ernest Hemingway, copyright 1949 by Charles Scribner's Sons.

William Sloane Associates for "Sherwood Anderson: An American as Artist" from *Sherwood Anderson* by Irving Howe, published by William Morrow and Co., copyright 1951 by William Sloane Associates.

University of Chicago Press for "Franz Kafka" from *Rage for Order,* by Austin Warren, copyright 1948 by University of Chicago Press.

The Viking Press for "Reality in America" and "Freud and Literature" from *The Liberal Imagination: Essays on Literature and Society,* by Lionel Trilling, copyright 1950 by Lionel Trilling.

Yale University Press for "Date Line: 1934" and "A Stray Document" from *Make It New,* by Ezra Pound, copyright 1935 by Ezra Pound.

The following magazines and their editors are likewise thanked for material that has appeared in their pages:

Accent, for "Literature as an Institution" by Harry Levin, VI, 159–165, Spring 1946.

The Atlantic Monthly, for "Shaw at Ninety" by Eric Bentley, CLXXVIII, 109–115, July 1946.

The Bookman, for "Experiment in Criticism" by T. S. Eliot, LXX, 225–233, November 1929, and "Poetry and Propaganda" by T. S. Eliot, LXX, 595–602, February 1930.

College English, for an earlier version of several portions of Cleanth Brooks's essay, "Irony as a Principle of Structure," which were adapted from his essay "Irony and 'Ironic' Poetry" in *College English,* IX, No. 5, 231–237, February 1948.

Ethics, for "I. A. Richards on the Art of Interpretation" by R. S. Crane, LIX, No. 2, Part I, 112–126, January 1949 (copyright 1949 by the University of Chicago Press).

Harper's Magazine, for "Gertrude Stein: A Self-Portrait" by Katherine Anne Porter, CXCV, 519–528, December 1947.

The Hound and Horn, for "Eugene O'Neill" by Francis Fergusson, III, 145–160, January 1930; for "The Later Poetry of W. B. Yeats" by Theodore Spencer, VII, 164–175, October 1933; and for "Henry James as a Characteristic American" by Marianne More, VII, 363–372, April 1934.

The Hudson Review, for "From Poe to Valéry" by T. S. Eliot, II, 327–342, Autumn 1949.

The Kenyon Review, for "Hemingway" by Robert Penn Warren, IX, 1–28, Winter 1947.

The Nation, for "Individualism and the American Writer" by Newton Arvin, CXXXIII, 391–393, October 14, 1931; for "The Austerity of George Kelly," CXXXVII, 240–242, August 30, 1933, and "The Dramatic Variety of Sidney Howard," CXXXVII, 294–295, September 13, 1933, both by Joseph Wood Krutch; for "James on a Revolutionary Theme" by Louise Bogan, CXLVI, 471–474, April 23, 1938; and for "The End of the Line" by Randall Jarrell, CLIV, 222–228, February 21, 1942.

The New Republic, for "Street Scene by Elmer Rice," LVII, 296–298, January 30, 1929, "*Mourning Becomes Electra* by Eugene O'Neill," LXVIII, 352–355, November 11, 1931, and "*Winterset* by Maxwell Anderson," LXXXIV, 365, November 6, 1935, all by Stark Young; for "John Dos Passos: The Poet and the World" by Malcolm Cowley, LXX, 303–305, April 27, 1932, and LXXXVIII, 34, September 9, 1936; for part of "A Literalist of the Imagination" by Morton Dauwen Zabel, LXXXIII, 370, August 7, 1935; for "Sinclair Lewis" by Robert Cantwell, LXXXVIII, 296–301, October 21, 1936; for "William Faulkner" by Robert Penn Warren, CXV, 176–180, 234–237, August 12 and 26, 1946; for three essays by W. H. Auden entitled "Heretics," C, 373–374, November 1, 1939, "The Poet of the Encirclement," CIX, 579–581, October 25, 1943, and "A Knight of the Infinite," CXI, 223–224, October 21, 1944; and for "William James and Henry James: 'Our Passion is our Task' " by Alfred Kazin, CVIII, 216–218, February 15, 1943.

Partisan Review, for "The Public vs. the Late Mr. William Butler Yeats" by W. H. Auden, VI, 46–51, Spring 1939; for "The Americanism of Van Wyck Brooks" by F. W. Dupee, VI, 69–85, Summer 1939; for "The Cult of Experience in American Writing" by Philip Rahv, VII, 412–424, November–December 1940; for "An Approach to Melville" by Richard Chase, XIV, 285–294, May–June 1947; for "The Literary Dictatorship of T. S. Eliot" by Delmore Schwartz, XVI, 119–137, February 1949; and for "The End of Modern Literature: Existentialism and Crisis" by William Barrett, XVI, 942–950, September 1949.

Poetry: A Magazine of Verse, for "Robinson Jeffers" by Yvor Winters, XXXV, 279–286, February 1930; for "A Literalist of the Imagination" by Morton Dauwen Zabel, XLVII, 326–336, March 1936; for "Private Experience and Public Philosophy" by William Phillips and Philip Rahv, XLVIII, 98–105, May 1936; and for "The Poetry of Wallace Stevens" by Marianne Moore, XLIX, 268–273, February 1937.

The Sewanee Review, for "Robert Frost: or, The Spiritual Drifter as Poet" by Yvor Winters, LVI, 564-569, Autumn 1948; and for "Scott Fitzgerald and the Imaginative Possession of American Life" by Arthur Mizener, LIV, 66-86, Winter 1946.

The Symposium, for "Paul Valéry" by Philip Blair Rice, I, 206–220, April 1930; and for "Virginia Woolf: The Novel of Sensibility" by William Troy, III, 53–63, 153–166, January and April, 1932.

The Yale Review, for "Willa Cather" by E. K. Brown, XXXVI (new series), 77–92, September 1946.

Besides the above essays reprinted directly from magazines, certain essays in this book, later incorporated in their original or in a revised form in books by their authors and here reprinted in that form, originally appeared in magazines, as follows: *The American Review,* New York ("How to Read 'Lycidas'" by Paul Elmer More); *The Atlantic Monthly* ("Our Cultural Humility" by Randolph Bourne, and "Marxism and Literature" by Edmund Wilson); *The Bookman* ("Thomas Mann and André Gide" by Kenneth Burke); *The Dial,* New York ("Penitent Art" by George Santayana, and "Psychology and Form" by Kenneth Burke); *The Egoist,* London ("Tradition and the Individual Talent" by T. S. Eliot); *The Forum,* New York ("The Critic and American Life" by Irving Babbitt); *The Freeman,* New York ("The Critical Movement in America" by Van Wyck Brooks); *Harper's Monthly,* New York ("The Question of a Criterion" in *Criticism and Fiction* by William Dean Howells); *The Hound and Horn* ("Notes on E. E. Cummings' Language" by R. P. Blackmur, and "Hart Crane" by Allen Tate); *The Kenyon Review* ("T. S. Eliot: The *Four Quartets*" by F. O. Matthiessen, and part of "Freud and Literature" by Lionel Trilling, the expanded form of this essay having later appeared in *Horizon,* London); *Literature,* London and New York ("The Question of the Opportunities" by Henry James); *The Nation* ("Ezra Pound" by Allen Tate, and part of "Reality in America" by Lionel Trilling); *The New Republic* ("James Joyce" and "T. S. Eliot" by Edmund Wilson); *The New Review,* London ("Criticism" by Henry James); *The New York Herald-Tribune: Books* ("How to Read" by Ezra Pound); *The New York Tribune* ("The Great Form" by Henry James, later republished in the *Times Literary Supplement,* London), *Partisan Review* (part of "Reality in America" by Lionel Trilling); *Poetry,* Chicago (part of "A Stray Document" by Ezra Pound); *Scrutiny,* Cambridge, England ("Tragic Philosophy" by George Santayana); *The Southern Review,* Baton Rouge, Louisiana ("Franz Kafka" by Austin Warren).

Certain essays that appeared in the 1937 edition of this book and are also in the present edition subsequently appeared in published volumes or were later reprinted in new books by their authors: thus Allen Tate's "Hart Crane" and "Ezra Pound," here taken from his *Reactionary Essays on Poetry and Ideas* as published by Charles Scribner's Sons in 1936, have recently been included in his *On the Limits of Poetry,* published by Swallow Press & William Morrow & Co., New York, 1948; Horace Gregory's "D. H. Lawrence: The Posthumous Reputation," first printed in *Literary Opinion in America* in 1937, has now been included in his *The Shield of Achilles,* published by Harcourt, Brace and Company, Inc. in 1944; Robert Cantwell's "Sinclair Lewis," here reprinted from *The New Republic,* reappeared in *After the Genteel Tradition,* edited by Malcolm Cowley and published by W. W. Norton and Company of New York, 1937; Stark Young's three essays, here reprinted from *The New Republic,* were included in his *Immortal Shadows,* published by Charles Scribner's Sons, New York, in 1948.

The material in some of the essays in this new edition of *Literary Opinion in America,* here reprinted from magazines, has been adapted or reworked in books by their authors: Eric Bentley's "Shaw at Ninety," here reprinted from *The Atlantic Monthly,* was reworked in his book *Bernard Shaw* (New Directions, 1947); the material in Richard Chase's "An Approach to Melville," here reprinted from *Partisan Review,* was incorporated in a different form in his book *Herman Melville* (New York: The Macmillan Company, 1949); that in Philip Rahv's "The Cult of Experience in American Writing," here reprinted from *Partisan Review,* was revised and expanded in his book *Image and Idea* (New Directions, 1949). The substance of Harry Levin's "Literature as an Institution," here reprinted from *Accent,* will be incorporated in his book *The Gates of Horn,* to be published by the Oxford University Press.

For special favors in the making of the book in its two editions I am indebted to R. P. Blackmur, Cleanth Brooks, Van Wyck Brooks, Kenneth Burke, T. S. Eliot, Horace Gregory, Harry Levin, H. L. Mencken, Marianne Moore, Paul Elmer More, Katherine Anne Porter, Philip Rahv, John Crowe Ransom, George Santayana, Lionel Trilling, Robert Penn Warren, and Edmund Wilson; as also to Professor Benedict Einarson, and to Miss Rosalind Lohrfinck, secretary to Mr. Mencken.

A NOTE ON THE TEXTS: In view of the liberal and unstable conditions of English orthography, a rigorous uniformity has not been imposed on the texts reproduced in this volume. Practices of capitalization and punctuation, which are largely a privilege of style, have usually been left unchanged. Spellings (except in the case of obvious errors or misprints which have been silently corrected) have been permitted to stand in the variant forms allowed by the dictionary, though consistency within individual essays has been attempted. Thus such variants as *criticize—criticise, enquiry—inquiry, defense—defence,* etc., have been allowed. It should be noted that one important word appears in its two permitted spellings: *aesthetic* and *esthetic* (so also *aesthetics—esthetics; aesthete—esthete,* etc.). The frequent employment of both these usages in the essays, sometimes even in their titles or in titles quoted within essays, has made insistence on a uniform spelling seem inadvisable. It is trusted that the reader will not be confused by this, and will recognize the word under either spelling. Forms of possessives have also been allowed to stand: thus *James's* and *James'*, *Yeats's* and *Yeats'*, etc. Standard practice has been applied to titles, however: titles of books and whole works have been set in italics; those of short, partial, or subordinate works have been set inside quotation marks and in Roman type.

The dates printed below the titles of the essays show as closely as possible when they were first written or published. Several of the authors have brought their discussions more nearly up to date by revision, or have added notes by way of observing recent aspects of their topics. Where essays have been otherwise or extensively revised, the fact is noted in the credit-lines at the end of the essays. The editor's footnotes (except for a few supplying dates or bibliographical details) are marked as such; footnotes not thus marked are by the authors of the essays. The value of these discussions lies partly in what they show of developments in literature and criticism during the sixty years covered by the book, and it has not been considered advisable consistently to alter essays that do this to advantage.

Introduction: Criticism in America

I

OURS, we are told, is an age of criticism. The fact, so far as it is one, has been disputed by some as illusory, by others as unfortunate, by still others as inimical to the prosperity of literature. But there can be no question that the age itself is critical—critical in its conditions and critical in the kind of intelligence they exact and stimulate. The Socratic principle that the life that remains uncriticized is not worth living has become an axiom of the times, a proverb among moralists, a necessity enforced by public events, a cardinal motive in the serious forms of literature, a habit of the contemporary mind. Even those who question the claims of criticism, or hold that it is "based upon the decay of the art criticized," or take refuge in simpler kinds of virtue or idealism, are obliged to recognize its necessity in the responsibilities of the modern intelligence. A condition once seen by Johnson as a distant prospect, by Coleridge as a remote possibility, by Poe and Lowell as a cognate to serious creation in the arts, by Henry James as an obligation of a mature culture, has become a prevalent feature of creative activity, education, and political society alike. It has, indeed, made so prominent what one recent critic has called "one of the most aggressive, hardest-working, and portentous critical movements the history of literature has known" that we may be encouraged to believe that criticism has become what one of its least expected defenders—Whitman —once called it: "a majestic office, perhaps an art, perhaps even a church."

Whatever the case, the critic of literature today occupies a position of remarkable advantages, of a kind almost unknown to his ancestors. He finds himself in an office of wide influence and in command of almost unlimited opportunities and public attention. No special conditions of locality or intellectual climate are needed to make his rank in the community an important one, or his work difficult. He deals with ideas in a state of unrest and with causes at crucial odds with one another, all of which pass through his hands in the form of books. His energies are spurred by every possible stimulus from other fields of activity—by the experiments of history and philosophy and by the researches of social and psychological science—but when these aids arrive they are likely to prove more confusing than helpful. He is expected to be everything but himself: patriot, moralist, and humanitarian; reformer, revolutionist, and prophet. Where once he was accused of "not knowing enough," he is now likely to know too much for his own good about everything but his craft, or about everything that makes his craft a baffling one to master. He is a recognized arbiter of opinion, but he serves a public whose needs are as difficult to determine as his own means of satisfying them are difficult to reduce to to an exact method or science. His office is so easily and commonly reduced to the cruder uses of journalism and propaganda that it is easy to forget that it can also be one of the most important in the well-being of society, and one of the few trustworthy indexes we have to the prosperity of intelligence and culture.

This is true in any country, but there are reasons for claiming a special importance for American criticism during the past half century. It forms the record of a nation's education, of its arrival at a point of moral maturity and at the responsibility of justifying its claims to a cultural and spiritual destiny of its own. This function would give dramatic force to any body of writing, and American criticism has become, in the hundred years since the day of Poe and Emerson, as dramatic in its local and political circumstances, in its pride of duty and purpose, as any activity of the age. It has found itself divided between the claims of tradition and those of an emancipation whose first promise was to simplify those claims or dismiss them altogether. When Emerson wrote *The American Scholar* and Whitman his preface to *Leaves of Grass* and *Democratic Vistas* it was possible to announce that hope confidently; it has been periodically renewed; but the day for an easy confidence is over. Art, for one thing, has refused to be simplified. For another, criticism has not been allowed to acquire much complacency. Its tools and methods, whatever their firmness or refinement, repeatedly prove inadequate to the strain laid upon them. No sooner is a royal road to critical wisdom charted than its progress becomes impeded by disputes and conflicts. In the United States this problem is thrown into a relief more difficult to visualize in European countries. For at the same moment that the creative energies of the nation have appeared at their height, the need of a critical discipline has announced itself with vigorous emphasis. The resulting conflict has made American criticism a battleground of ideals and purposes, as crowded with faction and argument as any to be seen in the countries of the West.

American criticism has seldom been primarily literary, and only a small part of it is so today. It has been ethical and moral, social and regional, political and religious. The special claims of art have, in fact, been obliged to put up a struggle for recognition. This condition existed in the past as an accepted fact, in spite of the protests of men like Poe, Lowell, and Henry James. But it has been equally present during the past quarter century, whatever gains in taste and sophistication may be boasted. When there appeared, toward the end of the Nineteenth Century, a "critical movement in American life," literature played a part in it with manners, morals, and social institutions, but usually a subordinate part. The nation, arriving at a sufficient political isolation and economic independence, began to loosen its protective armor of suspicion and self-esteem, and relaxed its vigilance over the contempt of foreigners and the irreverence of its own satirists. It allowed its "giddy minds" to turn from foreign quarrels and defensives to a healthy doubt about native life and its productions in manners and art. But this change did not come easily or without meeting resistance.

Once such irreverence was frankly considered sacrilegious. The hardpan of American complacency dulled the pick of anyone who tried to break it up. Poe was one of these. His attacks on the crusted dogmatism of his literary overlords and contemporaries crop up everywhere in his essays and reviews: "It is folly to assert, as some at present are fond of asserting, that the Literature of any nation or age was ever injured by plain speaking on the part of critics. As for American Letters, plain speaking about *them* is, simply, the one thing needed. They are in a condition of absolute quagmire." He fired his concentrated anger at the immediate tyrants in the field, the "Literati of New York," whose flourishing descendants have testified for the ensuing nine decades to the small effect of his demolitions. Lowell was more decorous in his sense of the same shortcomings; Emerson admitted them to Carlyle; and Hawthorne offered one of his earliest biographers, the young Henry James, a special case of the American author who, though acutely conscious of aesthetic standards, was doomed to labor on their behalf in an atmosphere from which serious aesthetic curiosity was almost totally banished, either by the philosophic ambitions of Boston and Concord or by a fatuous veneration of "the gentleman or the lady who has written a book." In his day an adulation of almost Renaissance-like fervor was accompanied by an artistic stolidity of equal proportions. "If the tone of the American world is in some respects provincial, it is in none more so than in this matter of the exaggerated homage rendered authorship. The gentleman or the lady who has written a book is in many circles the object of an admiration too indiscriminating to operate as an encouragement to good writing." James was writing in 1879 about conditions half a century earlier, but his remarks are open to more recent application:

There is no reason to suppose that this was less the case fifty years ago; but fifty years ago, greatly more than now, the literary man must have lacked the comfort and inspiration of belonging to a class. The best things come, as a general thing, from the talents that are members of a group; every man works better when he has companions working in the same line, and yielding the stimulus of suggestion, comparison, emulation. Great things of course have been done by solitary workers; but they have usually been done with double the pains they would have cost if they had been produced in more genial circumstances. The solitary worker loses the profit of example and discussion; he is apt to make awkward experiments; he is in the nature of the case more or less of an empiric. The empiric may, as I say, be treated by the world as an expert; but the drawbacks and discomforts of empiricism remain to him, and are in fact increased by the suspicion that is mingled with his gratitude, of a want in the public taste of a sense of the proportion of things.

If this isolation afflicted the American artist it was equally the lot of the honest critic, who lacked even the consolations of hero worship. He was likely to spend his thrift in wrangling with patriotic citizens and the regimented high priests of popular journalism, the Griswolds and Bryants of the hour. Melville said "I feel an exile here," and escaped into the created world of his imagination; Thoreau had the protection of Walden and his resolute individualism; Hawthorne himself was not prevented from writing his books by the critical poverty around him; and Emily Dickinson had her own way of keeping the "admiring bog" of the inept at a distance. But the critic, with his more practical business to perform, found himself shut out of the inner circles of literary influence. Poe's complaints come to mind again, a modern version of Ben Jonson's in *Timber*:

In a criticism of Bryant I was at some pains in pointing out the distinction between popular "opinion" of the merits of contemporary authors, and that held and expressed of them in private literary society. The former species of "opinion" can be called "opinion" only by courtesy. It is the public's own, just as we consider a book our own when we have bought it. In general, this opinion is adopted from the journals of the day, and I have endeavored to show that the cases are rare indeed in which these journals express any other sentiment about books than such as may be attributed directly or indirectly to the authors of the books. The most "popular," the most "successful" writers among us (for a brief period, at least) are, ninety-nine times out of a hundred, persons of mere address, perseverance, effrontery—in a word, busy-bodies, toadies, quacks. These people easily succeed in *boring* editors (whose attention is too often entirely engrossed by politics or other "business" matter) into the admission of favorable notices written or caused to be written by interested parties—or, at least, into the admission of *some* notice *where*, under ordinary circumstances, *no* notice would be given at all. In this way ephemeral "reputations" are manufactured which, for the most part, serve all the purposes designated—that is to say, the putting of money into the purse of the quack and the quack's publisher; for there never was a quack who could be brought to comprehend the value of mere fame. Now, men of genius will not resort to these manoeuvres, because genius involves in its very essence a scorn of chicanery; and thus for a time the quacks always get the advantage of them, both in respect to pecuniary profit and what *appears* to be public esteem.

This paradox, of homage for authors serving to cripple authorship, has always been the invention of journalism, commercial interest, and social coteries. It was never so depressing as in the middle of the Nineteenth Century, when it offered a special kind of critical confusion to the writers who formed what present-day historians have honored as our literary "golden day." It was a day whose true luminaries were likely to show, either by private seclusion or the sectarianism of groups and farms, the artist's instinctive withdrawal from the indignities of the public literary market or such disgusts as taxed Poe's intelligence in New York. It did the further damage of making critical discrimination appear incompatible with creative achievement at the very moment when such collaboration was necessary to the health of American literature. The visionary imagination of Whitman repelled Henry James, and the prophetic passion of Melville appalled the more aesthetic poets of his generation. The same division came to exist within the temperaments of individual writers, notably in such ambivalent and contradictory talents as Henry Adams. It created in other writers so open a contempt for American standards in art that they saved themselves by going abroad. The exile from American society had already, in Hawthorne, Thoreau, and Emily Dickinson, taken the form of the recluse. He now became an expatriate. The migrations of Whistler, James, and Lafcadio Hearn provided a model of escape from the practical responsibilities of American literature that remained feasible down to the years of mass exodus to Paris after the First World War.

The real task of criticism, however, does not fall on the conscience of the creative writer, even in an age like the present one when the artist and critic often appear in the same person. For a wider reform of the critical intelligence there was required a more thoroughgoing education in literary standards than an artist usually has the patience to give. The success of such a program in America depended on the appearance of men who were willing to make criti-cism their lifework. Until the last two decades of the Nineteenth Century no such body of writers came into view. By 1880 and 1890, however, a general sense of this deficiency was apparent. An important labor was waiting to be performed. The skeptical spirit abroad in the land was stimulating and healthy, but it needed translation into positive criteria of value and taste. The hour had arrived for setting up an American school of criticism that would face the duty of reconciling intelligent artists to their native birthright, and yet of developing in both them and the public sounder principles of appreciation and judgment. When that moment was recognized the contemporary movement in American criticism had its beginnings.

II

The sponsors of an American criticism had several models of purpose to remember from the past. Poe argued equally for a "poetic principle" in art and for a more complete aesthetic education in critics. Emerson examined literature in the empirical spirit of his English contemporaries, Macaulay, Carlyle,

and Arnold, for evidences of that "peculiar fruit which each man was created
to bear" and which ripens out of his personal hopes and struggles. Lowell had
turned toward past masterpieces to find the qualities of moral character and
idealism by which the writers around him might be invigorated. Whitman
threw on poets his prophecy of the supreme humanitarian destiny of the
American nation, and called on critics to instruct and defend the poet blessed
with this mission. But these leaders had succeeded neither in founding schools
nor in winning followers, and they were too much at odds to arouse concerted
action among critics. What was needed was just such action, to coördinate dis-
senting views, instruct a new generation in the traditions of literature, and
agree on the means by which the best talents should translate them into timely
and active form. There was still missing a vital contact between the abstract
standards of culture and the living experience and craftsmanship to which
they were now to be applied.

It was one thing to see this program of action. It was another thing to act by
it. The critical intelligence was faced not only with the duty of harmonizing
tradition with the complexities of modern life, but with the need of an education in aesthetic principles that would apply less to the tested achievements of
the past than to the books of a new generation. It had to grasp such matters
as taste and style in better terms than the outworn usages of academic convention, and it had to acquire enough realism and sophistication to know what
they mean in contemporary terms. Critics, seeing this responsibility, would inevitably turn toward European countries and learn many of their best lessons
from older standards, but it was equally important that they should avoid the
fallacy of thinking that the mere importation of a foreign example would
bring such standards to the United States.

Henry James was the first critic to undertake this task, and he saw its difficulties more clearly than any other man of his generation. The fact that he did
not remain in America to complete his work is one of the tragedies of our literature—not by any failure of his in greatness, but by ours in sharing his intelligence more fully. As early as the 'sixties, when he had barely come of age,
he was a diligent reviewer of books for *The Nation, The North American Review*, and other New York journals. He canvassed the taste and sentiments of
the Victorian Age—the lady novelists and sentimental poets as soberly as
Goethe, Sainte-Beuve, and Arnold. In another ten years his ground had
shifted. He was looking for his bases in art and criticism. He studied Balzac
and the realists, Eliot and the moral problem in fiction, George Sand for her
imaginative and atmospheric methods, the new French naturalists for their
inventories of contemporary society. In ten years more his European education
was fairly complete. He had examined the contrasting purposes of the schools
of Paris—romantic, symbolist, and realist. He listened to the counsels of Flaubert, Turgenev, Daudet, and Zola. He wrote his book on Hawthorne and the

essays in *French Poets and Novelists* and *Partial Portraits*. He formed his friendship with Stevenson and arrived at his own creative maturity. He was perhaps the first American man of letters to follow a complete course of literary and critical education, to compare European writers and doctrines, to impose on his own craft and conscience an unprejudiced critical detachment.

He saw the modern creative problem in its two essential aspects: its oppression by social conflict and theories of scientific and moral determinism, and its acute subtilization by the defenses which the aesthetic techniques of the modern sensibility had set up against these oppressions. He saw modern criticism confronting the task of reconciling the real and the aesthetic, human life in "its unprejudiced identity" with the form and laws of art. That task was nowhere more urgent than in America, and during the 'eighties, when James still had the ambition of becoming an "American Balzac," he formulated his working principles as a critic. His critical doctrine had three clauses. He argued for subtlety and plasticity in the critic's sympathy as a first condition. As a second he demanded a tireless study of the vital experience upon which all art is based and its use as a test of material validity, since for him all art was "in basis moral." And he required finally a knowledge of how the intelligence of the artist stamps this material with its unmistakable impression of form and language, since that imprint constituted for James the "quality of mind" he looked for in any valid work of art.

He held to the mean in both art and criticism. He had an American's natural suspicion of cults and doctrine. He looked upon Gautier's "art for art" as an absurdity and upon naturalism as a "treacherous ideal." To him aesthetic quality was as indispensable as realistic documentation, but to insist on one without the other, or on either without the harmonizing presence of a moral conception, was futile. Criticism must begin where a work of imagination begins: with experience tangibly perceived.

To lend himself, to project himself and steep himself, to feel and feel till he understands, and to understand so well that he can say, to have perception at the pitch of passion and expression as embracing as the air, to be infinitely curious and incorrigibly patient, and yet plastic and inflammable and determinable, stooping to conquer and yet serving to direct—these are fine chances for an active mind, chances to add the idea of independent beauty to the conception of success. Just in proportion as he is sentient and restless, just in proportion as he reacts and reciprocates and penetrates, is the critic a valuable instrument.

He thus pleaded for training in critical sensibility. It alone leads the critic directly into contact with the work of art and with art's own sources. But one must not make the mistake of confusing what James said with what Pater taught in the conclusion of *The Renaissance*. Impressionism was at that time almost as unknown in America as it had been exaggerated in Europe, and it had a service to perform in bringing critics back to an intimate sense of art; but neither James nor his American friends—Lowell, Norton, Howells—had any intention of subscribing to its methods. They were too thoroughly bred in ethical seriousness. When James declared in *Partial Portraits* that "the deepest quality of a work of art will always be the quality of the mind of the producer," he meant that for both art and criticism "the moral sense and the artistic sense lie very close together." Only their combination will supply the intellect's abstract operations with the vitality of a union that makes such "quality" possible. "The critic's judgment," he repeated, "being in the last analysis an estimate of the artist's quality of mind, is at once moral and aesthetic." The persistent linking of these terms runs like a motive through James's essays. To separate the moral from the aesthetic is to rob either of its vital complement. Genuine "unity of the mind" exists in such "fusions and interrelations," with "every part of the stuff encircled in every other." That is the secret of aesthetic form, a writer's ultimate achievement—just as its elucidation is the secret of the critic's success, his highest responsibility. These precepts stayed with James from his critical coming-of-age until he finally assayed his own achievement by their light when writing, a quarter century later, the prefaces for the New York edition of his works.

American literature itself did not long remain, however, the subject matter of James's critical books. His removal from America after the disillusioning failure of his excursion into social realism in the 'eighties left the task in the hands of William Dean Howells and William Crary Brownell. In the new program of action Howells took the part of facts, Brownell that of ideals. Howells undertook to explain the foundations of American realism, Brownell the basis of taste and prudence necessary for the existence of cultural and literary achievement. Howells combined a frontier childhood with New England schooling, a study of past masters under the guidance of Lowell, Norton, and Aldrich with his own zest for art and history during European travels and consulships. But he found his roots in the ambition and vigor of the average American life, and he made the rationalization of its values the task of both his criticism and his novels.

He found two instruments at his service: the aesthetics of French naturalism (from whose rawer examples he recoiled, preferring the tempered version of Jane Austen or Tolstoy) and the scientific humanitarianism of the modern sociologists (which he studied not only in Mill, Comte, Spencer, Morris, and Bellamy, but in the social unrest of his middle years, the Pennsylvania coal strikes and Haymarket riots, "the slavery implicated in our liberty"). He defined the principles of this moral realism for critics in his essay in 1891, *Criticism and Fiction*. "Realism is nothing more and nothing less than the truthful treatment of material." He repudiated the aristocratic element in romanticism which "seeks to withdraw itself, to stand aloof, to be distinguished and not to be identified." Realism is the particular duty of the artist in the democratic society, for it enables him to feel "in every nerve the equality of things and the unity of men . . . to front the everyday world and catch the charm of its work-worn, careworn, brave, kindly face." To these doctrines Howells added two riders which locate him infallibly in his generation and define his critical limitations unmistakably. That realism is best which studies the "large cheerful average of health and success and happy life," since "the more smiling aspects of life" are "the more American." And that realism is most successful which rejects the deterministic science of the naturalists in favor of ethical judgment, since "morality penetrates all things, it is the soul of all things." Here Howells admitted his patriotic and ethical prejudices as frankly as his followers a quarter century later. He lacked their basis of special social doctrine, but he stuck to the conviction that unless a critic assumes such prejudices and makes them the source of his judgments, he fails in moral responsibility.

Brownell differed from Howells in many circumstances of temperament and training, but he agreed with him in one fundamental belief: the relation of art to life can be grasped only in terms of a realistic and practical dependence. His manner of demonstrating this principle was as different from Howells' as his sense of the spiritual deficiencies of the American people was different from Howells' firm confidence in their tough integrity. Brownell found his model in Arnold. He too became a priest of the cultural ideal, and he shared Arnold's combination of hope and pessimism in the face of the democratic future. He too believed that literature is a "criticism of life," and that criticism in turn "determines the relation of the two, and thus needs as close touch with life as with arts and letters." Yet the critic can do his work effectively only by a knowledge of ideal ends and standards. Standards, indeed, were Brownell's fetish, his touchstone to all worth. "To an intelligence fully and acutely alive, its own time must, I think, be more interesting than any other," he said; but the critic must go on "to discern and characterize the abstract qualities informing the concrete expression of the artist." "It is the *qualities* of the writer, painter, sculptor, and not the *properties* of their production that are his essential concern." Among his *American Prose Masters* he found only Cooper and James free of poverty in these qualities of experience and perception. Hawthorne "neglected imagination"; Emerson's "nature was flooded with light, but it lacked heat"; of Poe it was "impossible to make a great writer . . . because his writings lack the elements not only of great, but real literature. They lack substance." But the critic can also fail if he lacks emotional and aesthetic energy. Lowell for all his scholarship "was reflectively indolent." There is, in fact, only one cure for the imaginative poverty and degrading materialism of the times, and that is a cultural ideal. It alone saves the artist from the enervating antagonism of his physical and aesthetic faculties.

This solvent Brownell looked for in the sustaining and renewing influence of a firmly ethical civilization. His models for it he found in the "culture" defined by Arnold and in the aesthetic achievements of France. He studied *French Traits* with the patient but always half-ironical hope of importing them to the United States. No one but James had his skill in the judicious inspection of such a model, and no one but James had the greater powers of imagination that could show how ineffectual Brownell's fastidious discretion would turn out to be. For forty years he taught his moderate and urbane gospel of discipline, decorum, and intellectual tact. The heresies of "self-expression," naturalism, and impressionism he considered aberrations from a desired norm. He insisted so austerely on this norm, this admirable but ultimately abstract principle, that he lost his hold on the very "substance" he demanded in his prose masters. When he faced the literary productions of the new age around him, or when he attempted to understand tradition as a reality that is valid only by its success in surviving in the present, he proved almost abjectly incompetent. His urgent counsels on taste and sophistication impressed themselves on a few respectful followers but on almost none of the artists and craftsmen he wished to enlighten. Today his precisely phrased and austerely bound books are unread. But excepting only those of James, they provided the most serious formulation of the responsibility that must be exchanged between artist, critic, and public that America had yet seen, and some of their views have never been restated to better effect. They may be recalled some day when another effort at integrating social and aesthetic thought comes due. By comparison with the puerilities of academic convention around him (Henry Van Dyke, or Hamilton Wright Mabie with his "White List of Books") he survives with the distinction of sensitive tastes which these prudish culturists never thought it worth their while to envy.

Taste, in those bewildered years of the late Nineteenth Century, was a faculty so threatened by anemia when refined and so exhausted by garish and unprincipled crudity when robust, that it is small wonder the word came to be the trademark of ludicrous elegance and snobbery among satirists like Mark Twain. James Huneker made something else of it. He was perhaps the first sybarite of the arts in America. His appetite and energy made him a valuable agent in combating the dead weight of genteel and Puritanic intolerance, the smug cant of "propriety" that acted as a customs barrier to aesthetic importations of any kind. Like George Moore and Arthur Symons in England, he was an ambassador of the aesthetic movement. He lavished his admiration on anything new, exotic, or rebellious, and his cascades of fervent publicity swept before the American public the novelties of modern music, drama, painting, fiction, and ballet, not to mention the gastronomic luxuries of every café and hostelry on the Continent. He wrote about the arts as he wrote about foods and menus, and before their rich fare professed nothing but an unlimited epicurean capacity. His writings were the cosmopolite's text books and involved few critical subtleties. They offered a plain man's version of Pater's appetitive ideal and Anatole France's doctrine of aesthetic exposure. The critic must aim "to spill his soul," and "humbly to follow and register his emotions aroused by a masterpiece." He spared nothing in the way of epithets, enigmas, and paradoxes when he spilled his soul, and upon the ensuing flood his readers were buffeted by the complete carnival of modern insurgence in the arts. The sheer gastronomic pleasure of this feast was crowned by a kind of moral satisfaction in knowing that it was an affront to all the inhibitions and hostilities of the Puritan tradition. There was no need to discriminate special qualities in the items: they had the common quality of scorning the pure and the prurient.

For the sophisticated children of the Gilded Age and for a few more serious apprentices, Huneker was revered as a bringer of gifts. On the popular level his influence was rapid and enormous. On the critical value of his work little need be added. His foremost disciple has said that for him art was no longer "even by implication a device for improving the mind. It is wholly a magnificent adventure. The notion of it is what Huneker brought into American criticism, and it is for that bringing that he will be remembered." This, spoken in tribute by Mencken, speaks for itself. In any serious sense Huneker did not pretend to write criticism, even in his books on Liszt and Chopin. He wrote aesthetic publicity. He brought the fleshpots of modern art into a genteel society, startled the literary conventions out of their frozen molds, shocked the high priests of the Lyceum circuit, inducted a new generation of journalists into a colorful style and extravagant zest for the arts, and introduced an easy brand of impressionism into literary appreciation. He shaped the adolescent phase of a new critical attitude, and as such his labors are preserved in the shelf of books in which his enormous avidity and honest share of sensitive enthusiasm for music, literature, and painting are preserved. He is the child of his period, and to return to his books now, after the sobering events of the last thirty years, is to realize how much of a child he remains. But he may claim a tonic quality: he made American readers more keenly aware of international activities than Henry James managed to do. He probably ruined taste more expertly than James improved it, but he also created an appetite for the arts that had its due effect on the physical health and public prestige of the American artist.

Around the work of James and Brownell, Howells and Huneker, a sizeable critical activity went on between the 'nineties and 1912, but from it few lasting services may be isolated. Much of this writing came from academic quarters, another share was composed of newspaper reviews, most of which risked little in the way of dispute or defense of new talent, and another part struck out along independent lines which either ended at the impasse of theoretical vagueness or led back to conventional quarters. George Edward Woodberry was one critic who felt dissatisfaction in the stolid confines of the academic world and began to work toward freer purposes. He produced a series of volumes in which various critical positions were carefully scanned, the work of new critics plotted, and impending problems suggested. He also said much about the need of a new humanistic and realistic attitude toward values, and in such books as *America in Literature* (1903), *The Torch* (1905), *The Appreciation of Literature* (1910), and *Two Phases of Criticism* (1914) he provided the best surveys of the situation and of critical methods that existed in those years. But theory took him too far afield, and a lax belletristic idealism removed him from the irrepressible forces that were demanding expression. Brander Matthews had less of this. By combining a shrewd study of European dramatic criticism with a lively attention to the New York stage he lifted the criticism of drama over from the pontifical conservatism of William Winter's era to the brisk journalism soon to come from younger men.

By far the keenest refreshment of aesthetic interest to come from academic quarters, however, was supplied by George Santayana. His *Sense of Beauty* in 1896 claimed to be nothing but a new arrangement of "the scattered commonplaces of criticism into a system, under the inspiration of a naturalistic psychology." The last phrase of this apology explains the great influence the book and its sequels were to have on the study and appreciation of art in the United States. It was the first textbook to refurbish the classical routine of philosophical discourse and add the stimulation of a realistic motive. Santayana set aside the didactic and historical approach to art, and offered the psychological. He presented "aesthetic judgments as phenomena of mind and products of mental evolution." He combined his exposition with a vivid sense of his personal appreciation of the arts, and stepped gracefully over the barrier that separated the philosophical idealist of the American college from an active grasp of the work of art itself. When he distinguished the three orders of beauty as residing in material, in form, and in expression, he took these criteria out of the dark chamber of theory and made them applicable to existing masterpieces. And fourteen years later, in *Three Philosophical Poets,* he showed that figures like Lucretius, Dante, and Goethe could be used as opportunities for the collaboration between philosophical and literary criticism which was needed to rescue aesthetic teaching from endless and enfeebling conventionality. But the "inspiration of a naturalistic psychology" remained basic to Santayana's activity in this line. It gave him his popularity among realists and psychologists, and it provided a clue to a new line of reaction which was presently to put in an appearance and prepare a heated repudiation of his influence and affiliations. That reaction proceeded cautiously, built its attack conservatively, and took almost a quarter century before it faced the enemy of naturalism in open battle. In 1904 Paul Elmer More issued the first volume of his *Shelburne Essays,* and in 1908 Irving Babbitt began his campaign against romanticism with *Literature and the American College.*

III

The work of the critics who attempted to bridge the distance between Nineteenth Century habits and the experimental conditions of modern literature now appears, especially when we recall the difficulties of prejudice and conventionality they faced, to gain in courage and distinction. More's phrase in his 1904 volume—"Before we can have an American literature, we must have an American criticism"—is a sufficient warrant of this. But when a new revival of literary activity arrived around 1912 it took, like most cases of insurgence, the immediately preceding generation as its first object of attack. It announced two purposes: the demolition of the genteel tradition and a rediscovery of the American spirit. These served to indict as academic, unrealistic, or corruptive the labors of most of the elder critics still on the scene. Henry James then appeared as a deserter from a sacred trust, a shirker of his duty as an American, tainted by the effete and artificial influences of English society and French theory. Brownell and Woodberry became supreme examples of academic dry rot and polite formulation. Paul Elmer More fell under contempt as a dogged apologist for ethical dogma. Huneker, in spite of his more attractive personality and acceptable epicureanism of taste, was lamed by vulgar aestheticism and exhausting garrulity, incapable of getting a close view of the serious duties of the artist, and rendered helpless as a judge of either life or art by his welter of gross and indiscriminate enthusiasms. The young critics who now took the field were of an equally heady breed, but they professed very different purposes. Reality was to provide their basic standard, and the existing life of the United States their chief test of values. In one of his essays Van Wyck Brooks suggested the new attitude toward history: "On Creating a Usable Past." The title of one of his most successful books gave the new criticism its label: *America's Coming-of-Age.* He and his colleagues corrected More's dictum. They believed that before there could be either an American literature or an American criticism there must appear a fresh and realistic understanding of what America itself meant. What they produced was not criticism in any pure or technical sense. It was Americanization.

That it was to be a critical and practical kind of Americanization, escaping the weakness of earlier prophecies and panegyrics, was made clear in another of Brooks's volumes, *Letters and Leadership.* There he took up a clue furnished by John Macy in his *Spirit of American Literature* (1913) and gave it as his conclusion that "our life is, on all its levels, in a state of arrested development, that it has lost, if indeed it has ever possessed, the principle of growth." He credited this adolescence to the commercial and materialistic obsessions of the nation. "We are," he said, "the victims of a systematic process

of inverse selection so far as the civilizing elements in the American nature
are concerned. Our ancestral faith in the individual and what he is able to
accomplish (or in modern parlance, to 'put over') as the measure of all things,
has despoiled us of that science, art, philosophy, the self-subordinating service
of which is almost the measure of the highest happiness. In consequence of
this our natural capacities have been dissipated, they have become egocentric
and socially centrifugal and they have hardened and become fixed in the most
anomalous form." He sketched a program for the correction of this state of
affairs, if only to keep alive "the hope of a 'national culture' to come . . . in
order that America may be able in the future to give something to the rest
of the world that is better than what the world too generally means by 'Americanism.' " The elder critics whom he condemned as "unpractical" had done
little toward this end, chiefly because while "they say that we are emotional
. . . what they really object to is that we are emotional at all, the strength
of their own case resting wholly on the assumption that literature ought to
spring not from the emotions but from the intellect." They had fostered a
"fear of experience."

Such, in fact, is the deficiency of personal impulse, of the creative will, in
America, so overwhelming is the demand laid upon Americans to serve ulterior
and impersonal ends, that it is as if the springs of spiritual action had altogether
evaporated. Launched in a society where individuals and their faculties appear
only to pass away, almost wholly apart from and without acting upon one another,
our writers find themselves enveloped in an impalpable atmosphere that acts as a
perpetual dissolvent to the whole field of reality both within and without themselves, an atmosphere that invades every sphere of life and takes its discount from
everything that they can do, an atmosphere that prevents the formation of oases of
reality in the universal chaos.

In Brooks's program for critics, the new critical realism joined hands with
this corrected view of the American ideal. It was immediately taken as a call
to action both by the young critical talents of the prewar years and by a new
group of "journals of opinion" which appeared on the scene—*The New Republic, The Masses, The Liberator,* the renovated *Nation,* the more aesthetic
Seven Arts, and later *The Freeman.* These found an almost ideal condition
for their activities: the unrest and dislocation of the prewar years, the excitement and controversy that followed our entry into the conflict, and a flourishing literary revival that brought the work of insurgent poets and novelists to
reinforce what the critics hoped to achieve. Dreiser, Sandburg, Masters, Frost,
Lindsay, Willa Cather, and Robinson supplied object lessons for the new
critical text. The moment was alive with creative energy and rebellion, with
the hope of casting out the venerable American superstitions. These critical
journalists were able to boast that they saw the creative problem from the in-

side. They felt its motives and difficulties with the artist, instead of holding off in suspicion and condescending scorn.

"The older critics," said Randolph Bourne in his *History of a Literary Radical,* "long since disavowed the intention of discriminating among current writers. These men, who had to have an Academy to protect them, lumped the younger writers of verse and prose together as 'anarchic' and 'naturalistic,' and had become, in these latter days, merely peevish and querulous, protesting in favor of standards that no longer represented our best values. Everyone . . . bemoaned the lack of critics, but the older critics seemed to have lost all sense of hospitality and to have become tired and a little spitefully disconsolate, while the newer ones were too intent on their crusades against puritanism and philistinism to have time for a constructive pointing of the way." Bourne had nothing but contempt for academic standardizers or importers of foreign fashions, but he saw the unorthodox belligerents threatened by another danger. He saw, "on the one hand, Mr. Mencken and Mr. Dreiser and their friends, going heavily forth to battle with the Philistines, glorying in pachydermous vulgarisms that hurt the polite and cultivated young men of the old school." He saw "these violent critics, in their rage against Puritanism, becoming themselves moralists, with the same bigotry and tastelessness as their enemies." And he continued:

The older American critic was mostly interested in getting the proper rank and reverence for what he borrowed. The new critic will take what suits his community of sentiment. He will want to link up not with the foreign canon but with that group which is nearest in spirit to the effort he and his friends are making. The American has to work to interpret and portray the life he knows. He cannot be international in the sense that anything but the life in which he is soaked, with its questions and its colors, can be the material for his art. But he can be international—and must be—in the sense that he works with a certain hopeful vision of a "young world," and with certain ideal values upon which the younger men, stained and revolted by war, in all countries are agreeing.

The "international" element in this program was chiefly an attack on provincialism. It had its earlier sponsors in Henry James and Brownell, its immediate godfather in Huneker, its practical workers in exiles like Ezra Pound and T. S. Eliot. Critics like Spingarn and Santayana had also, for different reasons, advised a familiarity with the critical ideas that were circulating in Europe. For the realists and liberals, however, this plea for an international point of view was incidental, a supplementary means of fighting down the conservatives and "professors." Against such foes any weapon was useful, and European radicalism offered ripe experience in the tactics of battle. Ludwig Lewisohn told the young critics to look toward France, where "their battle was fought and won thirty years ago," or toward Germany, "where the heritage of Goethe's supreme vision made the battle needless." Spingarn pointed

toward the books of Croce. France was, as always, held up as a model of un-
shackled liberalism in art and thought. But the defenders of the "authentic
American" had work to do at home which no amount of internationalism and
foreign example would make easier.

A great deal of it was negative in character. They attacked prudery, decorum, politeness, and every other evil that might be safely ascribed to the
Puritans. But they also wanted to give American writers a genuine confidence
in their native materials, a pragmatic and disillusioned approach to the life
around them, a standard of honesty, and if possible a critical understanding
of their problems. With so many prejudices to correct, it is little wonder that
a critical basis for the new realism was never satisfactorily arrived at. The
gusto of the "debunking" movement had little patience for that. Brooks and
Bourne laid out a program, to which their colleagues, Robert Morss Lovett,
Robert Littell, Harriet Monroe, Francis Hackett, Max Eastman, Alfred
Kreymborg, Harold E. Stearns, and Lewis Mumford contributed their energies. Among them a dominating voice was heard; the cause found its most
entertaining spokesman in H. L. Mencken.

It is easy now, in rereading Mencken's books, to limit his performance to
low-comedy journalism. The pages teem with the follies of twenty-five of the
oddest years in American history and form a hilarious *Dunciad* of an age.
Mencken delivered his barrage against them with the energy of a Swift or
Voltaire. War-time jingoism, the Prohibition era, the "Monkey Trial" in
Tennessee, the pieties of the Bible Belt, the orgies of Coolidge prosperity, and
the endless prodigalities of the jazz age, the "alfalfa *Gelehrten*," and the
Booboisie now almost bury the high reputation he once held as a literary
influence who made *The Smart Set* and *The American Mercury* serious forces
in the lives of important writers. But one fact must be remembered: he aimed
less to be a critic than a commissary of literary materials. He ransacked American life to justify writers like Dreiser, Masters, Sandburg, Lardner, and Lewis,
and to show younger writers what the realistic and critical spirit had to work
on. He was an evangelist of the vulgar, as much of an artist in his display of
its phenomena as many of the novelists he praised. What Edmund Wilson
has pointed out must be recalled: that while

Brooks exposed the negative aspects of our literary tradition and urged us to
get away from our governesses, Mencken showed the positive value of our vulgar
heritage; and he did more than anyone else in his field to bring about that "coming-
of-age" for which Brooks sounded the hour. The publication of Mencken's *Book
of Prefaces* in 1917, with its remarkable essay on Dreiser and its assault on
"Puritanism as a Literary Force," was a cardinal event for the new American literature. Mencken did not precisely discover Dreiser, but he was able to focus him
clearly for the first time as a figure of dignity and distinction, because he ap-

preciated and made us taste the Americanism of Dreiser as Americanism, without attempting to write him down for not being something other than American. This *positive* treatment of Dreiser—so different from the negative attitude with which even sympathetic critics had in the past approached American writers like Mark Twain,—was really a weight that tipped the scales.

His test of a book was rough and pragmatic. He mingled his burly prejudices with an uninhibited impressionism derived from Huneker. It is not hard to imagine what this procedure amounted to when he tackled an author beyond his depth or taste—Henry James, Herman Melville, or any poet of subtle originality. But at another level he brought an enormous stimulation to the literary scene, and he took that to be his function as a critic. "The function of a genuine critic of the arts is to provoke the reaction between the work of art and the spectator. The spectator, untutored, stands unmoved; he sees the work of art, but it fails to make any intelligible impression on him; if he were spontaneously sensitive to it, there would be no need for criticism." The common assumption, that a critic "writes because he is possessed by a passion to advance the enlightenment, to put down error and wrong, to disseminate some specific doctrine: psychological, epistemological, historical, or aesthetic" is true "only of bad critics, and its degree of truth increases in direct ratio to their badness. Criticism at bottom is indistinguishable from skepticism." Mencken rejected the arguments for "constructive criticism" as based "upon the same false assumption, that immutable truths exist in the arts, and that the artist will be improved by being made aware of them. . . . Truth is something that is believed in completely only by persons who have never tried personally to pursue it to its fastnesses and grab it by the tail. . . . The true aim of a critic is certainly not to make converts. He must know that very few of the persons who are susceptible to conversion are worth converting."

These remarks, scattered throughout his essays, indicate the elements in his literary outlook: a contempt of popular taste, a suspicion of intellectual and a skepticism of dogmatic attitudes toward art, and an ambition to demolish any tradition that had fostered the delusions of ethical and ideal theory in literature. Most of that tradition he labeled Puritan, and he translated his contempt of its moral absolutes into a scorn of aesthetic absolutes. "The American, save in moments of conscious and swiftly lamented deviltry, casts up all ponderable values, including even the values of beauty, in terms of right and wrong," and the only cure for this habit was to demolish the entire basis of rational and authoritarian judgment. Under tenets like these, it was hardly to be expected that Mencken would bring his literary preferences to the test of analysis or exact discrimination. His usefulness was of a more elementary character. He wrote a history of American manners, howled into perdition the genteel superstitions of culture and dignity, and provided a basis for evaluating the realistic principle in fiction for what it was worth. His own criticism will probably be remembered chiefly for the humor that accompanied its purgative effects.

In Van Wyck Brooks another form of the patriotic motive appeared. It combined affection and skepticism as Mencken's did, but it was tempered to a soberer employment. His early books on the revision of American society— *The Wine of the Puritans* (1909), *America's Coming-of-Age* (1915), and *Letters and Leadership* (1918)—were intended as manifestoes and were accepted as such. Brooks never intended an assault on genuine American loyalties; his reverence for these was instinctive and sincere, and he did not consider cosmopolitanism a cure-all for cultural ingrowth and provincialism. He proposed first to indict the traitors within the gates, the defilers of the pioneer idealism and all who had nursed along the enfeebling conformism of the academic life. After that he would take his "usable past" and apply its lessons to the unrealized present. In two of his books these purposes were first demonstrated in practical terms—*The Ordeal of Mark Twain* (1920) and *The Pilgrimage of Henry James* (1925). Both these inheritors of the American tradition were depicted as unworthy of its promise—Twain through pessimism and a failure of personal integrity, James through temperamental restlessness and aesthetic over-refinement. Brooks had set up in his mind the standard of American honesty and fortitude which he was later to apply in *The Flowering of New England* and the histories that followed it. In it he found his prescription for the authentic American artist, the source of his usable past and his productive present. Any betrayal of its promise spelled for him the secret failure of the artist.

It is in his book on James that the defects of Brooks's argument appear most strikingly. Starting with his thesis, he broke the body of James to fit it. James's qualities of irony and self-criticism, his subtle pessimism on the condition of English society and French literature, his sense of catastrophe in the European moral order, his skeptical detachment and unforgotten American loyalties, are all simplified or neglected in order to push to its logical conclusion the argument that they were ultimately stultified by James's refusal to return to his native shores to live and write. The words and speeches of James's fictions are used to convey his own personal attitude, ostensibly to give an "effect of immediacy" but actually with the result of reading into his personal career a coherent fiction which an exact reading of his letters, the autobiographical books, or the major novels themselves would have rendered impossible. Yet the desired effect was achieved. *The Pilgrimage of Henry James* becomes a parable of the American artist's betrayal of his birthright. The patriotic motive inhibits the critical. A valuable project of revision and reclamation falters in the individual test. In the end Brooks was to prove more adept as a pictorial and anecdotal historian of the past than as a student of the present. His *Opinions of Oliver Allston* in 1941 showed clearly his alienation from all but the most traditional and conservative of contemporary talents. His labors finally settled down to the writing of a literary chronicle of the United States which began with *The Flowering of New England* in 1936, and to the winning of a greater popular recognition, if a less serious achievement, than his early challenges ever hoped to arrive at.

Among Brooks's followers Lewis Mumford became a versatile leader. He wanted not merely to recover a usable past but to apply it as speedily as possible to the existing distractions and doubts of literature. He looked for it in the same quarter as Brooks did—in the *Golden Day* of New England culture, from whose high moment he saw modern American wealth and materialism as a decline. He studied the Utopian symbol as a means of combining its philosophic vitality with the mystic or humanitarian vision of Emerson, Whitman, and Melville. He took "Whitman with his cosmic faith" and "Melville in his cosmic defiance" as his prophets, and believed that "they will guide us to a splendid future" where the techniques of civilization will cease to tyrannize over man and provide a richer opportunity for his self-fulfillment. Like many of his contemporaries, Mumford was stronger on the side of indictments than of affirmations. In *Sticks and Stones* (1924) and *The Brown Decades* (1931) he produced two of the best accounts of American art and architecture that have yet been written, and in these books he shows that the practical arts furnish him with safer examples for speculation than the literary. He has fallen too glibly into the prophet's role to be anything but restive and generalizing in his treatment of literary style and craftsmanship. "The social sciences will lie beneath the foundations of the New Jerusalem precisely in the fashion that the physical sciences now underlie the stony exterior of New York" is one of Mumford's observations; and another: "The future of our civilization depends upon our ability to select and control our heritage from the past, to alter our present attitudes and habits, and to project fresh forms into which our energies may be freely poured." The glow here is messianic, the accent Whitman's, the skepticism as facile as the self-assurance is quick, and instead of producing the focus of scrutiny and discrimination where critical values come to a point, Mumford's energies have radiated and explored. He has contributed to the background of aesthetic thought more than he has given that thought principles and a discipline to work by.

Under the guidance of these men several things were accomplished. The past was revived in colorful and intimate terms, even though the uses to which it was put were not very intelligently defined, or free of a great deal of the cant about progress, patriotism, and disillusionment that circulated so recklessly in the postwar years. The term "American" was stripped of dogmatic and academic accretions. Large areas of subject matter formerly considered out of polite artistic bounds were thrown open to conquest by writers. A necessary leaven of plain sense and active speech was added to the fare in which novelists dealt and critics dealt. Literature was brought to closer terms with experience and fortified by candor and audacity. It was reduced to those simpler necessities and practices which correct the laxities of academic idealism or aesthetic refinement, but which may also put up the deluding appearance of being self-sufficient and in no need of the intellectual benefits of aesthetic or philosophic discipline. In fact, this entire activity was so attractive to journalists that it became vulgarized beyond its own intentions. It made the writing of books seem as easy as talking about them. Under its influence American literature was strengthened, but as often reduced to facile and rapid-fire journalism, criticism meanwhile becoming equally loose in its language, haphazard in its terminology, indifferent in analysis, and complacently hostile to anything in the way of intellectual attitudes or aesthetic experimentation. The realists and Americanizers nagged pure art and ridiculed its defenders; they encouraged the flight of experimentalists to Paris; they scoffed at originality by calling it "cerebralism"; and they did their part in keeping the literary activity of the twenties on a fairly confused level.

However, they flourished in their day. *The Saturday Review of Literature* became one of their strongholds, *The American Mercury* another, and independent or creative journalism was kept at the distance of Greenwich Village (in *The Dial, Others,* and *The Little Review*), Chicago (in *Poetry*), or Europe (in *Secession, Broom,* and *Transition*). Occasionally this vein of American revivalism took on the colors of prophecy, as in Ludwig Lewisohn's *The Creative Life* and *Expression in America* or in Waldo Frank's *The Re-Discovery of America,* where the "great tradition" became a spectre of mystic and international proliferations. Nothing showed better than these heavy-handed conjurings how severely the realistic revival stood in need of critical direction from both social and artistic authorities if it was to be saved from bombast and rhetoric, or from a debasement of the American principle fully as debilitating as the genteel conventions which it had opposed. Such correction began to appear some years after the First World War. One of the most important manifestations of it came in the form of a regional principle in the study of tradition and art, shown particularly among the group of Southern critics—John Crowe Ransom, Donald Davidson, and Allen Tate—who combined literary study with cultural investigations and who had their first organ in *The Fugitive* of Nashville. Another, from a different quarter, appeared in the form of social criticism of the radical type, of which such writers as Upton Sinclair and V. F. Calverton were pioneer professors, but which was ultimately to develop a method much more formal and extreme (particularly under the tenets of Marxism) than these men had exhibited. In any case, the arrogance and visionary gusto of the realistic movement were its weakest features. They exposed it most readily to critical attack and soon brought it under contempt from several quarters of the literary scene.

IV

One of these was occupied by the students of modern aesthetics who first found their ideas or centered their activities abroad. Paris and London were already before the War of 1914 the accepted capitals of artistic experimentation; and a revision of aesthetic ideas was in progress there far removed from the academic influences and public indifference that made such activity out of place at home. The departure from American shores of Ezra Pound and T. S. Eliot was taken as a hint that their talents were indifferent to the revival of an American ideal or the promotion of new standards of social realism. Their loadstone was neither the real nor the humanitarian, it was art; and they turned toward the schools of Italy, Paris, and prewar London to learn their lessons and ultimately to become recognized as leaders of the experimental groups that flourished there.

The deficiencies of American criticism in aesthetic and technical understanding had long been a byword. Poe had issued the first indictments on this score, and in the 1840's John Lothrop Motley had published in *The North American Review* a series of essays presenting the man of letters as an artist and pleading, especially in an essay on Balzac, that fiction be respected as an art before it is tested for its ethical and social respectability. These arguments later formed the chief responsibility of Henry James, but before 1900 the instructions of aesthetic critics in France, Germany, and England found scant hospitality in the United States, Huneker's defense of their doctrines being held a matter of highly questionable taste. Impressionism was as little known to American critics as to American writers. The Harvard professor, Lewis E. Gates, was probably its only sympathetic interpreter among the elect. In his essay on "Impressionism and Appreciation," published in *Studies and Appreciations* in 1900, he introduced his readers to the special conditions and mysteries of the aesthetic experience. There he argued that

The history of literary criticism from Addison's day to our own is, if viewed in one way, the history of the ever-increasing refinement of the critic's sensorium; it is a growing tendency on the part of the critic to value, above all else, his own intimate personal relation to this or that piece of literature—a tendency that more and more takes the form of prizing the fleeting mood, the passing poignant moment of enjoyment in the presence of art, until at last certain modern critics refuse, on principle, to feel twice alike about the same poem.

"Impressionism," he said, "justifies itself historically. But more than this, it justifies itself psychologically; for it recognizes with peculiar completeness the vitalizing power of literature—its fashion of putting into play the whole nature of each reader it addresses and its consequent, unlimited, creative energy." Santayana had also aimed to combine the philosophical rationalization of art with modern principles of inductive psychology in determining the character of aesthetic experience, and in counteracting the academic and philosophical influence with a more practical training in sensibility. In 1910 these influences were challenged even more defiantly by J. E. Spingarn in a celebrated lecture on "The New Criticism." This was a manifesto for a completely new program among critics. Under the guidance of Croce he attempted to import into America an unsparing revision of the critical motive, described by his term "creative criticism," in which the appreciative faculties of the critic's trained sensibility would serve as a basis for testing and rationalizing the intuition of the work of art. "The New Criticism" made a clean sweep of existing conventions:

We have done with all the old Rules. . . . We have done with the *genres,* or literary kinds. . . . We have done with the comic, the tragic, the sublime, and an army of vague abstractions of their kind. . . . We have done with theory of style, with metaphor, simile, and all the paraphernalia of Graeco-Roman rhetoric. . . . We have done with all moral judgment of art as art. . . . We have done with the confusion between the drama and the theatre which has permeated dramatic criticism for over half a century. . . . We have done with technique as separate from art. . . . We have done with the history and criticism of poetic themes. . . . We have done with the race, the time, the environment of a poet's work as an element in Criticism. . . . We have done with the "evolution" of literature. . . . We have done with the old rupture between genius and taste.

This provided a much-needed ventilation of the critical classrooms and it served for a time its purpose in affronting the conservative forces. Unfortunately Spingarn never demonstrated by inspection and analysis the technique he desiderated, and his usefulness was confined to stirring up controversy. It was the general limitation of these men that they had little talent for specific analysis. They taught, corrected, and debated, but they gave their readers little practical training in literary methods and craftsmanship.

"Active criticism" of this sort was what Ezra Pound went abroad to learn when he left America in 1907 and began his forty-year career in Italy, England, and France. In the early days of his apprenticeship he stood for a militantly aesthetic standard in literary experimentation, a rescue of art from formulae and discreet abstraction. He was drawn toward critics and editors like Henry James, Remy de Gourmont, W. B. Yeats, T. E. Hulme, and Ford Madox Hueffer, who made less pretense of organizing a philosophic system out of their tastes and appreciations than of refreshing and extending these by constant study of the problems of form and style. He put himself to school, as poet and critic, among the experimental masters of the past and the nonconformist teachers of the present. On an eclectic principle he studied the Latin lyrists, the balladists of Provence and medieval Italy, the Elizabethan translators and classicists, and the Chinese manuscripts he inherited from Ernest Fenollosa, all with the same zest as he gave to the ideas of Gourmont in Paris and Hulme in London. His enthusiasm was so contagious that he himself was soon a recognized leader in innovation and critical pedagogy.

From Gourmont he heard the conversations on style and aesthetic form which were epitomized in an aphorism that gives focal expression to the liaison now set up between the impressionistic principle and the new aesthetic formalism: *"Ériger en lois ses impressions personnelles, c'est le grand effort d'un homme s'il est sincère."* From Hulme he took up a protest against the romantic, the sentimental, the formally vague and subjective, the relative and the abstract, which the author of the fragmentary *Speculations* offered as his prophecy of a revival of classic formalism in modern literature. This principle of form, however, had little to do with the revival of the Aristotelian laws. It gained its chief stimulation from a contemptuous opposition to the degenerate romanticism of late Victorian and contemporary writers. For that reason it made a necessity of experiment, and Pound's career became a continuous participation in unconventionality—in Imagism, in Vorticism, in the aesthetic laboratories of Paris, in Objectivism, in any activity that satisfied his demand for novelty, exploration, and invention. These labors he never gave the appearance of a system—and purposely so, since "systems become tyrannies overnight"; and although he later, and disastrously, worked toward arguments of social, political, and economic reform, his purpose was never primarily moral, except in the sense that aesthetic discipline demands an integrity beyond the formality of practical ethics. His book titles indicate his motives: *Instigations, Irritations, How to Read, The A. B. C. of Reading, Make It New.* All of these were written less to persuade than to irritate and thus to *apply* the authority of creative literature itself. When he defined his "categories" of criticism he opposed the ineffectuality of abstract dogma with the dynamic value of the actual literary text. For him there were five categories of criticism:

(1) Criticism by discussion, extending from mere yatter, logic-chopping, and description of tendencies up to the clearly defined record of procedures and an attempt to formulate more or less general principles. . . . (2) Criticism by translation. . . . (3) Criticism by exercise in the style of a given period. . . . (4) Criticism by music, meaning definitely the setting of a poet's words. . . . This is the most intense form of criticism save: (5) Criticism in new composition.

And "Criticism so far as I have discovered has two functions:"

(1) Theoretically it tries to forerun composition, to serve as gunsight, though there is, I believe, no recorded instance of this foresight having *ever* been of the

slightest use save to actual composers. I mean the man who formulates any forward reach of co-ordinating principle is the man who produces the demonstration. . . . (2) Excernment. The general ordering and weeding out of what has actually been performed. The elimination of repetitions. The work analogous to that which a good hanging committee or curator would perform in a National Gallery or in a biological museum; the ordering of knowledge so that the next man (or generation) can most readily find the live part of it, and waste the least possible time among obsolete issues.

Pound brought criticism back to an active study of texts more directly and unequivocally than impressionism ever aimed to do, and with none of the obstruction by scientific methods that I. A. Richards and his disciples have brought about. His arguments have suffered as much as his style from their explosive purposes; so much so, in fact, that where his later books do not sin by endless reiteration of the familiar clichés of his much-boasted iconoclasm, they become an indistinguishable clutter of classifications that do not classify and distinctions that confuse discrimination. But Pound's work, for all its violence, haphazardness, and shock tactics, or its tragic political consequences, has had the virtues that go with these deliberate offenses: it has been direct, energetic, experimental, and seminal. It has also had a virtue to which academic criticism can rarely pretend: it has been useful to writers. It is in his role as a teacher of writers that Pound's service has been greatest and his importance in the aesthetic thought of our times most decided.

T. S. Eliot shares this distinction, but for very different reasons of temperament and method. In him contemporary criticism again finds an influence reinforced at every point by poetic practice. It is in his ability to suggest a principle by pointing out an example that his short essays show their vitality. In *The Sacred Wood* of 1920 Eliot began his work by defining the defects in modern critical methods—the historical and deterministic leanings of Sainte-Beuve and Taine, the ethical bias of the American schools (especially in More and Babbitt), the facile suggestibility of the impressionists, the rhetorical taste of romanticists like Swinburne and Wyndham, the exaggerated common sense of journalists like Charles Whibley. He found instead his first lessons in the books of Gourmont, whom he called "the critical consciousness of a generation." He set out to bridge the gap between impressionism and reason in critical thought, and his critical program was an attempt to educate the exact and conscientious sensibility (which is as basic to genuine criticism as it is to poetic creation) through discipline in the ideal conditions and formal principles of art, and only then in the ulterior purposes which art may serve. Eliot was temperamentally as much an antiromantic as Hulme, and yet he knew that the classic discipline cannot be obtained in modern art or thought through academic exhumation. "One must be firmly distrustful of accepting Aristotle in a canonical spirit; this is to lose the whole living force of him." It was for this reason that he took Gourmont as a model: "He combined to a remarkable degree sensitiveness, erudition, sense of fact and sense of history, and generalizing power," and this combination of assets served Eliot in his definition of "the perfect critic."

He himself found comparison and the exactly discriminating epithet his two most useful tools in determining the quality of a piece of writing. Though his essays are notable for their aphoristic generalizations, he resisted assuming a doctrine or principle without subjecting it to the empirical proof of his text. With this stress on the necessity of exact textual scrutiny he reproved, especially in his earlier essays where he was still more closely concerned with aesthetic and less with metaphysical problems, the tendencies in modern criticism toward historical explanation, biographical irrelevancies, and the deterministic effects of scientific method or sociological theory. The authors around whom he wrote his best criticism—the Elizabethan dramatists, the metaphysical poets, Dante, Donne, Blake, Baudelaire, Valéry, and Pound— gave those essays on style and form a practical virtue which begins to dissipate as Eliot's criticism has become more philosophically ambitious. His belief in the "isolated superiority" of the artist to practical justification has been modified by his desire to bring the literary object into closer relation with its historical tradition, its moral environment, and its wider human conditions: by his wish, in other words, to explain The Use of Poetry and the Use of Criticism. But he remains one of the most fructifying elements in contemporary literary thought, as anxious as ever to keep criticism close to its specific duties. In one of his essays, on "Experiment in Criticism," he defined the need of a dialectic discipline which will establish the terminology and analytical methods of literary study and thus correct a deficiency in means which still cripples the work of literary students; and in "Religion and Literature," he makes a statement that should be as corrective of existing critical confusions as it serves to indicate the line his own critical career has followed: "The 'greatness' of literature cannot be determined solely by literary standards; though we must remember that whether it is literature or not can be determined only by literary standards."

It was on a basis of the disciplines proposed by Pound and Eliot that aesthetic criticism was rescued from vague and static generalization and stimulated by contact with the processes of the modern sensibility. That contact was lacking in men like Brownell and More, and its absence produced in their minds and tempers an inflexible decorum that did an even greater injustice to their own refinement of taste than it did to the books that fell under their inspection. It was the maintenance of precisely such a contact that now engaged a younger generation of critics. In 1920 The Dial was transformed from its senile condition of reactionary conservatism in Chicago to a new life of literary experimentation in New York, and for a decade it was the chief organ of aesthetic critics in America. With *The Criterion* of London it provided a standard for the careers of *The Hound and Horn, The Symposium, The Kenyon Review, The Sewanee Review,* and *The Hudson Review* that followed. Some of its contributors, like Conrad Aiken, Charles Trueblood, and Cuthbert Wright, adhered to the impressionist manner but keyed it to new effects by their verbal and imaginative skill in poetic analysis. The most brilliant descriptive talent of this kind appeared in Marianne Moore, who showed in her essays the same wit in selecting, discriminating, and combining the effects of an aesthetic object that she manifested in her poems.

Two other members of *The Dial's* circle carried their study of modern texts to a point of masterly exposition: Kenneth Burke by situating a book in its setting of ideas and moral influences—the "quality of mind" reduced to the basic structure and complexity of the writer's imagination; and Edmund Wilson by producing from the book in hand an illumination of the specific experience and environment that produced it. Burke, in fact, has been distinguished among contemporary American critics by the persistence and alertness of his training in ideas. It has made him less effective than many of his colleagues in the handling of the literary item. His practical grasp of stylistic and imaginative properties—in books like *Counter-Statement* (1931), *Permanence and Change* (1935), *Attitudes Toward History* (1937), *The Philosophy of Literary Form* (1941), *A Grammar of Motives* (1945), and *A Rhetoric of Motives* (1950)—is diverted by his larger effort to synthesize the aesthetic with the moral, psychological, political, and "strategic" functions of literature. But he has examined and corrected the method, tactics, and terminology of modern criticism to better effect than any other American writer. His use of scientific and psychological resources has led him to become predominantly a kind of literary phenomenologist, but no one has assessed and indicated the relevance of such resources better than he has, or more systematically.

Edmund Wilson took another direction. He fell heir to the historical method of the Nineteenth Century French critics of the line of Sainte-Beuve, Taine, and Renan. Like these he looked to literature for evidences of the social and moral forces that produced it—for the materials of, as he said, "what literary criticism ought to be—a history of man's ideas and imaginings in the setting of the conditions which have shaped them." Where this procedure has led most modern critics to a deterministic view of art, or to the cruder mechanization of art through sociological and political theory, Wilson kept it critically vigorous by his sensitive reading of the text before him, by a brilliant talent for narrative summary and exposition, and by seeing aesthetic and imaginative developments as something subtler than the social conditions which surround and at times coerce them. Wilson brought the realistic and the aesthetic attitudes into a working alliance. At one point his shift (though a strongly unorthodox one) to social and political sympathies, and his study of Marxist theory and action (*To the Finland Station*, 1940), removed him from his earlier alliance with French and aesthetic influences. But he kept the Marxist principle under alert suspicion. His study of the symbolist tradition in *Axel's Castle* (1931), one of the most valuable books in American criticism in this century, was followed by further volumes of studies—*The Triple Thinkers* (1938), *The Wound and the Bow* (1941)—in which psychological enquiry joined with his earlier aesthetic and social analysis. The result has been a long series of enquiries in which historical, Marxist, Freudian, and personal motives have been defined in a wide range of subjects, and some of the most suggestive essays of our time. This is neither an aesthetic nor an analytical criticism, but a study of literature in its human and cultural values —sometimes boldly conjectural, often inviting strenuous resistance, but always vivid, dramatically presented, focal, and stimulating, one of the most vigorous records of the experience of literature that the period has produced.

A different approach to poetic and literary problems appeared in Yvor Winters. He carried into his criticism the same severe scrutiny of verbal and formal structures that made his verse notable as an indication of changing motives and disciplines in poetry. His effort to analyze the form of modern poetry, to define its processes and find a terminology for them, to rescue both poetry and prose from the disorder of aimless experimentation, led him toward principles of a formal and conservative type. He was influenced at one point by the neoclassical arguments of Irving Babbitt; at another by classical and French models; at another by a vigorous interest of his own in the moral elements that have shaped or confused the European and American traditions in literature—thus his trenchant assessments of American individualism, "obscurantism," and modernism in such books as *Maule's Curse* (1938) and *The Anatomy of Nonsense* (1943). In *Primitivism and Decadence* (1936), as again in his collected papers in *In Defense of Reason* (1947), he provided one of the most austere and fruitful statements of the classical position, with its emphasis on intellectual and moral relevances in art, that has been written in the present century, or that has appeared in the recent criticism of any country. His work joins tradition with an intensely reverent personal conception of art in an argument that is seminal, corrective, assertively personal, yet formally and ethically ordered.

A similar sense of traditional disciplines, deliberately called "reactionary," has worked in the criticism of Allen Tate; but in him these disciplines took on wider cultural and historical reference, with specific application to the situation in modern society and morality as measured by the classic standard in Southern life. Here again the obligation of poetic analysis and formal method preceded the use of historical or moral arguments. By combining these issues he made his volume of *Reactionary Essays* (1936) an important demonstration of the problems a critic faces when he attempts to harmonize modern innovation or experiment with the formal order implicit in tradition; and the same joining of standards reappeared in his *Reason in Madness* (1941) and *On the Limits of Poetry* (1948). The principle at work is a principle of wholeness and integration, and while it has sometimes emphasized special phenomena in art—the idea of "tension," for instance—it has also animated a larger view of literature and culture which has yielded some of the liveliest attacks on utilitarian, deterministic, and philosophic irrelevances in the critical controversy of the past two decades. Again this is a criticism basically moral, philosophic, in its findings, but it has kept these findings relevant to literature through the vigor of a poetic sensibility and an acute intellectual energy.

The special distinction of R. P. Blackmur's criticism, on the other hand, lies in its elucidation of verbal and stylistic properties as clues to the quality of thought and imagination. No one except William Empson in England has carried this method to greater lengths of meticulous discrimination, and no one has shown greater patience or curiosity in linguistic, structural, and imaginative analysis. It is a method difficult to raise from the descriptive to the synthetic or judicial level, and Blackmur has not always arrived at this coördination. But the effort, whatever its success, would be worthless without the exacting scrutiny of technique that he has made in *The Double Agent* (1935), *The Expense of Greatness* (1940), and many succeeding essays. If his criticism remains indecisive at many points it is largely because he has realized so fully the complexity of the problems which an exact analysis of the text can impose on a critic.

It is in fact the thoroughness of their stylistic investigations, their rigorous study of the words, patterns, and structures of the literary object, that has not only removed the best of these aesthetic students from the irresponsible conjurings of the impressionists, but has made them far too conscious of all that is implied and involved in the creative process to bring it into easy alignment with social or moral formulae. In them the impressionist procedure is at once rationalized and corrected, and more utilitarian critical methods are revealed in their routine of inflexible prejudice and ineptitude.

V

The apparent hostility among the new critical schools after 1918 was to some extent deceptive. Beneath it there existed a secret treaty between realists and aesthetes, a recognition of the common enemy of reaction, and an implicit alliance of the kind that may be detected beneath the conflicting appearances of naturalism, impressionism, and symbolism in the French schools of the late Nineteenth Century. They joined in accepting the heritage of romanticism, however they may have varied in their use of it. They assumed the unity of man and nature on a monistic principle, and the common belief that this unity is to be realized initially through sensory and intuitive agencies. They differed chiefly in their notions of the means—the instruments of aesthetic experience and expression—by which the work of art conveys this unity. They were divided as craftsmen and temperaments, but not as believers, and the same may be said of the critics who adhered to them as prophets or defenders.

There was also a general agreement among them concerning the subject matter of art—its freedom from, its value in, moral purpose; and when a sudden reaction struck from another quarter, it threw them into an alliance more strenuous than their two decades of public debate and divergence had prepared them for. The enemy was held in check for a number of years, but he was not inactive. Books like *Democracy and Leadership, Rousseau and Romanticism,* and the eleven volumes of *Shelburne Essays* had been appearing for twenty years. Mencken had fulminated against the "gloomy humors" of Paul Elmer More for several decades, and Babbitt had raised the dust of controversy in both academic and public circles. But critics as a whole had relegated such vexations to the dustbins of the Victorian Age. They were as certain of their emancipation as they were that the day was over for reviving beliefs about the dualism of man and nature, of good and evil, of reason and instinct, or convictions about the distance that lies between the purely natural order of experience and the art which results only when prudence selects, judgment shapes, and the moral will gives ethical value to that experience. Those beliefs were implicit in the American moral tradition and a fear of their eruption was implied by Lewisohn's anthology of 1918, *A Book of Modern Criticism,* which came as a warning against the slumbering dragon of reaction; by Spingarn's manifesto of a decade earlier; and by a critical symposium printed in *The New Republic* in 1921, which formed a fresh defense of impressionism and liberal rebellion for the younger critics of the hour.

Meanwhile the reaction was organizing its forces. Its name, "Humanism," had already been accepted from Babbitt's teachings. It had representatives all over the country, chiefly on college faculties: Prosser Hall Frye promoted the cause in Nebraska; Norman Foerster in North Carolina; Robert Shafer in Ohio; a considerable phalanx in the strongholds of New England; and Stuart Sherman in Illinois before he finally confessed himself a renegade from the ranks, became a literary editor in New York, turned liberal, and lost the wit and geniality he had contributed to his first allegiance. The acknowledged leaders of these men remained More and Babbitt, who wrote the program and creed by which all of them, with due allowance for personal errors and deviations, swore.

It was a creed which defined one central enemy, the Romantic Movement; one chief source of grievance, Rousseau; one main purpose, the integration of literary criticism with ethical; and one chief means of deciding the quality of a work of literature, its validity in moral qualities. Inheriting the Puritan austerity of the early American fathers, it had skirted the skepticism of Emerson and his generation in such a way as to remain aloof from commitment to religious faith and dogma. It preferred the discipline not of theological beliefs but of the human norm, and it looked for salvation not by sacrificing personal energy to an acceptance of supernatural authority, but by enhancing its sense of human values through restraint and self-control. Art thus became a means of judging man's nature chiefly in the degree to which it expressed this discipline.

More published his first book of essays in 1904 and there, in an essay on "Criticism," he lamented in Nineteenth Century critics like Arnold not "any intrinsic want of efficiency in the critical spirit, not . . . any want of moral earnestness," but the fact that "these men were lacking in another direction: they missed a philosophy which could bind together their moral and their aesthetic sense, a positive principle besides the negative force of ridicule and irony; and missing this, they left criticism more easily subject to a one-sided and dangerous development"—that which promoted the modern heresies of "naturalism," impressionism, subjectivity, and moral anarchy. For him literary criticism was "the specific exercise of a faculty which works in many directions. All scholars, whether they deal with history or sociology or philosophy or language or, in the narrower use of the word, literature, are servants of the critical spirit, in so far as they transmit and interpret and mold the sum of experience from man to man and generation to generation."

The Humanist ethic gave More his binding principle. At first his sense of art and the artist's personality was vivid and penetrating, but as the *Shelburne Essays* mounted, his responsibility to "the sum of experience" subdued it more and more, until finally he turned away from literature and explored the historical background of modern humanism itself, attempting to integrate the Christian idea with the humanistic principle of Plato and the Greeks.

What he brought to American philosophic and ethical thought was one matter; what he contributed to criticism was another. He supplied a model of erudition and high seriousness that admitted no suspicion of purely aesthetic or vaguely cultural leanings. But unfortunately this model came to shed less and less light on either the contemporary world around him or the literature it produced; it stiffened his sensibilities as well as his integrity; and while he never erred through the pedantry of his younger colleagues, his confinement of acceptable art in the tight circle of his moral prejudice caused him to reject the very art that would really have invigorated and humanized his doctrines. He believed that "literature divorced from life is an empty pursuit," but his conceptions of literature's dependence on experience became as arbitrary and as remote from the moral struggles of his contemporaries as his sense of the "meaning of life" stopped short of the understanding that kindles in imagination or language the fire of an overwhelming conviction. His belief that such conviction had failed to appear in modern literature may have been a reflection of its failure in his own thought.

Irving Babbitt was always a keener controversialist than More, and to him fell the more polemical role in the Humanist revival that broke out late in the 'twenties. He was less a critic of books than of ideas, and the ideas he attacked inevitably led him back to the chief source of his vexations, Rousseau. He assayed creative works rarely, but made an exhaustive study of the influences and cultural circumstances that produce them—educational systems, political movements, religious bodies, academic standards, classical traditions, ethical beliefs. The modern condition of these he invariably deplored as anarchic and decadent. He accepted in his early years the classic ideal, and declared himself the enemy of all that opposed it under the romantic canon: democratic individualism, freedom of press and speech, free aesthetic experiment, any vestige of the eccentric or idiosyncratic in art or conduct. He formulated the tenets to which the younger Humanists subscribed—the ideals of wholeness, proportion, and the human norm; the constants of tradition as against the limiting "specialism" of the time-spirit; the discipline of reason, of imagination when controlled by reason, and of the virtues of restraint and humility which are the final evidence of the ethical dignity of man.

Babbitt's work had its aesthetic motive, and his prescription of virtues was intended to apply to criticism an instrument of discipline in the disordered world of modern culture. When he stated his rule for critics he made that much clear: the critic must "rate creation with reference to some standard set both above his own temperament and that of the creator. . . . He will begin to have taste only when he refers the creative expression and his impression of it to some standard that is set above both." This is a worthy precept for any kind of rational judgment, and Babbitt had the worthy intention of correcting by means of it the sterility and solipsism of critical license. But the validity of such a rule depends wholly on its grasp of the two terms it employs: the integrity of the "impression" gained from a literary investigation, and the authority of the "standard" to which it is referred. Babbitt's failure in sensibility was extreme: in his last book, *On Being Creative* (1931), he equated modern writers like Dreiser, Joyce, and Dos Passos with no effort at discriminating their qualities, and the standard he defined in Greek and Latin masterpieces proved so inert that he was incapable of sympathizing with, and therefore understanding, any but a few isolated or academic imitations of it in the past eight centuries. Babbitt's distinguished mind was a prey to this mechanistic and pharisaical inflexibility of doctrine; his critical limitations (as opposed to his scholarly and historical eminence) have been well pointed out by Yvor Winters: "His analysis of literary principles appears to me to be gravely vitiated by an almost complete ignorance of the manner in which the moral intelligence actually gets into poetry."

The battle over Humanism was unfortunately conducted in a mood too full of heat, rancor, and confusion to represent the issues involved fairly. Thus it appeared as a last stand of the Puritan tradition against the enemies that had multiplied around it. What it might have achieved in correcting the aimlessness and vulgarity of the more irresponsible talents around it was as much nullified by its own intolerance and imperviousness as by the violence of the forces it stirred to attack. There were looseness, irresponsibility, and crudity to reprove, and Humanism left certain good effects behind, even though they bore little resemblance to what Babbitt and More demanded. But it never attacked its problems squarely. It aimed to correct and guide the conflicts of the modern consciousness, but it succeeded chiefly in ignoring them. It reduced imaginative and creative processes to a mechanical routine. It missed the wider and profounder sympathy of a genuinely religious spirit and at the same time failed to grasp the struggles of the skeptical spirit in seeking a basis of values in experience. Thus it fell ambiguously between the rigor of realistic experience that has produced the valid thought of naturalist writers, and the genuine metaphysical convictions of Frenchmen like Gilson and Maritain, whose interpretations of Thomistic aesthetic doctrine were not for some time to encourage a similar activity in America. The controversy of 1929 and 1930 centered in serious issues, but these were reduced to the obtuse didacticism of the "genteel tradition," the pedantry and intolerance of an academic principle. When it died down it left the critical situation much as it found it, and another type of moral argument—that of the social critics and proletarian revolutionaries—took up the attack on such irresponsibility as was held to reside in realist and aesthetic liberalism. A new alignment of critics soon appeared, one closer to the specific conditions of modern writing and therefore more vigorous in its appeal to the public and in its grasp of the problems of imaginative literature.

VI

It was a more realistic attack that now rose against the free critical traffic of the 1920's. That decade ended under darker clouds than Humanism had conjured up. When the economic disaster of 1929 struck, it dropped its bolts on one of the most productive literary periods America had seen. The high hopes and privileges of the liberal generation were bent at a blow, and prophets of disaster—like Dreiser and Robinson—who had spoken in the hour of general illusion, found a new honor. From Paris the aesthetes returned with shorn incomes and roughly opened eyes, finding their historian in Malcolm Cowley, whose *Exile's Return* described their awakening from the "religion of art" to the realities of making a living in a jobless world. The confidences of 1912 or 1918 sank as swiftly as the graphlines on stockbrokers' charts. The realist and aesthetic critics found their claims diminishing under harsh dispute, and deserters from their ranks began to take up the study and defense of economic arguments. Humanism had reacted chiefly against the claims of naturalism, but the awakened sense of social responsibility in reformers took aesthetic and liberal doctrines as its chief object of attack. It was by this alignment of creeds that the major critical issues of the 1930's were defined.

The necessity in criticism of a social principle was not a new argument. Whitman, Howells, and Adams were three of its early prophets, and the liberals of Bourne's generation made it a dominant tenet in their program of critical realism. These pioneers, however, submitted too easily to the malady of the humanitarian ideal to satisfy their inheritors. They accepted the grandeurs of the American future in too mystical a spirit, compromising too easily with the hopes of rugged individualism or democratic culture, and holding aloof from commitment to more positive beliefs. These required in their simplest essentials an attack on the capitalistic monopoly and competitive license which Howells, whatever sense he may have had of the ethical defects of American society, considered the proper complement of democratic enterprise. The Nineteenth Century reformers most acceptable to the American way of life had been acceptable because they left their revolutionary counsels at a mid-point of compromise, and stopped short of imposing the technical and forcible reforms of economic socialism. Some books were written, however, outside the literary field which forecast those reforms in highly trenchant language, and these in time were to influence critics of sociological sympathies more than the manuals of their own craft. The most important of these was Thorstein Veblen's *Theory of the Leisure Class*. More recently American criticism itself had turned toward economic premises: Upton Sinclair published *The Industrial Republic* as early as 1907 and *Mammonart* as late as 1925; and his angle of literary interpretation was turned to more aesthetic uses by V. F. Calverton in his "sociological criticism of literature," *The Newer Spirit* (1925), and in *The Liberation of American Literature* (1930). Both these men were urging a social principle while their recent rivals were still absorbed by now-repudiated liberal or aesthetic allegiances. But the shortcomings now commonly charged against them on dialectic grounds were fully as obvious on aesthetic grounds when their books were first published. They made literature a function of the social order without having arrived at a realistic articulation of the creative imagination with social necessities, and at the same time without a technique of rationalization which could cope successfully with the subtleties of aesthetic, as opposed to economic, experience. Calverton, though he was later to express a healthy dislike of the mechanistic routine of the average Marxist interpretation, accepted too smoothly the deterministic procedure of Taine. The result is that his *Liberation of American*

Literature is chiefly interesting for the lengths to which it pushed a prejudice and a method.

The social line of criticism since 1930 has profited by a situation much more conducive to serious discipline than existed before. For one thing, controversy is sufficiently active to offset the extravagances of party politics. For another, the defenders of the aesthetic approach to literature have stirred themselves to a more severe line of reasoning in order to match the subtleties of the materialist dialectic, and thus benefited their own cause while challenging the extremes of its opposite. Again, fresh growths of socially motivated literature have revealed the pitfalls of propaganda so obviously as to provide a caution to critics who have defended this function in art too glibly. And finally, the profound economic distress of the times has aroused a general agreement on the moral ends of literature, spurred a critical examination of them, and established much more forcefully than formerly the necessity of seeing what constitutes the truth and integrity of a work of literature before it can produce its desired effects in social or moral regeneration. Obviously these benefits have been accompanied by corresponding evils. Critical activity has been distracted by false simplifications and partisan bias. Its magazines have substituted personal abuse for sober thinking, and eloquence for logic. There has flourished a loose contempt for whatever is out of momentary fashion, and a consequent discarding of many literary works that might enlighten the dispute (or even support the cause of their condemners) to far greater advantage than the shoddy tracts that are often seized upon as profoundly significant. And there has risen so slovenly and uncritical a warfare of terms and premises —debates over the "function" of art, "utility," "ideology," "mass consciousness," "bourgeois" versus "proletarian," and "autonomy" versus "propaganda" —that the mere communication of intelligence about these causes, lacking as it does the very discipline of logic or dialectic that is the boasted advantage of their exponents, has lapsed into dilemma and confusion.

The implications of this problem are too complex to admit of easy statement. But the responsibilities of criticism remain at the same time too emphatic and unmistakable to allow the term to be applied to nine-tenths of what has passed by that title in the journals and newspapers of the past eighteen years. (This is equally true, however, of other kinds of apologetic; it would be unjust to make the reservation against the social critic any severer than against the common types of religious or political.) Yet the work of a number of writers in this field shows exceptional distinction, either in historical analysis or in a careful discrimination of issues. On the historical side the best statements appear in the last chapter of Wilson's *Axel's Castle*, where the divergence of art and life, pure poetry and social realism, in modern literature is described; in Cowley's *Exile's Return*, where the same division in the lives of present-day artists and critics is defined; and in such literary memoirs as

Granville Hicks's *John Reed* or Joseph Freeman's *An American Testament,* which form sequels to the sort of biographical study of literary problems that Bourne wrote in his *Literary Radical.* The most ambitious attempt to bring the literary history of America into alignment with the Marxist tenets was that of Granville Hicks's *Great Tradition* (1933), but its coherence of argument and graphic distinction are soon rendered suspect by the facility with which it accepts or dismisses the writers of American literature according to the degree to which they satisfy his highly simplified and crudely applied proposition on the interdependence of literature and economic law. It is their talent in a more closely reasoned, more broadly and soundly perceptive kind of interpretation that has made the essays of Phillip Rahv, William Phillips, Dwight Macdonald, and their contributors to *Partisan Review* and *Politics* a notable improvement over those of Hicks, Michael Gold, Joshua Kunitz, and other onetime writers in *The New Masses, Mainstream,* and other official Marxist (meaning, eventually, official Stalinist) organs. Though Hicks and a number of other spokesmen resigned from official Marxism around 1939 or 1940, their successors have continued in the prescribed line of Marxist literary doctrine; but it remained for journals like *Partisan Review* and *Politics* to correct the abuses of "leftist" and socialist interpretation and to produce the keenest radical journalism that has yet appeared in the United States.

Kenneth Burke's interest in social relevances in literature reinforced that distinction. So did the contributions to political-literary controversy that came from the novelist James T. Farrell in *A Note on Literary Criticism* (1936), *The League of Frightened Philistines* (1945), *The Fate of Writing in America* (1946), and *Literature and Morality* (1947). These essays were prompted by the flagrant lapses in valid reasoning among social critics, but equally by the regressive nationalism, commercialism, and sentimental special pleading that succeeded to Marxist polemic in the 1940's. They formed a challenging reproof to offenders and a sketch of necessary corrections for extremists of both types. They served further to remind the serious public that an escape from the mechanical routine of the average social criticism has come from men who have known, by their own creative practice, the creative task too intimately to permit it to be humbled by propagandist or official assignments. Thus is the value of the poetic criticism of Robert Penn Warren, Austin Warren, Louise Bogan, Horace Gregory, Delmore Schwartz, John Berryman, Randall Jarrell, Cleanth Brooks, Rolfe Humphries, and (now that he has become an American) W. H. Auden; or the criticism of fiction by Robert Penn Warren, Katherine Anne Porter, William Troy, Lionel Trilling, Diana Trilling, Alfred Kazin, Richard Chase, Mark Schorer, Albert Guérard, Jr., Irving Howe, Robert Gorham Davis, and Isaac Rosenfeld.

The firmer activity in force among these critics has been motivated by such purposes as were announced fifteen years ago by Phillips and Rahv:

Unfortunately many misguided enthusiasts of revolution, effacing their own experience, take for their subject-matter the public philosophy as such, or attempt to adorn with rhetorical language conventionalized patterns of feeling and action. What they don't see is that these patterns are, in the final analysis, just as impersonal as the philosophy itself. . . . If there is to be an ever-fresh balance between the accent of the poet and the attitude he shares with other people, he must understand the connection between what is *real* to him as an individual and what is *real* to him as a partisan of some given philosophy.

A warning from official quarters came from Joseph Freeman in 1935, in his introduction to the anthology *Proletarian Literature in the United States*. Admitting the immaturity of a great share of the writing and criticism of his colleagues, he indicated how much caution and discipline is required there:

No party resolution, no government decree, can produce art, or transform an agitator into a poet. A party card does not automatically endow a communist with artistic genius. Whatever it is that makes an artist, as distinguished from a scientist or man of action, it is something beyond the power of anyone to produce deliberately. But once the artist is there, once there is the man with the specific sensibility, the mind, the emotions, the images, the gift of language which make the creative writer, he is not a creature in a vacuum.

And Newton Arvin, who during a quarter century has remained one of the steadiest and most mature inspectors of the social standard in literature, gave in 1931 an early hint toward the correction of abuses at both extremes of aesthetic autonomy and political doctrine:

The case for a proletarian literature is not always cogently stated or wisely defended—any more than the case against it. One must insist that to adopt the proletarian point of view does not mean, for a novelist, to deal solely with economic conflicts, or, for a poet, to be a voice only for protest, momentous as both these things are and *implicit* as they are bound to be. That a truly proletarian literature, for us in America at least, would mean a break with the mood of self-pity, with the cult of romantic separatism, with sickly subjectivism and melodramatic misanthropy —this much is almost too clear to deserve stating. But the duty of the critic is certainly not to file an order for a particular sort of fiction or poetry before the event; his duty is to clarify, as best he can, the circumstances in which fiction and poetry must take shape, and to rationalize their manifestations when they arrive. For the moment, the important thing is that American criticism should define its position: in the midst of so much confusion, so much wasted effort, so much hesitation, this will itself be an advance.

These statements, while perhaps embarrassingly elementary, indicated the uneasy conscience that existed among the critics of the Left during the 1930's. By the time that decade came to an end, the high tide of Marxist and political influence in criticism had spent itself and begun to recede. Some critics of its excesses—Max Eastman, or Farrell, or the editors of *Partisan Review* and

Politics, or Edmund Wilson in his essay "Marxism and Literature," to name men of differing standards—had learned the dangers of that excess through their close participation in the radical political movement. They had found, all of them, a genuine schooling in political and social thought through their alliance, but they had also discovered the discomforts, didacticism, and strait-jacketing mentality under which both literature and criticism labor when subjected to party or political pressures. The outbreak of war in 1939 and the momentary alliance of Marxism with Nazism counted for a good deal in the recoil from official Marxist pressure which many partisans and sympathizers showed around 1940. The ensuing decade of the 1940's was by no means to make the critical problem simpler, but its political confinement was broken; the pressure of a revived nationalism, Americanism, or propagandist sentiment presented a new difficulty on the popular level of writing and journalism. But the war years also showed, unexpectedly, a revival of faith in aesthetic and moral standards. The revival and rediscovery of Henry James was one sign of it. So was the work done by a new series of critical journals—*The Kenyon Review* under John Crowe Ransom, the now independent and anti-Stalinist *Partisan Review,* the renovated *Sewanee* under Tate's editorship, or more independent ventures like *Accent* in Illinois, the surrealist *View* in New York, the classical-aesthetic *Hudson Review.* What survived of Marxist argument became more and more confined to the waning *New Masses,* to its affiliate *Mainstream,* to the scholarly quarterly *Science and Society,* and to the official Communist columns of *The Daily Worker.* The radical "red decade" of the thirties had recorded in its agitations and controversies a profound conflict in modern society and politics. Criticism played a part in this, but in the 'forties it was to reassert and reclaim its more specific and proper province. A revival of aesthetic, but also of moral and philosophic, claims appeared among both writers and critics, and a new decade of revision and critical discipline began.

VII

By the time the contemporary movement in American literature arrived at the fifth decade of the present century, criticism was able to take stock of a progress that had enriched its work and methods in a number of essential ways. The techniques of historical research had matured both through gains in scholarship and through philosophic enquiry. Aesthetic attitudes had outgrown their earlier preciosity or immaturity and become sharpened by analysis and a disciplined discrimination. The social, economic, and political elements of art had been redefined through the controversies and pressures of modern social thought. Certain kinds of scientific technique and theory—those of psychology, psychoanalysis, of philological and semantic research, of logical analysis, of biography, of the economic interpretation of history—had contributed both suggestion and new materials to critical method. The competition and interaction of these methods among critics had spurred literary students to an energy of controversy, a liveliness of dispute, that made the profession of criticism one of the most challenging in the entire field of literature.

There can be little question that the criticism of the past quarter century will be recorded in American literature as one of its liveliest chapters. The critic of literature has joined his forces with those of the creative writer himself. It is scarcely disputable that it has been the poets and novelists of our time who have shown the most vigorous *critical* sensibility, who have written the most forceful works of an imaginative order. A condition true of France, England, and Germany has become true also of the United States. The function of literary criticism has been defined as the analysis and evaluation of the forces already at work in a living literature, rather than to provide the impetus for new work; but this is a conception no longer as tenable as it used to be. A sound criticism does both these things. The existence of an active, virtually an organized, criticism during the past two or three decades—a criticism in working harmony with the best of contemporary creation—is possibly the most convincing evidence of the special character and importance of American literature at the present stage of its history.

While the writers of this criticism, like their fellow workers in fiction, poetry, and drama, have continued in several distinct lines of intention and method that had already declared themselves as long ago as 1925, they were aware, by 1950, of a change in their status and responsibility. They had not abandoned the idea of the "new"—of aesthetic innovation, of moral and intellectual revision, of social and political enquiry—so insistent in the earlier flush of literary radicalism or innovation; but a decade like the 1940's, however arresting or discouraging to original effort, was bound to impress its crisis upon the minds of both writers and critics and to impose that crisis in terms of the morality, the responsibility, the human and active values, of their craft. Their problem best defined itself in the fact that critics rediscovered that their business was that of a craft or an art; that only by maintaining its rights and existence as such could it hope to survive for higher or ulterior ends.

The pioneers of modern American criticism had by 1940 disappeared or turned to concerns other than those of literature. Babbitt and More died in the 1930's; Santayana turned to his later philosophical summations and personal records; Mencken to philological research and to reminiscence; Van Wyck Brooks to history and conservatism; Eliot himself, in spite of his continuing work in poetry and a persistent interest in craftsmanship, to an increasing program of religious and cultural enquiry—*The Idea of a Christian Society, The Classics and the Man of Letters, The Man of Letters and the*

Future of Europe, Notes towards the Definition of Culture. While a new generation of American scholars—F. O. Matthiessen, Alfred Kazin, Newton
Arvin, Perry Miller, Lionel Trilling, Mark Van Doren, Allen Tate, Harry
Levin, F. W. Dupee—inspected the bases of American experience and its
bearing on cultural or literary achievement with a view to correcting or extending the arguments of their predecessors, Van Wyck Brooks, V. L. Parring-
ton, Randolph Bourne, Constance Rourke, and Edmund Wilson, the
specialist in criticism found himself facing the need for a new program of
purpose and strategy. The result was not a single program, of course, but a
series of programs whose radical divergences did not preclude a certain community of intention and effort.

The present situation in American criticism, at the mid-point of the Twentieth Century, may be described as falling into four or five fairly distinct lines
of activity. (1) There is a continuing investigation of the social and cultural
bases of literature, sequel to the critical realism that began around 1912 and
continued through the political and economic controversies of the 'thirties, but
which now attempts to bring such realism to terms with aesthetic and moral
claims: thus the work of men like Lionel Trilling and F. O. Matthiessen, of
Edmund Wilson in his later books, of Philip Rahv, William Phillips, William
Barrett, Eliseo Vivas, Alfred Kazin. (2) There is likewise a continuation of
the aesthetic line initiated by Pound and carried on by Eliot, now bent more
systematically than ever toward integrating the study of craftsmanship with
metaphysical or philosophic elements in literature: thus John Crowe Ransom
with his demand for an "ontological" criticism, Allen Tate with his principle
of "reaction" toward the unity of the moral tradition in art, Yvor Winters with
his emphasis on an order based on the responsibility of moral integrity and
reason, Austin Warren with another emphasis on the idea of "order," Cleanth
Brooks with his studies of the interaction of tradition and irony in modern
poetry. (3) The discipline of formal and textual analysis also continues, now
rejecting the empirical methods of I. A. Richards or the scientific claims of
logical, semantic, or pragmatic positivists in order to recover from classical
doctrine, from Aristotle, or from formal philosophy an approach of wider
range, eclectic choice, but aesthetic wholeness as a corrective to monistic
emphasis and as a source of values: thus the work of Kenneth Burke, of
Blackmur in certain of his recent undertakings, and of R. S. Crane and his
Chicago colleagues. (4) This discipline has an ally in a renewed effort to
apply criticism to the practical business of education by revising the teaching
of poetry and prose through making the given text an organism of craft and
values: thus Burke throughout his essays, Yvor Winters in his analysis of
styles and poetic forms, the textbooks of Cleanth Brooks and Robert Penn
Warren, the program of Ransom and his disciples, of Crane and his group,
and of the conferences, seminars, and projects that have brought criticism

more actively into the American college—Harvard, Chicago, Princeton, Stanford, Columbia, Yale, Iowa, Kenyon, Minnesota, Bennington—than was ever the case in its earlier history. (5) There is, further, the work of critics who are attempting to make viable in literary study the findings in related fields of enquiry—psychology, anthropology, semantics, history—with their disclosure of ethnic, mythic, and ritualistic elements that operate in art: thus the enquiries stimulated by scholars or theorists like Fraser, Freud, Rivers, Harrison, Jung, Spengler, and Malinowski, and carried into criticism by Americans like Burke, Wilson, Blackmur, W. H. Auden, Richard Chase, Stanley Edgar Hyman, Suzanne Langer, Joseph Campbell, Frederick Hoffman. And against these specialists in method there must be counted the students who aim to restore a broader program of human and realistic values to the examination of literature in order to correct the specialization of aesthetic, technical, and archetypal approaches: thus the defenders of a revived historical and humanistic view of literature—Harry Levin, Eric Bentley, Robert Gorham Davis, David Daiches, Alfred Kazin.

To name these phases of recent American criticism is, of course, to arrive at little more than rough approximations of the critical programs and positions now visible on the scene. To name exponents of them, as has been done above, is to suggest alliances of purpose where none may exist, or a simplicity of purpose and method which is unjustified. The critics named here are frequently at radical odds with one another in the specific intention and results of their work; a charting of their activity must allow for the injustice of suggesting a greater unity of motive, a simpler harmony of effort, than has actually been arrived at. Yet the programs here indicated are at work in American criticism today, and must account for the stimulating forces that compete in its advancement.

Also at work are certain fundamental problems that remain basic to the modern critic's task. The correction of the romantic and idealistic excesses of the native American tradition is one of them. Another is the correction of that "dissociation of sensibility" which Eliot defined thirty years ago as a radical liability of the modern intelligence as it expresses itself in art, and which, by his advocacy of the aesthetic and moral unity of literature, he followed Henry James in resisting. It remains today as essential a problem in the determination of values as it was when Eliot carried it forward out of the work of James, Gourmont, and Hulme, and gave it to his disciples as a basic responsibility of their task. A third concern of the critic is his resistance to the mechanistic and deterministic conceptions of art that descended to the Twentieth Century from the Nineteenth. Once such conceptions were historical or biological in origin; later they became economic, political, Marxist; later still they became psychological—Freudian, Jungian, Gestalt; more recently they have become anthropological, ethnic, and racial. Under whatever tenet, they have had the effect of forcing upon literature causal or conditioning references which tend ultimately to deny or reduce its aesthetic existence, and thus to impose on the critic the duty of recovering that existence in terms of its necessity, even its autonomy, as art. There can no longer be said to exist, as among earlier aesthetic or impressionist schools, any serious desire to make art or literature an isolated phenomenon, an absolute end in itself, a completely self-justifying or self-sustaining mode of experience; but there does persist, and now more seriously than ever, a passion to show art as possessing an integrity of its own, its own wholeness of existence and experience, a superiority to use and practical relevance. And this means that criticism today demands an aesthetic not arrived at by simplifying art through abstracting it from life but based on a relevance of art to life so continuous and inclusive as to make art the one valid means that remains to us of doing justice to the wholeness of experience and history. Thus the word *aesthetic* has come to imply a function, a responsibility, an inescapable commitment in the critic, that it never had in its earlier and more facile uses.

Perhaps no earlier space of fifty years has seen the conflict of so many critical schools as the half century which has been sketched here. America has felt the force and agitation of all of them, from those that have looked on art as no longer "even by implication a device for improving the mind" to those that recognize neither the artist nor the critic except in the role of moralist and reformer. This outline of developments has necessarily simplified the ideas of the critics it has discussed. It has barely suggested the problems in modern life and thought that have made their difficulties great. But it has attempted to trace a line of activity that brings us to the present moment, and even if it does little to solve the perplexities or answer the questions of those who go to criticism for guidance and advice, it may show why such perplexities exist; why, in fact, they exist in the critic himself and give his work, if he is faithful to the art and the age around him, its special importance in our time.

The title of critic is no longer allowed to the mere sampler of books, the enthusiast for art, the adventurer among masterpieces. Neither is it permitted to the custodian of academic convention, the official moralist, the protector of vested interests. A few men have written beautiful prose or forceful polemic in these roles, but real criticism comes much harder than that. It ranks next to art itself in the insight it commands into the intellectual and spiritual problems of an age and of humanity. It studies the most intense and subtle forms which those problems assume—the forms of literature. Unless the critic realizes that he is dealing with such problems in their fullest complexity, their most intense and vital focus of meaning, he is not likely to hold the respect of the serious reader or the serious artist, or to make a contribution to the intelligence of his contemporaries.

The difficulty with a great share of modern criticism is that it decides these problems long before it understands what literature makes of them. It looks for them in the shape of systematic argument, of practical statements of emotion and belief, of useful morality, applicable wisdom, or formulated conclusions. No definition of art was ever worth listening to that claimed for it no purpose but the rendering of the subtleties and conditions of human experience in such terms. That, however, is what many critics and readers continue to demand of it, and that is why they defeat their purposes as students of literature and do so little to advance the value of art, the intelligence of society, or even the causes they claim to defend.

The best contemporary critics, in America or elsewhere, have won their first distinction by refusing to be complacent, discreet, official, or easy to accept. Such virtues afflicted their calling when Poe, Whitman, and Henry James began to disturb the scene; whenever they regain prestige, criticism falls into pedantry, loses touch with art, lapses into abstract formulation or inert theory. Occasionally they threaten to return, but that danger is no longer so likely. Another has taken its place: the danger of making criticism, as well as art, the agent of propaganda, public morality, mass prejudice, or regimented opinion. When that kind of coercion succeeds, the critic falls into fully as great an impotence as when he submits to academic pedantry or polite discretion. However noble his cause, his claim to the title of critic is fully as spurious. He may express a rightful contempt of academic routine or the irresponsibilities of "impressionism" and "liberalism," but he may merely be shirking his own responsibility when he does so, and he is likely to have little of value to say about literature. Criticism has many obligations—to morality, to science, to philosophy, to society—but its one certain assurance of failure comes when it prefers these obligations to its first and primary duty—its contact with a living and active literature and with the forces in experience and the human personality that make such a literature possible.

We have had in our time a number of descriptions of the "perfect critic." If perfection is wanted or is to be kept in view as a possible goal, the simplest rule for it probably takes the form of requiring in the critic everything in the way of sensitiveness and perception, even of verbal skill, that the artist himself possesses. But the critic, instead of expressing his intelligence, explains it; instead of realizing it under the conditions of an art, he defines, examines, and justifies it by the laws of reason; instead of writing poetry or fiction, he decides why and how others have written them, and how successfully. It is only when he has made that decision to the fullest extent of his sensibility and intelligence that the critic can use his findings effectively and make his contribution to the living body of literature.

The American critic, arriving at the middle of the Twentieth Century, has as little right as ever to rest in pride or complacency, but he may at least take stock of an improvement in his status and office. He has succeeded in making criticism an active part of contemporary literature and culture. He may turn for support to a number of his fellow citizens—Henry James the first among them—who have not only assured him that his work is worth doing but have done a good deal to show him how it can be carried out. He lacks none of the conditions and challenges that are needed to keep his faculties alert, his equipment vigorous, and his purpose serious. He has made a tradition and defined a function for himself in the course of a hundred years which it has become his unmistakable duty to defend, to justify, and to keep alive. His work has not become easy. It has, however, become inescapable.

PART I

Situation and Prospectus

HENRY JAMES
Criticism
[1891]

IF LITERARY criticism may be said to flourish among us at all, it certainly flourishes immensely, for it flows through the periodical press like a river that has burst its dikes. The quantity of it is prodigious, and it is a commodity of which, however the demand may be estimated, the supply will be sure to be in any supposable extremity the last thing to fail us. What strikes the observer above all, in such an affluence, is the unexpected proportion the discourse uttered bears to the objects discoursed of—the paucity of examples, of illustrations and productions, and the deluge of doctrine suspended in the void; the profusion of talk and the contraction of experiment, of what one may call literary conduct. This, indeed, ceases to be an anomaly as soon as we look at the conditions of contemporary journalism. Then we see that these conditions have engendered the practice of "reviewing"—a practice that in general has nothing in common with the art of criticism. Periodical literature is a huge, open mouth which has to be fed—a vessel of immense capacity which has to be filled. It is like a regular train which starts at an advertised hour, but which is free to start only if every seat be occupied. The seats are many, the train is ponderously long, and hence the manufacture of dummies for the seasons when there are not passengers enough. A stuffed mannikin is thrust into the empty seat, where it makes a creditable figure till the end of the journey. It looks sufficiently like a passenger, and you know it is not one only when you perceive that it neither says anything nor gets out. The guard attends to it when the train is shunted, blows the cinders from its wooden face and gives a different crook to its elbow, so that it may serve for another run. In this way, in a well-conducted periodical, the blocks of *remplissage* are the dummies of criticism—the recurrent, regulated breakers in the tide of talk. They have a reason for being, and the situation is simpler when we perceive it. It helps to explain the disproportion I just mentioned, as well, in many a case, as the quality of the particular discourse. It helps us to understand that the "organs of public opinion" must be no less copious than punctual, that publicity must maintain its high standard, that ladies and gentlemen may turn an honest penny by the free expenditure of ink. It gives us a glimpse of the high figure

47

presumably reached by all the honest pennies accumulated in the cause, and throws us quite into a glow over the march of civilization and the way we have organized our conveniences. From this point of view it might indeed go far towards making us enthusiastic about our age. What is more calculated to inspire us with a just complacency than the sight of a new and flourishing industry, a fine economy of production? The great business of reviewing has, in its roaring routine, many of the signs of blooming health, many of the features which beguile one into rendering an involuntary homage to success-ful enterprise.

Yet it is not to be denied that certain captious persons are to be met who are not carried away by the spectacle, who look at it much askance, who see but dimly whither it tends, and who find no aid to vision even in the great light (about itself, its spirit, and its purposes, among other things) that it might have been expected to diffuse. "Is there any such great light at all?" we may imagine the most restless of the sceptics to inquire, "and isn't the effect rather one of a certain kind of pretentious and unprofitable gloom?" The vulgarity, the crudity, the stupidity which this cherished combination of the offhand re-view and of our wonderful system of publicity have put into circulation on so vast a scale may be represented, in such a mood, as an unprecedented inven-tion for darkening counsel. The bewildered spirit may ask itself, without speedy answer, What is the function in the life of man of such a periodicity of platitude and irrelevance? Such a spirit will wonder how the life of man survives it, and, above all, what is much more important, how literature resists it; whether, indeed, literature does resist it and is not speedily going down beneath it. The signs of this catastrophe will not in the case we suppose be found too subtle to be pointed out—the failure of distinction, the failure of style, the failure of knowledge, the failure of thought. The case is therefore one for recognizing with dismay that we are paying a tremendous price for the diffusion of penmanship and opportunity; that the multiplication of en-dowments for chatter may be as fatal as an infectious disease; that literature lives essentially, in the sacred depths of its being, upon example, upon per-fection wrought; that, like other sensitive organisms, it is highly susceptible of demoralization, and that nothing is better calculated than irresponsible pedagogy to make it close its ears and lips. To be puerile and untutored about it is to deprive it of air and light, and the consequence of its keeping bad company is that it loses all heart. We may, of course, continue to talk about it long after it has bored itself to death, and there is every appearance that this is mainly the way in which our descendants will hear of it. They will, how-ever, acquiesce in its extinction.

This, I am aware, is a dismal conviction, and I do not pretend to state the case gayly. The most I can say is that there are times and places in which it strikes one as less desperate than at others. One of the places is Paris, and one

---

CRITICISM — page 49

of the times is some comfortable occasion of being there. The custom of rough-and-ready reviewing is, among the French, much less rooted than with us, and the dignity of criticism is, to my perception, in consequence much higher. The art is felt to be one of the most difficult, the most delicate, the most occasional; and the material on which it is exercised is subject to selection, to restriction. That is, whether or no the French are always right as to what they do notice, they strike me as infallible as to what they don't. They publish hundreds of books which are never noticed at all, and yet they are much neater bookmakers than we. It is recognized that such volumes have nothing to say to the critical sense, that they do not belong to literature, and that the possession of the critical sense is exactly what makes it impossible to read them and dreary to discuss them—places them, as a part of critical experience, out of the question. The critical sense, in France, *ne se dérange pas*, as the phrase is, for so little. No one would deny, on the other hand, that when it does set itself in motion it goes further than with us. It handles the subject in general with finer finger-tips. The bluntness of ours, as tactile implements addressed to an exquisite process, is still sometimes surprising, even after frequent exhibition. We blunder in and out of the affair as if it were a railway station—the easiest and most public of the arts. It is in reality the most complicated and the most particular. The critical sense is so far from frequent that it is absolutely rare, and the possession of the cluster of qualities that minister to it is one of the highest distinctions. It is a gift inestimably precious and beautiful; therefore, so far from thinking that it passes overmuch from hand to hand, one knows that one has only to stand by the counter an hour to see that business is done with baser coin. We have too many small schoolmasters; yet not only do I not question in literature the high utility of criticism, but I should be tempted to say that the part it plays may be the supremely beneficent one when it proceeds from deep sources, from the efficient combination of experience and perception. In this light one sees the critic as the real helper of the artist, a torch-bearing outrider, the interpreter, the brother. The more the tune is noted and the direction observed the more we shall enjoy the convenience of a critical literature. When one thinks of the outfit required for free work in this spirit, one is ready to pay almost any homage to the intelligence that has put it on; and when one considers the noble figure completely equipped—armed *cap-à-pie* in curiosity and sympathy—one falls in love with the apparition. It certainly represents the knight who has knelt through his long vigil and who has the piety of his office. For there is something sacrificial in his function, inasmuch as he offers himself as a general touchstone. To lend himself, to project himself and steep himself, to feel and feel till he understands, and to understand so well that he can say, to have perception at the pitch of passion and expression as embracing as the air, to be infinitely curious and incorrigibly patient, and yet plastic and inflammable and determinable, stooping to conquer and serving to direct —these are fine chances for an active mind, chances to add the idea of independent beauty to the conception of success. Just in proportion as he is sentient and restless, just in proportion as he reacts and reciprocates and penetrates, is the critic a valuable instrument; for in literature assuredly criticism *is* the critic, just as art is the artist; it being assuredly the artist who invented art and the critic who invented criticism, and not the other way round.

And it is with the kinds of criticism exactly as it is with the kinds of art— the best kind, the only kind worth speaking of, is the kind that springs from the liveliest experience. There are a hundred labels and tickets, in all this matter, that have been pasted on from the outside and appear to exist for the convenience of passers-by; but the critic who lives *in* the house, ranging through its innumerable chambers, knows nothing about the bills on the front. He only knows that the more impressions he has the more he is able to record, and that the more he is saturated, poor fellow, the more he can give out. His life, at this rate, is heroic, for it is immensely vicarious. He has to understand for others, to answer for them; he is always under arms. He knows that the whole honor of the matter, for him, besides the success in his own eyes, depends upon his being indefatigably supple, and that is a formidable order. Let me not speak, however, as if his work were a conscious grind, for the sense of effort is easily lost in the enthusiasm of curiosity. Any vocation has its hours of intensity that is so closely connected with life. That of the critic, in literature, is connected doubly, for he deals with life at second-hand as well as at first; that is, he deals with the experience of others, which he resolves into his own, and not of those invented and selected others with whom the novelist makes comfortable terms, but with the uncompromising swarm of authors, the clamorous children of history. He has to make them as vivid and as free as the novelist makes *his* puppets, and yet he has, as the phrase is, to take them as they come. We must be easy with him if the picture, even when the aim has really been to penetrate, is sometimes confused, for there are baffling and there are thankless subjects; and we make everything up to him by the peculiar purity of our esteem when the portrait is really, like the happy portraits of the other art, a text preserved by translation.

From *Essays in London and Elsewhere* by Henry James. Copyright, 1893, by Harper & Brothers. Copyright, 1921, by Mrs. Henry James. Reprinted by permission of Harper & Brothers. First published in *The New Review*, Vol. IV (May, 1891), pp. 398–401, under the title "The Science of Criticism."

The Question of the Opportunities
[1898]

ANY fresh start of speech today on American literature seems to me so in-evitably a more direct and even a slightly affrighted look at the mere num-bers of the huge, homogeneous and fast-growing population from which the flood of books issues and to which it returns that this particular impression admonishes the observer to pause long enough on the threshold to be sure he takes it well in. Whatever the "literature" already is, whatever it may be destined yet to be, the public to which it addresses itself is of proportions that no other single public has approached, least of all those of the periods and societies to which we owe the comparatively small library of books that we rank as the most precious thing in our heritage. This question of numbers is brought home to us again and again with force by the amazing fortune apparently open now, any year, to the individual book—usually the lucky novel—that happens to please; by the extraordinary career, for instance, yesterday, of *Trilby*, or, today (as I hear it reported), of an historical fiction translated from the Polish and entitled *Quo Vadis?* It is clear enough that such a public must be, for the observer, an immense part of the whole ques-tion of the concatenation and quality of books, must present it in conditions hitherto almost unobserved and of a nature probably to give an interest of a kind so new as to suggest for the critic—even the critic least sure of where the chase will bring him out—a delicious rest from the oppressive *a priori*. There can be no real sport for him—if I may use the term that fits best the critical energy—save in proportion as he gets rid of *that*; and he can hardly fail to get rid of it just in the degree in which the conditions are vivid to his mind. They are, of course, largely those of other publics as well, in an age in which, everywhere, more people than ever before buy and sell, and read and write, and run about; but their scale, in the great common-schooled and news-papered democracy, is the largest and their pressure the greatest we see; their characteristics are magnified and multiplied. From these characteristics no intelligent forecast of the part played in the community in question by the printed and circulated page will suffer its attention too widely to wander.

Homogeneous I call the huge American public, with a due sense of the variety of races and idioms that are more and more under contribution to build it up, for it is precisely in the great mill of the language, our predominant and triumphant English, taking so much, suffering perhaps even so much, in the process, but giving so much more, on the whole, than it has to "put up" with, that the elements are ground into unity. Into its vast motherly lap the supreme speech manages somehow or other—with a robust indifference to trifles and shades—to see these elements poured; and just in this unique situation of the tongue itself we may surely find, if we attend, the interest of the drama and the excitement of the question. It is a situation that strikes me as presenting to the critic some of the strain and stress—those of suspense, of life, movement, change, the multiplication of possibilities, surprises, disappointments (emotions, whatever they may be, of the truth-hunter)—that the critic likes most to encounter. What may be, from point to point, noted as charming, or even as alarming, consequences? What forms, what colours, what sounds may the language take on or throw off in accommodating itself to such a growth of experience; what life may it—and most of all may the literature that shall so copiously testify for it—reflect and embody? The answer to these inquiries is simply the march of the critic's drama and the bliss, when not the misery, of that spectator; but while the endless play goes on the spectator may at least so far anticipate deferred conclusions as to find a savour in the very fact that it has been reserved not for French, not for German, not for Italian to meet fate on such a scale. That consciousness is an emotion in itself and, for large views, which are the only amusing ones, a great portent; so that we can surely say to ourselves that we shall not have been called upon to supply the biggest public for nothing.

To overflow with the same confidence to others is indeed perhaps to expose ourselves to hearing it declared improbable that we have been called upon to supply it, at any rate, for literature—the moral mainly latent in literature for the million, or rather for the fast-arriving billion, finding here inevitably a tempting application. But is not our instant rejoinder to that, as inevitably, that such an application is precipitate and premature? Whether, in the conditions we consider, the supply shall achieve sufficient vitality and distinction really to be sure of itself as literature, and to communicate the certitude, is the very thing we watch and wait to discover. If the retort to that remark be in turn that all this depends on what we may take it into our heads to *call* literature, we work round to a ground of easy assent. It truly does much depend on that. But that, in its order, depends on new light—on the new light struck out by the material itself, the distinguishable symptoms of which are the justification for what I have called the critic's happy release from the cramped posture of foregone conclusions and narrow rules. There will be no real amusement if we are postively prepared to be stupid. It is assuredly true that literature for the billion will not be literature as we have hitherto known it at its best. But if the billion give the pitch of production and circulation, they do something else besides; they hang before us a wide picture of opportunities—opportunities that would be opportunities still even if, reduced to the *minimum,* they should be only those offered by the vastness of the implied habitat and the complexity of the implied history.

It is impossible not to entertain with patience and curiosity the presumption that life so colossal must break into expression at points of proportionate frequency. These places, these moments will be the chances.

The first chance that, in the longer run, expression avails herself of may, of course, very well be that of breaking up into pieces and showing thereby that—as has been hitherto and in other parts of the world but imperfectly indicated—the public we somewhat loosely talk of as for literature or for anything else is really as subdivided as a chess-board, with each little square confessing only to its own *kind* of accessibility. The comparison too much sharpens and equalizes; but there are certainly, as on a map of countries, divisions and boundaries; and if these varieties become, to assist individual genius or save individual life, accentuated in American letters, we shall immediately to that tune be rewarded for our faith. It is, in other words, just from the very force of the conditions making for reaction in spots and phases that the liveliest appeal of future American production may spring—reaction, I mean, against the grossness of any view, any taste or tone, in danger of becoming so extravagantly general as to efface the really interesting thing, the traceability of the individual. Then, for all we know, we may get individual publics positively more sifted and evolved than anywhere else, shoals of fish rising to more delicate bait. That is a possibility that makes meanwhile for good humour, though I must hasten to add that it by no means exhausts the favourable list. We know what the list actually shows or what, in the past, it has mainly shown—New England quite predominantly, almost exclusively, the literary voice and dealing with little else than material supplied by herself. I have just been reading two new books that mark strikingly how the Puritan culture both used and exhausted its opportunity, how its place knows it no longer with any approach to the same intensity. Mrs. Fields' *Life and Letters of Harriet Beecher Stowe* and Mr. John Jay Chapman's acute and admirable *Emerson and Other Essays* (the most penetrating study, as regards his main subject, to my sense, of which that subject has been made the occasion) appear to refer to a past already left long behind, and are each, moreover, on this ground and on others, well worth returning to. The American world of to-day is a world of combinations and proportions different from those amid which Emerson and Mrs. Stowe could reach right and left far enough to fill it.

The note of the difference—at least of some of it—is sharply enough struck in an equally recent volume from which I have gathered many suggestions and that exhibits a talent distinctly to come back to—Mr. Owen Wister's *Lin McLean* (episodes in the career of a young "cattle-puncher"), in which the manners of the remoter West are worked into the general context, the American air at large, by a hand of a singularly trained and modern lightness. I but glance in passing, not to lose my thread, at these things; but

Mr. Owen Wister's tales (an earlier strong cluster of which, *Red Men and White,* I a year or two ago also much appreciated) give me a pretext for saying that, not inexplicably perhaps, a novelist interested in the general outlook of his trade may find the sharpest appeal of all in the idea of the chances in reserve for the work of the imagination in particular—the vision of the distinguishable poetry of things, whether expressed in such verse or (rarer phenomenon) in such prose as really does arrive at expression. I cannot but think that the American novel has in a special, far-reaching direction to sail much closer to the wind. "Business" plays a part in the United States that other interests dispute much less showily than they sometimes dispute it in the life of European countries; in consequence of which the typical American figure is above all that "business man" whom the novelist and the dramatist have scarce yet seriously touched, whose song has still to be sung and his picture still to be painted. He is often an obscure, but not less often an epic, hero, seamed all over with the wounds of the market and the dangers of the field, launched into action and passion by the immensity and complexity of the general struggle, a boundless ferocity of battle—driven above all by the extraordinary, the unique relation in which he for the most part stands to the life of his lawful, his immitigable womankind, the wives and daughters who float, who splash on the surface and ride the waves, his terrific link with civilization, his social substitutes and representatives, while, like a diver for shipwrecked treasure, he gasps in the depths and breathes through an air-tube.

This relation, even taken alone, contains elements that strike me as only yearning for their interpreter—elements, moreover, that would present the further merit of melting into the huge neighbouring province of the special situation of women in an order of things where to be a woman at all—certainly to be a young one—constitutes in itself a social position. The difficulty, doubtless, is that the world of affairs, as affairs are understood in the panting cities, though around us all the while, before us, behind us, beside us, and under our feet, is as special and occult a one to the outsider as the world, say, of Arctic exploration—as impenetrable save as a result of special training. Those who know it are not the men to paint it; those who might attempt it are not the men who know it. The most energetic attempt at portrayal that we have anywhere had—*L'Argent,* of Emile Zola—is precisely a warning of the difference between false and true initiation. The subject there, though so richly imagined, is all too mechanically, if prodigiously, "got up." Meanwhile, accordingly, the American "business man" remains, thanks to the length and strength of the wires that move him, *the* magnificent theme *en disponibilité.* The romance of fact, indeed, has touched him in a way that quite puts to shame the romance of fiction. It gives his measure for purposes of art that it was he, essentially, who embarked in the great war of

1861–65, and who, carrying it on in the North to a triumphant conclusion, went back, since business was his standpoint, to his very "own" with an undimmed capacity to mind it. When, in imagination, you give the type, as it exists to-day, the benefit of its great double lustre—that of these recorded antecedents and that of its preoccupied, systematic and magnanimous abasement before the other sex—you will easily feel your sense of what may be done with.its overflow.

To glance at that is, at the point to which the English-speaking world has brought the matter, to remember by the same stroke that if there be no virtue in any forecast of the prospect of letters, any sounding of their deeps and shallows that fails to take account of the almost predominant hand now exercised about them by women, the precaution is doubly needful in respect to the American situation. Whether the extraordinary dimensions of the public be a promise or a threat, nothing is more unmistakable than the sex of some of the largest masses. The longest lines are feminine—feminine, it may almost be said, the principal front. Both as readers and as writers on the other side of the Atlantic women have, in fine, "arrived" in numbers not equalled even in England, and they have succeeded in giving the pitch and marking the limits more completely than elsewhere. The public taste, as our fathers used to say, has become so largely *their* taste, their tone, their experiment, that nothing is at last more apparent than that the public cares little for anything that they cannot do. And what, after all, may the very finest opportunity of American literature be but just to show that they can do what the peoples will have ended by regarding as everything? The settlement of such a question, the ups and downs of such a process surely more than justify that sense of sport, in this direction, that I have spoken of as the privilege of the vigilant critic.

From *Literature*, published by *The Times* (London); American edition published by Harper & Brothers; Vol. II (March 26, 1898), pp. 356–358, where it appeared as an "American Letter" with the title as here printed. The essay was not reprinted by Henry James in his books.

The Great Form
[1889]

[In the summer of 1889 there was held, at Deerfield, Massachusetts, a summer
school on "The Novel," to which Henry James, then in England, was invited to
contribute, the appeal of the school's organizers having told him it was their object
to discuss and resist "the materialism of our present tendencies" in this form of literature. Henry James, unable to attend the sessions, participated by letter, his message being then published in full in the *New York Tribune* of Sunday, August 4,
1889, and summarized in briefer form in the *Critic* (New York) of August 17,
1889. This letter was rediscovered by Mr. Leon Edel and published by him in the
Times Literary Supplement (London) of July 29, 1939, with a note in which he
remarks that the letter "is interesting, for it is a reiteration, in concise form, of the
views set forth by James in his famous essay 'The Art of Fiction,' while being at
the same time probably the most concrete advice he ever vouchsafed his countrymen on novel-writing."]

I AM afraid I can do little more than thank you for your courteous invitation
to be present at the sittings of your delightfully sounding school of romance,
which ought to inherit happiness and honour from such a name. I am so
very far away from you that I am afraid I can't participate very intelligently
in your discussions, but I can only give them the furtherance of a dimly discriminating sympathy. I am not sure that I apprehend very well your apparent premise "the materialism of our present tendencies," and I suspect
that this would require some clearing up before I should be able (if even
then) to contribute any suggestive or helpful word. To tell the truth, I can't
help thinking that we already talk too much about the novel, about and
around it, in proportion to the quantity of it having any importance that we
produce. What I should say to the nymphs and swains who propose to con-
verse about it under the great trees at Deerfield is: "Oh, do something from
your point of view; an ounce of example is worth a ton of generalities; do
something with the great art and the great form; do something with life.
Any point of view is interesting that is a direct impression of life. You each
have an impression coloured by your individual conditions; make that into a
picture, a picture framed by your own personal wisdom, your glimpse of the
American world. The field is vast for freedom, for study, for observation, for
satire, for truth." I don't think I really do know what you mean by "ma-
terializing tendencies" any more than I should by "spiritualizing" or "ethe-
realizing." There are no tendencies worth anything but to see the actual or the

imaginative, which is just as visible, and to paint it. I have only two little words for the matter remotely approaching to rule or doctrine; one is life and the other freedom. Tell the ladies and gentlemen, the ingenious inquirers, to consider life directly and closely, and not to be put off with mean and puerile falsities, and be conscientious about it. It is infinitely large, various and comprehensive. Every sort of mind will find what it looks for in it, whereby the novel becomes truly multifarious and illustrative. That is what I mean by liberty; give it its head and let it range. If it is in a bad way, and the English novel is, I think, nothing but absolute freedom can refresh it and restore its self-respect. Hence these raw brevities and please convey to your companions, my dear sir, the cordial good wishes of yours and theirs,

HENRY JAMES

WILLIAM DEAN HOWELLS
The Question of a Criterion
[1891]

THE question of a final criterion for the appreciation of art is one that perpetually recurs to those interested in any sort of aesthetic endeavor. Mr. John Addington Symonds, in a chapter of *The Renaissance in Italy* treating of the Bolognese school of painting, which once had so great cry, and was vaunted the supreme exemplar of the grand style, but which he now believes fallen into lasting contempt for its emptiness and soullessness, seeks to determine whether there can be an enduring criterion or not; and his conclusion is applicable to literature as to the other arts. "Our hope," he says, "with regard to the unity of taste in the future then is, that all sentimental or academical seekings after the ideal having been abandoned, momentary theories founded upon idiosyncratic or temporary partialities exploded, and nothing accepted but what is solid and positive, the scientific spirit shall make men progressively more and more conscious of these *bleibende Verhältnisse,* more and more capable of living in the whole; also, that in proportion as we gain a firmer hold upon our own place in the world, we shall come to comprehend with more instinctive certitude what is simple, natural, and honest, welcoming with gladness all artistic products that exhibit these qualities. The perception of the enlightened man will then be the task of a healthy person who has made himself acquainted with the laws of evolution in art and in society, and is able to test the excellence of work in any stage from immaturity to decadence by discerning what there is of truth, sincerity, and natural vigor in it."

*   *   *   *   *

That is to say, as I understand, that moods and tastes and fashions change; people fancy now this and now that; but what is unpretentious and what is true is always beautiful and good, and nothing else is so. This is not saying that fantastic and monstrous and artificial things do not please; everybody knows that they do please immensely for a time, and then, after the lapse of a much longer time, they have the charm of the rococo. Nothing is more curious than the charm that fashion has. Fashion in women's dress, almost every fashion, is somehow delightful, else it would never have been the fashion; but if any one will look through a collection of old-fashioned plates, he must own that most fashions have been ugly. A few, which could be readily instanced, have been very pretty, and even beautiful, but it is doubtful if these have pleased the greatest number of people. The ugly delights as well as the beautiful, and not merely because the ugly fashion is associated with the young loveliness of the women who wear the ugly fashions, and wins a grace from them, not because the vast majority of mankind are tasteless, but for some cause that is not perhaps ascertainable. It is quite as likely to return in the fashions of our clothes and houses and furniture, and poetry and fiction and painting, as the beautiful, and it may be from an instinctive or a reasoned sense of this that some of the extreme naturalists have refused to make the old discrimination against it or to regard the ugly as any less worthy of celebration in art than the beautiful; some of them, in fact, seem to regard it as rather more worthy, if anything. Possibly there is no absolutely ugly, no absolutely beautiful; or possibly the ugly contains always an element of the beautiful better adapted to the general appreciation than the more perfectly beautiful. This is a somewhat discouraging conjecture, but I offer it for no more than it is worth; and I do not pin my faith to the saying of one whom I heard denying, the other day, that a thing of beauty was a joy forever. He contended that Keats's line should have read, "Some things of beauty are sometimes joys forever," and that any assertion beyond this was too hazardous.

* * * * *

In the mean time the average of criticism is not wholly bad with us. To be sure, the critic sometimes appears in the panoply of the savages whom we have supplanted on this continent; and it is hard to believe that his use of the tomahawk and the scalping-knife is a form of conservative surgery. It is still his conception of his office that he should assail with obloquy those who differ with him in matters of taste or opinion; that he must be rude with those he does not like, and that he ought to do them violence as a proof of his superiority. It is too largely his superstition that because he likes a thing it is good, and because he dislikes a thing it is bad; the reverse is quite possibly the case, but he is yet indefinitely far from knowing that in affairs of taste his personal preference enters very little. Commonly he has no principles, but only an assortment of prepossessions for and against; and this otherwise very perfect character is sometimes uncandid to the verge of dishonesty. He seems not to mind misstating the position of any one he supposes himself to disagree with, and then attacking him for what he never said, or even implied; the critic thinks this is droll, and appears not to suspect that it is immoral. He is not tolerant; he thinks it a virtue to be intolerant; it is hard for him to understand that the same thing may be admirable at one time and deplorable at another; and that it is really his business to classify and analyze the fruits of the human mind very much as the naturalist classifies the objects of his study, rather than to praise or blame them; that there is a measure of the same absurdity in his trampling on a poem, a novel, or an essay that does not please him as in the botanist's grinding a plant underfoot because he does not find it pretty. He does not conceive that it is his business rather to identify the species and then explain how and where the specimen is imperfect and irregular. If he could once acquire this simple idea of his duty he would be much more agreeable company than he now is, and a more useful member of society; though I hope I am not yet saying that he is not extremely delightful as he is, and wholly indispensable. He is certainly more ignorant than malevolent; and considering the hard conditions under which he works, his necessity of writing hurriedly from an imperfect examination of far more books, on a greater variety of subjects, than he can even hope to read, the average American critic—the ordinary critic of commerce, so to speak—is very well indeed. Collectively he is more than this; for the joint effect of our criticism is the pretty thorough appreciation of any book submitted to it.

*   *   *   *   *

The misfortune rather than the fault of our individual critic is that he is the heir of the false theory and bad manners of the English school. The theory of that school has apparently been that almost any person of glib and lively expression is competent to write of almost any branch of polite literature; its manners are what we know. The American, whom it has largely formed, is by nature very glib and very lively, and commonly his criticism, viewed as imaginative work, is more agreeable than that of the Englishman; but it is, like the art of both countries, apt to be amateurish. In some degree our authors have freed themselves from English models; they have gained some notion of the more serious work of the Continent; but it is still the ambition of the American critic to write like the English critic, to show his wit if not his learning, to strive to eclipse the author under review rather than illustrate him. He has not yet caught on to the fact that it is really no part of his business to display himself, but that it is altogether his duty to place a book in such a light that the reader shall know its class, its function, its character. The vast good-nature of our people preserves us from the worst effects of this criticism without principles. Our critic, at his lowest, is rarely malignant; and when he is rude or untruthful, it is mostly without truculence; I suspect that he is often offensive without knowing that he is so. If he loves a shining mark because a fair shot with mud shows best on that kind of target, it is for the most part from a boyish mischievousness quite innocent of malice. Now and then he acts simply under instruction from higher authority, and denounces because it is the tradition of his publication to do so.

In other cases the critic is obliged to support his journal's repute for severity, or for wit, or for morality, though he may himself be entirely amiable, dull, and wicked; this necessity more or less warps his verdicts.

The worst is that he is personal, perhaps because it is so easy and so natural to be personal, and so instantly attractive. In this respect our criticism has not improved from the accession of numbers of ladies to its ranks, though we still hope so much from women in our politics when they shall come to vote. They have come to write, and with the effect to increase the amount of little-digging, which rather superabounded in our literary criticism before. They "know what they like"—that pernicious maxim of those who do not know what they ought to like—and they pass readily from censuring an author's performance to censuring him. They bring a lively stock of misapprehensions and prejudices to their work; they would rather have heard about than known about a book; and they take kindly to the public wish to be amused rather than edified. But neither have they so much harm in them: they, too, are more ignorant than malevolent.

*   *   *   *   *

Our criticism is disabled by the unwillingness of the critic to learn from an author, and his readiness to mistrust him. A writer passes his whole life in fitting himself for a certain kind of performance; the critic does not ask why, or whether the performance is good or bad, but if he does not like the kind, he instructs the writer to go off and do some other sort of thing—usually the sort that has been done already, and done sufficiently. If he could once understand that a man who has written the book he dislikes, probably knows infinitely more about its kind and his own fitness for doing it than any one else, the critic might learn something, and might help the reader to learn; but by putting himself in a false position, a position of superiority, he is of no use. He ought, in the first place, to cast prayerfully about for humility, and especially to beseech the powers to preserve him from the sterility of arrogance and the deadness of contempt, for out of these nothing can proceed. He is not to suppose that an author has committed an offence against him by writing the kind of book he does not like; he will be far more profitably employed on behalf of the reader in finding out whether they had better not both like it. Let him conceive of an author as not in any wise on trial before him, but as a reflection of this or that aspect of life, and he will not be tempted to browbeat him or bully him.

The critic need not be impolite even to the youngest and weakest author. A little courtesy, or a good deal, a constant perception of the fact that a book is not a misdemeanor, a decent self-respect that must forbid the civilized man the savage pleasure of wounding, are what I would ask for our criticism, as something which will add sensibly to its present lustre.

I would have my fellow-critics consider what they are really in the world for. It is not, apparently, for a great deal, because their only excuse for being is that somebody else has been. The critic exists because the author first existed. If books failed to appear, the critic must disappear, like the poor aphis or the lowly caterpillar in the absence of vegetation. These insects may both suppose that they have something to do with the creation of vegetation; and the critic may suppose that he has something to do with the creation of literature; but a very little reasoning ought to convince alike aphis, caterpillar, and critic that they are mistaken. The critic—to drop the others—must perceive, if he will question himself more carefully, that his office is mainly to ascertain facts and traits of literature, not to invent or denounce them; to discover principles, not to establish them; to report, not to create.

It is so much easier to say that you like this or dislike that, than to tell why one thing is, or where another thing comes from, that many flourishing critics will have to go out of business altogether if the scientific method comes in, for then the critic will have to know something beside his own mind, which is often but a narrow field. He will have to know something of the laws of that mind, and of its generic history.

The history of all literature shows that even with the youngest and weakest author criticism is quite powerless against his will to do his own work in his own way; and if this is the case in the green wood, how much more in the dry! It has been thought by the sentimentalist that criticism, if it cannot cure, can at least kill, and Keats was long alleged in proof of its efficacy in this sort. But criticism neither cured nor killed Keats, as we all now very well know. It wounded, it cruelly hurt him, no doubt; and it is always in the power of the critic to give pain to the author—the meanest critic to the greatest author—for no one can help feeling a rudeness. But every literary movement has been violently opposed at the start, and yet never stayed in the least, or arrested, by criticism; every author has been condemned for his virtues, but in no wise changed by it. In the beginning he reads the critics; but presently perceiving that he alone makes or mars himself, and that they have no instruction for him, he mostly leaves off reading them, though he is always glad of their kindness or grieved by their harshness when he chances upon it. This, I believe, is the general experience, modified, of course, by exceptions.

Then, are we critics of no use in the world? I should not like to think that, though I am not quite ready to define our use. More than one sober thinker is inclining at present to suspect that aesthetically or specifically we are of no use, and that we are only useful historically; that we may register laws, but not enact them. I am not quite prepared to admit that aesthetic criticism is useless, though in view of its futility in any given instance it is hard to deny that it is so. It certainly seems as useless against a book that strikes the popular fancy, and prospers on in spite of condemnation by the best critics, as it is against a book which does not generally please, and which no critical favor can make acceptable. This is so common a phenomenon that I wonder it has never hitherto suggested to criticism that its point of view was altogether mistaken, and that it was really necessary to judge books not as dead things, but as living things—things which have an influence and a power irrespective of beauty and wisdom, and merely as expressions of actuality in thought and feeling. Perhaps criticism has a cumulative and final effect; perhaps it does some good we do not know of. It apparently does not affect the author directly, but it may reach him through the reader. It may in some cases enlarge or diminish his audience for a while, until he has thoroughly measured and tested his own powers. If criticism is to affect literature at all, it must be through the writers who have newly left the starting-point, and are reasonably uncertain of the race, not with those who have won it again and again in their own way. I doubt if it can do more than that; but if it can do that I will admit that it may be the toad of adversity, ugly and venomous, from whose unpleasant brow he is to snatch the precious jewel of lasting fame.

I employ this figure in all humility, and I conjure our fraternity to ask themselves, without rancor or offence, whether I am right or not. In this quest let us get together all the modesty and candor and impartiality we can; for if we should happen to discover a good reason for continuing to exist, these qualities will be of more use to us than any others in examining the work of people who really produce something.

From *Criticism and Fiction* by William Dean Howells (being the "Introduction," and Chapters I, VI, VII, VIII, and IX). Copyright, 1891, by Harper & Brothers. Based on material that originally appeared in *Harper's Monthly* ("The Editor's Study"), Vols. LXXII–LXXXI (February, 1886–October, 1890). The present title has been supplied by the editor.

JOHN JAY CHAPMAN
The Aesthetic
[1910]

THERE are two distinct functions of the mind with regard to art: first, the creative function; second, the enjoying function. The first is the role of the artist, the second, the rôle of the public. The difference between these two rôles is that in the artist's rôle the active part—the part that counts, the part that makes the beholder have sensations—is unconscious. The artist should be wholly creator, and not at all spectator. If, while he works, there is anything in him that applauds and enjoys as a spectator might do, this part will leave a touch of virtuosity, of self-consciousness, of exaggeration, in his work. If the matter be humorous, this exaggeration will perhaps appear in the form of smartness; if the matter be serious, as sentimentality or melodrama.

The artist must not try to enjoy his own work by foretaste, or he will injure it. His aesthetic sense must not be active during the hours of creation; it must be consumed in the furnace of unconscious intellectual effort. The *reductio ad absurdum* of the view here suggested would be somewhat as follows:—The supremely great artist would be indifferent to the fate of his own works, because he would not know they were great. The whole creature would have become so unconscious during the act of creation that there would be nothing left over which should return to mankind and say, "See this great work!" This seems to have happened in the case of Shakespeare.

It must be confessed that there are very great artists in whose work we find a self-conscious, self-appreciatory note. There is, at times, such a note in Dante, and in Goethe. And it seems to me that even here the note a little deflects our attention from the matter in hand. Not by reason of this element, but in spite of it, does their work prevail.

The practical lesson for any artist to draw from such an analysis as the present is the lesson of detachment, almost of indifference. An artist must trust his material. The stuff in hand is serious, delicate, self-determined and non-emotional. The organic, inner logic of the thing done may reach points of complexity, points of climax, which—except in the outcome—are incomprehensible. They must not be appreciated in the interim, but only obeyed.

In the final review, and at a distance they are to justify themselves, but not in the making.

The question of whether or not an artist has succeeded, whether or not he has made something that speaks, is one which it is generally impossible for the artist himself to answer. He cares too much, and he stands too near the material. Sometimes a man having immense experience, and having acquired that sort of indifference which grows out of a supernal success, can make a just estimate of one of his own later works; but, in general, the artist must stand mum and bite his nails if he wishes to find out what there was in him. Let him be perfectly assured that the truth of the matter will get to him, if he will only do nothing except desire the truth. Someone will say something not intended for his ears, which will reveal the whole matter. This is the hard, heroic course which wisdom dictates to all artists, except, perhaps, to those very gifted persons who by their endowment are already among the elect. Most men are obliged to mine in their endowment and draw it to the surface through years of hard labor. The pretty good artist has need of the fortitude and self-effacement of a saint.

Thus much of the creative side of art. Our conceptions of the subject, however, are colored by the emotional view proper to the grand public. The receptive function, the enjoying function, the aesthetic sense, as it is often called, is very generally supposed to be art itself. Almost all writing on art has been done by men who knew only the aesthetic side of the matter. Now the enjoyment of art is a very common, very conscious, very intense experience; and yet it is not a very serious affair compared to the creation of art. It does not affect the recipient to any such depths of his nature, as one might expect it to do, from the vividness of his feelings during the experience. It leaves in him, as a general rule, no knowledge about the art itself, no understanding of the rod he has been lashed with, no suspicion of the intellectual nature of the vehicle.

Aesthetic appreciation gives a man the illusion that he is being spiritually made over and enlarged; and yet that appreciation is capable of an absolute divorcement from the intellect. It is—to take the extreme case—very strong in sleep. Dr. Holmes has recorded, in his own felicitous way, the experience, common to sensitive people, of writing down a dream-poem at midnight and discovering in its place at dawn a few lines of incomprehensible rubbish. The aesthetic sense is easily intensified by stimulants, by tea, coffee and tobacco. Anything that excites the heart or stimulates the emotions—praise, happiness, success, change of scene, any relief from mental tension—is apt to give a man new and sudden entry into unexplored worlds of art. He thinks himself a new man. And yet this man stands, perhaps, in as great danger of loss as he does in hope of gain. It is not through receptivity, but through activity, that men are really changed.

How trivial men become who live solely in the appreciation of the fine arts all of us know. The American who lives abroad is an intensely receptive being; but he has divorced himself from the struggles of a normal social existence, from communal life and duty. His love of the fine arts does not save him, but seems rather to enfeeble him the more. No European can effect a similar divorce in his own life; for the European is living at home: his social and political obligations make a man of him. Besides this, the fine arts are an old story to the European; and he does not go mad about them, as the American Indian goes mad about whiskey. The European is immune to the aesthetic; and neither a fine wainscot nor a beautiful doorknob can have the same power over him that it may have over that zealous, high-strung, new discoverer of the old world, the American who begins to realize what good decoration really means. Let anyone who thinks that this impoverishment is a purely American disease read the description of the Stanhope family in Trollope's *Barchester Towers*. Here is the beefiest kind of a British county family, reduced to anemia by residence in Italy. Prolonged exile and mere receptivity have withdrawn the energy from the organs of these people.

It will be noticed that in those cases where art is an enfeebling influence there is always a hiatus between the public and the artist. Let us consider the case of the folk-song as sung by the peasants of Suabia. Such songs are written by one peasant and sung by the next. The author and the singer and the hearer are all one. To the audience the song is life and emotion, social intercourse, love, friendship, the landscape, philosophy, prayer, natural happiness. You can hardly differentiate, in this case, between the artist and the public: both are unconscious. But if you take that song and sing it in a London drawing-room, or on a ranch in Colorado, it will perform a very different function in the audience. To these foreigners the song is a pleasing opiate. They hold it like a warm animal to their breast. The Oxford pundit who raves over a Greek coin, the cold-hearted business magnate in New York who enjoys the opera—these people live in so remote a relation to the human causes, impulses, and conditions behind the arts they love, that their enjoyment is exotic: it is more purely receptive, more remote from personal experience than the enjoyment of any living and native art could be.

A certain sickness follows the indulgence in art that is remote from the admirer's environment. This slightly morbid side of aestheticism has been caricatured to the heart's content. The dilettante and the critic are well-known types. To a superficial view these men seem like enemies of the living artist. They are always standing ready to eat up his works as soon as they shall be born. Goethe thought criticism and satire the two natural enemies to all liberty, and to all poetry proceeding from a spontaneous impulse. And surely the massive authority of learned critics who know everything, and are yet ignorant of the first principles of their subject, hangs like an avalanche above the head of every young creator. We cannot, however, to-day proceed as if we were early Greeks, stepping forward in roseate unconsciousness. The critics and their hurdy-gurdy are a part of our life, and have been so for centuries.

The brighter side of the matter is that the aesthetic person, even when morbid, is often engaged in introducing new and valuable arts to his countrymen. The dilettante who brings home china and violins and Japanese bronzes is the precursor of the domestic artist.

We must now return to the two functions of art, and endeavor to bring them into some sort of common focus. We cannot hope to understand or to reconcile them perfectly. We cannot hope to know what art is. Art is life, and any expression of art becomes a new form of life. A merchant in Boston in 1850 travels in Italy, and brings home a Murillo. Some years later a highly educated dilettante discovers the Murillo in Boston, and writes his dithyrambs about it. Some years later still, there arises a young painter, who perhaps does not paint very well, and yet he is nearer to the mystery than the other two. All these men are parts of the same movement, and are essential to each other; though the contempt they feel for each other might conceal this from us, as it does from themselves. All of them are held together by an invisible attraction and are servants of the same force. This force it is which, in the future, may weld together a few enthusiasts into a sort of secret society, or may even single out some one man, and see and speak through him. Then, as the force passes, it will leave itself reflected in pictures, which remain as the record of its flight.

From *Learning and Other Essays* by John Jay Chapman, pp. 235–242. Moffat, Yard and Company, 1910.

RANDOLPH BOURNE
Our Cultural Humility
[1914]

IT WAS Matthew Arnold, read and reverenced by the generation immediately preceding our own, who set to our eyes a definition and a goal of culture which has become the common property of all our world. To know the best that had been thought and said, to appreciate the master-works which the previous civilizations had produced, to put our minds and appreciations in contact with the great of all ages,—here was a clear ideal which dissolved the mists in which the vaguenesses of culture had been lost. And it was an ideal that appealed with peculiar force to Americans. For it was a democratic ideal; everyone who had the energy and perseverance could reasonably expect to acquire by taking thought that orientation of soul to which Arnold gave the magic name of culture. And it was a quantitative ideal; culture was a matter of acquisition—with appreciation and prayerfulness perhaps, but still a matter of adding little by little to one's store until one should have a vision of that radiant limit, when one knew all the best that had been thought and said and pictured in the world.

I do not know in just what way the British public responded to Arnold's eloquence; if the prophetic wrath of Ruskin failed to stir them, it is not probable that they were moved by the persuasiveness of Arnold. But I do know that, coming at a time when America was producing rapidly an enormous number of people who were "comfortably off," as the phrase goes, and who were sufficiently awake to feel their limitations, with the broader horizons of Europe just opening on the view, the new doctrine had the most decisive effect on our succeeding spiritual history. The "land-of-liberty" American of the era of Dickens still exists in the British weeklies and in observations of America by callow young journalists, but as a living species he has long been extinct. His place has been taken by a person whose pride is measured not by the greatness of the "land of the free," but by his own orientation in Europe.

Already in the nineties, our college professors and our artists were beginning to require the seal of a European training to justify their existence. We appropriated the German system of education. Our millionaires began the collecting of pictures and the endowment of museums with foreign works of art. We began the exportation of school-teachers for a summer tour of Europe. American art and music colonies sprang up in Paris and Berlin and Munich. The movement became a rush. That mystical premonition of Europe, which Henry James tells us he had from his earliest boyhood, became the common property of the talented young American, who felt a certain starvation in his own land, and longed for the fleshpots of European culture. But the bourgeoisie soon followed the artistic and the semi-artistic, and Europe became so much the fashion that it is now almost a test of respectability to have traveled at least once abroad.

Underlying all this vivacious emigration, there was of course a real if vague thirst for "culture," and, in strict accord with Arnold's definition, the idea that somehow culture could be imbibed, that from the contact with the treasures of Europe there would be rubbed off on us a little of that grace which had made the art. So for those who could not travel abroad, our millionaires transported, in almost terrifying bulk and at staggering cost, samples of everything that the foreign galleries had to show. We were to acquire culture at any cost, and we had no doubt that we had discovered the royal road to it. We followed it, at any rate, with eye single to the goal. The naturally sensitive, who really found in the European literature and arts some sort of spiritual nourishment, set the pace, and the crowd followed at their heels.

This cultural humility of ours astonished and still astonishes Europe. In England, where "culture" is taken very frivolously, the bated breath of the American, when he speaks of Shakespeare or Tennyson or Browning, is always cause for amusement. And the Frenchman is always a little puzzled at the crowds who attend lectures in Paris on "How to See Europe Intelligently," or are taken in vast parties through the Louvre. The European objects a little to being so constantly regarded as the keeper of a huge museum. If you speak to him of culture, you find him frankly more interested in contemporaneous literature and art and music than in his worthies of the olden time, more interested in discriminating the good of today than in accepting the classics. If he is a cultivated person, he is much more interested usually in quarreling about a living dog than in reverencing a dead lion. If he is a French lettré, for instance, he will be producing a book on the psychology of some living writer, while the Anglo-Saxon will be writing another on Shakespeare. His whole attitude towards the things of culture, be it noted, is one of daily appreciation and intimacy, not that attitude of reverence with which we Americans approach alien art, and which penalizes cultural heresy among us.

The European may be enthusiastic, polemic, radiant, concerning his culture; he is never humble. And he is, above all, never humble before the culture of another country. The Frenchman will hear nothing but French music, read nothing but French literature, and prefers his own art to that of any other nation. He can hardly understand our almost pathetic eagerness to learn of the culture of other nations, our humility of worship in the presence of art that in no sense represents the expression of any of our ideals and motivating forces.

To a genuinely patriotic American this cultural humility of ours is somewhat humiliating. In response to this eager inexhaustible interest in Europe, where is Europe's interest in us? Europe is to us the land of history, of mellow tradition, of the arts and graces of life, of the best that has been said and thought in the world. To Europe we are the land of crude racial chaos, of skyscrapers and bluff, of millionaires and "bosses." A French philosopher visits us, and we are all eagerness to get from him an orientation in all that is moving in the world of thought across the seas. But does he ask about our philosophy, does he seek an orientation in the American thought of the day? Not at all. Our humility has kept us from forcing it upon his attention, and it scarcely exists for him. Our advertising genius, so powerful and universal where soap and biscuits are concerned, wilts and languishes before the task of trumpeting our intellectual and spiritual products before the world. Yet there can be little doubt which is the more intrinsically worth advertising. But our humility causes us to be taken at our own face value, and for all this patient fixity of gaze upon Europe, we get little reward except to be ignored, or to have our interest somewhat contemptuously dismissed as parasitic.

And with justice! For our very goal and ideal of culture has made us parasites. Our method has been exactly wrong. For the truth is that the definition of culture, which we have accepted with such devastating enthusiasm, is a definition emanating from that very barbarism from which its author recoiled in such horror. If it were not that all our attitude showed that we had adopted a quite different standard, it would be the merest platitude to say that culture is not an acquired familiarity with things outside, but an inner and constantly operating taste, a fresh and responsive power of discrimination, and the insistent judging of everything that comes to our minds and senses. It is clear that such a sensitive taste cannot be acquired by torturing our appreciations into conformity with the judgments of others, no matter how "authoritative" those judgments may be. Such a method means a hypnotization of judgment, not a true development of soul.

At the back of Arnold's definition is, of course, the implication that if we have only learned to appreciate the "best," we shall have been trained thus to discriminate generally, that our appreciation of Shakespeare will somehow spill over into admiration of the incomparable art of Mr. G. Lowes Dickinson. This is, of course, exactly to reverse the psychological process. A true appreciation of the remote and the magnificent is acquired only after the judgment has learned to discriminate with accuracy and taste between the good and bad, the sincere and the false, of the familiar and contemporaneous art and writing of every day. To set up an alien standard of the classics is merely to give our lazy taste a resting point, and to prevent forever any genuine culture.

This virus of the "best" rages throughout all our Anglo-Saxon campaign for culture. Is it not a notorious fact that our professors of English literature make no attempt to judge the work produced since the death of the last consecrated saint of the literary canon,—Robert Louis Stevenson? In strict accordance with Arnold's doctrine, they are waiting for the judgment upon our contemporaries which they call the test of time, that is, an authoritative objective judgment, upon which they can unquestioningly rely. Surely it seems as if the principle of authority, having been ousted from religion and politics, had found a strong refuge in the sphere of culture. This tyranny of the "best" objectifies all our taste. It is a "best" that is always outside of our native reactions to the freshnesses and sincerities of life, a "best" to which our spontaneities must be disciplined. By fixing our eyes humbly on the ages that are past, and on foreign countries, we effectually protect ourselves from that inner taste which is the only sincere "culture."

Our cultural humility before the civilizations of Europe, then, is the chief obstacle which prevents us from producing any true indigenous culture of our own. I am far from saying, of course, that it is not necessary for our arts to be fertilized by the civilizations of other nations past and present. The culture of Europe has arisen only from such an extensive cross-fertilization in the past. But we have passed through that period of learning, and it is time for us now to set up our individual standards. We are already "heir of all the ages" through our English ancestry, and our last half-century of European idolatry has done for us all that can be expected. But, with our eyes fixed on Europe, we continue to strangle whatever native genius springs up. Is it not a tragedy that the American artist feels the imperative need of foreign approval before he can be assured of his attainment? Through our inability or unwillingness to judge him, through our cultural humility, through our insistence on the objective standard, we drive him to depend on a foreign clientele, to live even in foreign countries, where taste is more confident of itself and does not require the label, to be assured of the worth of what it appreciates.

The only remedy for this deplorable situation is the cultivation of a new American nationalism. We need that keen introspection into the beauties and vitalities and sincerities of our own life and ideals that characterizes the French. The French culture is animated by principles and tastes which are as old as art itself. There are "classics," not in the English and Arnoldian sense of a consecrated canon, dissent from which is heresy, but in the sense that each successive generation, putting them to the test, finds them redolent of those qualities which are characteristically French, and so preserves them as a precious heritage. This cultural chauvinism is the most harmless of patriotisms; indeed it is absolutely necessary for a true life of civilization. And it can hardly be too intense, or too exaggerated. Such an international art exhibition as was held recently in New York, with the frankly avowed purpose of showing American artists how bad they were in comparison with the modern

French, represents an appalling degradation of attitude which would be quite impossible in any other country. Such groveling humility can only have the effect of making us feeble imitators, instead of making us assert, with all the power at our command, the genius and individuality which we already possess in quantity, if we would only see it.

In the contemporary talent that Europe is exhibiting, or even in the genius of the last half-century, one will go far to find greater poets than our Walt Whitman, philosophers than William James, essayists than Emerson and Thoreau, composers than MacDowell, sculptors than Saint-Gaudens. In any other country such names would be focuses to which interest and enthusiasms would converge, symbols of a national spirit about which judgments and tastes would revolve. For none of them could have been born in another country than our own. If some of them had their training abroad, it was still the indigenous America that their works expressed,—the American ideals and qualities, our pulsating democracy, the vigor and daring of our pioneer spirit, our sense of *camaraderie*, our dynamism, the big-heartedness of our scenery, our hospitality to all the world. In the music of MacDowell, the poetry of Whitman, the philosophy of James, I recognize a national spirit, "l'esprit américain," as superbly clear and gripping as anything the culture of Europe has to offer us, and immensely more stimulating, because of the very body and soul of to-day's interests and aspirations.

To come to an intense self-consciousness of these qualities, to feel them in the work of these masters, and to search for them everywhere among the lesser artists and thinkers who are trying to express the soul of this hot chaos of America,—this will be the attainment of culture for us. Not to look on ravished while our marvelous millionaires fill our museums with "old masters," armor, and porcelains, but to turn our eyes upon our own art for a time, shut ourselves in with our own genius, and cultivate with an intense and partial pride what we have already achieved against the obstacles of our cultural humility. Only thus shall we conserve the American spirit and saturate the next generation with those qualities which are our strength. Only thus can we take our rightful place among the cultures of the world, to which we are entitled if we would but recognize it. We shall never be able to perpetuate our ideals except in the form of art and literature; the world will never understand our spirit except in terms of art. When shall we learn that "culture," like the kingdom of heaven, lies within us, in the heart of our national soul, and not in foreign galleries and books? When shall we learn to be proud? For only pride is creative.

From *The History of a Literary Radical, and Other Essays* by Randolph Bourne, edited, with an Introduction, by Van Wyck Brooks. B. W. Huebsch, 1920. Reprinted by permission of B. W. Huebsch. First published in *The Atlantic Monthly*, Vol. CXIV (October, 1914), pp. 503–507.

JAMES GIBBONS HUNEKER
The Great American Novel
[1917]

WHEN the supreme master of the historical novel modestly confessed that he could do the "big bow-wow strain," but to Jane Austen must be accorded the palm of exquisite craftsmanship, there was then no question upon the critical map of the so-called "great American novel." Sir Walter Scott—to whom such authors of historical novels as Châteaubriand and his Martyrs, the *Salammbô* of Flaubert, and that well-nigh perfect fiction, *The History of Henry Esmond*, by Thackeray, yield precedence—might have achieved the impossible: the writing of a library, epitomising the social history of "These States"—as Walt Whitman would say. After Scott no name but Balzac's occurs to the memory; Balzac, who laid all France under his microscope (and France is all of a piece, not the checker-board of nationalities we call America). Even the mighty Tolstoy would have balked the job. And if these giants would have failed, what may be said of their successors? The idea of a great American novel is an "absolute," and nature abhors an absolute, despite the belief of some metaphysicians to the contrary. Yet the notion still obtains and inquests are held from time to time, and the opinions of contemporary novelists are taken toll of; as if each man and woman could give aught else but their own side of the matter, that side which is rightfully enough personal and provincial. The question is, after all, an affair for critics, and the great American novel will be in the plural; thousands perhaps. America is a chord of many nations, and to find the key-note we must play much and varied music.

While a novelist may be cosmopolitan at his own risk, a critic should be ever so. (Consider the names of such widely contrasted critical temperaments as Sainte-Beuve, Taine, De Gourmont, Matthew Arnold, Brandes, Swinburne, Arthur Symons, Havelock Ellis, Henry James, Gosse, and W. C. Brownell; all cosmopolitan as well as national.) The sublime tenuities of Henry James, like the black music of Michael Artzibashef, are questions largely temperamental. But the Russian is all Slavic, and no one would maintain that Mr. James shows a like ingrained nationalism. Nevertheless, he is American, though dealing only with a certain side of American life, the cosmopolitan phase. At his peril an American novelist sails eastward to describe

73

the history of his countrymen abroad. With the critic we come upon a different territory. He may go gadding after new mud-gods (the newest god invented by man is always the greatest), for the time being, and return to his native heath mentally refreshed and broadened by his foreign outing. Not so the maker of fiction. Once he cuts loose his balloon he is in danger of not getting home again.

Mr. James is a splendid case for us; he began in America and landed in England, there to stay. Our other felicitous example of cosmopolitanism is Henry Blake Fuller, the author of *The Chevalier of Pensieri-Vani* and *The Châtelaine of la Trinité,* who was so widely read in the nineties. After those charming excursions into a rapidly vanishing Europe Mr. Fuller reversed the proceeding of James; he returned to America and composed two novels of high artistic significance, *The Cliff Dwellers* and *With the Procession,* which, while they continued the realistic tradition of William Dean Howells, were also the forerunners of a new movement in America. It is not necessary to dwell now on *The Last Refuge,* or on that masterly book of spiritual parodies, *The Puppet-Booth.* But Mr. Fuller did not write the great American novel. Neither did Mr. Howells, nor Mr. James. Who has? No one. Is there such a thing? Without existing it might be described in Celtic fashion, this mythical work, as pure fiction. Let us admit for the sake of argument that if it were written by some unknown monster of genius, it would, like Lewis Carroll's Snark, turn into a Boojum.

Henry James has said that no one is compelled to admire any particular sort of writing; that the province of fiction is all life, and he has also wisely remarked that "when you have no taste you have no discretion, which is the conscience of taste," and may we add, when you have no discretion you perpetrate the shocking fiction with which America is deluged at this hour. We are told that the new writers have altered the old canons of bad taste, but *"plus ça change, plus c'est la même chose."* A liquorish sentimentality is the ever-threatening rock upon which the bark of young American novelists goes to pieces. (Pardon the mixed metaphor.) Be sentimental and you will succeed! We agree with Dostoievsky that in fiction, as well as in life, there are no general principles, only special cases. But these cases, could they not be typical? even if there are not types, only individuals. And are men and women so enthralled by the molasses of sentimentalism in life? Have the motion-pictures hopelessly deranged our critical values? I know that in America charity covers a multitude of mediocrities, nevertheless, I am loath to believe that all one reads in praise of wretched contemporary fiction is meant in earnest.

Well, *chacun à ses dégoûts!* The "thrilling" detective story, the romantic sonorities of the ice-cream-soda woman novelist?—with a triple-barrelled name, as Rudyard Kipling put it once upon a time—or that church of Heavenly Ennui, the historical novel—what a cemetery of ideas, all of them! An outsider must be puzzle-pated by this tumult of tasteless writing and worse observation. However, history in fiction may be a cavalcade of shining shadows, brilliant, lugubrious, dull, or joyful happenings; but where Thackeray succeeded multitudes have failed. Who shall bend the bow of that Ulysses? Native talent, subtle and robust, we possess in abundance; thus far it has cultivated with success in its own parochial garden—which is as it should be. The United States of Fiction. America is Cosmopolis.

II

As to the Puritanism of our present novels one may dare to say in the teeth of youthful protestants that it is non-existent. The pendulum has swung too far the other way. And as literary artists are rare, the result has not been reassuring. Zola seems prudish after some experiments of the younger crowd. How badly they pull off the trick. How coarse and hard and heavy their touch. Most of these productions read like stupid translations from a dull French original. They are not immoral, only vulgar. As old Flaubert used to say: such books are false, nature is not like that. How keenly he saw through the humbug of "free love"—a romantic tradition of George Sand's epoch—may be noted in his comment that Emma Bovary found in adultery all the platitudes of marriage. Ah! that much-despised, stupid, venerable institution, marriage! How it has been flouted since the days of Rousseau—the father of false romanticism and that stupefying legend, the "equality" of mankind. (O! the beautiful word, "equality," invented for the delectation of rudimentary minds.) A century and more fiction has played with the theme of concubinage. If the Nacquet divorce bill had been introduced a decade or so before it was in France, what would have become of the threatre of Dumas *fils*, or later, of the misunderstood woman in Ibsen's plays? All such tribal taboos make or unmake literature.

So, merely as a suggestion to ambitious youngsters, let the novelist of the future in search of a novelty describe a happy marriage, children, a husband who doesn't drink or gamble, a wife who votes, yet loves her home, her family, and knows how to cook. What a realistic bombshell he would hurl into the camp of sentimental socialists and them that believe a wedding certificate is like Balzac's *La Peau de Chagrin*—a document daily shrinking in happiness. Absurdities make martyrs, but of all the absurd and ineffectual martyrdoms that of running off with another's wife is usually the crowning one. "I don't call this very popular pie," said the little boy in Richard Grant White's story; and the man in the case is usually the first to complain of his bargain in pastry.

However, categories are virtually an avowal of mental impuissance, and all marriages are not made in heaven. In the kingdom of morality there are many mansions. When too late you may sport with the shade—not in the shade— of Amaryllis, and perhaps elbow epigrams as a lean consolation. That is your own affair. Paul Verlaine has told us that *"j'ai vécu énormement,"* though his living enormously did not prove that he was happy. Far from it. But he had at least the courage to relate his terrors. American novelists may agree with Dostoievsky that "everything in the world always ends in meanness"; or with Doctor Pangloss that all is for the best in the best of possible worlds. An affair of temperament. But don't mix the values. Don't confuse intellectual substances. Don't smear a fact with treacle and call it truth. Above all, don't preach. Impiety is an indiscretion, yet, don't be afraid to tell the truth. From Jane Austen and Walter Scott, the parents of the modern English novel, to many modern instances, fiction has thrived best on naked truth. All the rest is sawdust, tripe-selling, and sentimentalism. Didn't Mr. Roundabout declare in one of his famous papers that "Figs are sweet, but fictions are sweeter"? In our land we can't get the latter sweet enough. Altruism, Brotherhood of Man Uplifting. These are the shibboleths of the *"nouvelles couches sociales."* Prodigious!

III

J. K. Huysmans declared that in the land of books there are no schools; no idealism, realism, symbolism; only good writers and bad. Whistler said the same about painting and painters. Setting aside the technical viewpoint of such dicta, we fancy that our "best sellers" do not preoccupy themselves with the "mere writing" of their fictions, but they have developed a formidable faculty of preaching. Old-fashioned fiction that discloses personal charm, that delineates manners, or stirs the pulse of tragedy—not melodrama, is vanishing from publishers' lists. Are there not as many charming men and women perambulating the rind of the planet as there were in the days when Jane Austen, or Howells, or Turgenev wrote? We refuse to believe there are not; but there is little opportunity, in a word, no market, for the display of these qualities. The novel with a purpose, generally an unpleasant purpose, has usurped the rule of the novel of character and manners. Boanerges, not Balzac, now occupies the pasteboard pulpit of fiction.

I quoted Henry James to the effect that all life is the province of the novelist. Nevertheless, the still small garden wherein is reared the tender solitary flower does but ill represent the vaster, complicated forest of common humanity. The ivory tower of the cultivated egoist is not to be unduly admired; rather Zola's *La Terre* with its foul facts than a palace of morbid art. Withal, the didactic side of our fiction is overdone. I set it down to the humbug about the "masses" being opposed to the "classes." Truly a false antithesis. As if the French bourgeois were not a product of the revolution (poor bourgeois, always abused by the novelist). As if a poor man suddenly enriched didn't prove, as a rule, the hardest taskmaster to his own class. Consider the new-rich. What a study they afford the students of manners. A new generation has arisen. Its taste, intelligence, and culture; its canned manners, canned music—preferably pseudo-African—canned art, canned food, canned literature; its devotion to the mediocre—what a field for our aspiring young "secretaries to society."

Cheap prophylactics, political and religious—for religion is fast being butchered to make the sensational evangelists' holiday—are in vogue. They affect our fiction-mongers, who burn to avenge wrongs, write novels about the "downtrodden masses," and sermons on social evils—evils that have always existed, always will exist. Like the knife-grinder, story they have none to tell. Why write fiction, or what they are pleased to call fiction? Why not join the brave brigade of agitators and pamphleteers? The lay preachers are carrying off the sweepstakes. For them Mr. Howells is a superannuated writer. Would there were more like him in continence of speech, wholesomeness of judgment, nobility of ideals, and in the shrewd perception of character.

Fiction, too, is a fine art, though this patent fact has escaped the juvenile Paul Prys, who are mainly endeavouring to arouse class against mass. It's an old dodge, this equality theory, as old as Beelzebub, Lord of Flies. When all fruit fails, welcome envy and malicious slandering. When you have nothing else to write about, attack your neighbour, especially if he hath a much-coveted vineyard. Max Stirner, least understood of social philosophers, wrote, "Mind your own business," and he forged on the anvil of experience a mighty leading motive for the conduct of life. But our busy little penmen don't see in this golden motto a sufficient sentimental appeal. It doesn't flatter the "masses." Mr. Bryan a few years ago told us that we were all middle class. What is middle class? In Carlyle's day it was a "gigman"; in ours is it the owner of a "flivver"? But in the case of Snob vs. Mob, Snob always wins.

This twaddle about "democratic art" is the bane of our literature. There is only good art. Whether it deals with such "democratic" subjects as *L'Assommoir* or *Germinie Lacerteux*, or such "aristocratic" themes as those of D'Annunzio and Paul Bourget, it is the art thereof that determines the product. I hold no brief for the sterile fiction that is enrolled under the banner of "Art for Art." I go so far as to believe that a novelist with a beautiful style often allows that style to get in the way of human nature. Stained-glass windows have their use, but they falsify the daylight. A decorative style may suit pseudo-mediaeval romances, but for twentieth-century realism it is sadly amiss. Nor is the arterio-sclerotic school of psychological analysis to be altogether commended. It has been well-nigh done to death by Stendhal, Meredith, James, and Bourget; and it is as cold as a star. Flaubert urged as an objection to writing a novel, proving something that the other fellow can prove precisely the opposite. In either case selection plays the role.

The chief argument against the novel "with a purpose"—as the jargon goes —is its lack of validity either as a document or as art. A novel may be anything, but it must not be polemical. Zola has been, still is, the evil genius of many talented chaps who "sling ink," not to make a genuine book, but to create a sensation. Such writers lack patience, art, and direction. They always keep one eye on the box-office. Indeed, the young men and women of the day, who are squandering upon paper their golden genius, painfully resemble in their productions the dime novels once published by the lamented Beadle or the lucubrations in the Saturday weeklies of long ago. But in those publications there was more virility. The heroes then were not well-dressed namby-pambies; the villains were villainous; the detectives detected real crimes, and were not weavers of metaphysical abstractions like your latter-day miracle-workers of an impossible Scotland Yard; and the girls were girls, neither neurasthenic, nor did they outgolf all creation. The "new novelists still deal with the same raw material of melodrama. Their handling of love-episodes has much of the blaring-brass quality of old-fashioned Italian opera. They loudly twang the strings of sloppy sentiment, which evoke not music, but mush and moonshine. And these are our "motion-masters" to-day.

IV

There can be no objection to literature and life coming to grips. Letters should touch reality. Many a sturdy blow has been struck at abuses by pen-men masquerading behind fiction. No need to summon examples. As for realism—I deny there are commonplace people. Only those writers are commonplace that believe in the phrase. It is one of the paradoxes of art that the commonplace folk of Thackeray, Flaubert, or Anthony Trollope who delight us between covers would in life greatly bore us. The ennui is artistically suggested, though not experienced by the reader. It is the magic of the novelist, his style and philosophy, that make his creations vital.

Dostoievsky says there are no old women—to be sure he puts the expression in the mouth of the sensualist Karamazov—and as a corollary I maintain that nothing is uninteresting if painted by a master hand, from carrots to Chopin. As for the historical novel, there is *Sentimental Education* as a model, if you desire something epical in scale and charged with the modern ironic spirit. A Flaubertian masterpiece, this book, with its daylight atmosphere; the inimitable sound, shape, gait, and varied prose rhythms of its sentences, its marvellous gallery of portraits executed in the Dutch manner of Hals and Vermeer, its nearness to its environment, and its fidelity to the pattern of life. It is a true "historical" novel, for it is real—to employ the admirable simile of Mr. Howells.

No need to transpose the tragic gloom of Artzibashef to America; we are an optimistic people, thanks to our air and sky, political conditions, and the immigration of sturdy peasant folk. Yet we, too, have our own peculiar gloom and misery and social problems to solve. We are far from being the "shadowland" of fiction, as a certain English critic said. When I praise the dissonantal art of Michael Artzibashef it is not with the idea that either his style or his pessimism should be aped. That way unoriginality lies. But I do contend that in the practice of his art, its sincerity, its profundity, he might be profitably patterned after by the younger generation. Art should elevate as well as amuse. Must fiction always be silly and shallow? It need be neither sordid nor didactic.

William James put the matter in a nutshell when he wrote that "the whole atmosphere of present-day Utopian literature tastes mawkish and dish-watery to people who still keep a sense of life's more bitter flavours." And on this fundamentally sound note I must end my little sermon—for I find that I have been practising the very preaching against which I warned embryo novelists. But, then, isn't every critic a lay preacher?

From *Unicorns* by James Gibbons Huneker, pp. 82–95. Copyright, 1917, by Charles Scribner's Sons. Reprinted by permission of Charles Scribner's Sons.

VAN WYCK BROOKS
The Critical Movement in America
[1921]

IT WAS only the other day that America first came in for its effective share of self-criticism. The critical movement in America happened, as it were, over-night; and the critic in this country is still so new a type that we cannot be surprised if he is regarded as an undesirable alien, even a traitor. There is nothing else in all modern history like the unanimity of praise and confidence with which, by its passengers, the American Ship of State was launched and manned. In all our long nineteenth-century past, there was scarcely a breath of dissent, doubt, or censure: the semi-outlaw Whitman's *Democratic Vistas* was almost unique in this regard, for Emerson's and Lowell's strictures were lost in the flood of their social optimism. No wonder we became the most complacent of peoples. No wonder the tide of criticism rose at last.

One thinks of all this as one considers, for instance, such an alien point of reference as John Ruskin. To most of us, no doubt, Ruskin has always seemed a normal and familiar possession. Yet, as one reflects on his career, the thought comes to one's mind: How different this man was from anything the America of his day could have produced! Hear, for example, what Mr. Masefield recently said of him: "Ruskin, looking out upon his native land some eighty years ago, decided that he could not believe in it, that there was nothing spiritual there which he could trust, nor human work being done which he could share." Imagine a nineteenth-century American giving utterance to such a sentiment, the sentiment from which Ruskin's work sprang! Yet this was surely the animating sentiment of the greatest English literature of the century, even of Charles Dickens: who but Macaulay, of all the writers of England, was not filled, as regards the future of his people, with more or less fundamental doubts? And meanwhile the writers of America chanted a unanimous hymn to progress. They were happy, they were hopeful. They agreed, or seemed to agree, with the famous utterance of Edward Everett: "Our government is in its theory perfect, and in its operation it is perfect also. Thus we have solved the great problem in human affairs." Was this because the American life of their epoch was finer and more wholesome than English life? Because it contained a greater spiritual promise? Few in our generation would

80

affirm this. We know too well how fully justified were most of the European travelers' reflections on our old social life—which used to cause such resentment in American breasts: they were not malignant, those travelers' reflections, any more than the comments of the European critics and scholars—Ruskin himself, for instance—who looked upon "Americanism" as a poisonous growth that might well infect and destroy all civilization. And as we observe the complacency to which our national optimism gave birth, we ask ourselves whether this optimism was ever a symptom of health, whether it was not indeed the symptom of a great evil: the loss of a clear sense of the true values of life.

It is certain, in any case, that our criticism has suffered from the obvious necessity of making up for much lost time. We do not understand criticism, and this is because we have had so little of it. We have had no candid friends of our own race, no "national conscience," in short, such as every European people has had, for England is not unique in this respect: and, consequently, it was difficult a few years ago for most Americans to question the belief of Mr. Meredith Nicholson, for instance, that "if there is any manifestation on earth of a divine ordering of things, it is here in America." This is the sort of belief the Philistine majority in every country cherishes in its heart; it is the sort of belief that Matthew Arnold so well described as "vulgar, and not only vulgar but retarding," for retarding it surely is if, in order to go somewhere, to get somewhere, to advance, to develop, we must first have an inner conviction that we have not already arrived. If American life as we know it is indeed a manifestation of a divine ordering of things, there is nothing for us to do but to continue to manifest our divinity. But is our life divine? Is it so much better than the life of England, France, Germany, Russia that the comments of a Ruskin, a Renan, a Nietzsche would have been sheer impertinences on our side of the Atlantic? The prosperous middle class the world over looks upon itself and its own fatness with an overkindly eye; but America is the only modern country where, until recent years, the prosperous middle class has gone unchallenged, where the Philistines have never been aroused to a sense of their limitations. Heine never permitted the Germans to forget how much they had to learn; no one was ever more outspoken than Nietzsche in regard to "what the Germans lack." The French are complacent enough; but Renan never ceased to remind them of their "incurable religious mediocrity," of "the alternations of levity and dullness, of narrow timidity and foolish temerity" which are among the features of the French mind. Arnold, Ruskin, Carlyle, as we know, kept their guns steadily trained on the weaknesses of the English character; and while Ibsen lived how many illusions in regard to their peculiar superiority were the people of Norway suffered to cherish?

Merely to mention these names is to suggest how uniformly our American fur has been rubbed the right way. For while Emerson, Lowell, Whitman deplored the imperfections of our social life, their criticism was neither sustained nor drastic. Emerson was the incarnation of optimism and lived, besides, too much in a timeless world to concern himself with a single phase of history: this was not his rôle. Lowell was so conscious of that "certain condescension in foreigners" that he could not sufficiently draw the veil over the short-comings of his countrymen. And there was Howells, with his rosy vision of the American scene, all the more delusive because he professed an intransigent realism. There was even Henry James, whom nothing could have induced to live in America: did he not apologize in one of his prefaces for having spoken in terms of disrespect of a certain small city in Massachusetts, adding so much thereby to the ultimate obloquy of those who have since reproached our Gopher Prairies? These men, of course, were not primarily critics, and that is just the point; Thoreau was not primarily a critic; in fact, before the war we had no critics. Those who could not put up with our life in the East quietly went West, and those who could not put up with our life at all quietly went to Europe. No one stood still and spoke out; and after the Civil War, even the voices of the traveling foreigners who told the truth about many of our ways were cloaked and muffled. Everyone waited, waited, by common consent, to see how the great experiment of democracy was going to work out. We had sixty years of grace while the oracles were dumb.

We were, in a word, singularly unconscious. America "just growed"—in the manner of the British Empire perhaps, but certainly in a very different man-ner from England itself, or France or Germany. It grew by sheer activity, expansion, immigration, without forethought, afterthought, reflection of any kind. That is to say, since no population is ever aware of itself as a population, save perhaps in times of war, it had no governing and directing minority more conscious than the multitude, more conscious of human values, no class of thinkers who, while having no administrative authority, might yet have ex-ercised a real authority over popular opinion, interpreting the movements of society in the light of historical principles, and arousing in those who were intelligent and articulate a just sense of what was really happening. Who knew, for instance, that America was becoming an empire, apprehended this fact in all its implications? America never "meant" to become an empire, and few Americans know, even today, really know, I mean *apprehend,* that Amer-ica is an empire, with all the paraphernalia of imperialism. This change came automatically, as it were, because, contrary as it plainly was to the professed genius of the Republic, no strong, articulate minority showed the people what was taking place before their eyes. One has only to compare the feeble protests that arose throughout this country over the annexation of the Philippines with the outburst of resentment and remonstrance, of satire and impassioned poetry, evoked in England by the Boer War, to perceive the difference be-tween a conscious and an unconscious society; and the difference only widens when we remember that imperialism in the England of those days had been for generations a deliberate national policy.

So it was that after the Civil War our social history became an illustration of what might be called a policy of indifference. The individual stood aside and let things take their course. To a large extent, this has been true of our thought from the beginning: whether optimistic, as with Emerson and Whitman, or pessimistic, as with Henry Adams and Mark Twain, it has always tended to be fatalistic. It has assumed, or tended to assume, that things were "coming out all right," because Americans are Americans, or else that things were coming out all wrong, because nothing could stop them from doing so, because human life itself is a mistake, as Mark Twain thought, or because, as Henry Adams thought, evolution is merely a matter of thermodynamics. These attitudes are all fatalistic because they beg the question of human control or deny its possibility; and together they have formed the various strands of a national tradition in which the critical intellect has played scarcely any part whatever.˙That America must and will be perfect just by being itself, or that America is doomed and damned: these are the two poles between which, even to this day, our public opinion oscillates. The cultivated classes are too often convinced, although they keep their opinion to themselves, that the country is already doomed and damned. The rest are equally sure, not that the country will be, but that the country already is what Mr. Nicholson calls it; and they have plainly arrived at this opinion by lowering their human standards to a point where the great values of life do not exist. Mr. Nicholson, who speaks so complacently of the "divine ordering of things" in America, also says that a "town is better advertised by enlightened sanitary ordinances duly enforced than by the number of its citizens who are acquainted with the writings of Walter Pater. If Main Street knows," he adds, "what America is all about, and bathes itself and is kind and considerate of its neighbors, why not leave the rest on the knees of the gods?" Why, indeed, if we share Mr. Nicholson's indifference to the great human values? "We do not know," he says again, "we do not know but that in some far day a prowling New Zealander, turning up a banjo and a trap-drum amid the ruins of some American college, will account them nobler instruments than the lyre and lute." But why wait for the "ruins" of this American college? The ruins are with us already if we have lost a sense of the distinction between the trap-drum and the lyre and lute.

And the sense of this distinction has been lost, too largely lost, because criticism, in all these years, has failed to keep it alive. Mr. William Allen White has observed that he would like to collect the junior pessimists who are raking America with their criticism and duck them in the town-pump. One readily understands Mr. White's resentment, for he has himself gone through life without once being held up, without once being checked in his rampant career of self-congratulation over the virtues of Kansas. And Mr. White's resentment is widely shared; one constantly hears of apostles of good-Americanism who have "had about enough" of these junior pessimists. And it cannot be denied that for this resentment there exists a certain reason, for few indeed of the pessimists in question are not open to the retort that they are themselves no more essentially civilized than the civilization they attack. We are always well aware of what they hate; we are seldom aware at all of what they love, and only what they love can civilize us. This is true; yet, save for these same vipers, whose critical equipment is, one admits, defective, where else in America can we turn for criticism? The "best" magazines freely open their columns to Mr. Nicholson's and Mr. White's opinions; the "best" people, as we are led to suppose, delight in these opinions. At every adverse comment on our civilization the cry still goes up: But there is so much to be said on the other side! And no one questions this; what one asserts, and asserts, and asserts again, is that there is so much to be said on *this* side. If it were not for these vipers who have risen among us, we should all find ourselves intellectually on the level of the "man in the street" for whom Messrs. Nicholson and White are so proud to speak. The conservative reviews, as one might think, exist for the purpose of combating the radical reviews, giving aid and comfort to that false-Americanism, now dominant through the world, the rise and spread of which was the nightmare of those European critics of the nineteenth century whose standards they profess to uphold.

In short, before the emergence of our critical movement, the clear sense of the great values of life had long been submerged in America. For we are obliged to take Mr. White and Mr. Nicholson at their word and assume that they really do not know the difference between the trap-drum and the lyre and lute, or between the Valley of Democracy and the Kingdom of Heaven. We are even obliged to take at their word the defenders of some pseudo-American tradition who failed to challenge Edward Bok, for instance, when he adopted the word "Americanization" to describe a career that was throughout devoted, with whatever good intentions, to the vulgarization of American life. And we cannot expect that those who are color-blind to the great values of life, in the name of which criticism speaks, will see anything but animus in this criticism, or regard it as anything but insulting. This indeed would be true if our criticism were ten times more certain of its values than it is: we know that Mr. White would as readily duck a Ruskin as a Mencken. For Americans are not accustomed to plain speaking. We cherish a romantic view of our activities, and an American spade, to most of us, is not a spade at all: it is a sword, an implement of knighthood, and to call it a spade is to challenge our fondest prepossessions. The romantic soul dwells in the region of hyperbole, and its virtues are not the virtues of understatement. This fact explains the apparent censoriousness of much of our recent social criticism. Some of this criticism has really been censorious, it has been so by reaction; but much of it has only appeared censorious. If we had been accustomed to a realistic view of affairs, and a true historic sense of human values, we should have accepted this criticism and even rejoiced in it.

For we know how America appears in the eyes of the world. The Japanese poet, Mr. Yone Noguchi, is the spokesman of contemporary humanity when he describes our country as "floating comfortably on the ocean all by itself, as if a well-fed seal or lazy iceberg." And those who have an interest in America, its true life, its true historic rôle, are aware that such a posture is a perilous posture. No doubt, in the beginning, this uncritical attitude, this attitude of uncriticised faith and hope, contributed much to our dawning civilization. A new country is obliged to affirm its existence, to believe in itself against all comers. If the America of three generations ago had seen itself as Europeans saw it, as its own cultivated minds saw it in the privacy of their souls, it would have lost heart; for with nations as with individuals nothing is more paralyzing than a premature self-consciousness. Our old writers were surely aware of all that was imperfect in our society, but they were aware also that too much cannot be expected of a new country. They saw, moreover, that America was too deeply in the grip of unusual natural forces for criticism to have much effect upon it; for, as Frederick Turner pointed out in his study of *The Frontier in American History,* the development of American civilization in the nineteenth century exhibited a constant return to primitive conditions on a continually advancing frontier-line. Our social development was always beginning again *de novo* on the frontier, and this largely prevented Americans even in the settled areas from retaining a firm hold upon civilized values. And so our old writers, convinced of the futility of criticism, turned their reluctant energies in other directions. Meanwhile, with few exceptions, the immigrants from the Old World belonged to the inarticulate classes; and for them it was enough, or seemed enough, that the New World afforded them opportunities, of an economic sort, which they had not possessed in the Old. We know how these immigrants expressed themselves. Such works as *The Promised Land* and *The Making of an American* contributed immensely to our national self-esteem; and, what is more to the point, in the absence of native spokesmen who might have maintained the sense of human values, they served as the final proof in American eyes that our civilization was superior in all essentials to the civilization of Europe. In this realm, the realm of self-congratulation, it never rains but it pours.

Because of these peculiar circumstances, our social history differs from that of any of the European countries. We have never conceived it as possible to shape our social life. This social life has grown and changed so rapidly, so many racial strains have merged themselves in it, so many territories have opened before it, this life has indeed existed in such a flux that the idea of molding it has scarcely entered our calculations. It was this that prevented for so long the development of criticism in America. We know how quietistic Hawthorne was regarding every prospect of social change: we know his fear, embodied in the character of Hollingsworth, of tampering with "the natural order of things." A similar diffidence inhibited Mark Twain, and surely this was one of the reasons that led Henry Adams to hide his life and restrained him from coming forward as the critic he plainly wished to be. They felt, these gifted men, that the only course for them was to stand aside and watch the American process—some in faith, others in despair, and more and more in despair, as they saw how little the process contemplated of what to them was important for civilization. For they felt that they could never shape the process, or control it in any way. Yet the longer the process continued, the more it became apparent that Americans, in so far as they were Americans who piqued themselves on their "Americanism," were ceasing to desire, were ceasing even to be able to desire, consciously and with their minds and wills, any goals in life except the goals that were placed before them by the world of trade. Yes, even to the point where their perceptions had come to rest on a purely physical plane.

But *autres temps, autres mœurs.* We have nourished ourselves on hope in America, where we should have nourished ourselves on desire. Many have hoped for America, few have desired for America. And desire is the mother of intention. And desire cannot come without criticism. "It is an *idea,*" as John Eglinton says, for which we wait. "Without an idea man is frivolous, dissatisfied, despicable. With an idea the long-hoarded initiatives of his nature are liberated, he strains forward to new consummations." Criticism, so silent in the past, is vocal now in America; and why should it be vocal if there were not within it a sudden faith in the ability of Americans to shape their destiny, to mold it and give it form, to ride things as things have ridden them? The division between the two great camps of modern American writers is a division between those who are still satisfied with a national state of adolescence and those who exact of America the traits and responsibilities of maturity; and if the latter appear a little rough and importunate, it is because they are obliged to shake out of a deep sleep a population that should have been kept awake by an unbroken succession of gentle proddings. The recent damming-up of our social energies, through the closing of the frontier at the West and the slackening of immigration at the East, enables us really for the first time to submit to a candid scrutiny our prepossessions in regard to property and every other fundamental issue, to desire a great and beautiful corporate life. How scattered our forces have been! We have taken pleasure, it seems, in making machines of men; and repudiating the vision of a good society, we have not discouraged our finest intellects from giving up society as a bad job and devoting to the material periphery the passion they might have devoted to human beings. Our thought has been centrifugal instead of centripetal; it has gone out to the frame, it has never fixed itself upon the picture.

The great social thinkers, the great critics have given us a sense of society as a whole, and of man as a social animal, capable of molding his environment towards a humane ideal. And Ruskin, as Lawrence Binyon says, might well have taken as his motto the lines of Blake:

> I will not cease from mental fight,
> Nor shall my sword sleep in my hand,
> Till we have built Jerusalem
> In England's green and pleasant land.

American criticism, too, is capable of such a vision. But this is certain, American criticism will never attain its object as long as it fails to conceive, as something ever-present in its purview, the "green and pleasant land" it contemplates. The great critics have always convinced the world in spite of the prepossessions of the world; it is their ability to do so that makes these critics great and worthy of attention, for unless they speak with reasonableness and human understanding they confess in their own words that they do not possess that in the name of which they pretend to speak. No doubt, for many years in this country the critics and the unconverted public are destined to wage the blindest kind of warfare; for the critical attitude in our general mind has perished from disuse. But as long as this continues let us remember that our work is only a kind of spadework, which antecedes the real task of criticism. To forget this is to have lost the battle. For Amiel expressed the just motto of critics in those memorable words: "Truth should not merely conquer, it should win."

From *Sketches in Criticism* by Van Wyck Brooks, pp. 11-25. Copyright, 1932, by E. P. Dutton & Co. Reprinted by permission of the author and publishers. An earlier form of this material appeared in *The Freeman* ("A Reviewer's Notebook"), Vol. IV (Oct. 12, 1921), pp. 118-119, and other issues of that year.

PART II

Versions of Tradition and Responsibility

T. S. ELIOT

Tradition and the Individual Talent

[1919]

IN ENGLISH writing we seldom speak of tradition, though we occasionally apply its name in deploring its absence. We cannot refer to "the tradition" or to "a tradition"; at most, we employ the adjective in saying that the poetry of So-and-so is "traditional," or even "too traditional." Seldom, perhaps, does the word appear except in a phrase of censure. If otherwise, it is vaguely approbative, with the implication, as to the work approved, of some pleasing archaeological reconstruction. You can hardly make the word agreeable to English ears without this comfortable reference to the reassuring science of archaeology.

Certainly the word is not likely to appear in our appreciations of living or dead writers. Every nation, every race, has not only its own creative, but its own critical turn of mind; and is even more oblivious of the shortcomings and limitations of its critical habits than of those of its creative genius. We know, or think we know, from the enormous mass of critical writing that has appeared in the French language the critical method or habit of the French; we only conclude (we are such unconscious people) that the French are "more critical" than we, and sometimes even plume ourselves a little with the fact, as if the French were the less spontaneous. Perhaps they are; but we might remind ourselves that criticism is as inevitable as breathing, and that we should be none the worse for articulating what passes in our minds when we read a book and feel an emotion about it, for criticising our own minds in their work of criticism. One of the facts that might come to light in this process is our tendency to insist, when we praise a poet, upon those aspects of his work in which he least resembles anyone else. In these aspects or parts of his work we pretend to find what is individual, what is the peculiar essence of the man. We dwell with satisfaction upon the poet's difference from his predecessors, especially his immediate predecessors; we endeavor to find something that can be isolated in order to be enjoyed. Whereas if we approach a poet without this prejudice we shall often find that not only the best, but the most individual parts of his work may be those in which the dead poets, his ancestors, assert their immortality most vigorously. And I do not mean the impressionable period of adolescence, but the period of full maturity.

Yet if the only form of tradition, of handing down, consisted in following the ways of the immediate generation before us in a blind or timid adherence to its successes, "tradition" should positively be discouraged. We have seen many such simple currents soon lost in the sand; and novelty is better than repetition. Tradition is a matter of much wider significance. It cannot be inherited, and if you want it you must obtain it by great labor. It involves, in the first place, the historical sense, which we may call nearly indispensable to anyone who would continue to be a poet beyond his twenty-fifth year; and the historical sense involves a perception, not only of the pastness of the past, but of its presence; the historical sense compels a man to write not merely with his own generation in his bones, but with a feeling that the whole of the literature of Europe from Homer and within it the whole of the literature of his own country has a simultaneous existence and composes a simultaneous order. This historical sense, which is a sense of the timeless as well as of the temporal and of the timeless and of the temporal together, is what makes a writer traditional. And it is at the same time what makes a writer most acutely conscious of his place in time, of his own contemporaneity.

No poet, no artist of any art, has his complete meaning alone. His significance, his appreciation is the appreciation of his relation to the dead poets and artists. You cannot value him alone; you must set him, for contrast and comparison, among the dead. I mean this as a principle of esthetic, not merely historical, criticism. The necessity that he shall conform, that he shall cohere, is not onesided; what happens when a new work of art is created is something that happens simultaneously to all the works of art which preceded it. The existing monuments form an ideal order among themselves, which is modified by the introduction of the new (the really new) work of art among them. The existing order is complete before the new work arrives; for order to persist after the supervention of novelty, the *whole* existing order must be, if ever so slightly, altered; and so the relations, proportions, values of each work of art toward the whole are readjusted; and this is conformity between the old and the new. Whoever has approved this idea of order, of the form of European, of English literature will not find it preposterous that the past should be altered by the present as much as the present is directed by the past. And the poet who is aware of this will be aware of great difficulties and responsibilities.

In a peculiar sense he will be aware also that he must inevitably be judged by the standards of the past. I say judged, not amputated, by them; not judged to be as good as, or worse or better than, the dead; and certainly not judged by the canons of dead critics. It is a judgment, a comparison, in which two things are measured by each other. To conform merely would be for the new work not really to conform at all; it would not be new, and would therefore not be a work of art. And we do not quite say that the new is more valuable because it fits in; but its fitting in is a test of its value—a test, it is true, which can only be slowly and cautiously applied, for we are none of us infallible judges of conformity. We say: it appears to conform, and is perhaps individual, or it appears individual, and may conform; but we are hardly likely to find that it is one, and not the other.

To proceed to a more intelligible exposition of the relation of the poet to the past: he can neither take the past as a lump, an indiscriminate bolus, nor can he form himself wholly on one or two private admirations, nor can he form himself wholly upon one preferred period. The first course is inadmissible, the second is an important experience of youth, and the third is a pleasant and highly desirable supplement. The poet must be very conscious of the main current, which does not at all flow invariably through the most distinguished reputations. He must be quite aware of the obvious fact that art never improves, but that the material of art is never quite the same. He must be aware that the mind of Europe—the mind of his own country—a mind which he learns in time to be much more important than his own private mind—is a mind which changes, and that this change is a development which abandons nothing *en route,* which does not superannuate either Shakespeare, or Homer, or the rock drawing of the Magdalenian draughtsman. That this development, refinement perhaps, complication certainly, is not, from the point of view of the artist, any improvement. Perhaps not even an improvement from the point of view of the psychologist or not to the extent which we imagine: perhaps only in the end based upon a complication in economics and machinery. But the difference between the present and the past is that the conscious present is an awareness of the past in a way and to an extent which the past's awareness of itself cannot show.

Someone said: "The dead writers are remote from us because we *know* so much more than they did." Precisely, and they are that which we know.

I am alive to a usual objection to what is clearly part of my programme for the *métier* of poetry. The objection is that the doctrine requires a ridiculous amount of erudition (pedantry), a claim which can be rejected by appeal to the lives of poets in any pantheon. It will even be affirmed that much learning deadens or perverts poetic sensibility. While, however, we persist in believing that a poet ought to know as much as will not encroach upon his necessary receptivity and necessary laziness, it is not desirable to confine knowledge to whatever can be put into a useful shape for examinations, drawing-rooms, or the still more pretentious modes of publicity. Some can absorb knowledge, the more tardy must sweat for it. Shakespeare acquired more essential history from Plutarch than most men could from the whole

British Museum. What is to be insisted upon is that the poet must develop
or procure the consciousness of the past and that he should continue to develop this consciousness throughout his career.

What happens is a continual surrender of himself as he is at the moment to
something which is more valuable. The progress of an artist is a continual
self-sacrifice, a continual extinction of personality.

There remains to define this process of depersonalization, and its relation
to the sense of tradition. It is in this depersonalization that art may be said
to approach the condition of science. I, therefore, invite you to consider, as
a suggestive analogy, the action which takes place when a bit of finely
filiated platinum is introduced into a chamber containing oxygen and sulphur
dioxide.

II

Honest criticism and sensitive appreciation are directed not upon the poet
but upon the poetry. If we attend to the confused cries of the newspaper critics
and the *susurrus* of popular repetition that follows, we shall hear the names
of poets in great numbers; if we seek not Blue-book knowledge but the
enjoyment of poetry, and ask for a poem, we shall seldom find it. I have
tried to point out the importance of the relation of the poem to other poems
by other authors, and suggested the conception of poetry as a living whole of
all the poetry that has ever been written. The other aspect of this Impersonal
theory of poetry is the relation of the poem to its author. And I hinted, by an
analogy, that the mind of the mature poet differs from that of the immature
one not precisely in any valuation of "personality," not being necessarily more
interesting, or having "more to say," but rather by being a more finely perfected medium in which special, or very varied, feelings are at liberty to enter
into new combinations.

The analogy was that of the catalyst. When the two gases previously mentioned are mixed in the presence of a filament of platinum, they form
sulphurous acid. This combination takes place only if the platinum is present;
nevertheless the newly formed acid contains no trace of platinum, and the
platinum itself is apparently unaffected; has remained inert, neutral, and unchanged. The mind of the poet is the shred of platinum. It may partly or
exclusively operate upon the experience of the man himself; but the more
perfect the artist, the more completely separate in him will be the man who
suffers and the mind which creates; the more perfectly will the mind digest
and transmute the passions which are its material.

The experience, you will notice, the elements which enter the presence of
the transforming catalyst, are of two kinds: emotions and feelings. The effect
of a work of art upon the person who enjoys it is an experience different in
kind from any experience not of art. It may be formed out of one emotion,

or may be a combination of several; and various feelings, inhering for the writer in particular words or phrases or images, may be added to compose the final result. Or great poetry may be made without the direct use of any emotion whatever: composed out of feelings solely. Canto XV of the *Inferno* (Brunetto Latini) is a working up of the emotion evident in the situation; but the effect, though single as that of any work of art, is obtained by considerable complexity of detail. The last quatrain gives an image, a feeling attaching to an image which "came," which did not develop simply out of what precedes, but which was probably in suspension in the poet's mind until the proper combination arrived for it to add itself to. The poet's mind is, in fact, a receptacle for seizing and storing up numberless feelings, phrases, images, which remain there until all the particles which can unite to form a new compound are present together.

If you compare several representative passages of the greatest poetry you see how great is the variety of types of combination, and also how completely any semi-ethical criterion of "sublimity" misses the mark. For it is not the "greatness," the intensity, of the emotions, the components, but the intensity of the artistic process, the pressure, so to speak, under which the fusion takes place, that counts. The episode of Paolo and Francesca employs a definite emotion, but the intensity of the poetry is something quite different from whatever intensity in the supposed experience it may give the impression of. It is no more intense, furthermore, than Canto XXVI, the voyage of Ulysses, which has not the direct dependence upon an emotion. Great variety is possible in the process of transmutation of emotion: the murder of Agamemnon, or the agony of Othello, gives an artistic effect apparently closer to a possible original than the scenes from Dante. In the *Agamemnon*, the artistic emotion approximates to the emotion of an actual spectator; in *Othello* to the emotion of the protagonist himself. But the difference between art and the event is always absolute; the combination which is the murder of Agamemnon is probably as complex as that which is the voyage of Ulysses. In either case there has been a fusion of elements. The ode of Keats contains a number of feelings which have nothing particular to do with the nightingale, but which the nightingale, partly, perhaps, because of its attractive name, and partly because of its reputation, served to bring together.

The point of view which I am struggling to attack is perhaps related to the metaphysical theory of the substantial unity of the soul: for my meaning is, that the poet has, not a "personality" to express, but a particular medium, which is only a medium, and not a personality, in which impressions and experiences combine in peculiar and unexpected ways. Impressions and experiences which are important for the man may take no place in the poetry, and those which become important in the poetry may play quite a negligible part in the man, the personality.

I will quote a passage which is unfamiliar enough to be regarded with
fresh attention in the light—or darkness—of these observations:

> And now methinks I could e'en chide myself
> For doating on her beauty, though her death
> Shall be revenged after no common action.
> Does the silkworm expend her yellow labours
> For thee? For thee does she undo herself?
> Are lordships sold to maintain ladyships
> For the poor benefit of a bewildering minute?
> Why does yon fellow falsify highways,
> And put his life between the judge's lips,
> To refine such a thing—keeps horse and men
> To beat their valours for her? . . .

In this passage (as is evident if it is taken in its context) there is a combination
of positive and negative emotions: an intensely strong attraction toward
beauty, and an equally intense fascination by the ugliness which is contrasted with it and which destroys it. This balance of contrasted emotion is in
the dramatic situation to which the speech is pertinent, but that situation
alone is inadequate to it. This is, so to speak, the structural emotion, provided
by the drama. But the whole effect, the dominant tone, is due to the fact that
a number of floating feelings, having an affinity to this emotion by no means
superficially evident, have combined with it to give us a new art emotion.

It is not in his personal emotions, the emotions provoked by particular
events in his life, that the poet is in any way remarkable or interesting. His
particular emotions may be simple, or crude, or flat. The emotion in his
poetry will be a very complex thing, but not with the complexity of the emotions of people who have very complex or unusual emotions in life. One error,
in fact, of eccentricity in poetry is to seek for new human emotions to express;
and in this search for novelty in the wrong place it discovers the perverse.
The business of the poet is not to find new emotions, but to use the ordinary
ones, and, in working them up into poetry, to express feelings which are not
in actual emotions at all. And emotions which he has never experienced
will serve his turn as well as those familiar to him. Consequently, we must believe that "emotion recollected in tranquillity" is an inexact formula. For it is
neither emotion nor recollection, nor, without distortion of meaning, tranquillity. It is a concentration, and a new thing resulting from the concentration, of
a very great number of experiences which to the practical and active person
would not seem to be experiences at all; it is a concentration which does not
happen consciously or of deliberation. These experiences are not "recollected,"
and they finally unite in an atmosphere which is "tranquil" only in that it is
a passive attending upon the event. Of course, this is not quite the whole
story. There is a great deal, in the writing of poetry, which must be conscious

and deliberate. In fact, the bad poet is usually unconscious where he ought to be conscious, and conscious where he ought to be unconscious. Both errors tend to make him "personal." Poetry is not a turning loose of emotion, but an escape from emotion; it is not the expression of personality, but an escape from personality. But, of course, only those who have personality and emotions know what it means to want to escape from these things.

III

ὁ δὲ νοῦς ἴσως θειότερόν τι καὶ ἀπαθές ἐστιν.[1]

This essay proposes to halt at the frontier of metaphysics or mysticism, and confine itself to such practical conclusions as can be applied by the responsible person interested in poetry. To divert interest from the poet to the poetry is a laudable aim: for it would conduce to a juster estimation of actual poetry, good and bad. There are many people who appreciate the expression of sincere emotion in verse, and there is a smaller number of people who can appreciate technical excellence. But very few know when there is an expression of *significant* emotion, emotion which has its life in the poem, and not in the history of the poet. The emotion of art is impersonal. And the poet cannot reach this impersonality without surrendering himself wholly to the work to be done. And he is not likely to know what is to be done unless he lives in what is not merely the present, but the present moment of the past, unless he is conscious, not of what is dead, but of what is already living.

From *Selected Essays, 1917–32* by T. S. Eliot, pp. 3–11. Copyright, 1932. Reprinted by permission of Harcourt, Brace and Company, Inc. Reprinted from *The Sacred Wood* (1920). First published in *The Egoist* (London), Vol. VI (September–October, 1919), pp. 54–55, and (November–December, 1919), pp. 72–73.

Poetry and Propaganda
[1930]

THE text for this paper is taken from Whitehead's *Science and the Modern World,* page 127:

The literature of the nineteenth century, especially its English poetic literature, is a witness to the discord between the esthetic intuitions of mankind and the mechanism of science. Shelley brings vividly before us the elusiveness of the eternal ob-

[1] Aristotle, *De Anima,* I. 4, 408b29: "mind is, no doubt, something more divine and impassible" (J. A. Smith, Oxford translation). (Editor's note.)

jects of sense as they haunt the change which infects underlying organisms. Wordsworth is the poet of nature as being the field of enduring permanences carrying
within themselves a message of tremendous significance. The eternal objects are
also there for him,

> The light that never was, on sea or land.

Both Shelley and Wordsworth emphatically bear witness that nature cannot be
divorced from its esthetic values; and that these values arise from the cumulation,
in some sense, of the brooding presence of the whole onto its various parts. Thus
we gain from the poets the doctrine that a philosophy of nature must concern itself
at least with these six notions: change, value, eternal objects, endurance, organism,
interfusion.

So far Professor Whitehead. Now I must insist clearly at the beginning that
what I have to say has nothing to do with this book as a whole, or with Mr.
Whitehead's theory as a whole: I am not here judging or valuing his theory or
his method or his results. I am concerned only with this one chapter, which
is called "The Romantic Reaction," and only with this one passage in that
chapter. And only, therefore, with two specific questions: can poetry be
cited to *prove* anything? and to what extent can it even be cited to *illustrate*
anything?

It appears to me that Mr. Whitehead is here summoning Shelley and
Wordsworth to *prove* something in connection with what he calls a "philosophy of nature"; that is what his words *thus we gain from the poets the
doctrine that,* seem to me to mean; even if the author did not mean that, it is
at least what many of his readers must have taken it to mean.

When so distinguished a scientist and philosopher makes this use of poetry,
a great many people will follow him, in the belief that anyone who can
understand symbolic logic must certainly understand anything so simple as
poetry. And indeed I must say that in the earlier part of his book Mr. Whitehead does prepare us to consent to any use of literature he may choose to
make: his knowledge and appreciation of history and literature are so great,
and his summaries and reviews of historical processes and periods so very skillful, his allusions so apt, that we are charmed into assent. Nevertheless, I believe that the passage I have just read is nonsense, and dangerous nonsense at
that. Consider first how really remarkable it is that we should

> . . . gain from the poets the doctrine that a philosophy of nature must concern
> itself at least with these six notions: change, value, eternal objects, endurance,
> organism, interfusion.

There are, to begin with, two steps in Whitehead's legerdemain. He has
quoted, and discussed generally, two poets of one period, Shelley and Wordsworth. These two then become "the poets"; would any beginner in scientific
inquiry ever exhibit such a perfect example of imperfect induction? And then

the poets are said to demonstrate that a philosophy of nature must be concerned at least with the six concepts mentioned.

Let us take the first sentence:

The literature of the nineteenth century, especially its English poetic literature,
is a witness to the discord between the esthetic intuitions of mankind and the
mechanism of science.

To call the whole of English poetry of the nineteenth century to witness such
a generality is certainly rash, and the meaning of the sentence is not clear.
It might mean that the great English poets were all *aware* of this discord between intuitions and mechanism. In this form the statement might be true of
the author of *In Memoriam*. But how far is it true of Browning or Swinburne,
and as far as it may be true how significant is it in their respective views of
life? But perhaps Mr. Whitehead means merely that poets, by affirming the
reality of values, are denying by implication the sufficiency of a mechanistic
philosophy. But in this form the statement is too comprehensive, for it applies
to all artists at every time, as they all have affirmed the validity of esthetic intuitions. And in the proposition there are two terms to be examined, "esthetic
intuitions," and "the mechanism of science"; and we must then consider in
what way there can be any "discord" between terms so disparate.

That poor old creature, "mechanistic philosophy" or "materialism" has been
in our time thoroughly repudiated by its old friends the scientists, and receives
no kindness from anyone but a few liberal theologians. It is not of course quite
the same thing as "the mechanism of science": the latter is strictly merely
the corpus of pre-Einstein and pre-Rutherford physical theory, which has been
rejected more or less by physicists on the good ground that it does not account
for all the facts—not on the doubtful ground that it offends poetic intuitions.
The mechanism of science is not the same thing as a *philosophy* based on
that science, which would assert that physical science would explain the
whole universe, and that what would not be explained in this way was unworthy of notice. But in any case, I find myself in the curious position of
having to defend the "mechanism of science," which is no friend of mine,
against an eminent scientist.

Are we to suppose that a mechanistic philosophy is fundamentally antagonistic to the esthetic intuitions of mankind? That is certainly surprising, as
some works of literary art seem to have been built upon it. The philosophy,
such as it is, of Thomas Hardy's novels, seems to be based upon the mechanism
of science. I think it is a very bad philosophy indeed, and I think that Hardy's
work would be better for a better philosophy, or none at all; but there it is:
has he not exploited determinism to extract his esthetic values from the contemplation of a world in which values do not count? There is a more important poet than Hardy, who is Lucretius. We cannot deny "esthetic in-

tuitions" to Lucretius. His world was mechanical enough, in all conscience; and just because it was, Lucretius gets the particular emotional values that he does get. We may admit therefore a discord between the mechanism of science and *some* esthetic intuitions; but then we shall have to say that *every* philosophy is discordant with *some* intuitions. The new philosophy of Professor Eddington, for instance, is discordant with some of the intuitions of all Christians except members of the Society of Friends; the philosophy of Dante is not the ideal ground on which to reap the intuitions of Wordsworth.

So far I have not questioned the term "esthetic intuitions"; but this term is beset with ambiguity and vagueness. I suppose that Mr. Whitehead means such intuitions as are more or less common to mankind, but of which the artist is the most sensitive receiver, and without which he would not have the material for great art. But however we define the term, there is a gulf, and I think an impassable one, between the intuitions of poets *as such*, and any particular philosophy, or even any philosophical direction rather than any other. The existence of art certainly implies the reality of values, but that does not take us anywhere, and certainly points to no philosophic theory of value.

If I examined each of the sentences I should quickly grow tedious, so I will pass now to the last of them:

Thus we gain from the poets the doctrine that a philosophy of nature must concern itself at least with these six notions: change, value, eternal objects, endurance, organism, interfusion.

The first question is, if we get all this from the poets, where do the poets get it? Take *change* and *endurance,* for which Mr. Whitehead is so obliged to Shelley. Shelley, I suspect, got them where everybody else has got them in the end—that is, from Plato. The reality of eternal objects sounds to me much more like Plato than a discovery of Shelley, or all the romantic poets together. I do not deny the possibility that Shelley may have had a fresh intuition of these things, but Plato did get there first. And also it is very difficult to spot these intuitions: Shelley must have had an esthetic intuition that there is no God, and that the Christian religion is an odious lie; for he could hardly have reached such passionate conviction on the subject from mere reasoning. (Of course it is possible that he read Rousseau and Voltaire, or even Godwin.) Even if we gain the doctrine in question from *the poets,* we hardly needed to have gone to the poets for that. And in passing, I wonder whether the concept of *organism* is so fundamental to a philosophy of nature as Mr. Whitehead supposes. We may get a better term some day, or we may even return to Aristotle, who knew as much about what this term represents as anybody.

At the very best, Mr. Whitehead is, I think, confusing the *persuasive* power of poetry with evidence of truth. He is transferring to poetry, as a scientist, that credulity which previous generations, including some poets, are said to have bestowed upon science.

Professor Whitehead may serve as a warning that a man may be one of the greatest living exponents of formal logic, and yet be quite helpless in a field with which he is not familiar. I should not however have devoted this space merely to the churlish pleasure of attacking a famous man; but because I believe that the theory of poetry implicit in Whitehead's chapter is dangerous, because we could prove by it, choosing our examples judiciously, almost anything we like. I also believe, what is a related point which I cannot deal with here, that Mr. Whitehead errs by his ignorance of theology just as he errs by his not having thought seriously enough about poetry.

Now among those persons who have thought directly about poetry—and indeed some of them are greatly indebted to Mr. Whitehead and Mr. Russell for their logical training—there have arisen lately two interesting views. One is that of Mr. Montgomery Belgion, in one chapter of his recent book *Our Present Philosophy of Life*. His theory is that the *literary* artist—he is not concerned with the other arts—is what he calls an "irresponsible propagandist." That is to say, every writer adopts a view or theory of life; his choice may have been more or less justified or capricious, may be more or less right, may be true or false: it happens to be the view which suits *him;* he makes use of it as material for his literary art. The effect of the work of literary art is always to *persuade* the reader to accept that view or theory. This persuasion is always illicit. That is to say, that the reader is always led to believe something, and that assent is hypnotic—the art of the presentation seduces the reader: even if what he is led to believe is right to believe, the reader has been *mis*lead into believing it. This theory is, as you see, rather depressing, and is remotely similar to that of Plato, who ejected the poets from his ideal republic; but it is neither fantastic nor easy to overthrow.

The other theory is that of Mr. I. A. Richards, as expressed particularly in his recent book *Practical Criticism*. Mr. Richards holds that while it is probably necessary for the poet to believe something, in order to write his poetry—although he inclines to think that a further step will be made when the poet believes nothing—the ideal reader will appreciate the poetry in a state of mind which is not belief, but rather a temporary suspension of disbelief. The one critic would say, you see, that you will value Dante more highly if you are a Catholic; or alternatively, that if you are enchanted by the poetry of Dante you will probably become a Catholic. Mr. Richards would say, I think, that the more you know about what Dante believed or more exactly the more you know about the philosophy of life on which Dante's poem is based—leaving out of account the question of what and how Dante himself believed—the better: but that when you are enjoying Dante's poem to the full as poetry, you cannot be said either to believe, or to doubt, or to disbelieve, its scholastic philosophy. So you *ought* to be able to appreciate, as literature, *all* literature, of whatever place, race or time.

These two theories are not so antithetical as they at first seem. Mr. Belgion is more concerned with what actually does happen; he says that, whether you know it or not, you tend to believe, you are *influenced,* by any author whose form of expression you admire. Mr. Richards is less concerned with the actual than with the ideal reader: he says, in effect, this may happen, but in so far as it does happen your reaction is impure; you *ought not* to be affected in this way: it is possible and it is right to enjoy poetry as poetry, and you merely use in the reading the philosophy of the author; just as the author was using, unconsciously, that philosophy in order to write the poetry.

In a note to a recent essay which I have published on Dante, I made a first attempt to criticise both views, and to find some way of mediation between the truth of both. I am now making a fresh start.

First of all no art, and particularly and especially no literary art, can exist in a vacuum. We are, in practice, creatures of divers interests, and in many of our ordinary interests there is no obvious coherence. Read, for instance, the information given by those personages in *Who's Who* who condescend to fill in that space of the form marked *Recreations*. There is no apparent relation, to fabricate a specimen, between breeding prize Persian cats and racing toy yachts. This is one extreme of the scale. At the other end, we do tend, I am sure, to unify our interests. To suppose that anyone likes only the *best* poetry, and that he likes all of the best poetry equally, and that he likes all of the second-best poetry in a second-best liking, and so on until he detests all of the worst poetry equally, is to suppose a monster. I do not suppose that there ever has been, or ever will be, a critic of any art, whose appreciation was a separate faculty, quite judicious and wholly isolated from his other interests and his private passions: if there was, is or will be, he was, is or will be a bore with nothing at all to say. And yet, on the other hand, there is no worse bore, and no more futile critic, than the one who renounces all objective standards in order to recount his own reactions. "A voyage among masterpieces" is, I believe, the phrase that Anatole France used to describe his own criticism, implying that it was merely an account of his own feelings—yet the phrase itself admits that the masterpieces were there as masterpieces, before the voyage began.

But this apparent paradox—this need of aiming at one thing in order to do another—this apparent gospel of hypocrisy or self-deception, is right, because it is in the nature of the human soul and embodies its need and craving for perfection and unity. We do tend, I think, to organize our tastes in various arts into a whole; we aim in the end at a theory of life, or a view of life, and so far as we are conscious, to terminate our enjoyment of the arts in a philosophy, and our philosophy in a religion—in such a way that the personal to oneself is fused and completed in the impersonal and general, not extinguished, but enriched, expanded, developed, and more itself by becoming more something not itself.

There is, according to my view, not *one,* but a *series,* of appreciators of poetry. One of the errors, I think, of critical theory, is to conceive one hypothetical poet on the one hand, and one hypothetical reader on the other. It is perhaps a less dangerous error than to have no hypotheses at all. My point is that the legitimate motives of the poet, and also the legitimate responses of the reader, vary very widely, but that there is a possible order in the variations. In my series let us put Mr. Belgion at one end of the scale and Mr. Richards at the other. The one extreme is to like poetry merely for what it has to say: that is, to like it merely because it voices our own beliefs or prejudices—which is of course to be quite indifferent to the *poetry* of the poetry. The other extreme is to like the poetry because the poet has manipulated his material into perfect art, which is to be indifferent to the material, and to isolate our enjoyment of poetry from life. The one extreme is not enjoyment of poetry at all, the other is enjoyment of an abstraction which is merely *called* poetry. But between these extremes occurs a continuous range of appreciations, each of which has its limited validity.

The validity of this range of appreciations is confirmed by our examination of the impulses of different poets. We may for convenience contrast three different types. There is the philosophic poet like Lucretius and Dante, who accepts one philosophy of life, so to speak, in advance, and who constructs his poem on one idea. There is the poet like Shakespeare, or possibly Sophocles, who accepts current ideas and makes use of them, but in whose work the question of belief is much more baffling and evasive. There is finally another type, of which we might take Goethe as an example, who neither quite accepts a particular view of the whole, nor merely sees views of life to make poetry out of, but who in himself more or less combines the functions of philosopher and poet—or perhaps Blake; poets who have their own ideas and definitely believe them.

Some poets are of so mixed a type that it is impossible to say how far they write their poetry because of what they believe, and how far they believe a thing merely because they see that they can make poetry out of it. And if I am justified in allowing this range of possible motives to the true poet (and an analogous range to the true reader of poetry) then Mr. Belgion's and Mr. Richards' theories must be considerably modified. For the "irresponsible propaganda" is sometimes less irresponsible, and sometimes less propaganda. Lucretius and Dante, for instance, are what Mr. Belgion would call propagandists, certainly, but they are particularly conscious and responsible ones: you have only to read what Dante says in the *Convivio* and in his letter to Can-Grande to understand what his purpose was.

Milton was also a deliberate propagandist; but here we must allow for another difference. The philosophies of Lucretius and Dante, different as they are from each other, are still potent to influence mankind. I cannot imagine any reader today being affected in his theological views by Milton. The reason is, I think, that Lucretius and Dante are each summing up and restating in great poetry two views which are central to the history of the mind of western man; whereas Milton is merely restating in great poetry a view which was very largely his own invention, or his own concoction, and which represents an eccentric heresy revived in his own mind. In Milton it is much easier to separate the greatness of the poetry from the thought, serious as it is, behind that poetry. Milton, therefore, is much more apprehensible from the Richards point of view; because in reading Milton we are, I think, rapt by the splendid verse without being tempted to believe the philosophy or theology. In considering whether a literary artist is an irresponsible propagandist or not, we have therefore to take into account both varieties of intention, and varieties of effect in time. Milton may, I feel, have had this powerful influence at one time which I feel that Lucretius and Dante can have at any time; but I do not believe that he has it now. And in general, the element of propaganda in the actual effect of any piece of literature upon us will depend either upon the permanence of the doctrine, or upon its nearness to us in time. The effect of a book like *The Way of All Flesh* was, I am sure, for the generation immediately following Butler much what he intended; for the next generation it is not at all the same.

You will infer, perhaps, that we must come to the conclusion that it is impossible to enjoy (or judge) a work of art as such, until sufficient time has elapsed for its doctrines to be quite out of date: so that we merely inspect and accept them, as Mr. Richards would have us do: wait a few hundred years, and we shall know how good any piece of literature is. There are several reasons why this simple solution will not do. One is that when an author is so remote from us, in time or in race, that we know nothing of his material and cannot at all understand his beliefs, we cannot appreciate his work as poetry. To enjoy Homer as poetry, we need a good deal more than Greek vocabulary and Greek accidence and syntax; and the more we saturate ourselves in the life of the ancient Greeks, the more we attempt to recreate imaginatively their world, the better we understand and enjoy the poetry of that world. Another reason is that time, alas, does not necessarily bring detachment. It may merely substitute for a set of prejudices favorable to the poet, another set unfavorable to him. It is interesting to read the comments of Mr. Richards' students, as set forth in *Practical Criticism,* on Donne's great sonnet "At the round world's imagined corners. . . ." Some of the misunderstanding is due, I believe, not so much to ignorance of the theology of Donne's time, as to these students' more or less conscious acceptance of another set of beliefs current in our own time.

I have called Lucretius and Dante *responsible propagandists*. But there are some poets whom it is a strain to think of as propagandists at all. Take Shakespeare. He is never, like the former, expounding one definite philosophical system. I am aware that many attempts have been made, and will be made, to expound in clear prose the theory of life which Shakespeare is supposed to have held; and that any number of views of life have been extracted from Shakespeare. I do not say that such attempts are illegitimate or altogether futile; it is a natural tendency to philosophize on Shakespeare just as it is to philosophize on the world itself. Only, the philosophy of Shakespeare is quite a different thing from that of Dante; it really has more in common with, let us say, the philosophy of Beethoven. That is to say, those of us who love Beethoven find in his music something that we call its meaning, though we cannot confine it in words; but it is this meaning which fits it in, somehow, to our whole life; which makes it an emotional exercise and discipline, and not merely an appreciation of virtuosity. Shakespeare does certainly influence us; but as he influences each man according to his own education, temperament and sensibility, and as we have no clue to the relation of his influence upon any one mind with what Shakespeare actually meant, it is almost fantastic to call it propaganda.

When we come to Mr. Whitehead's mentors, Shelley and Wordsworth, the situation is again different. Judging from their effect upon Mr. Whitehead, we should certainly call them irresponsible propagandists. But I suspect that their influence upon such a mind as Mr. Whitehead's is in direct ratio to the vagueness of their ideas, or to the fact that they take certain things for granted, instead of expounding them. The orthodox Christian, for example, is hardly likely to take Dante as proving Christianity; the orthodox materialist is hardly likely to adduce Lucretius as evidence of materialism or atomism. What he will find in Dante or in Lucretius is the *esthetic* sanction: that is, the partial justification of these views of life by the art to which they give rise. And there is no doubt that we are all of us powerfully influenced by the esthetic sanction; and that any way or view of life which gives rise to great art is for us more plausible than one which gives rise to inferior art or to none. And on the other hand I do not believe that a Christian can fully appreciate Buddhist art, or vice versa.

But Mr. Whitehead was not, I suspect, making this use, which I consider legitimate, of the esthetic sanction. You do not get this by going to the poets for maxims or gnomic sayings, or by attributing to them some inspiration as of the Delphic oracle. You can only say: this or that poet had used these ideas to make poetry, and has accordingly shown that these ideas can and do give rise to certain values. These ideas consequently are valid not merely in a theory, but can be integrated into life through art. But in order to do this we are obliged to value first the art of a Shelley or a Wordsworth. How complete, how intelligent, how well understood, is the philosophy used by the poet, how completely does he realize it poetically; where does he get it from, how much of life does it cover? Such questions we must ask first. And what poetry proves about any philosophy is merely its possibility for being lived—for life includes both philosophy and art.

But, we may ask, is the greatness, the comprehensiveness of the philosophy in any actual or theoretical relation to the greatness of the poetry? Actually, we may find a poet giving greater validity to an inferior philosophy, by realizing it more fully and masterfully in literary art, and another employing a better philosophy and realizing it less satisfactorily. Yet we can hardly doubt that the "truest" philosophy is the best material for the greatest poet; so that the poet must be rated in the end both by the philosophy he realizes in poetry and by the fullness and adequacy of the realization. For poetry—here and so far I am in accord with Mr. Richards—is not the assertion that something is true, but the making that truth more fully real to us; it is the creation of a sensuous embodiment. It is the making the Word Flesh, if we remember that for poetry there are various qualities of Word and various qualities of Flesh. Of course, as I said above, for some kinds of poetry it is necessary that the poet himself should believe the philosophy of which he is making use. I do not wish however to overemphasize the importance of the philosophy, or to speak of it as if it was the exclusive material. What we find when we read Lucretius or Dante is that the poet has effected a fusion between that philosophy and his natural feelings, so that the philosophy becomes real, and the feelings become elevated, intensified and dignified.

And we must remember that part of the *use* of poetry for human beings is similar to their use for philosophy. When we study philosophy as a humane discipline we do not do so merely in order to pick out one which we shall adopt as "true," or either to confect a philosophy of our own out of all philosophies. We do so largely for the exercise in assumption or entertaining ideas; for the enlargement and exercise of mind we get by trying to penetrate a man's thought and think it after him, and then passing out of that experience to another. Only by the exercise of understanding without believing, so far as that is possible, can we come in full consciousness to some point where we believe *and* understand. Similarly with the experience of poetry. We aim ideally to come to rest in some poetry which shall realize poetically what we ourselves believe; but we have no contact with poetry unless we can pass in and out freely, among the various worlds of poetic creation. In practice, our literary judgment is always fallible, because we inevitably tend to overestimate a poetry which embodies a view of life which we can understand and which we accept; but we are not really entitled to prize such poetry so highly unless we also make the effort to enter those worlds of poetry in which we are alien. Poetry cannot prove that anything is *true;* it can only create a variety of wholes composed of intellectual and emotional constituents, justifying the emotion by the thought and the thought by the emotion: it proves successively, or fails to prove, that certain worlds of thought and feeling are *possible.* It provides intellectual sanction for feeling, and esthetic sanction for thought.

From *The Bookman, LXX* (February, 1930), pp. 595–602. Reprinted by permission of author and editor. The essay has not been reprinted by the author.

GEORGE SANTAYANA

Penitent Art

[1922]

ART is like a charming woman who once had her age of innocence in the nursery, when she was beautiful without knowing it, being wholly intent on what she was making or telling or imagining.

Then she has had a season of .passion and vanity, when having discovered how beautiful she was, she decked herself out in all possible pomp and finery, invented fashion after fashion to keep admiration alive, and finally began to put on rouge and false hair and too much scent, in the hope of still being a belle at seventy.

But it sometimes happens, during her long decline, that she hears a call to repentance, and thinks of being converted. Naturally, such a fine lady cannot give up her carriage; she is obliged occasionally to entertain her old friends at dinner, and to be seen now and then at the opera. Habit and the commitments she has in the world, where no function is complete without her, are too strong for her to be converted suddenly, or altogether; but henceforth something in her, in her most sensitive and thoughtful hours, upbraids her for the hollowness of her old airs and graces. It is really a sorry business, this perpetual presence of being important and charming and charmed and beautiful.

Art seems to be passing at present through a lenten mood of this sort. Not all art, of course: somebody must still manufacture official statues and family portraits, somebody must design apartment houses, clubs, churches, skyscrapers, and stations. Visible through the academic framework of these inevitable objects, there is often much professional learning and judgment; there is even, sometimes, a glint of poetic life, or a suggestion of exotic beauty. In Mr. Sargent's painting, for instance, beneath the photographic standards of the studio, we often catch a satirical intention, or a philosophic idea, or love of the sensuous qualities in the model and in the accessories; a technical echo of Velasquez and Goya, though without plastic vitality or dramatic ease; a sort of Van Dyck, as it were, for the days of Edward VII; the dreadful lapse in refinement not being greater, perhaps, than is requisite for the documentary value of a true mirror of fashion in the later age. Taste of the old honest worldly sort is far from dead; it is found still in milliners and designers of fashionable garments, of furniture and ornaments. All this luxurious traditional art is as far as possible from repentance. Yet as the Magdalene was potentially a saint—perhaps always a saint really—so the most meretricious contrivances in the arts may sometimes include and betray the very principle of redemption, which is love; in this case the love of beauty. For example, here is the Russian ballet, doubling the dose of luxurious stimulation in every direction, erotic, tragic, historical, and decorative; yet see how it glides at times into simplicity, and in spite of all the paraphernalia of expert estheticism, issues in forms of unmistakably penitent art, like pure color and caricature.

I call pure color and caricature penitent art, because it is only disappointment in other directions that drives artists back to these primary effects. By an austere and deliberate abstinence from everything that naturally tempts them, they achieve in this way a certain peace; but they would far rather have found it by genuinely recovering their naïveté. Sensuous splendor and caricature would then have seemed to them not the acme of abstract art, but the obvious truth of things; they would have doted on puppets and pantomime as a child dotes on dolls, without ever noticing how remote they are from reality. In the nineteenth century some romantic artists, poets, and philosophers actually tried being rebaptized, hoping that a fresh dip in the Jordan might rejuvenate them; but it was of no use. The notion of *recovering innocence* is a contradiction in terms; conversion can only initiate a non-natural life of grace; death must intervene before corruption can put on incorruption. That age was accordingly an age of revivals, of antiquaries, nothing in art and religion but retrospective; it was progressive only in things material and in the knowledge of them. Even its philosophical idealism and psychology were meant to be historical and descriptive of facts, literary and egotistical as the view of the facts might be. Romanticism thought it was exquisitely sensitive to the spirit of remote things, but in reality it was sensitive only to material perspectives, to costume and stage-setting; it grew sentimental over legends and ruins, and being moonstruck, thought it was imbibing the spirit of the past. But the past had not been consciously romantic; what the ancients actually thought and felt was understood much better before the nineteenth century than since; for formerly they were regarded simply as men, essentially contemporary—which comes much nearer the truth. Of course, the passion that can drive people to such earnest affectations must be itself genuine. Keats or Ruskin or Oscar Wilde had abundant vitality and expressed, each in his studied archaism, the profound helplessness that beset him; but what was vital in them was some sensuous or moral or revolutionary instinct of their own, such as in Shelley had existed pure; only in them it was contorted by their terrible preoccupation with being early, or rich, or choice. They were hypnotized by dead beauty; and not having invention nor influence enough

to remodel their own age, they fled from it to exotic delights, sometimes primitive, sometimes luxurious, sometimes religious, and sometimes all these things
at once. Similarly the revivals in architecture and in the minor crafts expressed a genuine love of color, ornament, and beauty; they gave the snobbish
middle classes a taste of cheap luxury; they could sip culture in a teacup. Yet
the particular fashions revived were unstable; each successive affectation had
hardly ceased to seem exquisite when it began to look foolish. Art at best is
subject to fashion, because there is a margin of arbitrary variation in its forms,
even when their chief lines are determined by their function; but in revived
art fashion is all; it is a fancy dress, unsatisfying even in the glamour of the
ballroom, which we are positively ashamed to be seen in in the morning.

Fortunately revivals now seem to be over. Ruins and museums are interesting to the antiquary; they stir the historical imagination, and dazzle us here
and there with some ray of living beauty, like that of a jewel; but they cannot
supply inspiration. In art, in poetry, unless you become as a little child you
cannot enter the kingdom of heaven. Little children is what artists and poets
are now striving hard to be; little children who instead of blowing a tin
trumpet blow by chance through a whole orchestra, but with the same
emotion as the child; or who, instead of daubing a geometrical skeleton with
a piece of chalk, can daub a cross-eyed cross-section of the entire spectrum or
a compound fracture of a nightmare. Such is Cubism: by no means an inexpert or meaningless thing. Before you can compose a chaos or paint the un-
namable, you must train yourself to a severe abstention from all practical
habits of perception; you must heroically suppress the understanding. The
result, when the penance is genuinely performed, has a very deep and recondite charm; you revert to what the spinal column might feel if it had a
separate consciousness, or to what the retina might see if it could be pain-
lessly cut off from the brain; lights, patterns, dynamic suggestions, sights and
memories fused together, hypnotic harmonies such as may visit a vegetative
or even mineral sensibility; you become a thousand prisms and mirrors reflect-
ing one another. This is one kind of esthetic repentance. Vain, vain, it says to
itself, was the attempt to depict or beautify external objects; let material things
be what they will; what are they to the artist? Nature has the urgency of life,
which art cannot rival; it has the lure, the cruelty, of actual existence, where
all is sin and confusion and vanity, a hideous strife of forms devouring one
another, in which all are mutilated and doomed. What is that to the spirit?
Let it confess its own impotence in that field, and abandon all attempts to
observe or preserve what are called *things:* let it devote itself instead to cleansing the inside of the cup, to purifying its sensibility, which is after all what
nature plays upon when she seems to us to be beautiful. Perhaps in that way
spirit may abstract the gold of beauty and cast the dross away—all that alloy
of preoccupation with material forms and external events and moral senti-

ments and vain animal adventures which has so long distracted the misguided artist, when he could paint the whole world and had lost his own soul. It is always the play of sensibility, and nothing else, that lends interest to external themes; and it was an evil obsession with alien things that dragged sensibility into a slavery to things which stifled and degraded it: *salvation lies in emancipating the medium.*

To renounce representation, or be representative only by accident, is accordingly one sort of penitent art; but there is another sort, more humble and humorous. This second sort makes no attempt to resist the impulse to observe and to express external things. It does not proudly imagine that the medium, which is the human contribution to representation, can be sufficient unto itself. On the contrary, in its sensuous orchestration it is content to be rudimentary, to work in clay or in wood, and to dress in homespun. It is all feeling, all childlike tenderness, all sense of life. Persons and animals fascinate it. At the same time, warned by the fate of explicit poets and realistic painters, it does not attempt, in its portraiture, to give more than a pregnant hint, some large graphic sign, some profound caricature. Don't be rhetorical, it says; don't try to be exhaustive; all that is worth saying can be said in words of one syllable. Look long, and be brief. It is not in their material entirety and detail that things penetrate to the soul, but in their simple large identity, as a child knows his mother, nurse, or dog. Fresh inchoate forms, voices draped in mantles, people the mind, and return to it in dreams. Monsters and dwarfs were the first gods; the half, said a Greek proverb, is better than the whole. The implicit is alone important where life is concerned: nothing is more eloquent than an abstract posture, an immovable single gesture. Let art abandon reproduction and become indication. If it threatens thereby to become caricature, know that profound art can never be anything else. If men, when seen truly, take on the aspect of animals or puppets, it is because they are animals and puppets at bottom. But all caricature need not be unkind; it may be tender, or even sublime. The distortion, the single emphasis, the extreme simplification may reveal a soul which rhetoric and self-love had hidden in a false rationality. The absurd is the naked truth, the pathetic appeal of sheer fact, attempting to come into existence, like a featherless chick peeping out of its eggshell. All this pompous drapery of convention was a disguise; strip it away. Do not make maps of your images; make companions of them, make idols. Be reticent, emphatic, moody, bold; *salvation lies in caricature.*

Accustomed as they are to revivals, some critics have called this form of esthetic penance a revival of savage art; but the mood is reversed. Savages were never rudimentary on purpose; they were not experimenting in the distortion or simplification of forms; much less, of course, did they voluntarily eliminate all representation of objects in order to deepen sensibility for the medium. They simply painted as well as they could. We have got far beyond that. Penitent art, childish as it may seem at times, is a refinement, perhaps an over-refinement; it is not so much crude or incompetent, as ascetic or morbid. It is also sometimes a little vulgar; because one of the forms of caricature and self-revelation is to be brutal, to flaunt what is out of place, what spoils the picture. Tragedy used to be noble; there is a new refinement in seeing how often it is ignoble; there is a second tragedy in that. Perhaps what we regard at first sight as a terrible decline in art may be sometimes the awakening of this sort of self-scorn. See how ugly I am, it cries, how brutish, common, and deformed! There are remains of sculpture and paintings of the late Roman Empire in some respects like our latest experiments. The decorative splendor (which was very marked) is lost; we miss the colored marbles, the gold, the embroideries, the barbaric armor and jewels; but the stunted pathetic human figures remain in crowds. It seems that the spirit had no joy in man any more; it hid him in hieratic garments or pityingly recorded his gregarious misery. He was a corpse laid out in pontifical vestments. We too are dying; but in nature the death of one thing is commonly the birth of another. Instead of decorating a Byzantine sanctuary, our artists do penance in a psychological desert, studying their own sensations, the mysteries of sheer light and sound; and as music was long ago divorced from poetry and instrumental music from singing, so a luxurious but strident art is detaching itself from everything but its own medium. This on the decorative side; in representation the same retrenchment stops at another level. Representation too has a psychological medium; fancy must create the images which the observer or reproducer of things conceives to be their forms. These images are not the forms of things at all; not only is their perspective created by the observer, but their character, when it is truly considered, is amazingly summary, variable, and fantastic—a mere wraith, a mere hint, a mere symbol. What we suppose we see, what we *say* things look like, is rather an inventory, collected in memory and language, of many successive observations; it is discursive study, registered perhaps in discursive painting. But as the total composition never was nor ever could be a living image, so its parts are not images any longer; in being arrested they have acquired new boundaries and lost half their primitive essence. We may paint the things we see, we cannot arrest the images by which we see them; all we can do—if the images and not the things are what interest us—is to paint something that, by some occult trick of optics, may revive the image in some particular; and then, although the picture when studied discursively may not resemble the thing at all, it may bring back to us, as it were by scent, the feeling which the thing originally gave us; and we may say that it has caught the *spirit* of the thing. It is the medium that in such a case animates the object, and seems to obscure it; and this medium which we call sense in so far as things affect us through it, we call spirit in so far as it modifies our view of the things. The more we transform things in seeing them, the more we seem to spiritualize them and turn them into forms of our own sensibility, regarding the living image in us as the dramatic essence of the object. It is the business of science to correct this illusion; but the penitent artist—who has taken refuge in the spirit and is not striving to stretch his apprehension into literal truth, since the effort to depict things discursively has proved a vain and arid ambition—the penitent artist is content with the rhythms, echoes, or rays which things awaken within him; and in proportion as these reverberations are actually renewed, the poem remains a cry, the story a dream, the building a glimpse, the portrait a caricature.

From *Obiter Scripta* by George Santayana, pp. 151–161. Copyright, 1936, by Charles Scribner's Sons. Reprinted by permission of the author and publishers. First published in *The Dial*, Vol. LXXIII (July, 1922), pp. 25–31.

Tragic Philosophy
[1936]

IN COMPARING a passage from *Macbeth* with one from the *Paradiso*, Mr. T. S. Eliot tells us that poetically the two are equally good, but that the philosophy in Shakespeare is inferior. By what standard, I am tempted to ask, may the poetic value of different types of poetry in different languages be declared equal? By the equal satisfaction, perhaps, that fills the critic's mind? But the total allegiance of a mature person, his total joy in anything, can hardly be independent of his developed conscience and his sense for ultimate realities. He cannot be utterly enchanted by what he feels to be trivial or false. And if he is not utterly enchanted, how should he recognize the presence of the supremely beautiful? Two passages could hardly be pronounced equal in poetic force if the ultimate suggestions of the one were felt to be inferior to those of the other.

Admitting, then, that poetry expressing an inferior philosophy would to that extent be inferior poetry, we may ask this further question: In what respect other than truth may philosophies be called inferior or superior? Perhaps in being more or less poetical or religious, more or less inspired? Sometimes a philosophy may spring up imaginatively, and in that sense may be inspired rather than strictly reasoned or observed, as the myths of Plato are inspired; but nobody would call such inspired philosophy *superior* unless he felt it to spring from the total needs and total wisdom of the heart; and in that case he would certainly believe, or at least hope, that this superior philosophy was true. How then should the poetic expression of this inspired philosophy not be conspicuously superior as poetry, and more utterly enchanting, than the expression of any other philosophy?

Let me postpone generalities, and turn to the passages in question.

Lady Macbeth is dead. Macbeth foresees his own end. All the prophecies flattering his ambition have been fulfilled, and after the mounting horror of his triumph he stands at the brink of ruin. Surveying the whole in a supreme moment, he consents to his destiny.

> Tomorrow, and tomorrow and tomorrow
> Creeps in this petty pace from day to day
> To the last syllable of recorded time;
> And all our yesterdays have lighted fools
> The way to dusty death. Out, out, brief candle!
> Life's but a walking shadow; a poor player
> That struts and frets his hour upon the stage,
> And then is heard no more. It is a tale
> Told by an idiot, full of sound and fury,
> Signifying nothing.

Mr. Eliot says that this philosophy is derived from Seneca; and it is certain that in Seneca's tragedies, if not in his treatises, there is a pomp of diction, a violence of pose, and a suicidal despair not unlike the tone of this passage. But would Seneca ever have said that life signified nothing? It signified for him the universal reign of law, of reason, of the will of God. Fate was inhuman, it was cruel, it excited and crushed every finite wish; yet there was something in man that shared that disdain for humanity, and triumphed in that ruthless march of order and necessity. Something superior, not inferior, Seneca would have said; something that not only raised the mind into sympathy with the truth of nature and the decrees of heaven, but that taught the blackest tragedy to sing in verse. The passions in foreseeing their defeat became prophets, in remembering it became poets; and they created the noblest beauties by defying and transcending death.

In Seneca this tragic philosophy, though magnificent, seems stilted and forced; it struts rhetorically like an army of hoplites treading down the green earth. He was the last of ancient tragedians, the most aged and withered in his titanic strength; but all his predecessors, from Homer down, had proclaimed the same tragic truths, softened but not concealed by their richer medium. Some of them, like Virgil, had rendered those truths even more poignant precisely by being more sensitive to the loveliness of perishable things. After all, the same inhuman power that crushes us, breeds us and feeds us; life and death are but two aspects of the same natural mutation, the same round of seed-time and harvest. And if all human passions must be fugitive, they need not all be unamiable: some are merry in their prime, and even smile at their own fading. An accident of ritual led the ancients to divide tragedy sharply from comedy; I think it has been a happy return to nature in modern dramatists and novelists to intermingle the two. Comic episodes abound in the most tragic experience, if only we have the wit to see them; and even the tragic parts are in reality relieved by all sorts of compensations that stimulate our sense of life and prompt us to high reflection. What greater pleasure than a tear that pays homage to something beautiful and deepens the sense of our own profundity?

Not every part of this classic philosophy re-echoes in the pessimism of Macbeth. Shakespeare was not expressing, like Seneca, a settled doctrine of his own or of his times. Like an honest miscellaneous dramatist, he was putting into the mouths of his different characters the sentiments that, for the moment, were suggested to him by their predicaments. Macbeth, who is superstitious and undecided, storms excessively when he storms; there is something feverish and wild in his starts of passion, as there is something delicate in his perceptions. Shakespeare could give rein in such a character to his own subtle fancy in diction and by-play, as well as in the main to the exaggerated rhetoric proper to a stage where everybody was expected to declaim, to argue, and to justify sophistically this or that extravagant impulse. So at this point in Macbeth, where Seneca would have unrolled the high maxims of orthodox Stoicism, Shakespeare gives us the humors of his distracted hero; a hero nonplussed, confounded, stultified in his own eyes, a dying gladiator, a blinded lion at bay. And yet intellectually—and this is the tragedy of it—Macbeth is divinely human, rational enough to pause and survey his own agony, and see how brutish, how insignificant, it is. He sees no escape, no alternative; he cannot rise morally above himself; his philosophy is that there is no philosophy, because, in fact, he is incapable of any.

Shakespeare was a professional actor, a professional dramatist; his greatness lay there, and in the gift of the gab; in that exuberance and joy in language which everybody had in that age, but he supremely. The Renaissance needed no mastering living religion, no mastering living philosophy. Life was gayer without them. Philosophy and religion were at best like travels and wars, matters for the adventurer to plunge into, or for the dramatist to describe; never in England or for Shakespeare central matters even in that capacity, but mere conventions or tricks of fancy or moods in individuals. Even in a Hamlet, a Prospero or a Jacques, in a Henry VI or an Isabella, the poet feels no inner loyalty to the convictions he rehearses; they are like the cap and bells of his fools; and possibly if he had been pressed by some tiresome friend to propound a personal philosophy, he might have found in his irritation nothing else to fall back upon than the animal despair of Macbeth. Fortunately we may presume that burgherly comfort and official orthodoxy saved him from being unreasonably pressed.

That which a mastering living philosophy or religion can be, we may see at once by turning to the passage from Dante. In the lowest circle of Paradise, that of the inconstant moon, dwells the spirit of Piccarda, a lady who, having once been a nun but having been carried off and married by force, when later she became a widow preferred to continue her life in the world rather than return to her convent. Dante asks her if those who dwell in this part of Heaven ever desire to go higher, so as to see more and to love more. And she replies, No: for the essence of religious love is union with the order of creation. Perfect happiness would be impossible, if we were not perfectly happy in what God has given us; and in his will is our peace.

> Frate, la nostra volontà quieta
> > Virtù di carità, che fa volerne
> > Sol quel ch'avemo, e d'altro non ci asseta
> Se disiassimo esser più superne,
> > Foran discordi gli nostri disiri
> > Dal voler di colui che qui ne cerne;
> Che vedrai non capere in questi giri,
> > S'essere in carità è qui necesse,
> > E se la sua natura ben rimiri.
> Anzi è formale ad esto beato esse
> > Tenersi, dentro a la divina voglia,
> > Per ch'una fansi nostre voglie stesse;
> Si che, come noi sem di soglia in soglia
> > Per questo regno, a tutto il regno piace
> > Com' a lo re ch'a suo voler ne invoglia.
> E'n la sua volontade è nostra pace:
> > Ell'è quel mare al qual tutto si move
> > Ciò ch'ella crea e che natura face.
> Chiaro mi fu allor come ogni dove
> > In cielo è paradiso, e sì la grazia
> > Del sommo ben d'un modo non vi piove.[1]

[1] "Brother, the quality of love stilleth our will,
  and maketh us long only for what we have,
  and giveth us no other thirst.
Did we desire to be more aloft, our longings
  were discordant from his will who here
  assorteth us,
and for that, thou wilt see, there is no room
  within these circles, if of necessity we have
  our being here in love, and if thou think again
  what is love's nature.
Nay, it is the essence of this blessed being to
  hold ourselves within the divine will, whereby
  our own wills are themselves made one.
So that our being thus, from threshold unto
  threshold throughout the realm, is a joy to all

I questioned at the beginning whether the poetic value of unlike things could be pronounced equal: and if now I compare this whole passage with the passage from Macbeth I find that to my sense they are incommensurable. Both are notable passages, if that is all that was meant; but they belong to different poetic worlds, appealing to and developing different sides of the mind. And there is more than disparity between these two worlds; there is contrariety and hostility between them, in as much as each professes to include and to subordinate the other, and in so doing to annul its tragic dignity and moral finality. For the mood of Macbeth, religion and philosophy are insane vapors; for the mood of Dante, Macbeth is possessed by the devil. There is no possible common ground, no common criterion of truth, and no common criterion even of taste or beauty. We might at best say that both poets succeed in conveying what they wish to convey, and that in that sense their skill is equal: but I hardly think this is true in fact, because in Shakespeare the medium is rich and thick and more important than the idea; whereas in Dante the medium is as unvarying and simple as possible, and meant to be transparent. Even in this choice passage, there are stretches of pure scholastic reasoning, not poetical at all to our sensuous and romantic apprehension; yet the studious and rapt poet feels himself carried on those wings of logic into a paradise of truth, where choir answers choir, and everything is beautiful. A clear and transparent medium is admirable, when we love what we have to say; but when what we have to say is nothing previously definite, expressiveness depends on stirring the waters deeply, suggesting a thousand half-thoughts, and letting the very unutterableness of our passion become manifest in our disjointed words. The medium then becomes dominant: but can this be called success in expression? It is rather success in making an impression, if the reader is impressed; and this effect seems essentially incomparable with that of pure lucidity and tireless exact versification in one chosen form. To our insecure, distracted, impatient minds, the latter hardly seems poetry.

Voltaire said that Dante's reputation was safe, because nobody read him. Nowadays that is hardly true; all superior persons read him a little or read a great deal about him. He sets tempting problems for professional critics and antiquarians, and he appeals to archaistic taste, that flies for refuge into the fourth dimension, to everything that seems pure and primitive. But as living poetry, as a mold and stimulus for honest feeling, is Dante for us at all com-

the realm as to the king, who draweth our
    wills to what he willeth;
and his will is our peace; it is that sea to
    which all moves that it createth and that nature maketh."
Clear was it then to me how everywhere in heaven
is Paradise, even though the grace of the chief
Good doth not rain there after one only fashion.
        Paradiso, III, 70-90. (Wicksteed's translation)

parable to Shakespeare? Shakespeare, in passages such as this from *Macbeth*, is orchestrated. He trills away into fancy: what was daylight a moment ago, suddenly becomes a candle: we are not thinking or reasoning, we are dreaming. He needs but to say "all our yesterdays," and presently the tedium of childhood, the tedium of labor and illness, the vacancy of friendships lost, rise like vague ghosts before us, and fill us with a sense of the unreality of all that once seemed most real. When he mentions "a poor player" we think at once of the poet himself, because our minds are biographical and our sympathies novelesque; we feel the misery and the lurid contrasts of a comedian's life; and the existence that just now seemed merely vain, now seems also tempestuous and bitter. And the rhythms help; the verse struts and bangs, holds our attention suspended, obliges our thoughts to become rhetorical, and brings our declamation round handsomely to a grand finale. We should hardly have found courage in ourselves for so much passion and theatricality; but we bless Shakespeare for enabling us still to indulge in such emotions, and to relieve ourselves of a weight that we hardly knew we were carrying.

Nothing of the sort in the Italian: the simplest language, the humble vernacular, made pungent and to us often obscure only by an excess of concision and familiarity, or by allusions to events then on everybody's tongue. Dante allows his personal fortunes and hatreds to crop out in many places, perhaps quickening the interest of the modern gossip-loving reader. Yet these are incidental indiscretions, which the poet's own conscience might have regarded as blemishes. His work as a whole, and in intention, is that of a consecrated mind. A single thread of thought guides him; the eye is focused on pure truth, on human wills illustrating the divine laws against which they profess to rebel; hell in the heart of earth, and earth enveloped in celestial harmonies. No occasion, as in modern edifying works, to avoid mentioning things unpleasant or to explain them away. Every detail is noted, not bashfully or apologetically but with zest; when anything is wicked, its wickedness is exhibited and proved for our instruction. We learn the scientific complexity of the moral world, all plain facts, demonstrable truths, principles undoubted and certified. Mastered and chastened by this divine dispensation, what need should we feel of verbal opulence or lurid rhetoric? Not one rare epithet, not one poetic plum; instead, a childlike intellectual delight in everything being exact, limpid, and duly named, and dovetailed perfectly into everything else. Each word, each rhyme, files dutifully by in procession, white verses, three abreast, like choristers, holding each his taper and each singing in turn his appointed note. But what sweetness in this endless fugue, what simple exactitude, what devout assurance; and how unanimously these humble voices, often harsh and untutored if taken singly, rise together into a soaring canticle! The poetry, you might say, of industrious children, careful to make no mistake, but having nothing of their own to say, or not daring to say it. And indeed Dante's mind is busy, learned, and intense; exact even in allegory, as in a sort of heraldry; yet this very minuteness and pedantry are the work of love. Never was heart more tender or subtle or passionate; only that its intensity is all turned towards metaphysical joys, and transferred to an inward spiritual heaven.

I doubt whether either the beauty or the weakness of such poetry can be understood without understanding the nature of religion, as neither religious people nor irreligious people are likely to do; not the irreligious, because of insensibility, and not the religious because of delusion. Still, a disinterested student, say of the origins of Christianity, ought to understand. Religion is not essentially a supplement to common knowledge or natural affection on the same level as the latter: it is not essentially a part of rational life, adjusted however gropingly to cosmic or social influences, and expressing them and their effect. Religion is rather a second life, native to the soul, developed there independently of all evidence, like a waking dream: not like dreams coming in sleep and composed largely of distorted waking impressions, but an autonomous other life, such as we have also in music, in games, and in imaginative love. In religion the soul projects out of her own impulses, especially when these are thwarted, the conditions under which she will regard herself as living. If she need salvation, she will posit a savior; if the thought of death offends her, she will posit resurrection or even immortality; if she is troubled at the injustice of fortune, she will posit previous crimes or original sins of her own, to explain her misery. If in general she wishes to impose her will where she is impotent, she will utter that will in prayers or imprecations, and posit an invisible power inclined to listen, and able to help.

Now such an inner fountain of life and thought is evidently akin to poetic inspiration. As in poetry, so in religion, imagination evokes a more or less systematic invisible world in which the passions latent in the soul may work themselves out dramatically. Yet there are differences. The profane poet is by instinct a naturalist. He loves landscape, he loves love, he loves the humor and pathos of earthly existence. But the religious prophet loves none of these things. It is precisely because he does not love them that he cultivates in himself, and summons the world to cultivate, a second more satisfying life, more deeply rooted, as he imagines, in the nature of things. Earthly images therefore interest him only as symbols and metaphors, or as themes for denunciation. He is hardly a poet in the ordinary sense, except in so far as (like Milton, for instance) he may owe a double allegiance, and be a profane poet altogether when he is a poet at all. Religion is often professed and intellectually accepted without ever having flowered in the soul, or being suspected to have any kinship with poetry. It may have withered into a forced and angry metaphysics or semi-political party doctrine, poetically deplorable.

The opposite is the case in Dante, whose poetry is essentially religious, as his religion is essentially poetical. We are in the presence of an overpowering inspiration, become traditional, become also learned and quasi-scientific, but still kindled by moral passion and fertile in poetic ideas. The Hebrew prophets had begun by denouncing that which was and proclaiming that which should be; but that which should be could evidently never become actual without a miracle and a total revolution in the world; so that prophecy turned to eschatology and to expectation of a Messiah. At this point pagan streams of inspiration began to mingle with the Hebraic stream. Perhaps the Messiah had already come. Perhaps he was to be no conquering monarch, but a god in disguise. Perhaps he had been crucified, as the spirit is always crucified. Perhaps his kingdom was not of this world. Were there not reports that Jesus, who had been crucified, had been seen, risen from the dead? Would he not surely come again with glory in the clouds of heaven? Transfigured by this new spiritual faith, many current legends and maxims were ascribed to Jesus, and beautifully set down in the Gospels. The fathers worked out the theology. The saints repeated the miracles and explored all the phases of ascetic and mystical experience. Nothing remained but for Dante, with exquisite fidelity and minuteness, to paint a total picture of the Christian universe. The whole substance of that universe was poetry; only the details could threaten to become prosaic; but his danger was removed, in the more important places, by Dante's extraordinary sensitiveness. He had had a revelation of his own in childhood, interrupted later by the false glare of the world, but finally restored in the form of religious wisdom and consecration. The fresh dew of poetry and love trembled upon everything. Indeed, for our modern feeling the picture is too imaginative, too visionary, soaked too much in emotion. In spite of the stern historical details, when we rub our eyes and shake off the spell, the whole thing seems childishly unreal. We can understand why Mr. Eliot feels this to be a "superior" philosophy; but how can he fail to see that it is false?

Inspiration has a more intimate value than truth and one more unmistakably felt by a sensitive critic, since inspiration marks a sort of spring-tide in the life of some particular creature, whereas truth impassively maps the steady merciless stretches of creation at large. Inspiration has a kind of truth of its own, truth to the soul; and this sincerity in intuition, however private and special it might be, would never conflict with the truth of things, if inspiration were content to be innocently free and undogmatic, as in music or lyric poetry. The inmost vegetative impulses of life might then come to perfect flower, feeling and celebrating their own reality without pretending to describe or command reality beyond, or giving any hostages to fortune. But unfortunately animals cannot long imitate the lilies of the field. Where life is adventurous, combative and prophetic, inspiration must be so too. Ideas, however spontaneous, will then claim to be knowledge of ulterior facts, and will be in constant danger of being contradicted by the truth. Experience, from being lyrical, will become tragic; for what is tragedy but the conflict between inspiration and truth? From within or, as we may fancy, from above, some passionate hope takes shape in the mind. We fall in love or hear a voice from heaven; new energies seem to leap up within us; a new life begins crowding the old life out, or making it seem dreary or wicked. Even when inspiration is not moral, but merely poetical, it kindles a secret fire and an inner light that put vulgar sunshine to shame. Yet not for long, nor for ever; unless we passionately shut ourselves up in the *camera obscura* of our first inspiration, and fear the darkness of other lights. The more profound and voluminous that first inspiration was, the more complete at last will be our astonishment and despair. We shall cry with *Le Cid*:

> Percé jusque au fond du cœur
> D'une atteinte imprévue aussi bien que mortelle . . .
> Je demeure immobile, et mon âme abattue
> Cède au coup qui me tue.

Tragedy must end in death: for any immortality which the poet or his hero may otherwise believe in is irrelevant to the passion that has absorbed him. That passion, at least, dies, and all he cares for dies with it. The possibility of ulterior lives or alien interests destined in future to agitate the world makes no difference to this drama in this soul; and the mention of those irrelevant sequels to ruin, and to this ruin, and to this tragic acceptance of ruin, would tinkle with a ghastly mockery at this supreme moment, when a man is entering eternity, his measure taken, his heart revealed, and his pride entire.

These considerations may help us to understand why Shakespeare, although Christianity was at hand, and Seneca, although a Platonic philosophy was at hand, based like Christianity on moral inspiration, nevertheless stuck fast in a disillusioned philosophy which Mr. Eliot thinks inferior. They stuck fast in the facts of life. They had to do so, whatever may have been their private religious convictions, because they were dramatists addressing the secular mind and concerned with the earthly career of passionate individuals, of inspired individuals, whose inspirations contradicted the truth and were shattered by it. This defeat, together with a proud and grandiloquent acceptance of it, is final for the tragic poet. His philosophy can build only on such knowledge of the world as the world can give. Even in the seventeenth century, when Christian orthodoxy was most severe, most intellectual, and most dominant, also most courtly and presentable to the worldly mind, Christianity was nevertheless strictly banished from the stage, except in a few expressly religious plays written for young ladies. Both Christian and pagan personages talked and felt throughout like thoroughly unregenerate mortals. To have allowed religion to shift the scenes, override the natural passions of men, and reverse the moral of the story, would have seemed an intolerable anti-climax.

Nor does even Dante, who calls his vision a comedy, really escape this tragic reality. Existence is indeed a comedy, in that it is a series of episodes, each blind and inconclusive, though often merry enough, but all having their justi-fication beyond themselves, in a cosmic music which they help to make with-out knowing it. Nonetheless, the individual souls in Dante's hell and heaven speak the language of tragedy, either in desperate pride or in devout self-surrender. In either case, in eternity, they have no further hopes, fears, or ambitions. Their lives *there* are simply the full knowledge of what their lives had been *here*. If the *Divine Comedy* had not had in it this sublime note of recollection, if it had attempted to describe new adventures and fanciful Utopias succeeding one another *ad infinitum*, it would not have been divine at all, but only a romantic medley like the second part of *Faust*. In Dante the hurly-burly is rounded out into a moral tale, into a joyful tragedy, with that sense of finality, of eternity, which Christian eschatology had always pre-served.

I can think of only one tragedy in which religion might well play a leading part, and that is the tragedy of religion itself. The point would be to show that a second life of pure inspiration, freely bred in the soul out of moral impulses, must sooner or later confront the cold truth. The illusions then surrendered would not lose their poetic value, since their source would remain alive in the soul; and the element of deception involved might disappear insensibly, as it did in paganism, yielding with a good grace to an impartial philosophy. Such a philosophy need not be in the least hostile to inspiration. There is inspira-tion wherever there is mind. The sensuous images and categories of thought on which common knowledge relies are themselves poetic and wholly original in form, being products of a kind of inspiration in the animal organism. But they are controlled in their significance and application by experiment in the field of action. Higher fictions are more loosely controlled by the experience of the heart. They are less readily revived or communicated. They flare up into passionate prophecies, take themselves for revealed truths, and come more often to a tragic end.

From *The Works of George Santayana,* Triton Edition, Vol. II, pp. 275–288. Copyright, 1936, by Charles Scribner's Sons. Reprinted by per-mission of the author and publishers. First pub-lished in *Scrutiny* (Cambridge, England), Vol. IV (March, 1936), pp. 365–376.

J. E. SPINGARN
The American Critic
[1922]

WHEN I wrote the essays which were collected in a volume bearing the sub-title of "Essays on the Unity of Genius and Taste," the pedants and the professors were in the ascendant, and it seemed necessary to emphasize the side of criticism which was then in danger, the side that is closest to the art of the creator. But now the professors have been temporarily routed by the dilettanti, the amateurs, and the journalists, who treat a work of the imagination as if they were describing fireworks or a bullfight (to use a phrase of Zola's about Gautier); and so it is necessary now to insist on the discipline and illumination of knowledge and thought—in other words, to write an "Essay on the Divergence of Criticism and Creation."

American criticism, like that of England, but to an even greater extent, suffers from a want of philosophic insight and precision. It has neither inherited nor created a tradition of esthetic thought. Golden utterances there have been aplenty—utterances wise, or acute, or daring enough to confound those who refuse to recognize the American spirit except where they find a faded moralism—utterances that anticipate the most modern concepts of criticism throughout the world. To this American ancestry of my own thought I "point with pride." How can we forget Jefferson's literary Declaration of Independence, with its contempt for "the artificial canons of criticism" and its insistence that the only test of literary excellence is whether a work gives pleasure and is "animating, interesting, attaching"—even though the idea of pleasure no longer sums up for us the whole spiritual world of art? How can we forget Poe's conception of poetry as "the rhythmical creation of beauty" and of beauty as having "no concern whatever either with Duty or with Truth"; of Emerson's kindred idea that beauty, no less than truth, is "an ultimate end," and his definition of criticism, with its striking challenge, "Here was a new mind, and it was welcome to a new style"? Margaret Fuller believed like Goethe that the best critics "enter into the nature of another being and judge his work by its own law, but having done so, having ascertained his design and the degree of his success in fulfilling it, they do also know how to put this aim in its place and how to judge its relations," and said of Lowell as a poet that "his interest in the moral questions of the day has supplied the want of vitality in himself"; and yet even Lowell, as a critic, has clearly defined "the difference between what appeals to our esthetic or to our moral sense, between what is judged of by our taste or by our conscience." The author of our first formal treatise on esthetics, Moffat's *Introduction to the Study of Aesthetics,* published before the Civil War, and his successor, John Bascom, whose *Aesthetics* was contemporary with the battle of Antietam, write in the same spirit; for the former, "Art, in itself considered, is neither moral nor immoral; it belongs to an entirely separate class of things," while the latter insists that the processes of reasoning and judgment "have no power over Beauty," which is arrived at by the faculty of "internal intuition." Whether these ideas are false or true, one thing is clear: they are thoroughly American, and even though momentarily forgotten, are an integral part of the heritage of American criticism.

If we have forgotten these utterances, it is because they have remained more or less isolated, and their implications but half apprehended; they have never been consolidated into a body of thought or imposed themselves as a state of mind on American critics. For virtually all of us every critical problem is a separate problem, a problem in a philosophic vacuum, and so open for discussion to any astute mind with a taste for letters. Realism, classicism, romanticism, imagism, impressionism, expressionism, and other terms or movements as they spring up, seem ultimate realities instead of matters of very subordinate concern to any philosophy of art—mere practical programs which bear somewhat the same relation to esthetic truth that the platform of the Republican Party bears to Aristotle's *Politics* or Marx's *Capital.*

As a result, critics are constantly carrying on a guerrilla warfare of their own in favor of some vague literary shibboleth or sociological abstraction, and discovering anew the virtues or vices of individuality, modernity, Puritanism, the romantic spirit or the spirit of the Middle West, the traditions of the pioneer, and so on ad infinitum. This holds true of every school of American criticism, "conservative" or "radical"; for nearly all of them a disconnected body of literary theories takes the place of a real philosophy of art. "Find an idea and then write about it" sums up the average American writer's conception of criticism. There are even those who conceive this scattering of casual thoughts as the sole duty of a critic, on the extraordinary assumption that in this dispersion of thought and power the critic is "expressing himself" as an "artist." Now, while the critic must approach a work of literature without preconceived notion of what that individual work should attempt, he cannot criticize it without some understanding of what all literature attempts. The critic without an esthetic is a mariner without chart, compass, or knowledge of navigation; for the question is not where the ship should go or what cargo it should carry, but whether it is going to arrive at any port at all without sinking.

Criticism is essentially an expression of taste, or that faculty of imaginative sympathy by which the reader or spectator is able to relive the vision created by the artist. This is the soil without which it cannot flourish; but it attains its end and becomes criticism in the highest sense only when taste is guided by knowledge and rises to the level of thought, for then, and only then, does the critic give us something that the artist as artist cannot give. Of these three elements, implicit in all real criticism, the professors have made light of taste, and have made thought itself subservient to knowledge, while the dilettanti have considered it possible to dispense with both knowledge and thought. But even dilettante criticism is preferable to the dogmatic and intellectualist criticism of the professors, on the same grounds that Sainte-Beuve is superior to Brunetière, or Hazlitt to Francis Jeffrey; for the dilettante at least meets the mind of the artist on the plane of imagination and taste, while the intellectualist or moralist is precluded by his temperament and his theories from ever understanding the primal thrill and purpose of the creative act.

Back of any philosophy of art there must be a philosophy of life, and all esthetic formulae seem empty unless there is richness of content behind them. To define criticism without defining art, to define art without distinguishing it from philosophy and history, and to make this distinction without some understanding of the meaning of philosophy and history themselves, can only be compared with the mythical tasks of Tantalus. So that the critic, like the poet or the philosopher, has the whole world to range in, and the farther he ranges in it, the better his work will be. Yet this does not mean that criticism, in so far as it remains criticism of the arts of expression, should focus its attention on morals, history, life, instead of on the forms into which the artist transforms them. Art has something else to give us; and to seek moral or economic theories in it is to seek moral or economic theories, but not art. It is true that art is the product of human personality, and that personality has little meaning when divorced from moral personality, that is, from some actual or imaginative sense of moral values; but out of that moral personality must be created an aqueduct or an airplane, a treatise on logic or chemistry, a poem or a picture, and a host of other products whose excellence must be judged by their own standards, without reference to ethics. The personality behind the poem or the picture is merely, as it were, inchoate material and not the new and essential *form* that distinguishes the work of art. Even in the larger sense in which a poem may be said to be moral in so far as it aims at unity and order, at some relation with the whole of life, we may ask whether the esthetic order is identical with the moral order, or whether we have not here two commensurate but not identical planes or aspects of life.

But "to those who cannot understand the voice of Nature or Poetry, unless it speak in apothegms, and tag each story with a moral," as Margaret Fuller put it nearly eighty years ago, "I have nothing to say." A critic guilty of the incredible assertion that Goethe almost failed of being a great poet merely because he makes Mephistopheles say, "I am the spirit that denies," may be a distinguished moralist, but has completely failed to apprehend the meaning both of criticism and of poetry. The United States is the only civilized country where moral judgment takes precedence over esthetic judgment when face to face with a work of art; France, Germany, and Italy liberated themselves from this faded obsession long ago, except for a few unimportant reactionary cliques; even in England critics of authority hesitate to make moral standards the first and foremost tests of critical judgment. Yet this is precisely what divides the two chief schools of American criticism, the moralists and the anti-moralists, though even among the latter masquerade some whose only quarrel with the moralists is the nature of the moral standards employed. The seeds of a more fruitful tradition had been planted in our earlier criticism, as we have seen, but the seed had been left to wither and bore no ample fruit.

The main forces that have influenced the present clashes in the American attitude toward literature seem to be three. There is first of all the conception of literature as a moral influence, a conception which goes back to the Graeco-Roman rhetoricians and moralists, and after pervading English thought from Sidney to Johnson, finds its last stronghold today among the American descendants of the Puritans. There is, secondly, the Shavian conception of literature as the most effective instrument for the conversion of the world to a new Weltanschauung, to be judged by the novelty and freshness of its ideas, a conception particularly attractive to the school of young reformers, radicals, and intellectuals whose interest in the creative imagination is secondary, and whose training in esthetic thought has been negligible; this is merely an obverse of the Puritan moralism, and is tainted by the same fundamental misconception of the meaning of the creative imagination. And there is finally the conception of literature as an external thing, a complex of rhythms, charm, technical skill, beauty without inner content, or mere theatrical effectiveness, which goes back through the English Nineties to the French Seventies, when the idea of the spiritual autonomy of art—that "beauty is its own excuse for being"—was distorted into the merely mechanical theory of "art for art's sake"; the French have a special talent for narrowing esthetic truths into hard-and-fast formulae, devoid of their original nucleus of philosophic reality, but all the more effective on this account for universal conquest as practical programs.

All three of these conceptions have their element of truth, but all three are inadequate and incomplete. Works of literature, as mere documents, provide important material for history; the winged words of great poets have had a profound moral and social influence; the prophetic quality of the imagination gives its message an explosive force; and the technique of art is part of the material out of which the artist fashions his creations. All this the historian of culture may, indeed must, take into consideration; out of these elements the moralist or the esthete may draw material for his studies; yet to rest the case here is to ignore the essential problem of art. Pity the poor esthete, for whom art, in any of its single outer manifestations, is the whole life of the spirit; pity the poor moralist for whom the life of the spirit in one of its highest moments is cribbed and confined by a narrow theory of the meaning of art and life. It may be difficult to tell which of them misses the most; yet who can doubt that when we meet them in practical life the error of the moralist seems the nobler of the two? And how could it be otherwise—for it is precisely in the life of action that we seek for the guiding star of moral values, which the esthete attempts to evade in assuming that the ideal freedom of the artist as an artist is one with the practical duty of the artist as a man. But in the ideal world of art moralism must always find itself homeless and dispossessed. The very nature of poetry must forever be a bitter challenge to those who have only this narrow single standard; and there is no other way out except that of Plato, who because of the "immorality" of poetry banishes all poets forever from the ideal Republic. Of all the moralistic critics, Plato is one of the very few who are thoroughly consistent.

The apparent paradox which none of these critics face is that the Weltanschauung of the creative artist, his moral convictions, his views on intellectual, economic, and other subjects, furnish the content of his work and are at the same time the chief obstacles to his artistic achievement. Out of morals or philosophy he has to make, not morals or philosophy, but poetry; for morals and philosophy are only a part, and a small part, of the whole reality which his imagination has to encompass. The man who is overwhelmed with moral theories and convictions would naturally find it easiest to become a moralist, and moralists are prosaic, not poetic. A man who has strong economic convictions would find it easiest to become an economist or economic reformer, and economic theory as well as practice is also the prose of life, not the poetry. A man with a strong philosophic bias would find it easiest to become a pure thinker, and the poet's visionary world topples when laid open to the cold scrutiny of logic. A poet is a human being, and therefore likely to have convictions, prejudices, preconceptions, like other men; but the deeper his interest in them is, the easier it is for him to become a moralist, economist, philosopher, or what not, and the harder (without the divine aid of the Muses) to transcend them and to become a poet.

But if the genius of the poet (and by poet I mean any writer of imaginative literature) is strong enough, it will transcend them, pass over them by the power of the imagination, which leaves them behind without knowing it. It has been well said that morals are one reality, a poem is another reality, and the illusion consists in thinking them one and the same. The poet's conscience as a man may be satisfied by the illusion, but woe to him if it is not an illusion, for that is what we tell him when we say, "He is a moralist, not a poet." Such a man has merely expressed his moral convictions, instead of *leaping over and beyond them* into that world of the imagination where moral ideas must be interpreted from the standpoint of poetry, or the artistic needs of the characters portrayed, and not by the logical or reality value of morals. When we say with Emerson that beauty, like truth, is "an ultimate end," the narrow moralist or the man of practical mind assumes that we are giving advice to the dilettante trifler in verse (who is not an artist at all) instead of attempting to define the essential secret of the art of Aeschylus and Dante, Shakespeare and Goethe, Milton and Racine, and all their high compeers, classic and romantic, in the ancient and modern world. But how can we solve that secret if we see no difference whatever between their art and the thought of a Plato or Spinoza, the moral illumination of an Emerson or Franklin, or the noble exaltation of the Gettysburg Address? The critic who has missed that difference has missed everything. By ignoring one of the vital elements necessary to form a synthesis, he has even missed the power of understanding their essential unity in the life of the spirit.

That is what we mean when we say that this "leaping over" is the test of all art, that it is inherent in the very nature of the creative imagination. It explains a myriad problems. It explains, for example, how Milton the moralist started out to make Satan a demon and how Milton the poet ended by making him a hero; and from this "hymning of the devil" we learn how our moralistic critics cannot understand even a Puritan poet. From another angle, it explains the blindness of the American critic who recently objected to the "loose thinking" of Carl Sandburg's poem, *Smoke and Steel,* in which steel is conceived as made of "smoke and blood," and who propounded this question to the Walrus and the Carpenter: "How can smoke, the lighter refuse of steel, be one of its constituents, and how can the smoke which drifts away from the chimney and the blood which flows in the steelmaker's veins be correlates in their relation to steel?"

Where shall we match this precious gem? Over two centuries ago, Othello's cry after the death of Desdemona,

> O heavy hour,
> Methinks it should now be a huge eclipse
> Of sun and moon!

provoked another intellectualistic critic to inquire whether "the sun and moon can bothe together be so hugely eclipsed in any one heavy hour whatsoever"; but Rymer has been called "the worst critic that ever lived" for applying tests like these to the poetry of Shakespeare. Over a century ago a certain Abbé

Morellet, unmoved by the music of Chateaubriand's description of the moon—

She pours forth in the woods this great secret of melancholy which she loves to recount to the old oaks and the ancient shores of the sea—

asked his readers: "How can the melancholy of night be called a secret; and if the moon recounts it, how is it still a secret; and how does she manage to recount it to the old oaks and the ancient shores of the sea rather than to the deep valleys, the mountains, and the rivers?" And so when Macbeth, stung by his agony into immortal eloquence—"tomorrow and tomorrow and tomorrow" —finds time but a petty pace that has lighted fools the way to dusty death, and life itself nothing but a tale

> Told by an idiot, full of sound and fury,
> Signifying nothing,

can we not imagine some of our own professors, for whom Art is but a pretty page serving King Virtue and Queen Truth, crying out in disdain: "And it is this passage, gentlemen, in which a false and immoral conception of life is expounded, that some of the so-called esthetic critics consider the highwater mark of poetry"? Or if we cannot imagine it, it is only because the passage is not by a modern poet without the prestige of Shakespeare's fame.

These are simply exaggerations of the inevitable consequence of subjecting the world of the imagination to the moods and tests of actual life. "Sense, sense, nothing but sense!" cried a great Austrian poet, "as if poetry in contrast with prose were not always a kind of divine nonsense. Every poetic image bears within itself its own certain demonstration that logic is not the arbitress of art." And Alfieri spoke for every poet in the world when he said of himself, "Reasoning and judging are for me only pure and generous forms of feeling." The trained economist, philosopher, or moralist, examining the ideas of a poet, is always likely to say: "These are not clearly thought out or logical ideas; they are just a poet's fancy or inspiration"; and the sneer of the expert may be the final praise of the poet. To give us a vision of reality, and not reality, imagination rather than thought or morals, is the eternal mission of the artist. To forego that vision is to miss one of the highest moments of the life of the spirit. No other experience can serve as a substitute; no life that has not known it can regard itself as completely fulfilled.

These are some of the elementary reasons why those who demand of the poet a definite code of morals or manners, the ready-made standards of any society, however great, that is bounded by space or time—"American ideals," or "Puritanism," or on the other side, "radical ideas"—seem to me to show their incompetence as critics. Life, teeming life, with all its ardors and agonies, is the only limit within which the poet's vision can be cabined and confined; and all we ask of him is that he create a new life in which the imagination can breathe and move as naturally as our practical selves can live in the world of reality. How can we expect illumination from critics who share the "typical American business man's" inherent inability to live in the world of fantasy which the poets have created, without the business man's ability to face the external facts of life and mould them to his will? These men are schoolmasters, pedants, moralists, policemen, but neither critics nor true lovers of the spiritual food that art provides. To the creative writers of America I should give a wholly different message from theirs. I should say to them: "Express what is in you, all that serene or turbulent vision of multitudinous life which is yours by right of imagination, trusting in your own power to achieve discipline and mastery, and leave the theoretical discussion of 'American ideals' to statesmen, historians, and philosophers, with the certainty that if you truly express the vision of your highest self, the statesmen, historians, and philosophers of the future will point to your work as a fine expression of the 'American ideals' you have helped to create. Do not wait for the flux of time to create a society that you can copy, but create your own society; and if you are a great writer it will be a Great Society, which the world will never cease to live in and to love. For you America must always be not old but new, something unrealised, something to be created and to be given as an incredible gift to a hundred million men. Courage is the birthright of the poet as much as of the soldier or statesman; and courage in trusting your imagination is to you the very breath of life. But mastery of the imagination, and not mere submission to it, must be your goal; for how can the true artist express himself in terms of slavery rather than power? By giving what is best in him to his art, the American artist serves America best."

A profound inner reform is needed in order that the critics of America may prepare themselves adequately to interpret this new literature, to separate the chaff from the wheat, and in so doing to purify and ennoble the taste and enlarge the imaginative sympathies of a whole people.

The first need of American criticism today is education in esthetic thinking. It needs above all the cleansing and stimulating power of an intellectual bath. Only the drenching discipline that comes from mastery of the problems of esthetic thought can train us for the duty of interpreting the American litera- ture of the future. The anarchy of impressionism is a natural reaction against the mechanical theories and jejune text-books of the professors, but it is a temporary haven and not a home. The haphazard empiricism of English criti- cism and the faded moralism of some of our own will serve us no more. We must desert these muddy waters, and seek purer and deeper streams. For the conception of the critic as censor or as eulogist we must substitute the con- ception of the critic as esthetic thinker. In a country where philosophers urge men to cease thinking, it may be the task of the critic to revivify and reorganize thought.

The second need of American criticism can be summed up in the word scholarship—that discipline of knowledge which will give us at one and the same time a wider international outlook and a deeper national insight. One will spring from the other, for the timid colonial spirit finds no place in the heart of the citizen of the world; and respect for native talent, born of a surer knowledge, will prevent us alike from overrating its merits and from holding it too cheap. For the lifeless pedantry of the antiquarians, who think that tradition actually lives in monuments, heirlooms, dead ancestors, and printed books, we must substitute the illumination of a humane scholarship, which realizes that learning is but a quest for the larger self and that tradition is a state of the soul. Half-knowledge is either too timid or too cocksure; and only out of the spiritual discipline that is born of intellectual travail and adventure can come a true independence of judgment and taste.

For taste is after all both the point of departure and the goal; and the third and at this moment the greatest need of American criticism is a deeper sensibility, a more complete submission to the imaginative will of the artist, before attempting to rise above it into the realm of judgment. The critic is not a man seated on a block of ice watching a bright fire, or how could he realize the full force of its warmth and power? If there is anything that American life can be said to give least of all, it is training in taste. There is a deadness of artistic feeling, which is sometimes replaced or disguised by a fervor of sociological obsession, but this is no substitute for the faculty of imaginative sympathy which is at the heart of all criticism. By taste, I mean, of course, not the "good taste" of the dilettante or the amateur collector, or taste in its eighteenth-century sense, but that creative moment of the life of the spirit which the artist and the enjoyer of art share alike. For this the ardor of the reformer, the insight of the historian, even the moral passion of the saint is no substitute; for taste, or disciplined esthetic enjoyment, is the only gateway to the critic's judgment, and over it is a flaming signpost, "Critic, abandon all hope when this gate is shut."

This is your task, critics of America—to see that Plato's dream of banishing poets from the ideal Republic does not come true. It is your chief duty, against moralist and hedonist and utilitarian alike, to justify the ways of the artist to Americans. In a land where virtuous platitudes have so often been mistaken for poetry, it is your task to explain the real meaning of the esthetic moment for the higher lives of men. But no one knows better than I that you cannot rest satisfied even with this. For the modern critic has learnt to distinguish clearly between art, philosophy, history, religion, morals, not for the purpose of denying but of establishing their essential unity in the life of the spirit. Those who deny this unity and those who would substitute for it a muddle-headed if well-meaning confusion are alike the Enemy. Though you reject the criticism in which art is forever measured and tested by the moralist's rigid rules and justified by virtues that are not her own, still less can you be satisfied with the criticism in which "ideas" are struck out in random and irresponsible flashes like sparks from the anvil of a gnome. You cannot be satisfied with anything but truth—that whole truth which is life— even in the service of art and beauty.

From *Creative Criticism and Other Essays* by J. E. Spingarn, pp. 123–147. Copyright, 1931, by J. E. Spingarn. Reprinted by permission of Harcourt, Brace and Company, Inc. First published in *Civilization in the United States: An Enquiry by Thirty Americans,* edited by Harold E. Stearns. Harcourt, Brace and Company, Inc., 1922.

IRVING BABBITT

The Critic and American Life

[1928]

A FREQUENT remark of the French about Americans is: "They're children"; which, interpreted, means that from the French point of view Americans are childishly uncritical. The remark is relevant only in so far as it refers to general critical intelligence. In dealing with the special problems of a commercial and industrial society, Americans have shown that they can be abundantly critical. Certain Americans, for example, have developed a critical keenness in estimating the value of stocks and bonds that is nothing short of uncanny.[1] The very persons, however, who are thus keen in some particular field are, when confronted with questions that call for general critical intelligence, often puerile. Yet in an age like the present, which is being subjected to a constant stream of propaganda in everything from the choice of religion to its cigarettes, general critical intelligence would seem desirable.

As a matter of fact, most persons aspire nowadays to be not critical but creative. We have not merely creative poets and novelists, but creative readers and listeners and dancers. Lately a form of creativeness has appeared that may in time swallow up all the others—creative salesmanship. The critic himself has caught the contagion and also aspires to be creative. He is supposed to become so when he receives from the creation of another, conceived as pure temperamental overflow, so vivid an impression that, when passed through his temperament, it issues forth as a new creation. What is eliminated in both critic and creator is any standard that is set above temperament, and that therefore might interfere with their eagerness to get themselves expressed.

This notion of criticism as self-expression is important for our present subject, for it has been adopted by the writer who is, according to the

[1] This was written before the collapse of the great common stock bubble in the autumn of 1929. It then became evident that what the financial leaders of the "Boom" period lacked was not so much expertness in their own field as general critical intelligence—especially some working knowledge of the ways of Nemesis. There were, of course, honorable exceptions. The late Paul M. Warburg showed that he was one of them when he remarked, apropos of the so-called business cycle, that "it is a subject for psychologists rather than for economists." [What is involved] "is the answer to the question: How long—in industry, commerce and finance—does the memory of painful experiences prevent human greed and conceit from regaining control, etc."

Encyclopedia Britannica,[2] "The greatest critical force in America"—Mr. H. L. Mencken. Creative self-expression, as practiced by himself and others, has, according to Mr. Mencken, led to a salutary stirring up of the stagnant pool of American letters: "Today for the first time in years there is strife in American criticism. . . . Heretics lay on boldly and the professors are forced to make some defense. Often going further they attempt counterattacks. Ears are bitten off, noses are bloodied. There are wallops both above and below the belt."

But it may be that criticism is something more than Mr. Mencken would have us believe, more in short than a squabble between Bohemians, each eager to capture the attention of the public for his brand of self-expression. To reduce criticism indeed to the satisfaction of a temperamental urge, to the uttering of one's gustos and disgustos (in Mr. Mencken's case chiefly the latter) is to run counter to the very etymology of the word which implies discrimination and judgment. The best one would anticipate from a writer like Mr. Mencken, possessing an unusual verbal virtuosity and at the same time temperamentally irresponsible, is superior intellectual vaudeville. One must grant him, however, certain genuine critical virtues—for example, a power of shrewd observation within rather narrow limits. Yet the total effect of his writing is nearer to intellectual vaudeville than to serious criticism.

The serious critic is more concerned with achieving a correct scale of values and so seeing things proportionately than with self-expression. His essential virtue is poise. The specific benefit he confers is to act as a moderating influence on the opposite insanities between which mankind in the lump is constantly tending to oscillate—oscillations that Luther compares to the reelings of a drunken peasant on horseback. The critic's survey of any particular situation may very well seem satirical. The complaint that Mr. Mencken is too uniformly disgruntled in his survey of the American situation rather misses the point. Behind the pleas for more constructiveness it is usually easy to detect the voice of the booster. A critic who did not get beyond a correct diagnosis of existing evils might be very helpful. If Mr. Mencken has fallen short of being such a diagnostician, the failure is due not to his excess of severity but to his lack of discrimination.

The standards with reference to which men have discriminated in the past have been largely traditional. The outstanding fact of the present period, on the other hand, has been the weakening of traditional standards. An emergency has arisen not unlike that with which Socrates sought to cope in ancient Athens. Anyone who is untraditional and seeks at the same time to be discriminating must almost necessarily own Socrates as his master. As is well known, Socrates above all sought to be discriminating in his use of general

[2] Thirteenth edition. In the fourteenth edition we are informed that Mr. Mencken is a satirist rather than a critic.

terms. Before allowing one's imagination and finally one's conduct to be controlled by a general term, it would seem wise to submit it to a Socratic scrutiny.

It is, therefore, unfortunate that at a time like the present, which plainly calls for a Socrates, we should instead have got a Mencken. One may take as an example of Mr. Mencken's failure to discriminate adequately, his attitude towards the term that for several generations past has been governing the imagination of multitudes—democracy. His view of democracy is simply that of Rousseau turned upside down, and nothing, as has been remarked, resembles a hollow so much as a swelling. A distinction of which he has failed to recognize the importance is that between a direct or unlimited and a constitutional democracy. In the latter we probably have the best thing in the world. The former, on the other hand, as all thinkers of any penetration from Plato and Aristotle down have perceived, leads to the loss of liberty and finally to the rise of some form of despotism. The two conceptions of democracy involve not merely incompatible views of government but ultimately of human nature. The desire of the constitutional democrat for institutions that act as checks on the immediate will of the people implies a similar dualism in the individual—a higher self that acts restrictively on his ordinary and impulsive self. The partisan of unlimited democracy on the other hand is an idealist in the sense the term assumed in connection with the so-called romantic movement. His faith in the people is closely related to the doctrine of natural goodness proclaimed by the sentimentalist of the eighteenth century and itself marking an extreme recoil from the dogmas of total depravity. The doctrine of natural goodness favors the free temperamental expansion that I have already noticed in speaking of the creative critic.

It is of the utmost importance, however, if one is to understand Mr. Mencken, to discriminate between two types of temperamentalist—the soft and sentimental type, who cherishes various "ideals" and the hard, or Nietzschean type, who piques himself on being realistic. As a matter of fact, if one sees in the escape from traditional controls merely an opportunity to live temperamentally, it would seem advantageous to pass promptly from the idealistic to the Nietzschean phase, sparing oneself as many as possible of the intermediary disillusions. It is at all events undeniable that the rise of Menckenism has been marked by a certain collapse of romantic idealism in the political field and elsewhere. The numerous disillusions that have supervened upon the War have provided a favoring atmosphere.

The symptoms of Menckenism are familiar: a certain hardness and smartness and disposition to rail at everything that, rightly or wrongly, is established and respected; a tendency to identify the real with what Mr. Mencken terms "the cold and clammy facts" and to assume that the only alternative to facing these facts is to fade away into sheer romantic unreality. These and similar traits are becoming so widely diffused that, whatever one's opinion of Mr. Mencken as a writer and thinker, one must grant him representativeness. He is a chief prophet at present of those who deem themselves emancipated but who are, according to Mr. Brownell, merely unbuttoned.

The crucial point in any case is one's attitude towards the principle of control. Those who stand for this principle in any form or degree are dismissed by the emancipated as reactionaries or, still graver reproach, as Puritans. Mr. Mencken would have us believe that the historical Puritan was not even sincere in his moral rigorism, but was given to "lamentable transactions with loose women and fiery jugs." This may serve as a sample of the assertions, picturesquely indiscriminate, by which a writer wins immediate notoriety at the expense of his permanent reputation. The facts about the Puritan happen to be complex and need to be dealt with very Socratically. It has been affirmed that the point of view of the Puritan was stoical rather than truly Christian, and the affirmation is not wholly false. The present discussion of the relationship between Puritanism and the rise of capitalism with its glorification of the acquisitive life also has its justification. It is likewise a fact that the Puritan was from the outset unduly concerned with reforming others as well as himself, and this trait relates him to the humanitarian meddler or "wowser" of the present day, who is Mr. Mencken's pet aversion.

Yet it remains true that awe and reverence and humility are Christian virtues and that there was some survival of these virtues in the Puritan. For a representative Puritan like Jonathan Edwards they were inseparable from the illumination of grace, from what he terms a "divine and supernatural light." In the passage from the love and fear of God of an Edwards to the love and service of man professed by the humanitarian, something has plainly dropped out, something that is very near the center. What has tended to disappear is the inner life with the special type of control it imposes. With the decline of this inner control there has been an increasing resort to outer control. Instead of the genuine Puritan we then have the humanitarian legalist who passes innumerable laws for the control of people who refuse to control themselves. The activity of the uplifters is scarcely suggestive of any "divine and supernatural light." Here is a discrimination of the first importance that has been obscured by the muddy thinking of our half-baked intelligentsia. One is thus kept from perceiving the real problem, which is to retain the inner life, even though one refuse to accept the theological nightmare with which the Puritan associated it. More is involved in the failure to solve this problem than the Puritan tradition. It is the failure of our contemporary life in general. Yet, unless some relation is reached by a full and free exercise of the critical spirit, one remains a mere modernist and not a thoroughgoing and complete modern; for the modern spirit and the critical spirit are in their essence one.

What happens, when one sets out to deal with questions of this order

without sufficient depth of reflection and critical maturity, may be seen in
Mr. Sinclair Lewis's *Elmer Gantry*. He has been lured from art into the
writing of a wild diatribe which, considered even as such, is largely beside
the mark. If the Protestant Church is at present threatened with bankruptcy,
it is not because it has produced an occasional Elmer Gantry. The true reproach it has incurred is that, in its drift toward modernism, it has lost its
grip not merely on certain dogmas, but simultaneously on the facts of human
nature. It has failed above all to carry over in some modern and critical form
the truth of a dogma that unfortunately receives much support from these
facts—the dogma of original sin. At first sight Mr. Mencken would appear to
have a conviction of evil—when, for example, he reduces democracy in its
essential aspect to a "combat between jackals and jackasses"—that establishes
at least one bond between him and the austere Christian.

The appearance, however, is deceptive. The Christian is conscious above
all of the "old Adam" in himself; hence his humility. The effect of Mr.
Mencken's writing, on the other hand, is to produce pride rather than humility, a pride ultimately based on flattery. The reader, especially the young and
callow reader, identifies himself imaginatively with Mr. Mencken, and conceives of himself as a sort of morose and sardonic divinity surveying from
some superior altitude an immeasurable expanse of "boobs." This attitude will
not seem especially novel to anyone who has traced the modern movement.
One is reminded in particular of Flaubert, who showed a diligence in collecting bourgeois imbecilities comparable to that displayed by Mr. Mencken in
his *Americana*. Flaubert's discovery that one does not add to one's happiness
in this way would no doubt be dismissed by Mr. Mencken as irrelevant, for
he has told us that he does not believe in happiness. Another discovery of
Flaubert's may seem to him more worthy of consideration. "By dint of railing
at idiots," Flaubert reports, "one runs the risk of becoming idiotic oneself."

It may be that the only way to escape from the unduly complacent cynicism
of Mr. Mencken and his school, is to reaffirm once more the truths of the inner life. In that case it would seem desirable to disengage, so far as possible,
the principle of control on which the inner life finally depends from mere
creeds and traditions and assert it as a psychological fact; a fact, moreover,
that is neither "cold" nor "clammy." The coldness and clamminess of much
so-called realism arises from its failure to give this fact due recognition. A
chief task, indeed, of the Socratic critic would be to rescue the noble term
"realist" from its present degradation. A view of reality that overlooks the element in man that moves in an opposite direction from mere temperament,
the specifically human factor, in short, may prove to be singularly one-sided. Is
the Puritan, John Milton, when he declares that "he who reigns within himself and rules passions, desires, and fears is more than a king," less real than
Mr. Theodore Dreiser when he discourses in his peculiar dialect of "those rear-

ranging chemisms upon which all the morality and immorality of the world
is based"?

As a matter of fact, according to the degree and nature of the exercise of
the principle of control, one may distinguish two main types of realism which
may be denominated respectively religious and humanistic: as the principle
of control falls into abeyance, a third type tends to ˌemerge, which may be
termed naturalistic realism. That the decline of the traditional controls has
been followed by a lapse to the naturalistic level is indubitable. The characteristic evils of the present age arise from unrestraint and violation of the
law of measure and not, as our modernists would have us believe, from the
tyranny of taboos and traditional inhibitions. The facts cry to heaven. The
delicate adjustment that is required between the craving for emancipation
and the need of control has been pointed out once for all by Goethe, speaking
not as a Puritan, but as a clear-eyed man of the world. Everything, he says,
that liberates the spirit without a corresponding growth in self-mastery is pernicious. This one sentence would seem to cover the case of our "flaming youth"
rather completely.

The movement in the midst of which we are still living was from its inception unsound in its dealing with the principle of control. It is vain to
expect from the dregs of this movement what its "first sprightly running failed
to give." Mr. Carl Sandburg speaks of the "marvelous rebellion of man at all
signs reading *Keep off*." An objection to this purely insurrectional attitude is
that, as a result of its endless iteration during the past century and more, it has
come to savor too strongly of what has been called the "humdrum of revolt."
A more serious objection to the attitude is that it encourages an unrestricted
and merely temperamental liberty which, paradoxically enough, at first sight
affords the modern man no avenue of escape from the web that is being
woven about him by the scientific determinist.

Realists of the current type are in point of fact intimately allied with the
psychologists—glandular, behavioristic, and psychoanalytical—who, whatever
their divergences among themselves, unite in their deterministic trend and
therefore class fundamentally with both religious and humanistic realists.
The proper method of procedure in defending the freedom of the will would
seem to insist upon it as a fact of experience, a fact so primary that the position of the determinist involves an evasion of one of the immediate data of
consciousness in favor of a metaphysical dream. What is genuinely experimental in naturalistic psychology should of course be received with respect;
but the facts of which it takes account in its experiments are unimportant
compared with the facts it either neglects or denies. Practically it is running
into grotesque extremes of pseudo-science that make it a shining mark for
the Socratic critic.

Here at all events is the issue on which all other issues finally hinge; for until the question of moral freedom—the question of whether man is a responsible agent or only the plaything of his impulses and impressions—is decided, nothing is decided; and to decide the question under existing circumstances calls for the keenest critical discrimination. Creation that is not sufficiently supported by such discrimination is likely to prove premature.

One may illustrate from Mr. Dreiser's *American Tragedy*, hailed in certain quarters as the "Mount Everest" of recent fiction. He has succeeded in producing in this work something genuinely harrowing; but one is harrowed to no purpose. One has in more than full measure the tragic qualm but without the final relief and enlargement of spirit that true tragedy succeeds somehow in giving, and that without recourse to explicit moralizing. It is hardly worth while to struggle through eight hundred and more very pedestrian pages to be left at the end with a feeling of sheer oppression. The explanation of this oppression is that Mr. Dreiser does not rise sufficiently above the level of "rearranging chemisms," in other words, of animal behavior. Tragedy may admit fate—Greek tragedy admits it—but not of the naturalistic variety. Confusion on this point may compromise in the long run the reputations of writers more eminent that Mr. Dreiser—for example, of Thomas Hardy. Fatalism of the naturalistic type is responsible in large measure for the atmosphere of futility and frustration that hangs heavily over so much contemporary writing. One finally comes to feel with a recent poet that "dust" is the common source from which

> . . . stream
> The cricket's cry and Dante's dream.

Anyone who admits reality only in what derives from the dust, whether in a cricket or Dante, must, from the point of view of the religious or the humanistic realist, be prepared to make substantial sacrifices. In the first place, he must sacrifice the depth and subtlety that arise from the recognition in some form of the duality in man's nature. For the interest that may rise from the portrayal of the conflict between a law of the spirit and a law of the members, the inordinate interest in sex for its own sake promoted by most of the so-called realists is a rather shabby substitute. A merely naturalistic realism also involves the sacrifice of beauty in almost any sense of that elusive term. Closely related to this sacrifice is the sacrifice of delicacy, elevation, and distinction. The very word realism has come to connote the opposite of these qualities. When we learn, for example, that someone has written a realistic study of a great man, we are sure in advance that he has devoted his main effort to proving that "Plutarch lied." The more the great man is reduced to the level of commonplace or worse, the more we feel he has been "humanized."

Mr. Sherwood Anderson has argued ingeniously that, inasmuch as we ourselves are crude, our literature, if it is not to be unreal and fictitious, should be crude likewise. But the writer who hopes to achieve work of importance cannot afford to be too deeply immersed in the atmosphere of the special place and passing moment. Still less can he afford to make us feel, as writers like Mr. Anderson and Mr. Dreiser and Mr. Sinclair Lewis do, that, if there were any lack of vulgarity in what they are depicting, they would be capable of supplying the defect from their own abundance. More is involved here than the mere loss of distinction. We have come, indeed, to the supreme sacrifice that every writer must make who does not transcend a naturalistic realism. He must forego the hope of the enduring appeal—the hope that every writer worthy of his salt cherishes in some degree. In the absence of humanistic or religious standards, he is prone to confound the real with the welter of the actual, and so to miss the "grandeur of generality."

Certain books in the current mode are so taken up with the evanescent surfaces of life that they will survive, if at all, not as literature but as sociological documents. The very language in which they are written will, in a generation or two, require a glossary. So far from imposing an orderly pattern on the raw material of experience, they rather emphasize the lack of pattern. The resulting effect, to borrow a phrase from the late Stephen Crane, who has had a marked influence on the recent movement, is that of a "cluttered incoherency." As an extreme example of this tendency one may cite *Manhattan Transfer,* by John Dos Passos. In the name of reality Mr. Dos Passos has perpetrated a literary nightmare. Such a work would seem to have slight value even as a sociological document; unless, indeed, one is prepared to admit that contemporary Manhattan is inhabited chiefly by epileptic Bohemians.

"It is as much a trade," says La Bruyère, "to make a book as it is to make a clock"; in short, literature is largely a matter of technique. The technique of *Manhattan Transfer* is as dubious as its underlying philosophy. Neither can be justified save on the assumption that the aim of art is to exaggerate the clutter and incoherency of the mundane spectacle instead of eliciting its deeper meaning. Technique counts for even more in poetry than in prose. It would be possible to base on technical grounds alone a valid protest against the present preposterous overestimate of Walt Whitman. Fundamental questions need, in these very untraditional days, to be critically elucidated with a view to right definition if the poet is not to lack technique or still worse, if he is not, like certain recent practitioners of free verse, to be hagridden by a false technique. It evidently concerns both the form and substance of poetry, whether one define it with Aristotle as the portrayal of representative human action, or whether one define it with Mr. Carl Sandburg as a "mystic, sensuous mathematics of fire, smokestacks, waffles, pansies, people, and purple sunsets."

There is no doubt much in America of today that suggests a jazzy impressionism. Still our naturalistic deliquescence has probably not gone so far as one might infer from poetry like that of Mr. Sandburg or fiction like that of Mr. Dos Passos. The public response to some of the realistic novels has been considerable: allowance must be made however for the *succès de scandale*, also for the skill attained by the modern publisher in the art of merchandising. The reputation of certain books one might mention may be regarded as a triumph of "creative" advertising. What has been created is a mirage of masterpieces where no masterpieces are. It is well also to remember in regard to some of the works that have been most discussed that, so far from being an authentic reflection of the American scene, they are rather a belated echo of certain European movements. For it is as certain that in our literary and artistic modes we follow Europe—usually at an interval of from five to forty years—as it is that we lead Europe in our bathtubs and sanitary plumbing. Anyone who resided in Paris in the nineties and later in America, will, as I can testify from personal experience, have the sense of having lived through the same literary fads twice. Mr. Dreiser reminds one of Zola and his school. The technique of Mr. Dos Passos recalls that of the Goncourts. Our experimenters in free verse have followed in the wake not merely of Walt Whitman but of the French symbolists, and so on.

We shall presently begin to hear of certain new developments in French literature and critical thought that point, though indecisively as yet, to a radical departure from what has been the main current since the eighteenth century and in some respects since the Renaissance. It is well that we should become familiar with the writers who reveal in different ways this latest trend —notably with Maritain, Maurras, Lasserre, Seillière, and Benda; for they give evidence of a quality of cerebration that is rare in our own literati. At the same time we should not adopt with our usual docility the total outlook of any of these writers: for no one of them has worked out a point of view exactly adapted to our requirements. In general, it is not fitting that a great nation at the very height of its power should go on indefinitely trailing after Europe. It is time for us to initiate something of our own. This does not mean that we should proceed forthwith to inbreed our own "originality." It means almost the exact opposite. The most original thing one could do nowadays would be to question the whole theory of originality as mere temperamental overflow and self-expression that has prevailed from the "geniuses" of the eighteenth century down to one of our youthful and very minor bards who aspires to "spill his bright illimitable soul."

A genuinely critical survey would make manifest that the unsatisfactoriness of our creative effort is due to a lack of the standards that culture alone can supply. Our cultural crudity and insignificance can be traced in turn to the inadequacy of our education, especially our higher education. Mr. Mencken's attack on the "professors" is therefore largely justified; for if the professors were performing their function properly Mr. Mencken himself would not be possible. One must add in common justice that the professors themselves, or at least some of them, are becoming aware that all is not well with existing conditions. One could not ask anything more perspicacious than the following paragraph from a recent report of Committee G to the American Association of University Professors:

American education has suffered from the domination, conscious or unconscious, direct or indirect, of political and sentimental, as well as educational, theories that are demonstrably false. If the views of some men are to prevail the intellectual life of the country is doomed; everybody except the sheer idiot is to go to college and pursue chiefly sociology, nature study, child study, and community service—and we shall have a society unique only in its mediocrity, ignorance, and vulgarity. It will not do to dismiss lightly even so extreme a view as this; it is too indicative. Such influences are very strong, their pressure is constant; and if education has largely failed in America, it has been due primarily to them.

In short, as a result of the encroachments of an equalitarian democracy, the standards of our higher education have suffered in two distinct particulars: first, as regards the quality of students; second, as regards the quality of the studies these students pursue. The first of these two evils is generally recognized. There is even some prospect of remedial measures. Certain institutions, Harvard, for example, without being as yet severely selective, are becoming more critical of the incompetent student. On the other hand, there seems to be less hope than ever of any righting of the second and more serious evil—the failure to distinguish qualitatively between studies. The main drift is still towards what one may term a blanket degree. (Dartmouth, for example, has just merged its bachelor of arts and bachelor of science.) Yet rather than blur certain distinctions it would have been better, one might suppose, to use up all the letters of the alphabet devising new degrees to meet the real or supposed educational needs of the modern man. To bestow the A.B. degree indiscriminately on a student for whom education has meant primarily a specialization in chemistry and one for whom it has meant primarily an assimilation of the masterpieces of Greek literature is to empty it of any effective meaning. At the present rate, indeed, the time may come when the A.B. degree will not throw much more light on the cultural quality of its recipient than it would if, as has been suggested, it were bestowed on every American child at birth.

It goes without saying that those who have been lowering and confusing educational standards have been profuse in their professions of "service." A critical examination, not merely of American education, but of American life at the present time, will almost necessarily hinge on this term. The attitude of the Socratic critic toward it is not to be confounded with that of Mr. Mencken and the "hardboiled" contingent. "When a gang of real estate agents," says Mr. Mencken, "bond salesmen, and automobile dealers get together to sob for Service, it takes no Freudian to surmise that someone is about to be swindled." But if one entertains doubts about this current American gospel, why waste one's ammunition on any such small fry? Other and more exalted personages than the members of the Rotary Club at Zenith have, in Mr. Mencken's elegant phrase, been "yipping for Service." If one is to deal with this idea of service Socratically, one needs to consider it in relation to the two figures who have rightly been taken to be most representative in our cultural background—Benjamin Franklin and Jonathan Edwards. Franklin's idea of service is already humanitarian. Edwards' idea is still traditionally Christian—service not of man but of God. What Franklin stood for is flourishing prodigiously at the present moment, so much so that he may perhaps be defined in his chief line of influence as the great superrotarian. What Edwards stood for is, on the other hand, largely obsolete or survives only in the form of habits, which, lacking doctrinal support, are steadily declining along with the whole Puritan culture.

Intermediary types are possible. One may in one's character reflect the Puritan background and at the same time in one's idea of service derive rather from Franklin. Precisely that combination is found in the most influential of our recent educational leaders—the late President Eliot. A legitimate admiration for his personal qualities should not interfere with the keenest critical scrutiny of his views about education, for the two things stand in no necessary connection. Practically this means to scrutinize the humanitarian ideal that he probably did more than any other man of his generation to promote. In this respect most of the heads of our institutions of learning have been and still are understudies of President Eliot.

In an address on the occasion of his ninetieth birthday President Eliot warned his hearers against introspection, lest it divert them from a whole-hearted devotion to service. Between this attitude and a religious or humanistic attitude there is a clash of first principles. Both humanism and religion require introspection as a prerequisite of the inner life and its appropriate activity. With the disappearance of this activity what is left is the outer activity of the utilitarian, and this leads straight to the one-sided cult of material efficiency and finally to the standardization that is, according to nearly all foreign critics and many of our own, a chief American danger. We cannot return to the introspection of the Puritan. We shudder at the theology an Edwards would impose as the condition of his "divine and supernatural light." Yet it does not follow, as I have already suggested, that we should reject the inner life along with this theology. One may recognize innumerable advantages in the gospel of service and yet harbor an uneasy suspicion withal that in the passage from the old religion to the modern humanitarian dispensation something vital has disappeared, something from which neither the outer working of the utilitarian nor again the expansive sympathy of the sentimentalist can offer an equivalent.

The problem of the inner life is very much bound up with two other problems that are now pressing for solution in our higher education and have as yet found none: the problem of the specialist and the problem of leisure. The man of leisure is engaged in an inner and specifically human form of activity, a form that is, according to Aristotle, needful if he is to compass the end of ends—his own happiness. The question is whether one should consent like the specialist to forego this activity and to live partially and as a mere instrument for the attainment of some outer end—even though this end be the progress of humanity. We are beginning to hear a great deal nowadays about the "menace" of leisure. It has been estimated that with the prefecting of mechanical devices the man of the future will be able to satisfy his material wants by working not more than four hours a day. It is vain to anticipate that the rank and file will use this release from outer activity intelligently unless the leaders, notably those in high academic station, show the way. The notion of true leisure is the ultimate source of the standards of any education that deserves to be called liberal. When even a few of our college and university presidents show that they are thinking to some purpose on the nature of leisure it will be time enough to talk of "America's coming of age."

As it is, our institutions of learning seem to be becoming more and more hotbeds of "idealism." Their failure, on the whole, to achieve standards as something quite distinct from ideals, on the one hand, and standardization, on the other, may prove a fact of sinister import for the future of American civilization. The warfare that is being waged at the present time by Mr. Sinclair Lewis and others against a standardized Philistinism continues in the main the protest that has been made for several generations past by the temperamentalists, hard or soft, against the mechanizing of life by the utilitarian. This protest has been, and is likely to continue to be, ineffectual. The fruitful opposite of the standardized Philistine is not the Bohemian, nor again the hard temperamentalist or superman, as Mr. Mencken conceives him, but the man of leisure. Leisure involves an inner effort with reference to standards that is opposed to the sheer expansion of temperament, as it is to every other form of sheer expansion.

Perhaps a reason why the standards of the humanist are less popular in this country than the ideals of the humanitarian is that these standards set bounds to the acquisitive life; whereas it seems possible to combine a perfect idealism with an orgy of unrestricted commercialism. It is well for us to try to realize how we appear to others in this matter. Our growing unpopularity abroad is due no doubt in part to envy of our material success, but it also arises from the proneness of the rest of the world to judge us, not by the way we feel about ourselves, but by our actual performance. If we are in our own eyes a nation of idealists, we are, according to a recent French critic, M. André Siegfried,[3] a "nation of Pharisees." The European, M. Siegfried would have us believe,

[3] See his volume *Les États-Unis d'aujourd'hui* (1927), translated under the title *America Comes of Age.*

still has a concern for the higher values of civilization, whereas the American is prepared to sacrifice these values ruthlessly to mass production and material efficiency.

It is easy to detect under this assumption the latest form of a "certain condescension in foreigners." The breakdown of cultural standards is European as well as American. It is not clear that M. Siegfried himself has an adequate notion of the form of effort that can alone serve as a counterpoise to the one-sided activity of the utilitarian. At the same time his anatomy of our favorite ideal of service is not without interest. This ideal opposes no effective barrier to our expansiveness. An unchecked expansiveness on the national scale is always imperialistic. Among the ingredients of a possible American imperialism M. Siegfried enumerates the American's "great self-satisfaction, his rather brutal sense of his own interests, and *the consciousness, still more dangerous, of his 'duties' towards humanity."* M. Siegfried admits however that our imperialism is likely to be of a new and subtle essence, not concerned primarily with territorial aggrandizement.

A proper discussion of M. Siegfried's position as well as of other issues I have been raising would transcend the limits of an essay. My end has been accomplished if I have justified in some measure the statement with which I started as to the importance of cultivating a general critical intelligence. James Russell Lowell's dictum that before having an American literature we must have an American criticism was never truer than it is today. The obvious reply to those who call for more creation and less criticism is that one needs to be critical above all in examining what now passes for creation. A scrutiny of this kind would, I have tried to show, extend beyond the bounds of literature to various aspects of our national life and would converge finally on our higher education.

We cannot afford to accept as substitute for this true criticism the self-expression of Mr. Mencken and his school, unless indeed we are to merit the comment that is, I am told, made on us by the South Americans: "They are not a very serious people!" To be sure, the reader may reflect that I am myself a critic, or a would-be critic. I can only express the hope that, in my magnifying of the critical function, I do not offer too close a parallel to the dancing-master of Molière who averred, it will be remembered, that "all the mistakes of men, the fatal reverses that fill the world's annals, the shortcomings of statesmen, and the blunders of great captains arise from not knowing how to dance."

From *On Being Creative* by Irving Babbitt, pp. 201–234. Houghton Mifflin Company, 1932. Reprinted by permission. First published in *The Forum*, Vol. LXXIX (February, 1928), pp. 161–176.

PAUL ELMER MORE

How to Read "Lycidas"

[1936]

AFTER passing, as I might say, through the valley of the shadow of death, after months of physical prostration so abject that reading of any sort was beyond the strength of a depleted brain, the poet to whom I turned instinctively with the first renewal of health was Milton. And so I have been reading Milton again and books about him, with the old zest I had as a boy, and with an added joy of almost tremulous excitement such as a miser might feel at the rediscovery of a treasure of gold stolen from him and long buried out of sight. But with this delight have been mingled certain scruples which had troubled me in the old days and for which I had never found quite a satisfactory answer. Again, as many times before, on laying down one of the poems the familiar words of Tennyson would come unbidden to my mind:

> O mighty-mouth'd inventor of harmonies,
> O skill'd to sing of Time or Eternity,
>   God-gifted organ-voice of England,
>   Milton, a name to resound for ages.

Of the mighty harmonies there would be no doubt; God-gifted voice certainly; organ-voice certainly, for those who have ears to hear. If anyone in English, Milton had the divine craft of words, the mastery of sonorous speech. His is not Shakespeare's incalculable gift; it lacks the element of magic that captures us in Shakespeare; it is, or soon after his earliest experiments it was, an art that came by reflection, and as we read him we imagine that we might by equal deliberation attain the same perfection—only we never do attain it. And something of this distinction Milton himself seems to have felt when he wrote of Shakespeare:

> For whil'st to th' shame of slow-endeavoring Art
> Thy easie numbers flow.

The same distinction, I think, was present to Irving Babbitt when he spoke, as I have heard him do more than once, of his experience in quoting. It was Babbitt's custom in the first draught of his essays to cite from memory,

146

and then, before printing, to verify the quotation by reference to the text. He would find occasionally that even his retentive memory had slipped and that he had substituted a word of his own for the poet's. And sometimes, he would say, he could not see that the substitution was inferior to the original— except in the case of Shakespeare. He never made a change in Shakespeare's language but some force or charm was lost. That was not so even with Milton. Such a difference exists between the seemingly careless spontaneity and the elaborated art of our two supreme masters of poetical diction; and he would be a rash judge who should say that the advantage was all on one side or the other.

But to return to the question that vexed my mood of acquiescent joy. God-gifted organ-voice Milton possessed in full measure—but "voice of England"? Does he speak for the whole of England, or, that being scarcely possible, does he speak for the heart of England, giving articulate expression to that central quality which has made England what we know and love? And by his influence did he maintain that balance and moderation, that sense of law enveloping the individual, which made a Falkland a true type of the Englishman that was to be? Here the question begins with style, but extends beyond mere style to psychology and to principles of government and life.

Now, if there be any hesitation with me to accept Milton's style as the norm of good English, it is certainly not on the ground of that "dissociation of sensibility" which draws a school of modern critics and poets to repudiate what may be called the Miltonic line of development and to seek their parentage in Shakespeare and Donne and the "Metaphysicals." If I understand what the leader of that Choir means by this rather obscure phrase, it is that Milton by conscious choice and judgment dissociated his mind from one whole range of perceptions, refusing to respond to them emotionally as unrelated to a fixed theory of values, and by the same deliberate act of selection created a more or less artificial language, whereas the poets proceeding from Donne held their sensibility open to any and every perception and employed words to convey the sharp immediate impression of each fact of sense and experience without discrimination. The distinction is valid, and it is interesting; for the "modernist" in poetry it is of vital significance. But I am not sure that the "dissociation of sensibility," so taken, has been the source of dead monotony and of verbal unreality in our literature; and I am sure that if Milton failed in national leadership it was not for this reason. Rather I should say that his influence in this respect has made for sanity and form and for limitations which are characteristically English. Rather I should maintain that Milton's failure, so far as he failed, was owing to something essentially un-English, or only partially English, to something belonging to his individual temperament, which passed into his philosophy of life and diverted the love of liberty, which was the central driving force of all his being, into a morbid and isolating passion. Here too Milton was clear-headed in his application of the law to others, but curiously perverse when his own interests were affected. In the second of the sonnets on the book called *Tetrachordon,* he berates his fellow countrymen as "Owles and Cuckoos, Asses, Apes and Doggs" for the very reason that they have lost the true meaning of liberty, while they

> . . . bawle for freedom in this senceless mood,
> And still revolt when truth would set them free.
> License they mean when they cry libertie;
> For who loves that, must first be wise and good;
> But from that mark, how far they roave we see
> For all this wast of wealth, and loss of blood.

That is sound doctrine, but—alas to say it!—Milton did not see how apt would be the retort, *de te fabula;* how easy the reply: License he meant when he cried liberty.

This book called *Tetrachordon,* written by Milton himself, was the second of his treatises on divorce, and is a bitter invective against those who, by opposing the facile freedom of marital separation, enslave the soul under man-made laws, forgetting that which "makes us holiest and likest to God's immortal image," and, for the law of liberty, setting up "that which makes us most conformable and captive to civil and subordinate precepts: . . . although indeed no ordinance, human or from heaven, can bind against the good of man." By "the good of man," as Mr. Tillyard observes in his comment on the passage, Milton means what elsewhere he calls "nature"—damnable word, I add, into which have been distilled all the fallacies of human wit through thousands of years. If you track the word down through its many ambiguities, you will discover that in the end it signifies that which a man temperamentally and personally desires as distinguished from that which is prescribed for him by human rule or divine precept. So it was that Milton, fretted and humiliated because his wife, finding existence with him intolerable, left him and ran away home—so it was that incontinently he rebelled against the human divine laws of marriage and wrote his pleas for freedom of divorce as complying with natural law and the good of man. If ever there was a case of liberty becoming license, it was here. However they may have differed in other respects, in this quality Milton resembled Shelley: they both identified what they desired at any moment with the natural good of man; they both made self-righteousness the law of right.

That was the beginning of Milton's public career and of his prose writings, and it was typical of what ensued. If the bishops in any way interfered with his personal idea of worship, then down with episcopacy and away with the Church; if the monarchical form of government hampered his political independence, then down with monarchy and away with the Constitution.

There is no more painful reading in English literature than these apologies for
free divorce and regicide which occupied the greatest genius of the age between "Lycidas" and *Paradise Lost,* and the style in which they are written is
as heavy and un-English as their spirit is perverse. There are purple patches
scattered through these treatises, which are all that most readers know of
Milton's prose and which would give the impression that he is as magnificent
here as in his verse; but if these passages are examined it will be found that,
taken apart from their context, they are expressions of a personal ambition,
legitimate in itself and magnificent in its devotion to the aim of a poet, while
all about them floats and rages a sea of rebellious discontent. I will not endorse
Hilaire Belloc's sweeping condemnation of the prose in his study of *Milton,*
but as a whole it must be admitted to form a repellent body of reading. Following the ideas of the tractates through the surging verbiage, one is reminded of
the monsters in the account of creation, "wallowing unweildie" in

> . . . the vast immeasurable Abyss
> Outrageous as a Sea, dark, wasteful, wilde,
> Up from the bottom turn'd by furious windes.

There is something disconcerting in the spectacle of a supreme artist, as Milton
was in his verse, so losing his craftsmanship in another medium; what I would
insist on is that the very style of his prose has a close relation to the fact that
when he passes from imagination to theory his voice is not that of his people
but of an exasperated individual. The seventeenth century, with all its greatness, is an age of frustration, filled with fine promises that, except in the field
of science, came to no fruition, replete with noble utterance that somehow
failed to convince. In the Church, in the State, in society, the one thing
needed and not found was a commanding genius that should have indeed the
voice of England. It is the tragedy of the time that he who had the genius so
to speak should have wasted his energies in querulous complaints against what
was, and in the future was to show itself, the true spirit of the land. In a word
that spirit may be decribed precisely as liberty, not license, as centrality, not
dissent.

But I am not concerned to pass judgment on Milton's character and its effect
upon his work as a whole; that is a longer theme than I care now to discuss.
What I started out to do was to consider one small piece of his output, the
"Lycidas," and to ask myself how it should be read. To this question, at least
in its acuter form, I was moved by chancing to take up at the same time Mr.
Tillyard's estimation of the poem and Dr. Johnson's. As a whole I should regard Mr. Tillyard's *Milton* as about the best book we have on the man and the
poet, a study admirable for its scholarship and discrimination, and particularly
notable for its treatment of the philosophical problems raised by *Paradise Lost,*
such as Milton's conception of the nature of evil and the cause of man's fall.

Now to Mr. Tillyard " 'Lycidas' is the last and greatest English poem of Milton's youth; though shorter, it is greater than *Comus*, written with newly won but complete mastery and expressing a mental experience both valuable and profound." That is a sentiment with which my own reaction is in perfect accord; indeed, I should go further and hold it to be the greatest short poem of any author in English, the very criterion and touchstone of poetical taste.

Yet with that opinion I have felt bound to remember the sweeping condemnation of Johnson, to whom "the diction" of the poem "is harsh, the rhymes uncertain, and the numbers unpleasing." It is without passion and without art. In part no doubt Johnson's lack of appreciation can be set down to his known deficiency in the higher faculty of imagination. His comment on the diction and rhythm does nothing more than indicate a certain insensitiveness to the finer and more delicate effects of poetry in general. But one cannot read the whole essay without perceiving that his hostile criticism of the art of "Lycidas" sprang not so much from his miscomprehension and esthetic obtuseness as from hostility to the poet and to all that Milton as a man stood for. Touching Milton's plea for looser laws of divorce, the neglect of which by the ruling Presbyterians turned him against that sect, Johnson observes, and justly: "He that changes his party by his humor is not more virtuous than he that changes it by his interest; he loves himself rather than truth." As for the political tirades, Johnson in his attack ran true to form: "Milton's republicanism was . . . founded in an envious hatred of greatness, and a sullen desire of independence. . . . He hated monarchs in the State, and prelates in the Church; for he hated all whom he was required to obey. . . . He felt not so much the love of liberty as repugnance to authority." Now for myself I do not like Belloc's summary and contemptuous characterization of Milton as "a man rotten with the worst vices: falsehood and pride"; for somehow one shrinks from using such language of a very great poet. To Johnson's charge, on the contrary, I can subscribe without reservation (indeed I have already said much the same thing in weaker language), and I do not see how the charge, in substance, can be countered by any impartial student of Milton's life. But to Johnson the faults of the man were ruinous to the earlier work of the poet, and he denounced "Lycidas" because he read into it the author's ecclesiastical and political heresies; whereas I must reject the maker whilst admiring what he has made. And there the difficulty lies—or has lain for me: how can one so combine detestation and love? how can one make so complete a separation between Milton the destroyer of Church and State, and Milton the creative artist? how is one to read "Lycidas"?

That particular difficulty, it will be observed, opens up into one of the major problems of criticism in general: the relation between the content of a poem and the art of a poem independent of its content. In the beginning, when that distinction first presented itself to the Greek mind, it took a very simple form and indeed scarcely provoked any doubt: the *Iliad* and the *Odyssey* were valued theoretically, not for their charm and interest, but because in them the statesman, the soldier, the athlete, the man who desired to live honorably, could find the wisest precepts and the best models. For later times, and for us of the West, the principle involved was formulated by Horace in his famous saying that the most successful poet was he who knew how to mix the *utile* and the *dulce*. What Horace meant by the *dulce* is clear enough; it is just that in a poem which gives pleasure to a reader. And what he meant by the *utile* is equally clear; it is that in a poem from which we draw instruction. So in one of the *Epistles* he tells a friend, held in Rome by the practice of declaiming, no doubt about the schools of philosophy, that he is in the country reading Homer, who is a better teacher than all the philosophers:

> Qui, quid sit pulchrum, quid turpe, quid utile, quid non,
> Plenius ac melius Chrysippo et Crantore dicit.

In exactly that form the question reached the Renaissance critics, with the emphasis still heavily on the *utile*. So Puttenham, to cite a single example, thinks it necessary to preface his treatise on *The Arte of English Poesie* with a long apology, wherein is shown how "poets were the first priests, the first prophets, the first Legislators and politicians in the world," as seen in Homer, Orpheus, Amphion, and the rest. You are back a thousand years and more, and might be reading one of the ancient Greek commentators. But a change came with the advent of the romantic movement. The *utile* and the *dulce* took on a new significance, and the old division was sharpened to something like an absolute contrast between two irreconcilable criteria of excellence. The *utile* was broadened so as to embrace the whole substance of a poem whether instructive or not, its sense or meaning. The *dulce* on the other hand was refined to a conception of pure poetry, the quintessence of art, as a sort of abstract entity which could be felt and judged somehow apart from any articulate thought or story conveyed; indeed the ideal poem would be a succession of beautiful words with no meaning at all.

Such a thesis, baldly stated, is manifestly bare nonsense; but practically the early romantics applied it to criticism by taking "Kubla Khan" as the ideal poem, because, while the content was no more than the shimmering matter of a dream, it reeked of that mysterious entity called pure poetry. And it was not so long ago that the theory flared up again in France under the impulse of the Abbé Brémond's monograph on *La Poésie pure*. The discussion that ensued was confused by the Abbé's association of esthetic rapture with a mystical view of the function of prayer. More illuminating, to me at least, is T. S. Eliot's pursuit and final rejection of the same ideal of absolute poetry. In his earlier essays, particularly those on Seneca, Shakespeare, and Dante, you will see him tentatively using this *ignis fatuus* as the ultimate standard of value.

In the first of those studies he ranks Shakespeare and Dante together as the supreme poets of the world, and the two are equally great though the Italian has taken up into the *Commedia* the profoundest wisdom of human experience as expounded in the Thomistic theology, whereas the Englishman has no interpretation of life's riddle beyond the stale platitudes of Seneca. "Perhaps it was Shakespeare's special rôle in history to have effected this peculiar union—perhaps it is a part of his special eminence to have expressed an inferior philosophy in the greatest poetry." It is true that Mr. Eliot has his reservations in supporting this romantic dream of pure poetry, which came to him from certain, as I think unfortunate, associations in the period before he had fully found himself, and which has haunted him all through his years of self-development. It is more important to note that in his latest enunciation he has worked himself quite clear of the disturbing inheritance. There lies before me now his recently published volume of *Essays Ancient and Modern,* and in the opening paragraph of one of the "modern" (that is, hitherto unprinted) essays I am held by this sentence: "The 'greatness' of literature cannot be determined solely by literary standards; though we must remember that whether it is literature or not can be determined only by literary standards." That I take to be a complete truth perfectly formulated; and the whole essay on "Religion and Literature" is a masterly application of this sentence to modern currents in verse and fiction. It is the critic come to full maturity after years of probation.

And so, to apply this canon of taste to "Lycidas," it may be possible for a young man, enamored of the sheer beauty of words and untroubled as yet by the graver issues of life, to enjoy the marvelous art of the poem with no thought of what the poem means if connected with the poet's place in the world of ideas and action. But such a rupture between the form and the substance of literature cannot long be maintained with the ripening of experience. Sooner or later we are bound to make up our account with that law of taste so ably formulated: "The 'greatness' of literature cannot be determined solely by literary standards; though we must remember that whether it is literature or not can be determined only by literary standards." That "Lycidas" is literature, poetry and not mere verse, depends on the language, the images, the form, on that mysterious working of the imagination which we can feel but cannot ultimately analyze or adequately describe; that it is great literature must depend on the junction of such qualities with nobility of content. And such nobility is there, in full measure.

The poem is an elegy prompted by the drowning of a college friend of the author. It has been the complaint of more than one critic that the expression of grief has little of that warmth which might be expected from such a subject. Dr. Johnson can find no "effusion of real passion, for passion runs not after remote allusions and obscure opinions." Against this charge of frigidity

Mr. Tillyard contends with great acumen that the true theme of the poem is not the death of Edward King at all, but the possible death of the poet himself. Milton was writing just before he set out on his voyage to Italy, when such an adventure was more or less perilous, and the possibility of shipwreck and drowning might very well have occupied his mind. So taken, the charge of coldness towards a friend might be changed to one of cowardice or egotism. But Milton was no coward and, however he may have shown himself elsewhere, the note of egotism is relieved by the artful, though doubtless unconscious transference of anxiety for himself to sorrow for another. And it was not the mere termination of life that made him anxious, but the fear that his one all-absorbing ambition might so be left unfulfilled. To understand his state of mind and the emotion that was impelling him to write, the elegy should be read in the light of those passages of self-dedication scattered through his prose works. These purple patches laid upon the coarse cloth of controversy are too well-known to need repeating here. The keynote is given by the words inserted in the gross *Apology for Smectymnuus*:

He who would not be frustrate of his hope to write well hereafter in laudable things, ought himself to be a true poem; that is, a composition and pattern of the best and honourablest things; not presuming to sing high praises of heroic men, or famous cities, unless he have in himself the experience and the practice of all that which is praiseworthy.

And joined with this personal ambition was the conviction that no loftier or purer service could be rendered to one's country and to the world than such a work as he was preparing himself to produce. Under the spell of a great heroic poem the mind of the people would respond in efforts towards great and heroic living. That was Milton's faith. It was the spirit of the reformer engrafted upon the temperament of the artist. In such a profession, wherein personal glory is identified with public welfare, pride with humility, there lurks, let us admit, a subtle danger; to fall short of brilliant success must leave the professor a monument of ridicule, like the mountains in labor that brought forth only a mouse. But, on the other hand, such a purpose, if carried through valiantly to a successful issue, makes the ordinary ambition of the artist and poet to appear in comparison no more than a cheap parade of vanity. And Milton had the courage of conviction and the genius to succeed. In the history of English letters there is nothing like this determination carried through from youth to age except the solemn dedication of Wordsworth to a similar purpose. All this must be read into "Lycidas." Under the pretext of grief for the loss of a comrade in hope the poem is in reality as it were the quintessence of those prose passages through which there speaks a self-confidence as sublime as it was justified.

It is in the light of this life-long ambition that we should read the savage

attack on the abuses in Church and State which raises the note of elegy to
the "higher mood" of righteous indignation:

> Last came and last did go,
> The Pilot of the *Galilean* lake . . .
> He shook his Miter'd locks, and stern bespake,
> How well could I have spar'd for thee, young swain,
> Anow of such as for their bellies sake,
> Creep and intrude, and climb into the fold? . . .
> But that two-handed engine at the door,
> Stands ready to smite once, and smite no more.

And apart from any theory of episcopacy and royalty the abuses were there
and cried out for remedy. Laud knew them as well as did Baxter, Charles as
well as Cromwell; but none but Milton possessed the "dread voice" which—
alas, but for defects of temper!—might have done so much to set them right.

In this light also we should interpret the allegorical symbolism of the poem:

> The hungry Sheep look up, and are not fed.

To Dr. Johnson all this masquerade of sheep and shepherds is "easy, vulgar,
and therefore disgusting," a cheap device of images without passion and without art. Johnson had good reason to be suspicious of a *genre* that has invited
so many weak poets to indulge in flim-flam. But he should not have forgotten
how all through the Old Testament, from the call that came to Amos, "who
was among the herdmen of Tekoa," and all through the New Testament, from
the angelic vision that broke upon the shepherds who were "abiding in the
field" about Bethlehem to the parable that Jesus spake to his disciples, "I am
the good shepherd and know my sheep,"—how all through the Bible this
pastoral allegory of the Church runs like the very music of religion.

These were the thoughts that haunted the memory of the poet when he
linked himself with his friend as shepherds:

> Together both, ere the high Lawns appear'd
> Under the opening eye-lids of the morn,
> We drove a field.

Together they were practicing their "rural ditties" in preparation for the
louder chant that was to stir the nation from its ignoble lethargy, when one
of the twain was washed away by the sounding sea, and his voice forever si-
lenced. And what if a like fate awaited the other, who also was about to start
on a voyage? "What boots it with incessant care . . . to meditate the thankless Muse," of what avail to "live laborious dayes," when, just as we

> . . . think to burst out into sudden blaze,
> Comes the blind *Fury* with th' abhorred shears,
> And slits the thin spun life?

"But not the praise," he exclaims; the reward and the outcome are not confined to this world nor are they measured by success "on mortal soil," but in heaven before the "witness of all judging *Jove*." I do not know how others are affected, but I can never peruse the climax of the poem without a thrill such as scarcely any other verses of the language excite.

> Weep no more, woful Shepherds weep no more,
> For *Lycidas* your sorrow is not dead,
> Sunk though he be beneath the watry floor,
> So sinks the day-star in the Ocean bed,
> And yet anon repairs his drooping head,
> And tricks his beams, and with new spangled Ore,
> Flames in the forehead of the morning sky:
> So *Lycidas* sunk low, but mounted high,
> Through the dear might of him that walk'd the waves
> Where other groves, and other streams along,
> With *Nectar* pure his oozy Lock's he laves,
> And hears the unexpressive Nuptiall Song,
> In the blest Kingdoms meek of joy and love.
> There entertain him all the Saints above,
> In solemn troops, and sweet Societies
> That sing, and singing in their glory move,
> And wipe the tears for ever from his eyes.

Milton always rang true when he wrote of the world to come, but never before nor after did he attain quite this elevation, or achieve so realistic an expression of the invisible mysteries wrapt in the future. A few of his contemporaries possessed this power of giving substance to the hopes of eternity —notably Vaughan—but none of them approach the master. And in later times the art was simply lost. Choose the best of the moderns, Newman for instance in *The Dream of Gerontius,* and they will appear cold and unconvincing beside Milton. Nor did any of the great poets of the earlier ages of faith quite equal him in this field. I would not compare the few lines of an elegy with the mighty structure of Dante's *Paradiso,* but for myself at least there is no single incident in Dante's voyage through the celestial spheres that touches me with the shock of actuality like that which I feel when I read "Lycidas." I am not competent to explain by what devices, by what choice of words, Milton obtains his sublime effect. It would be easy of course, if it seemed worth while, to point to the rich manipulation of vowel sounds in this or that verse, to note the startling obviousness of the allusion to the might of him that walked the waves, but the final alchemy of art escapes such an analysis; indeed I question whether any skill of criticism can penetrate to the heart of that mystery of the word which we call inspiration, and leave at that. But one phase of Milton's method impresses me: the fact that his images are bor-

rowed from the simplest commonplaces of faith—the return of dawn after the
sinking of the sun in the ocean stream, the tears wiped away, the heavenly
choiring of the blest. A comparison of Newman's attempt to translate the
subtler speculations of theology into a poetic account of the soul's awakening
after death shows how inevitably right was Milton's choice. There are regions
of spiritual experience where the untutored imagination of the people goes
deeper into reality than all the groping wisdom of philosophy.

One thing in the end is certain, the "greatness" of "Lycidas" is determined
by an intimate marriage of form and matter, expression and substance. He
who would read the poem worthily must see this, and must be equally sensitive to the delicacy of its art and to the sublimity of its ideas. This does not
mean that he will forget or slur over the disagreeable traits of the poet's character or the repulsiveness of his ecclesiastical and political theories. But for
our good fortune what repels us in the man and roused Johnson to a fury of
protest is reserved for his prose and is excluded from his poetry—not completely indeed, for, not to mention the more outrageous sonnets, occasionally
the bitterness of his disappointed soul breaks out in his later works, yet to
such an extent that it is not impossible to keep the poet and the controversialist
apart as two almost separate powers. That divorce has its unhappy aspect; for
one thing it debars Milton, in his total effect, from being accepted as the voice
of England. But it leaves to him the high credit of having raised in *Paradise
Lost,* to the honor of his native land, the one monumentally successful product of that humanistic culture of the Renaissance in which originality of
genius and faithfulness to the classical tradition are combined in perfect union.
And for "Lycidas" there is this further apology, that the elegy was composed
before Milton's splendid spirit of liberty was exacerbated by opposition into
petulant license, when his personal pride flamed with a yet undiverted zeal
to make of his own life a true poem and so to train himself for creating such
a work of art as would lift his people from the ugly slough of faction and greed,
where they were grovelling, into the finer atmosphere where pure religion and
the love of beauty might flourish together.

From *On Being Human* by Paul Elmer More, pp.
184–202. Princeton University Press. Copyright,
1936. Reprinted by permission. First published
in *The American Review,* Vol. VII (May,
1936), pp. 140–158.

H. L. MENCKEN

The American Novel

[1924]

IT IS an ancient platitude of historical criticism that great wars and their sequelae are inimical to the fine arts, and particularly to the arts of letters. The kernel of truth in it lies in the obvious fact that a people engaged in a bitter struggle for existence have no time for such concerns, which demand not only leisure but also a certain assured feeling of security, well-being and self-sufficiency—in brief, the thing often called aristocratic (or sometimes intellectual) detachment. No man ever wrote good poetry with his wife in parturition in the next room, or the police preparing to raid his house, or his shirt-tail afire. He needs to be comfortable to do it, and if not actually comfortable, then at all events safe. Wars tend to make life uncomfortable and unsafe—but not, it must be observed, inevitably and necessarily, not always and invariably. A bitter and demoralizing struggle goes with wars that are lost, and the same struggle goes with wars that are won only by dint of stupendous and ruinous effort, but it certainly does not go with wars that are won easily. These last do not palsy and asphyxiate the artist, as he is palsied and asphyxiated by cholera morbus, suits for damages or marriage. On the contrary, they pump him full of ozone, and he is never more alive and lively than following them.

I point to a few familiar examples. The Civil War, as everyone knows, bankrupted the South and made life a harsh and bitter struggle for its people, and especially for the gentler and more civilized minority of its people. In consequence, the South became as sterile artistically, after Lee's surrender, as Mexico or Portugal, and even today it lags far behind the North in beautiful letters, and even further behind in music, painting and architecture. But the war, though it went on for four years, strained the resources of the North very little, either in men or in money, and so its conclusion found the Northerners very rich and cocky, and full of a yearning to astonish the world, and that yearning, in a few decades, set up a new and extremely vigorous American literature, created an American architecture of a revolutionary character, and even laid the first courses of American schools of music and painting.

Mark Twain, Walt Whitman, Henry James, and William Dean Howells, all
of them draft dodgers in the war itself, were in a very real sense products of
the war, for they emerged as phenomena of the great outburst of creative energy that followed it, and all of them, including even James, were as thoroughly American as Jay Gould, P. T. Barnum, or Jim Fisk. The stars of the
national letters in the years before the war had been Americans only by geographical accident. About Emerson there hung a smell of Königsberg and
Weimar; Irving was simply a New York Englishman; Poe was a citizen of No
Man's Land; even Hawthorne and Cooper, despite their concern with American themes, showed not the slightest evidence of an American point of view.
But Mark Twain, Howells and Whitman belonged to the Republic as pal-
pably as Niagara Falls or Tammany Hall belonged to it, and so did James,
though the thought horrified him and we must look at him through his brother
William to get the proof. Turn now to Europe. France, harshly used in the
war of 1870–71, was sterile for a decade, but the wounds were not deep, and
recovery was in full swing by 1880. Germany, injured scarcely at all, produced
Nietzsche almost before the troops got home, and was presently offering an
asylum and an inspiration to Ibsen, preparing the way for the reform and
modernization of the theatre, and making contributions of the utmost value
to practically all of the arts and sciences. Spain, after the Armada, gave the
world Cervantes and then expired; England produced Shakespeare and
founded a literature that is not surpassed in history.

What has thus happened over and over again in the past—and I might pile
up examples for pages—may be in process of repetition today, and under our
very noses. All Europe, plainly enough, is in a state of exhaustion and depression, and in no department of human activity is the fact more visible than in
that of the arts. Not only are the defeated nations, Russia, Germany, and
Austria, producing nothing save a few extravagant eccentricities; there is also
a great lowness of spirit in the so-called victorious nations, for their victory was
almost as ruinous as defeat. France, as after 1870, is running to a pretentious
and artificial morbidity in letters, and marking time in music and painting;
Italy is producing little save psychopathological absurdities by such mounte-
banks as D'Annunzio and Papini; even England shows all the signs of profound fatigue. The great English writers of the age before the war are passing.
Meredith is gone; Hardy has put up his shutters; Kipling went to wreck in
the war itself; Conrad is dead; Shaw, once so agile and diverting, becomes a
seer and prophet. Nor is there any sign of sound progress among the younger
men. Arnold Bennett, a star of brilliant promise in 1913, is today a smoking
smudge. Wells has ceased to be an artist and become a prophet in the Sunday
supplements. Masefield has got no further than he was on August 2, 1914.
The rest of the novelists are simply chasing their own tails. The Georgian
poets, having emerged gloriously during the war, now disappear behind their

manners. Only a few women, led by May Sinclair, and a few iconoclastic young men, led by Aldous Huxley, are still indubitably alive.

It seems to me that, in the face of this dark depression across the water, the literary spectacle on this side takes on an aspect that is extremely reassuring, and even a bit exhilarating. For the first time in history, there begins to show itself the faint shadow of a hope that, if all goes well, leadership in the arts, and especially in all the art of letters, may eventually transfer itself from the eastern shore of the Atlantic to the western shore. Our literature, as I have more than once pointed out in the past, is still oppressed by various heavy handicaps, chiefly resident in the failure of the new aristocracy of money to function as an aristocracy of taste. The artist among us is still a sort of pariah, beset by public contempt on the one hand and by academic enmity on the other; he still lacks the public position that his brothers enjoy in older and more civilized countries. Nevertheless, it must be obvious to everyone that his condition tends to improve materially—that, in our own time, it has improved materially—that though his rewards remain meager, save in mere money, his freedom grows steadily greater. And it must be obvious, too, that he begins to show that that increasing freedom is not wholly wasted upon him—that he knows how to use it, and is disposed to do so with some gusto. What all the younger American writers have in common is a sort of new-found elasticity or goatishness, a somewhat exaggerated sense of aliveness, a glowing delight in the spectacle before them, a vigorous and naïve self-consciousness. The schoolmaster critics belabor them for it, and call it a disrespect for tradition, and try to put it down by denouncing it as due to corrupt foreign influences. But it is really a proof of the rise of nationalism—perhaps of the first dawn of a genuine sense of nationality. No longer imitative and timorous, as most of their predecessors were, these youngsters are attempting a first-hand examination of the national scene, and making an effort to represent it in terms that are wholly American. They are the pioneers of a literature that, whatever its defects in the abstract, will at least be a faithful reflection of the national life, that will be more faithful, indeed, in its defects than in its merits. In England the novel subsides into formulae, the drama is submerged in artificialities, and even poetry, despite occasional revolts, moves toward scholarliness and emptiness. But in America, since the war, all three show the artless and superabundant energy of little children. They lack, only too often, manner and urbanity; it is no wonder that they are often shocking to pedants. But there is the breath of life in them, and that life is far nearer its beginning than its end.

The causes of all this are not far to seek. The American Legion is right: we won the war. It cost us nothing in men; it brought us a huge profit in money; as Europe has gone down, we have gone up. Moreover, it produced a vast discharge of spiritual electricity, otherwise and more injuriously dissipated in the countries more harshly beset. The war was fought ignobly; its first and most obvious effect was to raise up a horde of cads, and set them in authority as spokesmen of the nation. But out of that swinishness there was bound to come reaction, and out of the reaction there was bound to flow a desire to re-examine the whole national pretension—to turn on the light, to reject old formulae, to think things out anew and in terms of reality. Suddenly the old houses of cards came tumbling down, and the professors inhabiting them ran about in their nightshirts, bawling for the police. The war, first and last, produced a great deal more than John Dos Passos' *Three Soldiers*. It also produced Lewis' *Babbitt*, and Cabell's *Jurgen*, and Fergusson's *Capitol Hill* and O'Neill's *The Emperor Jones*. And, producing them, it ended an epoch of sweetness and light.

II

The young American literatus of today, with publishers ready and eager to give him a hearing, can scarcely imagine the difficulties which beset his predecessor of twenty years ago; he is, indeed, far too little appreciative of the freedom he has, and far too prone to flee from hard work to the solace of the martyr's shroud. When I first began practice as a critic, in 1908, there was yet plenty of excuse for putting it on. It was a time of almost inconceivable complacency and conformity. Hamilton Wright Mabie was still alive and still taken seriously, and all the young pedagogues who aspired to the critical gown imitated him in his watchful stupidity. This camorra had delivered a violent wallop to Theodore Dreiser eight years before, and he was yet suffering from his bruises; it was not until 1911 that he printed *Jennie Gerhardt*. Miss Harriet Monroe and her gang of new poets were still dispersed and inarticulate; Miss Amy Lowell, as yet unaware of Imagism, was writing polite doggerel in the manner of a New England schoolmarm; the reigning dramatists of the nation were Augustus Thomas, David Belasco, and Clyde Fitch; Miss Cather was imitating Mrs. Wharton; Hergesheimer had six years to go before he'd come to *The Lay Anthony;* Cabell was known only as one who provided the text·for illustrated gift-books; the American novelists most admired by most publishers, by most readers and by all practicing critics were Richard Harding Davis, Robert W. Chambers, and James Lane Allen. It is hard indeed, in retrospect, to picture those remote days just as they were. They seem almost fabulous. The chief critical organ of the Republic was actually the Literary Supplement of the *New York Times. The Dial* was down with diabetes in Chicago; *The Nation* was made dreadful by the gloomy humors of Paul Elmer More; *The Bookman* was even more saccharine and sophomoric than it is today. When the mild and pianissimo revolt of the middle 90's—a feeble echo of the English revolt—had spent itself, the Presbyterians marched in and took possession of the works. Most of the erstwhile revoltés boldly took the veil—notably Hamlin Garland. No novel that told the truth about life as Americans were living it, no poem that departed from the old patterns, no play that had the merest ghost of an idea in it had a chance. When, in 1908, Mrs. Mary Roberts Rinehart printed a conventional mystery story which yet managed to have a trace of sense in it, it caused a sensation. And when, two years later, Dr. William Lyon Phelps printed a book of criticism in which he actually ranked Mark Twain alongside Emerson and Hawthorne, there was as great a stirring beneath the college elms as if a naked fancy woman had run across the campus. If Hergesheimer had come into New York in 1908 with *Cytherea* under his arm, he would have worn out his pantaloons on publishers' benches without getting so much as a polite kick. If Eugene O'Neill had come to Broadway with *The Hairy Ape*, he would have been sent to Edward E. Rose to learn the elements of his trade. The devilish and advanced thing, in those days, was for the fat lady star to give a couple of matinées of Ibsen's *A Doll's House*.

A great many men and a few women addressed themselves to the dispersal of this fog. Some of them were imaginative writers who found it simply impossible to bring themselves within the prevailing rules; some were critics; others were young publishers. As I look back, I can't find any sign of concerted effort; it was, in the main, a case of each on his own. The more contumacious of the younger critics, true enough, tended to rally 'round Huneker, who, as a matter of fact, was very little interested in American letters, and the young novelists had a leader in Dreiser, who, I suspect, was quite unaware of most of them. However, it was probably Dreiser who chiefly gave form to the movement, despite the fact that for eleven long years he was silent. Not only was there a useful rallying-point in the idiotic suppression of *Sister Carrie*; there was also the encouraging fact of the man's massive immovability. Physically and mentally he loomed up like a sort of headland—a great crag of basalt that no conceivable assault seemed able to touch. His predecessor, Frank Norris, was of much softer stuff. Norris, had he lived longer, would have been wooed and ruined, I fear, by the Mabies, Boyntons, and other such Christian critics, as Garland had been wooed and ruined before him. Dreiser, fortunately for American letters, never had to face any such seduction. The critical schoolmarms, young and old, fell upon him with violence the moment he appeared above the horizon of his native steppe, and soon he was the storm center of a battle-royal that lasted nearly twenty years. The man himself was solid, granitic, without nerves. Very little cunning was in him and not much bellicose enterprise, but he showed a truly appalling tenacity. The pedagogues tried to scare him to death, they tried to stampede his partisans and they tried to put him into Coventry and get him forgotten, but they failed every time. The more he was reviled, sneered at, neglected, the more resolutely he stuck to his formula. That formula is now every serious American novelist's formula. They all try to write better than Dreiser, and not a few of them succeed, but they all follow him in his fundamental purpose—to make the novel true. Dreiser added something, and here following him is harder: he tried to make the novel poignant—to add sympathy, feeling, imagination to understanding. It will be a long while before that enterprise is better managed than he managed it in *Jennie Gerhardt*.

Today, it seems to me, the American imaginative writer, whether he be novelist, poet or dramatist, is quite as free as he deserves to be. He is free to depict the life about him precisely as he sees it, and to interpret it in any manner he pleases. The publishers of the land, once so fearful of novelty, are now so hospitable to it that they constantly fail to distinguish the novelty that has hard thought behind it from that which has only some Village mountebank's desire to stagger the wives of Rotarians. Our stage is perhaps the freest in the world—not only to sensations, but also to ideas. Our poets get into print regularly with stuff so bizarre and unearthly that only Christian Scientists can understand it. The extent of this new freedom, indeed, is so great that large numbers of persons appear to be unable to believe in it; they are constantly getting into sweats about the taboos and inhibitions that remain, for example, those nourished by comstockery. But the importance and puissance of comstockery, I believe, is quite as much over-estimated as the importance and puissance of the objurgations still hurled at sense and honesty by the provincial professors of American Idealism, the Genius of America, and other such phantasms. The Comstocks, true enough, still raid an occasional book, particularly when their funds are running low and there is need to inflame Christian men, but that their monkeyshines ever actually suppress a book of any consequence I very much doubt. The flood is too vast for them. Chasing a minnow with desperate passion, they let a whole school of whales go by. In any case, they confine their operations to the single field of sex, and it must be plain that it is not in the field of sex that the hottest battles against the old American manner have been fought and won. *Three Soldiers* was far more subversive of that manner than all the stories of sex ever written in America—and yet *Three Soldiers* came out with the imprint of one of the most respectable American publishers, and was scarcely challenged. *Babbitt* scored a victory that was still easier, and yet more significant, for its target was the double one of American business and American Christianity; it set the whole world to laughing at two things that are far more venerated in the United States than the bodily chastity of women. Nevertheless, *Babbitt* went down so easily that even the alfalfa *Gelehrten* joined in whooping for it, apparently on the theory that praising Lewis would make the young of the national species forget Dreiser. Victimized by their own craft, the *Gelehrten* thus made a foul attack upon their own principles, for if their principles did not stand against just such anarchistic and sacrilegious books, then they were without any sense whatever, as was and is, indeed, the case.

I shall not rehearse the steps in the advance from *Sister Carrie,* suppressed and proscribed, to *Babbitt,* swallowed and hailed. The important thing is that, despite the caterwauling of the Comstocks and the pedagogues, a reasonable freedom for the serious artist now prevails—that publishers stand ready to print him, that critics exist who are competent to recognize him and willing to do battle for him, and that there is a large public eager to read him. What use is he making of his opportunity? Certainly not the worst use possible, but also certainly not the best. He is free, but he is not yet, perhaps, worthy of freedom. He lets the popular magazine, the movie and the cheap-John publisher pull him too hard in one direction; he lets the vagaries of his politics pull him too hard in another. Back in 1908 I predicted the destruction of Upton Sinclair the artist by Upton Sinclair the visionary and reformer. Sinclair's bones now bleach upon the beach. Beside them repose those of many another man and woman of great promise—for example, Winston Churchill. Floyd Dell is on his way—one novel and two doses of Greenwich Village psychology. Her-gesheimer writes novelettes for the *Saturday Evening Post.* Willa Cather has won the Pulitzer Prize—a transaction comparable to the election of Charles W. Eliot to the Elks. Masters turns to prose that somehow fails to come off. Dreiser, forgetting his trilogy, experiments rather futilely with the drama, the essay, free verse. Fuller renounces the novel for book reviewing. Tarkington is another Pulitzer prizeman, always on the verge of first-rate work but always falling short by an inch. Many of the White Hopes of ten or fifteen years ago perished in the war, as surely victims of its slaughter as Rupert Brooke or Otto Braun; it is, indeed, curious to note that practically every American author who moaned and sobbed for democracy between the years 1914 and 1919 is now extinct. The rest have gone down the chute of the movies.

But all this, after all, may signify little. The shock troops have been piled up in great masses, but the ground is cleared for those that follow. Well, then, what of the youngsters? Do they show any sign of seizing their chance? The answer is yes and no. On the one hand there is a group which, revolving 'round *The Bookman,* talks a great deal and accomplishes nothing. On the other hand there is a group which, revolving 'round *The Dial* and *The Little Review,* talks even more and does even less. But on the third hand, as it were, there is a group which says little and saws wood. There seems to be little in common between its members, no sign of a formal movement, with its blague and its bombast, but all of them have this in common: that they owe both their opportunity and their method to the revolution that followed *Sister Carrie.* Most of them are from the Middle West, but they are distinct from the Chicago crowd, now degenerated to posturing and worse. They are sophisticated, disillusioned, free from cant, and yet they have imagination. The raucous protests of the evangelists of American Idealism seem to have no more effect upon them than the advances of the Expressionists, Dadaists, and other such café-table prophets. Out of this dispersed and ill-defined group, I believe, something will come. Its members are those who are free from the the two great delusions which, from the beginning, have always cursed American letters: the delusion that a work of art is primarily a moral document, that its purpose is to make men better Christians and more docile cannon-fodder, and the delusion that it is an exercise in logic, that its purpose is to prove something. These delusions, lingering beyond their time, are responsible for most of the disasters visible in the national literature today—the disasters of the radicals as well as those of the 100 per cent. dunderheads. The writers of the future, I hope and believe, will carefully avoid both of them.

Reprinted from *Prejudices: Fourth Series* by H. L. Mencken, pp. 278–293, by permission of Alfred A. Knopf, Inc. Copyright, 1924, by Alfred A. Knopf, Inc.

EZRA POUND

Date Line

[1934]

CRITICISM has at least the following categories, differing greatly in the volume of their verbal manifestation, and not equally zoned.

1. Criticism by discussion, extending from mere yatter, logic-chopping, and description of tendencies up to the clearly defined record of procedures and an attempt to formulate more or less general principles.

Aristotle being neither poet nor complete imbecile contented himself with trying to formulate some of the general interior and exterior relations of work already extant.

He has presumably the largest bastard family of any philosopher. Ninkus, Pinkus and Swinky all try to say what the next writer must do.

Dante who was capable of executing the work and of holding general ideas, set down a partial record of procedures.

2. Criticism by translation.

3. Criticism by exercise in the style of a given period.

As you would not seriously consider a man's knowledge of tennis until he either could make or had made some sort of show in a tournament, so we can assume that until a man can actually control a given set of procedures there must be many elements in them of which he has but an imperfect knowledge.

This introduces almost a personal note, or at least a long-delayed reply to carpers who objected to my spending three days in translating Fontenelle on the grounds that I should have been "doing original work and not wasting my energies in translation." They took the *Divagation* as a proof that I was merely gathering daisies.

4. Criticism via music, meaning definitely the setting of a poet's words; e.g. in *Le Testament*, Villon's words, and in *Cavalcanti*, I have set Guido's and Sordello's. In the famous caricature of Edward and Alfonso, seated on a bench in the Bois, the elder monarch remarks to the younger: "A votre âge j'étais

seulement Prince de Galles, c'est le seul moyen de bien connaître Paris."

This is the most intense form of criticism save:

5. Criticism in new composition.

For example the criticism of Seneca in Mr. Eliot's *Agon* is infinitely more alive than in his essay on Seneca.

Years ago I made the mistake of publishing a volume (*Instigations*) without blatantly telling the reader that the book had a design. Coming after an era of gross confusion and irrelevance, wherein malicious camouflage is infinitely more general than any sort of coherence whatsoever, such violent rupture with the general public habit is perfectly useless, and may, for all I know, be unfair to those readers who inhabit a middle zone between effulgent intellect and *les cuistres*.

There would have been no point in asking indulgence as long as the appearances were so greatly against one, I mean so long as the appearance of mere haphazard gave ground for argument, and the reader of ill-will had ample basis for hostile demonstration.

II

Criticism so far as I have discovered has two functions:

1. Theoretically it tries to forerun composition, to serve as gun-sight, though there is, I believe, no recorded instance of this foresight having EVER been of the slightest use save to actual composers. I mean the man who formulates any forward reach of co-ordinating principle is the man who produces the demonstration.

The others who use the principle learn usually from the example, and in most cases merely dim and dilute it.

I think it will usually be found that the work outruns the formulated or at any rate the published equation, or at most they proceed as two feet of one biped.

2. Excernment. The general ordering and weeding out of what has actually been performed. The elimination of repetitions. The work analogous to that which a good hanging committee or a curator would perform in a National Gallery or in a biological museum;

The ordering of knowledge so that the next man (or generation) can most readily find the live part of it, and waste the least possible time among obsolete issues.

"Admitted that it had nothing to do with life but said that it couldn't be changed, therefore I did not take the course." (Letter from Cambridge student, Nov. 1933. The letter referred to economics and not to literature, but it is too

good an example of the academic, of the, alas, "university" spirit to leave un-
used.)

It is impossible to deal with the whole question of education, "culture,"
paideuma, in one volume of literary criticism. What Mr. Eliot calls "Para
something or other" need not for a few hundred pages concern us, save to say
that University education during my time failed from lack of attention to its
circle of reference:

(a) Society in general.
(b) The general intellectual life of the nation.

I take it this was equally true of England, the U.S.A. and several other
nations with which I have had less painful experience.

We have passed from the time wherein it was possible to illude oneself by
a "glittering" or other generality. The contemporary philosopher on the Greek
model with one profound (? if any) central (more or less) intuition and a
lot of unverified hypotheses, analogies, uninspected detail, no longer inveigles
serious attention. Philosophy since Leibnitz (at least since Leibnitz) has been
a weak trailer after material science, engaging men of tertiary importance.

It is not to be expected that the knowledge of the human consciousness, or
its most efficient registering material, language, can dispense with progress in
method at least par with that of the particular sciences, nor that any one individual can escape all the limitations of his confrères. No biologist expects
to formulate a WHOLE new biology. At best he expects to explore a limited
field, to improve the knowledge of certain details, and, if lucky, to clarify the
relations of that field, both in regard to the field itself, and to its exterior
reference.

You don't necessarily expect the bacilli in one test tube to "lead to" those
in another by a mere logical or syllogistic line. The good scientist now and
then discovers similarities, he discovers family groups, similar behaviour in
presence of like reagents, etc. Mark Carleton "the great" improved American
wheat by a series of searches. I see no reason why a similar seriousness should
be alien to the critic of letters.

Language is not a mere cabinet curio or museum exhibit. It does definitely
function in all human life from the tribal state onward. You cannot govern
without it, you cannot make laws without it. That is you make laws, and they
become mere mare's nests for graft and discussion. "The meaning has to be
determined," etc.

There are other means of direct human communication but they are all
narrowly zoned to their *specific* departments, plastic directness, mathematical
relations (in music, or engineering), and in borderline territory where a little
very clear language has to be used along with the "technical" expression.
(Even if it be only to label the photograph or the slide.) However much you
accept of Frobenius' theory of *paideuma* as general and overreaching, over-

stretching the single man, whether you take this as literal fact, or as convenient modus of correlation, the spoken idiom is not only a prime factor, but certainly one of the most potent, progressively so as any modality of civilization ages. Printed word or drum telegraph are neither without bearing on the aggregate life of the folk. As language becomes the most powerful instrument of perfidy, so language alone can riddle and cut through the meshes. Used to conceal meaning, used to blur meaning, to produce the complete and utter inferno of the past century . . . discussion of which would lead me out of the bounds of this volume . . . against which, SOLELY a care for language, for accurate registration by language avails. And if men too long neglect it their children will find themselves begging and their offspring betrayed. Summaries of my conclusions after thirty years' search are now available (*How to Read, ABC of Reading*).

From *Make It New,* by Ezra Pound, pp. 3–7.
Yale University Press, 1935. Copyright, 1935.
By permission of the publishers and the author.

A Stray Document
[1913; 1934]

THE "Don'ts" in the following reprint had a plain utilitarian purpose in that they were intended as a rejection slip to be used by a trade paper. They are aimed at the faults most prevalent of poetry as we found it 1905–1912.

Naturally the second clause in the Imagist triad was the first to be avoided. That really did require a little thought and consciousness, and was promptly followed by various more wordy formulae designed to avoid the trouble.

It is not to be expected that a great number of people in any age will be able to maintain an interesting tenseness in verbal manifestation, any more than we are likely to be beset by a large herd of great draughtsmen or an overwhelming swarm of composers capable of great melodic invention.

A RETROSPECT

In the spring or early summer of 1912, "H. D.," Richard Aldington and myself decided that we were agreed upon the three principles following:

1. Direct treatment of the "thing" whether subjective or objective.
2. To use absolutely no word that does not contribute to the presentation.
3. As regarding rhythm: to compose in the sequence of the musical phrase, not in sequence of a metronome.

Upon many points of taste and of predilection we differed, but agreeing upon these three positions we thought we had as much right to a group name as a number of French "schools" proclaimed by Mr. Flint in the August number of Harold Munro's magazine for 1911.

This school was later "joined" or "followed" by numerous people who, whatever their merits, do not show any signs of agreeing with the second specification. *Vers libre* has become as prolix and as verbose as any of the flaccid varieties of verse that preceded it. It has brought in faults of its own. The actual language and phrasing in it is often as bad as that of our elders, without having even the excuse that the words are shoveled in to fill a metrical pattern or to complete the noise of a rhyme-sound. Whether or no the phrases followed by the followers are musical must be left to the reader's decision. At times I can find a marked metre in *"vers libres,"* as stale and hackneyed as any pseudo-Swinburnian, at times the writers seem to follow no musical structure whatever. But it is, on the whole, good that the field should be ploughed. A few excellent poems have come from the new method, thereby is it justified.

Criticism is not a circumscription or a set of prohibitions. It offers fixed points of departure. It may startle a dull reader into alertness. That little of it which is good is to be found mostly in stray phrases; an older artist helping a younger in great measure by rules of thumb or cautions gained by experience.

A FEW DON'TS

An "Image" is that which presents an intellectual and emotional complex in an instant of time. I use the term "complex" rather in the technical sense employed by the newer psychologist, such as Hart, though we might not agree absolutely in our application.

It is the presentation of such a "complex" instantaneously which gives that sense of sudden liberation; that sense of freedom from time limits and space limits; that sense of sudden growth, which we experience in the presence of the greatest works of art.

It is better to present one Image in a lifetime than to produce voluminous works.

All this, however, some may consider open to debate. The immediate necessity is to tabulate A LIST OF DON'TS for those beginning to write verses. I can not put all of them into Mosaic negative.

To begin with, consider the three propositions (demanding direct treatment, economy of words, and the sequence of the musical phrase), not as dogma—never consider anything as dogma—but as the result of long contemplation, which, even if it is someone else's contemplation, may be worth consideration.

Pay no attention to the criticism of men who have never themselves written a notable work. Consider the discrepancies between the actual writing of the Greek poets and dramatists, and the theories of the Graeco-Roman grammarians, concocted to explain their metres.

LANGUAGE

Use no superfluous word, no adjective, which does not reveal something. Don't use such an expression as "dim lands *of peace.*" It dulls the image. It mixes an abstraction with the concrete. It comes from the writer's not realizing that the natural object is always the *adequate* symbol.

Go in fear of abstractions. Do not re-tell in mediocre verse what has already been done in good prose. Don't think any intelligent person is going to be deceived when you try to shirk all the difficulties of the unspeakably difficult art of good prose by chopping your composition into line lengths.

What the expert is tired of to-day the public will be tired of tomorrow.

Don't imagine that the art of poetry is any simpler than the art of music, or that you can please the expert before you have spent at least as much effort on the art of verse as the average piano teacher spends on the art of music.

Be influenced by as many great artists as you can, but have the decency either to acknowledge the debt outright, or to try to conceal it.

Don't allow "influence" to mean merely that you mop up the particular decorative vocabulary of some one or two poets whom you happen to admire. A Turkish war correspondent was recently caught red-handed babbling in his dispatches of "dove-gray" hills, or else it was "pearl-pale." I can not remember.

Use either no ornament or good ornament.

RHYTHM AND RHYME

Let the candidate fill his mind with the finest cadences he can discover, preferably in a foreign language[1] so that the meaning of the words may be less likely to divert his attention from the movement; e.g., Saxon charms, Hebridean Folk Songs, the verse of Dante, and the lyrics of Shakespeare—if he can dissociate the vocabulary from the cadence. Let him dissect the lyrics of Goethe coldly into their component sound values, syllables long and short, stressed and unstressed, into vowels and consonants.

It is not necessary that a poem should rely on its music, but if it does rely on its music that music must be such as will delight the expert.

Let the neophyte know assonance and alliteration, rhyme immediate and rhyme delayed, simple and polyphonic, as a musician would expect to know harmony and counterpoint and all the minutiae of his craft. No time is too great to give to these matters or to any one of them, even if the artist seldom have need of them.

[1] This is for rhythm; his vocabulary must of course be found in his native tongue.

Don't imagine that a thing will "go" in verse just because it's too dull to go in prose.

Don't be "viewy"—leave that to the writers of pretty little philosophic essays. Don't be descriptive; remember that the painter can describe a landscape much better than you can, and that he has to know a deal more about it.

When Shakespeare talks of the "Dawn in russet mantle clad" he presents something which the painter does not present. There is in this line of his nothing that one can call description; he presents.

Consider the way of the scientists rather than the way of an advertising agent for a new soap.

The scientist does not expect to be acclaimed as a great scientist until he has *discovered* something. He begins by learning what has been discovered already. He goes from that point onward. He does not bank on being a charming fellow personally. He does not expect his friends to applaud the results of his freshman class work. Freshmen in poetry are unfortunately not confined to a definite and recognizable class room. They are "all over the shop." Is it any wonder "the public is indifferent to poetry"?

Don't chop your stuff into separate *iambs*. Don't make each line stop dead at the end, and then begin every next line with a heave. Let the beginning of the next line catch the rise of the rhythm wave, unless you want a definite longish pause.

In short, behave as a musician, a good musician, when dealing with that phase of your art which has exact parallels in music. The same laws govern, and you are bound by no others.

Naturally, your rhythmic structure should not destroy the shape of your words, or their natural sound, or their meaning. It is improbable that, at the start, you will be able to get a rhythm-structure strong enough to affect them very much, though you may fall a victim to all sorts of false stopping due to line ends and caesurae.

The musician can rely on pitch and the volume of the orchestra. You can not. The term harmony is misapplied to poetry; it refers to simultaneous sounds of different pitch. There is, however, in the best verse a sort of residue of sound which remains in the ear of the hearer and acts more or less as an organ-base.

A rhyme must have in it some slight element of surprise if it is to give pleasure; it need not be bizarre or curious, but it must be well used if used at all.

Vide further Vildrac and Duhamel's notes on rhyme in *Technique Poétique.*

That part of your poetry which strikes upon the imaginative *eye* of the reader will lose nothing by translation into a foreign tongue; that which appeals to the ear can reach only those who take it in the original.

Consider the definiteness of Dante's presentation as compared with Milton's rhetoric. Read as much of Wordsworth as does not seem too unutterably dull.

If you want the gist of the matter go to Sappho, Catullus, Villon, Heine when he is in the vein, Gautier when he is not too frigid; or, if you have not the tongues, seek out the leisurely Chaucer. Good prose will do you no harm, and there is good discipline to be had by trying to write it.

Translation is likewise good training, if you find that your original matter "wobbles" when you try to rewrite it. The meaning of the poem to be translated can not "wobble."

If you are using a symmetrical form, don't put in what you want to say and then fill up the remaining vacuums with slush.

Don't mess up the perception of one sense by trying to define it in terms of another. This is usually only the result of being too lazy to find the exact word. To this clause there are possibly exceptions.

The first three simple proscriptions will throw out nine tenths of all the bad poetry now accepted as standard and classic; and will prevent you from many a crime of production.

". . . *Mais d'abord il faut être un poète*," as MM. Duhamel and Vildrac have said at the end of their little book, *Notes sur la Technique Poétique*.

Since March, 1913, Ford Madox Hueffer has pointed out that Wordsworth was so intent on the ordinary or plain word that he never thought of hunting for *le mot juste*.

John Butler Yeats has handled or man-handled Wordsworth and the Victorians, and the criticism, contained in letters to his son, is now printed and available.

From *Make It New: Essays* by Ezra Pound, pp. 335–341. Yale University Press, 1935. Reprinted by permission. "A Few Don'ts" first appeared as "A Few Don'ts by an Imagist" in *Poetry: A Magazine of Verse*, Vol. I (March, 1913), pp. 200–206.

How to Read

(PART II: OR WHAT MAY BE AN INTRODUCTION TO METHOD)

[1929]

IT IS as important for the purpose of thought to keep language efficient as it is in surgery to keep tetanus bacilli out of one's bandages.

In introducing a person to literature one would do well to have him examine works where language is efficiently used; to devise a system for getting directly and expeditiously at such works, despite the smoke-screens erected by half-knowing and half-thinking critics. To get at them, despite the mass of dead matter that these people have heaped up and conserved round about them in the proportion: one barrel of sawdust to each half-bunch of grapes.

Great literature is simply language charged with meaning to the utmost possible degree.

When we set about examining it we find that this charging has been done by several clearly definable sorts of people, and by a periphery of less determinate sorts.

(a) *The inventors*, discoverers of a particular process or of more than one mode and process. Sometimes these people are known, or discoverable; for example, we know, with reasonable certitude, that Arnaut Daniel introduced certain methods of rhyming, and we know that certain finenesses of perception appeared first in such a troubadour or in G. Cavalcanti. We do not know, and are not likely to know, anything definite about the precursors of Homer.

(b) *The masters*. This is a very small class, and there are very few real ones. The term is properly applied to inventors who, apart from their own inventions, are able to assimilate and co-ordinate a large number of preceding inventions. I mean to say they either start with a core of their own and accumulate adjuncts, or they digest a vast mass of subject-matter, apply a number of known modes of expression, and succeed in pervading the whole with some special quality or some special character of their own, and bring the whole to a state of homogeneous fulness.

(c) *The diluters*, those who follow either the inventors or the "great writers," and who produce something of lower intensity, some flabbier variant, some diffuseness or tumidity in the wake of the valid.

(d) (And this class produces the great bulk of all writing.) The men who do more or less good work in the more or less good style of a period. Of these the delightful anthologies, the song books, are full, and choice among them is the matter of taste, for you prefer Wyatt to Donne, Donne to Herrick, Drummond of Hawthornden to Browne, in response to some purely personal sympathy, these people add but some slight personal flavour, some minor variant of a mode, without affecting the main course of the story.

At their faintest *"Ils n'existent pas, leur ambiance leur confert une existence."* They do not exist: their ambience confers existence upon them. When they are most prolific they produce dubious cases like Virgil and Petrarch, who probably pass, among the less exigent, for colossi.

(e) *Belles Lettres*. Longus, Prévost, Benjamin Constant, who are not exactly "great masters," who can hardly be said to have originated a form, but who have nevertheless brought some mode to a very high development.

(f) And there is a supplementary or sixth class of writers, the starters of crazes, the Ossianic Macphersons, the Gongoras whose wave of fashion flows over writing for a few centuries or a few decades, and then subsides, leaving things as they were.

It will be seen that the first two classes are the more sharply defined: that the difficulty of classification for particular lesser authors increases as one descends through the list, save for the last class, which is again fairly clear.

The point is, that if a man know the facts about the first two categories, he can evaluate almost any unfamiliar book at first sight. I mean he can form a just estimate of its worth, and see how and where it belongs in this schema.

As to crazes, the number of possible diseases in literature is perhaps not very great, the same afflictions crop up in widely separated countries without any previous communication. The good physician will recognize a known malady, even if the manifestation be superficially different.

The fact that six different critics will each have a different view concerning what author belongs in which of the categories here given, does not in the least invalidate the categories. When a man knows the facts about the first two categories, the reading of work in the other categories will not greatly change his opinion about those in the first two.

LANGUAGE

Obviously this knowledge cannot be acquired without knowledge of various tongues. The same discoveries have served a number of races. If a man have not time to learn different languages he can at least, and with very little delay, be told what the discoveries were. If he wish to be a good critic he will have to look for himself.

Bad critics have prolonged the use of demoded terminology, usually a terminology originally invented to describe what had been done before 300 B.C., and to describe it in a rather exterior fashion. Writers of second order have often tried to produce works to fit some category or term not yet occupied in their own local literature. If we chuck out the classifications which apply to the outer shape of the work, or to its occasion, and if we look at what actually happens, in, let us say, poetry, we will find that the language is charged or energized in various manners.

That is to say, there are three "kinds of poetry":

MELOPOEIA, wherein the words are charged, over and above their plain meaning, with some musical property which directs the bearing or trend of that meaning.

PHANOPOEIA, which is a casting of images upon the visual imagination.

LOGOPOEIA, "the dance of the intellect among words," that is to say, it employs words not only for their direct meaning, but it takes count in a special way of habits of usage, of the context we *expect* to find with the word, its usual concomitants, of its known acceptances, and of ironical play. It holds the aesthetic content which is peculiarly the domain of verbal manifestation, and cannot possibly be contained in plastic or in music. It is the latest come, and perhaps most tricky and undependable mode.

The *melopoeia* can be appreciated by a foreigner with a sensitive ear, even though he be ignorant of the language in which the poem is written. It is practcially impossible to transfer or translate it from one language to another, save perhaps by divine accident, and for half a line at a time.

Phanopoeia can, on the other hand, be translated almost, or wholly, intact. When it is good enough, it is practically impossible for the translator to destroy it save by very crass bungling, and the neglect of perfectly well-known and formulatable rules.

Logopoeia does not translate; though the attitude of mind it expresses may pass through a paraphrase. Or one might say, you can *not* translate it "locally," but having determined the original author's state of mind, you may or may not be able to find a derivative or an equivalent.

PROSE

The language of prose is much less highly charged, that is perhaps the only availing distinction between prose and poesy. Prose permits greater factual presentation, explicitness, but a much greater amount of language is needed. During the last century or century and a half, prose has, perhaps for the first time, perhaps for the second or third time, arisen to challenge the poetic pre-eminence. That is to say, *Un Coeur Simple,* by Flaubert, is probably more important than Théophile Gautier's *Carmen,* etc.

The total charge in certain nineteenth-century prose works possible surpasses the total charge found in individual poems of that period; but that merely indicates that the author has been able to get his effect cumulatively, by a greater heaping up of factual data; imagined fact, if you will, but nevertheless expressed in factual manner.

By using several hundred pages of prose, Flaubert, by force of architectonics, manages to attain an intensity comparable to that in Villon's *Heaulmière,* or his prayer for his mother. This does not invalidate my dissociation of the two terms: poetry, prose.

In *phanopoeia* we find the greatest drive toward utter precision of word; this art exists almost exclusively by it.

In *melopoeia* we find a contrary current, a force tending often to lull, or to distract the reader from the exact sense of the language. It is poetry on the borders of music, and music is perhaps the bridge between consciousness and the unthinking sentient or even insentient universe.

All writing is built up of these three elements, plus "architectonics" or "the form of the whole," and to know anything about the relative efficiency of various works one must have some knowledge of the maximum already attained by various authors, irrespective of where and when.

It is not enough to know that the Greeks attained to the greatest skill in *melopoeia*, or even that the Provençaux added certain diverse developments and that some quite minor, nineteenth-century Frenchmen achieved certain elaborations.

It is not quite enough to have the general idea that the Chinese (more particularly Rihaku and Omakitsu) attained the known maximum of *phanopoeia*, due perhaps to the nature of their written ideograph, or to wonder whether Rimbaud is, at rare moments, their equal. One wants one's knowledge in more definite terms.

It is an error to think that vast reading will automatically produce any such knowledge or understanding. Neither Chaucer with his forty books, nor Shakespeare with perhaps half a dozen, in folio, can be considered illiterate. A man can learn more music by working on a Bach fugue until he can take it apart and put it together, than by playing through ten dozen heterogeneous albums.

You may say that for twenty-seven years I have thought consciously about this particular matter, and read or read at a great many books, and that with the subject never really out of my mind, I don't yet know half there is to know about *melopoeia*.

There are, on the other hand, a few books that I still keep on my desk, and a great number that I shall never open again. But the books that a man needs to know in order to "get his bearings," in order to have a sound judgment of any bit of writing that may come before him, are very few. The list is so short, indeed, that one wonders that people, professional writers in particular, are willing to leave them ignored and to continue dangling in mid-chaos emitting the most imbecile estimates, and often vitiating their whole lifetime's production.

Limiting ourselves to the authors who actually invented something, or who are the "first known examples" of the process in working order, we find:

OF THE GREEKS: Homer, Sappho. (The "great dramatists" decline from Homer and depend immensely on him for their effects; their "charge," at its highest potential, depends so often, and so greatly on their being able to count on their audience's knowledge of the *Iliad*. Even Aeschylus is rhetorical.)

OF THE ROMANS: As we have lost Philetas, and most of Callimachus, we may suppose that the Romans added a certain sophistication; at any rate, Catullus, Ovid, Propertius, all give us something we cannot find now in Greek authors.

A specialist may read Horace if he is interested in learning the precise demarcation between what can be learned about writing, and what cannot. I mean that Horace is the perfect example of a man who acquired all that is acquirable, without having the root. I beg the reader to observe that I am being exceedingly iconoclastic, that I am omitting thirty established names for every two I include. I am chucking out Pindar, and Virgil, without the slightest compunction. I do not suggest a "course" in Greek or Latin literature, I name a few isolated writers; five or six pages of Sappho. One can throw out at least one-third of Ovid. That is to say, I am omitting the authors who can teach us no new or no more effective method of "charging" words.

OF THE MIDDLE AGES: The Anglo-Saxon *Seafarer,* and some more cursory notice of some medieval narrative, it does not so greatly matter what narrative, possibly the *Beowulf,* the *Poema del Cid,* and the sagas of *Grettir* and *Burnt Nial.* And then, in contrast, troubadours, perhaps thirty poems in Provençal, and for comparison with them a few songs by Von Morungen, or Wolfram von Essenbach, and von der Vogelweide; and then Bion's *Death of Adonis.*

From which mixture, taken in this order, the reader will get his bearings on the art of poetry made to be sung; for there are three kinds of *melopoeia:* (1) that made to be sung to a tune; (2) that made to be intoned or sung to a sort of chant; and (3) that made to be spoken; and the art of joining words in each of these kinds is different, and cannot be clearly understood until the reader knows that there are three different objectives.

OF THE ITALIANS: Guido Cavalcanti and Dante; perhaps a dozen and a half poems of Guido's, and a dozen poems by his contemporaries, and the *Divina Commedia.*

In Italy, around the year 1300, there were new values established, things said that had not been said in Greece, or in Rome or elsewhere.

VILLON: After Villon and for several centuries, poetry can be considered as *fioritura,* as an efflorescence, almost an effervescence, and without any new roots. Chaucer is an enrichment, one might say a more creamy version of the "matter of France," and he in some measure preceded the verbal richness of the classic revival, but beginning with the Italians after Dante, coming through the Latin writers of the Renaissance, French, Spanish, English, Tasso, Ariosto, etc., the Italians always a little in the lead, the whole is elaboration, medieval basis, and wash after wash of Roman or Hellenic influence. I mean one need not read any particular part of it for purpose of learning one's comparative values.

If one were studying history and not poetry, one might discover the medieval mind more directly in the opening of Mussato's *Ecerinus* than even in Dante. The culture of Chaucer is the same which went contemporaneously into Ferrara, with the tongue called *"francoveneto."*

One must emphasize one's contrasts in the quattrocento. One can take Villon as pivot for understanding them. After Villon, and having begun before his time, we find this *fioritura,* and for centuries we find little else. Even in Marlowe and Shakespeare there is this embroidery of language, this talk about the matter, rather than presentation. I doubt if anyone ever acquired discrimination in studying "The Elizabethans." You have grace, richness of language, abundance, but you have probably nothing that isn't replaceable by something else, no ornament that wouldn't have done just as well in some other connection, or for which some other figure of rhetoric couldn't have served, or which couldn't have been distilled from literary antecedents.

The "language" had not been heard on the London stage, but it had been heard in the Italian law courts, etc.; there were local attempts, all over Europe, to teach the public (in Spain, Italy, England) Latin diction. "Poetry" was considered to be (as it still is considered by a great number of drivelling imbeciles) synonymous with "lofty and flowery language."

One Elizabethan specialist has suggested that Shakespeare, disgusted with his efforts, or at least despairing of success, as a poet, took to the stage. The drama is a mixed art; it does not rely on the charge that can be put into the word, but calls on gesture and mimicry and "impersonation" for assistance. The actor must do a good half of the work. One does no favour to drama by muddling the two sets of problems.

Apologists for the drama are continually telling us in one way or another that drama either cannot use at all, or can make but a very limited use of words charged to their highest potential. This is perfectly true. Let us try to keep our minds on the problem we started with, i.e., the art of writing, the art of "charging" language with meaning.

After 1450 we have the age of *fioritura*; after Marlowe and Shakespeare came what was called a "classic" movement, a movement that restrained without inventing. Anything that happens to mind in England has usually happened somewhere else first. Someone invents something, then someone develops, or some dozens develop a frothy or at any rate creamy enthusiasm or over-abundance, then someone tries to tidy things up. For example, the estimable Pleiad emasculating the French tongue, and the French classicists, and the English classicists, etc., all of which things should be relegated to the subsidiary zone: period interest, historical interest, bric-à-brac for museums.

At this point someone says: "O, but the ballads." All right, I will allow the voracious peruser a half-hour for ballads (English and Spanish, or Scotch, Border, and Spanish). There is nothing easier than to be distracted from one's point, or from the main drive of one's subject by a desire for utterly flawless equity and omniscience.

Let us say, but strictly in parenthesis, that there was a very limited sort of *logopoeia* in seventeenth- and eighteenth-century satire. And that Rochester and Dorset may have introduced a new note, or more probably re-introduced an old one, that reappears later in Heine.

Let us also cut loose from minor details and minor exceptions: the main fact is that we "have come" or that "humanity came" to a point where verse-writing can or could no longer be clearly understood without the study of prose-writing.

Say, for the sake of argument, that after the slump of the Middle Ages, prose "came to" again in Machiavelli; admit that various sorts of prose had existed, in fact nearly all sorts had existed. Herodotus wrote history that is literature, Thucydides was a journalist. (It is a modern folly to suppose that vulgarity and cheapness have the merit of novelty; they have always existed, and are of no interest in themselves.)

There had been bombast, oratory, legal speech, balanced sentences, Ciceronian impressiveness; Petronius had written a satiric novel, Longus had written a delicate nouvelle. The prose of the Renaissance leaves us Rabelais, Brantôme, Montaigne. A determined specialist can dig interesting passages, or sumptuous passages, or even subtle passages out of Pico, the medieval mystics, scholastics, Platonists, none of which will be the least use to a man trying to learn the art of "charging language."

I mean to say that from the beginning of literature up to 1750 A.D., poetry was the superior art, and was so considered to be, and if we read books written before that date we find the number of interesting books in verse at least equal to the number of prose books still readable; and the poetry contains the quintessence. When we want to know what people were like before 1750, when we want to know that they had blood and bones like ourselves, we go to the poetry of the period.

But, as I have said, this *"fioritura* business" set in. And one morning Monsieur Stendhal, not thinking of Homer, or Villon, or Catullus, but having a very keen sense of actuality, noticed that "poetry," *la poésie,* as the term was then understood, the stuff written by his French contemporaries, or sonorously rolled at him from the French stage, was a damn nuisance. And he remarked that poetry, with its bagwigs and its bobwigs, and its padded calves and its periwigs, its "fustian à la Louis XIV," was greatly inferior to prose for conveying a clear idea of the diverse states of our consciousness (*"les mouvements du coeur"*).

And at that moment the serious art of writing "went over to prose," and for some time the important developments of language as means of expression were the developments of prose. And a man cannot clearly understand or justly judge the value of verse, modern verse, any verse, unless he have grasped this.

From *Polite Essays* by Ezra Pound, pp. 166–179. New Directions, 1938. Reprinted by permission. *How to Read* first appeared serially in *The New York Herald-Tribune* (*Books*) for January 13, 20, and 27, 1929, and in book form as here printed, from Desmond Harmsworth, London, in 1931.

PART III
The Individual Talent

EDMUND WILSON

James Joyce

[1931]

JAMES JOYCE's first work of fiction, the volume of short stories called *Dubliners,* was finished in 1904 and was to have been brought out by a Dublin publisher; but for a combination of reasons, including the supposed impropriety of certain of the stories, the introduction by name of the Dublin shops, restaurants and pubs, and some disrespectful references to Queen Victoria and Edward VII on the part of one of the characters, the Irish publishers could never bring themselves to publish the book until it had first been brought out in England in 1914, ten years after it had been written. *A Portrait of the Artist as a Young Man* was published first in New York in 1916. Neither of these books had much in common with the English fiction then being written: the typical novelists of that time were H. G. Wells and Arnold Bennett, and Joyce was not in the least like either. In their recent literary renaissance the Irish had been closer to the Continent than to London; and James Joyce, like George Moore, was working in the tradition, not of English, but of French fiction. *Dubliners* was French in its objectivity, its sobriety and its irony, at the same time that its paragraphs ran with a music and a grace quite distinct from the taut metallic quality of Maupassant and Flaubert. And *A Portrait of the Artist as a Young Man,* coming at a time when the public was already surfeited with the early histories of sensitive young men—the Edward Ponderevos, the Clayhangers, the Jacob Stahls, the Michael Fanes—not only was able to attract attention, but had the effect of making most of these books look psychologically superficial and artistically shoddy.

Ulysses was published in Paris in 1922. It had originally been conceived as a short story for *Dubliners,* and was to have been called "Mr. Bloom's Day in Dublin" or something of the sort. But this idea was afterwards combined with the further history of Stephen Dedalus, the hero of the autobiographical *Portrait of the Artist as a Young Man. Ulysses,* however, in its final form as a volume of seven hundred-odd large pages, took shape as something entirely different from either of Joyce's earlier books, and it must be approached from a different point of view than as if it were merely, like the others, a straight work of Naturalistic fiction.

The key to *Ulysses* is in the title—and this key is indispensable if we are to appreciate the book's real depth and scope. Ulysses, as he figures in the *Odyssey*, is a sort of type of the average intelligent Greek: among the heroes, he is distinguished for cunning rather than for exalted wisdom, and for common sense, quickness and nerve rather than for, say, the passionate bravery of an Achilles or the steadfastness and stoutness of a Hector. The *Odyssey* exhibits such a man in practically every situation and relation of an ordinary human life—Ulysses, in the course of his wanderings, runs the whole gauntlet of temptations and ordeals and through his wits he survives them all to return at last to his home and family and to reassert himself there as master. The *Odyssey* thus provides a classical model for a writer attempting a modern epic of the ordinary man—and a model particularly attractive to a modern writer by reason of the apparently calculated effectiveness, the apparent sophistication, of its form. By a device suggestive of some of the novels of Conrad, Homer has framed the wanderings of Ulysses between an introductory group of books in which our interest is aroused in the hero before we meet him by Telemachus' search for his lost father, and a culminating group of books which present dramatically and on a larger scale the wanderer's return home.

Now the *Ulysses* of Joyce is a modern *Odyssey*, which follows closely the classical *Odyssey* in both subject and form; and the significance of the characters and incidents of its ostensibly Naturalistic narrative cannot properly be understood without reference to the Homeric original. Joyce's Telemachus of the opening books is Stephen Dedalus—that is, Joyce himself. The Dedaluses, as we have already learned from *A Portrait of the Artist as a Young Man*, are a shabby-genteel family of Dubliners. Stephen's father, Simon Dedalus, has run through a great variety of employments to end up as nothing in particular, a drinker, a decayed sport, an amateur tenor, a well-known character of the bars. But Stephen has been given a good education at a Jesuit college, and we have seen him, at the end of the earlier novel, on the point of leaving for France to study and write. At the beginning of *Ulysses*, he has been back in Dublin a year: he had been summoned home from Paris by a telegram that his mother was dying. And now, a year after her death, the Dedalus family, already reduced to poverty, has become completely demoralized and disintegrated. While Stephen's young sisters and brothers have hardly enough to eat, Simon Dedalus makes the rounds of the pubs. Stephen, who has always resented his father, feels now that in effect he has none. He is more isolated in Dublin than ever. He is Telemachus in search of a Ulysses. His friend, the medical student, Buck Mulligan, with whom he is living in an old tower on the coast and who believes himself to share Stephen's artistic tastes and intellectual interests, really humiliates him by patronizing him and turns to ridicule his abilities and ambitions. He is Antinous, the boldest of Penelope's suitors, who, while Ulysses is away, tries to make himself master of his house and mocks at Telemachus. Stephen has announced at the end of the earlier book that he is going forth "to forge in the smithy of my soul the uncreated conscience of my race"; and now he has returned to Dublin baffled and disinherited—his life with Mulligan is dissolute and unproductive. Yet as Telemachus finds friends and helpers, so Stephen is reminded by the old woman who brings the milk for breakfast in the tower of that Ireland whose uncreated conscience it is still his destiny to forge: "Old and secret . . . maybe a messenger." She is Athene in the guise of Mentor who provides Telemachus with his ship; and the memory of Kevin Egan, an Irish exile in Paris, is the Menelaus who speeds him on his way.

The scene now shifts, as it does in the *Odyssey,* to the lost Ulysses himself. Joyce's Ulysses is a Dublin Jew, an advertisement canvasser named Bloom. Like Stephen, he dwells among aliens: a Jew and the son of a Hungarian father, he is still more or less of a foreigner among the Irish; and a man of something less than mediocre abilities, but of real sensibility and intelligence, he has little in common with the other inhabitants of the lower middle-class world in which he lives. He has been married for sixteen years to the buxom daughter of an Irish army officer, a professional singer, of prodigious sexual appetite, who has been continually and indiscriminately unfaithful to him. They have had one daughter, who is already growing up and apparently going the way of her mother; and one son, of whom Bloom had hoped that he might resemble, that he might refine upon, himself, but who died eleven days after he was born. Things have never been the same between the Blooms since the death of this son; it is now more than ten years since Bloom has attempted complete intercourse with his wife—it is as if the birth of the sickly Rudy had discouraged him and made him doubt his virility. He is aware that his wife has lovers; but he does not complain or try to interfere—he is even resigned to her accepting money from them. He is a Ulysses with no Telemachus and cut off from his Penelope.

We now follow Bloom's adventures on the day of June 16, 1904 (the whole of *Ulysses* takes place within less than twenty-four hours). Lotus-eaters allure him; he is affrighted by Laestrygonians. He assists at the burial of an Elpenor and descends with him in imagination to the underworld; he suffers from the varying favor of an Aeolus. He escapes by ruse from the ferocity of a Cyclops and he disengages himself through prudence from the maiden charms of a Nausicaa. And he emerges finally a man again from the brothel of a Circe who had transformed him into a swine.

The comings and goings of Stephen during the day are woven in and out among the wanderings of Bloom: the two encounter each other twice but do not recognize each other. Both men, we become aware, are constantly accompanied and oppressed by ideas which they have tried to dismiss from their minds: the family situation of each really lies back of and explains all that he does that day. In Stephen's case, it is only a few days from the anniversary of his mother's death, and he is haunted by the memory of it: she had begged him on her deathbed to kneel down and pray for her soul and, in rebellion against the Catholic education which had disciplined and maimed his spirit, jealous of the independence he had won and in fear of the past to which he had returned, he had cruelly refused and had allowed her to die without the comfort of believing that he had repented of his apostasy. But now that she is dead, this incident tortures him. He has in the early morning reproached Mulligan—accusing really himself—for something the latter had said about Stephen's mother at the time of her death which Stephen had overheard and resented; and, as he has looked out upon the bright morning sea, the pathos and horror of her life have become suddenly vivid to him—he has been dragged back to relive all that she had suffered. Then, "No, mother!" he has cried out within himself as he thrust her memory down out of his mind, "let me be and let me live!" But through his whole bitter and baffled day, it is his helpless feeling of guilt toward his mother, his hopeless discouragement and disgust with his father, which govern all his thoughts and movements. When he teaches school, he brings the class to a close by a hysterical joke about "the fox burying his grandmother under a hollybush," and in a stupid boy who cannot do his sums he can see now only his own graceless youth which his mother had shielded from the world. After school, he has gone to walk on the beach and has contemplated paying a visit to the family of a maternal uncle whom he despises, as if he could do penance in this fashion for his hardness to his mother and somehow make it up to her now by kindness to her wretched relatives; but again the counter-impulse which had proved too strong on the former occasion comes into play to block his intention: his mind drifts off to other things and he walks beyond where he should have turned. The artist still conflicts with the son—the two are irreconcilable: he sets out to compose a poem, but the poem itself breaks down and he is left gazing at a silent homing ship.—Visiting the library later in the day, he improvises a long, pretentious lecture on the relation of Shakespeare to his father—a lecture which has little to do with Shakespeare, but a good deal to do with Stephen himself.

And as Stephen is ridden by thoughts of his parents, so Bloom is ridden by thoughts of his wife. He has seen Molly at breakfast get a letter which he suspects—and suspects rightly—to be from Blazes Boylan, a flashy buck about town who is managing a concert tour for her and with whom she is having a love affair. All day he has to change the subject when Boylan's name is mentioned—all day he avoids meeting him in the street. In the afternoon, while Bloom is eating at the Ormond Hotel, Boylan comes into the bar, gets a drink and sets off to call on Mrs. Bloom, and when he has gone, Bloom hears the men in the bar talking and laughing about Molly's easy favors. And the conversation, later on in the pub, about Boylan's having won money in a boxing-match—in spite of Bloom's gently insistent efforts to induce the company to talk about tennis—is one of the incidents which give rise to an antagonism between Bloom and the rest of the company and eventually to the quarrel between the Cyclops-Citizen and Bloom. At the end of the Nausicaa episode, the voice of the cuckoo-clock from the priest's house tells Bloom that he is now a cuckold.

In the evening, Bloom goes to a maternity hospital to inquire after the wife of a friend who has been having a hard delivery: there he meets and recognizes Stephen, who is drinking with the medical students. In the *Odyssey*, the final shipwreck of Ulysses and his subsequent misfortunes are the result of the impiety of his companions, who in defiance of all his warnings have killed and eaten the Oxen of the Sun. So Bloom is pained by the impiety of the medical students as they joke obscenely about childbirth and maternity. On the part of Stephen, whose mother died only a year ago, this levity seems especially shocking, but Stephen's very feeling of guilt about her makes him particularly blasphemous and brutal. Yet Bloom has himself in his own way offended against the principle of fertility by his recent prolonged neglect of Molly: the Calypso who has detained him since his shipwreck is the nymph who hangs in his bedroom and whom he makes the object of amorous fantasies. It is this sin against fertility which—at the hour when Mrs. Bloom is entertaining Boylan—has landed Bloom on the Phaeacian strand indulging in further erotic daydreams in connection with little Gerty MacDowell, the Nausicaa of the Dublin beach.

When Mrs. Purefoy's child has finally been born, the party rushes out to a public house; and, later on—after a drunken altercation between Dedalus and Buck Mulligan at the tram station, in which Antinous and Telemachus apparently dispute over the key to the tower and Telemachus goes away homeless—Stephen, with one of his companions and with Bloom following some distance behind, proceeds to a brothel. Both, by this time, are pretty drunk—though Bloom, with his invincible prudence, is not so drunk as Stephen. And in their drunkenness, in the sordid gaslight and to the tune of the mechanical piano of the brothel, their respective preoccupations emerge fully for the first time since the morning into their conscious minds: Bloom beholds himself, in a hideous vision, looking on at Blazes Boylan and Molly, an abject cuckold, the laughing-stock of the world; and there rises suddenly in Stephen's imagination the figure of his dead mother come back from the grave to remind him of her bleak disheartened love and to implore him to pray for her soul. But again he will not, cannot, acquiesce; in a desperate drunken gesture, intolerably torn by his conflict of impulses, by his emotions which deadlock each other, he lifts his stick and smashes the chandelier—then rushes out into the street, where he gets embroiled with two English Tommies and knocked down. Bloom has followed and, as he bends over Stephen, beholds an appari-

tion of his own dead son, little Rudy, as Bloom would have had him live to be
—learned, cultivated, sensitive, refined: such a youth, in short, as Stephen
Dedalus. Ulysses and Telemachus are united.

Bloom picks Stephen up and takes him first to a coffee-stand, then home
to his own house. He tries to talk to him of the arts and sciences, of the general
ideas which interest him; but Stephen is morose and exhausted and makes
little response. Bloom begs him to spend the night—to come and live with
them, but Stephen declines and presently takes his leave. Bloom goes up, goes
to bed with Molly, describes to her his adventures of the day, and soon drops
off to sleep.

But Bloom's encounter with Stephen is to affect both Stephen's life and
the relations between the Blooms. To have rescued and talked with Stephen
has somehow restored Bloom's self-confidence. He has gotten into the habit
in the past of cooking breakfast for Molly in the morning and bringing it to
her in bed—it is the first thing we have seen him doing at the beginning of the
day; but tonight, before he goes to sleep, he gives her to understand that he
expects her to get breakfast next morning herself and to bring it up to him.
This amazes and disconcerts Mrs. Bloom, and the rest of the book is the record
of her meditations as she lies awake thinking over Bloom's homecoming. She
has been mystified by his recent behavior, and her attitude toward him now
is at first a mixture of jealousy and resentment. She congratulates herself upon
the fact that, if Bloom neglects her nowadays, her needs are ably supplied by
Blazes Boylan. But as she begins to ruminate on the possibility of Stephen
Dedalus's coming to live with them, the idea of Blazes Boylan's coarseness becomes intolerable to her: the thought of Stephen has made her fastidious,
and, rapidly becoming very tender about him, she prefigures a relation between them of an ambiguous but intimate character, half-amorous, half-
maternal. Yet it is Bloom himself who has primarily been the cause of this
revolution in Molly's mind: in telling her about Stephen, he has imposed
upon her again his own values; in staying away from the house all day and
coming back very late at night, and in asking for his breakfast in bed, he has
reasserted his own will. And she goes back in her mind over her experience
of Bloom—their courtship, their married life. She remembers how, when she
had promised to marry him, it had been his intelligence and his sympathetic
nature, that touch of imagination which distinguished him from other men,
which had influenced her in his favor—"because he understood or felt what
a woman is and I knew I could always get around him"; and on the day when
he had first kissed her, he had called her "a flower of the mountain." It is in
the mind of his Penelope that this Ulysses has slain the suitors who have been
disputing his place.

As for Stephen, unresponsive as he has seemed to Bloom's interest and cor-
diality, he has at last, none the less, found in Dublin someone sufficiently

sympathetic to himself to give him the clew, to supply him with the subject, which will enable him to enter imaginatively—as an artist—into the common life of his race. It is possible that Molly and Bloom, as a result of Bloom's meeting with Stephen, will resume normal marital relations; but it is certain that Stephen, as a result of this meeting, will go away and write *Ulysses*. Buck Mulligan has told us that the young poet says he is going "to write something in ten years": that was in 1904—*Ulysses* is dated at the end as having been begun in 1914.

II

This is the story of *Ulysses* in the light of its Homeric parallel; but to describe the book in such a way gives no idea of what it is really like—of its psychological and technical discoveries or of its magnificent poetry.

Ulysses is, I suppose, the most completely "written" novel since Flaubert. The example of the great prose poet of Naturalism has profoundly influenced Joyce—in his attitude toward the modern bourgeois world and in the contrast implied by the Homeric parallel of *Ulysses* between our own and the ancient world, as well as in an ideal of rigorous objectivity and of adaptation of style to subject—as the influence of that other great Naturalistic poet, Ibsen, is obvious in Joyce's single play, *Exiles*. But Flaubert had, in general, confined himself to fitting the cadence and the phrase precisely to the mood or object described; and even then it was the phrase rather than the cadence, and the object rather than the mood, with which he was occupied—for mood and cadence in Flaubert do not really vary much: he never embodies himself in his characters nor identifies his voice with theirs, and as a result, Flaubert's own characteristic tone of the somber-pompous-ironic becomes, in the long run, a little monotonous. But Joyce has undertaken in *Ulysses* not merely to render, with the last accuracy and beauty, the actual sights and sounds among which his people move, but, showing us the world as his characters perceive it, to find the unique vocabulary and rhythm which will represent the thoughts of each. If Flaubert taught Maupassant to look for the definitive adjectives which would distinguish a given cab-driver from every other cab-driver at the Rouen station, so Joyce has set himself the task of finding the precise dialect which will distinguish the thoughts of a given Dubliner from those of every other Dubliner. Thus the mind of Stephen Dedalus is represented by a weaving of bright poetic images and fragmentary abstractions, of things remembered from books, on a rhythm sober, melancholy and proud; that of Bloom by a rapid staccato notation, prosaic but vivid and alert, jetting out in all directions in little ideas growing out of ideas; the thoughts of Father Conmee, the Rector of the Jesuit college, by a precise prose, perfectly colorless and orderly; those of Gerty-Nausicaa by a combination of school-girl colloquialisms with the jargon of cheap romance; and the ruminations of Mrs.

Bloom by a long, unbroken rhythm of brogue, like the swell of some profound sea.

Joyce takes us thus directly into the consciousness of his characters, and in order to do so, he has availed himself of methods of which Flaubert never dreamed—of the methods of Symbolism. He has, in *Ulysses,* exploited together, as no writer had thought to do before, the resources both of Symbolism and of Naturalism. Proust's novel, masterly as it is, does perhaps represent a falling over into decadence of psychological fiction: the subjective element is finally allowed to invade and to deteriorate even those aspects of the story which really ought to be kept strictly objective if one is to believe that it is actually happening. But Joyce's grasp on his objective world never slips: his work is unshakably established on Naturalistic foundations. Where *A la Recherche du Temps Perdu* leaves many things vague—the ages of the characters and sometimes the actual circumstances of their lives, and—what is worse—whether they may not be merely bad dreams that the hero has had; *Ulysses* has been logically thought out and accurately documented to the last detail: everything that happens is perfectly consistent, and we know precisely what the characters wore, how much they paid for things, where they were at different times of the day, what popular songs they sang and what events they read of in the papers, on June 16, 1904. Yet when we are admitted to the mind of any one of them, we are in a world as complex and special, a world sometimes as fantastic or obscure, as that of a Symbolist poet—and a world rendered by similar devices of language. We are more at home in the minds of Joyce's characters than we are likely to be, except after some study, in the mind of a Mallarmé or an Eliot, because we know more about the circumstances in which they find themselves; but we are confronted with the same sort of confusion between emotions, perceptions and reasonings, and we are likely to be disconcerted by the same sort of hiatuses of thought, when certain links in the association of ideas are dropped down into the unconscious mind so that we are obliged to divine them for ourselves.

But Joyce has carried the methods of Symbolism further than merely to set a Naturalistic scene and then, in that frame, to represent directly the minds of his different characters in Symbolistic monologues like *Prufrock* or *L'Après-midi d'un Faune.* And it is the fact that he has not always stopped here which makes parts of *Ulysses* so puzzling when we read them for the first time. So long as we are dealing with internal monologues in realistic settings, we are dealing with familiar elements merely combined in a novel way—that is, instead of reading, "Bloom said to himself, 'I might manage to write a story to illustrate some proverb or other. I could sign it, Mr. and Mrs. L. M. Bloom,' " we read, "Might manage a sketch. By Mr. and Mrs. L. M. Bloom. Invent a story for some proverb which?" But as we get further along in *Ulysses,* we find the realistic setting oddly distorting itself and deliquescing, and we are astonished at the introduction of voices which seem to belong neither to the characters nor to the author.

The point is that of each of his episodes Joyce has tried to make an independent unit which shall blend the different sets of elements of each—the minds of the characters, the place where they are, the atmosphere about them, the feeling of the time of day. Joyce had already, in *A Portrait of the Artist*, experimented, as Proust had done, in varying the form and style of the different sections to fit the different ages and phases of his hero—from the infantile fragments of childhood impressions, through the ecstatic revelations and the terrifying nightmares of adolescence, to the self-possessed notations of young manhood. But in *A Portrait of the Artist*, Joyce was presenting everything from the point of view of a single particular character, Dedalus; whereas in *Ulysses* he is occupied with a number of different personalities, of whom Dedalus is no longer the center, and his method, furthermore, of enabling us to live in their world is not always merely a matter of making us shift from the point of view of one to the point of view of another. In order to understand what Joyce is doing here, one must conceive a set of Symbolistic poems, themselves involving characters whose minds are represented Symbolistically, depending not from the sensibility of the poet speaking in his own person, but from the poet's imagination playing a rôle absolutely impersonal and always imposing upon itself all the Naturalistic restrictions in regard to the story it is telling at the same time that it allows itself to exercise all the Symbolistic privileges in regard to the way it tells it. We are not likely to be prepared for this by the early episodes of *Ulysses*: they are as sober and as clear as the morning light of the Irish coast in which they take place: the characters' perceptions of the external world are usually distinct from their thoughts and feelings about them. But in the newspaper office, for the first time, a general atmosphere begins to be created, beyond the specific minds of the characters, by a punctuation of the text with newspaper heads which announce the incidents in the narrative. And in the library scene, which takes place in the early afternoon, the setting and people external to Stephen begin to dissolve in his apprehension of them, heightened and blurred by some drinks at lunchtime and by the intellectual excitement of the conversation amid the dimness and tameness of the library—"Eglintoneyes, quick with pleasure, looked up shybrightly. Gladly glancing, a merry puritan, through the twisted eglantine." Here, however, we still see all through Stephen's eyes—through the eyes of a single character; but in the scene in the Ormond Hotel, which takes place a couple of hours later—our reveries absorb the world about us progressively as daylight fades and as the impressions of the day accumulate—the sights and sounds and the emotional vibrations and the appetites for food and drink of the late afternoon, the laughter, the gold-and-bronze hair of the barmaids, the jingling of Blazes Boylan's car on his way to visit Molly Bloom, the ringing of the hoofs of the horses of the viceregal cavalcade clanging in through the open window, the ballad sung by Simon Dedalus, the sound of the piano accompaniment and the comfortable supper of Bloom—though they are not all, from beginning to end, perceived by Bloom himself—all mingle quite un-Naturalistically in a harmony of bright sound, ringing color, poignant indistinct feeling and declining light. The scene in the brothel, where it is night and where Dedalus and Bloom are drunk, is like a slowed-up moving-picture, in which the intensified vision of reality is continually lapsing into phantasmagoric visions; and the let-down after the excitement of this, the lassitude and staleness of the cabman's shelter where Bloom takes Stephen to get him some coffee, is rendered by a prose as flavorless, as weary and as banal as the incidents which it reports. Joyce has achieved here, by different methods, a relativism like that of Proust: he is reproducing in literature the different aspects, the different proportions and textures, which things and people take on at different times and under different circumstances.

III

I do not think that Joyce has been equally successful with all these technical devices in *Ulysses;* but before it will be possible to discuss them further, we must approach the book from another point of view.

It has always been characteristic of Joyce to neglect action, narrative, drama, of the usual kind, even the direct impact on one another of the characters as we get it in the ordinary novel, for a sort of psychological portraiture. There is tremendous vitality in Joyce, but very little movement. Like Proust, he is symphonic rather than narrative. His fiction has its progressions, its developments, but they are musical rather than dramatic. The most elaborate and interesting piece in *Dubliners*—the story called "The Dead"—is simply a record of the modification brought about during a single evening in the relations of a husband and wife by the man's becoming aware, from the effect produced on the woman by a song which she has heard at a family party, that she has once been loved by another man; *A Portrait of the Artist as a Young Man* is simply a series of pictures of the author at successive stages of his development; the theme of *Exiles* is, like that of "The Dead," the modification in the relations of a husband and wife which follows the reappearance of a man who has been the wife's lover. And *Ulysses* again, for all its vast scale, is simply the story of another small but significant change in the relations of yet another married couple as a result of the impingement on their household of the personality of an only slightly known young man. Most of these stories cover a period of only a few hours, and they are never carried any further. When Joyce has explored one of these situations, when he has established the small gradual readjustment, he has done all that interests him.

All, that is, from the point of view of ordinary incident. But though Joyce almost entirely lacks appetite for violent conflict or vigorous action, his work is prodigiously rich and alive. His force, instead of following a line, expands itself in every dimension (including that of Time) about a single point. The world of *Ulysses* is animated by a complex inexhaustible life: we revisit it as we do a city, where we come more and more to recognize faces, to understand personalities, to grasp relations, currents and interests. Joyce has exercised considerable technical ingenuity in introducing us to the elements of his story in an order which will enable us to find our bearings: yet I doubt whether any human memory is capable, on a first reading, of meeting the demands of *Ulysses*. And when we reread it, we start in at any point, as if it were indeed something solid like a city which actually existed in space and which could be entered from any direction—as Joyce is said, in composing his books, to work on the different parts simultaneously. More than any other work of fiction, unless perhaps the *Comédie Humaine, Ulysses* creates the illusion of a living social organism. We see it only for twenty hours, yet we know its past as well as its present. We possess Dublin, seen, heard, smelt and felt, brooded over, imagined, remembered.

Joyce's handling of this immense material, his method of giving his book a shape, resembles nothing else in modern fiction. The first critics of *Ulysses* mistook the novel for a "slice of life" and objected that it was too fluid or too chaotic. They did not recognize a plot because they could not recognize a progression; and the title told them nothing. They could not even discover a pattern. It is now apparent, however, that *Ulysses* suffers from an excess of design rather than from a lack of it. Joyce has drawn up an outline of his novel, of which he has allowed certain of his commentators to avail themselves, but which he has not allowed them to publish in its entirety (though it is to be presumed that the book on *Ulysses* which Mr. Stuart Gilbert has announced will include all the information contained in it);[1] and from this outline it appears that Joyce has set himself the task of fulfilling the requirements of a most complicated scheme—a scheme which we could scarcely have divined except in its more obvious features. For even if we had known about the Homeric parallel and had identified certain of the correspondences—if we had had no difficulty in recognizing the Cyclops in the ferocious professional Fenian or Circe in the brothel-keeper or Hades in the cemetery—we should never have suspected how closely and how subtly the parallel had been followed—we should never have guessed, for example, that when Bloom passes through the National Library while Stephen is having his discussion with the literary men, he is escaping, on the one hand, a Scylla—that is, Aristotle, the rock of Dogma; and, on the other, a Charybdis—Plato, the whirlpool of Mysticism; nor that, when Stephen walks on the seashore, he is re-enacting the com-

---

[1] Stuart Gilbert's book *James Joyce's Ulysses* appeared in 1930 (London: Faber & Faber; New York: Alfred A. Knopf).

bat with Proteus—in this case, primal matter, of whose continual transforma-
tions Stephen is reminded by the objects absorbed or washed up by the sea,
but whose forms he is able to hold and fix, as the Homeric Proteus was held
and vanquished, by power of the words which give him images for them. Nor
should we have known that the series of phrases and onomatopoetic syllables
placed at the beginning of the Sirens episode—the singing in the Ormond
Hotel—and selected from the narrative which follows, are supposed to be
musical themes and that the episode itself is a fugue; and though we may have
felt the ironic effect of the specimens of inflated Irish journalism introduced
at regular intervals in the conversation with the patriot in the pub—we should
hardly have understood that these had been produced by a deliberate technique of "gigantism"—for, since the Citizen represents the Cyclops, and since
the Cyclops was a giant, he must be rendered formidable by a parade of all
the banalities of his patriotic claptrap swollen to gigantic proportions. We
should probably never have guessed all this, and we should certainly never
have guessed at the ingenuity which Joyce has expended in other ways. Not
only, we learn from the outline, is there an elaborate Homeric parallel in
Ulysses, but there is also an organ of the human body and a human science
or art featured in every episode. We look these up, a little incredulously, but
there, we find, they all actually are—buried and disguised beneath the realistic
surface, but carefully planted, unmistakably dwelt upon. And if we are tipped
off, we are able further to discover all sorts of concealed ornaments and emblems: in the chapter of the Lotus-Eaters, for example, countless references to
flowers; in the Laestrygonians, to eating; in the Sirens, puns on musical terms;
and in Aeolus, the newspaper office, not merely many references to wind but,
according to Mr. Gilbert—the art featured in this episode being Rhetoric—
some hundred different figures of speech.

Now the Homeric parallel in *Ulysses* is in general pointedly and charm-
ingly carried out and justifies itself: it does help to give the story a universal
significance and it enables Joyce to show us in the actions and the relations of
his characters meanings which he perhaps could not easily have indicated in
any other way—since the characters themselves must be largely unaware of
these meanings and since Joyce has adopted the strict objective method, in
which the author must not comment on the action. And we may even accept
the arts and sciences and the organs of the human body as making the book
complete and comprehensive, if a little laboriously systematic—the whole of
man's experience in a day. But when we get all these things together and
further complicated by the virtuosity of the technical devices, the result is
sometimes baffling or confusing. We become aware, as we examine the outline, that when we went through *Ulysses* for the first time, it was these organs
and arts and sciences and Homeric correspondences which sometimes so discouraged our interest. We had been climbing over these obstacles without

knowing it, in our attempts to follow Dedalus and Bloom. The trouble was that, beyond the ostensible subject and, as it were, beneath the surface of the narrative, too many other subjects and too many different orders of subjects were being proposed to our attention.

It seems to me difficult, then, not to conclude that Joyce elaborated *Ulysses* too much—that he tried to put too many things into it. What is the value of all the references to flowers in the Lotus-Eaters chapter, for example? They do not create in the Dublin streets an atmosphere of lotus-eating—we are merely puzzled, if we have not been told to look for them, as to why Joyce has chosen to have Bloom think and see certain things, of which the final explanation is that they are pretexts for mentioning flowers. And do not the gigantic interpolations of the Cyclops episode defeat their object by making it impossible for us to follow the narrative? The interpolations are funny in themselves, the incident related is a masterpiece of language and humor, the idea of combining them seems happy, yet the effect is mechanical and annoying: in the end we have to read the whole thing through, skipping the interpolations, in order to find out what has happened. The worst example of the capacities for failure of this too synthetic, too systematic, method seems to me the scene in the maternity hospital. I have described above what actually takes place there as I have worked it out, after several readings and in the light of Joyce's outline. The Oxen of the Sun are "Fertility"—the crime committed against them is "Fraud." But, not content with this, Joyce has been at pains to fill the episode with references to real cattle and to include a long conversation about bulls. As for the special technique, it seems to me in this case not to have any real appropriateness to the situation, but to have been dictated by sheer fantastic pedantry: Joyce describes his method here as "embryonic," in conformity to the subject, maternity, and the chapter is written as a series of parodies of English literary styles from the bad Latin of the early chronicles up through Huxley and Carlyle, the development of the language corresponding to the growth of the child in the womb. Now something important takes place in this episode—the meeting between Dedalus and Bloom—and an important point is being made about it. But we miss the point because it is all we can do to follow what is happening at the drinking-party, itself rather a confused affair, through the medium of the language of the *Morte d'Arthur*, the seventeenth-century diaries, the eighteenth-century novels, and a great many other kinds of literature in which we are not prepared at the moment to be interested. If we pay attention to the parodies, we miss the story; and if we try to follow the story, we are unable to appreciate the parodies. The parodies have spoiled the story; and the necessity of telling the story through them has taken most of the life out of the parodies.

Joyce has as little respect as Proust for the capacities of the reader's attention; and one feels, in Joyce's case as in Proust's, that the *longueurs* which

break our backs, the mechanical combinations of elements which fail to coalesce, are partly a result of the effort of a supernormally energetic mind to
compensate by piling things up for an inability to make them move.

We have now arrived, in the maternity hospital, at the climactic scenes of
the story, and Joyce has bogged us as he has never bogged us before. We shall
forget the Oxen of the Sun in the wonderful night-town scene which follows
it—but we shall be bogged afterwards worse than ever in the interminable
let-down of the cabman's shelter and in the scientific question-and-answer
chapter which undertakes to communicate to us through the most opaque and
uninviting medium possible Dedalus's conversation with Bloom. The night-
town episode itself and Mrs. Bloom's soliloquy, which closes the book, are,
of course, among the best things in it—but the relative proportions of the other
three latter chapters and the jarring effect of the pastiche style sandwiched
in with the straight Naturalistic seem to me artistically absolutely indefensible. One can understand that Joyce may have intended the colorless and
tiresome episodes to set off the rich and vivid ones, and also that it is of the
essence of his point of view to represent the profoundest changes of our lives
as beginning naturally between night and morning without the parties' ap-
preciating their importance at the time; but a hundred and sixty-one more or
less deliberately tedious pages are too heavy a dead weight for even the brilliant flights of the other hundred and ninety-nine pages to carry. Furthermore,
Joyce has here half-buried his story under the virtuosity of his technical devices. It is almost as if he had elaborated it so much and worked over it so long
that he had forgotten, in the amusement of writing parodies, the drama which
he had originally intended to stage; or as if he were trying to divert and over-
whelm us by irrelevant entertainments and feats in order that we might not
be dissatisfied with the flatness—except for the drunken scene—of Dedalus's
final meeting with Bloom; or even perhaps as if he did not, after all, quite
want us to understand his story, as if he had, not quite conscious of what he
was doing, ended by throwing up between us and it a fortification of solemn
burlesque prose—as if he were shy and solicitous about it, and wanted to
protect it from us.

IV

Yet even these episodes to which I have objected contribute something valuable to *Ulysses*. In the chapter of parodies, for example, Joyce seems to be
saying to us: "Here are specimens of the sort of thing that man has written
about himself in the past—how naïve or pretentious they seem! I have broken
through these assumptions and pretences and shown you how he must recognize himself today." And in the question-and-answer chapter, which is written
entirely from the conventional point of view of science and where we are
supplied with every possible physical, statistical, biographical and astronom-

ical fact about Stephen's visit to Bloom: "This is all that the twentieth-century man thinks he knows about himself and his universe. Yet how mechanical and rigid this reasoning seems when we apply it to Molly and Bloom—how inadequate to explain them!"

For one of the most remarkable features of *Ulysses* is its interest as an investigation into the nature of human consciousness and behavior. Its importance from the point of view of psychology has never, it seems to me, been properly appreciated—though its influence on other books and, in consequence, upon our ideas about ourselves, has already been profound. Joyce has attempted in *Ulysses* to render as exhaustively, as precisely and as directly as it is possible in words to do, what our participation in life is like—or rather, what it seems to us like as from moment to moment we live. In order to make this record complete, he has been obliged to disregard a number of conventions of taste which, especially in English-speaking countries, have in modern times been pretty strictly observed, even by the writers who have aimed to be most scrupulously truthful. Joyce has studied what we are accustomed to consider the dirty, the trivial and the base elements in our lives with the relentlessness of a modern psychologist; and he has also—what the contemporary Naturalist has seldom been poet enough for—done justice to all those elements in our lives which we have been in the habit of describing by such names as love, nobility, truth and beauty. It is curious to reflect that a number of critics—including, curiously enough, Arnold Bennett—should have found Joyce misanthropic. Flaubert is misanthropic, if you like—and in reproducing his technique, Joyce sometimes suggests his acrid tone. But Stephen, Bloom and Mrs. Bloom are certainly not either unamiable or unattractive—and for all their misfortunes and short-comings, they inspire us with considerable respect. Stephen and Bloom are played off a little against the duller and meaner people about them; but even these people can scarcely be said to be treated with bitterness, even when, as in the case of Buck Mulligan or the elder Dedalus, Stephen's feeling about them is bitter. Joyce is remarkable, rather, for equanimity: in spite of the nervous intensity of *Ulysses*, there is a real serenity and detachment behind it—we are in the presence of a mind which has much in common with that of a certain type of philosopher, who in his effort to understand the causes of things, to interrelate the different elements of the universe, has reached a point where the ordinary values of good and bad, beautiful and ugly, have been lost in the excellence and beauty of transcendent understanding itself.

I believe that the first readers of *Ulysses* were shocked, not merely by Joyce's use of certain words ordinarily excluded today from English literature, but by his way of representing those aspects of human nature which we tend to consider incongruous as intimately, inextricably mingled. Yet the more we read *Ulysses*, the more we are convinced of its psychological truth, and the more we are amazed at Joyce's genius in mastering and in presenting, not through analysis or generalization, but by the complete recreation of life in the process of being lived, the relations of human beings to their environment and to each other; the nature of their perception of what goes on about them and of what goes on within themselves; and the interdependence of their intellectual, their physical, their professional and their emotional lives. To have traced all these interdependences, to have given each of these elements its value, yet never to have lost sight of the moral through preoccupation with the physical, nor to have forgotten the general in the particular; to have exhibited ordinary humanity without either satirizing it or sentimentalizing it—this would already have been sufficiently remarkable; but to have subdued all this material to the uses of a supremely finished and disciplined work of art is a feat which has hardly been equaled in the literature of our time.

In Stephen's diary in *A Portrait of the Artist,* we find this significant entry apropos of a poem by Yeats: "Michael Robartes remembers forgotten beauty and, when his arms wrap her round, he presses in his arms the loveliness which has long faded from the world. Not this. Not at all. I desire to press in my arms the loveliness which has not yet come into the world."

And with *Ulysses,* Joyce has brought into literature a new and unknown beauty. Some readers have regretted the extinction in the later Joyce of the charming lyric poet of his two little books of poems and the *fin de siècle* prose writer of the *fin de siècle* phases of *A Portrait of the Artist as a Young Man* (both the prose and verse of the early Joyce showed the influence of Yeats). This poet is still present in *Ulysses:* "Kind air defined the coigns of houses in Kildare Street. No birds. Frail from the housetops two plumes of smoke ascended, pluming, and in a flaw of softness softly were blown." But the conventions of the romantic lyric, of "esthetic" *fin de siècle* prose, even of the esthetic Naturalism of Flaubert, can no longer, for Joyce, be made to accommodate the reality of experience. The diverse elements of experience are perceived in different relations and they must be differently represented. Joyce has found for this new vision a new language, but a language which, instead of diluting or doing violence to his poetic genius, enables it to assimilate more materials, to readjust itself more completely and successfully than that of perhaps any other poet of our age to the new self-consciousness of the modern world. But in achieving this, Joyce has ceased to write verse. I have suggested, in connection with Valéry and Eliot, that verse itself as a literary medium is coming to be used for fewer and fewer and for more and more special purposes, and that it may be destined to fall into disuse. And it seems to me that Joyce's literary development is a striking corroboration of this view. His prose works have an artistic intensity, a definitive beauty of surface and of form, which make him comparable to the great poets rather than to most of the great novelists.

Joyce is indeed really the great poet of a new phase of the human consciousness. Like Proust's or Whitehead's or Einstein's world, Joyce's world is always
changing as it is perceived by different observers and by them at different
times. It is an organism made up of "events," which may be taken as infinitely
inclusive or infinitely small and each of which involves all the others; and
each of these events is unique. Such a world cannot be presented in terms of
such artificial abstractions as have been conventional in the past: solid institutions, groups, individuals, which play the parts of distinct durable entities
—or even of solid psychological factors: dualisms of good and evil, mind and
matter, flesh and spirit, instinct and reason; clear conflicts between passion
and duty, between conscience and interest. Not that these conceptions are left
out of Joyce's world: they are all there in the minds of the characters; and the
realities they represent are there, too. But everything is reduced to terms of
"events" like those of modern physics and philosophy—events which make up
a "continuum," but which may be taken as infinitely small. Joyce has built
out of these events a picture, amazingly lifelike and living, of the everyday
world we know—and a picture which seems to allow us to see into it, to follow its variations and intricacies, as we have never been able to do before.

Nor are Joyce's characters merely the sum of the particles into which their
experience has been dissociated: we come to imagine them as solidly, to feel
their personalities as unmistakably, as we do with any characters in fiction;
and we realize finally that they are also symbols. Bloom himself is in one of
his aspects the typical modern man: Joyce has made him a Jew, one supposes,
partly in order that he may be conceived equally well as an inhabitant of any
provincial city of the European or Europeanized world. He makes a living by
petty business, he leads the ordinary middle-class life—and he holds the conventional enlightened opinions of the time: he believes in science, social reform and internationalism. But Bloom is surpassed and illuminated from
above by Stephen, who represents the intellect, the creative imagination; and
he is upheld by Mrs. Bloom, who represents the body, the earth. Bloom leaves
with us in the long run the impression that he is something both better and
worse than either of them; for Stephen sins through pride, the sin of the
intellect; and Molly is at the mercy of the flesh; but Bloom, though a less
powerful personality than either, has the strength of humility. It is difficult
to describe the character of Bloom as Joyce finally makes us feel it: it takes
precisely the whole of *Ulysses* to put him before us. It is not merely that Bloom
is mediocre, that he is clever, that he is commonplace—that he is comic, that
he is pathetic—that he is, as Rebecca West says, a figure of abject "squatting"
vulgarity, that he is at moments, as Foster Damon says, the Christ—he is all
of these, he is all the possibilities of that ordinary humanity which is somehow
not so ordinary after all; and it is the proof of Joyce's greatness that, though
we recognize Bloom's perfect truth and typical character, we cannot pigeon-

hole him in any familiar category, racial, social, moral, literary or even—because he does really have, after all, a good deal in common with the Greek Ulysses—historical.

Both Stephen and Molly are more easily describable because they represent extremes. Both are capable of rising to heights which Bloom can never reach. In Stephen's rhapsody on the seashore, when he first realizes his artist's vocation, in *A Portrait of the Artist as a Young Man,* we have had the ecstasy of the creative mind. In the soliloquy of Mrs. Bloom, Joyce has given us another ecstasy of creation, the rhapsody of the flesh. Stephen's dream was conceived in loneliness, by a drawing apart from his fellows. But Mrs. Bloom is like the earth, which gives the same life to all: she feels a maternal kinship with all living creatures. She pities the "poor donkeys slipping half asleep" in the street of Gibraltar, as she does "the sentry in front of the governor's house . . . half roasted" in the sun; and she gives herself to the bootblack at the General Post Office as readily as to Professor Goodwin. But, none the less, she will tend to breed from the highest type of life she knows: she turns to Bloom, and, beyond him, toward Stephen. This gross body, the body of humanity, upon which the whole structure of *Ulysses* rests—still throbbing with so strong a rhythm amid obscenity, commonness and squalor—is laboring to throw up some knowledge and beauty by which it may transcend itself.

These two great flights of the mind carry off all the ignominies and trivialities through which Joyce has made us pass: they seem to me—the soaring silver prose of the one, the deep embedded pulse of the other—among the supreme expressions in literature of the creative powers of humanity: they are, respectively, the justifications of the woman and the man.

V

Since finishing *Ulysses,* Joyce has been engaged upon another work, about half of which has been published in the transatlantic monthly, *Transition.*[2] It is not possible to judge this book properly in the imperfect form in which it has appeared. It is intended as a sort of complement to *Ulysses;* Joyce has explained that, as *Ulysses* deals with the day and with the conscious mind, so his new work is to deal with the night and with the subconscious. The whole book is apparently to occupy itself with the single night's sleep of a single character. Joyce has already exhibited in *Ulysses* a unique genius for

[2] In 1931. This then unfinished work of Joyce's was known as *Work in Progress* until it was published in its completed form as *Finnegans Wake* in 1939. Mr. Wilson's essay on the whole book appears as "The Dream of H. C. Earwicker" in his volume *The Wound and the Bow,* pages 243-271 (Boston, 1941; new edition, New York, 1947). Among other discussions of *Finnegans Wake,* the following may be mentioned here: *An Exagmination . . . of "Work in Progress,"* by various writers (Paris, 1929; Norfolk, Conn., 1937); *James Joyce,* by Harry Levin (Norfolk, Conn., 1941); and *A Skeleton Key to Finnegans Wake,* by Joseph Campbell and Henry Morton Robinson (New York, 1944). (Editor's note, 1950.)

the representation of special psychological states: I know of nothing else in literature, for example, like the drunken night-town scene, with its astounding recreation of all the deliriums, dazes, gibberings, exaltations and hallucinations of drunkenness. And Joyce's method of rendering the phases of sleep is similar to his methods in the Circe episode. But he is here attempting something even more difficult, and his way of doing it raises an important question in regard to all Joyce's later work. Joyce, as I have said, always nowadays represents the consciousness of his characters directly: but his method of representing consciousness is to let you overhear his characters talking to themselves. Joyce's people think and feel exclusively in terms of words, for Joyce himself thinks in terms of words. This is partly due, no doubt, to his defective eyesight, which of late years has become so serious as to make it difficult for him to work. There is an interesting passage in *A Portrait of the Artist* in which Joyce himself discusses this aspect of his writing:

He drew forth a phrase from his treasure and spoke it softly to himself:
—A day of dappled seaborne clouds.—
The phrase and the day and the scene harmonized in a chord. Words. Was it their colors? He allowed them to glow and fade, hue after hue: sunrise gold, the russet and green of apple orchards, azure of waves, the greyfringed fleece of clouds. No, it was not their colors: it was the poise and balance of the period itself. Did he then love the rhythmic rise and fall of words better than their associations of legend and color? Or was it that, being as weak of sight as he was shy of mind, he drew less pleasure from the reflection of the glowing sensible world through the prism of a language many colored and richly storied than from the contemplation of an inner world of individual emotions mirrored perfectly in a lucid supple periodic prose?

And in *Ulysses* we hear the characters far more plainly than we see them: Joyce supplies us with descriptions of them in sparse, scrupulous phrases, one trait here, another there. But the Dublin of *Ulysses* is a city of voices. Who has a clear idea of how Bloom or Molly Bloom looks?—and should we have a clear idea of Stephen if we had never seen photographs of Joyce? But their eternally soliloquizing voices become our intimate companions and haunt us long afterwards.

Joyce already seems sometimes, in *Ulysses,* to go a little beyond the probabilities in the vocabulary which he allows Bloom to command. When Bloom, in the drunken scene, for example, imagines himself giving birth to "eight male yellow and white children," all "with valuable metallic faces" and each with "his name printed in legible letters on his shirt-front: Nasodoro, Goldfinger, Chrysostomos, Maindorée, Silversmile, Silberselber, Vifargent, Panargyros" —we have difficulty in believing that he would have been learned enough for this. Yet I do not suppose that Joyce means us to think of Bloom as actually formulating these words in his mind: it is the author's way of conveying in words a vision which on the part of Bloom must have been a good deal less distinct, or at least a good deal less literary, than this. Now, in his new book, Joyce has tried to make his hero express directly in words, again, states of mind which do not usually in reality make use of words at all—for the subconscious has no language—the dreaming mind does not usually speak—and when it does, it is more likely to express itself in the looking-glass language of "Jabberwocky" than in anything resembling ordinary speech. Joyce's attempts to write the language of dreams have a good deal in common with those of Lewis Carroll; but the difference between his new novel and the Alice books is that, whereas in the Alice books it is the author who is supposed to be telling in straight English the adventures which his heroine thinks she is having and the literary language peculiar to dreams appears only in a poem which she reads, in Joyce's book he is plunging us directly into the consciousness of the dreamer itself, which is presented, without explanations by the author, entirely in the Jabberwocky language. The book is thus more easily comprehensible to literary people than to people who are not "word-minded," whose minds do not habitually breed words in response to sensations, emotions and thoughts. Yet it is worth making the effort to understand, because what Joyce is trying to do is both artistically and psychologically extremely interesting, and it may be that he will turn out to have written the most remarkable piece of dream-literature in existence.

The best way to understand Joyce's method is to note what goes on in one's own mind when one is just dropping off to sleep. Images—or words, if one thinks in words like Joyce—which were already in the conscious mind will suddenly acquire an ominous significance which has nothing to do with their ordinary functions; some vivid incident which may have taken place just before one went to bed will begin to swell with a meaning, an emotion, which at first we do not recognize because it has come up from the submerged part of the mind and is attempting to pass itself off in the clothes of an immediate experience—because it is dissociated from the situation out of which it originally arose. Or conversely, one may rid oneself of a troublesome abstract idea with which one has been preoccupied by allowing it to transform itself into some innocuous concrete image more easily dismissed from the attention: the page of a philosophical book, for example, where one had been continually stumbling over phrases and terms may vanish on the threshold of sleep in the guise of a spotted man, the spots having substituted themselves for the impenetrable words and phrases. And so the images which our waking mind would keep distinct from one another incongruously mix in our sleep with an effect of perfect congruity. A single one of Joyce's sentences, therefore, will combine two or three different meanings—two or three different sets of symbols; a single word may combine two or three. Joyce has profited, in inventing his dream-language, by Freud's researches into the principles which govern the language actually spoken in dreams: certain people, it appears, do make up "portmanteau-words" in their sleep; but we are not, I take it, to suppose that Joyce's hero necessarily frames all these sentences to himself. Except when he dreams he is reading something or carrying on a conversation, the language is merely a literary equivalent for sleeping states not even articulate in fancy. Nor are we to assume that Joyce's sleeper is actually master of all the languages or understands all the allusions of which Joyce makes him avail himself in his dream. We are now at a level below particularized languages—we are in the region whence all languages arise and where the impulses to all acts have their origin.

The hero of the night's sleep in question is, we gather, a man named H. C. Earwicker, a Norwegian or descendant of Norwegians, living in Dublin. He seems to have attempted a number of occupations—to have been a postman, to have worked in Guiness's Brewery, to have kept a hotel and a shop. He is married and has children, but has apparently been carrying on a flirtation with a girl named Anna Livia. This, along with other lapses from respectability associated with it in his mind, troubles his conscience and his repose. We are introduced, at the very beginning, into Earwicker's drowsing consciousness, and we have to make what we can of the names, the shapes, and above all, of the voices, which fill that dim and shifting world—they combine and recombine, they are always changing into one another—but as we go on, we find the same themes recurring and we begin to be able to understand them in relation to one another—we become familiar with the character of Earwicker—we begin to guess at his condition and history. We identify Maggie and the children, the house in which they live, the four old men with the donkey, Earwicker's drunken misdemeanors and his fear of being caught by the police, the washerwomen gathering up their washing, Anna Livia on the bank of the Liffey, the Hill of Howth, the tree and the stone. But none of these elements is seen clearly or objectively—they are all aspects, the dramatic projection of aspects, of Earwicker himself: men and women, old and young, stronger and weaker, river and mountain, tree and stone—it is the dreamer who speaks or is spoken to, who sees or is seen, in all of them. The old men come to admire him as he is sleeping on the mountainside, but in a moment it is Earwicker himself who is talking about himself; or he splits up into two personalities, one of whom bullies or accuses the other. He is coming out of a pub into the street with a party of drunken companions, many people are standing about but the revelers do not care how much attention they attract: they egg on one of their number to sing but the song turns out to be a recital of all Earwicker's failures and sins—he has proved himself a fool and a swindler to the derision of all Dublin, his wife is going to read him the Riot Act. Or he sets out very sweetly to explain something by a fable of "the Mookse and the Gripes": the Mookse comes swaggering up to the Gripes, who is hanging on a tree—a sort of altercation takes place, and it turns into rather a painful re-enactment of one of Earwicker's encounters with the police —but dusk falls and the washerwomen come out and carry off the Mookse and the Gripes, who are now merely two pieces of laundry.

One of the most remarkable parts which have so far appeared is the *allegro* conclusion to the first of the four long sections which are to make up the completed work. (Joyce has allowed it to be published separately in a little book called *Anna Livia Plurabelle.*) Here the washerwomen have become identified with the stone and elm on the river bank—we hear them gossiping about Anna Livia, who is both the girl with whom the hero is in love and the river Liffey; and their gossip is the voice of the river itself, light, rapid, incessant, almost metrical, now monotonously running on one note, now impeded and synocopated, but vivaciously, interminably babbling its indistinct rigmarole story, half-unearthly, half-vulgarly human, of a heroine half-legendary, half-real:

Oh tell me all about Anna Livia! I want to hear all about Anna Livia. Well, you know Anna Livia? Yes, of course, we all know Anna Livia. Tell me all. Tell me now. You'll die when you hear. . . . Tell me, tell me, how cam she camlin through all her fellows, the neckar she was, the diveline? Linking one and knocking the next, tapting a flank and tipting a jutty and palling in and pietaring out and clyding by on her eastway. Waiwhou was the first thurever burst? . . . She says herself she hardly knows whuon the annals her graveller was, a dynast of Leinster, a wolf of the sea, or what he did or how blyth she played or how, when, why, where and who offon he jumnpad her. She was just a young thin pale soft shy slim slip of a thing then, sauntering, by silvamoonlake, and he was a heavy trudging lurching lieabroad of a Curraghman, making his hay for whose sun to shine on, as tough as the oaktrees (peats be with them!) used to rustle that time down by the dykes of killing Kildare, that forstfellfoss with a plash across her. She thought she's sankh neathe the ground with nymphant shame when he gave her the tigris eye!

As darkness falls between stone and elm, the voices grow husky and vague:

And ho! Hey? What all men. Hot? His tittering daughters of Whawk?
Can't hear with the waters of. The chittering waters of. Flittering bats, fieldmice, bawk talk. Ho! Are you not gone ahome? What Tom Malone? Can't hear with bawk of bats, all the liffeying waters of. Ho, talk save us. My foos won't moos. I feel as old as yonder elm. A tale told of Shaun or Shem? All Livia's daughtersons. Dark hawks hear us. Night! Night! My ho head halls. I feel as heavy as yonder stone. Tell me of John or Shaun? Who were Shem and Shaun the living sons or daughters of? Night now! Tell me, tell me, tell me, elm! Night night! Tell me tale of stem or stone. Beside the rivering waters of, hitherandthithering waters of. Night!

Night is just falling in this first section of the book, and the shadow of the past, the memory presumably of the day before, darkens the hero's sleep—the vulgarities of his waking life oppress him and pursue him; but after midnight, as dawn approaches, as he becomes dimly aware of the first light, the dream begins to brighten and to rise unencumbered. If I am not mistaken, the middle-aged Earwicker reverts to the period of his youth, once again he is carefree, attractive, well-liked—his spirit turns refreshed to the new day. Are we to leave him on the verge of waking or are we finally to see the fantasies of the dream closed down into the commonplace fate which we have already been able to divine?

This new production of Joyce's exaggerates the qualities we have noted in *Ulysses*. There is even less action than in *Ulysses*. Joyce has set out with certain definite themes and the themes are evidently all to have their developments, but these developments take a long time. We make progress—we pass from night to morning—and no doubt, when the whole book is before us, we shall see that some sort of psychological drama has been played out in Earwicker's mind—but, as we progress, we go round and round. And whereas in *Ulysses* there is only one parallel, in this new book there are a whole set: Adam and Eve, Tristan and Isolde, Swift and Vanessa, Cain and Abel, Michael and Lucifer, Wellington and Napoleon. The multiplication of references does, to be sure, deepen and extend the significance of Earwicker: he and Anna Livia are the eternal woman and the eternal man, and during the early hours of heaviness and horror of Earwicker's dream, he is an Adam fallen from grace —to be redeemed, Joyce is said to have announced, with the renewal of the morning light. And it would seem that Joyce has provided plausible reasons for the appearance of all these personages in his hero's dream: Napoleon and Wellington have gotten in by way of the Wellington monument in the Phoenix Park, near which one of Earwicker's misdemeanors has been committed; and Michael and Lucifer—it appears from the last installment published, in which Earwicker is partly waked up toward morning by the crying of one of his children—by a picture on the bedroom wall. Yet the effect of the superposition, one upon the other, of such a variety of parallels seems sometimes less to enrich the book than to give it a mere synthetic complication. Joyce is again, we come to the conclusion, trying to do too many things at once. The style he has invented for his purpose works on the principle of a palimpsest: one meaning, one set of images, is written over another. Now we can grasp a certain number of such suggestions simultaneously, but Joyce, with his characteristic disregard for the reader, apparently works over and over his pages, packing in allusions and puns. This appears clearly from the different versions which have been published in various places of the Anna Livia Pluribelle section. (I have given in an appendix three stages of the same passage from this.) Joyce has improved it in making the texture denser, but this enrichment also obscures the main outlines and somewhat over-solidifies and impedes the dim ambiguous fluidity of the dream—especially when it takes the form of introducing in the final version puns on the names of some five hundred rivers. And so soon as we are aware of Joyce himself systematically embroidering on his text, deliberately inventing puzzles, the illusion of the dream is lost.

Yet, on the whole, this illusion is created and kept up with extraordinary success. There is a curious fascination about becoming gradually acquainted with a character whom we know only from the inside and from his dreams. And without the complications of his vocabulary, Joyce would no doubt never be able to paint for us with so sensitive and sure a hand the turbid life of that mental half-world where the unconscious is merged with the conscious—as without his machinery of history and myth, he would not be able to give his subject any poetic freedom of significance beyond the realistic framework which holds it firm. We are to see in H. C. Earwicker Everyman (he imagines his initials standing for Here Comes Everybody). We are to find in his dream all human possibilities—for out of that human nature, that psychological plasm, which swims dark and deep beneath the surface of the meager words, the limited acts, the special mask, of one man's actual day-time career, all history and myth have arisen—victim and conqueror, lover and beloved, childhood and old age—all the forms of human experience. And what humor, what imagination, what poetry, what psychological wisdom, Joyce has put into Earwicker's dream! I have offered the criticisms above only tentatively and without assurance: when we come to think about what we take at first to be the defects in Joyce's work, we find them so closely involved with the depth of his thought and the originality of his conception that we are obliged to grant them a certain necessity. And whatever difficulties we may have with this book in its present fragmentary and incomplete state, I feel confident that, when we read it as a whole, we shall find, not only that it is not unworthy—as the snappers at the heels of genius have been so eager and prompt to assert—of the great master of letters who wrote it, but that he is still at the height of his power.

From *Axel's Castle* by Edmund Wilson, pp. 191–236. Charles Scribner's Sons. Copyright, 1931. Reprinted by permission of the author and publishers. An earlier version of this essay appeared in *The New Republic*, Vol. LXI (December 18, 1929), pp. 84–93.

T. S. Eliot

[1931]

I HAVE noted the similarity between the English seventeenth-century poets and the French nineteenth-century Symbolists. The poetry of T. S. Eliot has, in our own time, brought together these two traditions, as it is Eliot who, so far as I know, has for the first time called attention to their resemblance. "The form," he says, "in which I began to write, in 1908 or 1909, was directly drawn from the study of Laforgue together with the later Elizabethan drama; and I do not know anyone who started from exactly that point."

I have so far, in discussing the early Symbolists, spoken chiefly of Mallarmé. But T. S. Eliot derived, as he indicates, from a different branch of the Symbolist tradition. In 1873 there had appeared in Paris a book of poems called *Les Amours Jaunes*, by a writer who signed himself Tristan Corbière. *Les Amours Jaunes* was received with complete indifference, and scarcely more than a year after it appeared, the author died of consumption. Only thirty at the time of his death, Tristan Corbière had been an eccentric and very maladjusted man: he was the son of a sea captain who had also written sea stories and he had had an excellent education, but he chose for himself the life of an outlaw. In Paris, he slept all day and spent the nights in the cafés or at his verses, greeting at dawn the Paris harlots as they emerged from the station house or the hotel with the same half-harsh, half-tender fellow-feeling for the exile from conventional society which, when he was at home in his native Brittany, caused him to flee the house of his family and seek the company of the customs-men and sailors—living skeleton and invalid as he was, performing prodigies of courage and endurance in the navigation of a little cutter which he sailed by preference in the worst possible weather. He made a pose of his unsociability and of what he considered his physical ugliness, at the same time that he undoubtedly suffered over them. Melancholy, with a feverishly active mind, full of groanings and vulgar jokes, he used to amuse himself by going about in convict's clothes and by firing guns and revolvers out the window in protest against the singing of the village choir; and on one occasion, on a visit to Rome, he appeared in the streets in evening dress, with a mitre on his head and two eyes painted on his forehead, leading a pig decorated with ribbons. And Corbière's poetry was a poetry of the outcast: often colloquial and homely, yet with a rhetoric of fantastic slang; often with the manner of slapdash doggerel, yet sure of its own morose artistic effects; full of the parade of romantic personality, yet incessantly humiliating itself with a self-mockery scurrilous and savage, out of which, as Huysmans said, would sometimes rise without warning "a cry of sharp pain like the breaking of a 'cello string"—Corbière's verse brought back into French poetry qualities which had been alien to its spirit since François Villon's day.

So outlandish did Corbière appear even from the point of view of the Romantics that he was dismissed, when he was noticed at all, as not merely unseemly but insane—till Paul Verlaine, in 1883, did him honor in a series of articles *Les Poètes Maudits*, which was one of the important critical events in the development of Symbolism. Verlaine himself, a more accomplished artist, but a less original and interesting personality, had been strongly influenced by *Les Amours Jaunes*—he seems, indeed, to have caught over from Corbière, not only certain artistic effects, but even something of his own poetic personality, his peculiar accent of wistful naïveté: compare Corbière's "Rondels pour Après" with Verlaine's sonnet which begins, "L'espoir luit comme un brin de paille dans l'étable"; or "Paria" with "Casper Hauser."

But another French poet, Jules Laforgue, nineteen years younger than Corbière, had independently developed a tone and technique—poignant-ironic, grandiose-slangy, scurrilous-naïve—which had much in common with Corbière's. Laforgue was the son of a schoolmaster and, for all his non-chalance in handling rudely the conventions of French poetry, much more a professional man of letters than Corbière. Laforgue even errs through preci-osity in his fashion; what with Corbière seems a personal and inevitable, if eccentric, manner of speech, in Laforgue sounds self-conscious and deliberate, almost sometimes a literary exercise. He was tubercular, as Corbière was also, and dead at twenty-seven—and his gentleness and sadness are still those of a sick well-cared-for child; his asperities, his surprising images, his coquetries, his cynicism, and his impudence, are still those of a clever schoolboy. La-forgue's friends procured him a post as reader to the Empress Augusta of Germany; and, falling under the spell of German philosophy, he brought its jargon into his verse, contributing thereby to Symbolism perhaps the one element of obscurity which it had lacked.

Yet Laforgue is a very fine poet and one of the most remarkable of the Symbolists. He and Corbière had introduced a new variety of vocabulary and a new flexibility of feeling. With Mallarmé, it may be said that, on the whole, it is the imagery, not the feeling, which is variable: though some-times playful, he is classical in the sense (as Yeats and Valéry are) that he sustains a certain grandeur of tone. But it is from the conversational-ironic, rather than from the serious-esthetic, tradition of Symbolism that T. S. Eliot derives. Corbière and Laforgue are almost everywhere in his early work. The emphatic witty quatrains of Corbière, with their sudden lapses into tenderness or pathos, are heard again in the satiric verse of Eliot: a poem like "Mr. Eliot's Sunday Morning Service" would hardly, one imagines, have been written without Corbière's "Rapsodie Foraine." And as "Conversation Galante" derives clearly from certain poems in Laforgue's "Complaintes" and "Imitation de Notre-Dame la Lune," so the more elaborate "Portrait of a Lady" and "The Love Song of J. Alfred Prufrock" follow closely the longer poems of Laforgue. Compare the conclusion of "Prufrock" with the conclusion of the early version of Laforgue's poem "Légende":

> I grow old . . . I grow old . . .
> I shall wear the bottoms of my trousers rolled.

Shall I part my hair behind? Do I dare to eat a peach!
I shall wear white flannel trousers, and walk upon the beach,
I have heard the mermaids singing, each to each.

I do not think that they will sing to me.

I have seen them riding seaward on the waves
Combing the white hair of the waves blown back
When the wind blows the water white and black.

We have lingered in the chambers of the sea
By sea-girls wreathed with seaweed red and brown
Till human voices wake us, and we drown.

*   *   *   *   *

      Hier l'orchestre attaqua
      Sa dernière polka

      Oh! L'automne, l'automne!
        Les casinos
        Qu'on abandonne
      Remisent leurs pianos! . . .

Phrases, verroteries,
Caillots de souvenirs.
Oh! comme elle est maigrie!
Que vais-je devenir? . . .

      Adieu! Les filles d'ifs dans les grisailles
      Ont l'air de pleureuses de funerailles
      Sous l'autan noir qui veut que tout s'en aille.

            Assez, assez,
          C'est toi qui as commencé.

Va, ce n'est plus l'odeur de tes fourrures.
Va, vos moindres clins d'yeux sont des parjures.
Tais-toi, avec vous autres rien ne dure.

           Tais-toi, tais-toi,
          On n'aime qu'une fois . . .

Here it will be seen that Eliot has reproduced Laforgue's irregular metrical
scheme almost line for line. Furthermore, the subject of Laforgue's poem—the
hesitations and constraints of a man either too timid or too disillusioned to

make love to a woman who provokes his ironic pity at the same time that she
stirs gusts of stifled emotion—has a strong resemblance to the subjects of
"Prufrock" and the "Portrait of a Lady." And in another poem, "La Figlia
Che Piange," Eliot has adapted a line of Laforgue's: "Simple et sans foi
comme un bonjour"—"Simple and faithless as a smile and shake of the hand."
He has even brought over into English some of the unstressed effect of French
verse: how different, for example, is the alexandrine of Eliot's just quoted
from the classical English alexandrine "which like a wounded snake drags
its slow length along" or "with sparkless ashes loads an unlamented urn."
(In his exhaustive *Influence du Symbolisme Français sur la Poésie Américaine
de 1910 à 1920*, M. René Taupin has shown the influence of Gautier also in
Eliot's satiric poems: "The Hippopotamus," it appears, is almost a transcript
of a hippopotamus by Gautier, and the "Grishkin is nice" passage in "Whis-
pers of Immortality" repeats a "Carmen est maigre" of Gautier.)

It must not be supposed, however, that Eliot is not original or that he is
not the equal of either of his masters. Those longer and more elaborate poems
—"Derniers Vers" in the collected edition—which Laforgue was constructing
at the time of his death out of more fragmentary and less mature work are
certainly his most important performances: through his masterly flexibility of
vocabulary and metric, he has here achieved one of the definitive expressions
of the pathetic-ironic, worldly-esthetic moods of the *fin de siècle* temperament.
Yet, though Eliot has, in certain obvious respects, applied Laforgue's formula
so faithfully, he cannot properly be described as an imitator because he is
in some ways a superior artist. He is more mature than Laforgue ever was,
and his workmanship is perfect in a way that Corbière's and Laforgue's were
rarely. T. S. Eliot's peculiar distinction lies, as Clive Bell has said, in his
"phrasing." Laforgue's images are often far-fetched and inappropriately
grotesque: his sins in this respect are really very closely akin to those of the
English metaphysical poets; but Eliot's taste is absolutely sure—his images
always precisely right. And the impression that Eliot leaves, even in these
earliest poems, is clear, vivid and unforgettable: we do not subordinate him to
his Symbolist predecessors any more than, when we find him, as in "Gerontion," writing in the rhythms of late Elizabethan blank verse, we associate
him with Middleton or Webster.

When we come to examine Eliot's themes, we recognize something which
we have found already in Laforgue, but which appears in Eliot in a more intense form. One of the principal preoccupations of Flaubert—a great hero of
Eliot's, as of Eliot's fellow-poet, Ezra Pound's—had been the inferiority of the
present to the past: the Romantics had discovered the possibilities of the historical imagination; with their thirst for boldness, grandeur, and magnificence,
they had located these qualities in past epochs—especially the Middle Ages
and the Renaissance. And Flaubert, who shared with the Romantics this

appetite for the gorgeous and the untamed, but who constrained himself,
also, to confront the actual nineteenth-century world, pursued two parallel
lines of fiction which lent significance and relief to each other. On the one
hand, he reconstructed, in *Salammbô* and in *La Tentation de Saint-Antoine*,
the splendid barbarities of the pagan world and the heroic piety of the early
Christian; and on the other, he caricatured, in *Madame Bovary*, in *L'Education Sentimentale* and in *Bouvard et Pécuchet*, the pusillanimity and mediocrity of contemporary bourgeois France. This whole point of view of Flaubert's
—summed up, as it were, in *Trois Contes*, where the three periods are contrasted in one book—was profoundly to affect modern literature. We shall
find it later on in Joyce; but in the meantime we must note its reappearance
in the poetry of Eliot. Eliot, like Flaubert, feels at every turn that human life is
now ignoble, sordid or tame, and he is haunted and tormented by intimations
that it has once been otherwise. In "Burbank with a Baedeker: Bleistein with
a Cigar," the young American tourist in Venice, superseded in his affair with
the Princess Volupine by a vulgar Austrian Jew, meditates on the clipped
wings and pared claws of the Lion of St. Mark's, the symbol of the old arrogant Venice and of the world where such a city was possible. In "A Cooking
Egg," the poet demands, after a call upon a very mild, dull spinster: "Where
are the eagles and the trumpets?" and himself returns the saddened answer:
"Buried beneath some snow-deep Alps." In "Lune de Miel," the Middle
Western American travelers, stifled with the summer heat and devoured by
the bedbugs of Ravenna, are contrasted with the noble crumbling beauty of
the old Byzantine church less than a league away, of which they are totally
unaware and to which they have apparently no relation; and in "Mr. Eliot's
Sunday Morning Service," the combined grossness and aridity of the modern
clergymen is contrasted with the pure and fresh religious feeling of a picture
of the baptism of Christ by "a painter of the Umbrian school." In the best and
most effective of these poems, "Sweeney Among the Nightingales," the poet,
during a drowsy, idiotic and mildly sinister scene in some low dive, where
two of the girls are supposed to be plotting against one of the men, remembers,
at the sound of nightingales singing, the murder of Agamemnon in Aeschylus:

> The host with someone indistinct
> Converses at the door apart,
> The nightingales are singing near
> The Convent of the Sacred Heart,

> And sang within the bloody wood
> When Agamemnon cried aloud,
> And let their liquid siftings fall
> To stain the stiff dishonoured shroud.

The present is more timid than the past: the bourgeois are afraid to let themselves go. The French had been preoccupied with this idea ever since the first days of Romanticism; but Eliot was to deal with the theme from a somewhat different point of view, a point of view characteristically American. For T. S. Eliot, though born in St. Louis, comes from a New England family and was educated at Harvard; and he is in some ways a typical product of our New England civilization. He is distinguished by that combination of practical prudence with moral idealism which shows itself in its later developments as an excessive fastidiousness and scrupulousness. One of the principal subjects of Eliot's poetry is really that regret at situations unexplored, that dark rankling of passions inhibited, which has figured so conspicuously in the work of the American writers of New England and New York from Hawthorne to Edith Wharton. T. S. Eliot, in this respect, has much in common with Henry James. Mr. Prufrock and the poet of the "Portrait of a Lady," with their helpless consciousness of having dared too little, correspond exactly to the middle-aged heroes of *The Ambassadors* and "The Beast in the Jungle," realizing sadly too late in life that they have been living too cautiously and too poorly. The fear of life, in Henry James, is closely bound up with the fear of vulgarity. And Eliot, too, fears vulgarity—which he embodies in the symbolic figure of "Apeneck Sweeney"—at the same time that he is fascinated by it. Yet he chafes at the limitations and pretenses of the culture represented by Boston—a society "quite uncivilized," as he says, "but refined beyond the point of civilization." He has some amusing satiric poems about old New England ladies—in one of which he reflects on his way to the house of his Cousin Harriet, how

> . . . evening quickens faintly in the street,
> Wakening the appetites of life in some
> And to others bringing the *Boston Evening Transcript*.

And the "Portrait of a Lady," whether the scene be laid in Boston or in London, is essentially a poem of that New England society "refined beyond the point of civilization": from the Lady, who serves tea among lighted candles—"an atmosphere of Juliet's tomb"—with her dampening efforts at flattery and flirtation through the medium of cultured conversation—her slightly stale and faded gush about Chopin and her memories of Paris in the spring—the poet is seized with an impulse to flee:

> I take my hat: how can I make a cowardly amends
> For what she has said to me?
> You will see me any morning in the park
> Reading the comics and the sporting page.
> Particularly I remark
> An English countess goes upon the stage,

> A Greek was murdered at a Polish dance,
> Another bank defaulter has confessed.
> I keep my countenance,
> I remain self-possessed
> Except when a street piano, mechanical and tired,
> Reiterates some worn-out common song
> With the smell of hyacinths across the garden
> Recalling things that other people have desired.

But he is always debating things with his conscience: his incurable moral solicitude makes him wonder:

> Are these ideas right or wrong?

So Mr. Prufrock in the room where

> . . . women come and go
> Talking of Michelangelo,

wistfully asks himself:

> Shall I say, I have gone at dusk through narrow streets
> And watched the smoke that rises from the pipes
> Of lonely men in shirt-sleeves, leaning out of windows? . . .

And Mr. Prufrock wonders also whether he should not put a question to his lady—but he never gets to the point of putting it.

II

But Eliot's most complete expression of this theme of emotional starvation is to be found in the later and longer poem called *The Waste Land* (1922). The Waste Land of the poem is a symbol borrowed from the myth of the Holy Grail: it is a desolate and sterile country ruled by an impotent king, in which not only have the crops ceased to grow and the animals to reproduce, but the very human inhabitants have become incapable of having children. But this sterility we soon identify as the sterility of the Puritan temperament. On the first pages we find again the theme of the girl with the hyacinths (themselves a symbol for the rearisen god of the fertility rites who will save the rainless country from drouth) which has already figured in "La Figlia Che Piange" and "Dans le Restaurant"—a memory which apparently represents for the poet some fulfillment foregone in youth and now agonizingly desired; and in the last pages it is repeated. We recognize throughout *The Waste Land* the peculiar conflicts of the Puritan turned artist: the horror of vulgarity and the shy sympathy with the common life, the ascetic shrinking from sexual experience and the distress at the drying up of the springs of sexual emotion, with the straining after a religious emotion which may be made to take its place.

Yet though Eliot's spiritual and intellectual roots are still more firmly fixed in New England than is, I believe, ordinarily understood, there is in *The Waste Land* a good deal more than the mere gloomy moods of a New Englander regretting an emotionally undernourished youth. The colonization by the Puritans of New England was merely an incident in that rise of the middle class which has brought a commercial-industrial civilization to the European cities as well as to the American ones. T. S. Eliot now lives in London and has become an English citizen; but the desolation, the esthetic and spiritual drouth, of Anglo-Saxon middle-class society oppresses London as well as Boston. The terrible dreariness of the great modern cities is the atmosphere in which *The Waste Land* takes place—amidst this dreariness, brief, vivid images emerge, brief pure moments of feeling are distilled; but all about us we are aware of nameless millions performing barren office routines, wearing down their souls in interminable labors of which the products never bring them profit—people whose pleasures are so sordid and so feeble that they seem almost sadder than their pains. And this Waste Land has another aspect: it is a place not merely of desolation, but of anarchy and doubt. In our post-war world of shattered institutions, strained nerves and bankrupt ideals, life no longer seems serious or coherent—we have no belief in the things we do and consequently we have no heart for them.

The poet of *The Waste Land* is living half the time in the real world of contemporary London and half the time in the haunted wilderness of the medieval legend. The water for which he longs in the twilight desert of his dream is to quench the spiritual thirst which torments him in the London dusk; and as Gerontion, "an old man in a dry month," thought of the young men who had fought in the rain, as Prufrock fancied riding the waves with mermaids and lingering in the chambers of the sea, as Mr. Apollinax has been imagined drawing strength from the deep sea-caves of coral islands—so the poet of *The Waste Land*, making water the symbol of all freedom, all fecundity and flowering of the soul, invokes in desperate need the memory of an April shower of his youth, the song of the hermit thrush with its sound of water dripping and the vision of a drowned Phoenician sailor, sunk beyond "the cry of gulls and the deep sea swell," who has at least died by water, not thirst. The poet, who seems now to be traveling in a country cracked by drouth, can only feverishly dream of these things. One's head may be well stored with literature, but the heroic prelude of the Elizabethans has ironic echoes in modern London streets and modern London drawing-rooms: lines remembered from Shakespeare turn to jazz or refer themselves to the sound of phonographs. And now it is one's personal regrets again—the girl in the hyacinth garden—"the awful daring of a moment's surrender which an age of prudence can never retract"—the key which turned once, and once only, in the prison of inhibition and isolation. Now he stands on the arid plain

again, and the dry-rotted world of London seems to be crumbling about him
—the poem ends in a medley of quotations from a medley of literatures—like
Gérard de Nerval's "Desdichado," the poet is disinherited; like the author of
the *Pervigilium Veneris,* he laments that his song is mute and asks when the
spring will come which will set it free like the swallow's; like Arnaut Daniel,
in Dante, as he disappears in the refining fire, he begs the world to raise a
prayer for his torment. "These fragments I have shored against my ruins."

The Waste Land, in method as well as in mood, has left Laforgue far behind. Eliot has developed a new technique, at once laconic, quick, and precise, for representing the transmutations of thought, the interplay of perception and reflection. Dealing with subjects complex in the same way as those
of Yeats' poem "Among School-Children" and Valéry's "Cimetière Marin,"
Eliot has found for them a different language. As May Sinclair has said of
Eliot, his "trick of cutting his corners and his curves makes him seem obscure
when he is clear as daylight. His thoughts move very rapidly and by astounding cuts. They move not by logical stages and majestic roundings of the full
literary curve, but as live thoughts move in live brains." Let us examine, as
an illustration, the lovely nightingale passage from *The Waste Land.* Eliot
is describing a room in London:

> Above the antique mantel was displayed
> As though a window gave upon the sylvan scene
> The change of Philomel, by the barbarous king
> So rudely forced; yet there the nightingale
> Filled all the desert with inviolable voice
> And still she cried, and still the world pursues,
> "Jug Jug" to dirty ears.

That is, the poet sees, above the mantel, a picture of Philomela changed to
a nightingale, and it gives his mind a moment's swift release. The picture is
like a window opening upon Milton's earthly paradise—the "sylvan scene,"
as Eliot explains in a note, is a phrase from "Paradise Lost"—and the poet
associates his own plight in the modern city, in which some "infinitely gentle,
infinitely suffering thing," to quote one of Eliot's earlier poems, is somehow
being done to death, with Philomela, raped and mutilated by Tereus. But in
the earthly paradise, there had been a nightingale singing: Philomela had
wept her woes in song, though the barbarous king had cut out her tongue—
her sweet voice had remained inviolable. And with a sudden change of tense,
the poet flashes back from the myth to his present situation:

> And still she *cried,* and still the world *pursues,*
> "Jug Jug" to dirty ears.

The song of birds was represented in old English popular poetry by such outlandish syllables as "Jug Jug"—so Philomela's cry sounds to the vulgar. Eliot

has here, in seven lines of extraordinary liquidity and beauty, fused the picture, the passage from Milton and the legend from Ovid, into a single moment of vague poignant longing.

The Waste Land is dedicated to Ezra Pound, to whom Eliot elsewhere acknowledges a debt; and he has here evidently been influenced by Pound's *Cantos*. The Waste Land, like the *Cantos*, is fragmentary in form and packed with literary quotation and allusion. In fact, the passage just discussed above has a resemblance to a passage on the same subject—the Philomela-Procne myth—at the beginning of Pound's Fourth Canto. Eliot and Pound have, in fact, founded a school of poetry which depends on literary quotation and reference to an unprecedented degree. Jules Laforgue had sometimes parodied, in his poems, the great lines of other poets—

> O Nature, donne-moi la force et le courage
> De me croire en âge . . .

And Eliot had, in his early poetry, introduced phrases from Shakespeare and Blake for purposes of ironic effect. He has always, furthermore, been addicted to prefacing his poems with quotations and echoing passages from other poets. But now, in The Waste Land, he carries this tendency to what one must suppose its extreme possible limit: here, in a poem of only four hundred and three lines (to which are added, however, seven pages of notes), he manages to include quotations from, allusions to, or imitations of, at least thirty-five different writers (some of them, such as Shakespeare and Dante, laid under contribution several times)—as well as several popular songs; and to introduce passages in six foreign languages, including Sanskrit. And we must also take into consideration that the idea of the literary medley itself seems to have been borrowed from still another writer, Pound. We are always being dismayed, in our general reading, to discover that lines among those which we had believed to represent Eliot's residuum of original invention had been taken over or adapted from other writers (sometimes very unexpected ones: thus, it appears now, from Eliot's essay on Bishop Andrewes, that the first five lines of "The Journey of the Magi," as well as the "word within a word, unable to speak a word" of "Gerontion," had been salvaged from Andrewes's sermons; and the "stiff dishonoured shroud" of "Sweeney Among the Nightingales" seems to be an echo of the "dim dishonoured brow" of Whittier's poem about Daniel Webster). One would be inclined *a priori* to assume that all this load of erudition and literature would be enough to sink any writer, and that such a production as The Waste Land must be a work of second-hand inspiration. And it is true that, in reading Eliot and Pound, we are sometimes visited by uneasy recollections of Ausonius, in the fourth century, composing Greek-and-Latin macaronics and piecing together poetic mosaics out of verses from Virgil. Yet Eliot manages to be most effective precisely—in The Waste Land—where he might be expected to be least original—he succeeds in conveying his meaning, in communicating his emotion, in spite of all his learned or mysteriout allusions, and whether we understand them or not.

In this respect, there is a curious contrast between Eliot and Ezra Pound. Pound's work *has* been partially sunk by its cargo of erudition, whereas Eliot, in ten years' time, has left upon English poetry a mark more unmistakable than that of any other poet writing English. It is, in fact, probably true at the present time that Eliot is being praised too extravagantly and Pound, though he has deeply influenced a few, on the whole unfairly neglected. I should explain Eliot's greater popularity by the fact that, for all his fragmentary method, he possesses a complete literary personality in a way that Pound, for all his integrity, does not. Ezra Pound, fine poet though he is, does not dominate us like a master imagination—he rather delights us like a miscellaneous collection of admirably chosen works of art. It is true that Pound, in spite of his inveterate translating, is a man of genuine originality—but his heterogeneous shorter poems, and the heterogeneous passages which go to make his longer ones, never seem to come together in a whole—as his general prose writing gives scrappy expression to a variety of ideas, a variety of enthusiasms and prejudices, some ridiculous and some valid, some learned and some half-baked, which, though valuable to his generation as polemic, as propaganda and as illuminating casual criticism, do not establish and develop a distinct reasoned point of view as Eliot's prose-writings do. T. S. Eliot has thought persistently and coherently about the relations between the different phases of human experience, and his passion for proportion and order is reflected in his poems. He is, in his way, a complete man, and if it is true, as I believe, that he has accomplished what he has credited Ezra Pound with accomplishing—if he has brought a new personal rhythm into the language— so that he has been able to lend even to the borrowed rhythms, the quoted words, of his great predecessors a new music and a new meaning—it is this intellectual completeness and soundness which has given his rhythm its special prestige.

Another factor which has probably contributed to Eliot's extraordinary success is the essentially dramatic character of his imagination. We may be puzzled by his continual preoccupation with the possibilities of a modern poetic drama—that is to say, of modern drama in verse. Why, we wonder, should he worry about drama in verse—why, after Ibsen, Hauptmann, Shaw and Chekhov, should he be dissatisfied with plays in prose? We may put it down to an academic assumption that English drama ended when the blank verse of the Elizabethans ran into the sands, until it occurs to us that Eliot himself is really a dramatic poet. Mr. Prufrock and Sweeney are characters as none of the personages of Pound, Valéry or Yeats is—they have become a part of our modern mythology. And most of the best of Eliot's poems are based on unexpected dramatic contrasts: *The Waste Land* especially, I am sure, owes a large part of its power to its dramatic quality, which makes it peculiarly effective read aloud. Eliot has even tried his hand at writing a play,[1] and the two episodes from "Wanna Go Home, Baby" which he has published in *The Criterion* seem rather promising. They are written in a sort of jazz dramatic meter which suggests certain scenes of John Howard Lawson's *Processional*; and there can be no question that the future of drama in verse, if it has any future, lies in some such direction. "We cannot reinstate," Eliot has written, "either blank verse or the heroic couplet. The next form of drama will have to be a verse drama, but in new verse forms. Perhaps the conditions of modern life (think how large a part is now played in our sensory life by the internal combustion engine!) have altered our perception of rhythms. At any rate, the recognized forms of speech-verse are not as efficient as they should be; probably a new form will be devised out of colloquial speech."

In any case, that first handful of Eliot's poems, brought out in the middle of the War (1917) and generally read, if at all, at the time, as some sort of modern *vers de société*, was soon found, as Wyndham Lewis has said, to have had the effect of a little musk that scents up a whole room. And as for *The Waste Land*, it enchanted and devastated a whole generation. Attempts have been made to reproduce it—by Aldington, Nancy Cunard, etc.—at least a dozen times. And as Eliot, lately out of Harvard, assumed the rôle of the middle-aged Prufrock and today, at forty, in one of his latest poems, "The Song of Simeon," speaks in the character of an old man "with eighty years and no tomorrow"—so "Gerontion" and *The Waste Land* have made the young poets old before their time. In London, as in New York, and in the universities both here and in England, they for a time took to inhabiting exclusively barren beaches, cactus-grown deserts, and dusty attics overrun with rats—the only properties they allowed themselves to work with were a few fragments of old shattered glass or a sparse sprinkling of broken bones. They had purged themselves of Masefield as of Shelley for dry tongues and rheumatic joints. The dry breath of the Waste Land now blighted the most amiable country landscapes; and the sound of jazz, which had formerly seemed jolly, now inspired only horror and despair. But in this case, we may forgive the young for growing prematurely decrepit: where some of even the finest intelligences of the elder generation read *The Waste Land* with blankness or laughter, the young had recognized a poet.

III

As a critic, Eliot occupies today a position of distinction and influence equal in importance to his position as a poet. His writings have been comparatively

[1] Eliot's further work in drama has since appeared: *The Rock* in 1934, *Murder in the Cathedral* in 1935, *The Family Reunion* in 1939. A fourth play in poetic form, *The Cocktail Party*, was produced at the Edinburgh Festival in the summer of 1949 and was published in book form in 1950. (Editor's note, 1950.)

brief and rare—he has published only four small books of criticism[2]—yet he has probably affected literary opinion, during the period since the War, more profoundly than any other critic writing English. Eliot's prose style has a kind of felicity different from that of his poetic style; it is almost primly precise and sober, yet with a sort of sensitive charm in its austerity—closely reasoned and making its points with the fewest possible words, yet always even, effortless and lucid. In a reaction against the impressionistic criticism which flourished at the end of the century and which had survived into our own time—the sort of criticism which, in dealing with poetry, attempts to reproduce its effect by having recourse to poetic prose—T. S. Eliot has undertaken a kind of scientific study of esthetic values: avoiding impressionistic rhetoric and *a priori* esthetic theories alike, he compares works of literature coolly and tries to distinguish between different orders of artistic effects and the different degrees of satisfaction to be derived from them.

And by this method, Eliot has done more than perhaps any other modern critic to effect a revaluation of English literature. We sometimes follow his literary criticism with the same sort of eagerness and excitement with which we follow a philosophical inquiry. Professor Saintsbury has played in literature much the same sort of rôle that he has played as a connoisseur of wines, that of an agreeable and entertaining guide of excellent taste and enormous experience; Edmund Gosse, often intelligent and courageous in dealing with French or Scandinavian writers, could never quite, when it came to English literature, bring himself to drop his official character of Librarian of the House of Lords—his attitude was always a little that of the Beef Eater in the Tower of London, who assumes the transcendent value of the Crown Jewels which he has been set to guard and does not presume to form a personal opinion as to their taste or their respective merits; and the moral passion of Paul Elmer More has ended by paralyzing his esthetic appreciation. But T. S. Eliot, with an infinitely sensitive apparatus for esthetic appreciation, approaching English literature as an American, with an American's peculiar combination of avidity and detachment and with more than the ordinary English critic's reading in the literatures, ancient and modern, of the Continent, has been able to succeed as few writers have done in the excessively delicate task of estimating English, Irish and American writers in relation to one another, and writers in English in relation to writers on the Continent. The extent of Eliot's influence is amazing: these short essays, sent out without publicity as mere scat-

[2] In 1931. Eliot has since issued four further volumes: *The Use of Poetry and the Use of Criticism* (1933), *After Strange Gods* (1934), *Elizabethan Essays* (1934), and *Essays Ancient and Modern* (1936). He has also published two books of speculative prose: *The Idea of a Christian Society* (1939) and *Notes towards the Definition of Culture* (1948). Certain later critical papers and lectures have likewise appeared, usually in pamphlet form: *The Music of Poetry* (1942), *The Classics and the Man of Letters* (1942), *What is a Classic?* (1945), *The Man of Letters and the Future of Europe* (1945), *Milton* (1947), *From Poe to Valéry* (1948). See Appendix IV. (Editor's note, 1950.)

tered notes on literature, yet sped with so intense a seriousness and weighted
with so wide a learning, have not only had the effect of discrediting the academic clichés of the text-books, but are even by way of establishing in the
minds of the generation now in college a new set of literary clichés. With the
ascendancy of T. S. Eliot, the Elizabethan dramatists have come back into
fashion, and the nineteenth-century poets gone out. Milton's poetic reputation
has sunk, and Dryden's and Pope's have risen. It is as much as one's life is
worth nowadays, among young people, to say an approving word for Shelley
or a dubious one about Donne. And as for the enthusiasm for Dante—to
paraphrase the man in Hemingway's novel, there's been nothing like it since
the Fratellinis!

Eliot's rôle as a literary critic has been very similar to Valéry's in France:
indeed, the ideas of the two men and their ways of stating them have corresponded so closely that one guesses they must influence each other a good
deal. Like Valéry, Eliot believes that a work of art is not an oracular outpour-
ing, but an object which has been constructed deliberately with the aim of
producing a certain effect. He has brought back to English criticism something of that trenchant rationalism which he admires in the eighteenth century, but with a much more catholic appreciation of different styles and points
of view than the eighteenth century allowed. The Romantics, of course, fare
badly before this criticism. Vague sentiment vaguely expressed, rhetorical
effusion disguising bad art—these Eliot's laconic scorn has nipped. For him,
Byron is "a disorderly mind, and an uninteresting one": Keats and Shelley
"not nearly such great poets as they are supposed to be"; whereas the powers
of Dryden are "wider, but no greater than those of Milton." Just as Valéry
lately protested in a lecture that he was unable to understand the well-known
lines of Alfred de Musset:

> Les plus désespérés sont les chants les plus beaux,
> Et j'en sais d'immortels qui sont de purs sanglots,

so Eliot, in an essay on Crashaw, has confessed, with a certain supercilious-
ness, his inability to understand the following stanza from Shelley's "Skylark":

> Keen as are the arrows
>   Of that silver sphere
> Whose intense lamp narrows
>   In the white dawn clear,
> Until we hardly see—we feel that it is there.

"For the first time, perhaps," says Eliot, "in verse of such eminence, sound
exists without sense."

It will be seen that Eliot differs from Valéry in believing that poetry should
make "sense." And he elsewhere, in his essay on Dante in *The Sacred Wood*,

remonstrates with Valéry for asserting that philosophy has no place in poetry. Yet Eliot's point of view, though more intelligently reasoned and expressed, comes down finally to the same sort of thing as Valéry's and seems to me open to the same sort of objection. Eliot's conclusion in respect to the relation of philosophy to poetry is that, though philosophy *has* its place in poetry, it is only as something which we "see" among the other things with which the poet presents us, a set of ideas which penetrate his world, as in the case of the *Divina Commedia*: in the case of such a poet as Lucretius, the philosophy sometimes seems antagonistic to the poetry only because it happens to be a philosophy "not rich enough in feeling . . . incapable of complete expansion into pure vision." Furthermore, "the original form of philosophy cannot be poetic": the poet must use a philosophy already invented by somebody else. Now, though we may admire the justice of Eliot's judgments on the various degrees of artistic success achieved by Dante, Lucretius and others, it becomes plainer and plainer, as time goes on, that the real effect of Eliot's, as of Valéry's, literary criticism, is to impose upon us a conception of poetry as some sort of pure and rare esthetic essence with no relation to any of the practical human uses for which, for some reason never explained, only the technique of prose is appropriate.

Now this point of view, as I have already suggested in writing about Paul Valéry, seems to me absolutely unhistorical—an impossible attempt to make esthetic values independent of all the other values. Who will agree with Eliot, for example, that a poet cannot be an original thinker and that it is not possible for a poet to be a completely successful artist and yet persuade us to accept his ideas at the same time? There is a good deal in Dante's morality which he never got out of the Scholastics, as, for all we know, there may be a good deal in Lucretius which he never got out of Epicurus. When we read Lucretius and Dante, we are affected by them just as we are by prose writers of eloquence and imagination—we are compelled to take their opinions seriously. And as soon as we admit that prose writing may be considered on the same basis with verse, it becomes evident that we cannot, in the case of Plato, discriminate so finely as to the capacity of his philosophy for being "expanded into pure vision" that we are able to put our finger on the point where the novelist or poet stops and the scientist or metaphysician begins; nor, with Blake any more than with Nietzsche and Emerson, distinguish the poet from the aphorist. The truth is, of course, that, in Lucretius' time, verse was used for all sorts of didactic purposes for which we no longer consider it appropriate—they had agricultural poems, astronomical poems, poems of literary criticism. How can the *Georgics*, the *Ars Poetica* and Manilius be dealt with from the point of view of the capacity of their material for being "expanded into pure vision"? To modern readers, the subjects of the *Georgics*—bee-keeping, stock-raising, and so forth—seem unsuitable and sometimes annoying in verse;

yet for Virgil's contemporaries, the poem must have been completely successful —as, indeed, granted the subject, it is. Nor does it follow that, because we are coming to use poetry for fewer and fewer literary purposes, our critical taste is becoming more and more refined, so that we are beginning to perceive for the first time the true, pure and exalted function of poetry: that is, simply, as Valéry says, to produce a "state"—as Eliot says, to afford a "superior amusement." It is much more likely that for some reason or other, verse as a technique of literary expression is being abandoned by humanity altogether—perhaps because it is a more primitive, and hence a more barbarous technique than prose. Is it possible to believe, for example, that Eliot's hope of having verse reinstated on the stage—even verse of the new kind which he proposes— is likely ever to be realized?

The tendency to keep verse isolated from prose and to confine it to certain highly specialized functions dates in English at least from the time of Coleridge, when, in spite of the long narrative poems which were fashionable, verse was already beginning to fall into disuse. Coleridge defined a poem as "that species of composition which is opposed to works of science by proposing for its *immediate* object pleasure, not truth; and from all other species (having *this* object in common with it), it is discriminated by proposing to itself such delight from the *whole,* as is compatible with a distinct gratification from each component part." Poe, who had doubtless read Coleridge on the subject, wrote thirty years later that there was no such thing as a long poem, that "no very long poem would ever be popular again," etc. Eliot and Valéry follow Coleridge and Poe in their theory as well as in their verse, and they seem to me to confuse certain questions by talking as if the whole of literature existed simultaneously in a vacuum, as if Homer's and Shakespeare's situations had been the same as Mallarmé's and Laforgue's, as if the latter had been attempting to play the same sort of rôles as the former and could be judged on the same basis. It is inevitable, of course, that we should try to arrive at absolute values through the comparison of the work of different periods—I have just praised Eliot for his success at this—but it seems to me that in this particular matter a good many difficulties would be cleared up if certain literary discussions could be removed from the artificially restricted field of verse—in which it is assumed that nothing is possible or desirable but a quintessential distillation called "poetry," and that that distillation has nothing in common with anything possible to obtain through prose—to the field of literature in general. Has not such a great modern novel as *Madame Bovary,* for example, at least as much in common with Virgil and Dante as with Balzac and Dickens? Is it not comparable from the point of view of intensity, music and perfection of the parts, with the best verse of any period? And we shall consider Joyce in this connection later.

With all gratitude, therefore, for the salutary effect of Eliot's earlier criticism in curbing the carelessness and gush of the aftermath of Romanticism, it seems plain that the anti-Romantic reaction is leading finally into pedantry and into a futile estheticism. "Poetry," Eliot wrote in *The Sacred Wood*, "is not a turning loose of emotion, but an escape from emotion; it is not the expression of personality, but an escape from personality. But, of course, only those who have personality and emotion know what it means to want to escape from them." This was valid, and even noble in 1920 when *The Sacred Wood* was published; but today, after ten years of depersonalized and over-intellectualized verse, so much of it written in imitation of Eliot, the same sort of thing in the mouths of Eliot's disciples sounds like an excuse for *not* possessing emotion and personality.

Yet, in spite of the weaknesses of Eliot's position as he has sometimes been driven to state it dogmatically, he has himself largely succeeded in escaping the vices which it seems to encourage. The old nineteenth-century criticism of Ruskin, Renan, Taine, Sainte-Beuve, was closely allied to history and novel writing, and was also the vehicle for all sorts of ideas about the purpose and destiny of human life in general. The criticism of our own day examines literature, art, ideas and specimens of human society in the past with a detached scientific interest or a detached esthetic appreciation which seems in either case to lead nowhere. A critic like Herbert Read makes dull discriminations between different kinds of literature; a critic like Albert Thibaudet discovers dull resemblances between the ideas of philosophers and poets; a critic like I. A. Richards writes about poetry from the point of view of a scientist studying the psychological reactions of readers; and such a critic as Clive Bell writes about painting so exclusively and cloyingly from the point of view of the varying degrees of pleasure to be derived from the pictures of different painters that we would willingly have Ruskin and all his sermonizing back. And even Virginia Woolf and Lytton Strachey have this in common with Clive Bell that they seem to feel they have done enough when they have distinguished the kind of pleasure to be derived from one kind of book, the kind of interest to be felt in one kind of personality, from the kind to be found in another. One is supposed to have read everything and enjoyed everything and to understand exactly the reasons for one's enjoyment, but not to enjoy anything excessively nor to raise an issue of one kind of thing against another. Each of the essays of Strachey or Mrs. Woolf, so compact yet so beautifully rounded out, is completely self-contained and does not lead to anything beyond itself; and finally, for all their brilliance, we begin to find them tiresome.

Now there is a good deal in T. S. Eliot of this pedantry and sterility of his age. He is very much given, for example, to becoming involved in literary Houses-that-Jack-Built: "We find this quality occasionally in Wordsworth," he will write, "but it is a quality which Wordsworth shares with Shenstone rather than with Collins and Gray. And for the right sort of enjoyment of

Shenstone, we must read his prose as well as his verse. The 'Essays on Men and Manners' are in the tradition of the great French aphorists of the seventeenth century, and should be read with the full sense of their relation to Vauvenargues, La Rochefoucauld and (with his wider range) La Bruyère. We shall do well to read enough of Theophrastus to understand the kind of effect at which La Bruyère aimed. (Professor Somebody-or-other's book on 'Theophrastus and the Peripatetics' gives us the clew to the intellectual atmosphere in which Theophrastus wrote and enables us to gauge the influences on his work—very different from each other—of Plato and Aristotle.)" At this rate (though I have parodied Eliot), we should have to read the whole of literature in order to appreciate a single book, and Eliot fails to supply us with a reason why we should go to the trouble of doing so. Yet against the background of the criticism of his time, Eliot has stood out unmistakably as a man passionately interested in literature. The real intensity of his enthusiasm makes us forget the primness of his tone; and his occasional dogmatism is redeemed by his ability to see beyond his own ideas, his willingness to admit the relative character of his conclusions.

IV

But if Eliot, in spite of the meagreness of his production, has become for his generation a leader, it is also because his career has been a progress, because he has evidently been on his way somewhere, when many of his contemporaries, more prolific and equally gifted, have been fixed in their hedonism or despair. The poet of *The Waste Land* was too serious to continue with the same complacence as some of his contemporaries inhabiting that godforsaken desert. It was certain he would not stick at that point, and one watched him to see what he would do.

This destination has now, however, become plain. In the preface to the new 1928 edition of *The Sacred Wood*, poetry is still regarded as a "superior amusement," but Eliot reports on his part "an expansion or development of interests." Poetry is now perceived to have "something to do with morals, and with religion, and even with politics perhaps, though we cannot say what." In *For Lancelot Andrewes*, published in the same year, Eliot declares himself a classicist in literature, an Anglo-Catholic in religion and a royalist in politics, and announces that he has in preparation "three small books" treating to these subjects and to be called respectively "The School of Donne," "The Principles of Modern Heresy," and "The Outline of Royalism." There follows a slender selection of essays, which hint quietly at what may be expected.

We must await the further exposition of Eliot's new body of doctrine before it will be possible to discuss it properly. In the meantime, we can only applaud his desire to formulate a consistent central position, at the same time that we may regret the unpromising character of the ideals and institutions which he invokes. One cannot but recognize in Eliot's recent writings a kind of reactionary point of view which had already been becoming fashionable among certain sorts of literary people—a point of view which has much in common with that of the neo-Thomists in France and that of the Humanists in America. "Unless by civilizations," writes Eliot, "you mean material progress, cleanliness, etc. . . . if you mean a spiritual coördination on a high level, then it is doubtful whether civilization can endure without religion, and religion without a church." Yet you can hardly have an effective church without a cult of Christ as the son of God; and you cannot have such a cult without more willingness to accept the supernatural than most of us today are able to muster. We feel in contemporary writers like Eliot a desire to believe in religious revelation, a belief that it would be a good thing to believe, rather than a genuine belief. The faith of the modern convert seems to burn only with a low blue flame. "Our literature," Eliot has himself recently made a character in a dialogue say, "is a substitute for religion, and so is our religion." From such a faith, uninspired by hope, unequipped with zeal or force, what guidance for the future can we expect?

One cannot, however, doubt the reality of the experience to which Eliot testifies in his recent writings—though it seems to us less an Anglo-Catholic conversion than a reawakening of the New Englander's conscience, of the never quite exorcised conviction of the ineradicable sinfulness of man. Eliot admires Machiavelli because Machiavelli assumes the baseness of human nature as an unalterable fact; and he looks for light to the theologians who offer salvation, not through economic readjustment, political reform, education or biological and psychological study, but solely through "grace." Eliot apparently today regards "Evil" as some sort of ultimate reality, which it is impossible either to correct or to analyze. His moral principles seem to me stronger and more authentic than his religious mysticism—and his relation to the Anglo-Catholic Church appears largely artificial. The English seventeenth-century divines whose poetry and sermons he admires so much, upon whom he seems so much to depend for nourishment, exist in a richer, a more mysterious, a more heavily saturated atmosphere, in which even monumental outlines are blurred; Eliot himself is stiffer and cooler, more intent, more relentless, more clear. He has his own sort of graciousness, but he seems, as the phrase is, a little thin-lipped. His religious tradition has reached him by way of Boston.

In any case, Eliot's new phase of piety has brought with it a new humility. He apologizes in his 1928 preface for the "assumption of pontifical solemnity" which he now detects in *The Sacred Wood*, and his recent little book on Dante (a most admirable introduction) not merely surprises but almost embarrasses us by the modesty with which Eliot professes to desire nothing but to be of use to beginners and to tell us of a few of the beautiful things which he has found in the great poet. I will not say that this humility has enfeebled his poetry. The three devout little poems which he has published as Christmas cards since "The Hollow Men" announced the nadir of the phase of sterility and despair given such effective expression in *The Waste Land,* seem comparatively uninspired; but the long poem or group of poems, *Ash-Wednesday* (1930), which follows a scheme somewhat similar to that of *The Waste Land,* is a not unworthy successor to it.

The poet begins with the confession of his bankruptcy:

> Because I do not hope to turn again
> Because I do not hope
> Because I do not hope to turn
> Desiring this man's gift and that man's scope
> I no longer strive to strive towards such things
> (Why should the agèd eagle stretch its wings?)
> Why should I mourn
> The vanished power of the usual reign? . . .
>
> Because these wings are no longer wings to fly
> But merely vans to beat the air
> The air which is now thoroughly small and dry
> Smaller and dryer than the will
> Teach us to care and not to care
> Teach us to sit still.
>
> Pray for us sinners now and at the hour of our death
> Pray for us now and at the hour of our death.

There follow passages in which the prayer is apparently answered: the poet's contrition and pious resignation are rewarded by a series of visions which first console then lighten his heart. We find an imagery new for Eliot, a symbolism semi-ecclesiastical and not without a Pre-Raphaelite flavor: white leopards, a Lady gowned in white, junipers and yews, "The Rose" and "The Garden," and jeweled unicorns drawing a gilded hearse: these are varied by an interlude which returns to the imagery and mood of *The Waste Land,* and a swirling churning anguished passage which suggests certain things of Gertrude Stein's. At last the themes of the first section recur: the impotent wings of the agèd eagle seem to revive, as,

> From the wide window toward the granite shore
> The white sails still fly seaward, seaward flying
> Unbroken wings.
> And the lost heart stiffens and rejoices
> In the lost lilac and the lost sea voices
> And the weak spirit quickens to rebel
> For the bent golden-rod and the lost sea smell
> Quickens to recover
> The cry of quail and the whirling plover

And the blind eye creates
The empty forms between the ivory gates
And smell renews the salt savour of the sandy earth . . .

The broken prayer, at once childlike and mystically subtle, with which the poem ends seems to imply that the poet has come closer to the strength and revelation he craves: grace is about to descend.

> Blessèd sister, holy mother, spirit of the fountain,
>   spirit of the garden,
> Suffer us not to mock ourselves with falsehood
> Teach us to care and not to care
> Teach us to sit still
> Even among these rocks,
> Our peace in His will
> And even among these rocks
> Sister, mother
> And spirit of the river, spirit of the sea,
> Suffer me not to be separated
>
> And let my cry come unto Thee.

The literary and conventional imagery upon which *Ash-Wednesday* so largely relies and which is less vivid because more artificial than that of Eliot's earlier poems, seems to me a definite feature of inferiority; the "devil of the stairs" and the "shape twisted on the banister," which are in Eliot's familiar and unmistakable personal vein, somehow come off better than the jeweled unicorn, which incongruously suggests Yeats. And I am made a little tired at hearing Eliot, only in his early forties, present himself as an "agèd eagle" who asks why he should make the effort to stretch his wings. Yet *Ash-Wednesday*, though less brilliant and intense than Eliot at his very best, is distinguished by most of the qualities which made his other poems remarkable: the exquisite phrasing in which we feel that every word is in its place and that there is not a word too much; the metrical mastery which catches so naturally, yet with so true a modulation, the faltering accents of the supplicant, blending the cadences of the liturgy with those of perplexed brooding thought; and, above all, that "peculiar honesty" in "exhibiting the essential sickness or strength of the human soul" of which Eliot has written in connection with Blake and which, in his own case, even at the moment when his psychological plight seems most depressing and his ways of rescuing himself from it least sympathetic, still gives him a place among those upon whose words we reflect with most interest and whose tones we remember longest.

From *Axel's Castle* by Edmund Wilson, pp. 93–131. Charles Scribner's Sons. Copyright, 1931. Reprinted by permission of the author and publishers. An earlier and shorter version of this essay appeared in *The New Republic*, Vol. LX (November 13, 1929), pp. 341–349.

ALLEN TATE
Hart Crane
[1932]

THE career of Hart Crane will be written by future critics as a chapter in the neo-symbolist movement. A historical view of his poetry at this time would be misleading and incomplete. Like most poets of his age in America, Crane discovered Rimbaud through Eliot and the Imagists; it is certain that long before he had done any of his best work he had come to believe himself the spiritual heir of the French poet. While it is true that he mastered the symbolist use of fused metaphor, it is also true that this is a feature of all poetic language. Whether Crane's style is symbolistic, or should, in many instances like the first six or seven stanzas of "The River," be called Elizabethan, is a question that need not concern us now.

Between *The Bridge* and *Une Saison d'Enfer* there is little essential affinity. Rimbaud achieved "disorder" out of implicit order, after a deliberate cultivation of "derangement," but in our time the disintegration of our intellectual systems is accomplished. With Crane the disorder is original and fundamental. That is the special quality of his mind that belongs peculiarly to our own time. His esthetic problem, however, was more general; it was the historic problem of romanticism.

Harold Hart Crane, one the great masters of the romantic movement, was born in Garrettsville, Ohio, on July 21, 1899. His birthplace is a small town near Cleveland, in the old Western Reserve, a region which, as distinguished from the lower portions of the state, where people from the southern up-country settled, was populated largely by New England stock. He seems to have known little of his ancestry, but he frequently said that his maternal forebears had given Hartford, Connecticut, its name, and that they went "back to Stratford-on-Avon"—a fiction surely, but one that gave him distinct pleasure. His formal education was slight. After the third year at high school, when he was fifteen, it ended, and he worked in his father's candy factory in Cleveland, where the family had removed in his childhood. He repeatedly told me that money had been set aside for his education at college, but that it had been used for other purposes. With the instinct of genius he read the great poets, but he never acquired an objective mastery of any literature, or even of the history of his country—a defect of considerable interest in a poet whose most ambitious work is an American epic.

In any ordinary sense Crane was not an educated man; in many respects he was an ignorant man. There is already a Crane legend, like the Poe legend—it should be fostered because it will help to make his poetry generally known —and the scholars will decide that it was a pity that so great a talent lacked early advantages. It is probable that he was incapable of the discipline of a formal classical education, and probable too that the eclectic education of his time would have scattered and killed his talent.

His poetry not only has defects of the surface, it has a defect of vision; but its great and peculiar value cannot be separated from its limitations. Its qualities are bound up with a special focus of the intellect and sensibility, and it would be foolish to wish that his mind had been better trained or differently organized.

The story of his suicide is well known. The information that I have seems authentic, but it is incomplete and subject to excessive interpretation. Toward the end of April, 1932, he embarked on the S.S. *Orizaba* bound from Vera Cruz to New York. On the night of April 26 he got into a brawl with some sailors; he was severely beaten and robbed. At noon the next day, the ship being in the Caribbean a few hours out of Havana, he rushed from his stateroom clad in pajamas and overcoat, walked through the smoking-room out onto the deck, and then the length of the ship to the stern. There without hesitation he made a perfect dive into the sea. It is said that a life-preserver was thrown to him; he either did not see it or did not want it. By the time the ship had turned back he had disappeared. Whether he forced himself down—for a moment he was seen swimming—or was seized by a shark, as the captain believed, cannot be known. After a search of thirty-five minutes his body was not found, and the *Orizaba* put back into her course.

In the summer of 1930 he had written to me that he feared his most ambitious work, *The Bridge,* was not quite perfectly "realized," that probably his soundest work was in the shorter pieces of *White Buildings,* but that his mind, being once committed to the larger undertaking, could never return to the lyrical and more limited form. He had an extraordinary insight into the foundations of his work, and I think this judgment of it will not be refuted.

From 1922 to 1928—after that year I saw him and heard from him irregularly until his death—I could observe the development of his style from poem to poem; and his letters—written always in a pure and lucid prose—provide a valuable commentary on his career. This is not the place to bring all this material together for judgment. As I look back upon his work and its relation to the life he lived, a general statement about it comes to my mind that may throw some light on the dissatisfaction that he felt with his career

It will be a judgment on the life and works of a man whom I knew for ten years as a friend.

Suicide was the sole act of will left to him short of a profound alteration of his character. I think the evidence of this is the locked-in sensibility, the insulated egoism, of his poetry—a subject I shall return to. The background of his death was dramatically perfect: a large portion of his finest imagery was of the sea, chiefly the Caribbean:

> O minstrel galleons of Carib fire,
> Bequeath us to no earthly shore until
> Is answered in the vortex of our grave
> The seal's wide spindrift gaze toward paradise.

His verse is full of splendid images of this order, a rich symbolism for an implicit pantheism that, whatever may be its intrinsic merit, he had the courage to vindicate with death in the end.

His pantheism was not passive and contemplative, it arose out of the collision between his own locked-in sensibility and the ordinary forms of experience. Every poem is a thrust of that sensibility into the world: his defect lay in his inability to face out the moral criticism implied in the failure to impose his will upon experience.

The Bridge is presumably an epic. How early he had conceived the idea of this poem and the leading symbolism, it is difficult to know: certainly as early as February, 1923. Up to that time, with the exception of "For the Marriage of Faustus and Helen" (1922), he had written only short poems, but most of them, "Praise for an Urn," "Black Tambourine," "Paraphrase," and "Emblems of Conduct," are among his finest work. It is a mistake then to suppose that all of *White Buildings* is early experimental writing; a large portion of that volume, and perhaps the least successful part of it, is made up of poems written after *The Bridge* was begun. "Praise for an Urn" was written in the spring of 1922—one of the finest elegies by an American poet—and although his later development gave us a poetry that the period would be much the less rich for not having, he never again had such perfect mastery of his subject—because he never again knew precisely what his subject was.

Readers familiar with "For the Marriage of Faustus and Helen" admire it by passages, but the form of the poem, in its framework of symbol, is an abstraction empty of any knowable experience. It is a conventional revival of the kind of diction that a young poet picks up in his first reading. Crane, I believe, felt that this was so; and he became so dissatisfied not only with the style of the poem, which is heavily influenced by Eliot and Laforgue, but with the "literary" character of the symbolism, that he set about the greater task of writing *The Bridge*. He had looked upon his "Faustus and Helen" as an answer to the cultural pessimism of the school of Eliot, and *The Bridge* was to be an even more complete answer.

There was a fundamental mistake in Crane's diagnosis of Eliot's problem. Eliot's "pessimism" grows out of an awareness of the decay of the individual consciousness and its fixed relations to the world; but Crane thought that it was due to something like pure "orneryness," the unwillingness to "share with us the breath released," the breath being a new kind of freedom that he identified emotionally with the age of the machine. This vagueness of purpose, in spite of the apparently concrete character of the Brooklyn Bridge, which became the symbol of his epic, he never succeeded in correcting. The "bridge" stands for no well-defined experience; it differs from the Helen and Faust symbols only in its unliterary origin. I think Crane was deceived by this difference, and by the fact that Brooklyn Bridge is "modern," and a fine piece of "mechanic." His more ambitious later project permitted him no greater degree of formal structure than the more literary symbolism of his youth.

The fifteen parts of *The Bridge* taken as one poem suffer from the lack of a coherent structure, whether symbolistic or narrative: the coherence of the work consists in the personal quality of the writing—in mood, feeling, and tone. In the best passages Crane has a perfect mastery over the qualities of his style; but it lacks an objective pattern of ideas elaborate enough to carry it through an epic or heroic work. The single symbolistic image, in which the whole poem centers, is at one moment the actual Brooklyn Bridge; at another, it is any bridge or "connection"; at still another, it is a philosophical pun, and becomes the basis of a series of analogies.

In "Cape Hatteras," the aeroplane and Walt Whitman are analogous "bridges" to some transcendental truth. Because the idea is variously metaphor, symbol, and analogy, it tends to make the poem static. The poet takes it up, only to be forced to put it down again *when the poetic image of the moment is exhausted*. The idea does not, in short, fill the poet's mind; it is the starting point for a series of short flights, or inventions connected only in analogy—which explains the merely personal passages, which are obscure, and the lapses into sentimentality. For poetic sentimentality is emotion undisciplined by the structure of events or ideas of which it is ostensibly a part. The idea is not objective and articulate in itself; it lags after the poet's vision; it appears and disappears; and in the intervals Crane improvises, often beautifully, as in the flight of the aeroplane, sometimes badly, as in the passage on Whitman in the same poem.

In the great epic and philosophical works of our tradition, notably the *Divine Comedy,* the intellectual groundwork is not only simple philosophically; we not only know that the subject is personal salvation, just as we know that Crane's is the greatness of America; we are also given the complete

articulation of the idea down to the slightest detail, and we are given it objectively apart from anything that the poet is going to say about it. When the
poet extends his perception, there is a further extention of the groundwork
ready to meet and discipline it, and compel the sensibility of the poet to stick
to the subject. It is a game of chess; neither side can move without consulting
the other. Crane's difficulty is that of modern poets generally: they play the
game with half of the men, the men of sensibility, and because sensibility can
make any move, the significance of all moves is obscure.

If we subtract from Crane's idea its periphery of sensation, we have left
only the dead abstraction, the Greatness of America, which is capable of
elucidation neither on the logical plane nor in the generally accepted idea of
America.

The theme of *The Bridge* is, in fact, an emotional simplification of a
subject-matter that Crane did not, on the plane of narrative and idea, simplify
at all. The poem is emotionally homogeneous and simple—it contains a single
purpose; but because it is not structurally clarified it is emotionally confused.
America stands for a passage into new truths. Is this the meaning of American
history? The poet has every right to answer yes, and this he has done. But
just what in America or about America stands for this? Which American
history? The historical plot of the poem, which is the groundwork on which
the symbolic bridge stands, is arbitrary and broken, where the poet would have
gained an overwhelming advantage by choosing a single period or episode, a
concrete event with all its dramatic causes, and by following it up minutely,
and being bound to it. In short, he would have gained an advantage could he
have found a subject to stick to.

Does American culture afford such a subject? It probably does not. After
the seventeenth century the sophisticated history of the scholars came into
fashion; our popular, legendary chronicles come down to us only from the remoter European past. It was a sound impulse on Crane's part to look for an
American myth, some simple version of our past that lies near the center of
the American consciousness; a heroic tale with just enough symbolism to give
his mind both direction and play. The soundness of his purpose is witnessed
also by the kind of history in the poem: it is inaccurate, and will not at all
satisfy the sticklers for historical fact. It is the history of the motion picture,
of naïve patriotism. This is sound; for it ignores the scientific ideal of historical truth-in-itself, and looks for a cultural truth which might win the spontaneous allegiance of the people. It is on such simple integers of truth, not
of fact but of religious necessity, that men unite. The American mind was
formed by the eighteenth-century Enlightenment, which broke down the
European truths, and gave us a temper deeply hostile to the making of new
religious truths of our own.

The impulse in *The Bridge* is religious, but the soundness of an impulse is no warrant that it will create a sound art form. The form depends on too many factors beyond the control of the poet. The age is scientific and pseudo-scientific, and our philosophy is John Dewey's instrumentalism. And it is possibly this circumstance that has driven the religious attitude into a corner where it lacks the right instruments for its defense and growth, and where it is in a vast muddle about just what these instruments are. Perhaps this dis-unity of the intellect is responsible for Crane's unphilosophical belief that the poet, unaided and isolated from the people, can create a myth.

If anthropology has helped to destroy the credibility of the myths, it has shown us how they rise; their growth is mysterious from the people as a whole. It is probable that no one man ever put myth into history. It is still a nice problem among higher critics whether the authors of the Gospels were de-liberate myth-makers, or whether their minds were simply constructed that way; but the evidence favors the latter. Crane was a myth-maker, and in an age favorable to myths he would have written a mythical poem in the act of writing an historical one.

It is difficult to agree with those critics who find his epic a single poem, and as such an artistic success. It is a collection of lyrics, the best of which are not surpassed by anything in American literature. The writing is most distinguished when Crane is least philosophical, *when he writes from sensa-tion.* "The River" has some blemishes toward the end, but by and large it is a masterpiece of order and style; it alone is enough to place Crane in the front rank of American poets, living or dead. Equally good, but less ambitious are the "Proem: to Brooklyn Bridge," and "Harbor Dawn," and "The Dance" from the section called "Powhatan's Daughter."

These poems bear only the loosest relation to the symbolic demands of the theme; they contain allusions to the historical pattern or extend the slender structure of analogy running through the poem. They are primarily lyrical, and each has its complete form. The poem "Indiana," written presumably to complete the pattern of "Powhatan's Daughter," does not stand alone, and is one of the most astonishing performances ever made by a poet of Crane's genius. "The Dance" gives us the American background for the coming white man, and "Indiana" carries the stream of history to the pioneer West. It is a nightmare of sentimentality. Crane is at his most "philosophical" in a theme in which he feels no poetic interest whatever.

The structural defect of *The Bridge* is due to this functional contradiction of purpose. In one of his best earlier poems, "The Wine Menagerie," he ex-claims: "New Thresholds, new Anatomies!"—new sensation, but he could not subdue the new sensation to a symbolic form.

His pantheism is necessarily a philosophy of sensation without point of view. An epic is a judgment of human action, an implied evaluation of a civilization, a way of life. In *The Bridge* the civilization that contains the sub-

way hell of the section called "The Tunnel" is the same civilization that contains the aeroplane that the poet apostrophizes in "Cape Hatteras": there is
no reason why the subway should be a fitter symbol of damnation than the
aeroplane: both were produced by the same mentality on the same moral
plane. There is a concealed, meaningless analogy between, on the one hand,
the height of the plane and the depth of the subway, and, on the other,
"higher" and "lower" in the religious sense. At one moment Crane faces his
predicament of blindness to any rational order of value, and knows that he is
damned; but he cannot face it long, and he tries to rest secure upon the intensity of sensation.

To the vision of the abyss in "The Tunnel," a vision that Dante passed
through midway of this mortal life, Crane had no alternative: when it became
too harrowing he cried to his Pocahontas, a typically romantic and sentimental
symbol:

> Lie to us—dance us back our tribal morn!

It is probably the most perfect word of romanticism in this century. When
Crane saw that his leading symbol, the bridge, would not hold all the material
of his poem, he could not sustain it ironically, in the classical manner, by
probing its defects; nor in the personal sections, like "Quaker Hill," does he
include himself in his Leopardian denunciation of life. He is the blameless
victim of a world whose impurity violates the moment of intensity, which
would otherwise be enduring and perfect. He is betrayed, not by a defect of
his own nature, but by the external world; he asks of nature, perfection—requiring only of himself, intensity. The persistent, and persistently defeated
pursuit of a natural absolute places Crane at the center of his age.

Alternately he asserts the symbol of the bridge and abandons it, because
fundamentally he does not understand it. The idea of bridgeship is an elaborate blur leaving the inner structure of the poem confused.

Yet some of the best poetry of our times is in *The Bridge*. Its inner confusion is a phase of the inner cross-purposes of the time. Crane was one of
those men whom every age seems to select as the spokesmen of its spiritual
life; they give the age away. The accidental features of their lives, their place
in life, their very heredity, seem to fit them for the rôle: even their vices contribute to their preparation. Crane's biographer will have to study the early
influences that confirmed him in narcissism, and thus made him typical of
the rootless spiritual life of our time. The character formed by those influences
represents an immense concentration, and becomes almost a symbol, of American life in this age.

Crane's poetry has incalculable moral value: it reveals our defects in their
extremity. I have said that he knew little of the history of his country. It was
not a mere defect in education, but a defect, in the spiritual sense, of the

modern mind. Professor Charles A. Beard has immense information about American history, but understands almost none of it: Crane lacked the sort of indisputable understanding of his country that a New England farmer has who has never been out of his township. *The Bridge* attempts to include all American life, but it covers the ground with seven-league boots, and like a sightseer, sees nothing. With reference to its leading symbol, it has no subject matter. The poem is the effort of a solipsistic sensibility to locate itself in the external world, to establish points of reference.

It seems to me that by testing out his capacity to construct a great objective piece of work, in which his definition of himself should have been perfectly articulated, he brought his work to an end. I think he knew that the structure of *The Bridge* was finally incoherent, and for that reason—as I have said— he could no longer believe in even his lyrical powers; he could not return to the early work and take it up where he had left off. Far from "refuting" Eliot, his whole career is a vindication of Eliot's major premise—that the integrity of the individual consciousness has broken down. Crane had, in his later work, no individual consciousness: the hard firm style of "Praise for an Urn," which is based upon a clear-cut perception of moral relations, and upon their ultimate inviolability, begins to disappear when the poet goes out into the world and finds that the simplicity of a child's world has no universal sanction. From then on, instead of the effort to define himself in the midst of almost overwhelming complications—a situation that might have produced a tragic poet—he falls back upon the intensity of consciousness, rather than clarity, for his center of vision. And that is romanticism.

His world had no center, and the compensatory action that he took is responsible for the fragmentary quality of his most ambitious work. This action took two forms, the blind assertion of the will, and the blind desire for self-destruction. The poet did not face his first problem, which is to define the limits of his personality and to objectify its moral implications in an appropriate symbolism. Crane could only assert a quality of will against the world, and at each successive failure of the will he turned upon himself. In the failure of understanding—and understanding, for Dante, was a way of love— the romantic modern poet of the age of science attempts to impose his will upon experience and to possess the world.

It is this impulse of the modern period that has given us the greatest romantic poetry: Crane instinctively continued the conception of the will that was the deliberate discovery of Rimbaud. A poetry of the will is a poetry of sensation, for the poet surrenders to his sensations of the object in his effort to identify himself with it, and to own it. Some of Crane's finest lyrics—those written in the period of *The Bridge*—carry the modern impulse as far as you will find it anywhere in the French romantics. "Lachrymae Christi" and "Passage," though on the surface made up of pure images without philosophical meaning of the sort explicit in *The Bridge,* are the lyrical equivalents of the epic: the same kind of sensibility is at work. The implicit grasp of his material that we find in "Praise for an Urn" the poet exchanged for an external, random symbol of which there is no possibility of realization. *The Bridge* is an irrational symbol of the will, of conquest, of blind achievement in space; its obverse is "Passage," whose lack of external symbolism exhibits the poetry of the will on the plane of sensation; and this is the self-destructive return of the will upon itself.

Criticism may well set about isolating the principle upon which Crane's poetry is organized. Powerful verse overwhelms its admirers, and betrays them into more than technical imitation. That is one of the arguments of Platonism against literature; it is the immediate quality of an art rather than its whole significance that sets up schools and traditions. Crane not only ends the romantic era in his own person; he ends it logically and morally. Beyond Crane no future poet can go. (This does not mean that the romantic impulse may not rise and flourish again.) The finest passages in his work are single moments in the stream of sensation; beyond the moment he goes at peril; for outside it there lies the discrepancy between the sensuous fact, the perception, and its organizing symbol—a discrepancy that plunges him into chaos and sentimentality. A true symbol has in it, within the terms of its properties, all the qualities that the artist is able to attribute to it. But the "bridge" is empty and static, it has no inherent content, and the poet's attribution to it of the qualities of his own moral predicament is arbitrary. That explains the fragmentary and often unintelligible framework of the poem. There was neither complete action nor ordered symbolism in terms of which the distinct moments of perception could be clarified.

This was partly the problem of Rimbaud. But Crane's problem was nearer to the problem of Keats, and *The Bridge* is a failure in the sense that *Hyperion* is a failure, and with comparable magnificence. Crane's problem, being farther removed from the epic tradition, was actually more difficult than Keats', and his treatment of it was doubtless the most satisfactory possible in our time. Beyond the quest of pure sensation and its ordering symbolism lies the total destruction of art. By attempting an extreme solution of the romantic problem, Crane proved that it cannot be solved.

From *Reactionary Essays on Poetry and Ideas* by Allen Tate, pp. 26–42. Charles Scribner's Sons. Copyright, 1936. Reprinted by permission of the author and publishers. First published, in part, in *The Hound and Horn,* Vol. V (July–September, 1932), pp. 612–619. Recently included in *On the Limits of Poetry* by Allen Tate (New York: Swallow Press & William Morrow & Co., 1948).

Ezra Pound
[1931]

> and as for text we have taken it
> from that of Messire Laurentius
> and from a codex once of the Lords Malatesta . . .

ONE is not certain who Messire Laurentius was; one is not very certain that it makes no difference. Yet one takes comfort in the vast range of Mr. Pound's obscure learning, which no one man could be expected to know much about. In this great work[1] one is continually uncertain, as to space, time, history. The codex of the Lords Malatesta would be less disconcerting than Laurentius— if we were sure it existed—for more than half of the thirty cantos contain long paraphrases or garbled quotations from the correspondence, public and private, of the Renaissance Italians, chiefly Florentine and Venetian. About a third of the lines are versified documents. Another third are classical allusions, esoteric quotations from the ancients, fragments of the Greek poets with bits of the Romans thrown in; all magnificently written into Mr. Pound's own text. The rest is contemporary—anecdotes, satirical pictures of vulgar Americans, obscene stories, evenings in low Mediterranean dives, and gossip about amazing rogues behind the scenes of European power. The three kinds of material in the cantos are antiquity, the Renaissance, and the modern world. They are combined on no principle that seems in the least consistent to a first glance. They appear to be mixed in an incoherent jumble, or to stand up in puzzling contrasts.

This is the poetry which, in early and incomplete editions, has had more influence on us than any other of our times; it has had an immense "underground" reputation. And deservedly. For even the early reader of Mr. Pound could not fail to detect the presence of a new poetic form in the individual cantos, though the full value and intention of this form appears for the first time in the complete work. It is not that there is any explicit feature of the whole design that is not contained in each canto; it is simply that Mr. Pound must be read in bulk; it is only then that the great variety of his style and the apparent incoherence turn into order and form. There is no other poetry like the *Cantos* in English. And there is none quite so simple in form. The form is, in fact, so simple that almost no one has guessed it, and I suppose it will

[1] *A Draft of XXX Cantos,* by Ezra Pound. Paris: The Hours Press, 1930; New York: Farrar and Rinehart, 1933. Further installments of the Cantos appeared in the following years: *A Draft of Cantos XXXI–XLI, The Fifth Decad of Cantos, etc.,* the latest being *The Pisan Cantos* (1948) and a complete collection of all the Cantos to date (also in 1948). (Editor's note, 1950.)

continue to puzzle, perhaps to enrage, our more academic critics for a generation to come. But this form by virtue of its simplicity remains inviolable to critical terms: even now it cannot be technically described.

I begin to talk like Mr. Pound, or rather like the way in which most readers think Mr. Pound writes. The secret of his form is this: conversation. The cantos are talk, talk, talk; not by anyone in particular to anyone else in particular; they are just rambling talk. At least each canto is a cunningly devised imitation of a polite conversation, in which no one presses any subject very far. The length of breath, the span of conversational energy, is the length of canto. The conversationalist pauses; there is just enough left hanging in the air to give him a new start; so that the transitions between the cantos are natural and easy.

Each canto has the broken flow and the somewhat elusive climax of a good monologue: because there is no single speaker, it is a many-voiced monologue. That is the method of the poems—though there is another quality of the form that I must postpone for a moment—and *that is what the poems are about.*

There are, as I have said, three subjects of conversation—ancient times, Renaissance Italy, and the present—but these are not what the cantos are about. They are not about Italy, nor about Greece, nor are they about us. They are not about anything. But they are distinguished poetry. Mr. Pound himself tells us:

> And they want to know what we talked about?
>   *"de litteris et de armis, praestantibus ingeniis,*
> Both of ancient times and our own; books, arms,
> And men of unusual genius
> Both of ancient times and our own, in short the usual subjects
> Of conversation between intelligent men."

II

There is nothing in the cantos more difficult than that. There is nothing inherently obscure; nothing too profound for any reader who has enough information to get to the background of all the allusions in a learned conversation. But there is something that no reader, short of some years of hard textual study, will understand. This is the very heart of the cantos, the secret of Mr. Pound's poetic character, which will only gradually emerge from a detailed analysis of every passage. And this is no more than our friends are constantly demanding of us; we hear them talk, and we return to hear them talk, and we return to hear them again, but we never know what they talk about; we return for that mysterious quality of charm that has no rational meaning that we can define. It is only after a long time that the order, the direction, the rhythm of the talker's mind, the logic of his character as distinguished from anything logical he may say—it is a long time before this begins to take on form for us. So with Mr. Pound's cantos. It is doubtless easier for us (who are trained in the more historic brands of poetry) when the poems are about God, Freedom, and Immortality, but there is no reason why poetry should not be so perplexingly simple as Mr. Pound's, and be about nothing at all.

The ostensible subjects of the cantos—ancient, middle, and modern times —are only the materials round which Mr. Pound's mind plays constantly; they are the screen upon which he throws a beautiful, flowing quality of poetic thought. Now in conversation the memorable quality is a sheer accident of character, and is not designed; but in the cantos the effect is deliberate, and from the first canto to the thirtieth the set tone is maintained without a single lapse.

It is this tone, it is this quality quite simply, which is the meaning of the cantos, and although, as I have said, it is simple and direct, it is just as hard to pin down, it is as hidden in its shifting details, as a running, ever-changing conversation. It cannot be taken out of the text; and yet the special way that Mr. Pound has of weaving his three materials together, of emphasizing them, of comparing and contrasting them, gives us a clue to the leading intention of the poems. I come to that quality of the form which I postponed.

The easiest interpretation of all poetry is the symbolic method: there are few poems that cannot be paraphrased into a kind of symbolism, which is usually false, being by no means the chief intention of the poet. It is very probable, therefore, that I am about to falsify the true simplicity of the cantos into a simplicity that is merely convenient and spurious. The reader must bear this in mind, and view the slender symbolism that I am going to read into the cantos as a critical shorthand, useful perhaps, but which when used must be dropped.

One of the finest cantos is properly the first. It describes a voyage:

> And then went down to the ship,
> Set keel to breakers, forth on the godly sea, and
> We set up mast and sail on that swart ship,
> Bore sheep aboard her, and our bodies also
> Heavy with weeping, and winds from sternward
> Bore us out onward with bellying canvas,
> Circe's this craft, the trim-coifed goddess.

They land, having come "to the place aforesaid by Circe"—whatever place it may be—and Tiresias appears, who says:

"Odysseus
Shalt return through spiteful Neptune, over dark seas,
Lose all companions." And then Anticlea came.
Lie quiet Divus. I mean, that is, Andreas Divus,
In officina Wecheli, 1538, out of Homer.
And he sailed, by Sirens and thence outward and away
And unto Circe.

Mr. Pound's world is the scene of a great Odyssey, and everywhere he lands it is the shore of Circe, where men "lose all companions" and are turned into swine. It would not do at all to push this hint too far, but I will risk one further point: Mr. Pound is a typically modern, rootless, and internationalized intelligence. In the place of the traditional supernaturalism of the older and local cultures, he has a cosmopolitan curiosity which seeks out marvels, which are all equally marvelous, whether it be a Greek myth or the antics in Europe of a lady from Kansas. He has the bright, cosmopolitan *savoir faire* which refuses to be "taken in": he will not believe, being a traditionalist at bottom, that the "perverts, who have set money-lust before the pleasures of the senses," are better than swine. And ironically, being modern and a hater of modernity, he sees all history as deformed by the trim-coifed goddess.

The cantos are a book of marvels—marvels that he has read about, or heard of, or seen; there are Greek myths, tales of Italian feuds, meetings with strange people, rumors of intrigues of state, memories of remarkable dead friends like T. E. Hulme, comments on philosophical problems, harangues on abuses of the age; the "usual subjects of conversation between intelligent men."

It is all fragmentary. Now nearly every canto begins with a bit of heroic antiquity, some myth, or classical quotation, or a lovely piece of lyrical description in a grand style. It invariably breaks down. It trails off into a piece of contemporary satire, or a flat narrative of the rascality of some Italian prince. This is the special quality of Mr. Pound's form, the essence of his talk, the direction of these magnificent conversations.

For not once does Mr. Pound give himself up to any single story or myth. The thin symbolism from the Circe myth is hardly more than a leading tone, an unconscious prejudice about men which he is not willing to indicate beyond the barest outline. He cannot believe in any of them, not even in his own power of imagining them out to a conclusion. None of his myths is compelling enough to draw out his total intellectual resources; none goes far enough to become a belief or even a momentary faith. They remain marvels to be looked at, but they are meaningless, the wrecks of civilization. His powerful juxtapositions of the ancient, the Renaissance, and the modern worlds reduce all three elements to an unhistorical miscellany, timeless and without origin, and no longer a force in the lives of men.

III

And that is the peculiarly modern quality of Mr. Pound. There is a certain likeness in this to another book of marvels, those stories of late antiquity known to us as *The Golden Ass*. The cantos are a sort of *Golden Ass*. There is a likeness, but there is no parallel beyond the mere historical one: both books are the production of worlds without convictions and given over to a hard secular program. Here the similarity ends. For Mr. Pound is a powerful reactionary, a faithful mind devoted to those ages when the myths were not merely pretty, but true. And there is a cloud of melancholy irony hanging over the cantos. He is persuaded that the myths are only beautiful, and he drops them after a glimpse, but he is not reconciled to this estheticism: he ironically puts the myths against the ugly specimens of modern life that have defeated them. But neither are the specimens of modernity worthy of the dignity of belief:

> She held that a sonnet was a sonnet
> And ought never to be destroyed
> And had taken a number of courses
> And continued with hope of degrees and
> Ended in a Baptist learnery
>> Somewhere near the Rio Grande.

I am not certain that Mr. Pound will agree with me that he is a traditionalist; nor am I convinced that Mr. Pound, for his part, is certain of anything under heaven but his genius for poetry. He is probably one of two or three living Americans who will be remembered as poets of the first order. Yet there is no reason to infer from that that Mr. Pound, outside his craft, or outside his conversation, knows in the least what he is doing or saying. He is and always has been in a muddle of revolution; and for some appalling reason he identifies his crusade with liberty—liberty of speech, liberty of press, liberty of conduct—in short, liberty. I do not mean to say that either Mr. Pound or his critic knows what liberty is. Nevertheless, Mr. Pound identifies it with civilization and intelligence, of the modern and scientific variety. And yet the ancient cultures, which he so much admires, were, from any modern viewpoint, hatched in barbarism and superstition. One is entitled to the suspicion that Mr. Pound prefers barbarism, and that by taking up the rôle of revolution against it he has bitten off his nose to spite his face. He is the confirmed enemy of provincialism, never suspecting that his favorite, Lorenzo the Magnificent, for example, was provincial to the roots of his hair.

This confusion runs through the cantos, and it makes the irony that I have spoken of to a certain extent unconscious. For as the apostle of humane culture, he constantly discredits it by crying up a rationalistic enlightenment. It would appear from this that his philosophical tact is somewhat feminine, and that, as intelligence, it does not exist. His poetic intelligence is of the finest: and if he doesn't know what liberty is, he understands poetry, and how to write it. This is enough for one man to know. And the thirty *Cantos* are enough to occupy a loving and ceaseless study—say a canto a year for thirty years, all thirty to be read every few weeks just for the tone.

From *Reactionary Essays on Poetry and Ideas* by Allen Tate, pp. 43–51. Charles Scribner's Sons. Copyright, 1936. Reprinted by permission of the author and publishers. First published as "Ezra Pound's Golden Ass" in *The Nation*, Vol. CXXXII (June 10, 1931), pp. 632–634. Recently included in *On the Limits of Poetry* by Allen Tate (New York: Swallow Press & William Morrow & Co., 1948).

KENNETH BURKE
Thomas Mann and André Gide
[1930]

WHEN Gustav von Aschenbach, the hero of Thomas Mann's *Death in Venice*, was about thirty-five years of age, he was taken ill in Vienna. During the course of a conversation, one keen observer said of him: "You see, Aschenbach has always lived like this," and the speaker contracted the fingers of his left hand into a fist; "never like this," and he let his hand droop comfortably from the arm of a chair. It is with such opening and closing of the hand that this essay is to deal.

In the early writings of both Mann and Gide the characters are exceptional, though always in keeping with our metaphor. Mann's concern is with serious and lonely fellows, deviations from type, who are over-burdened with a feeling of divergency from their neighbors. In stories like "Der Bajazzo" the deformations are more mental, but generally the subject is simplified by his imagining characters who are physically extravagant. There is Tobias Mindernickel, whose ill-dressed, gaunt, ungainly figure excites the persecution of all healthy children. He buys a little puppy, and names it Esau. They become inseparable, but one day Esau leaps for food, is accidentally wounded by a knife which Tobias is holding, whereupon Tobias nurses his puppy with great tenderness. After some days it is cured, it no longer lies gazing at him with bewildered, suffering eyes, it leaps down from its sick-bed, goes racing about with full delight in its puppyhood, with no thought that it is showing how it no longer needs Tobias's morbid tenderness. It is a cheerful little mutt—and maddened at his loss, Tobias plunges his knife into it again, then forlornly gathers its dying body in his arms. Similarly, there is the little Herr Friedemann, who, humble as he is, can by the course of his story be still further humiliated and, in the very act of taking his life, grovels. Mann also writes of an abnormally fat man, who worships his adulterous wife abjectly, and falls dead of apoplexy at a particularly comical moment, topples like a collapsing building, when he feels the full weight of the indignities which have been heaped upon him. And Piepsam, Herr Gottlob Piepsam, a decayed alcoholic, a victim of life if there ever was one, is insulted as he goes to visit the grave of his wife. On the path to the cemetery he is passed by a boy on a bicycle, the merest

child who is too happy to be anything but well-meaning, yet Piepsam resents
him and works himself into a fatal rage—the story being told fancifully, even
cheerfully. After Piepsam has been bundled off in an ambulance, one feels
how brightly the sun is shining.

These outsiders (Mann later took over the word "outsider" from the English) appear under many guises. They watch, they compare themselves with
others to their own detriment, they are earnest to the point of self-disgust,
and they are weighted with vague responsibilities. In "Tonio Kröger" the
concept has matured. Tonio's divergencies are subtler. As a writer, he observes the unliterary with nostalgia. Vacillating by temperament, one might
almost say vacillating by profession, he seeks simple people, who form for him
a kind of retrogressive ideal. He does not fraternize with them, he spies upon
them. A Bohemian, he distrusts Bohemianism. He watches these others, awed
by the healthiness, or the ease, of their satisfaction. It is a kind of inverted
praising, since he envies them for qualities which he himself has outgrown.
And it is melancholy.

Against this earnestness, this non-conforming mind's constant preoccupation
with conformity, we find in the early writings of Gide much the same rotten
elegance as characterizes Wilde's *The Picture of Dorian Gray*. Religious
thinking is perverted to produce an atmosphere of decay and sinfulness. There
is the Baudelairean tendency to invoke Satan as redeemer. Even in a work as
late as *Les Nourritures terrestres*, we find a crooked evangelism, calling us to
vague and unnatural revelations. These artificial prophecies, with a rhetorical,
homiletic accent which Gide has since abandoned, suggest a kind of morbid
Whitmanism. In place of expansion across an unpeopled continent, we have
a pilgrimage through old, decaying cities, erotic excitations at the thought of
anonymity and freedom among the ruins of other cultures. The hero who
cries out to Nathaniel is seeking, not the vigor of health, but the intensity of
corruption. The mood, if I understand it correctly, has by now lost much of
its immediacy, but in his later works Gide has shown it capable of great re-
adaptation; what we find earlier, in an archaistic terminology, is subsequently
transformed into something wholly contemporary.

The most thorough contrast between these writers probably arises from the
juxtaposition of Mann's *Death in Venice* and Gide's *The Immoralist*. Gustav
von Aschenbach is nationally respected as a master of his calling. Parts of his
works are even among the prescribed reading of school children. His austerity,
his "morality of production," is emphasized. Aschenbach has clearly erected a
structure of external dignity in keeping with the sobriety, the earnestness,
which he has brought to the business of writing. But he is now undergoing a
period of enervation. He finds that he cannot tackle his page with the necessary zest. As a purely therapeutic measure, he permits himself a trip to Venice,
and here becomes fascinated by a young Polish boy, Tadzio, who is living at

the same hotel. In his shy and troubled contemplation of this boy he finds an absorption which is painful, but imperious. Von Aschenbach remains outwardly the man of dignity honored by his nation—he does not, as I recall, ever exchange a word with this Tadzio, whose freshness, liquidity, immaturity, are the sinister counterpart of the desiccation of Aschenbach's declining years. But inwardly he is *notwendig liederlich und Abenteurer des Gefühls.* Necessarily dissolute—an adventurer of the emotions—the words are Mann's, when discussing this book in his *Betrachtungen eines Unpolitischen* years afterwards. We thus find again the notion that the artist faces *by profession* alternatives which are contrary to society. The theme of Aschenbach's gloomy infatuation coexists with the theme of the plague—and we observe the elderly man's erotic fevers metamorphose gradually into the fevers of incipient cholera. A poignant and inventive passage describing his cosmetic treatment at the hands of a barber is followed by Aschenbach's delirious remembrance of lines from the *Phaedrus,* wherein Socrates is speaking words of courtship and metaphysics indiscriminately, a merging which Aschenbach makes more pronounced by his own diseased reworking of the Platonic dialogue. A few pages later "a respectably shocked world" receives the news of his death.

The same themes, sickness and sexual vagary, underlie Gide's *The Immoralist.* Michel, after being at the verge of death and being nursed by his bride into vigorous health, subtly drives her to her own grave. Throughout the novel he is profuse in his tenderness, he is almost hysterically attentive to her, but at the same time he is steadily destroying her—and during the final march of her illness he takes her on that savage pilgrimage from city to city which inevitably results in her death. There has been a young Arab on the fringes of this plot, an insolent fellow who first charmed Michel by stealing from his wife. The reader places him unmistakably as a motive in this unpunishable murder. Despite the parallelism between *Death in Venice* and *The Immoralist,* the emphasis is very different. Whereas in Mann we feel most the sense of resistance, of resignation to the point of distress, and Aschenbach's dissolution is matched by a constant straining after self-discipline, in Gide we hear a narrator who relates with more than pride, with something akin to positive advocacy, the unclean details of his life. *"Je vais vous parler longuement de mon corps,"* he opens one chapter in a tone which I sometimes regret he has seen fit to drop from his later work; there is no mistaking its connotations; it is the accent of evangelism, of pleading.

Buddenbrooks and *Lafcadio's Adventure* do not fall in corresponding stages of their author's developments. *Buddenbrooks,* a remarkably comprehensive realistic novel of life in North Germany, comes much earlier. But the same contrast in attitude is apparent. We might interpret *Buddenbrooks* as having the theme of "Tonio Kröger" greatly subtilized and ramified. This "fall of a family" through four generations is also the "growth of an artist" through four generations. What is lost in health and moral certitude is gained in questioning and conscientiousness, in social and esthetic sensitiveness, until we arrive at little Hanno the musician, who, like Aschenbach, finally mingles inspiration with disease, as we watch his improvisations become the first symptoms of the typhoid fever that is to result in his death. In *Lafcadio's Adventure*, however, we meet with a brilliant type of villainy, an "esthetic criminal" who commits crimes for pure love of the art. The character of Lafcadio is perhaps Gide's most remarkable discovery. It suggests a merging of Stendhal's Julien Sorel with those criminals of Dostoevsky whose transgressions are inexplicable from the standpoint of utilitarian purpose.

In *Lafcadio's Adventure* Gide makes a notable change in nomenclature, recasting his "corruption" in more characteristically contemporary molds of thought. The transgressions have become "secular," advancing from sin to crime. If theology remains, it is relegated to a more superficial function; it becomes background, the story being built about a swindle whereby certain picturesque crooks fleece Catholic pietists. Lafcadio, who remembers five uncles but no father, has placed villainy on a distinguished and difficult plane. The author endows him with accomplishments somewhat lavishly, perhaps even a bit credulously; he seems eager that our sympathies be with this experimenter in crime, who can look upon kindly and vicious acts as almost interchangeable:

The old woman with the little white cloud above her head, who pointed to it and said: "It won't rain today!" that poor shrivelled old woman whose sack I carried on my shoulders (he had followed his fancy of travelling on foot for four days across the Apennines, between Bologna and Florence, and had slept a night at Covigliajo) and whom I kissed when we got to the top of the hill . . . one of what the *curé* of Covigliajo would have called my "good actions." I could just as easily have throttled her—my hand would have been as steady—when I felt her dirty wrinkled skin beneath my fingers . . . Ah! how caressingly she stroked and dusted my coat collar and said "*figlio mio! carino!*" . . . I wonder what made my joy so intense when afterwards—I was still in a sweat—I lay down on the moss— not smoking though—in the shade of that big chestnut-tree. I felt as though I could have clasped the whole of mankind to my heart in my single embrace—or strangled it, for that matter.

We shall not reconstruct here that gratuitous murder which recommends the hero particularly to our attention when poor Fleurissoire, attracted by this pleasant-seeming lad, chooses to seat himself in the same compartment with him and unknowingly excites Lafcadio to homicidal criticism. Gide exacts a very complex reception on the part of the reader. He asks us to observe a moral outrage committed by a charming scoundrel to whose well-being we are considerably pledged. Fleurissoire is the butt of much injustice in this book but it is Lafcadio, insolent, despotic, with his mercurial slogan "what would happen if . . ." who earns our suffrage.

The war ends, the mythical post-war period begins, and Thomas Mann issues *The Magic Mountain*, Gide *The Counterfeiters*. Our contrast is by no means imperiled. Mann shows how for seven years, during his illness in the mountains, Hans Castorp has lain exposed to moral questionings. While each day observing his temperature and eating five enormous meals to combat the wastage of his phthisis, he is privileged to hear the grave problems of our culture aired by sparring critics, themselves diseased, who speak with much rhetorical and dialectic finish. In particular, a humanist and a Jesuit altercate for his benefit, until Mynheer Peeperkorn enters (a much grander version of Herr Klöterjahn in the story "Tristan") and routs them both by his inarticulate vitality. He is life, himself ailing, to be sure, but magnificent and overwhelming while he lasts—and Castorp's melancholy respect for him is, in a matured and complex form, Tonio Kröger's respect for the burghers whom he watched with aloof humility. Castorp has the attitude of a student. Under ordinary circumstances he would probably have been unthinking, but he is made sensitive by his illness and his seven years' elevation above the century. He amasses greater understanding chapter by chapter, or at least learns to play one statement against another—until once more we come to that bewildered fever which marks the close of both *Buddenbrooks* and *Death in Venice*. At the last, as we see him on the battlefield, advancing to the aimless business of slaughter, simplified, regimented, unquestioning, we comprehend his evasion. For years he has been uncertain—he now embraces the arbitrary certainty of war. "Moralism, pessimism, humor"—these three qualities, whose interrelation Mann himself has stressed, are the dominant traits of this momentous novel, a summarization book, a comprehensive and symbolic work to be included in the world's literature of last wills and testaments.

To turn from *The Magic Mountain* to *The Counterfeiters* is to turn from brooding to shrewdness. Cruelty, malice, sensuality, intrigue—such elements are assiduously welded into an entertaining volume, of much subtle literary satisfaction. The reader of *The Magic Mountain* may have to deal with the fruits of complexity on the part of the author, but he receives them simply. The reader of *The Counterfeiters* finds complexity unresolved—he is not even at liberty to differentiate between the absurd and the beautiful. He is left fluctuant, in great tenuousness of moral values. The book contains Gide's development from sin to crime, and reaffirms his sympathy with deviations from the average ethical stock.

Returning to Aschenbach, ill at the age of thirty-five in Vienna, we find ourselves with correspondences for the closed and opened hand. It seems that Mann, who himself has situated the mainspring of his work in conscientiousness, is like his protagonist Aschenbach, with the hand contracted. And Gide,

whose works could readily be taken by the immature or the trivial as invitations to the most unscrupulous kinds of living, who masters an air of suave
corruption beyond any possible corrupt act, Gide can be the hand relaxed.
Gewissenhaftigkeit, Einsamkeit—loneliness, the sense of responsibility—are
Mann's words; but as the most distinctive device for Gide, I would quote from
his Journal the triptych: *"nouveauté, vice, art."*

Our primary purpose, however, in establishing this distinction between the
conscientious and the corrupt is to destroy it. One need not read far in the
writings of Gide to discover the strong ethical trait which dominates his thinking. Perhaps no other modern writer has quoted the New Testament so
frequently, or shown such readiness to settle secular issues by formulas drawn
from religion. His critical work on Dostoevsky, with its theological distinction
between the psychology of humility and the psychology of humiliation, is
throughout an exercise in moral sensitiveness. And his Lafcadio is a mass of
categorical imperatives. We learn from entries in his diary how, with the
athleticism of an anchorite, he plunges a knife into his side for penance, one
thrust "for having beaten Protos at chess," another thrust "for having answered before Protos," four thrusts "for having cried at hearing of Faby's
death." Faby was one of his "uncles." Protos was his master in adventure, his
accomplished rival, and Lafcadio punished himself, it seems, for not having
been disdainful enough to let Protos win. Lafcadio's lamentable conduct
might even be derived from an excess of scruples, though these scruples are
peculiar to himself.

"I began to feel," Gide has written on this subject in his autobiography, *Si
le Grain ne meurt,* "that perhaps all men's obligations were not the same, and
that God himself might well abhor the uniformity which nature protests but
towards which the Christian ideal seems to lead us in aiming to bring nature
under control. I could concede none but an individual morality, its imperatives
sometimes in conflict with those of other moralities. I was persuaded that each
person, or at least each one of the elect, had to play a rôle on earth, which was
wholly his own and did not resemble any other. And every attempt to submit
to a general rule became treason in my eyes, yes, treason which I likened to
that great unpardonable sin against the Holy Ghost, since the individual lost
his precise, irreplaceable significance, his 'savor.'"

We should also consider Gide's *Strait is the Gate,* which constructs a sympathetic idyll out of the perverse rigors of chastity. As Alissa is courted by
Jerome, the two progress into a difficult relationship, obscuring their sensual
attraction in a state of pietistic exaltation. Jerome seeks her patiently and un-
erringly—and with the vocabulary of nobility she beckons to him while continually delaying the time of their union. At first she can offer logical pretexts for this delay, but as they are one by one removed she retreats behind

the subterfuges of her faith, and with the assistance of Biblical quotations, morbidly chosen, she remains to the end difficult, pure, intact, a treasure, while loving Jerome with hysterical effusiveness. From the standpoint of its genesis the book is doubtless a companion piece to *The Immoralist*. Both are perverse studies in the frustration of heterosexual union, the one with the connotations of corruption, the other with connotations of great conscientiousness. When bringing them together, we see that Alissa's moral sensitiveness was no greater than that of Michel. Similarly we should recall in *The Counterfeiters* the brutal letter which the bastard Bernard Profitendieu writes to his nominal father, a dutifully vicious letter, and the first step, we might say, in the growth of Bernard's affection.

Has not Mann, on the other hand, spoken with fervor of a "sympathy with the abyss," an admitting of the morally chaotic, which he considers not merely the prerogative, but the duty, of the artist? Aschenbach is committed to conflict: whatever policy he decides upon for his conduct, he must continue to entertain disintegrating factors in contemplation. That practical "virtuous" procedure which silences the contrary is not allowed him. He must contain dissolution. In "the repellent, the diseased, the degenerate," Mann situates the ethical. Distinguishing between the moral and the virtuous, he finds that the moralist is "exposed to danger" and "resists no evil." As essential components of art he names "the forbidden, the adventurous, scrutiny, and self-abandonment." Defining sin as doubt, he pleads for sinfulness. His work might be called an epistemology of dignity, for he never relinquishes the love of dignity, and never ceases to make the possession of it difficult.

Mann has defined the problematical as the proper sphere of art ("art is the problematical sphere of the human"). In any event, the problematical is the sphere of his own art. Implicit in his work there is a cult of conflict, a deliberate entertaining of moral vacillation, which could not permit a rigid standard of judgments. He has said that the artist must contain his critic, must recognize the validity of contraries. This attitude could make such simple certainty as moral indignation impossible. It would imply exposure to mutually exclusive codes of conduct, diverse modes of behavior. Esthetically, as he himself has said, he finds the unification of this attitude in irony, which merges the sympathetic and antipathetic aspects of any subject. Unlike the satirist, the standpoint of the ironist is shifting—he cannot maintain a steady attack—by the standards of military morale he is treacherous; he belittles the things he lives for, and with melancholy praises what he abandons. He is equally tentative towards *Leben*, life, nature, and *Geist*, spirit, the intellectual order erected above life. The vigor of the pamphleteer is denied him. To the Rooseveltian mind he is corrosive—wherefore that "sympathy with the abyss" which anyone of rigid criteria, of sure distinctions between the admirable and the reprehensible, must feel as corrupting, and which Mann himself, approaching from the attitude of alien criticism, chose to designate as "dissolute." The ironist is essentially impure, even in the chemical sense of purity, since he is divided. He must deprecate his own enthusiasms, and distrust his own resentments. He will unite waveringly, as the components of his attitude, "dignity, repugnance, the problematical art."

To the slogan-minded, the ralliers about a flag, the marchers who convert a simple idea into a simple action, he is an "outsider." Yet he must observe them with nostalgia, he must feel a kind of awe for their fertile assurance, even while remaining on the alert to stifle it with irony each time he discovers it growing in unsuspected quarters within himself. It will continue to rise anew, for man has a tremendous fund of certainty—and one will find only too little of Mann's best ironic manner in his essays written during the war, or will find it without its counterpart of melancholy. Yet I grant that the slogans of his opponents were enough to infuriate any subtle man in his position; the temporary disorientation which turned him away from the ironist and towards the pamphleteer is readily understandable. In *The Magic Mountain,* however, the author has recovered from his citizenship to become again the artist. Castorp descends, not to a specific European war, but to regimentation, to the relief, even the suicidal relief, of the slogan-minded. He, the hero, represents the ultimate betrayal of his author's own most serious message. After years of vacillation he seeks the evasion of a monastery, though in these secular days, when the power of theology has dwindled, the dogmatic certainties for which people are burned will more often be those of patriotism, and the equivalent of churchly penance becomes the advance in numbers under arms.

What Mann does with irony, Gide parallels with experimentalism, with curiosity. He views any set code of values with distrust, because it implies the exclusion of other codes. He speculates as to "what would happen if . . ." He is on guard lest the possible be obscured by the real. In his autobiography we find him, characteristically, considering a whole civilization gratuitously different from our own:

"I thought of writing the imaginary history of a people, a nation, with wars, revolutions, changes of administration, typical happenings. . . . I wanted to invent heroes, sovereigns, statesmen, artists, an artistic tradition, an apocryphal literature, explaining and criticising movements, recounting the evolution of forms, quoting fragments of masterpieces. . . . And all to what purpose? To prove that the history of man could have been different—our habits, morals, customs, tastes, judgments, standards of beauty could have all been different—and yet the humanity of mankind would remain the same."

By recalling *Gulliver's Travels,* we see again how far removed we are from satire. Perhaps, in a much simpler and more lyrical form, Gide did write this book. I refer to *La Symphonie pastorale,* where he speculates upon a world foreign to him, an arbitrary world so far as this author is concerned, the world of blindness. He even contrives to forget his own knowledge, as when his blind heroine, trying to meditate her way into the world of sight, surmises that sunlight must be like the humming of a kettle.

Perhaps one may interpret Gide's "corruption" too literally. I do not believe that his work can be evaluated properly unless we go beyond the subject-matter to the underlying principles. His choice of material even implies a certain obscurantism, assuming a sophistication on the part of the reader whereby the reader would not attempt too slavishly to become the acting disciple of his author's speculations. Surely Gide would be the first to admit that we could not build a very convenient society out of Lafcadios, however admirable they are. I should take the specific events in Gide as hardly more than symbols: their parallel in life would not be the enacting of similar events, but the exercising of the complex state of mind which arises from the contemplation of such events with sympathy. To live a life like the life in Gide's books would be to commit under another form the very kind of exclusion which he abhors—Lafcadio is for the pious, he is not for poisoners and forgers. Nor must one, in placing this author's malice, forget his *Travels in the Congo*, with its protests against the systematic injustice meted out to the Negroes at the hands of the concessionaires.[1]

Irony, novelty, experimentalism, vacillation, the cult of conflict—are not these men trying to make us at home in indecision, are they not trying to humanize the state of doubt? A philosopher has recently written of this new wilderness we now face, a wilderness not of nature, but of social forces. Perhaps there is an evasion, a shirking of responsibility, in becoming certain too quickly, particularly when our certainties involve reversions to an ideology which has the deceptive allurement of tradition. To seek the backing of the past may be as cowardly as to seek the backing of the many, and as flattering to our more trivial needs of conformity. Need people be in haste to rebel against the state of doubt, when doubt has not yet permeated the organs of our body, the processes of our metabolism, the desire for food and companionship, the gratification with sun and water? There is a large reserve of physical unquestioning, and until we find this reserve itself endangered by the humiliation of tentative living and unauthoritative thinking, are we compelled to reach out impetuously for set criteria? Since the body is dogmatic, a generator

[1] It is doubtful, I grant, whether Gide arrived at his useful position through wholly untrammelled motives. The Olympian result shows traces of troubled, Orphic beginnings. It seems likely that his concern with homosexuality, and his struggle for its "recognition," early gave him a sense of divergence from the social norms among which he lived, and in time this sense of divergence was trained upon other issues. In seeking, let us say, to defend a practice which society generally considered reprehensible, he came to defend practices which society considered more reprehensible—as a child who resented a cruel father might end by slaying the king.

of belief, society might well be benefited by the corrective of a disintegrating art, which converts each simplicity into a complexity, which ruins the possibility of ready hierarchies, which concerns itself with the problematical, the experimental, and thus by implication works corrosively upon those expansionistic certainties preparing the way for our social cataclysms. An art may be of value purely through preventing a society from becoming too assertively, too hopelessly, itself.

From *Counter-Statement* by Kenneth Burke, pp. 116–135. Harcourt, Brace and Company, Inc. Copyright, 1931. Reprinted by permission of Harcourt, Brace and Company, Inc. First published in *The Bookman,* Vol. LXXI (June, 1930), pp. 257–264.

W. H. AUDEN
Makers of Modern Poetry

A KNIGHT OF THE INFINITE
(*Gerard Manley Hopkins*)
[1944]

BIOGRAPHIES of the great masters are unnecessary. Living in humdrum domestic bliss with their gifts, their huge families are their whole story. Resembling each other more than they resemble anyone else, their lives seem too atypical to illuminate either their age or the human heart. The artists whom we want to know personally, and Hopkins is one, are those whose relation to their art is romantically difficult, full of rows, infidelities, miscarriages, strain, and Miss Ruggles deserves our thanks for a neat, competent job.[1] Both as an eccentric poet and as a Jesuit, Hopkins invites an all-or-none response, but she manages remarkably well to keep her balance. Apart from a few careless phrases out of the Poetry Appreciation Class, e.g., "the stanzas seem to rock and rend themselves in a long ecstatic intolerable shudder, an all but physical movement," her comments on his poems are sensible and suggestive, and in her treatment of his faith, she has so far succeeded in concealing her own beliefs that this reader may be quite wrong in suspecting that she finds Jowett more congenial than Pusey.

There are two eternal classes of men, the Knight and the Bourgeois, Don Quixote and Sancho Panza, Holmes and Watson, Pascal and Montaigne, the man who is capable of excess, and the man who is not. Each needs the other: the Knight needs the Bourgeois to nurse him and laugh at him, the Bourgeois needs the Knight as a subject for absolute devotion. Alone, since the former can never remember the finite and the latter can never perceive the infinite, each becomes a killer, the Knight by violence because he begins to despise life, the Bourgeois by sneers because he begins to fear death.

The pure types, the ideal comradeship, are, of course, to be found only in books, but in fuzzy, faint forms they occur quite often in real life, and the friendship of Hopkins and Bridges is one example.

[1] *Gerard Manley Hopkins: A Life*, by Eleanor Ruggles. New York: W. W. Norton & Company, 1944.

Bridges was a poet and if it has always been difficult for a poet not to think of himself as a Knight—since the Romantic movement it has become almost impossible—how could a refined esthete, educated at Eton and Oxford, be, nevertheless, a Sancho Panza? Bridges' devotion, therefore, to a man whose heroic rejection of the esthetic he could not understand, his preservation and publication of greater poems than his own which it lay completely in his power to suppress, is extraordinary and enormously to his credit. Hopkins' other friend, Dixon, was a minor Knight, so that their relationship is less surprising but more touching. "Can I do anything? I have said something of the institution of your society in my next volume of Church history, which is not yet published. I could very well give an abrupt footnote about your poems, if you thought good. You may think it odd for me to propose to introduce you into the year 1540, but I know how to do it." The lance is only an umbrella, but the voice is Don Quixote's.

The affectionate exasperation of the Bourgeois is one form in which the Knight finds the necessary corrective for his excess; another is the impersonal discipline of an order, military or monastic, and among such, the most uncompromising is the Society of Jesus. It is unequivocally Catholic, yet prefers as recruits those who by nature are protestant, not conformist; hence its double insistence that the will shall be surrendered, but that the surrender shall be a free choice. It demands the monastic virtues of chastity and poverty, and then demands as well the military virtues of an active life in the world; hence its exercises in the *use* of images, in contrast to the conventional contemplative training in their rejection.

Compared with his fellow-novice Kerr, a cheerful old bruiser and Crimean veteran, Hopkins, unbusinesslike, rather sissy, must have seemed to his superiors unpromising material, and very probably they shook their heads over him to the end. It cannot, after all, have been easy for the officials of an order founded to preach and teach, to be enthusiastic over one who from the pulpit compared the seven sacraments of Mother Church to the seven teats of a milch-cow, and in the classroom, "from a quixotic sense of justice towards members who failed to attend, refused to allow his examination questions to refer to his lectures, so that students only came to find out what would not be set."

What the Society of Jesus did for Hopkins is clearer: it did not make him happy—only Wales could do that—it prevented him from writing much and from finishing even the little he did get written, but it turned an esthete, no better or worse than half a dozen bright young men of the sixties and seventies, into a serious and unique artist.

In the child who wailed when shut up with his sick brother, "Cyril has become so ugly," one hears the voice of Wilde; in the undergraduate's journal, "She had made a call, she had met the Miss Finlayson, she had

done some shopping, she had been round half the place and seen the naked-
ness of the land, and now it struck her how hateful was Clapham. Especially
she abominated the Berlin woolshop," the voice of Firbank; and there are
lines in his weaker poems like "The Bugler's First Communion," which show
how constantly he had to struggle against that confusion of the religious
with the erotic to which Whitman succumbed. Again, there was in Hopkins,
as in most people whose senses are abnormally acute, an impulse towards
their *dérèglement*. To a skinny boy who, to compare his endurance with a
shipwrecked sailor's can go without water for a week (some say three), the
road that Masoch and Sade took is always open. It is precisely to such natures
that Loyola's exercises are designed to give meaning and purpose, and "The
Wreck of the Deutschland" is Hopkins' witness to their success.

Miss Ruggles points out how directly much of that poem derives from his
experiences as a novice in his Long Retreat. The objective wreck of the ship
is counterpointed with the subjective breaking of the self-loving will. (Someone could make a comparative study of "The Deutschland" with other poems
dealing with disastrous sea-trips, like "Un Voyage à Cythère," or "Le Voyage"
of Baudelaire, and with the death of the self, like Rimbaud's *Une Saison en
Enfer*.)

Miss Ruggles also draws attention to the intellectual support that the neglected philosophy of Duns Scotus gave to Hopkins' feeling for esthetic
uniqueness. Here, as in so much else, Hopkins was ahead of fashion, and
translators from the German *Existenz* school might, for instance, find a worse
equivalent than *inscape* for that stumper *Dasein*.

He didn't matter: he had a silly face; he was a martyr to piles; he bored
his congregations and was a joke to his students; he fiddled around with
Egyptian and with Welsh and with Gregorian music; he wrote a few poems
which his best friends couldn't understand and which would never be published; after forty-four years he died. Yes, like Don Quixote. His poems gloss
over none of the suffering and defeat, yet when we read them, as when we
read Cervantes, the final note is not the groan of a spiritual Tobacco Road,
but the cry of gratitude which Hopkins once heard a cricketer give for a
good stroke, "Arrah, sweet myself!"

From *The New Republic*, Vol. CXI (August 21,
1944), pp. 223-224. Reprinted by permission
of the author and editors.

HERETICS

(Rimbaud and Lawrence)

[1939]

A COMPARISON of these two books proves very clearly the impossibility of writing about someone you dislike.[1] Miss Starkie is just as critical of her subject as Mr. Tindall is of his—she whitewashes nothing—but she loves Rimbaud and he does not love Lawrence. Pascal regarded Montaigne as an enemy, but he recognized his greatness; whereas when one has finished reading Mr. Tindall, one feels: "If that is all that Lawrence was, why bother to write a whole book about him?"

It is not that Mr. Tindall's remarks are unjust or untrue; they are acute as far as they go, but nowhere does he give any sign of recognizing that Lawrence was not only, like thousands of others, a neurotic, but also a uniquely gifted writer who owes his influence for good or evil to his gift. It is significant that Mr. Tindall concentrates on the novels and philosophical works, pays a grudging tribute to the travel books but does not discuss them, and ignores completely the poems and short stories, which are Lawrence's best work. Lawrence thought of himself primarily as a poet, and said that he wrote the novels mainly for money. One may reasonably argue that, gifted or not, he was a heretic whose pernicious influence must be destroyed, but any study of heresy requires a definition of orthodoxy, and on that subject Mr. Tindall is reticent; the most that emerges is a sort of nineteenth-century liberal rationalism, which is by now a very vulnerable position.

Miss Starkie's interest in Rimbaud as a poet makes such a statement on her part less necessary, but as a matter of fact it emerges far more clearly. Her general thesis, though elaborated with all the detailed scholarship which her study of Baudelaire has led one to expect from her, is simple: Rimbaud conceived of the poet as a pure *voyant*, and of poetry as a mystical exercise through which he could become God. When he realized that, however far one may push the disorganization of the senses, the self cannot be eliminated from the creative act, he abandoned writing and attempted self-annihilation by leading what he imagined to be the "ordinary" life, but his idea of this was as extravagant as his previous overvaluation of poetry. Miss Starkie brings out very clearly the pathetic inefficiency of his later years; as a man of action he was a self-tortured failure, for no one can live by will alone.

Mr. Tindall sees Lawrence as a romantic irrationalist intent on the founding of a private religion, and condemns him for not separating his art from his

[1] *Arthur Rimbaud*, by Enid Starkie. New York: W. W. Norton & Company, 1939, and *D. H. Lawrence and Susan His Cow*, by William York Tindall. New York: Columbia University Press, 1939.

beliefs. If we must have religion, he would rather it were kept in church where it can do no harm. I do not believe such a separation is possible. Lawrence's beliefs were certainly heretical, but so were the beliefs of the mechanistic science from which they were a reaction. Lawrence is artistically successful where they fail, and vice versa. No writer has been more illuminating about birds, beasts and flowers; few have been sillier about those areas of human life where conscious planning is necessary.

At any moment in history there always is an orthodoxy, i.e., the sum of human knowledge forms an interdependent whole, but today the specialization of function inseparable from an industrialized society makes its conscious formulation extremely difficult. One method of approach is through a study of eccentric deviations, of their differences and resemblances: to such an approach Mr. Tindall will be useful but Miss Starkie indispensable.

Rimbaud and Lawrence have much in common. Both their mothers married beneath them, both had mother-fixations, both combined a personal messianic arrogance with attacking Christian individualism, both were attracted by Eastern mysticism and primitive peoples, both were inveterate wanderers. But there are significant differences. Rimbaud was born a Catholic in an anti-clerical country at a time when dogmatic scientific materialism was still unchallenged; Lawrence was born a non-conformist, and, by the time he reached maturity, science had abandoned all claim to give an objective picture of reality. While Rimbaud went from extreme individualism, a belief in poetry and a mystic technique, to an extreme collectivism and a belief in engineering and textbooks, from the Cabala to Comte, Lawrence changed essentially little during his life. To understand either, one must see them as sensitive individuals in an atomized industrial society, seeking an orthodoxy, a universally valid faith. Their protest against the atomization is linked to a belief that science was responsible.

When the Catholic world picture was replaced by the Protestant, science took over the public worlds of neutral matter, and art and religion the individual private worlds of value and emotion. However much they might grumble, the early romantics were really content enough; they had their worlds to themselves. But by Rimbaud's time both worlds were already over-populated and demanding *Lebensraum*. Science, biology in particular, was invading art and religion, and the rhetorical romanticism of de Musset was no longer possible. Poetry was being pushed closer and closer toward the dark corner of the unconscious where, since expression is a conscious activity, it would be impossible to write. Unless an *Anschluss* of the two worlds took place which would enable men to "enjoy truth in one body and soul," art must perish. Rimbaud saw this and gave up art for activism; Verlaine did not, and I think that this was the basic reason which made their marriage impossible.

But just when its complete victory seemed assured, science voluntarily re-treated. Hitherto it had confidently affirmed that its truth was objectively real and independent of all considerations of human value and feeling. Now it came more and more to regard its statements not as eternal truths but as "as if" conveniences for organizing its experience. In his extremely important Harvard lectures, recently published under the title, *The Place of Value in a World of Fact,* Professor Köhler has a dream encounter with a modern physicist:

"What is an electron?" he asks.

"A volume of space that resists the approach of more electrons and attracts protons."

"What is a proton?"

"A volume of space that resists the approach of more protons and attracts electrons."

"But what is in these volumes?"

"I could not tell you. Nobody knows."

This is worse than Henry James dialogue. And on every part the attack on objectivity has been carried on, by the Marxists, by the psychoanalysts, by the anthropologists.

Encouraged by this, the poets recovered their nerve. In a curious way the relative positions of poetry and science became reversed; now it was the scientists who showed the caution and self-criticism of Mathew Arnold, while the poets displayed all the dogmatic self-confidence, the *concupiscence d'esprit* of T. H. Huxley. Lawrence, striking his solar plexus as someone tried to explain to him the Copernican theory, and crying, "But I don't feel it here," is typical of the new attitude. So is modern political propaganda. Works like *A Fantasia of the Unconscious* or Yeats's *A Vision* are not humble attempts at private myths, but are designed as the new and only science. Seeing the abuses of our civilization and ascribing them, quite wrongly, to science, they imagine at the same time that science has rejected itself and given its blessing to a nihilistic subjectivism. This is untrue. Modern science is becoming more and more isomorphic: it sees the subject-object relation as an indissoluble unity. If the nature of the subject determines its perception of the object, the nature of the subject is equally determined by the existence of the object. The formulation of truth can never be absolute, but neither is truth nonexistent nor anything we like to make it.

In his essays on Wagner and Freud, Thomas Mann points out that a backward looking toward the night, the folk-soul, death, can be not only reactionary but also an indispensable preparation for a new step forward. The effect of this attraction depends upon whether or not it is harnessed to a will to serve enlightenment. Artists are always vulnerable to reaction because, unlike science, art has no objective practical end to control its excesses.

The only corrective for the artist lies within himself, not in his gift, which is neutral to reaction or progress, but in his self-knowledge of his weaknesses and the abdication of the desire to avenge them. Goethe was the last individual to attempt to formulate an orthodoxy, to effect a synthesis of human knowledge. Today such a thing is impossible: it is idle to suppose that the dialects of the various specialists will ever coalesce into a common tongue, but we shall not despair if we realize that they are all only different angles of approach to the same single field, and that among these techniques art has a responsible and not unimportant place.

From *The New Republic*, Vol. C (November 1, 1939), pp. 373–374. Reprinted by permission of the author and editors.

THE POET OF THE ENCIRCLEMENT

(Rudyard Kipling)

[1943]

ART, as the late Professor R. G. Collingwood pointed out, is not Magic, i.e., a means by which the artist communicates or arouses his feelings in others, but a mirror in which they may become conscious of what their own feelings really are: its proper effect, in fact, is disenchanting.

By significant details it shows us that our present state is neither as virtuous nor as secure as we thought, and by the lucid pattern into which it unifies these details, its assertion that order is *possible*, it faces us with the command to make it *actual*. In so far as he is an artist, no one, not even Kipling,[1] is intentionally a magician. On the other hand, no artist, not even Eliot, can prevent his work being used as magic, for that is what all of us, highbrow and lowbrow alike, secretly want Art to be. Between the schoolmaster who quoted "If," and the undergraduate who quoted "The Waste Land," there was not so much difference. Had the former really read his poem, he would have had to say, "Yes, *if*. Unfortunately, I do not keep my head . . . etc. I realize now that I am not a man." Instead, of course, he said, "Admirably put. That's exactly what the boys need to realize." Similarly, had the undergraduate really read his poem, he would have had to say: "Now I realize I am not the clever young man I thought, but a senile hermaphrodite. Either I must recover or put my head in the gas-stove." Instead, of course, he said, "That's wonderful. If only they would read this, Mother would understand why I

[1] *A Choice of Kipling's Verse.* Made by T. S. Eliot with an Essay on Rudyard Kipling. New York: Charles Scribner's Sons, 1943.

can't stay home nights, and Father would understand why I can't hold a job."

If today the war makes people discover that Kipling is good, it will be an excellent thing, but if at the same time they start saying that Eliot is "defeatist," it will prove that they have not discovered a poet, but only changed their drug to suit the new climate.

In his essay, Mr. Eliot draws a distinction between poetry and verse:

> For other poets—at least, for some other poets—the poem may begin to shape itself in fragments of musical rhythm, and its structure will first appear in terms of something analogous to musical form. . . . What fundamentally distinguishes his (Kipling's) "verse" from "poetry" is the subordination of musical interest. . . . There is a harmonics of poetry which is not merely beyond the range of the poems —it would interfere with the intention.

This distinction is real and neatly describes the difference between the kind of poetry written by Eliot and the kind written by Kipling, but, so defined, there are more verse or ballad writers and fewer poets, I think, than Mr. Eliot seems to imply. Ben Jonson, for instance, who wrote out a prose draft which he then versified, Dunbar, Butler's *Hudibras*, most of Burns, Byron's *Don Juan*, etc.

I mention this only because I agree with Mr. Eliot that Kipling is an odd fish, but doubt if his capacity to write great verse is a sign of this.

What is it then, that makes Kipling so extraordinary? Is it not that while virtually every other European writer since the fall of the Roman empire has felt that the dangers threatening civilization came from *inside* that civilization (or from inside the individual consciousness), Kipling is obsessed by a sense of dangers threatening from *outside*?

Others have been concerned with the corruptions of the big city, the *ennui* of the cultured mind; some sought a remedy in a return to Nature, to childhood, to Classical Antiquity; others looked forward to a brighter future of liberty, equality and fraternity: they called on the powers of the subconscious, or prayed for the grace of God to inrupt and save their souls; they called on the oppressed to arise and save the world. In Kipling there is none of this, no nostalgia for a Golden Age, no belief in Progress. For him civilization (and consciousness) is a little citadel of light surrounded by a great darkness full of malignant forces and only maintained through the centuries by everlasting vigilance, will-power and self-sacrifice. The philosophers of the Enlightenment shared his civilization-barbarism antithesis, but their weapon was reason, i.e., coming to consciousness, whereas for Kipling too much thinking is highly dangerous, an opening of the gates to the barbarians of melancholia and doubt. For him the gates are guarded by the conscious Will (not unlike the Inner Check of Irving Babbitt).

Poem after poem, under different symbolic disguises, presents this same situation of the danger without, the anxiety of encirclement—by inanimate forces, the Picts beyond the Roman Wall:

> No indeed! We are not strong
> But we know Peoples that are.
> Yes, and we'll guide them along
> To smash and destroy you in War.
> We shall be slaves just the same,
> Yes, we have always been slaves,
> But you—you will die of the shame,
> And then we shall dance on your graves.

The Danes, the Dutch, the Huns, the "new-caught sullen peoples, half devil and half child," even the Female of the Species—by inanimate forces, Karela, the club-footed vine, the sea:

> Coming, like stallions they paw with their hooves,
> going, they snatch with their teeth,

the ice

> Once and again as the Ice came South
> The glaciers ground over Lossiemouth

and by Spiritual Powers:

> They builded a tower to shiver the sky and wrench
> the stars apart,
> Till the Devil grunted behind the bricks: "It's
> striking, but is it Art?"

> Very softly down the glade runs a waiting watching shade
> And the whisper spreads and widens far and near,
> And the sweat is on thy brow, for he passes even now—
> He is Fear, O little Hunter, he is Fear.

It is noteworthy that the *interested* spirits are all demonic; the Divine Law is aloof.

Given such a situation, the important figure in society is, of course, the man on guard, and it is he who, in one form or another, from the sentry on the Afghanistan frontier to the gardener

> Grubbing weeds from gravel paths with broken dinner knives

is the Kipling hero. Unlike the epic hero, he is always on the *defensive*. Thus Kipling is interested in engineering, in the weapons which protect man against the chaotic violence of nature, but not in physics, in the intellectual *discovery* that made the weapons possible.

His ethics and his politics are those of a critical emergency, which is why it is impossible to classify them under conventional party labels, for they presuppose a state where differences of opinion are as irrelevant as they are to a soldier in a foxhole, and, in so far as they apply at all, apply to everyone, Democrat, Nazi or Communist.

Of the guardians, Kipling has profound understanding. He knows that most of them are prodigal sons, given to drink and fornication, acquainted with post-dated checks, now cruel, now sentimental, and he does not try to present them as nice people. But when he turns from them to the Sons of Mary whom they are paid to guard (the shift from religious to social meaning is significant), his vision becomes dim and his touch uncertain, for his interest is not really in them, but only in their relation to the sons of Martha, so that what he sees is either too soft, the exile's nostalgic daydream of Mom and the roses round the door, or too hard, the sentry's resentful nightmare of the sleek and slack stay-at-homes dining and wining while he and his sufferings are forgotten.

Kipling has been rightly praised for his historical imagination, but it is questionable if historical is the right word. If by history we mean *irreversible* temporal changes as contrasted with the cyclical and reversible changes of Nature, then Kipling's imaginative treatment of the past is an affirmation of Nature and a denial of History, for his whole concern is to show that the moment of special emergency is everlasting:

> As it will be in the future, it was at the birth of Man—
> There are only four things certain since Social Progress began.
> That the Dog returns to his Vomit and the Sow returns to her Mire,
> And the Burnt Fool's bandaged finger goes wabbling back to the Fire.

But if Nature and History are the same, how can Nature and Man, the Jungle and the City, be opposed to each other, as Kipling is clearly certain that they are? If one asks him "What is civilization?" he answers, "The People living under the Law, who were taught by their fathers to discipline their natural impulses and will teach their children to do the same":

> This we learned from famous men,
>   Knowing not its uses,
> When they showed, in daily work
> Man must finish off his work—
> Right or wrong his daily work
>   And without excuses

in contrast to the barbarian who is at the mercy of his selfish appetites. But if one asks him "What is this Law and where does it come from?" he refers one back to Nature, to the Darwinian law of the Jungle, "Be Fit," or to the Newtonian law of the Machine:

> We are not built to comprehend a lie
> We can neither love nor pity nor forgive.
> If you make a slip in handling us, you die.

One might almost say that Kipling had to concentrate his attention and ours upon the special emergency in order to avoid the embarrassment of this paradox, for it is precisely when We are threatened by Them that we can naturally think of the ethical relation between Me and You as one of self-sacrifice, and the ethical relation between Us and Them as one of self-interest. It is precisely when civilization is in mortal danger that the immediate necessity to defend it has a right to override the question of just what it is we are defending.

It may not be too fanciful, either, to see in the kind of poetry Kipling wrote, the esthetic corollary of his conception of life. His virtuosity with language is not unlike that of one of his sergeants with an awkward squad:

> Said England unto Pharaoh: "You've had miracles before
>   When Aaron struck your rivers into blood,
> But if you watch the sergeant he can show you something more
>   He's a charm making riflemen from mud."
> It was neither Hindustani, French or Coptics,
>   It was odds and ends and leavings of the same
> Translated by a stick (which is really half the trick)
>   And Pharaoh hearkened to Sergeant Whatsisname.

Under his will, the vulgarest words learn to wash behind their ears and to execute complicated movements at the word of command, but they can hardly be said to learn to think for themselves. His poetry is arid; personally, I prefer this to the damp poetry of self-expression, but both are excesses.

His poems in their quantity, their limitation to one feeling at a time, have the air of brilliant tactical improvisations to overcome sudden unforeseen obstacles, as if, for Kipling, experience were not a seed to cultivate patiently and lovingly, but an unending stream of dangerous feelings to be immediately mastered as they appear.

No doubt his early experiences of India gave him a sense of the danger of Nature which it is hard for a European to realize (though easier perhaps for an American), but these are not sufficient to explain the terror of demons, visible and invisible, which gives his work its peculiar excitement, any more than the English Civil War expresses Hobbes's terror of political disorder. Nor does it matter particularly what the real cause may have been. The "mirror" that Kipling holds out to us is one in which, if we see anything, we see vague, menacing shapes which can be kept away by incessant action but can never be finally overcome:

> Heart may Fail, and Strength outwear, and Purpose turn
>   to Loathing

But the everyday affair of business, meals and clothing
Builds a bulkhead 'twixt Despair and the Edge of Nothing.

I get it as well as you—oo—oo
If I haven't enough to do—oo—oo
We all get hump,
Camelions hump,
Kiddies and grown-ups too.

From *The New Republic,* Vol. CIX (October 25,
1943), pp. 579–581. Reprinted by permission
of the author and editors.

THE PUBLIC VS. THE LATE MR. WILLIAM BUTLER YEATS

[1939]

THE PUBLIC PROSECUTOR:

Gentlemen of the Jury. Let us be quite clear in our minds as to the nature of this case. We are here to judge, not a man, but his work. Upon the character of the deceased, therefore, his affectations of dress and manner, his inordinate personal vanity, traits which caused a fellow countryman and former friend to refer to him as the greatest literary fop in history, I do not intend to dwell. I must only remind you that there is usually a close connection between the personal character of a poet and his work, and that the deceased was no exception.

Again I must draw your attention to the exact nature of the charge. That the deceased had talent is not for a moment in dispute; so much is freely admitted by the prosecution. What the defense are asking you to believe, however, is that he was a great poet, the greatest of this century writing in English. That is their case, and it is that which the prosecution feels bound most emphatically to deny.

A great poet. To deserve such an epithet, a poet is commonly required to convince us of these things: firstly a gift of a very high order for memorable language, secondly a profound understanding of the age in which he lived, and thirdly a working knowledge of and sympathetic attitude towards the most progressive thought of his time.

Did the deceased possess these? I am afraid, gentlemen, that the answer is, no.

On the first point I shall be brief. My learned friend, the counsel for the defense, will, I have no doubt, do his best to convince you that I am wrong. And he has a case, gentlemen. O yes, a very fine case. I shall only ask you to apply to the work of the deceased a very simple test. How many of his lines can you remember?

Further, it is not unreasonable to suppose that a poet who has a gift for language will recognize that gift in others. I have here a copy of an Anthology edited by the deceased entitled *The Oxford Book of Modern Verse*. I challenge anyone in this court to deny that it is the most deplorable volume ever issued under the imprint of that highly respected firm which has done so much for the cause of poetry in this country, The Clarendon Press.

But in any case you and I are educated modern men. Our fathers imagined that poetry existed in some private garden of its own, totally unrelated to the workaday world, and to be judged by pure aesthetic standards alone. We know that now to be an illusion. Let me pass, then, to my second point. Did the deceased understand his age?

What did he admire? What did he condemn? Well, he extolled the virtues of the peasant. Excellent. But should that peasant learn to read and write, should he save enough money to buy a shop, attempt by honest trading to raise himself above the level of the beasts, and O, what a sorry change is there. Now he is the enemy, the hateful huxter whose blood, according to the unseemly boast of the deceased, never flowed through *his* loins. Had the poet chosen to live in a mud cabin in Galway among swine and superstition, we might think him mistaken, but we should admire his integrity. But did he do this? O dear no. For there was another world which seemed to him not only equally admirable, but a deal more agreeable to live in, the world of noble houses, of large drawing rooms inhabited by the rich and the decorative, most of them of the female sex. We do not have to think very hard or very long, before we shall see a connection between these facts. The deceased had the feudal mentality. He was prepared to admire the poor just as long as they remained poor and deferential, accepting without protest the burden of maintaining a little Athenian band of literary landowners, who without their toil could not have existed for five minutes.

For the great struggle of our time to create a juster social order, he felt nothing but the hatred which is born of fear. It is true that he played a certain part in the movement for Irish Independence, but I hardly think my learned friend will draw your attention to that. Of all the modes of self-evasion open to the well-to-do, Nationalism is the easiest and most dishonest. It allows to the unjust all the luxury of righteous indignation against injustice. Still, it has often inspired men and women to acts of heroism and self-sacrifice. For the sake of a free Ireland the poet Pearse and the countess Markiewicz gave their all. But if the deceased did give himself to this movement, he did so with singular moderation. After the rebellion of Easter Sunday 1916, he wrote a poem on the subject which has been called a masterpiece. It is. To succeed at such a time in writing a poem which could offend neither the Irish Republicans nor the British army was indeed a masterly achievement.

And so we come to our third and last point. The most superficial glance at the last fifty years is enough to tell us that the social struggle towards greater equality has been accompanied by a growing intellectual acceptance of the scientific method and the steady conquest of irrational superstition. What was the attitude of the deceased towards this? Gentlemen, words fail me. What are we to say of a man whose earliest writings attempted to revive a belief in fairies and whose favorite themes were legends of barbaric heroes with unpronounceable names, work which has been aptly and wittily described as Chaff about Bran!

But you may say, he was young; youth is always romantic; its silliness is part of its charm. Perhaps it is. Let us forgive the youth, then, and consider the mature man, from whom we have a right to expect wisdom and common sense. Gentlemen, it is hard to be charitable when we find that the deceased, far from outgrowing his folly, has plunged even deeper. In 1900 he believed in fairies; that was bad enough; but in 1930 we are confronted with the pitiful, the deplorable spectacle of a grown man occupied with the mumbo-jumbo of magic and the nonsense of India. Whether he seriously believed such stuff to be true, or merely thought it petty, or imagined it would impress the public, is immaterial. The plain fact remains that he made it the centre of his work. Gentlemen, I need say no more. In the last poem he wrote, the deceased rejected social justice and reason, and prayed for war. Am I mistaken in imagining that somewhat similar sentiments are expressed by a certain foreign political movement which every lover of literature and liberty acknowledges to be the enemy of mankind?

THE COUNSEL FOR THE DEFENSE:

Gentlemen of the Jury. I am sure you have listened with as much enjoyment as I to the eloquence of the prosecution. I say enjoyment because the spectacle of anything well-done, whether it be a feat of engineering, a poem, or even an outburst of impassioned oratory, must always give pleasure.

We have been treated to an analysis of the character of the deceased which for all I know, may be as true as it is destructive. Whether it proves anything about the value of his poetry is another matter. If I may be allowed to quote my learned friend. "We are here to judge, not a man but his work." We have been told that the deceased was conceited, that he was a snob, that he was a physical coward, that his taste in contemporary poetry was uncertain, that he could not understand physics and chemistry. If this is not an invitation to judge the man I do not know what is. Does it not bear an extraordinary resemblance to the belief of an earlier age that a great artist must be chaste? Take away the frills, and the argument of the prosecution is reduced to this:

"A great poet must give the right answers to the problems which perplex his generation. The deceased gave the wrong answers. Therefore the deceased was not a great poet." Poetry in such a view is the filling up of a social quiz; to pass with honours the poet must score not less than 75%. With all due respect to my learned friend, this is nonsense. We are tempted so to judge contemporary poets because we really do have problems which we really do want solved, so that we are inclined to expect everyone, politicians, scientists, poets, clergymen, to give us the answer, and to blame them indiscriminately when they do not. But who reads the poetry of the past in this way? In an age of rising nationalism, Dante looked back with envy to the Roman Empire. Was this socially progressive? Will only a Catholic admit that Dryden's "The Hind and the Panther" is a good poem? Do we condemn Blake because he rejected Newton's theory of light, or rank Wordsworth lower than Baker, because the latter had a deeper appreciation of the steam engine?

Can such a view explain why

> Mock Emmet, Mock Parnell
> All the renown that fell

is good; and bad, such a line as

> Somehow I think that you are rather like a tree

In pointing out that this is absurd, I am not trying to suggest that art exists independently of society. The relation between the two is just as intimate and important as the prosecution asserts.

Every individual is from time to time excited emotionally and intellectually by his social and material environment. In certain individuals this excitement produces verbal structures which we call poems; if such a verbal structure creates an excitement in the reader, we call it a good poem. Poetic talent, in fact, is the power to make personal excitement socially available. Poets, i.e., persons with poetic talent, stop writing good poetry when they stop reacting to the world they live in. The nature of that reaction, whether it be positive or negative, morally admirable or morally disgraceful, matters very little; what is essential is that the reaction should genuinely exist. The later Wordsworth is not inferior to the earlier because the poet had altered his political opinions, but because he had ceased to feel and think so strongly, a change which happens, alas, to most of us as we grow older. Now, when we turn to the deceased, we are confronted by the amazing spectacle of a man of great poetic talent, whose capacity for excitement not only remained with him to the end, but actually increased. In two hundred years when our children have made a different and, I hope, better social order, and when our science has developed out of all recognition, who but a historian will care a button whether the deceased was right about the Irish Question or wrong about the transmigration of souls? But because the excitement out of which his poems arose was genuine, they will still, unless I am very much mistaken, be capable of exciting others, different though their circumstances and beliefs may be from his.

However, since we are not living two hundred years hence, let us play the schoolteacher a moment, and examine the poetry of the deceased with reference to the history of our time.

The most obvious social fact of the last forty years is the failure of liberal capitalist democracy, based on the premises that every individual is born free and equal, each an absolute entity independent of all others. And that a formal political equality, the right to vote, the right to a fair trial, the right of free speech, is enough to guarantee his freedom of action in his relations with his fellow men. The results are only too familiar to us all. By denying the social nature of personality, and by ignoring the social power of money, it has created the most impersonal, the most mechanical and the most un-equal civilization the world has ever seen, a civilization in which the only emotion common to all classes is a feeling of individual isolation from every-one else, a civilization torn apart by the opposing emotions born of economic injustice, the just envy of the poor and the selfish terror of the rich.

If these latter emotions meant little to the deceased, it was partly because Ireland compared with the rest of western Europe was economically backward, and the class struggle was less conscious there. My learned friend has sneered at Irish Nationalism, but he knows as well as I that Nationalism is a neces-sary stage towards socialism. He has sneered at the deceased for not taking arms, as if shooting were the only honorable and useful form of social action. Has the Abbey Theatre done nothing for Ireland?

But to return to the poems. From first to last they express a sustained pro-test against the social atomisation caused by industrialism, and both in their ideas and their language a constant struggle to overcome it. The fairies and heroes of the early work were an attempt to find through folk tradition a binding force for society; and the doctrine of Anima Mundi found in the later poems is the same thing, in a more developed form, which has left purely local peculiarities behind, in favor of something that the deceased hoped was universal; in other words, he was working for a world religion. A purely religious solution may be unworkable, but the search for it is, at least, the result of a true perception of a social evil. Again, the virtues that the deceased praised in the peasantry and aristocracy, and the vices he blamed in the com-mercial classes were real virtues and vices. To create a united and just society where the former are fostered and the latter cured is the task of the politician, not the poet.

For art is a product of history, not a cause. Unlike some other products, technical inventions for example, it does not re-enter history as an effective agent, so that the question whether art should or should not be propaganda is unreal. The case for the prosecution rests on the fallacious belief that art ever makes anything happen, whereas the honest truth, gentlemen, is that, if not a poem had been written, not a picture painted, not a bar of music composed, the history of man would be materially unchanged.

But there is one field in which the poet is a man of action, the field of language, and it is precisely in this that the greatness of the deceased is most obviously shown. However false or undemocratic his ideas, his diction shows a continuous evolution towards what one might call the true democratic style. The social virtues of a real democracy are brotherhood and intelligence, and the parallel linguistic virtues are strength and clarity, virtues which appear even more clearly through successive volumes by the deceased.

The diction of *The Winding Stair* is the diction of a just man, and it is for this reason that just men will always recognize the author as a master.

From *The Partisan Review*, Vol. VI (Spring, 1939), pp. 46–51. Reprinted by the permission of the author and editors.

THEODORE SPENCER

The Later Poetry of W. B. Yeats

[1933]

A DISTINGUISHED critic, Mr. Yvor Winters, has recently compared the poetry of W. B. Yeats with the poetry of T. Sturge Moore.[1] His remarks are challenging and need to be discussed. In his opinion, Moore is a greater poet than Yeats; he says that Yeats, at crucial moments, suffers from the "fundamental post-Romantic defect, the abandonment of logic," that Yeats achieves a "factitious coherence," is guilty of intellectual confusion, and is an "unregenerate Romantic." These adverse criticisms sum up very well the case against Yeats as an important poet, and the reason they need to be discussed by anyone concerned with Yeats' poetry is that they have a plausibility which may make them a serious obstacle to a satisfactory judgment of Yeats' position.

There is not much to be said about the first of them. To say that Moore is a better poet than Yeats seems to me meaningless, and I cannot imagine any standards of criticism by which such a statement can be defended. In subtlety of rhythm, in intensity, in richness of verbal association, in force, in everything which implies an original and individual style, the later poems of Yeats are superior to anything by Moore. Compare, for example, the opening lines of Moore's sonnet, "Apuleius Meditates," which Mr. Winters praises very highly, with the opening of Yeats' sonnet on Leda and the Swan. This is Moore:

> An old tale tells how Gorgo's gaze distilled
> Horror to petrify men's mobile limbs:
> Endymion's moonlit beauty never dims,
> Hard-frozen as the fond chaste goddess willed.

And Yeats:

> A sudden blow: the great wings beating still
> Above the staggering girl, her thighs caressed
> By the dark webs, her nape caught in his bill,
> He holds her helpless breast upon his breast.

[1] "T. Sturge Moore," by Yvor Winters. *The Hound and Horn*, Vol. VI, No. 3 (April–June, 1933), pages 534–545.

There is an important distinction illustrated here, a distinction which applies to other poetry than that of Moore and Yeats. It is the distinction between the poetry of revery and the poetry of immediacy. I do not, of course, mean by the poetry of revery poetry which is written necessarily about past events; what I am describing, to put it loosely, is the associative climate into which we feel the poet has moved when he got himself ready for writing, and in which he has remained during the composition of the poem. Even without the revealing phrase "An old tale tells," which begins Moore's sonnet, we know from the rhythm, the fairly obvious and hence unregenerated adjectives, that the subject is being viewed from a distance, that it is not apprehended immediately. The poet and his material have not passed through a period of "intimate welding"; they have been contiguous, not fused. But, "A sudden blow: the great wings beating still": here the poet has put the reader in the midst of the action; the subject is not considered and contemplated from outside; we are convinced that the matter has been so vividly an essential part of the poet's experience, that it becomes, if we are reading with the proper attention, an equally vivid part of the reader's experience too.

The distinction between these two ways of regarding the subject matter of a poem becomes obvious if we think of Wordsworth's famous definition of the origin of poetry. "It takes its origin," he says, "from emotion recollected in tranquillity; the action is contemplated till, by a species of reaction, the tranquillity gradually disappears, and an emotion, kindred to that which was before the subject of contemplation, is gradually produced, and does itself actually exist in the mind." It is the last part of this sentence, the part usually left unquoted, which is important. Without the disappearance of tranquillity no good poem can be written, and the trouble with the kind of poetry I have called the poetry of revery is that when we are reading it we feel the tranquillity is still there; the "emotion which was before the subject of contemplation" has not turned up. It is because we never feel like this about Shakespeare that we consider Shakespeare so great a poet, and it is because we often feel like this about Tennyson, that Tennyson's reputation is dubious.

The difference between immediate poetry and the poetry of revery is a reflection of a difference in poetic temperament, and like all differences in temperament it shows itself in a number of ways. One does not expect that a temperament addicted to revery will seek for startling words or for arrangements of images and thoughts that will surprise the mind. Revery in any form not being a function of the human personality as a whole, its aim, when expressed in poetry, will be to lull rather than excite, to describe, or even lament, as beautifully as possible, rather than to assert or protest. Not that poetry of this kind is without intensity; one has only to think of sections *liv* to *lvi* of *In Memoriam*; but it is not the intensity of immediacy, of anger, or of satire, because it is not an intensity which fully includes the intellect.

Of course the contrast between these two kinds of poetic temperament may be carried too far, and one can waste one's time in putting various poets into the various categories they imply, which is foolish because in many cases it is impossible to draw a satisfactory line between them. The reason I mention the matter at all is that it throws an interesting light on the poetry of Yeats. He is a striking example of a man whose poetic development has been from the one way of writing to the other, of a man who has tried to move from a partial to a complete way of looking at the experience he is putting into words. This change, and the success with which he has brought it about, is one of the reasons why his later poetry is so interesting, and is one of the facts which justify the assertion that Yeats is the greatest of living English poets.

The point can be made clearer if we compare one of his earlier poems, "The Sad Shepherd," with one written about forty years later, the poem, "Coole Park, 1929," in *Words for Music Perhaps*.[2] "The Sad Shepherd" begins:

> There was a man whom Sorrow named his friend,
> And he, of his high comrade Sorrow dreaming,
> Went walking with slow steps along the gleaming
> And humming sands, where windy surges wend.

There is little, except its rhythm, to recommend that. It is typical writing of an "unregenerate Romantic." The weak personification of Sorrow, the phrase "high comrade" (this emotive use of the adjective "high" is usually suspicious), the inaccuracy and looseness of the rhyme word "wend"—all these make bad writing, for they are the result of soft feeling and of practically no thinking at all. And the poem, with the exception of the closing lines, gets worse as it goes on. It is an excellent example of the poetry of revery at its weakest; of poetry written not with the object imaginatively vivid and sharp before the mind's eye, but written, so to speak, from memory, with the object wrapped in the falsifying haze of illusion, the kind of illusion that flourishes, like algae in a stagnant pool, when the mind is not stirring.

Bad poetry like this can be found in any age, and the kind of mistiness that makes it bad depends on the particular literary conventions of the time. The minor poets of the eighteenth century had a chilly poetic diction which hampered clarity, and the minor poets of the '90's had little clarity because they used a poetic diction which, one is tempted to say, was too warm. Closely connected with this, and in fact inseparable from it, they had a languorous and evasive habit of feeling, which is as dangerous to good writing as it is difficult to get rid of. What makes Yeats so worthy of admiration is that he did get rid of it. He tells us, in his *Autobiographies,* how, by sleeping upon a board (or at least by thinking of sleeping upon a board), by making his

---

[2] *Words for Music Perhaps and Other Poems,* by W. B. Yeats. Dublin: Cuala Press, 1932. (In *Collected Poems.* New York: Macmillan Co. 1933.)

rhythms "faint and nervous," by contemplating the Dantesque image, by changing his subject matter and his vocabulary, he struggled to make his poems bare and clear, and expressive of the whole man. That he has succeeded is one reason why Mr. Winters' comparison of his verse to Sturge Moore's seems to me so imperceptive. His "quarrel with himself," to use his own phrase, has made Yeats a great poet, with a style of communicating his experience which is authentic and individual, whereas the style of Sturge Moore, careful craftsman though he be, never rises above the commonplace.

It is, of course, an over-simplification of the truth to say that Yeats has entirely turned from one way of writing to the other. He has not lost, he has enriched and perfected, the sensitive rhythms which were at the beginning the best thing about his style. What has happened is that Yeats has taught himself to give the exactly right, and hence unsentimentalized, emotional tone to what he wants to say. "I tried," he says in his preface (1925) to the collected edition of his early poems, "after the publication of the *Wanderings of Oisin* to write of nothing but emotion, and in the simplest language, and now I have had to go through it all, cutting out or altering passages that are sentimental from lack of thought." Few poets have had more difficulties to escape from, more veils of unreality to break through—or, to change the metaphor, more intangible vapors to condense into solids—than Yeats. The late Romanticism of the '90's, Irish super-nationalism, the use of occult symbols, reliance upon a private metaphysical system; any one of these might have been the ruin of a lesser talent. But Yeats, in spite of what at times seemed unavoidable disaster, has triumphantly survived. Perhaps a life of action, and the anger it has sometimes generated—anger is an excellent emotion, if aimed at the right things, for a poet to cultivate—has helped to put iron into his style. At any rate, even when writing about the past, Yeats is no longer a poet of revery, in the sense that I have defined. That is the point I want to make by referring to his poem "Coole Park, 1929."

> I meditate upon a swallow's flight,
> Upon an aged woman and her house:
> A sycamore and lime tree lost in night
> Although that western cloud is luminous,
> Great works constructed there in nature's spite
> For scholars and for poets after us,
> Thoughts long knitted into a single thought,
> A dance-like glory that those walls begot.

At first sight this stanza would seem to be an excellent example of revery. The poet is looking back upon the past, the tone is not "active," the rhythm is appropriate for retrospection. But on a more careful reading, it will be seen that every image is at once individually specific and symbolically general in

its reference, that no word can be changed except for the worse, and that the
climax of the last line is prepared for by the contrasting images and symbols
that have gone before. And how admirably the poem continues:

> There Hyde before he had beaten into prose
> That noble blade the Muses buckled on,
> There one that ruffled in a manly pose
> For all his timid heart, there that slow man,
> That meditative man John Synge and those
> Impetuous men Shawe-Taylor and Hugh Lane,
> Found pride established in humility,
> A scene well set and excellent company.
>
> They came like swallows and like swallows went,
> And yet a woman's powerful character
> Could keep a swallow to its first intent;
> And half a dozen in formation there
> That seemed to whirl upon a compass point
> Found certainly upon the dreaming air. . . .

It is tempting to quote the whole poem, but I will leave the last stanza unquoted—though with its swelling rhythm and superb rhetoric it is the finest
of all—in hopes that what I have already quoted will send the reader to the
book itself.

There are other poems of this kind in *Words for Music Perhaps,* and I
should like to call attention particularly to "The Burning Tree" and to "Coole
Park and Ballylee, 1932," both written, like "Coole Park, 1929," in ottava
rima, and both containing that reverberative haunting quality which Yeats,
in such a masterly way, can give to his rhythms. Equally striking, and equally
masterly, is the way Yeats uses, in these latest poems, the individual word to
its fullest effect. He has always been able, as the result of his control over
rhythm, to emphasize any word he pleased, but the word itself has not always
been the final word for its context. Now, with his more recent intensity of
vision, his control of focus, the individual word has that combination of immediate exactness with potential expansion which is the mark of great poetry.
Yeats is particularly successful with adjectives; I can think of few poets who
in this respect are his equals. Consider, for example, his use of the word
"resinous" in the last line of the following stanza; it is the end of the final
chorus to his play "Resurrection":

> Everything that man esteems
> Endures a moment or a day;
> Love's pleasure drives his love away,
> The painter's brush consumes his dreams;
> The herald's cry, the soldier's tread

> Exhaust his glory and his might:
> Whatever flames upon the night
> Man's own resinous heart has fed.

We have only to compare with this an earlier expression of a similar idea to see how far Yeats has progressed. I quote from "The Happy Shepherd (1889)."

> Nor seeks; for this is also sooth;
> To hunger fiercely after truth,
> Lest all thy toiling only breed
> New dreams, new dreams; there is not truth
> Saving in thine own heart . . .

That is rhythmically effective, but little more; there are too many unnecessary words ("nor," "also," "only," etc.), and nowhere is there the concreteness and inevitability of the later poem.

II

The second part of the present volume consists of a number of short poems and songs, many of them built around a figure whom Yeats at first called Cracked Mary, but who now appears as Crazy Jane; an old woman who sings of the wild ineradicable love she had in her youth. I can best give the the quality of these poems by quotation.

> I know, although when looks meet
> I tremble to the bone,
> The more I leave the door unlatched
> The sooner love is gone,
> For love is but a skein unwound
> Between the dark and dawn.
>
> A lonely ghost the ghost is
> That to God shall come;
> I—love's skein upon the ground,
> My body in the tomb—
> Shall leap into the light lost
> In my mother's womb.
>
> But were I left to lie alone
> In an empty bed,
> The skein so bound us ghost to ghost
> When you turned your head
> Passing on the road that night,
> Mine would walk, being dead.

The technique of this is very interesting. The spondee at the end of the first lines of the first and second stanzas (why does it not occur in the third as well?), the interlocking rhymes, by which the third line of one stanza rhymes with the fifth line of the stanza preceding, the cumulative effect of the triple rhyme, all these form a technical triumph which widens the limits of English poetry.

A further technical device, used very often in these poems, is the refrain, and I should like to examine for a moment the way Yeats handles it, for with its help, he gives a remarkable muscle and pungency to his verse form, and there is much to be learned, by a practicing versifier, from the success of his experiments.

There are, generally speaking, three chief ways in which the refrain has been used by English poets. The first is that found in popular ballads, and to a less extent in Elizabethan songs. Here the effect achieved is rhythmical poignancy and contrast; the repetition of a meaningless phrase, unrelated to the subject of the poem, and balanced in a different rhythm, can first create a kind of rhythmical suspense, and then resolve it:

> There were twa sisters in a bower,
> *Edinburgh, Edinburgh,*
> There were twa sisters in a bower,
> *Sterling for aye;*
> There were twa sisters in a bower,
> There cam a knight to be their wooer,
> *Bonnie St. Johnston stands upon Tay.*

Or it can produce rhythmical variety alone, as in Elizabethan songs:

> Ho ho, ho ho, this world doth pass
> Right merrily, I'll be sworn,
> When many an honest Indian ass
> Goes for a unicorn.
> *Tara-diddle-deino; this is idle feino.*

> Tee-hee, tee-hee, O sweet delight,
> He tickles this age who can
> Call Tullia's ape a marmosite,
> And Leda's goose a swan.
> *Tara-diddle-deino; this is idle feino.*

The second use of the refrain is to bind together and intensify the chief subject-matter of the poem. In the earliest English example, the Anglo-Saxon "Deor's Lament," the repeated words, "That passed over, so may this," by which the poet refers to past calamities in relation to his own, connect the various incidents under one emotional roof, and give unity to what would otherwise be an unrelated series of incidents. Milton, imitating Virgil, uses this device with great success in his "Epitaphium Damonis," where the repetition, at irregular intervals, of the words, "Ite domum impasti, domino iam non vacat, agni," has a singularly haunting effect.

And there is a third, more sophisticated way of using the refrain to be found in the marriage songs of Spenser. Keeping the standard rhythm of the poem, it supplies a background of natural description, and it places the action in a definite environment: "Sweete Themmes! runne softlie, till I end my song." A notable use of this method has been made by Hardy, in a poem called "The Sacrilege," where the refrain descriptive of Nature, "And Dunkery frowned on Exon Moor," changes from gloomy to gay, or rather (characteristically) from gay to gloomy, according to the events in the story.

I make these somewhat pedantic classifications because they throw light on what Yeats has done. He has used the refrain in all three ways, and with each use has broadened its possibilities. We can find the first in "Crazy Jane Reproved," the second in "Crazy Jane on God," and the third in "Three Things." But even more interesting are the poems in which he has used the refrain in two or three ways at the same time.

> Bring me to the blasted oak
> That I, midnight upon the stroke,
> *All find safety in the tomb,*
> May call down curses on his head
> Because of my dear Jack that's dead
> "Cockscomb" was the least he said
> *The solid man and the cockscomb.*

Here we have a combination of the first and second methods: the indirect allusion, *All find safety in the tomb,* grows into a necessary reference; by binding the poem together and giving it rhythmical variety—*The solid man and the cockscomb*—the refrain adds intensity, and the result is that we have, not a single note, as we should have if the refrain were missing, but a chord.

Frequently, as here, Yeats chooses for a refrain some general statement upon which the poem itself is a specific comment. An admirable example is the poem "Crazy Jane Grown Old Looks at the Dancers," where the line, *Love is like the lion's tooth,* repeated at the end of each stanza, is both a statement of a general truth and a representation of the fierceness of the old woman's remembered passion. In fact there is no better example of Yeats' genius than the way in which he chooses his refrains to give this double effect; it was essential to find the right words, and in nearly every poem, Yeats has found them. In his use of this device, as in everything else, we find the later Yeats making his poems a reflection of a complete experience, not of a discrete layer of experience only. Comparison with the earlier poems is again illuminating,

and it is interesting to compare a poem called "Running to Paradise" (1914),
where the refrain gives merely a rhythmical variety, though it is very effective
and surprising, with either of the poems I have just mentioned, where the
refrain gives emotional vividness and tautness as well.

In my opinion the finest of all these poems is the one called "I am of Ireland," where the refrain is used more elaborately, with a more subtle rhythmical sway, than anywhere else. In fact it is difficult to tell which is the refrain
and which is the chief part of the poem; the refrain is at once a voice and an
echo, a question and a reply, and the fusion between the two takes place in
that deep part of consciousness, or perhaps unconsciousness, which only true
poetry can spring from or can reach. I quote the poem in full, for only by
doing so can I hope to explain why I find it so moving.

> "I am of Ireland,
> And the Holy Land of Ireland,
> And time runs on" cried she,
> "Come out of charity
> Come dance with me in Ireland."
>
> One man, one man alone
> In that outlandish gear,
> One solitary man
> Of all that rambled there
> Had turned his stately head,
> "That is a long way off,
> And time runs on," he said
> "And the night grows rough."
>
> "I am of Ireland
> And the Holy Land of Ireland
> And time runs on," cried she.
> "Come out of charity
> And dance with me in Ireland."
>
> "The fiddlers are all thumbs,
> Or the fiddle string accursed,
> The drums and the kettle drums
> And the trumpets all are burst
> And the trombone," cried he,
> "The trumpet and trombone,"
> And cocked a malicious eye
> "But time runs on, runs on."
>
> "I am of Ireland
> And the Holy Land of Ireland

> And time runs on," cried she.
> "Come out of charity
> And dance with me in Ireland."

III

I have written at some length about the technique of Yeats' poetry because a deep respect for Yeats as a craftsman is necessary to a proper understanding of his work. But his craftsmanship would hardly be worth mentioning if it were an end in itself; what is significant about these later poems is that the substitution, to use Yeats' own description, of "sound for sense and ornament for thought," which was the fault of his early style, has given place to vigor and toughness, to a style where thought is substance and not accident, and which is able to communicate, in an entirely individual way, important emotions. It remains to enquire what these are.

About ten years ago, it appeared likely that Yeats was in danger of losing himself in a tangle of occult metaphysics; he published a book on the subject called *A Vision*, "which book," to use Chaucer's words,

> Spak muchel of the operaciouns
> Touchynge the eighte and twenty mansiouns
> That longen to the moone, and swich folye
> As in oure dayes is nat worth a flye,

and he wrote several poems which depended, if they were to be understood, on a fable connected with the philosophy described in this volume. And though Yeats has since remarked (1929) that nearly all of *A Vision* "fills me with shame," he also attributes to the experience behind it the fact that his poetry has gained in "self-possession and power."

This is doubtless true, and it is therefore unfair to apply Chaucer's words too literally to *A Vision*. At the present time a poet must take what external aid he can find to plan the structure and symbolism of his poetry; but if he is a good poet the mechanics will obviously be more helpful to him than to the reader, and most of the time they will be out of sight. This is what occurs in Yeats' later poems; specific references to the philosophy of *A Vision* are very scarce, only an occasional metaphor is derived from it, and the subject matter of the poems is not a private world of dreams, as the most acute of contemporary English critics once feared it would be, but the subject matter of all great poetry.

That, to be sure, is a very loose statement, for the subject matter of great poetry is a difficult and complex thing to define. But if one were pressed for a definition, the reply would be, I believe, that at the bottom of all great poetry, as at the bottom of all human experience, lies the problem of the relation between the transient and the permanent, expressed in innumerable

ways, and regarded from innumerable angles. In mystical poetry, such as
Dante's, the permanent is found and described as the center of experience, for
it is the object of both emotion and thought; in Shelley's poetry it is sought
for by the mind, but found only temporarily, for it is discovered by the emotions alone; while in Shakespeare, though the sense of permanence is nearly
always somewhere in the background, it is change, not permanence, the
Many, not the One, that is emphasized, and the passion, as in *Lear,* can play
itself out in the dark. Today, as has been frequently said ("What are all those
fish that lie gasping on the strand?"), the flux itself seems the only thing that
does not change, and to seek a pattern of permanence elsewhere appears an
impossible task. *A Vision* is such an attempt, and the apparent intractability of
its philosophy for poetry is significant. Yet without such an attempt Yeats'
later poetry would lose its richness and its "power." The philosophy may not
be acceptable to others, but to Yeats it represents a sense of values which recognizes the importance of the permanent, and without such recognition all
statements about life, whether in poetry or prose, are shallow.

The chief subject matter of these poems is the passing of youth into age,
of passion into death.

> Earth in beauty dressed
> Awaits returning spring.
> All true love must die,
> Alter at the best
> Into some lesser thing.
> Prove that I lie.
>
> Such bodies lovers have,
> Such exacting breath
> That they touch or sigh.
> Every touch they give
> Love is nearer death.
> Prove that I lie.

It is a poetry of change, striving for stability, for transmutation into "monuments of unaging intellect." And though both the ephemeral and the lasting
are continually brought to our attention, it is the passing of the ephemeral
that remains most vivid to us. One might expect, as a result, that the prevailing tone would be one of pathos, but this is not true; the emotions here expressed go deeper than pathos, and slight as these poems are, they leave in
the mind an impression of tragedy.

I trust that I have said enough to show that I consider Yeats' poetry to have
more than a contemporary value. It does not, as Mr. Winters says it does,
abandon logic; it springs from a deeper well than mere logic ever swam in,
and its coherence is far from "factitious." Even if we may sometimes feel that

an individual poem is not entirely successful, the great majority of these
poems do not grow commonplace with familiarity, nor are they easily forgotten. On the contrary they sing into the memory, and we feel, after contemplating them, that Yeats did himself no more than justice when he once
wrote:

> There is not a fool can call me friend,
> And I may dine at journey's end
> With Landor and with Donne.

From *The Hound and Horn,* Vol. VII (October–
December, 1933), pp. 164–175. Reprinted by
permission.

F. O. MATTHIESSEN

T. S. Eliot: The Four Quartets

[1943]

In the course of an artist's development certain phases may detach themselves and challenge comprehension as completed wholes. Eliot has rounded out such a cycle with *Little Gidding,* and we are now able to see the full significance of the experiments with structure which he inaugurated in *Burnt Norton* eight years previously.[1] He speaks of the four poems which form this cycle as "quartets," and has evolved for them all the same kind of sequence of five parts with which he composed *Burnt Norton. The Waste Land* was also composed in this fashion, but the contrast is instructive. In his earlier desire for intense concentration the poet so eliminated connectives that *The Waste Land* might be called an anthology of the high points of a drama. It was as though its author had determined to make his poem of nothing but Arnold's "touchstones," or had subscribed to Poe's dictum that no longer poem could exist than one to be read at a sitting. In the intervening years Eliot has given further thought to the problem, and he has recently concluded that "in a poem of any length there must be transitions between passages of greater and lesser intensity, to give rhythm of fluctuating emotion essential to the musical structure of the whole." He has also enunciated "a complementary doctrine" to that of Arnold's "touchstones": the test of a poet's greatness by "the way he writes his less intense but structurally vital matter."

None of the four quartets is much more than half as long as *The Waste Land,* but he has included in them all transitional passages that he would previously have dismissed as "prosaic." His fundamentally altered intention is at the root of the matter. The dramatic monologues of Prufrock or Gerontion or of the various *personae* of *The Waste Land* have yielded to gravely modulated meditations of the poet's own. The vivid situations of his *Inferno* have been followed by the philosophic debates of his *Purgatorio.* He has made quite explicit the factors conditioning his new structures in the essay from which I

[1] Before appearing in collected form in 1943, Eliot's *Four Quartets* appeared as separate booklets, as follows: "Burnt Norton" in 1941, "East Coker" in 1940, "The Dry Salvages" in 1941, "Little Gidding" in 1942. Thus these titles are printed here in italics. Similarly, "Triumphal March" appeared in separate book form in 1931, "Journey of the Magi" in 1927, and the essay "The Music of Poetry" in 1942. (Editor's note, 1950.)

have just quoted, *The Music of Poetry*. As is always the case with Eliot, this essay throws the most relevant light upon his poetic intentions, and is thus a further piece of refutation to those who persist in the fallacy that there is no harmony beween his "revolutionary" creative work and his "traditionalist" criticism.

Looking back now over the past generation, he finds the poetry of our period to be best characterized by its "search for a proper modern colloquial idiom." He develops the same theme near the close of *Little Gidding* where he envisages the right equilibrium between "the common word" and "the formal word." Only through their union of opposites do we get

> The complete consort dancing together.

Eliot, no less than the later Yeats, has helped to restore to poetry the conversational tones which had been muffled by the ornamental forms and diction of the end of the century. But now Eliot is thinking of the other partner to the union, and remarks that "when we reach a point at which the poetic idiom can be stabilized, then a period of musical elaboration can follow." Just as Donne, in his later work, returned to the formal pattern of the sonnet which he had mocked in the broken rhythms of his early lyrics, so Eliot now believes that there is such a "tendency to return to set, and even elaborate patterns" after any period when they have been laid aside.

The present phase of his own return seems to have started with *New Hampshire* and *Virginia*, the short musical evocations which grew out of his renewed impressions of America in the early nineteen thirties. The impulse to write a series of such place-name poems led on in turn to the more ambitious *Burnt Norton*, which borrows its title from a Gloucestershire manor near which Eliot has stayed. The titles of the other three quartets indicate more intimate relationships: East Coker, in Somerset, is where the Eliot family lived until its emigration in the mid-seventeenth Century to the New England coast; the Dry Salvages, a group of rocks off Cape Ann, mark the part of that coast which the poet knew best as a boy; Little Gidding, the seat of the religious community which Nicholas Ferrar established and with which the names of George Herbert and Crashaw are associated, is a shrine for the devout Anglican, but can remind the poet also that

> History is now and England.[1]

[1] By including in *Little Gidding* a refrain from Juliana of Norwich—

> Sin is Behovely, but
> All shall be well, and
> All manner of thing shall be well—

Eliot also aimed, as he has said, "to escape any suggestion of historical sentimentality about the seventeenth century by this reiterated reference to the fourteenth century and therefore to get more bearing on the present than would be possible if the relation was merely between the present and one particular period of the past."

The rhythmical pattern of *Burnt Norton* is elaborated far beyond the delicate melodies of the brief "Landscapes." Eliot seems to have found in the interrelation of its five parts a type of structure which satisfied him beyond his
previous experiments. For he has adhered to it with such remarkably close
parallels in the three succeeding quartets that a description of the structure of
one of them involves that of all, and can reveal the deliberateness of his intentions. In each case the first part or movement might be thought of as a
series of statements and counterstatements of a theme in lines of an even
greater irregularity than those of the late Jacobean dramatists. In each of these
first movements a "landscape" or presented scene gives a concrete base around
which the poet's thoughts gather.

The second movement opens with a highly formal lyric: in *The Dry Salvages* this is a variant of a sestina, rising from the clang of the bell buoy; in
Little Gidding each of the three eight-line stanzas ends with a refrain—and
thus does Eliot signalize his own renewal of forms that would have seemed
played out to the author of *Prufrock*. In the other two poems he has also illustrated a remark which he has been repeating in his recent essays, that "a
poem, or a passage of a poem, may tend to realize itself first as a particular
rhythm before it reaches expression in words." The lyric in *Burnt Norton*—
which is echoed perhaps too closely in *East Coker*—is as pure musical incantation as any Eliot has written. Not only does its opening image, "Garlic and
sapphires in the mud," take its inception from Mallarmé's line "Tonnerre et
rubis aux moyeux"; but the rhythm of the poem in which that line occurs,
M'introduire dans ton histoire, seems also to have haunted Eliot's ear until
it gave rise to a content which, with the exception of its opening line, is
wholly different from Mallarmé's.

Following the lyric in the second movement, Eliot has relaxed his rhythms
for a sudden contrast; and in *The Dry Salvages*, and especially in *East Coker*,
has carried his experiment with the prosaic virtually over the border into
prose:

> That was a way of putting it—not very satisfactory:
> A periphrastic study in a worn-out poetical fashion,
> Leaving one still with the intolerable wrestle
> With words and meanings. The poetry does not matter.
> It was not (to start again) what one had expected.

The sharp drop from incantation is designed to have the virtue of surprise;
but it would seem here to have gone much too far, and to have risked the
temporary collapse of his form into the flatness of a too personal statement.
The variant in *Little Gidding* substitutes for such a sequence a modified terza
rima, where the poet uses instead of rhyme a sustained alternation of masculine and feminine endings, in a passage that makes the strongest testimony
for the value of formal congruence.

What the third parts have in common is that each is an account of movement. In *Burnt Norton* it is a descent into the London underground, which
becomes also a descent into the dark night of the soul. In *East Coker* the allusion to Saint John of the Cross is even more explicit. The poet's command
to his soul to

> be still and wait without hope,
> For hope would be hope of the wrong thing,

borrows its sequence of paradoxes directly from tht text of the 16th Century
Spanish mystic. In *The Dry Salvages* where the concluding charge is

> Not fare well
> But fare forward, voyagers,

the doctrine of action beyond thought of self-seeking is, again explicitly, what
Krishna urged to Arjuna on the field of battle; and we recall Eliot's remarking,
in his essay on Dante, that "the next greatest philosophical poem" to *The
Divine Comedy* within his experience was the *Bhagavad-Gita*. In *Little Gidding* the passage of movement is the terza rima passage at the close of the
second part, and the deliberately prosaic lines open the third section. The
movement described is the "dead patrol" of two air raid wardens.

The versification in these third parts is the staple for the poems as a whole,
a very irregular iambic line with many substitutions, of predominantly four or
five beats, but with syllables ranging from six to eighteen. The fourth movement, in every case, is a short lyric, as it was in *The Waste Land*. The fifth
movement is a resumption and resolution of themes, and becomes progressively more intricate in the last two poems, since the themes are cumulative
and are all brought together at the close of *Little Gidding*.

It seems doubtful whether at the time of writing *Burnt Norton*, just after
Murder in the Cathedral, Eliot had already projected the series. His creative
energies for the next three years were to be largely taken up with *The Family
Reunion*, which, to judge from the endless revisions in the manuscript, caused
him about as much trouble as anything he has done. With *East Coker* in the
spring of 1940 he made his first experiment in a part for part parallel with an
earlier work of his own. Again Donne's practice is suggestive: when he had
evolved a particularly intricate and irregular stanza, he invariably set himself
the challenge of following it unchanged to the end of his poem. But in as-
signing himself a similar problem for a poem two hundred lines long, Eliot
has tried something far more exacting, where failure could be caused by the
parallels becoming merely mechanical, and by the themes and rhythms becoming not subtle variations but flat repetitions. *East Coker* does indeed have
something of the effect of a set piece. Just as its high proportion of prosaic
lines seems to spring from partial exhaustion, so its resumption of themes

from *Burnt Norton* can occasionally sound as though the poet was merely imitating himself. But on the whole he had solved his problem. He had made a renewal of form that was to carry him successively in the next two years through *The Dry Salvages* and *Little Gidding*. The discrimination between repetition and variation lies primarily in the rhythm; and these last two poems reverberate with an increasing musical richness.

A double question that keeps insisting itself through any discussion of these structures is the poet's consciousness of analogies with music, and whether such analogies are a confusion of arts. One remembers Eliot's comment on Lawrence's definition of "the essence of poetry" for our age "of stark and un-lovely actualities" as a "stark, bare, rocky directness of statement." "This speaks to me," Eliot remarked a decade ago, "of that at which I have long aimed in writing poetry"; and he drew an analogy with the later quartets of Beethoven. This does not mean that he has ever tried to copy literally the ef-fects of a different medium. But he knows that poetry is like music in being a temporal rather than a spatial art; and he has by now thought much about the subject, as the concluding paragraph of *The Music of Poetry* shows:

I think that a poet may gain much from the study of music: how much tech-nical knowledge of musical form is desirable I do not know, for I have not that technical knowledge myself. But I believe that the properties in which music con-cerns the poet most nearly, are the sense of rhythm and the sense of structure. I think that it might be possible for a poet to work too closely to musical analogies: the result might be an effect of artificiality.

But he insists—and this has immediate bearing on his own intentions—that "the use of recurrent themes is as natural to poetry as to music." He has worked on that assumption throughout his quartets, and whether he has proved that "there are possibilities of transitions in a poem comparable to the different movements of a symphony or a quartet," or that "there are possibil-ities of contrapuntal arrangement of subject-matter," can be known only through repeated experience of the whole series. All I wish to suggest here is the pattern made by some of the dominant themes in their interrelation and progression.

Burnt Norton opens as a meditation on time. Many comparable and con-trasting views are introduced. The lines are drenched with reminiscences of Heraclitus' fragments on flux and movement. Some of the passages on dura-tion remind us that Eliot listened to Bergson's lectures at the Sorbonne in the winter of 1911 and wrote an essay then criticizing his *durée réelle* as "simply not final." Other lines on the recapture of time through consciousness suggest the aspect of Bergson that most stimulated Proust. But the chief contrast around which Eliot constructs this poem is that between the view of time as a mere continuum, and the difficult paradoxical Christian view of how man lives both "in and out of time," how he is immersed in the flux and yet can penetrate to the eternal by apprehending timeless existence within time and above it. But even for the Christian the moments of release from the pressures of the flux are rare, though they alone redeem the sad wastage of otherwise unillumined existence. Eliot recalls one such moment of peculiar poignance, a childhood moment in the rose garden—a symbol he has previously used, in many variants, for the birth of desire. Its implications are intricate and even ambiguous, since they raise the whole problem of how to discriminate between supernatural vision and mere illusion. Other variations here on the theme of how time is conquered are more directly apprehensible. In dwelling on the extension of time into movement, Eliot takes up an image he had used in *Triumphal March:* "at the still point of the turning world." This notion of "a mathematically pure point" (as Philip Wheelwright has called it) seems to be Eliot's poetic equivalent in our cosmology for Dante's "unmoved Mover," another way of symbolising a timeless release from the "outer compulsions" of the world. Still another variation is the passage on the Chinese jar in the final section. Here Eliot, in a conception comparable to Wallace Stevens' "Anecdote of the Jar," had suggested how art conquers time:

> Only by the form, the pattern,
> Can words or music reach
> The stillness, as a Chinese jar still
> Moves perpetually in its stillness.

Burnt Norton is the most philosophically dense of the series, and any adequate account of Eliot's development of his themes would demand detailed analysis. With the opening phase of *East Coker,* "In my beginning is my end," he has extended his meditation on time into history. In such a phrase, which is close to Heraclitus' "The beginning and the end are common," the poet has also indicated the recurrent attraction he feels to the reconciliation of opposites which characterizes that pre-Socratic philosopher. Eliot is using these words in a double sense. He is thinking historically—as the first section goes on to make clear, he is thinking back to the conception of order and harmony as propounded by a 16th Century Thomas Elyot in his *Booke named the Governour.* And near the close of the poem, the overtones of history and of family are blended in the phrase, "Home is where one starts from." But the continuity with which he is concerned is not simply that of race. He is also thinking in religious terms—in my beginning, in my birth, is implied my end, death; yet, in the Christian reversal of terms, that death can mean rebirth, and the culminating phrase of *East Coker* is "In my end is my beginning."

As his thought becomes involved with the multiple meanings of history, with how the moments of significance and illumination bisect "the world of time," he dwells also on the course of the individual history, and his reflections become deeply personal as he confronts the disappointments of old age. He weighs the "limited value" of what can be learned from experience, since its accustomed pattern may restrict and blind us to what comes with the "new and shocking" moment. When the soul is sick, it can learn only through humility, only if it accepts the paradox which is developed both by St. John of the Cross and by Marvell in his *Dialogue Between the Soul and Body,* that "Our only health is the disease." Man may come to the end of his night of dark vacancy only if he learns that he "must go by the way of dispossession."

The three middle sections of *East Coker* are as somber as anything Eliot has written, and culminate in his pronouncing his career which has fallen between two wars as "twenty years largely wasted." The danger of such a declaration is that it risks false humility, and the inertness of these lines contrasts unsatisfactorily with the comparable passage in *Burnt Norton* on what is gained through form. But the contrast is structurally deliberate, and with the phrase, "Home is where one starts from," there comes the quickening reflection that old men should be explorers "into another intensity/ For a further union." What they must pass through is such "empty desolation" at the sea's, and in developing that image in the concluding lines of *East Coker,* the poet prepares the most thrilling transition of the whole series. For *The Dry Salvages* opens with a contrast between the river and the sea, between the two forces that have most conditioned Eliot's sense of rhythm. For nationalist critics of the Van Wyck Brooks school who declare that Eliot has broken away from his roots since he has not included in his poems realistic details from the Middle West, it could be profitable to note that the river is "the big river,"—at first the frontier, then the "useful, untrustworthy" conveyor of shipping, then a problem to be solved by the bridge builder, and at last "almost forgotten" by the city dwellers. This passage gives an insight into the sources of a poet's rhythm; and into how he penetrates for his material beneath all surface details, in order to repossess his essential experience. The significance of the river for Eliot shows in what he wrote to a St. Louis paper in 1930:

I feel that there is something in having passed one's childhood beside the big river, which is incommunicable to those who have not. Of course my people were Northerners and New Englanders, and of course I have spent many years out of America altogether; but Missouri and the Mississippi have made a deeper impression on me than any other part of the world.

The contrapuntal balance of sea and river reinforces, throughout *The Dry Salvages,* the themes of time and movement. And yet the underlying changelessness of the sea beneath its tides, with its tolling bells measuring "time not our time," underscores also the contrasting theme of the timeless. History is again dwelt on, and is now discerned as not just the blind corridor it seemed to Gerontion, since "Time the destroyer is time the preserver." This perception gives foundation for Krishna's counsel of disinterested action. Then, after the bell buoy's "perpetual angelus" has resounded through the lyrical fourth movement, as it had in the sestina at the opening of the second, Eliot makes his most complete articulation of what can be involved in "the intersection of the timeless with time." By allusions to the rose garden and to the other moments of illumination that he has symbolized in the three poems so far, he suggests the common basis of such moments in their "hints" of grace. He goes farther, and states that such "hints" lead also to the central truth in his religious convictions:

> But to apprehend
> The point of intersection of the timeless
> With time, is an occupation for the saint—
> No occupation either, but something given
> And taken, in a lifetime's death in love,
> Ardour and selflessness and self-surrender.
> For most of us, there is only the unattended
> Moment, the moment in and out of time,
> The distraction fit, lost in a shaft of sunlight,
> The wild thyme unseen, or the winter lightning,
> Or the waterfall, or music heard so deeply
> That it is not heard at all, but you are the music
> While the music lasts. These are only hints and guesses,
> Hints followed by guesses; and the rest
> Is prayer, observance, discipline, thought and action.
> The hint half guessed, the gift half understood, is Incarnation.
> Here the impossible union
> Of spheres of existence is actual,
> Here the past and future
> Are conquered and reconciled. . . .

The doctrine of Incarnation is the pivotal point on which Eliot's thought has swung well away from the 19th Century's romantic heresies of Deification. The distinction between thinking of God become Man through the Saviour, or of Man becoming God through his own divine potentialities, can be at the root of political as well as of religious belief. Eliot has long affirmed that Deification, the reckless doctrine of every great man as a Messiah, has led ineluctably to Dictatorship. What he has urged in his *Idea of a Christian Society,* is a reestablished social order in which both governors and governed find their completion in their common humility before God. The above passage, therefore, compresses, at the climax of *The Dry Salvages,* the core of Eliot's thought on time, on history, and on the destiny of man.

The content of *Little Gidding* is most apparently under the shadow of the war. But it underlines what Eliot declared in a recent essay on "Poetry in War-time," that the more permanently valuable war poetry of 1914–18 was "more of sadness and pity than of military glory." The secluded chapel enforces thoughts of pilgrimage and prayer, but a further reflection on history carries the poet to the realization that

> We cannot restore old policies
> Or follow an antique drum.

If "history may be servitude, history may be freedom," and

> Here the intersection of the timeless moment
> Is England and nowhere. Never and always.

In the final movement he resumes successively all his major themes, opening with "The end is where we start from." This leads into another passage on words and form, since "every sentence is an end and a beginning," "every poem an epitaph." Comparably, every action is a step towards death, but may likewise be a step towards redemption. Once again we have a recognition of the potentialities of history far more resolute than what was seen in the tired backward look in *East Coker*. For now the poet affirms that

> We shall not cease from exploration
> And the end of all our exploring
> Will be to arrive where we started
> And know the place for the first time.

What we will know is ·adumbrated through allusions that take us back through the series, back to "the source of the longest river," back, indeed, to the moment of release that he evoked in "New Hampshire," to "the children in the apple tree." But the completion of that glimpsed vision, as was the case with Dante's childhood love for Beatrice, must be sought through full maturity, through

> A condition of complete simplicity
> (Costing not less than everything).

The value of Eliot's device of incremental repetition hinges most on this final section of *Little Gidding*, since there is hardly a phrase that does not recall an earlier passage in the series. Some readers may object that this makes too much for a circular movement, with insufficient resolution at the close. In one sense this is true, but only in as much as the questions on which the poet is meditating are endless in their recurrent urgency. And such structural recurrence of themes, as Proust also found, is the chief device by which the writer can convey the recapture of time. The concluding lines mount to final-ity in their enunciation that all

> shall be well
> When the tongues of flame are in-folded
> Into the crowned knot of fire
> And the fire and the rose are one.

Out of their context these lines may seem to be merely a decorative allusion to Dante's paradise. But once you have observed the central rôle that fire plays, intermittently through the series and dominantly in *Little Gidding*, the potential reconciliation of the flames of destruction with the rose of light is weighted with significance. A glance at Eliot's varied symbolic use of fire can also give us an opportunity to examine more closely than we have so far the texture of the poetry he has developed through the structures of his quartets.

The lyric at the opening of the second part of *Little Gidding* recounts the successive death of the elements. It versifies, with amplification, a sentence of Heraclitus that dwells both on the ceaseless flux and on the reconciliation of opposites, "Fire lives in the death of air, and air in the death of fire; water lives in the death of earth, and earth in the death of water." We can observe again the lasting impression made on the poet's consciousness by this philosopher, concerning whom he recorded in his student's notebook of thirty years ago: "By God he meant fire." But the fire in this lyric, and in the terza rima lines which follow it, is not the fire of creation:

> In the uncertain hour before the morning
> Near the ending of interminable night
> At the recurrent end of the unending
> After the dark dove with the flickering tongue
> Had passed below the horizon of his homing. . . .

The "dark dove" is the bird that haunts now all our skies; its "flickering tongue" is the airman's fire of destruction. The figures who meet "between three districts when the smoke arose" and who tread "the pavement in a dead patrol" need no annotation of their function. But Eliot is occupied here with other meetings as well. It is no usual fellow warden whom he encounters but "a familiar compound ghost." This "ghost" is akin, as some phrases show, to Brunetto Latini, whose meeting with Dante in Hell is one of the passages which has impressed Eliot most. A characteristic of Eliot's poetic thought ever since *Ash Wednesday* has been to make free transitions from the *Inferno* to the *Purgatorio;* and the last words spoken in this "disfigured street" as the day is breaking, are advice to the poet that he cannot escape from the "exasperated spirit" of old age,

> unless restored by that refining fire
> Where you must move in measure, like a dancer.

And here, in the image of the dance—as Theodore Spencer has remarked to me—one also moves in anticipation beyond the searing flames of purgatory to the radiant spheres of paradise.

The other chief passage on fire in *Little Gidding* is the fourth movement, as impressive a lyric as any Eliot has produced:

> The dove descending breaks the air
> With flame of incandescent terror
> Of which the tongues declare
> The one discharge from sin and error.
> The only hope or else despair
>   Lies in the choice of pyre or pyre—
>   To be redeemed from fire by fire.
>
> Who then devised the torment? Love.
> Love is the unfamiliar Name
> Behind the hands that wove
> The intolerable shirt of flame
> Which human power cannot remove.
>   We only live, only suspire
>   Consumed by either fire or fire.

The control of the range of meanings here is masterly. On one level, the choice in the first stanza is between destruction and destruction, for as "the tongues" on both sides declare it is either "we" or "they," the "incandescent terror" must blot out either London or Berlin. But the descending dove is, more profoundly, that of annunciation, and "the tongues" of prophecy declare the terms of our possible redemption. The poem reaches the heart of its meaning in the heavily stressed end-word of the opening line of the second stanza. That most familiar word is yet unfamiliar to mankind, which "cannot bear very much reality." We can hardly face the fact that love is essentially not release but suffering; and that the intolerable burden of our desires—our Nessus shirt—can be removed by nothing within our power, but solely through grace. All we have is the terms of our choice, the fire of our destructive lusts or the inscrutable terrible fire of divine Love.

The poetry of purgation, as Eliot has observed, is ordinarily less exciting than that of either damnation or beatitude, but this lyric transcends such limitation through its fervor. The encounter between the air raid wardens is the other most dramatic passage in the poem. Since it marks Eliot's first experiment with terza rima, it carries further the long series of his debts to Dante. But its method follows more particularly the lesson of another master. The "forgotten, half-recalled" figure is evoked by the device of multiple reference which Henry James used in his "ghost" stories. The figure, "too strange . . .

for misunderstandings," suggests not only Brunetto Latini or Arnaut Daniel. When he reminds Eliot how their common concern with speech impelled them "to purify the dialect of the tribe," he virtually translates from Mallarmé's *Le Tombeau d'Edgar Poe* ("donner un sens plus pur aux mots de la tribu"), and indicates that he may be thought of as any of Eliot's dead masters. When he proceeds to disclose "the gifts reserved for age," it is interesting to recall that Eliot's bitter "Lines for an Old Man" contain in the manuscript the epigraph, "to Stéphane Mallarmé."

It may be objected that such a range of suggestion detracts from dramatic singleness. It is more certainly true that Eliot, from the time of his earliest poems, has been more successful in posing a dramatic moment than in developing a sustained action. It may also be charged that he betrays a limitation of content in comparison with some of the other strange meetings that he recalls. Whereas the lines spoken by Brunetto Latini are, as Eliot himself has said, Dante's "testimony of a loved master of arts"; and Wilfred Owen's hallucinated pitiful encounter was with no less than the enemy he had killed; the main burden that Eliot's "ghost" has to convey is the impotent lacerations of growing old.

It has been charged against Eliot ever since his conversion that his content has been tenuous; but the range of reflection and feeling in the quartets alone should serve to give a persuasive refutation. The trouble has been that whereas Eliot's earlier poetry was difficult in form, his later work is difficult in thought. The reader of *Gerontion* had to learn how to supply the missing connectives. The reader of the quartets finds a sufficiently straightforward logic, but is confronted with realms of discourse largely unfamiliar to a secular age. Sustained knowledge of the dark night of the soul is a rare phase of mystical experience in any age; and it is at that point that agnostic and atheist readers have been most severe in demanding whether Eliot's lines express anything more than mere literary allusions. The severity is desirable, but it should not be forgotten that authentic poetry often takes us into experiences equally remote from our ordinary hours, as in Oedipus' vision at Colonnos, in Rilke's *Duino Elegies,* or in almost the whole *Paradiso.* Misconceptions of Eliot's content may be avoided if we remain aware, at least, of what he is aiming to do. As our examination of the structures of his quartets has borne out, the greatest change from his earlier poems is that his intentions now are only intermittently dramatic. Or rather, he has tried to concentrate his desire for drama into his two plays; and what he has produced in his quartets is what in the 17th Century would have been called meditations. Yet the most striking change in the texture of his verse is his abandonment of the devices that he learned from Donne and the other metaphysicals. The qualities for which he now aspires are those of a less popular 17th Century master, Lancelot Andrewes, whose "spiritual discipline" he has contrasted with Donne's broken intensity. The three attributes of Andrewes' style that Eliot singled out for praise can belong to poetry as well as to prose: "ordonnance, or arrangement and structure, precision in the use of words, and relevant intensity." Those attributes seemed very far from the poetical aims of "The Hollow Men" which he had written the year before in his essay on Andrewes; but something comparable to the "purely contemplative" emotion he found in Andrewes is what he now wants most to express.

The measure of an author's attraction for Eliot can always be read in what that author has taught him about the development of his medium; and it is notable that the passage which Eliot cited to show how Andrewes' spiritual reflections can yet force "a concrete presence upon us," provided him with the starting point of his own *Journey of the Magi*. Another sentence ("Let us then make this so accepted a time in itself twice acceptable by our accepting . . ."), which illustrated how Andrewes did "not hesitate to hammer, to inflect, even to play upon a word for the sake of driving home its meaning," gave Eliot a similar word-play in *Burnt Norton* ("There they were as our guests, accepted and accepting"), and stimulated him to such an independent development as the startling

Distracted from distraction by distraction.

Those who demand that a poet's content should be immediately useful will take no satisfaction in Eliot's belief that the poet in wartime should as a man "be no less devoted to his country than other men," but that "his first duty as a poet is towards his native language, to preserve and to develop that language." To the nationalist critics that will seem to beg the question of content altogether. But the cheapness of Van Wyck Brooks's opinion that Eliot is a poet of little hope, less faith, and no charity, should be substantially refuted by the lyric on the kinds of love alone. But such a lyric does not exist alone; it rises organically as the summation of one of Eliot's profoundest themes. And those who are suspicious of the inertness of the passages which urge the soul to wait in the dark without hope, should remember that the final declaration, even in *East Coker,* is that

We must be still and still moving.

The reconciliation of opposites is as fundamental to Eliot as it was to Heraclitus. Only thus can he envisage a resolution of man's whole being. The "heart of light" that he glimpsed in the opening movement of *Burnt Norton* is at the opposite pole from the "Heart of Darkness," from which he took the epigraph for "The Hollow Men." Essential evil still constitutes more of Eliot's subject-matter than essential good, but the magnificent orchestration of his themes has prepared for that paradisal glimpse at the close, and thereby makes it no decorative allusion, but an integrated climax to the content no less than to the form. Such spiritual release and reconciliation are the chief reality for which he strives in a world that has seemed to him increasingly threatened with new dark ages.

From *The Achievement of T. S. Eliot* by F. O. Matthiessen, pp. 177–195. Copyright, 1947, by Oxford University Press, Inc. Reprinted by permission of the author and publishers. First published in *The Kenyon Review* as "Eliot's Quartets," Vol. V (Spring, 1943), pp. 161–178.

R. P. BLACKMUR

Notes on E. E. Cummings' Language

[1930]

In his four books of verse, his play, and the autobiographical *Enormous Room*,[1] Mr. Cummings has amassed a special vocabulary and has developed from it a special use of language which these notes are intended to analyze and make explicit. Critics have commonly said, when they understood Mr. Cummings' vocabulary at all, that he has enriched the language with a new idiom; had they been further interested in the uses of language, they would no doubt have said that he had added to the general sensibility of his time. Certainly his work has had many imitators. Young poets have found it easy to adopt the attitudes from which Mr. Cummings has written, just as they often adopt the superficial attitudes of Swinburne and Keats. The curious thing about Mr. Cummings' influence is that his imitators have been able to emulate as well as ape him; which is not so frequently the case with the influence of Swinburne and Keats. Mr. Cummings is a school of writing in himself; so that it is necessary to state the underlying assumptions of his mind, and of the school which he teaches, before dealing with the specific results in poetry of those assumptions.

It is possible to say that Mr. Cummings belongs to the anticulture group; what has been called at various times vorticism, futurism, dadaism, surrealism, and so on.[2] Part of the general dogma of this group is a sentimental denial of the intelligence and the deliberate assertion that the unintelligible is the only object of significant experience. These dogmas have been defended with considerable dialectical skill, in the very practical premise that only by presenting the unintelligible as viable and actual *per se* can the culture of the *dead intelligence* (Brattle Street, the Colleges, and the Reviews) be shocked into sentience. It is argued that only by denying to the intelligence its function of discerning quality and order, can the failures of the intelligence be overcome; that if we take things as they come without remembering what has gone before or guessing what may come next, and if we accept these

[1] As of 1930. There would seem little modification of these notes necessary because of *Eimi* or the subsequent volumes of verse.

[2] The reader is referred to the late numbers *Transition* for a serial and collaborative expression of the latest form which this group has assumed: the Battle of the Word.

things at their face value, we shall know life, at least in the arts, as it really is. Nothing could be more arrogant, and more deceptively persuasive to the childish spirit, than such an attitude when held as fundamental. It appeals to the intellect which wishes to work swiftly and is in love with immediate certainty. A mind based on it accepts every fragment of experience as final and every notion as definite, yet never suffers from the delusion that it has learned anything. By an astonishing accident, enough unanimity exists among these people to permit them to agree among themselves; to permit them, even, to seem spiritually indistinguishable as they appear in public.

The central attitude of this group has developed, in its sectaries, a logical and thoroughgoing set of principles and habits. In America, for example, the cause of the lively arts has been advanced against the ancient seven; because the lively arts are necessarily immediate in appeal and utterly transitory. Thus we find in Mr. Cummings' recent verse and in his play *Him* the side show and the cabaret set up as "inevitable" frames for experience. Jazz effects, tough dialects, tough guys, slim hot queens, barkers, fairies, and so on, are made into the media and symbols of poetry. Which is proper enough in Shakespeare where such effects are used ornamentally or for pure play. But in Cummings such effects are employed as substance, as the very mainstay of the poetry. There is a continuous effort to escape the realism of the intelligence in favor of the realism of the obvious. What might be stodgy or dull because not properly worked up into poetry is replaced by the tawdry and by the fiction of the immediate.

It is no great advantage to get rid of one set of flabby generalities if the result is merely the immersion of the sensibility in another set only super-ficially less flabby. The hardness of the tough guy is mostly in the novelty of the language. There is no hardness in the emotion. The poet is as far from the concrete as before. By denying the dead intelligence and putting on the heresy of unintelligence, the poet only succeeds in substituting one set of unnourished conventions for another. What survives, with a deceptive air of reality, is a surface. That the deception is often intentional hardly excuses it. The surface is meant to clothe and illuminate a real substance, but in fact it is impenetrable. We are left, after experiencing this sort of art, with the certainty that there was nothing to penetrate. The surface was perfect; the deceit was childish; and the conception was incorrigibly sentimental: all be-cause of the dogma which made them possible.

If Mr. Cummings' tough-guy poems are excellent examples of this senti-mentality, it is only natural that his other poems—those clothed in the more familiar language of the lyric—should betray even more obviously, even more perfectly, the same fault. There, in the lyric, there is no pretense at hardness of surface. We are admitted at once to the bare emotion. What is most strik-ing, in every instance, about this emotion is the fact that, in so far as it exists at all it is Mr. Cummings' emotion, so that our best knowledge of it must be, finally, our best guess. It is not an emotion resulting from the poem; it existed before the poem began and is a result of the poet's private life. Besides its inspiration, every element in the poem, and its final meaning as well, must be taken at face value or not at all. This is the extreme form, in poetry, of romantic egoism: whatever I experience is real and final, and whatever I say represents what I experience. Such a dogma is the natural counterpart of the denial of the intelligence.

Our interest is not in the abstract principle, but in the results of its application in poetry. Assuming that a poem should in some sense be understood, should have a meaning apart from the poet's private life, either one of two things will be true about any poem written from such an attitude as we have ascribed to Mr. Cummings. Either the poem will appear in terms so conventional that everybody will understand it—when it will be flat and no poem at all; or it will appear in language so far distorted from convention as to be inapprehensible except by lucky guess. In neither instance will the poem be genuinely complete. It will be the notes for a poem, from which might flow an infinite number of possible poems, but from which no particular poem can be certainly deduced. It is the purpose of this paper to examine a few of the more obvious types of distortion which Mr. Cummings has practiced upon language.

The question central to such a discussion will be what kind of meaning does Mr. Cummings' poetry have; what is the kind of equivalence between the language and its object? The pursuit of such a question involves us immediately in the relations between words and feelings, and the relations between the intelligence and its field in experience—all relations which are precise only in terms themselves essentially poetic—in the feeling for an image, the sense of an idiom. Such relations may only be asserted, may be judged only tentatively, only instinctively, by what seems to be the disciplined experience, but what amounts, perhaps, only to the formed taste. Here criticism is appreciation. But appreciation, even, can take measures to be certain of its grounds, and to be full should betray the constant apprehension of an end which is the necessary consequence, the proper rounding off, of just those grounds. In the examination of Mr. Cummings' writings the grounds will be the facts about the words he uses, and the end will be apprehended in the quality of the meaning his use of these words permits.

There is one attitude towards Mr. Cummings' language which has deceived those who hold it. The typographical peculiarities of his verse have caught and irritated public attention. Excessive hyphenation of single words, the use of lower case "i," the breaking of lines, the insertion of punctuation between the letters of a word, and so on, will have a possible critical importance to the textual scholarship of the future; but extensive consideration of these peculiarities today has very little importance, carries almost no reference to the meaning of the poems. Mr. Cummings' experiments in typography merely extend the theory of notation by adding to the number, *not* to the *kind,* of conventions the reader must bear in mind, and are dangerous only because since their uses cannot readily be defined, they often obscure rather than clarify the exact meaning. No doubt the continued practice of such notation would produce a set of well-ordered conventions susceptible of general use. At present the practice can only be "allowed for," recognized in the particular instance, felt, and forgotten: as the diacritical marks in the dictionary are forgotten once the sound of the word has been learned. The poem, after all, only takes wing on the page. It persists in the ear.[3]

Considering typographical peculiarities for our present purposes as either irrelevant or unaccountable, there remain the much more important peculiarities of Mr. Cummings' vocabulary itself; of the poem *after* it has been read, as it is in the mind's ear, as it is on the page only for reassurance and correction.

If a reader, sufficiently familiar with these poems not to be caught on the snag of novelty, inspects carefully any score of them no matter how widely scattered, he will especially be struck by a sameness among them. This sameness will be in two sorts—a vagueness of image and a constant recurrence of words. Since the one depends considerably upon the other, a short list of some of Mr. Cummings' favorite words will be a good preliminary to the examination of his images. In *Tulips and Chimneys* words such as these occur frequently: thrilling, flowers, serious, absolute, sweet, unspeaking, utter, gradual, ultimate, final, serene, frail, grave, tremendous, slender, fragile, skillful, carefully, musical, intent, young, gay, untimid, incorrigible, groping, dim, slow, certain, deliberate, strong, chiselled, subtle, tremulous, perpetual, crisp, perfect, sudden, faint, strenuous, minute, superlative, keen, ecstatic, fleet, delicious stars, enthusiastic, capable, dull, bright. In listing these as favorite words, it is meant that these words do the greater part of the work in the poems where they occur; these are the words which qualify the subject-matter of the poems, and are sometimes even the subjects themselves. Observe that none of them, taken alone, are very concrete words; and observe that many of them are the rather abstract, which is to say typical, names for precise qualities, but are not, and cannot be, as orginally important words

---

[3] It is not meant to disparage Mr. Cummings' inventions, which are often excellent, but to minimize an exaggerated contemporary interest. *A Survey of Modernist Poetry* by Laura Riding and Robert Graves, is a study in original punctuation and spelling. Their point is made by printing sonnet 129 in its original notation beside a modern version; the point being that Shakespeare knew what he was doing and that his editors did not.

in a poem, very precise or very concrete or very abstract: they are middling words, not in themselves very much one thing or the other and should be useful only with respect to something concrete in itself.

If we take Mr. Cummings' most favored word "flower" and inspect the uses to which he puts it, we should have some sort of key to the kind of poetry he writes. In *Tulips and Chimneys* the word "flower" turns up, to a casual count, forty-eight times, and in &, a much smaller volume, twenty-one times. We have among others the following: smile like a flower; riverly as a flower; steeped in burning flowers; last flower; lipping flowers; more silently than a flower; snow flower; world flower; softer than flowers; forehead a flight of flowers; feet are flowers in vases; air is deep with flowers; slow supple flower of beauty; flower-terrible; flower of thy mouth; stars and flowers; mouth a new flower; flower of silence; god's flowers; flowers of reminding; dissonant flowers; flower-stricken air; Sunday flower; tremendous flower; speaking flower; flowers of kiss; futile flowers, etc., etc. Besides the general term there is a quantity of lilies and roses, and a good assortment of daisies, pansies, buttercups, violets and chrysanthemums. There are also many examples of such associated words as "petals" and "blooms" and "blossoms," which, since they are similarly used, may be taken as alternative to flowers.

Now it is evident that this word must attract Mr. Cummings' mind very much; it must contain for him an almost unlimited variety and extent of meaning; as the mystic says God, or at least as the incomplete mystic repeats the name of God to every occasion of his soul, Mr. Cummings in some of his poems says flower. The question is, whether or not the reader can possibly have shared the experience which Mr. Cummings has had of the word; whether or not it is possible to discern, after any amount of effort, the precise impact which Mr. Cummings undoubtedly feels upon his whole experience when he uses the word. "Flower" like every other word not specifically the expression of a logical relation, began life as a metaphor, as a leap from feeling to feeling, as a bridge in the imagination to give meaning to both those feelings. Presumably, the amount of meaning possible to the word is increased with each use, but only the meaning *possible*. Actually, in practice, a very different process goes on. Since people are occupied mostly with communication and argument and conversation, with the erection of discursive relationships, words are commonly spoken and written with the least possible meaning preserved, instead of the most. History is taken for granted, ignored or denied. Only the outsides of words, so to speak, are used; and doubtless the outsides of words are all that the discursive intellect needs. But when a word is used in a poem it should be the sum of all its appropriate history made concrete and particular in the individual context; and in poetry all words act *as if* they were so used, because the only kind of meaning poetry can have requires that all its words resume their full life: the full life being modified and made unique by the *qualifications* the words perform one upon the other in the poem. Thus even a very bad poem may seem good to its author, when the author is not an acute critic and believes that there is life in his words merely because there was life (and a very different sort of life, truly) in the feelings which they represent. An author should remember, with the Indians, that the reality of a word is anterior to, and greater than, his use of it can ever be; that there is a perfection to the feelings in words to which his cannot hope to attain, but that his chief labor will be toward the approximation of that perfection.

We sometimes speak of a poet as a master of his words, and we sometimes say that a man's poetry has been run away with by words—meaning that he has not mastered his words but has been overpowered by his peculiar experience of certain among them. Both these notions are commonly improper, because they represent misconceptions of the nature of poetry in so far as they lay any stress upon originality, or lack of it, in the poet's use of words. The only mastery possible to the poet consists in that entire submission to his words which is perfect knowledge. The only originality of which the poet is properly capable will be in the choice of order, and even this choice is largely a process of discovery rather than of origination. As for words running away with a poet or poem, it would be more accurate to say that the poet's *ideas* had run away with him than his words.

This is precisely what has occurred to Mr. Cummings in his use of the word "flower" as a maid of all work. The word has become an idea, and in the process has been deprived of its history, its qualities, and its meaning. An idea, the intellectual pin upon which a thought is hung, is not transmissible in poetry as an important element in the poem and ought only to be employed to pass over, with the greatest possible velocity, the area of the uninteresting (what the poet was not interested in). That is, a poem whose chief intent was the notation of character and yet required a descriptive setting might well use for the description such vague words as space and time, but could not use such words as goodness or nobleness without the risk of flatness. In Mr. Cummings' poetry we find the contrary; the word "flower," because of the originality with which he conceives it, becomes an idea and is used to represent the most interesting and most important aspect of his poem. Hence the center of the poem is permanently abstract and unknowable for the reader, and remains altogether without qualifications and concreteness It is not the mere frequency of use that deadens the word flower into an idea; it is the kind of thought which each use illustrates in common. By seldom saying *what* flower, by seldom relating immitigably the abstract word to the specific experience, the content of the word vanishes; it has no inner mystery, only an impenetrable surface.

This is the defect, the essential deceit, we were trying to define. Without questioning Mr. Cummings, or any poet, as to sincerity (which is a personal attitude, irrelevant to the poetry considered) it is possible to say that when in any poem the important words are forced by their use to remain impenetrable, when they can be made to surrender nothing actually to the senses—then the poem is defective and the poet's words have so far deceived him as to become ideas merely.[4] Mr. Cummings is not so much writing poetry, as he is dreaming, idly ringing the changes of his reveries.

Perhaps a small divagation may make clearer the relation of these remarks to Mr. Cummings' poems. Any poetry which does not consider itself as much of an art and having the same responsibilities to the consumer as the arts of silversmithing or cobbling shoes—any such poetry is likely to do little more than rehearse a waking dream. Dreams are everywhere ominous and full of meaning; and why should they not be? They hold the images of the secret self, and to the initiate dreamer betray the nerve of life at every turn, not through any effort to do so, or because of any inherited regimen, but simply because they cannot help it. Dreams are like that—to the dreamer the maximal limit of experience. As it happens, dreams employ words and pictorial images to fill out their flux with a veil of substance. Pictures are natural to everyone, and words, because they are prevalent, seem common and inherently sensible. Hence, both picture and word, and then with a little stretching of the fancy the substance of the dream itself, seem expressible just as they occur—as things created, as the very flux of life. Mr. Cummings' poems are often nothing more than the report of just such dreams. He believes he knows what he knows, and no doubt he does. But he also believes, apparently, that the words which he encourages most vividly to mind are those most precisely fitted to put his poem on paper. He transfers the indubitable magic of his private musings from the cell of his mind, where it is honest incantation, to the realm of poetry. Here he forgets that poetry, so far as it takes a permanent form, is written and is meant to be read, and that it cannot be a mere private musing. Merely because his private fancy furnishes his liveliest images, is the worst reason for assuming that this private fancy will be approximately experienced by the reader or even indicated on the printed page.

But it is unfair to limit this description to Mr. Cummings; indeed, so limited, it is not even a description of Mr. Cummings. Take the *Oxford Book of English Verse*, or any anthology of poems equally well known, and turn

[4] It should be confessed that for all those persons who regard poetry only as a medium of communication, these remarks are quite vitiated. What is communicated had best remain as abstract as possible, dealing with the concrete as typical only; then "meaning" will be found to reside most clearly in the realm of ideas, and everything will be given as of equal import. But here poetry is regarded not at all as communication but as expression, as statement, as presentation of experience, and the emphasis will be on what is made known concretely. The question is not what one shares with the poet, but what one knows in the poem.

from the poems printed therein of such widely separated poets as Surrey, Crashaw, Marvell, Burns, Wordsworth, Shelley, and Swinburne, to the collected works of these poets respectively. Does not the description of Mr. Cummings' mind at work given above apply nearly as well to the bulk of this poetry as to that of Mr. Cummings, at least on the senses' first immersion? The anthology poems being well known are conceived to be understood, to be definitely intelligible, and to have, without inspection, a precise meaning. The descent upon the collected poems of all or of any one of these authors is by and large a descent into tenuity. Most of their work, most of any poet's work, with half a dozen exceptions, is tenuous and vague, private exercises or public playthings of a soul in verse. So far as he is able, the reader struggles to reach the concrete, the solid, the definite; he must have these qualities, or their counterparts among the realm of the spirit, before he can understand what he reads. To translate such qualities from the realm of his private experience to the conventional forms of poetry is the problem of the poet; and the problem of the reader, likewise, is to come well equipped with the talent and the taste for discerning the meaning of those conventions as they particularly occur. Neither the poet's casual language nor the reader's casual interlocution is likely to be much help. There must be a ground common but exterior to each: that is the poem. The best poems take the best but not always the hardest reading; and no doubt it is so with the writing. Certainly, in neither case are dreams or simple reveries enough. Dreams are natural and are minatory or portentous; but except when by accident they fall into forms that fit the intelligence, they never negotiate the miracle of meaning between the poet and the poem, the poem and the reader.

Most poetry fails of this negotiation, and it is sometimes assumed that the negotiation was never meant, by the poet, to be made. For the poet, private expression is said to be enough; for the reader, the agitation of the senses, the perception of verbal beauty, the mere sense of stirring life in the words, are supposed sufficient. If this defense had a true premise—if the poet did express himself to his private satisfaction—it would be unanswerable; and to many it is so. But I think the case is different, and this is the real charge against Mr. Cummings: the poet does not ever express himself privately. The mind cannot understand, cannot properly know its own musings until those musings take some sort of conventional form. Properly speaking, a poet, or any man, cannot be adequate to himself in terms of himself. True consciousness and true expression of consciousness must be external to the blind seat of consciousness—man as sensorium. Even a simple image must be fitted among other images, and conned with them, before it is understood. That is, it must take a form in language which is highly traditional and conventional. The genius of the poet is to make the convention apparently disappear into the use to which he puts it.

Mr. Cummings and the group with which he is here roughly associated, the anti-culture or anti-intelligence group, persists to the contrary. Because experience is fragmentary as it strikes the consciousness it is thought to be essentially discontinuous and therefore essentially unintelligible except in the fragmentary form in which it occurred. They credit the words they use with immaculate conception and there hold them unquestionable. A poem, because it happens, must mean something and mean it without relation to anything but the private experience which inspired it. Certainly it means something, but not a poem; it means that something exciting happened to the writer and that a mystery is happening to the reader. The fallacy is double: they believe in the inexorable significance of the unique experience; and they have discarded the only method of making the unique experience into a poem —the conventions of the intelligence. As a matter of fact they do not write without conventions, but being ignorant of what they use, they resort most commonly to their own inefficient or superficial conventions—such as Mr. Cummings' flower and doll. The effect is convention without substance; the unique experience becomes a rhetorical assurance.

If we examine next, for the sake of the greatest possible contrast, one of the "tough" poems in Is 5, we will find a similar breach with the concrete. The use of vague words like "flower" in the lyrical poems as unexpanded similes, is no more an example of sentimental egoism than the use of vague conventions about villains. The distortion differs in terms but is essentially identical.

Sometimes the surface of the poem is so well constructed that the distortion is hard to discover. Intensity of process occasionally triumphs over the subject. Less frequently the subject itself is conceived directly and takes naturally the terms which the language supplies. The poem numbered "One-XII" in Is 5 is an example in so far as the sentimental frame does not obscure the process.

> now dis "daughter" uv eve (who aint precisely slim) sim
> ply don't know duh meanin uv duh woid sin in
> not disagreeable contras tuh dat not exactly fat
> "father" (adjustin his robe) who now puts on his flat hat.

It is to be noted in this epigram, that there is no inexorable reason for either the dialect or the lapses from it into straight English. No one in particular is speaking, unless it be Mr. Cummings slumming in morals along with he-men and lady social workers, and taking it for granted that the dialect and the really refined language which the dialect exercises together give a setting. There are many other poems in Is 5, more sentimental and less successful, where the realism is of a more obvious sort; not having reference to an ideal so much as to a kind of scientific reality. That is, there is an effort to ground an emotion, or the facts which make the emotion, in the style of the character to whom the emotion happens. It is the reporter, the man with the good ear for spoken rhythms, who writes out of memory. The war poems and the poem about Bill and his chip ("One-XVI") are examples. Style in this sense (something laid on) is only an attribute; is not the man; is not the character. And when it is substituted for character, it is likely to be sentimental and melodramatic. That is, the emotion which is named in the poem (by one of its attributes) is in excess of its established source (that same attribute). There is a certain immediate protection afforded to this insufficiency by the surface toughness, by the convention of burlesque; as if by mocking oneself one made sure there was something to mock. It is a kind of trickery resulting from eager but lazy senses; where the sensation itself is an excess, and appears to have done all the work of intuition and intelligence; where sensation seems expert without incorporation into experience. As if sensation could be anything more than the idea of sensation, so far as poetry goes, without being attached to some central body of experience, genuinely understood and *formed* in the mind.

The intrusion of science into art always results in a sentimental realism and always obfuscates form when that science is not kept subordinate to the qualitative experience of the senses—as witness the run of sociological novels. The analogues of science, where conventions are made to do the work of feeling instead of crowning it, are even more dangerous. Mr. Cummings' tough guy and his hard-boiled dialects are such analogues.

Mr. Cummings has a fine talent for using familiar, even almost dead words, in such a context as to make them suddenly impervious to every ordinary sense; they become unable to speak, but with a great air of being bursting with something very important and precise to say. "The bigness of cannon is *skilful* . . . enormous rhythm of *absurdity* . . . *slimness* of *evenslicing* eyes are chisels . . . electric Distinct face haughtily vital *clinched* in a swoon of *synopsis* . . . my friend's being continually whittles *keen* careful futile *flowers*," etc. With the possible exception of the compound *evenslicing* the italicized words are all ordinary words; all in normal contexts have a variety of meaning both connotative and denotative; the particular context being such as to indicate a particular meaning, to establish precisely a feeling, a sensation or a relation.

Mr. Cummings' contexts are employed to an opposite purpose in so far as they wipe out altogether the history of the word, its past associations and general character. To seize Mr. Cummings' meaning there is only the free and *uninstructed* intuition. Something precise is no doubt intended; the warrant for the belief is in the almost violent isolation into which the words are thrown; but that precision can seldom, by this method, become any more than just that "something precise." The reality, the event, the feeling, which we will allow Mr. Cummings has in mind, is not sensibly in the word It is one thing for meaning to be difficult, or abstruse—hidden in its heart, that is. "Absent thee from *felicity* a while," Blake's "Time is the mercy of eternity" are reasonable examples; there the mystery is inside the words. In Mr. Cummings' words the mystery flies in the face, is on the surface; because there is no inside, no realm of possibility, of essence.

The general movement of Mr. Cummings' language is away from communicable precision. If it be argued that the particular use of one of the italicized words above merely makes the word unique, the retort is that such uniqueness is too perfect, is sterile. If by removing the general sense of a word the special sense is apotheosized, it is only so at the expense of the general sense itself. The destruction of the general sense of a word results in the loss of that word's individuality; for in practice the character of a word (which is its sense) is manifest only in good society, and meaning is distinguished only by conventional association. Mr. Cummings' use of words results in a large number of conventions, but these conventions do not permeate the words themselves, do not modify their souls or change their fates; they cannot be adopted by the reader because they cannot be essentially understood. They should rather be called inventions.

If we take a paragraph from the poem beginning on page thirty in *Is 5*, we will discover another terminus of the emotional habit of mind which produced the emphasis on the word "flower" in *Tulips and Chimneys*.

the Bar. tinking luscious jugs dint of ripe silver with warmlyish wetflat splurging smells waltz the glush of squirting taps plus slush of foam knocked off and a faint piddle-of-drops she says I ploc spittle what the lands thaz me kin in no sir hopping sawdust you kiddo he's a palping wreaths of badly Yep cigars who jim hin why gluey grins topple together eyes pout gestures stickily point made glints squinting who's a wink bum-nothing and money fuzzily mouths take big wobbly foot-steps every goggle cent of it get out ears dribbles sofe right old feller belch the chap hic summore eh chuckles skulch.

Now the point is that the effect of this whole paragraph has much in common with the effect of the word "flower." It is a flower disintegrated, and the parts are not component; so that by presenting an analysis of his image Mr. Cummings has not let us into its secret; the analysis is not a true analysis, because it exhibits, finally, what are still only the results, not the grounds, of his private conventions, his personal emotions. It is indubitable that the words are alive; they jostle, even overturn, the reader in the assurance of their vitality; but the notion of what their true vitality is remains Mr. Cummings' very own. The words remain emotive. They have a gusty air of being something, but they defeat themselves in the effort to say what, and come at last to a bad end, all fallen in a heap.

The easiest *explanation* of the passage would be to say that each separate
little collection of words in it is a note for an image; an abstraction, very keen
and lively in Mr. Cummings' mind, of something very precise and concrete.
Some of the words seem like a painter's notes, some a philologist's. But they
are all, as they are presented, notes, abstractions, ideas—with their concrete
objects unknown—except to the most arbitrary guess. The guess must be
arbitrary because of the quantity, not the quality, of the words employed. Mr.
Cummings is not here overworking the individual words, but by heaping so
many of them together he destroys their individuality. Meaning really residual
in the word is not exhausted, is not even touched; it must remain abstract and
only an emotional substitute for it can be caught. The interesting fact about
emotional substitutes in poetry, as elsewhere, is their thinness, and the inadequacy resulting from the thinness. The thinness is compulsory because they
can, so far as the poem is concerned, exist only as a surface; they cannot possess
tentacular roots reaching into, and feeding on, feelings, because the feelings
do not exist, are only present by legerdemain. Genuine emotion in poetry
perhaps does not *exist* at all; though it is none the less real for that, because a
genuine emotion does not need the warrant of existence: it is the necessary
result, in the mind, of a convention of feelings: like the notion of divine grace.

In *Tulips and Chimneys* (p. 109) there is a poem whose first and last lines
supply an excellent opposition of proper and improper distortion of language.

> the Cambridge ladies who live in furnished souls . . .
>   the
> moon rattles like a fragment of angry candy.

In the context the word "soul" has the element of surprise which is surprise
at *justness*; at *aptness*; it fits in and finishes off the notion of the line. "Furnished souls" is a good, if slight, conceit; and there is no trouble for the reader
who wishes to know what the line means: he has merely to *extend* his knowledge slightly, just as Mr. Cummings merely extended the sense of his language slightly by releasing his particular words in this particular order. The
whole work that the poet here demands of his reader is pretty well defined.
The reader does not have to *guess*; he is enabled to *know*. The reader is not
collecting data, he is aware of a meaning.

It would be unfair not to quote the context of the second line.

> . . . the Cambridge ladies do not care, above
> Cambridge if sometimes in its box of
> sky lavender and cornerless, the
> moon rattles like a fragment of angry candy.

We can say that Mr. Cummings is putting beauty next to the tawdry; juxta-
posing the dead with the live; or that he is being sentimentally philosophical

in verse—that is, releasing from inadequate sources something intended to be an emotion.[5]

We can go on illustrating Mr. Cummings' probable intentions almost infinitely. What Mr. Cummings likes or admires, what he holds dear in life, he very commonly calls flowers, or dolls, or candy—terms with which he is astonishingly generous; as if he thought by making his terms general enough their vagueness could not matter, and never noticed that the words so used enervate themselves in a kind of hardened instinct. We can understand what Mr. Cummings intended by "moon" and "candy" but in the process of understanding, the meaning of the words themselves disappears. The thrill of the association of "rattles" with "moon" and "angry" with "candy" becomes useless as a guide. "Rattles" and "angry" can only be continued in the meaning of the line if the reader supplies them with a force, a definiteness of suggestion, with which Mr. Cummings has not endowed them.

The distortion is here not a release of observation so keen that commonplace language would not hold it; it is not the presentation of a vision so complete that words must lose their normal meanings in order to suggest it. It is, on the contrary, the distortion of the commonplace itself; and the difficulty about a commonplace is that it cannot be known, it has no character, no fate, and no essence. It is a substitute for these.

True meaning (which is here to say knowledge) can only exist where some contact, however remote, is preserved between the language, forms, or symbols in which it is given and something concrete, individual, or sensual which inspired it; and the degree in which the meaning is seized will depend on the degree in which the particular concreteness is realized. Thus the technique of "meaning" will employ distortion only in so far as the sense of this concreteness is promoted by it. When contrast and contradiction disturb the ultimate precision of the senses the distortion involved is inappropriate and destructive. Mr. Cummings' line about the moon and candy does not weld a contradiction, does not identify a substance by a thrill of novel association. It leaves the reader at a loss: where it is impossible to *know,* after any amount of effort and good will, what the words mean. If it be argued that Mr. Cummings was not interested in meaning then Mr. Cummings is not a serious poet, is a mere collector of sensations, and can be of very little value to us. And to defend Mr. Cummings on the ground that he is in the pretty good company of Swinburne, Crashaw, and Victor Hugo, is partly to ignore the fact that by the same argument all four also enjoy the companionship of Edgar Guest. Such defense would show a very poor knowledge of the verses of Mr. Cummings, who is nothing if not serious in the attempt to exhibit precise knowledge. His in-

---

[5] That is, as the most common form of sentimentality is the use of emotion in *excess* of its impetus in the feelings, here we have an example of emotion which fails by a great deal to *come up* to its impetus. It is a very different thing from understatement, where the implications are always definite and where successful disarming.

terest in words and in their real meanings is probably greater than that of most poets of similar dimensions. He has consciously stretched syntax, word order, and meaning in just the effort to expand knowledge in poetry; and his failure is because he has gone too far, has lost sight of meaning altogether—and because, perhaps, the experience which he attempts to translate into poetry remained always personal to him and was never known objectively as itself. By his eagerness Mr. Cummings' relation to language has become confused; he has put down what has meant much to him and can mean little to us, because for us it is not put down—is only indicated, only possibly there. The freshness and depth of his private experience is not denied; but it is certain that, so far as its meaning goes, in the poetry into which he translated it, sentimentality, empty convention, and commonplace rule. In short, Mr. Cummings' poetry ends in ideas *about* things.

When Mr. Cummings resorts of language for the *thrill* that words may be made to give, when he allows his thrill to appear as an equivalent for concrete meaning, he is often more successful than when he is engaged more ambitiously. This is true of poets like Swinburne and Poe, Shelley and the early Marlowe: where the first pair depended almost as much upon *thrill* as Mr. Cummings in those poems where they made use of it at all, and where the second pair, particularly Marlowe, used their thrills more appropriately as ornament: where all four were most successful in their less ambitious works, though perhaps not as interesting. Likewise, today, there is the example of Archibald MacLeish, whose best lines are those that thrill and do nothing more. So that at least in general opinion Mr. Cummings is in this respect not in bad company. But if an examination of thrill be made, whether in Mr. Cummings' verse or in that of others, it will be shown that the use of thrill has at heart the same sentimental impenetrability that defeats the possibility of meaning elsewhere. Only here, in the realm of thrill, the practice is comparatively less illegitimate. Thrill, by itself, or in its proper place, is an exceedingly important element in any poem: it is the circulation of its blood, the *quickness* of life, by which we know it, when there is anything in it to know, most intimately. To use a word for its thrill is to resurrect it from the dead; it is the incarnation of life in consciousness; it is movement.[6]

---

[6] Cf. Owen Barfield's *Poetic Diction* (London, Faber and Gwyer, 1928), page 202. "For what is absolutely necessary to the present existence of poetry? Movement. The wisdom which she has imparted may remain for a time at rest, but she herself will always be found to have gone forward to where there is life, and therefore movement, *now*. And we have seen that the experience of aesthetic pleasure betrays the real presence of movement. . . . But without the continued existence of poetry, without a steady influx of new meaning into language, even the knowledge and wisdom which poetry herself has given in the past must wither away into a species of mechanical calculation. Great poetry is the progressive incarnation of life in consciousness." That is, we must know what thrills us; else being merely thrilled we are left gasping and aghast, like the little girl on the roller-coaster.

But what Mr. Cummings does, when he is using language as thrill, is not to resurrect a word from the dead: he more often produces an apparition, in itself startling and even ominous, but still only a ghost: it is all a thrill, and what it is that thrilled us cannot be determined. For example, in *XLI Poems*, the following phrases depend considerably for their effect upon the thrill that is in them: "Prisms of sharp *mind;* where strange birds *purr;* into the *smiling* sky *tense* with *blending;* ways cloaked with *renewal;* sinuous riot; *steeped* with burning flowers; little kittens who are called *spring;* electric Distinct face haughtily vital clinched in a *swoon* of synopsis; unreal *precise* intrinsic fragment of actuality; an orchid whose *velocity* is *sculptural;* scythe takes *crisply* the *whim* of thy *smoothness;* perpendicular taste; wet stars, etc., etc." (The italics are mine.)

Take especially the phrase, "scythe takes *crisply* the *whim* of thy *smoothness.*" We know in the poem that it is the scythe of death and that it is youth and beauty (in connection with love) that is to be cut off. So much is familiar, is very conventional; and so the conventional or dead emotion is placed before us; the educated reader receives it and reacts to it without a whimper. But Mr. Cummings must not have been content with presenting the conventional emotion in its conventional form; he felt bound to enliven it with metaphor, with overtones of the senses and the spirit: so that he substituted for the direct statement a rather indirect image combining three usually sensed words for the sake of the *thrill* the special combination might afford. As the phrase stands there is no precision in it. There is a great suggestion of precision about it—like men going off to war; but precisely *what* is left for the reader to guess, to supply from his own heart. By themselves *whim* and *smoothness* are abstract quality words; and in order for them to escape the tensity, the firm disposition, of concrete meaning, they should demand a particular reference.

Smoothness is probably the smoothness of the body and is used here as a kind of metonymy; but it may be pure metaphor and represent what is really to die—the spirit—taken in its physical terms; or it may be that all that is to be understood is a pure tautology. And so on. Even with this possible variety of reference, *smoothness* would not be very objectionable, were it the only word in the phrase used in this way, or were the other words used to clarify the *smoothness.* But we have also the noun *whim* bearing directly on *smoothness* and the adverb *crisply* which while it directly modifies *takes,* really controls the entire phrase. Taken seriously, *whim,* with reference to the smoothness of either the body or the spirit or the love it inspires, is to say the least a light word; one might almost say a "metrical" word, introduced to stretch the measure, or because the author liked the sound of it, or enjoyed whimsy. It diminishes without limiting the possibilities of *smoothness.* Because it is here, in the phrase, it is inseparable from the phrase's notion of smoothness; yet instead of assisting, tends to prevent what that notion of smoothness is from being divulged.

Crisply is even more difficult to account for; associated with a scythe it perhaps brings to mind the sound of a scythe in a hayfield, which is surely not the reference here intended; it would be very difficult for such a crispness to associate itself with death, which the scythe represents, or *whim,* or *smoothness* in either the spiritual or fleshly sense. If it implies merely a cleanness, a swiftness of motion in the apparition of death, some other word would have seemed better chosen. If this analysis be correct, the three words are unalterably combined by the force of *crisply* in such a way as to defeat the only possible sense their *thrilling* use would have had. They are, so to speak, only the notions of themselves and those selves must remain forever unknown. All we are left with in such a phrase as this is the strangeness which struck us on our first encounter; and the only difference is that the strangeness is the more intensified the more we prolong the examination. This is another test of poetry: whether we understand the *strangeness* of a poem or not.[7]

As it happens there is an exquisite example of the proper use of this strangeness, this thrill, in another poem of Mr. Cummings'; where he speaks of a cathedral before whose face "the streets turn *young* with rain." While there might be some question as to whether the use of *young* presents the only adequate image, there is certainly no question at all that the phrase is entirely successful: that is, the suggestive feeling in *young* makes the juncture, the emotional conjugation, of streets and rain transparent and perfect. This may be so because there is no element of essential contradiction, in the terms of feeling, between the emotional word *young* and the factual word *streets* and *rain;* or because, positively, what happens to the context by the insertion of *young* is, by a necessary leap of the imagination, something qualified. *Young* may be as abstract a word by itself, as purely relative and notional a word, as any other; but here it is brought into the concrete, is fixed there in a proper habitation. Just because reference is not commonly made either to young streets or young rain, the combination here effected is the more appropriate. The surprise, the contrast, which lend force to the phrase, do not exist in the poem; but exist, if at all, rather in the mind of the reader who did not foresee the slight stretch of his sensibility that the phrase requires—which the phrase

---

[7] *Poetic Diction, op. cit.,* pp. 197–8: "It (strangeness) is not synonymous with wonder; for wonder is our reaction to things which we are conscious of not quite understanding, or at any rate of understanding less than we had thought. The element of strangeness in beauty has the contrary effect. It arises from contact with a different kind of *consciousness* from our own, different, yet not so remote that we cannot partly share it, as indeed, in such a connexion, the mere word 'contact' implies. Strangeness, in fact, arouses wonder when we do not understand; aesthetic imagination when we do."

not only requires but necessitates. This then is a *strangeness* understood by its own viableness. No preliminary agreement of taste, or contract of symbols, was necessary.

The point is that Mr. Cummings did not here attempt the impossible, he merely stretched the probable. The business of the poet who deals largely with tactual and visual images, as Mr. Cummings does, for the meat of his work, is to escape the prison of his private mind; to use in his poem as little as possible of the experience that happened to him personally, and on the other hand to employ as much as possible of that experience as it is data.

It is idle for a critic to make the familiar statement that the mind of the writer is his work, or that "the style is the man," when by mind and man is meant the private experience of the author. So far as, in this sense, the mind *is* the work, or the style *is* the man, we can understand the work or the style only through an accidental unanimity; and what we understand is likely to be very thin—perhaps only the terms of understanding. For the author himself, in such circumstances, can have understood very little more. He has been pursuing the impossible, when the probable was right at hand; he has been transcending his experience instead of submitting to it. And this is just what Mr. Cummings does in the phrases quoted above.

It would be ungracious to suppose that as a poet "a swoon of synopsis" did not represent to Mr. Cummings a very definite and very suggestive image. But to assent to that image would be a kind of *tour de force;* the application of such assent would imply that because the words appear, and being words contain notions, they must in this particular instance exhibit the undeniable sign of interior feeling. The proper process of poetry designs exactly what the reader will perceive; that is what is meant when a word is said to be inevitable or *juste.* But this exactness of perception can only come about when there is an extreme fidelity on the part of the poet to his words as living things; which he can discover and control—which he must learn, and nourish, and stretch; but which he cannot invent. The unanimity in our possible experience of words implies that the only unanimity which the reader can feel in what the poet represents must be likewise exterior to the poet; must be somehow both anterior and posterior to the poet's own experience. The poet's mind, perhaps, is what he is outside himself with; is what he has learned; is what he knows; it is also what the reader knows. So long as he is content to remain in his private mind, he is unknowable, impenetrable, and sentimental. All his words perhaps must thrill us, because we cannot know them in the very degree that we sympathize with them. But the best thrills are those we have without knowing it.

This essay has proceeded so far on the explicit assumption that the poems of Mr. Cummings are unintelligible, and that no amount of effort on the part of the reader can make them less so. We began by connecting Mr. Cummings to two schools, or groups, which are much the same essentially—the anti-culture group which denies the intelligence, and the group, not limited to writers, of which the essential attitude is most easily defined as sentimental egoism or romantic idealism. Where these schools are most obviously identical is in the poetry they nourish; the avowed interest is the relentless pursuit of the actual in terms of the immediate as the immediate is given, without overt criticism, to the ego. Unintelligibility is a necessary consequence of such a pursuit, if by the intelligible we mean something concrete, qualified, perma-nent, and public. Poetry, if we understand it, is not in immediacy at all. It is not given to the senses or to the free intuition. Thus, when poetry is written as if its substance were immediate and given, we have as a result a distorted sensibility and a violent inner confusion. We have, if the poet follows his principles, something abstract, vague, impermanent, and essentially private. When every sensation and every word is taken as final and perfect, the sub-stance which sensations report and for which words must stand remains in-explicable. We can understand only by accident.

Of course there is another side to the matter. In a sense anyone can under-stand Mr. Cummings and his kind by the mere assertion that he does under-stand. Nothing else is needed but a little natural sympathy and a certain apt-ness for the resumption of a childish sensibility. In much the same way we understand a stranger's grief—by setting up a private and less painful simula-crum. If we take the most sentimental and romantic writers as they come, there will be always about their works an excited freshness, the rush of sensa-tion and intuition, all the ominous glow of immediacy. They will be eagerly at home in the mystery of life. Adroitness, expertness, readiness for any expe-rience, will enlighten their activities even where they most miserably fail. They are all actors, ready to take any part, for they put themselves, and noth-ing else, into every part they play. Commonly their real success will depend on the familiarity of the moments into which they sink themselves; they will depend on convention more than others, because they have nothing else to depend on.

So with the poetry of Mr. Cummings we might be altogether contented and pleased, were he himself content with the measure of his actual performance. But no poetry is so pretentious. No poetry ever claimed to mean more; and in making this claim it cannot avoid submitting itself, disastrously, to the criti-cism of the intelligence. So soon as we take it seriously, trying to discover what it really says about human destiny and the terms of love and death, we see how little material there is in this poetry except the assurance, made with con-tinuous gusto, that the material exists. We look at the poetry. Sometimes one word, in itself vague and cloudy, is made to take on the work of an entire philosophy—like flower. Sometimes words pile themselves up blindly, each defeating the purport of the others. No feeling is ever defined. No emotion betrays a structure. Experience is its own phantoms, and flows willy-nilly. With the reality of experience the reality of language is lost. No metaphor crosses the bridge of tautology, and every simile is unexpanded. All the *thought* is metonymy, yet the substance is never assigned; so in the end we have only the thrill of substance.

Such an art when it pretends to measure life is essentially vicarious; it is a substitute for something that never was—like a tin soldier, or Peter Pan. It has all the flourish of life and every sentimental sincerity. Taken for what it is, it is charming and even instructive. Taken solemnly, as it is meant to be, the distortion by which it exists is too much for it, and it seems a kind of baby-talk.

From *The Double Agent. Essays in Craft and Elucidation* by R. P. Blackmur, pp. 1–29. Arrow Editions. Copyright, 1935, by R. P. Blackmur. Reprinted by permission of the author. First published in *The Hound and Horn*, Vol. IV (January–March, 1931), pp. 163–192.

PHILIP BLAIR RICE
Paul Valéry
[1930]

M. PAUL VALÉRY has declared from time to time that his poetry is only an exercise. Perhaps this is but mock humility: in any case, his readers refuse to believe that verse so lovely as much of his can fail to be worth while for itself alone. Certainly no other poet enjoys an equal esteem in France today, and it was as a practitioner of *poésie pure* that he was elected to the French Academy, through the able publicity work of the Abbé Brémond. M. Valéry, furthermore, is one of the few poets of his nation who have been widely read abroad; floods of essays on his poetic technique have appeared in many languages.

But for once let us take the man at his word. He has versified only intermittently. He does not seem to care whether anyone reads his poetry or not: his volumes are issued in limited editions, which sell at four times their marked price as soon as they appear. This may be, as M. Souday suggests, merely "une espèce de coquetterie, de manège habile pour se faire désirer." Nevertheless it is difficult to read Valéry's works or to hear him speak without believing in his sincerity. Both his verse and his prose have centered around certain problems which for long periods of time have become so absorbing that he has given up poetical composition entirely. If his poetry is only an exercise, an exercise for what?

Before he was twenty, under Mallarmé's influence the poet began to write Symbolist verse, which appeared in the reviews of the cult. Then in 1894, at the age of twenty-three, Valéry was asked to do an essay on Leonardo. Ever since, he has been in quest of something, and the germs of that quest are to be found in the early *Introduction à la Méthode de Léonard de Vinci*. Valéry saw in Leonardo, so he later wrote, the "principal character of that *Comédie Intellectuelle* which has not hitherto found its poet, and which would be, to my taste, still more precious than the *Comédie Humaine,* and even than the *Divine Comedy*." The object of this study he stated as follows: "I felt that this master of his means, this possessor of design, of images, of calculation, had found the central attitude starting from which the undertakings of knowledge and the operations of art are equally possible, and a happy reciprocity between analysis and acts is singularly probable."

With Leonardo, then, the accepted example of the universal man, did Valéry's search begin. The universal man, he indicates, is not necessarily a jack-of-all-trades. In the first place, he is universal not in the sense of one who is able to do a little of everything but of one who attains to a balance of his faculties. This mental proportion enabled Leonardo, in both his art and his science, to discover universal laws. The secret of this man of the Renaissance lay in his ability to find relations between "things whose law of continuity escapes us." His method was what Valéry calls "construction," a word used "to designate more emphatically the problem of human intervention in the things of the world and to direct the reader's mind toward the logic of the subject, a material suggestion."

Valéry takes up Leonardo's paintings and his architectural and engineering works, showing that his hero sought objective standards for their construction. These standards are found in the geometrical aspects of composition, in the dictates of perspective and in Leonardo's fancy that "the air is filled with an infinite number of straight and radiating lines, intersecting and interweaving without ever borrowing each other's paths, and they represent for each object the true form of its explanation (or its essence)."

As the fine arts go farther from architecture, the more intractable "human element" becomes of increasing importance, and it is necessary to find a non-mathematical objectivity in valuing the work of art. For literature this is difficult and Valéry does little but adduce Poe's theory that the poem must be made not for the poet's own good pleasure, but according to psychological laws by which it will realise a common state in those who read it, even if the readers be taken as a choice few with a similar foundation of culture. "The function of the poet is not to be inspired himself, but to create inspiration in his readers," as M. Valéry later phrased it.

Universality, or objectivity, therefore, requires a discounting of the artist's personal eccentricities. Here Valéry breaks with the main Romantic tradition, which coddled the artist with the notion that all he had to do was to develop his individuality and let it drip over on paper or canvas. Valéry is struggling to escape from the subjectivism which infected the art and thought of the nineteenth century: "Our personality is only a *thing*, mutable and accidental. . . . All criticism is dominated by the superannuated principle that the man is the *cause* of the work—as the criminal in the eyes of the law is the cause of the crime. They are rather the effect!" Or again: "An artist pays for every genuine discovery with a decrease in the importance of his 'ego.' A *person* loses something of himself for everything beautiful he has created." The superior man, he reminds us, is never an "original," and the history of his life is wholly inadequate to explain his works.

If the works are so important, why did Leonardo leave so much unfinished? Valéry implies that even works are incidental to the great artist. "To live, and even to live well, is only a means for him. . . . To act is only an exercise. To love—I don't know if he can." All are subsidiary to the attainment of true universality, which is at the same time to achieve consciousness of self. What self is it that Valéry is trying to know? Not the individual self, the personality, certainly. The superior man, he believes, moves toward a state of pure consciousness, or the pure ego (*le moi pur*), which is identical with the knowledge of universal laws and relations. Rather than Hegelian, it is Spinozistic: Valéry arrives at something very like Spinoza's Intellectual Love of God. This conclusion, it should be remarked, was at most only implicit in the early *Introduction,* for it is first given full statement in the "Note and Digression" which he wrote as a preface to that essay in 1919.

We may, then, find it fruitful to approach Valéry's life work by taking it as the quest for universality. His success may be judged accordingly. From the beginning we find him torn by two seductions which perhaps are irreconcilable. He is lured by action—by the fulfillment and human balance achieved in shaping matter into some concrete embodiment of universal laws which have been discovered by the artist. On the other hand, the discovery of these laws itself seems at times to be the ultimate fulfillment. After long and vigorous travail, "pure consciousness"—this clear flash of a universal law from the hidden bosom of reality—brings an exaltation to which the making of any individual thing, however splendid, seems an anticlimax.

Which then, if either, is the universal man: the builder or the pure spirit? Our author vacillates.

II

In *Monsieur Teste,* which followed soon after the *Introduction,* Valéry swung toward asceticism. M. Teste, this extraordinary bourgeois, this impeccably precise talker, who does not even read, who merely observes and reflects, has attained a perfect working of the intellect. Everything about him—his voice, his bearing, his manner of eating, his absence of gesture—shows the complete abnegation of individuality. His room is the Platonic idea of a room: it contains nothing which bears the stamp of a personality; the chairs, the bed, the table, are as "general" as could be imagined. He spends his hours in contemplating such subjects as the nature of time and consciousness, and in finding the exact word to express his observations. That M. Teste left a deep impression on Valéry is obvious when one hears him speak: the lecture, no matter what the subject, flows with the lucidity and the seeming inevitability of a geometrical theorem.

M. Teste has achieved the "obstinate rigor," the *netteté désespérée* of Leonardo. But he is not the universal man in the sense of the builder. He does not act at all! Furthermore—but this is to raise another point—emotion and certain kinds of sensibility in him are starved by the intellect, the faculty of concepts, as they would not be in a mind that used all its functions. As a counterpoise to M. Teste, who has been called the *animus*, Valéry creates Mme. Teste, the *anima*. She says of her husband: "Quand il me revient de la profondeur! . . . Il retombe sur moi comme si j'étais la terre même!"

Yet the attractiveness of M. Teste for Valéry proved irresistible. For twenty years he gave himself to the exact disciplines. He studied the foundations of geometry, the nature of time, attention, formal logic, physiology. A few of the notes that Valéry took during his long reclusion have lately trickled into the magazines. More in the fashion of Pascal than of a systematic philosopher, they are inflections upon the personality, its metamorphoses, and its self-abnegating labor of creation.

At the end of this period Valéry, like André Gide, wished to pay "a last debt to the past." He planned to write *La Jeune Parque* in his earlier Symbolist manner. But his prepossession grew upon him. The poem is a long paean of the young Fate awakening to self-consciousness. Then came a scattering of essays and eventually another book of poems, *Charmes*. Among the most important of these works are the charming dialogues, *L'Âme et la Danse*, and *Eupalinos ou l'Architecte*. In the former, Socrates and his companions watch a ballet, giving the most exquisite description of it, and philosophizing upon its significance. Socrates finally decides that the dance does not represent a story, or an emotion such as love, but "the pure act of metamorphosis," "love as well as the sea, and life itself and thoughts." The dancer escapes entirely from her personality to become this pure act. When she comes out of her trance she says:

Asile, asile, ô mon asile, ô Tourbillon!—J'étais en toi, ô mouvement, en dehors de toutes choses.

After twenty years of silence the poet has proceeded from analysis to act, and he celebrates in this song of triumph. But further reflection, in *Eupalinos*, somewhat dampens his joy. The shades of Socrates and Phaedrus are discoursing in the dim Elysian fields. Their talk gradually shifts to the nature of beauty. Phaedrus quotes his friend, Eupalinos the architect, as saying that there are "buildings which sing"; these are the temples which are built for sheer beauty of form. A factory, on the other hand, talks; it is constructed for utility only. Music and architecture are held to be the supreme arts because of their "purity." Painting, for example, can never escape altogether into a world of its own. It must cover a given surface, and it cannot wholly avoid representing objects or persons. But a melody or a temple feigns to be nothing but itself; it expresses pure relations which have no necessary reference to any other created thing. Thus it attains a sort of universality, in that it is not bound to take any of the individual conformations in which the Demiurge left the world.

Architecture and music, then, have pure beauty. But another advantage is imputed to architecture which makes it superior to music—its "solidity or duration." Duration is inappropriate here, in one meaning of the word: Many of Socrates' sayings, for example, have endured, while the temples of Eupalinos are in ruins. And it is probable that Bach's music will be played long after the Mestrovic chapel in Cavtat will have been destroyed by shells. A temple, like a statue or a painting, can have more duration than a piece of music only by the fact that it exists continuously through time, while the music—though it may "subsist," or float in the realm of essence forever—is embodied but intermittently, that is, when it is played. Why one type of duration should be more sublime than the other is a question. Valéry's rather curious preference for architecture might be taken as a gesture of courtesy—he wrote *Eupalinos* for an architectural magazine—but the psychological explanation would perhaps be more just. After his long period of inactivity . .

> tant d'étrange
> Oisivité; mais pleine de pouvoir . . .

Valéry had come to glorify action in its most materialistic sense, the shaping of good solid earth and stone. At the end of the dialogue, Socrates, the mere talker, concluding that his life in the other world was misspent, evokes and praises anti-Socrates, the builder.

In the same way, doubtless, Valéry has found even his versifying unsatisfactory. A poet has something of the pure spirit's pitiful ineptitude. He performs overt actions, indeed, but to one enamored of "pure beauty," how unsatisfying are these scrawls and scratchings with a pencil! Affairs are even worse if the poet's handwriting is bad; he has not even the minor satisfaction of seeing his thoughts embodied in beautiful curves and flourishes. He yearns for the sculptor's chisel, test-tubes, the piano, brush, and canvas; any apparatus by which he could manipulate matter would give him release. And the ultimate product, a book, is but a receptacle for symbols, which as such are nothing to the senses: they speak to the mind in its terrible remoteness and isolation.

Yet the poet, and even the philosopher, is by Valéry's definition somewhat of a builder: "The builder whom I now conjure up finds before him, as chaos and primitive matter, precisely the order of the world that the Demiurge drew from the disorder of the beginning. Nature is formed and its elements are separated; but something compels him to consider this work as incomplete, and needing to be reworked and again put in motion, in order that it may be satisfying more specifically to mankind. Man begins his activity precisely at the point where the god left off." Valéry brought together images and ideas to combine them in a form which the Demiurge—Nature and mankind before him, that is—had never created; Socrates found universal laws about the human mind, the State, and logical reality, which until then had dwelt in limbo. And if the Athenians had only listened to him, perhaps his ideas, too, would have been embodied—not, it is true, in temples, but in human beings living beautifully and intelligently. The architect has no exclusive claim to be the Demiurge's successor.

III

The other question raised in the dialogue, that of the "purity" of the arts, is more important to the subject of the universal man. It was put rather well by Kant in the *Critique of Judgment,* when he made his distinction between free or pure beauty, and dependent beauty. Enjoyment of a flower or an arabesque, he says, presupposes no concept of what the object ought to be, whereas enjoyment of dependent beauty, such as that of a man or a horse (Kant even includes buildings—"be it church, palace, arsenal, or summer-house") "presupposes a concept of what the thing is to be, and consequently a concept of its perfection." Even Valéry's favorites, music and architecture, are not simon-pure arts. Music, for example, is not a mere pattern of sounds. It produces what may be called an emotional tone in the listener, or, more accurately, a developed emotional experience. To state the matter simply, and rather crudely, in Bach this emotional experience may be one of grandeur; in Mozart, of dignified joy or sadness; in Berlioz or Liszt, of fake heroism or barbaric disorder. The quality of the emotion communicated—to take the emotion alone—is one criterion for judging the worth of the music; and this emotion is akin to the emotions which enter into the rest of life. Likewise, it would be a very limited view of architecture that did not take into account its function, which in the case of the Greek temple involves the congruity of its meaning with that of the Olympian religion.

Valéry applied his esthetic ideas to his own art in the doctrine of *poésie pure,* which he derived, or thought he derived, from Poe through Baudelaire. What Poe was getting at in *The Poetic Principle,* the essay to which Valéry refers, and which Baudelaire plagiarized, may be summed up as follows: First, he tried to find the psychological laws governing the effect of the poem on the reader. In this he did not go much farther than to insist that a poem should not be too long to be read in a half-hour or an hour, because the poetic exaltation cannot be maintained for more than that span of time, and the unity of the effect is destroyed if the poem cannot be finished in one reading. Second, he objected to the didacticism of such moralists as Longfellow, on the basis of the old division of mental faculties into pure intellect, taste, and moral sense. Poetry should aim to satisfy "taste," and not to instruct or exhort. Its object is the attainment of "Supernal Loveliness." Poe says further (in his essay on Longfellow) that the test for specious poetry is to ask the question: "Might not this matter be as well or better handled in prose?" He does not object to narrative or drama as such, and he adds that "it does not follow that the incitements of Passion, the precepts of Duty, or even the lessons of Truth, may not be introduced into a poem, and with advantage; for they may subserve, incidentally, in various ways the general purposes of the work."

In spite of a dash of estheticism, Poe's concern was to keep the ethical and intellectual elements of a poem in their due proportion, and to ensure that the poem be primarily a poem, and not a scientific treatise or a tract. The doctrine of *poésie pure* would go still further. According to it, poetry aspires to the "pure state," in which science, morality, and history (including story-telling?) should be ruled out altogether, and poetry becomes sheer word-music. Valéry, indeed, has only dallied with this notion; he has never, as many of his encomiasts would have us believe, held to it strictly. Such absolute poetry, as Valéry realizes, is at best an ideal limit: "Rien de si pur ne peut coexister avec les conditions de la vie." Consequently, he decided to admit an element of thought, and to allow his verse to please the intellect as well as the ear. He had long cherished, in any event, the hope of writing the Comedy of Intellect. Poetic immaculateness would receive fewer stains in the high altitude of metaphyics than in the smoky region of conflicts between man and man. He treated such abstruse subjects as time and change (*Le Cimetière Marin, Palme*). In *Ébauche d'un Serpent,* he sang the strange emergence of life, desire, existence—all symbolized by the snake—from the infinite nothingness of the realm of essence, where

> L'univers n'est qu'un défaut
> Dans le pureté du Non-Être.

But his principal theme was the old one of the mind awakening to self-consciousness (*La Jeune Parque, Air de Sémiramis, Narcisse, La Pythie, La Fausse Morte,* etc.). This preoccupation led to the charge of Narcissism, although, of course, Valéry is far from making an idol of his own personality. His is rather an impersonal Narcissism of the intellect looking at its own conditions and workings. And the Narcissus of the poem died the moment he kissed the image of his own lips in the water. To a large extent, the poet has been concerned with the form of the mind's action—or rather, with the *fact* of its acting, and he has neglected its content.

IV

Just as Lucretius was the epic poet of Intellect, Valéry is the lyric. And this is no mean distinction. Criticism of a poet who has done well what he set out to do must always seem carping. Yet the critic in the long run has to ask: Why is this poet not the perfect poet? Although M. Valéry is, of course, much too modest ever to have claimed that he was trying to be the universal man, in his case the critic's question takes the form: What progress has he made toward that elusive ideal of his youth, universality?

His poetry has a wealth of music, a plenitude of ideas, poetically expressed. It has the rigor necessary to a true universality. Yet there is something lacking. As E. R. Curtius says: "Valéry's poetry oscillates between the icy region of a thought that is pure play with forms, and the dry fire of a sensibility that is pure impulsion and is directed toward no goal. It is the poetry of sensuous intellectuality. . . . The mean between intellect and sensation—the region of the soul and her beauty, in which we are accustomed to see the home of poetry and her beauty—is missing from Valéry. Here is, if you like, a void."[1] Those who would not use the word "soul" with the connotations that it has in the German language might prefer to rephrase Herr Curtius' criticism as follows: Is the universal poet to be a pure spirit or a rational animal? The pure spirit may spend his days intellectualizing his sensations; the rational animal, and the poet who is truly universal, would also take his themes from the wisdom of life. His model would be, not Leonardo, but another geometer-painter of the Renaissance, Piero della Francesca. With even greater purity of form than Leonardo's, Piero seized that moment of delicate equilibrium when human life was in the flower of a pagan fullness which had not yet lost the restraint of the Middle Ages. And so skillful was the artist that his humanism does not detract from the formal beauty of the work but fuses with it and gives it meaning. But a humanist Valéry is not: he does not live in a world of men.

Before a final judgment can be hazarded as to Valéry's success thus far in his arduous undertaking, it is necessary to consider *La Crise de l'Esprit* and the extract from the lecture given at Zürich in 1922, both of which are included in the *Variété*. Shaken from his delvings into psychology and esthetics, our author looks at some of the questions that confront civilization after the World War. He sets out to discover why the Europe of the past has been more than its geographical position alone would have made it—a mere cape on the mainland of Asia. Its pre-eminence he finds to have been due to the characteristics of the European man: "eager activity, ardent and disinterested curiosity, a happy blend of imagination and logical rigor, a certain scepticism which is yet not pessimistic, a mysticism without resignation."

But whatever unity there was in the mind of Europe has dissolved. Valéry shows us that European Hamlet looking down on the mental disorder of a continent, which is attributed to "the free coexistence in all cultivated minds of the most dissimilar ideas and the most opposed principles of life and knowledge. That is what characterizes the modern epoch." T. S. Eliot has spoken of the need for the construction of a new spiritual unity of the Occident, which would consist in a unified view of the world such as the Thomistic

[1] *Französischer Geist im Neuen Europa*, pp. 158–159.

system supplied for the Middle Ages. In this, what Valéry calls "principles of life" are probably more fundamental than the problems disputed at Geneva. Within his necessary limits, and in his concrete fashion, the poet too can contribute to this synthesis—perhaps a poet will be the first to sketch its outlines and to create its ritual and mythology. And thereby he may attain the sort of universality that is possible in our day.

V

For the last decade M. Valéry has relapsed into a poetic silence almost as complete as that which followed *Monsieur Teste*. He seems to have put his mind into some kind of order, and it may be that he is seeking an object worthy of its employment.

In his later poems the hymn of joy sung by the mind awakening becomes ever more triumphant. From the impure body of the Pythoness, writhing, panting, drunk, exhaling fumes from nostrils toughened by incense—

> A la fumée, à la fureur! . . .

. . . comes at last the voice of the god bringing with it

> Illumination, largesse!

We wait, expectantly, to learn if M. Valéry is addressing himself when the Dawn speaks to Semiramis:

> EXISTE! . . . Sois enfin toi-même! dit l'Aurore,
> O grande âme, il est temps que tu formes un corps!
> Hâte-toi de choisir un jour digne d'éclore,
> Parmi tant d'autres feux, tes immortels trésors!

From *The Symposium*, Vol. I (April, 1930), pp. 206–220. Reprinted by permission.

Note—Although my opinion of M. Valéry's success in his intellectual quest has not been modified greatly in the years since this essay was published, subsequent developments call for these comments: 1. Immediately after the publication of this essay, M. Valéry became prolific, and his works were issued in popular editions. 2. His new writings were not such as to fulfill the sanguine expectations suggested in the conclusion of the essay. 3. Although T. S. Eliot's dream of a new synthesis still seems to me a worthy ideal, I should not like to be taken as seconding anything Mr. Eliot has said since then about the content of that synthesis, its social and economic foundation, or the method of its attainment.—P. B. R., 1937.

(Valéry died in 1945. He continued to publish during the last years of his life: a new edition of *Regards sur le monde actuel,* his essays on contemporary history; several *discours* before the Académie Française; *Mélange; Mauvaises pensées et autres;* the final volumes of his five series of essays titled *Variété;* two volumes of another series titled *Tel quel;* a collected edition of his *Oeuvres complètes* in twelve volumes; etc., as well as the posthumous *Mon Faust* of 1946. Mr. Rice's essay stands here as it first appeared in 1930. [Editor's note, 1950.])

WILLIAM TROY

Virginia Woolf: The Novel of Sensibility

[1932]

Life is not a series of gig-lamps symmetrically arranged; but *a luminous halo, a semi-transparent envelope* surrounding us from the beginning of consciousness to the end.

Not only in rhythm and tone but also in the imponderable vagueness of its diction this statement has a familiar ring to the modern ear. The phrases in italics alone are sufficient to suggest its proper order and place in contemporary thought. For if this is not the exact voice of Henri Bergson, it is at least a very successful imitation. Dropped so casually by Mrs. Woolf in the course of a dissertation on the art of fiction, such a statement really implies an acceptance of a whole theory of metaphysics. Behind it lies all that resistance to the naturalistic formula, all that enthusiastic surrender to the world of flux and individual intuition, which has constituted the influence of Bergson on the art and literature of the past thirty years. Whether Mrs. Woolf was affected by this influence directly, or through the medium of Proust or some other secondary source, is not very important. The evidence is clear enough in her work that the fundamental view of reality on which it is based derives from what was the most popular ideology of her generation. What is so often regarded as unique in her fiction is actually less the result of an individual attitude than of the dominant metaphysical bias of a whole generation.

For members of that generation concerned with fiction the philosophy of flux and intuition offered a relief from the cumbersome technique and mechanical pattern of naturalism. (Against even such mild adherents to the doctrine as Wells and Bennett Mrs. Woolf raised the attack in *Mr. Bennett and Mrs. Brown.*) Moreover, the new philosophy opened up sources of interest for the novel which allowed it to dispense with whatever values such writers as George Eliot and Henry James had depended on in a still remoter period. Like naturalism, it brought with it its own version of an esthetic; it supplied a medium which involved no values other than the primary one of self-expression. Of course one cannot wholly ignore the helpful co-operation of psychoanalysis. But to distinguish between the metaphysical and the

324

psychological origins of the new techniques is not a profitable task. It is not difficult to understand how the subjective novel could have derived its assumptions from the one field, its method from the other. And the fusion between them had been completed by the time Mrs. Woolf published her little pamphlet. Everybody, in Rebecca West's phrase, was "doing" a novel in the period immediately following the World War. Everybody, that is to say, was writing a quasi-poetic rendition of his sensibility in a form which it was agreed should be called the novel.

Possessing a mind schooled in abstract theory, especially alert to the intellectual novelties of her own time, Mrs. Woolf was naturally attracted by a method which in addition to being contemporary offered so much to the speculative mind. But the deeper causes of the attraction, it is now evident, were embedded in Mrs. Woolf's own temperament of sensibility. The subjective mode is the only mode especially designed for temperaments immersed in their own sensibility, obsessed with its movements and vacillations, fascinated by its instability. It was the only mode possible for someone like Proust; it was alone capable of projecting the sensibility which because it has remained so uniform throughout her work we may be permitted to call Mrs. Woolf's own. Here it happens to be Bernard, in *The Waves,* speaking:

> A space was cleared in my mind. I saw through the thick leaves of habit. Leaning over the gate I regretted so much litter, so much unaccomplishment and separation, for one cannot cross London to see a friend, life being so full of engagements; nor take ship to India and see a naked man spearing fish in blue water. I said life had been imperfect, an unfinished phrase. It had been impossible for me, taking snuff as I do from any bagman met in a train, to keep coherency—that sense of the generations, of women carrying red pitchers to the Nile, of the nightingale who sings among conquests and migrations. . . .

But this might be almost any one of Mrs. Woolf's characters; and from such a passage we can appreciate how perfectly the subjective or "confessional" method is adapted to the particular sensibility reflected throughout her work.

And if we require in turn some explanation for this hieratic cultivation of the sensibility, we need only examine for a moment the nature and quality of the experience represented by most of her characters. From *The Voyage Out* to *The Waves* Mrs. Woolf has written almost exclusively about one class of people, almost one might say one type of individual, and that a class or type whose experience is largely vicarious, whose contacts with actuality have been for one or another reason incomplete, unsatisfactory, or inhibited. Made up of poets, metaphysicians, botanists, water-colorists, the world of Mrs. Woolf is a kind of superior Bohemia, as acutely refined and aristocratic in its way as the world of Henry James, except that its inhabitants concentrate on their sensations and impressions rather than on their problems of conduct.

(Such problems, of course, do not even exist for them since they rarely allow themselves even the possibility of action.) Life for these people, therefore, is painful less for what it has done to them than for what their excessive sensitivity causes them to make of it. Almost every one of them is the victim of some vast and inarticulate fixation: Mrs. Dalloway on Peter Walsh, Lily Briscoe in *To the Lighthouse* on Mrs. Ramsay, everyone in *The Waves* on Percival. All of them, like Neville in the last-named book, are listening for "that wild hunting-song, Percival's music." For all of them what Percival represents is something lost or denied, something which must remain forever outside the intense circle of their own renunciation. No consolation is left them but solitude, a timeless solitude in which to descend to a kind of self-induced Nirvana. "Heaven be praised for solitude!" cries Bernard toward the close of *The Waves*. "Heaven be praised for solitude that has removed the pressure of the eye, the solicitation of the body, and all need of lies and phrases." Through solitude these people are able to relieve themselves with finality from the responsibilities of living, they are able to complete their divorce from reality even to the extent of escaping the burden of personality. Nothing in Mrs. Woolf's work serves as a better revelation of her characters as a whole than these ruminations of Mrs. Ramsay in *To the Lighthouse*:

> To be silent; to be alone. All the being and the doing, expansive, glittering, vocal, evaporated; and one shrunk, with a sense of solemnity, to being oneself, a wedge-shaped core of darkness. . . . When life sank down for a moment, *the range of experience seemed limitless.* . . . Losing personality, one lost the fret, the hurry, the stir; and there rose to her lips always some exclamation of triumph over life when things came together in this peace, this rest, this eternity. . . .

What Mrs. Ramsay really means to say is that when life sinks down in this manner the range of *implicit* experience is limitless. Once one has abandoned the effort to act upon reality, either with the will or the intellect, the mind is permitted to wander in freedom through the stored treasures of its memories and impressions, following no course but that of fancy or simple association, murmuring Pillicock sat on Pillicock's Hill or Come away, come away, Death, "mingling poetry and nonsense, floating in the stream." But experience in this sense is something quite different from experience in the sense in which it is ordinarily understood in referring to people in life or in books. It does not involve that active impact of character upon reality which provides the objective materials of experience in both literature and life. And if it leads to its own peculiar triumphs, it does so only through a dread of being and doing, an abdication of personality and a shrinking into the solitary darkness.

Because of this self-imposed limitation of their experience, therefore, the characters of Mrs. Woolf are unable to *function* anywhere but on the single plane of the sensibility. On this plane alone is enacted whatever movement, drama, or tragedy occurs in her works. The movement of course is centrifugal, the drama unrealized, the tragedy hushed. The only truly dramatic moments in these novels are significantly enough precisely those in which the characters seem now and again to catch a single brief glimpse of that imposing world of fact which they have forsworn. The scenes we remember best are those like the one in *Mrs. Dalloway* in which the heroine, bright, excited and happy among the guests at her party, is brought suddenly face to face with the fact of death. Or like the extremely moving one at the end of *To the Lighthouse* in which Lily Briscoe at last breaks into tears and cries aloud the hallowed name of Mrs. Ramsay. In such scenes Mrs. Woolf is excellent; no living novelist can translate these nuances of perception in quite the same way; and their effect in her work is of an occasional transitory rift in that diaphanous "envelope" with which she surrounds her characters from beginning to end.

II

For the novelist of sensibility the most embarrassing of all problems, of course, has been the problem of form. From Richardson to Mrs. Woolf it has been the problem of how to reconcile something that is immeasurable, which is what experience as *feeling* very soon becomes, with something that is measured and defined, which has remained perhaps our most elementary conception of art. In the eighteenth century the impulse toward reconciliation was undoubtedly less acute than it has become today: Richardson and Sterne were working in a medium which did not yet make serious pretensions to being opposed to poetry and drama as a distinct art form. There was not yet a Flaubert or a Tolstoy, a Turgenev or a Henry James. Feeling was enough; and feeling was allowed to expand in volumes whose uncontrollable bulk was an eloquent demonstration of its immeasurability. But when at the turn of the present century, under distinguished philosophical auspices, feeling was restored to the novel, when the sensibility finally triumphed over the floundering nineteenth-century Reason, no such artistic insouciance was possible for anyone at all conscious of the literary tradition. In Proust we see the attempt to achieve form on a large scale through the substitution of a purely metaphysical system for the various collapsing frameworks of values—religious, ethical, and scientific—on which the fiction of the nineteenth century had depended. In Joyce it is through a substitution of quite a different kind, that of a particular myth from the remote literary past, that the effort is made to endow the treasures of the sensibility with something like the *integritas* of the classical estheticians. And in the case of Mrs. Woolf, who is in this respect representative of most of the followers of these two great contemporary exemplars, the pursuit of an adequate form has been a strenuous one from first to last.

In her earliest two books, to be sure, this strain is not too clearly apparent. But *The Voyage Out*, although an interesting novel in many respects, is notably deficient in what we usually designate as narrative appeal. In retrospect the excellence of the dialogue, the skill with social comedy, the objective portraiture of character—all traditional elements which Mrs. Woolf has since chosen to discard—seem remarkable. But already one can observe a failure or reluctance to project character through a progressive representation of motives, which provides the structure in such a novelist as Jane Austen, for example, whom Mrs. Woolf happens to resemble most in this novel. For an ordered pattern of action unfolding in time Mrs. Woolf substitutes a kind of spatial unity (the setting is a yacht at sea and later a Portuguese hotel), a *cadre,* so to speak, within which everything—characters, scenes and ideas— tends to remain fixed and self-contained. This would be an altogether true description if it were not for the promise of some larger development in the love affair that emerges at the end. But even here, in Mrs. Woolf's first novel, no fulfillment is allowed; death is invoked; death supplies a termination which might not otherwise be reached since none is inherent in the plan. *Night and Day* is an effort to write a novel on a thoroughly conventional model, and the result is so uncertain that we can understand the rather sudden turning to a newer method. It is as if Mrs. Woolf had persuaded herself by these experiments (how consciously we may judge from her essay *Mr. Bennett and Mrs. Brown*) that her view of personality did not at all coincide with the formal requirements of the conventional novel. Of course she was not alone in this discovery for there already existed the rudiments of a new tradition, whose main tendency was to dispense with form for the sake of an intensive exploitation of method.

Despite the number of artists in every field who assume that an innovation in method entails a corresponding achievement in form, method cannot be regarded as quite the same thing as form. For the novelist all that we can mean by method is embraced in the familiar phrase "the point of view." As his object is character his only method can be that by which he endeavors to attain to a complete grasp and understanding of that object. "Method" in fiction narrows down to nothing more or less than the selection of a point of view from which character may be studied and presented. The drastic shift in the point of view for which Henry James prepared English fiction has undeniably resulted in many noticeable effects in its form or structure. But it is not yet possible to declare that it has resulted in any *new* form. Dorothy Richardson, in the opening volume of *Pilgrimage,* was among the first to apply this new method but in none of the volumes which followed has she allied it to anything like a consistent form. What Mrs. Woolf absorbed from Miss Richardson, from May Sinclair and from James Joyce, all of whom had advanced its use before 1918, was therefore only method, and not form.

In the collection of sketches called *Monday or Tuesday* Mrs. Woolf definitely announced her affiliation with the new tradition. But such pieces as "Kew Gardens" and "The Mark on the Wall" were so slight in scope that they could make their appeal (like the essays of Lamb, for example) without the aid of any formal order or plan. Not until *Jacob's Room* does Mrs. Woolf attempt to use the method at any length, and in this book, with which her larger reputation began, we can first perceive the nature of the problem suggested by her work.

In one sense, the structure of *Jacob's Room* is that of the simplest form known to story-telling—the chronicle. From its intense pages one is able to detach a bare continuity of events: Jacob goes to the seashore, to Cambridge, to Greece, to the War. But what his creator is manifestly concerned with is not the relation of these events to his character, but their relation to his sensibility. The latter is projected through a poetic rendering of the dreams, desires, fantasies and enthusiasms which pass through his brain. The rendering is poetic because it is managed entirely by images, certain of which are recurrent throughout—the sheep's jaw with yellow teeth, "the moors and Byron," Greece. The theme also would seem to be a kind of poetic contrast between the outward passage of events and the permanence of a certain set of images in the mind. It happens that there is enough progression of outward events to give the book about as much movement as any other biographical (or autobiographical) chronicle. But one cannot point to any similar movement, any principle of progressive unity in the revelation of all that implicit life of the hero which makes up the substance of the book. As a sensibility Jacob remains the same throughout; he reacts in an identical fashion to the successive phenomena of his experience. Since he reacts only through his sensibility, since he does not act directly upon experience, he fails to "develop," in the sense in which characters in fiction usually develop. Instead of acting, he responds, and when death puts an end to his response, the book also comes to an end. "What am I to do with these?" his mother asks at the close, holding up an old pair of shoes, and this bit of romantic pathos is all the significance which his rich accumulation of dreams and suffering is made to assume in our minds.

In *Mrs. Dalloway* there is a much more deliberate use of recurrent images to identify the consciousness of each of the characters. The effort is not toward an integration of these images, for that would amount to something which is opposed to Mrs. Woolf's whole view of personality. It is toward no more than the emphasis of a certain rhythm in consciousness, which is obviously intended to supply a corresponding rhythm to the book as a whole. Moreover, in this work use is made for the first time of an enlarged image, a symbol that is fixed, constant and wholly outside the time-world of the characters. The symbol of Big Ben, since it sets the contrast between physical

time and the measureless duration of the characters' inner life, serves as a
sort of standard or center of reference. But neither of these devices, it should
be realized, has anything directly to do with the organization of character:
rhythm, the rhythm of images in the consciousness, is not the same thing as
an order of the personality; the symbol of Big Ben is no real center because
it exists outside the characters, is set up in contrast with them. By means of
these devices carried over from lyric poetry, a kind of unity is achieved which
is merely superficial or decorative, corresponding to no fundamental organization of the experience.

In her next book, however, Mrs. Woolf goes much further toward a fusion
of character and design. *To the Lighthouse,* which is probably her finest performance in every respect, owes its success not least to the completeness
with which the symbol chosen is identified with the will of every one of the
characters. The lighthouse is the common point toward which all their desires
are oriented; it is an object of attainment or fulfillment which gives direction
to the movements of their thought and sensibility; and since it is thus associated with them it gives a valid unity to the whole work. Moreover, alone
among Mrs. Woolf's works, *To the Lighthouse* has for its subject an action, a
single definite action, *"going* to the lighthouse," which places it clearly in the
realm of narrative. In fact, as narrative, it may be even more precisely clas-
sified as an *incident.* The sole objection that might be raised on esthetic
grounds is whether Mrs. Woolf's method has not perhaps caused her to extend her development beyond the inherent potentialities of this form. The
question is whether such a narrow structure can support the weight of the
material and the stress of its treatment. More relevant to the present question,
however, is the consideration that so much of the success of the book rests on
the unusually happy choice of symbol, one that is very specially adapted to the
theme, and not likely to be used soon again. Not many more such symbols occur to the imagination.

Certainly Mrs. Woolf does not make use of the same kind of symbol in
her next novel; for in *The Waves* she returns to the devices of rhythm and
symbolical contrast on which she depended in her earlier books. (*Orlando* is
not a novel, but a "biography," and has only to follow a simple chronological
order. Whatever hilarious variations its author plays on the traditional concept
of time do not affect her adherence to this simple order.) In *The Waves* Mrs.
Woolf again presents her characters through the rhythm of images in the
brain, again bases her structure on a contrast between these and a permanent
symbol of the objective world. There is, first of all, the image or set of images
which serves as a *motif* for each of the characters: for Louis, a chained beast
stamping on the shore, for Bernard, the willow tree by the river; for Neville,
"that wild hunting-song, Percival's music." And also there is the cumulative

image of each of their lives taken as a whole set in a parallel relationship to the movements of the sea.

Such a parallel, of course, is not an unfamiliar one. "Dwellers by the sea cannot fail to be impressed by the sight of its ceaseless ebb and flow," remarks Frazer in *The Golden Bough,* "and are apt . . . to trace a subtle relation, a secret harmony, between its tides and the life of man." What is unique is Mrs. Woolf's effort to expand what is usually no more than an intuition, a single association, a lyrical utterance to the dimensions of a novel. In one sense this is accomplished by a kind of multiplication: we are given six lyric poets instead of the usual one. For what Mrs. Woolf offers is a rendering of the subjective response to reality of six different people at successive stages in their lives. We are presented to them in childhood, adolescence, youth, early and late middle-age. *"The waves broke on the shore"* is the last line in the book, and from this we are probably to assume that at the close they are all dead. Such a scheme has the order of a chronicle, of a group of parallel biographies, but Mrs. Woolf is much more ambitious. Each period in her characters' lives corresponds to a particular movement of the sea; the current of their lives at the end is likened to its "incessant rise and fall and rise and fall again." In addition, the different periods correspond to the changing position of the sun in the sky on a single day, suggesting a vision of human lives *sub specie aeternitatis.* (The ancillary images of birds, flowers and wind intensify the same effect.) The theme is best summed up by one of the characters in a long monologue at the end: "Let us again pretend that life is a solid substance, shaped like a globe, which we turn about in our fingers. Let us pretend that we can make out a plain and logical story, so that when one matter is despatched —love for instance—we go on, in an orderly manner to the next. I was saying there was a willow tree. Its shower of falling branches, its creased and crooked bark had the effect of what remains outside our illusions yet cannot stay them, is changed by them for the moment, yet shows through stable, still, with a sternness that our lives lack. Hence the comment it makes; the standard it supplies, the reason why, as we flow and change, it seems to measure." In conception and form, in method and style, this book is the most poetic which Mrs. Woolf has yet written. It represents the extreme culmination of the method to which she has applied herself exclusively since *Monday or Tuesday.* It is significant because it forces the question whether the form in which for her that method has resulted is not essentially opposed to the conditions of narrative art.

For this form is unmistakably that of the extended or elaborated lyric; and criticism of these novels gets down ultimately to the question with what impunity one can confuse the traditional means of one literary form with the traditional means of another. This is no place to undertake another discussion of the difference between poetry and prose—or, more particularly, the difference between the lyrical and the narrative. It is a difference which we immediately recognize, and which criticism has always rightly recognized, even when it has not been altogether certain of its explanations. The least sensible of these explanations has undoubtedly been that which would make us believe that the difference between them is *qualitative*—that poetry deals with different things from prose, with the implication that the things of poetry are of higher order than those of prose. This is a snobbery which, fortunately in one sense, has been pretty well removed in our time, although unfortunately in another it has led to a different kind of confusion. And this is the confusion which consists in removing any *formal* distinctions between the two modes.

The objection to the lyrical method in narrative is that it renders impossible the peculiar kind of interest which the latter is designed to supply. By the lyrical method is meant the substitution of a group of symbols for the orderly working-out of a motive or a set of motives which has constituted the immemorial pattern of narrative art. Perhaps the simplest definition of symbols is that they are things used to stand for other things; and undoubtedly the most part of such a definition is the word "stand." Whatever operations of the imagination have gone on to produce them, symbols themselves become fixed, constant, and static. They may be considered as the end-results of the effort of the imagination to fix itself somewhere in space. The symbol may be considered as something *spatial*. Symbols are thus ordinarily used in lyric poetry, where the effort is to fix ideas, sentiments, or emotions. By themselves, of course, symbols in poetry are no more than so many detached, isolated and unrelated points in space. When projected separately, as in the poetry of the Imagist school, or in too great confusion, as in much contemporary poetry, they do not possess any necessary meaning or value to the intelligence: the worlds that they indicate are either too small or too large to live in. Moreover, whether separate or integrated into a total vision symbols are capable of being grasped, like any other objects of space, by a single and instantaneous effort of perception. The interval of time between their presentation and our response to them is ideally no longer than the time required for our reading of a poem. Even when their presentation is like a gradual exfoliation, as in certain poems by Donne and Baudelaire, for example, that time is never allowed to be too greatly prolonged. We do not require Poe's axiom that all lyrics must be brief to understand why they must be so. The symbols on which they are constructed can be perceived in a moment of time.

When narrative based itself on a simple chronological record of action, it was assured of a certain degree of interest. When, later, it based itself on an arrangement of action which corresponded to an orderly view of life or reality, it attained to the very high interest of a work of art. As long as it based itself firmly on action according to one pattern or another, it was certain of some degree of interest. To understand the nature of the satisfaction which we seem to take in the representation of reality in a temporal order we should have to know more about certain primitive elements of our psychology than science has yet been able to discover. It is enough to recognize that whatever the reasons this satisfaction is rooted in our sense of *time*. It is enough to realize that this is the basis of the appeal which narrative has made through the whole history of fiction, from the earliest fables of the race to the most complex "constructions" of Henry James. For this reason, for example, description has always occupied a most uncertain place in fiction. Description, which deals with things rather than events, interposes a space-world in the march of that time-world which is the subject of fiction. For this reason the use of poetic symbols in fiction, as in all Mrs. Woolf's work since *Monday or Tuesday*, seems to be in direct contradiction to the foundations of our response to that form.

III

Because it is in an almost continuous state of moral and intellectual relaxation that Mrs. Woolf's characters draw out their existence, they can be projected only through a more or less direct transcription of their consciousness. Such a qualification is necessary, however, for the method here is rarely if ever as direct as that of Joyce or his followers. Between the consciousness and the rendition of it there is nearly always interposed a highly artificial literary style. This style remains practically uniform for all the characters; it is at once individual and traditional. The effect of its elegant diction and elaborately turned periods is to make one feel at times as if these sad and lonely people were partly compensated for the vacuity of their lives by the gift of casting even their most random thoughts in the best literary tradition. For some of them, like Bernard in *The Waves* (or is it the author herself speaking?), language is more than a compensation; it has an absolute value in itself: "A good phrase, however, seems to me to have an independent existence." Others may go to religion, to art, to friendship, but Mrs. Woolf's people more often than not go "to seek among phrases and fragments something unbroken." It is as if they seek to net the world of time and change with a phrase, to retrieve the chaos with words. For this reason the presentation of character by Mrs. Woolf gets down finally to a problem of style, to the most beautiful arrangement of beautiful words and phrases.

Here also Mrs. Woolf is pre-eminently the poet; for as an unwillingness to use motives and actions led to her substitution of poetic symbols in their stead so is she also compelled to use a metaphorical rather than a narrative style. In this practice of course she is not without precedent; other novelists have relied on metaphor to secure their finest effects of communication. But while such effects are ordinarily used to heighten the narrative, they are never extended to the point where they assume an independent interest. In Mrs. Woolf's books metaphorical writing is not occasional but predominate; from the beginning it has subordinated every other kind; and it was inevitable that it should one day be segmented into the purely descriptive prose-poems of *The Waves*.

No sooner is the essentially poetic character of this writing admitted than one is confronted with the whole host of problems associated with the general problem of imagery in poetry. It happens, however, that the peculiar use of imagery in Mrs. Woolf's prose suggests among other things a particular distinction, and one which has not been often enough made, although it was recognized by both Coleridge and Baudelaire, a distinction between two kinds of sensibility.

Of the two kinds of sensibility that we can identify in examining works of poetry the first would seem to be incapable of receiving impressions except through the prism of an already acquired set of language symbols. It is as if poets with this type of sensibility are uncontrollably *determined* in the kind of response they can make to reality. And because they are so determined in their initial response they are determind also in their manner of expression. The original language-symbols, acquired through culture, training, or unconscious immersion in some tradition, are infinitely perpetuated in their writing. At its worst such writing is anemic and invertebrate, like the minor verse of any period or like the earlier work of many excellent poets. In such verse the language gives the effect of having occasioned the feeling more often than the feeling the language. At its most sophisticated, however, this verse is capable of achieving a certain superficial quality of distinction all its own. It is a quality of distinction undoubtedly made possible by the reduced effort to discover precise images to convey very definite and particular sensations or emotions. It may consist in the pure musicalization of language through the draining of all specific content from the imagery that we find in Mallarmé or (on a lower plane) in Swinburne. Or it may consist in that plastic manipulation of surfaces which is another department of the interesting verse of any period. The effect in either case is the same, that of a resuscitation rather than a re-creation of language.

The other type of sensibility, of course, is in the habit of receiving direct impressions, of forming images which possess the freshness, uniqueness, and body of the original object. It has the faculty of creating new language-symbols to convey what it has perceived or, as sometimes happens, of re-creating traditional symbols with enough force to make them serve again. (For used symbols are capable of being recharged, so to speak, under the pressure of the new emotion they are called upon to convey.) Only when the original perception is solid and clear is it able to crystallize into images capable of transmitting emotion; and only when the emotion is adequate are these images capable of creating or re-creating language. The difference is between language which is made its own object and language which is made to realize emotion by evoking particular objects of concrete experience. It is the difference between writing which secures a certain effectiveness through being recognizable in a particular tradition and writing which is an exact verbal equivalent for a precise emotion or set of emotions. It is the difference, among the writers of our time, between Conrad Aiken and T. S. Eliot, or between Thornton Wilder and Ernest Hemingway. And in the most characteristic lines of the best writers of any time it is this latter kind of sensibility that we can see at work. We see it in Antony's rebuke to Cleopatra:

> I found you as a morsel, cold upon
> Dead Caesar's trencher

or in Baudelaire's

> J'ai cherché dans l'amour un sommeil oublieux;
> Mais l'amour n'est pour moi qu'un matelas d'aiguilles

or in Yeats'

> I pace upon the battlements and stare
> On the foundations of a house, or where
> Tree, like a sooty finger, starts from the earth.

In prose fiction, when the language approaches the precision and density of poetry, it is a result of the same necessity on the part of author or character, under stress of exceptional feeling, to seize upon his experience for the particular image or images necessary to express his state. The only difference is that the images of fiction are likely to be less remote, less "difficult" perhaps, than those of poetry. And the reason of course is that the images are likely to arise out of the immediate background of the novel. No better example of this can be offered than in the speech in *Wuthering Heights* in which Catherine, in her delirium, shakes the feathers out of her pillow:

That's a turkey's . . . and this is a wild duck's; and this is a pigeon's. Ah, they put pigeons' feathers in the pillows—no wonder I couldn't die! . . . And here is a moor-cock's; and this—I should know it among a thousand—it's a lapwing's. Bonny bird; wheeling over our heads in the middle of the moor. It wanted to get to its nest, for the clouds had touched the swells, and it felt rain coming.

In Mrs. Woolf's novels, as replete with imagery as they are, the effect is never quite the same as in this passage from Emily Brontë. The images that pass through in her characters' minds are rarely seized from any *particular* background of concrete experience. There are few of them which we have not encountered somewhere before. They belong not so much to the particular character as to the general tradition of literature. The effect is of an insidious infiltration of tradition into the sensibility. And this effect is the same whether it is a straight description by the author, as in *To the Lighthouse*:

The autumn trees, ravaged as they are, take on the flash of tattered flags kindling in the gloom of cool cathedral caves where gold letters on marble pages describe death in battle and how bones bleach and burn far away on Indian sands. The autumn trees gleam in the yellow moonlight, in the light of harvest moons, the light which mellows the energy of labour, and smooths the stubble, and brings the wave lapping blue to the shore.

or a presentation of mood, as in *Mrs Dalloway*:

Fear no more, says the heart. Fear no more, says the heart, committing its burden to some sea, which sighs collectively for all sorrows, and renews, begins, collects, lets fall. And the body alone listens to the passing bee; the wave breaking; the dog barking, far away barking and barking.

or a translation of ecstasy, as in *The Waves*:

Now tonight, my body rises tier upon tier like some cool temple whose floor is strewn with carpets and murmurs rise and the altars stand smoking; but up above, here in my serene head, come only fine gusts of melody, waves of incense, while the lost dove wails, and the banners tremble above tombs, and the dark airs of midnight shake trees outside the open windows.

From such examples it should be apparent to what extent the sensibility here is haunted by the word-symbols of the past. The consciousness of each of these characters is a Sargasso Sea of words, phrases, broken relics of poetry and song. The phrases which rise to the surface are like bright shells resonant with the accumulated echoes of their past histories. Some of them have the familiar charm of cherished heirlooms; only a few retain completely whatever power to stir the imagination they may once have had. Almost all of them depend for their effect on their associations to the cultivated mind rather than on their ability to evoke the fullness and immediacy of concrete experience. And the reason of course is that there is insufficient experience of this sort anywhere reflected in the course of Mrs. Woolf's work.

It is also clear in such passages how Mrs. Woolf has come more and more to cultivate language for its own sake, to seek in phrases some "independent existence" which will give them an absolute beauty in themselves. But detached from experience as they are they attain to no more substantial beauty than that of a charming virtuosity of style. It is not the beauty but the cleverness of Mrs. Woolf's writing which is responsible for the final effect on the reader. "No woman before Virginia Woolf has used our language with such easy authority," wrote the late Sara Teasdale. Indeed few writers of either sex have written English with the same mastery of traditional resources, the same calculated effectiveness, the same facility. And when this facile traditionalism is allied with an appropriate subject, as in a frank burlesque like *Orlando,* the result is truly brilliant. It is only when it is used as the vehicle for significant serious thoughts and emotions, as in the larger portion of Mrs. Woolf's work, that its charm seems false, its authority invalid, and its beauty sterile.

It is only fair to point out what would seem to be a sincere self-questioning in the long monologue at the end of *The Waves.* Bernard, the inveterate phrasemonger, recalling the scene in which he and his friends first heard of Percival's death, remembers that they had compared him to a lily. "So the sincerity of the moment passed," Bernard cries, "so it had become symbolical; and that I could not stand. Let us commit any blasphemy of laughter and criticism rather than exude this lily-sweet glue; and cover him over with phrases." Perhaps it is too much to read into this lapse into sincerity on the part of a single character a confession of dissatisfaction by the author with the kind of language that she has been using all along in her work. But while such an interpretation may be too eager there is at least the implication that she is aware that reality when it is encountered is something far too important to be covered over with beautiful phrases. The vague hope is thrown out that in her later work she may finally be tempted to give us Percival himself, that she may spare him from death and allow him a more solid existence than he ever enjoyed in the minds and memories of his friends.

But no sooner is this idea expressed than one is reminded of the profound changes that would have to happen in Mrs. Woolf's whole metaphysical outlook before any such hope could be realized. For every element of her work that we have considered—her form, her method of characterization, her style even—is affected by the same fundamental view of personality at its root. These elements of form and of style can hardly be expected to change as long as the view which determines them remains unchanged. And nothing in Mrs. Woolf's recent work, it must be admitted, justifies the belief that this view is likely to be changed in the near future.

From *The Symposium*, Vol. III (January–March, 1932), pp. 53–63; and (April–June, 1932), pp. 153–166. Reprinted in this revision by permission of the author and editors.

KATHERINE ANNE PORTER

Gertrude Stein: A Self-Portrait

[1947]

. . . I want to say that just today I met Miss Hennessy and she was carrying, she did not have it with her, but she usually carried a wooden umbrella. This wooden umbrella is carved out of wood and looks like a real one even to the little button and the rubber string that holds it together. It is all right except when it rains. When it rains it does not open and Miss Hennessy looks a little foolish but she does not mind because it is after all the only wooden umbrella in Paris. And even if there were lots of others it would not make any difference.

Gertrude Stein: Everybody's Autobiography

WHEN Kahnweiler the picture dealer told Miss Stein that Picasso had stopped painting and had taken to writing poetry, she confessed that she had "a funny feeling" because "things belonged to you and writing belonged to me. I know writing belongs to me, I am quite certain," but still it was a blow. ". . . No matter how certain you are about anything belonging to you if you hear that somebody says it belongs to them it gives you a funny feeling."

Later she buttonholed Picasso at Kahnweiler's gallery, shook him, kissed him, lectured him, told him that his poetry was worse than bad, it was offensive as a Cocteau drawing and in much the same way, it was unbecoming. He defended himself by reminding her that she had said he was an extraordinary person, and he believed an extraordinary person should be able to do anything. She said that to her it was repellent sight when a person who could do one thing well dropped it for something else he could not do at all. Convinced, or defeated, he promised to give back writing to its natural owner.

Writing was no doubt the dearest of Miss Stein's possessions, but it was not the only one. The pavilion atelier in rue de Fleurus was a catchall of beings and created objects, and everything she looked upon was hers in more than the usual sense. Her weighty numerous divans and armchairs covered with dark, new-looking horsehair; her dogs, Basket and Pépé, conspicuous, special, afflicted as neurotic children; her clutter of small tables each with its own clutter of perhaps valuable but certainly treasured objects; her Alice B. Toklas; her visitors; and finally, ranging the walls from floor to ceiling, giving the impression that they were hung three deep, elbowing each other, canceling each other's effects in the jealous way of pictures, was her celebrated collection of paintings by her collection of celebrated painters. These were everybody of her time whom Miss Stein elected for her own, from her idol Picasso (kidnapped bodily from brother Leo, who saw him first) to miniscule Sir Francis Rose, who seems to have appealed to the pixy in her.

Yet the vaguely lighted room where things accumulated, where they appeared to have moved in under a compulsion to be possessed once for all by someone who knew how to take hold firmly, gave no impression of disorder. On the contrary, an air of solid comfort, of inordinate sobriety and permanence, of unadventurous middle-class domesticity—respectability is the word, at last—settled around the shoulders of the guest like a Paisley shawl, a borrowed shawl of course, something to be worn and admired for a moment and handed back to the owner. Miss Stein herself sat there in full possession of herself, the scene, the spectators, wearing thick no-colored shapeless woolen clothes and honest woolen stockings knitted for her by Miss Toklas, looking extremely like a handsome old Jewish patriarch who had backslid and shaved off his beard.

Surrounded by her listners, she talked in a slow circle in her fine deep voice, the word "perception" occurring again and again and yet again like the brass ring the children snatch for as their hobby horses whirl by. She was in fact at one period surrounded by snatching children, the literary young, a good many of them American, between two wars in a falling world. Roughly they were divided into two parties: those who were full of an active, pragmatic unbelief, and those who searched their own vitals and fished up strange horrors in the style of *transition*. The first had discovered that honor is only a word, and an embarrassing one, because it was supposed to mean something wonderful and was now exposed as meaning nothing at all. For them, nothing worked except sex and alcohol and pulling apart their lamentable midwestern upbringings and scattering the pieces. Some of these announced that they wished their writings to be as free from literature as if they had never read a book, as indeed too many of them had not up to the time. The *transition* tone was even more sinister, for though it was supposed to be the vanguard of international experimental thought, its real voice was hoarse, anxious, corrupted mysticism speaking in a thick German accent. The editor, Eugene Jolas, had been born in the eternally disputed land of Alsace, bilingual in irreconcilable tongues, French and German, and he spoke both and English besides with a foreign accent. He had no mother tongue, nor even a country, and so he fought the idea of both, but his deepest self was German: he issued frantic manifestoes demanding that language be reduced to something he could master, crying aloud in "defense of the hallucinative forces," the exploding of the verb, the "occult hypnosis of language," "chthonian grammar"; reason he hated, and defended the voice of the blood, the disintegration of syntax—with a special grudge against English—preaching like an American Methodist evangelist in the wilderness for "the use of a language which is a mantic instrument, and which does not hesitate to adopt a revolutionary attitude toward word syntax, going even so far as to invent a hermetic language, if necessary." The final aim was "the illumination of a collective reality and a totalistic universe." Meanwhile Joyce, a man with a mother tongue if ever there was one, and a master of languages, was mixing them in strange new forms to the delight and enrichment of language for good and all.

Miss Stein had no problems: she simply exploded a verb as if it were a soap bubble, used chthonian grammar long before she heard it named (and she would have scorned to name it), was a born adept in occult hypnosis of language without even trying. Serious young men who were having a hard time learning to write realized with relief that there was nothing at all to it if you just relaxed and put down the first thing that came into your head. She gave them a romantic name, the Lost Generation, and a remarkable number of them tried earnestly if unsuccessfully to live up to it. A few of them were really lost, and disappeared, but others had just painted themselves into a very crowded corner. She laid a cooling hand upon their agitated brows and asked with variations, What did it matter? There were only a few geniuses, after all, among which she was one, only the things a genius said made any difference, the rest was "just there," and so she disposed of all the dark questions of life, art, human relations, and death, even eternity, even God, with perfect Stein logic, bringing the scene again into its proper focus, upon herself.

Some of the young men went away, read a book, began thinking things over, and became the best writers of their time. Humanly, shamefacedly, they then jeered at their former admiration, and a few even made the tactical error of quarreling with her. She enjoyed their discipleship while it lasted, and dismissed them from existence when it ended. It is easy to see what tremendous vitality and direction there was in the arts all over the world; for not everything was happening only in France, for life was generated in many a noisy seething confusion in many countries. Little by little the legitimate line of succession appeared, the survivors emerged each with his own shape and meaning, the young vanguard became the Old Masters and even old hat.

In the meantime our heroine went on talking, vocally or on paper, and in that slow swarm of words, out of the long drone and mutter and stammer of her lifetime monologue, often there emerged a phrase of ancient native independent wisdom, for she had a shrewd deep knowledge of the commoner human motives. Her judgments were neither moral nor intellectual, and least of all aesthetic, indeed they were not even judgments, but simply her description from observation of acts, words, appearances giving her view; limited, personal in the extreme, prejudiced without qualification, based on assumptions founded in the void of pure unreason. For example, French notaries' sons have always something strange about them—look at Jean Cocteau. The Spaniard has a natural center of ignorance, all except Juan Gris. On the other hand, Dali had not only the natural Spanish center of ignorance, but still another variety, quite maligant, of his own. Preachers' sons do not turn out like other people—E. E. Cummings, just for one. Painters are always little short round men—Picasso and a crowd of them. And then she puts her finger lightly on an American peculiarity of our time: ". . . so perhaps they are right the Americans in being more interested in you than in the work you have done, although they would not be interested in you if you had not done the work you had done." And she remarked once to her publisher that she was famous in America not for her work that people understood but for that which they did not understand. That was the kind of thing she could see through at a glance.

It was not that she was opposed to ideas, but that she was not interested in anybody's ideas but her own, except as material to put down on her endless flood of pages. Like writing, opinion also belonged to Miss Stein, and nothing annoyed her more—she was easily angered about all sorts of things—than for anyone not a genius or who had no reputation that she respected, to appear to be thinking in her presence. Of all those GI's who swarmed about her in her last days, if any one showed any fight at all, any tendency to question her pronouncements, she smacked him down like a careful grandmother, for his own good. Her GI heroes Brewsie and Willie are surely as near to talking zombies as anything ever seen in a book, and she loved, not them, but their essential zombiness.

Like all talkers, she thought other people talked too much, and there is recorded only one instance of someone getting the drop on her—who else but Alfred Stieglitz? She sat through a whole session at their first meeting without uttering one word, a feat which he mentioned with surprised approval. If we knew nothing more of Stieglitz than this we would know he was a great talker. She thought that the most distressing sound was that of the human voice, other peoples' voices, "as the hoot owl is almost the best sound," but in spite of this she listened quite a lot. When she was out walking the dogs, if workmen were tearing up the streets she would ask them what they were doing and what they would be doing next. She only stopped to break the monotony of walking, but she remembered their answers. When a man passed making up a bitter little song against her dog and his conduct *vis-á-vis* lamp posts and house walls, she put it all down, and it is wonderfully good reporting. Wise or silly or nothing at all, down everything goes on the page with the air of everything being equal, unimportant in itself, important because it happened to her and she was writing about it.

II

She had not always been exactly there, exactly that. There had been many phases, all in consistent character, each giving way in turn for the next, of her portentous being. Ford Madox Ford described her, in earlier Paris days, as trundling through the streets in her high-wheeled American car, being a spectacle and being herself at the same time. And this may have been near the time of Man Ray's photograph of her, wearing a kind of monk's robe, her poll clipped, her granite front and fine eyes displayed at their best period.

Before that, she was a youngish stout woman, not ever really young, with a heavy shrewd face between a hard round pompadour and a round lace collar, looking more or less like Picasso's earliest portrait of her. What saved her then from a good honest husband, probably a stockbroker, and a houseful of children? The answer must be that her envelope was a tricky disguise of Nature, that she was of the company of Amazons which nineteenth-century America produced among its many prodigies: not-men, not-women, answerable to no function in either sex, whose careers were carried on, and how successfully, in whatever field they chose: they were educators, writers, editors, politicians, artists, world travelers, and international hostesses, who lived in public and by the public and played out their self-assumed, self-created roles in such masterly freedom as only a few early medieval queens had equaled. Freedom to them meant precisely freedom from men and their stuffy rules for women. They usurped with a high hand the traditional masculine privileges of movement, choice, and the use of direct, personal power. They were few in number and they were not only to be found in America, and Miss Stein belonged with them, no doubt of it, in spite of a certain temperamental passivity which was Oriental, not feminine. With the top of her brain she was a modern girl, a New Woman, interested in scientific experiment, historical research, the rational view; for a time she was even a medical student, but she could not deceive herself for long. Even during her four years at Radcliffe, where the crisp theories of higher education battled with the womb-shaped female mind (and they always afterward seemed foolish to her at Radcliffe) she worried and worried, for worrying and thinking were synonyms to her, about the meaning of the universe, the riddle of human life, about time and its terrible habit of passing, God, death, eternity, and she felt very lonely in the awful singularity of her confusions. Added to this, history taught her that whole civilizations die and disappear utterly, "and now it happens again," and it gave her a great fright. She was sometimes frightened afterward, "but now well being frightened is something less frightening than it was," but her ambiguous mind faced away from speculation. Having discovered with relief that all knowledge was not her province, she accepted rightly, she said, every superstition. To be in the hands of fate, of magic, of the daemonic forces, what freedom it gave her not to decide, not to act, not to accept any responsibility for anything—one held the pen and let the mind wander. One sat down and somebody did everything for one.

Still earlier she was a plump solemn little girl abundantly upholstered in good clothes, who spent her allowance on the work of Shelley, Thackeray, and George Eliot in fancy bindings, for she loved reading and *Clarissa Harlowe* was once her favorite novel. These early passions exhausted her; in later life she swam in the relaxing bath of detective and murder mysteries, because she liked somebody being dead in a story, and of them all Dashiell Hammett killed them off most to her taste. Her first experience of the real death of somebody had taught her that it could be pleasant for her too. "One morning we could not wake our father." This was in East Oakland, California. "Leo climbed in by the window and called out that he was dead in his bed and he was." It seems to have been the first thing he ever did of which his children, all five of them, approved. Miss Stein declared plainly they none of them liked him at all: "As I say, fathers are depressing but our family had one," she confessed, and conveys the notion that he was a bore of the nagging, petty sort, the kind that worries himself and others into the grave.

Considering her tepid, sluggish nature, really sluggish like something eating its way through a leaf, Miss Stein could grow quite animated on the subject of her early family life, and some of her stories are as pretty and innocent as lizards running over tombstones on a hot day in Maryland. It was a solid, getting-on sort of middle-class Jewish family of Austrian origin, Keyser on one side, Stein on the other: and the Keysers came to Baltimore about 1820. All branches of the family produced their individual eccentrics—there was even an uncle who believed in the Single Tax—but they were united in their solid understanding of the value of money as the basis of a firm stance in this world. There were incomes, governesses, spending money, guardians appointed when parents died, and Miss Stein was fascinated from childhood with stories about how people earned their first dollar. When, rather late, she actually earned some dollars herself by writing, it changed her entire viewpoint about the value of her work and of her own personality. It came to her as revelation that the only difference between men and four-footed animals is that men can count, and when they count, they like best to count money. In her first satisfaction at finding she had a commercial value, she went on a brief binge of spending money just for the fun of it. But she really knew better. Among the five or six of the seven deadly sins which she practiced with increasing facility and advocated as virtues, avarice became her favorite. Americans in general she found to be rather childish about money: they spent it or gave it away and enjoyed wastefully with no sense of its fierce latent power. "It is hard to be a miser, a real miser, they are as rare as geniuses it takes the same kind of thing to make one, that is time must not exist for them. . . . There must be a reality that has nothing to do with the passing of time. I have it and so had Hetty Green. . . ." and she found only one of the younger generation in America, a young man named Jay Laughlin, who had, she wrote, praising him, avarice to that point of genius which makes the true miser. She made a very true distinction between avarice, the love of getting and keeping, and love of money, the love of making and spending. There is a third love, the love of turning a penny by ruse, and this was illustrated by brother Michael, who once grew a beard to make himself look old enough to pass for a G. A. R. veteran, and so disguised he got a cut-rate railway fare for a visit home during a G. A. R. rally, though all the men of this family fought on the Confederate side.

The question of money and of genius rose simultaneously with the cheerful state of complete orphanhood. Her mother disappeared early after a long illness, leaving her little nest of vipers probably without regret, for vipers Miss Stein shows them to have been in the most Biblical sense. They missed their mother chiefly because she had acted as a buffer between them and their father, and also served to keep them out of each other's hair. Sister Bertha and Brother Simon were simple-minded by family standards, whatever they were, Brother Leo had already started being a genius without any regard for the true situation, and after the death of their father, Brother Michael was quite simply elected to be the Goat. He had inherited the family hatred of responsibility—from their mother, Miss Stein believed, but not quite enough to save him. He became guardian, caretaker, business manager, handy-man, who finally wangled incomes for all of them, and set them free from money and from each other. It is pleasant to know he was a very thorny martyr who did a great deal of resentful lecturing about economy, stamping and shouting around the house with threats to throw the whole business over and let them fend for themselves if they could not treat him with more consideration. With flattery and persuasion they would cluster around and get him back on the rails, for his destiny was to be useful to genius, that is, to Miss Stein.

She had been much attached to her brother Leo, in childhood they were twin souls. He was two years older and a boy, and she had learned from Clarissa Harlowe's uncle's letter that older brothers are superior to younger sisters, or any boy to any girl in fact. Though she bowed to this doctrine as long as it was convenient, she never allowed it to get in her way. She followed her brother's advice more or less, and in turn he waited on her and humored and defended her when she was a selfish lazy little girl. Later he made a charming traveling companion who naturally, being older and a man, looked after all the boring details of life and smoothed his sister's path everywhere. Still, she could not remember his face when he was absent, and once was very nervous when she went to meet him on a journey, for fear she might not recognize him. The one thing wrong all this time was their recurring quarrel about who was the genius of the two, for each had assumed the title and neither believed for a moment there was room for more than one in the family. By way of proving himself, brother Leo took the pavilion and atelier in the rue de Fleurus, installed himself well, and began trying hard to paint. Miss Stein, seeing all so cozy, moved in on him and sat down and began to write—no question of trying. "To try is to die," became one of her several hundred rhyming aphorisms designed to settle all conceivable arguments; after a time, no doubt overwhelmed by the solid negative force of that massive will and presence, her brother moved out and took the atelier next door, and went on being useful to his sister, and trying to paint.

But he also went on insisting tactlessly that he, and not she, was the born genius; and this was one of the real differences between them, that he attacked on the subject and was uneasy, and could not rest, while his sister reasoned with him patiently at first defending her title, regretting she could not share it. Insist, argue, upset himself and her as much as he liked, she simply, quietly knew with a Messianic revelation that she was not only a genius, but *the* genius, and sometimes, she was certain, one of not more than half a dozen real ones in the world. During all her life, whenever Miss Stein got low in her mind about anything, she could always find consolation in this beautiful knowledge of being a born genius, and her brother's contentiousness finally began to look like treason to her. She could not forgive him for disputing her indivisible right to her natural property, genius, on which all her other rights of possession were founded. It shook her—she worried about her work. She had begun her long career of describing "how every one who ever lived eats and drinks and loves and sleeps and talks and walks and wakes and forgets and quarrels and likes and dislikes and works and sits,"—everybody's autobiography, in fact, for she had taken upon herself the immense task of explaining everybody to himself, of telling him all he needed to know about life, and she simply could not have brother Leo hanging around the edges of this grandiose scheme pinching off bits and holding them up to the light. By and by, too, she had Alice B. Toklas to do everything for her. So she and her brother drifted apart, but gradually, like one of Miss Stein's paragraphs. The separation became so complete that once, on meeting her brother unexpectedly, she was so taken by surprise she bowed to him, and afterward wrote a long poem about it in which her total confusion of mind and feeling were expressed with total incoherence: for once, form, matter and style stuttering and stammering and wallowing along together with the agitated harmony of roiling entrails.

III

There are the tones of sloth, of that boredom which is a low-pressure despair, of monotony, of obsession, in this portrait; she went walking out of

boredom, she could drive a car, talk, write, but anything else made her nervous. People who were doing anything annoyed her: to be doing nothing, she
thought, was more interesting than to be doing something. The air of deathly
solitude surrounded her; yet the parade of names in her book would easily fill
several printed pages, all with faces attached which she could see were quite
different from each other, all talking, each taking his own name and person
for granted—a thing she could never understand. Yet she could see what they
were doing and could remember what they said. She only listened attentively
to Picasso—for whose sake she would crack almost any head in sight—so she
half-agreed when he said Picabia was the worst painter of all; but still, found
herself drawn to Picabia because his name was Francis. She had discovered
that men named Francis were always elegant, and though they might not
know anything else, they always knew about themselves. This would remind
her that she had never found out who she was. Again and again she would
doubt her own identity, and that of everyone else. When she worried about
this aloud to Alice B. Toklas, saying she believed it impossible for anyone
ever to be certain who he was, Alice B. Toklas made, in context, the most inspired remark in the whole book. "It depends on who you are," she said, and
you might think that would have ended the business. Not at all.

These deep-set, chronic fears led her to a good deal of quarreling, for when
she quarreled she seems to have felt more real. She mentions quarrels with
Max Jacob, Francis Rose, with Dali, with Picabia, with Picasso, with Virgil
Thomson, with Braque, with Bréton, and how many others, though she rarely
says just why they quarreled or how they made it up. Almost nobody went
away and stayed, and the awful inertia of habit in friendships oppressed her.
She was sometimes discouraged at the prospect of having to go on seeing certain persons to the end, merely because she had once seen them. The world
seemed smaller every day, swarming with people perpetually in movement, full
of restless notions which, once examined by her, were inevitably proved to be
fallacious, or at least entirely useless. She found that she could best get rid of
them by putting them in a book. "That is very funny if you write about any
one they do not exist any more, for you, so why see them again. Anyway,
that is the way I am."

But as she wrote a book and disposed of one horde, another came on, and
worried her afresh, discussing their ludicrous solemn topics, trying to understand things, and being unhappy about it. When Picasso was fretful because
she argued with Dali and not with him, she explained that "one discusses
things with stupid people but not with sensible ones." Her true grudge against
intelligent people was that they talked "as if they were getting ready to change
something." Change belonged to Miss Stein, and the duty of the world was to
stand still so that she could move about in it comfortably. Her top flight of
reasoning on the subject of intelligence ran as follows: "The most actively
war-like nations could always convince the pacifists to become pro-German.

That is because pacifists were such intelligent beings they could follow what any one is saying. If you follow what any one is saying then you are a pacifist you are a pro-German . . . therefore understanding is a very dull occupation."

Intellectuals, she said, always wanted to change things because they had an unhappy childhood. "Well, I never had an unhappy childhood, what is the use of having an unhappy anything?" Léon Blum, then Premier of France, had had an unhappy childhood, and she inclined to the theory that the political uneasiness of France could be traced to this fact.

There was not, of course, going to be another war (this was in 1937!), but if there was, there *would* be, naturally; and she never tired of repeating that dancing and war are the same thing "because both are forward and back," while revolution, on the contrary, is up and down, which is why it gets nowhere. Sovietism was even then going rapidly out of fashion in her circles, because they had discovered that it is very conservative, even if the Communists do not think so. Anarchists, being rarities, did not go out of fashion so easily. The most interesting thing that ever happened to America was the Civil War; but General Lee was severely to be blamed for leading his country into that war, just the same, because he must have known they could not win; and to her, it was absurd that any one should join battle in defense of a principle in face of certain defeat. For practical purposes, honor was not even a word. Still it was an exciting war and gave an interest to America which that country would never have had without it. "If you win you do not lose and if you lose you do not win." Even as she was writing these winged words, the Spanish Civil War, the Republicans against the Franco-Fascists, kept obtruding itself. And why? "Not because it is a revolution, but because I know so well the places they are mentioning and the things there they are destroying." When she was little in Oakland, California, she loved the big, nice American fires that had "so many horses and firemen to attend them," and when she was older, she found that floods, for one thing, always read worse in the papers than they really are; besides how can you care much about what is going on if you don't see it or know the people? For this reason she had Santa Teresa being indifferent to far-away Chinese while she was founding convents in Spain. William Seabrook came to see her to find out if she was as interesting as her books. She told him she was, and he discovered black magic in the paintings of Sir Francis Rose. And when she asked Dashiell Hammett why so many young men authors were writing novels about tender young male heroines instead of the traditional female ones, he explained that it was because as women grew more and more self-confident, men lost confidence in themselves, and turned to each other, or became their own subjects for fiction. This, or something else, reminded her several times that she could not write a novel, therefore no one could any more, and no one should waste time trying.

Somehow by such roundabouts we arrive at the important, the critical event ir all this eventful history. Success. Success in this world, here and now, was what Miss Stein wanted. She knew just what it was, how it should look and feel, how much it should weigh and what it was worth over the counter. It was not enough to be a genius if you had to go on supporting your art on a private income. To be the center of a recondite literary cult, to be surrounded by listeners and imitators and seekers, to be mentioned in the same breath with James Joyce, and to have turned out bales of titles by merely writing a 'half-hour each day: she had all that, and what did it amount to? There was a great deal more and she must have it. As to her history of the human race, she confessed: "I have always been bothered . . . but mostly . . . because after all I do as simply as it can, as commonplacely as it can say, what everybody can and does do; I never know what they can do, I really do not know what they are, I do not think that any one can think because if they do, then who is who?"

It was high time for a change, and yet it occurred at hazard. If there had not been a beautiful season in October and part of November 1932, permitting Miss Stein to spend that season quietly in her country house, the *Autobiography of Alice B. Toklas* might never have been written. But it was written, and Miss Stein became a best seller in America; she made real money. With Miss Toklas, she had a thrilling tour of the United States and found crowds of people eager to see her and listen to her. And at last she got what she had really wanted all along: to be published in the *Atlantic Monthly* and the *Saturday Evening Post*.

Now she had everything, or nearly. For a while she was afraid to write any more, for fear her latest efforts would not please her public. She had never learned who she was, and yet suddenly she had become somebody else. "You are you because your little dog knows you, but when your public knows you and does not want to pay you, and when your public knows you and does want to pay you, you are not the same you."

This would be of course the proper moment to take leave, as our heroine adds at last a golden flick of light to her self-portrait. "Anyway, I was a celebrity." The practical result was that she could no longer live on her income. But she and Alice B. Toklas moved into an apartment once occupied by Queen Christina of Sweden, and they began going out more, and seeing even more people, and talking, and Miss Stein settled every question as it came up, more and more. But who wants to read about success? It is the early struggle which makes a good story.

IV

She and Alice B. Toklas enjoyed both the wars. The first one especially being a lark with almost no one getting killed where you could see, and it ended so nicely too, without changing anything. The second was rather more serious. She lived safely enough in Bilignin throughout the German occupation, and there is a pretty story that the whole village conspired to keep her presence secret. She had been a citizen of the world in the best European tradition; for though America was her native land, she had to live in Europe because she felt at home there. In the old days people paid little attention to wars, fought as they were out of sight by professional soldiers. She had always liked the notion, too, of the gradual Orientalization of the West, the peaceful penetration of the East into European culture. It had been going on a great while, and all Western geniuses worth mentioning were Orientals: look at Picasso, look at Einstein. Russians are Tartars, Spaniards are Saracens—had not all great twentieth-century painting been Spanish? And her cheerful conclusion was, that "Einstein was the creative philosophic mind of the century, and I have been the creative literary mind of the century also, with the Oriental mixing with the European." She added, as a casual afterthought, "Perhaps Europe is finished."

That was in 1938, and she could not be expected to know that war was near. They had only been sounding practice *alertes* in Paris against expected German bombers since 1935. She spoke out of her natural frivolity and did not mean it. She liked to prophesy, but warned her hearers that her prophecies never came out right, usually the very opposite, and no matter what happened, she was always surprised. She was surprised again: as the nations of Europe fell, and the Germans came again over the frontiers of France for the third time in three generations, the earth shook under her own feet, and not somebody else's. It made an astonishing difference. Something mysterious touched her in her old age. She got a fright, and this time not for ancient vanished civilizations, but for this civilization, this moment; and she was quite thrilled with relief and gay when the American Army finally came in, and the Germans were gone. She did not in the least know why the Germans had come, but they were gone, and so far as she could see, the American Army had chased them out. She remembered with positive spread eagle patriotism that America was her native land. At last America itself belonged to Miss Stein, and she claimed it, in a formal published address to other Americans. Anxiously she urged them to stay rich, to be powerful and learn how to use power, not to waste themselves; for the first time she used the word "spiritual." Ours was a spiritual as well as a material fight; Lincoln's great lucid words about government of the people by the people for the people suddenly sounded like a trumpet through her stammering confession of faith; she wanted nothing now to stand between her and her newly discovered country. By great good luck she was born on the winning side and she was going to stay there. And we were not to forget about money as the source of power; "Remember the depression, don't be afraid to look it in the face and find out the reason why, if you don't find out the reason why you'll go poor and my God, how I would hate to have my native land go poor."

The mind so long shapeless and undisciplined could not now express any knowledge out of its long willful ignorance. But the heart spoke its crude urgent language. She had liked the doughboys in the other war well enough, but this time she fell in love with the whole American Army below the rank of lieutenant. She "breathed, ate, drank, lived GI's," she told them, and inscribed numberless photographs for them, and asked them all to come back again. After her flight over Germany in an American bomber, she wrote about how, so often, she would stand staring into the sky watching American war planes going over, longing to be up there again with her new loves, in the safe, solid air. She murmured, "Bless them, bless them."

It was the strangest thing, as if the wooden umbrella feeling the rain had tried to forsake its substance and take on the nature of its form; and was struggling slowly, slowly, much too late, to unfold.

From *Harper's Magazine*, Vol. CXCV (December, 1947), pp. 519–528. Reprinted by permission of the author and editors.

LOUISE BOGAN
James on a Revolutionary Theme
[1938]

FOR all the varied critical attention given, in the last twenty years, to the novels of Henry James, those of his middle period are seldom read. When they are read, their real intention is often missed or is interpreted in some peculiar, special way. F. R. Leavis has recently pointed out several flagrant misinterpretations of James (including the classic mistake made by the critic who thought Isabel Archer divorced her husband and married an American business man at the end of *The Portrait of a Lady*) and has explained the neglect of the early and middle James by the fact that readers, steered toward the works of the late, "difficult" period, and baffled by these, make no further investigation. The three books which, appearing in the center of James's career, fully exemplify the virtues of his early manner—*The Bostonians, The Princess Casamassima* and *The Tragic Muse*—are those most completely ignored.

The Princess Casamassima, it is true, has recently come in for some attention, since critics interested in novels concerned with revoluntionary activities have discovered that in this book James deals with revolutionaries in the financially depressed London of the '80's. Although I cannot claim to have unearthed every scrap of material written about this book, I have read a fair amount and can say that not one commentator has shown signs of understanding the design James has so clearly presented in it. Usually *The Princess* has been put down as a melodramatic and rather fumbling attempt at a novel dealing with a revolutionary theme.[1]

[1] In 1938. Since the present essay was written *The Princess Casamassima* has been discussed in other studies of Henry James: by F. O. Matthiessen in *Henry James: The Major Phase* (1944), by Osborn Andreas in *Henry James and the Expanding Horizon* (1948), by Elizabeth Stevenson in *The Crooked Corridor* (1949), etc., but particularly by Lionel Trilling in his Introduction to a new edition of the novel published by The Macmillan Company, New York, 1948, and now included in Mr. Trilling's book *The Liberal Imagination* (New York: The Viking Press, 1950), pp. 58–92. The earlier discussions of the novel to which Miss Bogan refers here are those in *The Pilgrimage of Henry James* by Van Wyck Brooks (1925), in *The Three Jameses: A Family of Minds* by C. Hartley Grattan (1932), and in "The School of Experience in the Early Novels" by Stephen Spender, *The Hound and Horn*, Vol. VII (April–June, 1934), pp. 417–433, this later incorporated in Spender's book *The Destructive Element* (1935). (Editor's note, 1950.)

Several good reasons exist for these critical misconceptions, but before we deal with them, it would be well to get clear in our minds, since one of the charges against the book is that its material has not been thoroughly grasped, exactly what degree of mastery over his material, of insight into his characters, James had reached when he wrote it. *The Princess* was probably written concurrently with *The Bostonians*. Both novels were complete failures when they appeared (in 1886). James believed in both books, although for reasons that remain obscure he did not include *The Bostonians* in the definitive New York edition. But *The Princess* was included, with a preface which delicately but firmly pointed up the book's intention.

During the '70's James had produced no completely successful long work. And certainly *Watch and Ward* (1878) and *Confidence* (1880) are not only the most clumsy novels ever signed by James but the most clumsy pieces of fiction ever signed by a man of genius. They display the unsure approach of the writer who is doing it all from the outside—from the notebook, the stiff plan, the bad guess. Through some spurt of development James, in 1881, wrote the finely balanced, deeply observed *Washington Square* and *The Portrait of a Lady*. He was now able to base his books upon his characters, as opposed to supporting the action with some artificial diagram of conduct. Each character now casts light and shadow and is in turn accented or illuminated by the darkness or brilliance of the others. James had not finished profiting from Balzac, but he was now Turgenev's intelligent pupil as well. The realistic method was becoming more effortless at the same time that the technique of suggestion took in more territory with greater ease. So that the chance of James's fumbling, at this period, any problem he put his hand to is small.

The Princess Casamassima, it is true, opens with a block of Balzacian realism mixed with Dickensian melodrama that is extremely hard for modern readers to accept. In the later chapters of the book detail and suspense are to be brought in with sureness and ease; every part of the situation is to be elucidated by that sure technical skill so characteristic of the pre-theater James. The first three chapters, however, are thick with underlining and filled with a kind of cardboard darkness. The characters are so overloaded with reasons that they closely approach the line dividing drama from burlesque. The delicate little boy called Hyacinth, the son of a French working girl, who is also a murderess, and an earl, her victim; Miss Pynsent, the tender old maid who has raised the child; Mr. Vetch, the battered fiddler with leanings toward anarchism—at first glance these appear cut out of whole cloth. And in spite of a few flashes of insight, the scene in which Hyacinth witnesses his mother's death in prison is dated and overcharged. Thus balked at the outset, it is little wonder that the reader expects to find a measure of falseness everywhere in the story.

Given the remarkable figure of Hyacinth and the remarkable fact of his sharply divided inheritance, what use does James make of them? It may be best to give the story in bare outline. Hyacinth, grown to young manhood, is apprenticed to M. Poupin, an exiled veteran both of '48 and the Commune. (Hyacinth's own maternal grandfather, James tells us at an early point, died on the Paris barricades.) Poupin teaches him revolutionary principles along with the trade (James considers it a minor art) of book-binding. The youth then meets the two people who are to bring about the crisis in his life. The Princess Casamassima, separated from her husband and footloose in London on her husband's money, first dazzles Hyacinth with her interest in revolutionary plots and then with her interest in himself. And Paul Muniment, son of a north-country miner, an active, realistic, and inscrutable worker deep in revolutionary activities, attracts the ardent boy. Hyacinth actually gives over his life to Muniment, promising in a moment of enthusiasm that he will be the instrument for an act of violence whenever the need arises. Muniment accepts his pledge and binds Hyacinth fully, by a vow taken before witnesses. Hyacinth tells the Princess, after she has given him some minor glimpses of the great world, of his origin and dedication. Miss Pynsent dies; her small legacy enables Hyacinth to go to the Continent. He comes back changed. What he has seen has convinced him that certain objects, of which he had no former notion, should be preserved, not destroyed. The Princess has meanwhile met Muniment. She brings her charm to bear on him, with the secondary purpose of extricating Hyacinth from his vow; but primarily to get herself deeper into true conspiratorial circles. Hyacinth, whose determination to do what he can to further the cause of the people remains unchanged in spite of his secret change of heart, thinks that the pair have cast him off. Then the call comes: a duke is to be assassinated and Hyacinth is picked by the mysterious instigator of these affairs to be the assassin. The revolutionary group, at this news, splits into two factions: those who wish to save Hyacinth and those who are willing to let matters take their course. Muniment, although he professes sympathy for Hyacinth and says that he is free to choose, does nothing. The Princess rushes to save the boy and to offer herself in his stead. She and a kind, methodical German conspirator meet at Hyacinth's lodgings. But the boy has already shot himself, with the revolver meant for the assassination.

Critics have construed this story according to the set of their own convictions. Van Wyck Brooks, for example, although appreciative of James's success with Poupin, Vetch, Miss Pynsent, and others, considers Hyacinth an insufferable little snob. And Hyacinth is, according to Brooks, an embodiment of James's own yearning after the glories of the British upper classes.

This unfortunate but remarkably organized youth . . . is conscious of nothing but the paradise of which he has been dispossessed. . . . In real life the last thing that would have occurred to a young man of Hyacinth's position would have been to "roam and wander and yearn" about the gates of that lost paradise: he would have gone to Australia, or vanished into the slums, or continued *with the utmost indifference* at his *trade* of binding books. But this attitude represents the feeling of Hyacinth's creator. [Italics mine.]

C. Hartley Grattan believes that Hyacinth's "sense of deprivation" vitiates the worth of his radical impulses:

The conviction that it is senseless to do anything, no matter how small the act, to destroy the upper classes leads to the climax of the novel in [Hyacinth's] suicide.

But Grattan admits James's insight into his material.

When the social-minded young English disinterred the book some years ago because of its theme, Stephen Spender wrote in *The Destructive Element*:

The observation of political types in this book is really remarkable and curiously undated . . . Paul Muniment . . . is a true revolutionary type. He has the egoism, the sense of self-preservation, the cynicism of a person who identifies himself so completely with a cause that he goes through life objectively guarding himself from all approach, as one might preserve for the supreme eventuality a very intricate and valuable torpedo.

Spender's evaluation of Hyacinth is this:

Hyacinth, with his strong leaning toward the upper classes and yet his feeling that he is somehow committed to the cause of the workers, might today have become a Socialist Prime Minister: a Ramsay MacDonald who . . . would dismay ·his followers by going over to the other side and becoming the most frequent visitor at large country houses and of dinners at Buckingham Palace.

Now Hyacinth, in the very essence of his character as James with great care and at considerable length presents it, could never become what Spender thinks he could become, any more than what Brooks thinks James should have made him become. Before turning to Hyacinth, let us examine the character of the Princess. Who is she? What is she? What has she been, and what is she likely to be? The development of her character must have meant a good deal to James since she is the only figure he ever "revived" and carried from one book to another.

She was Christina Light in *Roderick Hudson*, the character in that early work who evokes the mixed feelings of admiration and exasperation that James was later to call up through many of his women. She is the daughter of an Anglo-American shrew and adventuress who forces her, by a threat of scandal, into a marriage with the highest bidder. James managed to bring out, even at a time when his art was still imperfect, Christina's marred idealism and ignorant, rather than innocent, pride, so that they freshen every page on which she appears. The coarser and weaker people, in contrast with her straightforwardness, show up in a sorry way. Roderick Hudson, with whom she falls in love and whom she tries to galvanize into some kind of manhood, crumbles, after losing her, in much the same way, James makes us feel, as he would have crumbled had he won her. Brought up to deadening shifts, she has one flaw. She is not truly courageous. She marries the prince at once after receiving the shock of her mother's revelations.

In the later book she is the single person who is continuously presented from the outside. James never "goes behind" her. We are never told what she thinks or how she feels; we merely see her act. James clearly presupposes a knowledge in the reader of her early tragedy. To watch her casting her charm and enthusiasm about; to see her reacting more and more violently against her money and position; to see her—after Muniment has told her that it is her money alone which interests his circle, and has prophesied her certain return to her husband now that the Prince has stopped the flow of that money—rushing in desperation to offer herself as a substitute in the affair of the duke's assassination—all this can puzzle us if we know nothing of the beautiful girl who moved through the scenes of *Roderick Hudson*.

Now "the cleverest woman in Europe," she bears a grudge against society strong enough to force her into repudiation of everything her trained taste fully values. When Hyacinth bares his own tragedy to her, the relation of the two is lifted out of a stupid contrast between a revolutionary-minded woman of the world and a talented pauper. For what the Princess knows, as she listens to him, and what the reader should also know, is that she is herself a bastard. James, far from being taken in by it, deeply realizes that the life she represents is as undermined by the results of cruelty and passion, for all its beautiful veneer, as Hyacinth's own. Having failed in her youth to face a crisis and see it through, she knows in her heart that when she thinks of herself as "one of the numerous class who could be put on a tolerable footing only by a revolution," she is thinking dishonestly. It is her despair and her defects which push her toward extreme revolutionary enthusiasm, as much as her generosity of spirit. But in Hyacinth she recognizes—after she has emerged from her first sentimental ideas concerning him—complete devotion, consistency, and fineness. This boy "never makes mistakes," and is incapable of going back on a given promise. She shows him specimens of English county families, toward whom her own reaction is: "You know, people oughtn't to be both corrupt and dreary." But what Hyacinth tenders them, as he tenders her, beneath his devotion, is a kind of gentle pity.

For this son of a criminal and an aristocrat is not, as he has been made out to be, a little snob, an affected artisan with a divided nature and ambitions beyond his station. James, with every subtle device of his mature art, from the first sentence describing him to the last, shows the boy as an artist, a clear, sensitive intelligence, filled with the imagination "which will always give him the clue about everything." James has endowed him, indeed, with the finest qualities of his own talent; and this is what is meant when James says that Hyacinth had watched London "very much as I had watched it." Hyacinth is, like James, "a person on whom nothing is lost." If the character has a fault, it is that James has distilled too purely into his creature the sharp insight, the capacity for selfless devotion, the sense of proportion, the talent for self-mockery and gentle irony which seldom exist in genius without an admixture of cruder ingredients. But James wanted a cool and undistorting mirror to shine between the dark and violent world of the disinherited on the one hand and the preposterous world of privilege on the other. Such a clear lens (Maisie, Nanda) James was later to place in the center of psychological situations. He was never again to place it, and with the final polish of genius added, between social classes. For that matter it has never been placed there, up to the present, by anyone else, although Conrad, in *Under Western Eyes,* a book almost certainly modeled on *The Princess,* examined the revolutionary side of the picture through the intense spirit of Razumov. We are used, in fiction dealing with social problems, to the spectacle of the artist absorbed or deflected into one class or another. James kept Hyacinth detached to the end. And though the solution for the artist, in the insoluble situation James has constructed, is death, as the symbols of the two extremes he has instinctively rejected (after he knows that his own life must exist independently, apart from either) stand by his deathbed, we feel that what they both have been left to is not exactly life.

The book is full of wonderful moments. Short mention should be made of the ultimate opacity and brutality of Muniment, as he is shown in contrast not only to Hyacinth but to the more humane members of the revolutionary circle; of James's masterly analysis of Hyacinth's spiritual coming of age, resulting, on his return from abroad, in increased self-sufficiency and a more complete grasp of his art; of the complex rendering of Hyacinth's rejection of the thought of violence when his mother's murderous hands come before him; of the superb portraits of the solidly disillusioned Madame Grandoni, the morbidly jealous Prince, and those true fools and snobs—Captain Sholto and Muniment's horrible invalid sister. The scenes of submerged London have been praised. What is even more astonishing than these is James's knowledge of the relentless mechanisms of poverty—poverty's minutiae.

It is interesting to trace down the source of James's understanding of Muniment. We remember that the elder James was surrounded by socialists of the Fourier school, and that he "agreed with Fourier that vice and crime were the consequences of our present social order, and it would not survive them." The younger James had, no doubt, seen Muniment's counterpart multiplied about him, in Fourier's more fanatical followers, in his childhood.

"Very likely . . . all my buried prose will kick off its tombstones at once," James wrote to Howells in 1888. After, it would seem, Stendhal's hundred years.

From *The Nation,* Vol. CXLVI (April 23, 1938), pp. 471–474. Reprinted by permission of the author and editors.

ERIC BENTLEY
Shaw at Ninety
[1946]

ON THE twenty-sixth of July, Bernard Shaw will be ninety years old.[1] How should we—or he—feel about it? The ninetieth birthday of the man who once wrote, "Every man over forty is a scoundrel," is an ambiguous occasion. Ambiguous because he does not believe in celebrating any birthdays, let alone ninetieth birthdays. Ambiguous because, in the opinion of so many, Mr. Shaw has outlived his genius and even his usefulness. Ambiguous because, it is thought, the politics of the twentieth century has traveled far beyond the ken of Fabianism. Ambiguous because twentieth-century literature has taken quite a different turn since the days when Shavian drama was the latest thing. And yet, despite Mr. Shaw's indifference to celebrations, despite the indifference of my contemporaries to Mr. Shaw, I propose to celebrate the ninety-year span of this man's life by asking the Shavian question: What use has it been? To what end has Bernard Shaw lived?

Seventy years ago a young Irishman went to live in London. Another twenty years had to pass before London was fully aware of the fact that it possessed a new critic, a new novelist, a new thinker, a new wit, and—rarest of all—a new dramatist. In the first decade of the twentieth century Shaw's reputation swept across America and Central Europe. On the death of Anatole France in 1924 he was declared the leading Great Man of European letters. A new play by Shaw was a world event. Between 1923 and 1925 the part of Saint Joan was enacted by Winifred Lenihan in America, Sybil Thorndike in England, Ludmilla Pitoëff in Paris, Elisabeth Bergner in Berlin. On the occasion of his seventieth birthday a *New York Times* editorial declared Shaw "probably the most famous of living writers."

Soon the fame won by plays and books was doubled by the fame won by his films. Shaw's opinions on everything were reported in the press almost weekly. Has any other author ever been so famous during his lifetime? (Since 1905 many articles on Shaw have been published every year. Some forty whole books have been written about him.) True, none of his books has sold like *Gone With the Wind,* none of his plays has run as long as *Tobacco Road.*

[1] Written in 1946, on the occasion of Shaw's ninetieth birthday. (Editor's note.)

But even by the economic criterion, Shaw's career was "sounder" than any merely popular author's, for his books went on selling indefinitely and his plays returned to the stage again and again. True, as a "best-selling classic" Shaw does not rival Shakespeare or the Bible. But then it takes the death of its author to put the final seal of respectability upon a classic. And Shaw refuses to die.

If, as Freud says, the life of the artist is a quest for honor, riches, fame, love, and power, Shaw must be one of the most successful men who ever lived. Then why is he, rather obviously, a sad old man? Because he is sorry to leave a world which he has so brilliantly adorned? That is too shallow an explanation. Honor, riches, fame, the love of women, these he has been granted in abundance. Yet the striking thing about Shaw is his relative aloofness from all these worldly advantages. He talks about them all as if they belonged to somebody else.

But Freud mentioned a fifth goal: power. And this Shaw has only had to the same extent as any other rich writer, and that is to a very small extent indeed. Not that Shaw wanted to be Prime Minister or anything of that sort. The only time Shaw stood as candidate in a large-scale election his abstention from demagogy amounted to a Coriolanus-like repudiation of his electors. When the electors turned him down, they were returning a compliment.

This was not the kind of power Shaw wanted. Crude personal ambition is something he scarcely understands. What he did feel was the consciousness of great spiritual resources within him, the consciousness of a message—of, as he put it, being used by something larger than himself. When, therefore, people paid attention to the ego of Shaw and not to the message of Shaw, when they paid attention to the small and not to the large thing, that was for Shaw the ultimate catastrophe. More plainly put, Shaw's aim has been to change our minds and save civilization; but we are still in the old ruts and civilization has gone from bad to worse. For Shaw this must be the cardinal fact of his career. "I have produced no permanent impression because nobody has ever believed me."

Anyone who knows Shaw's aims and attitudes knows that this is as complete a confession of failure as old Carlyle's famous sentence: "They call me a great man now, but not one believes what I have told them." Three years after Carlyle's death Shaw wrote on behalf of the peaceful Fabians that "we had rather face a Civil War than such another century of suffering as this has been." And then came, of all things, the twentieth century, the age of Wilhelm II, Tojo, and Hitler! In 1932 Shaw was again addressing the Fabians. He said: "For forty-eight years I have been addressing speeches to the Fabian Society and to other assemblies in this country. So far as I can make out, those speeches have not produced any effect whatsoever."

"So what?" some will be content to say, reconciling themselves with cynical

ease to the ways of the world. Why should Shaw think he can change civilization by thinking, writing, and talking? This, says one of his Marxist critics, is
the "bourgeois illusion." Winston Churchill does not use the Marxist vocabulary, but his essay on Shaw, in *Great Contemporaries,* conveys the same contempt. He will accept Shaw only on condition that he does not ask to be taken
seriously. He ignored Shaw's repeated assertion: "The real joke is that I am in
earnest."

II

The fact that Shaw has been easy to brush off can be explained by the
method which he has used to spread his fame, a method he expounded forty
years ago with characteristic frankness:

> In order to gain a hearing it was necessary for me to attain the footing of a privi-
> leged lunatic with the license of a jester. My method has therefore been to take
> the utmost trouble to find the right thing to say and then say it with the utmost
> levity.

The lunatic jester was named "G. B. S.," a personage who from the start was
known to many more people than Bernard Shaw could ever hope to be, a
Very Funny Man, whose perversities were so outrageous that they could be
forgiven only under the assumption that they were not intended, whose views
and artistic techniques seemed to be arrived at by the simple expedient of in-
verting the customary. Unfortunately Bernard Shaw proved a sorcerer's ap-
prentice: he could not get rid of "G. B. S." The very method by which Shaw
made himself known prevented him from being understood. The paradox of
his career is that he should have had so much fame and so little influence.

So little influence? Is the phrase disparaging? After all, Shaw had an ap-
preciable influence at least on the generation of 1910. And yet even this is
hardly something that Shaw would congratulate himself upon, for it was
mainly negative. It represented only the superficial part of his teaching, his
anti-Victorianism. It was often the kind of influence he had positively to dis-
own—as in the case of the young criminal whose plea of being a disciple of
Shaw was later embodied in *The Doctor's Dilemma*. The attention Shaw attracts must not be confused with influence.

During the first decades "G. B. S." was a Dangerous Spirit, distinctly Me-
phistophelian, red-bearded, young, and aggressive. No kind of philosopher can
more easily be dismissed. Eugene O'Neill's play *Ah, Wilderness* portrays this
early Shavian "influence" as a sort of measles which the more literary high
school boy must have and then forget. After the First World War, the great
dividing line in Shaw's career, "G. B. S." was regarded as rather cute, a Santa
Claus if not a Simple Simon. William Archer crowned his long series of
attempts to discredit Shaw with a final blow: Shaw was a Grand Old Man.

"Not taking me seriously," said Shaw, "is the Englishman's way of refusing to face facts." And by "the Englishman" Shaw has always meant Monsieur Tout-le-monde. "What is wrong with the prosaic Englishman is what is wrong with the prosaic men of all countries: stupidity."

Before the First World War, Shaw was the leader of the *avant-garde*. After it he was the Grand Old Man—which meant that he had lost the support of the rebellious young. In 1898 Shaw had written: "I may dodder and dote; I may potboil and platitudinize; I may become the butt and chopping-block of all the bright original spirits of the rising generation; but my reputation shall not suffer; it is built up fast and solid, like Shakespeare's, on an impregnable basis of dogmatic reiteration." Like Shakespeare's! What an irony, for the man who wished to have, not literary prestige "like Shakespeare's," but *influence* like Voltaire's or Luther's. "I see there is a tendency," Shaw said in 1921, "to begin treating me like an archbishop. I fear in that case that I must be becoming a hopeless old twaddler."

The new "G. B. S." proved another spirit that could not be exorcised. And the new "G. B. S." was worse than the old, for fogies have even less influence than iconoclasts. The old critics had at least feared and scorned Shaw. An admirer of the new sort wrote: "But I do not believe that we will thus scorn him or forget him when the irritation of his strictures on events that are close to our hearts or to our pride is removed." Unfortunately, for Shaw's purposes, irritation to our hearts and our pride was desirable, while praise for the irritator was neither here nor there. If the undirected rebelliousness of Mencken —whose first book of criticism (1905) was also the first book ever written about Shaw—was only a negative and distorted Shavianism, that is the only sort of Shavianism that has as yet had any currency at all.

The people who have revered Shaw in his later years—revered him as patriarch, as senile prodigy—have not bothered to imbibe any of his teaching. This is best illustrated by the fact that Broadway, though always reluctant to stage anything but a new play, has revived old Shaw plays and made money with them, while his new plays were either left alone or played to half-empty houses. It was not that Shaw's new plays were so obviously inferior to his old plays. They were in any case much better plays than most of those on Broadway. It was that Shaw was no longer welcome as a living force. He was a Classic—that is, the author of plays old and awesome enough to be innocuous.

When Shaw won popular fame he lost his serious reputation. "The bright and original spirits of the rising generation" repudiated him and passed on. A *Nation* editorial of October, 1909, already reflects new departures: "The time has come . . . when the insolent Shavian advertising no longer fills us with astonishment or discovery, or disables our judgment from a cool inspection of the wares advertised. The youthful Athenians who darted most impetuously after his novelties are already hankering after some new thing. The deep young souls who looked to him as an evangelist are beginning to see through him and despair." The occasion of these patronizing remarks was the publication of Chesterton's brilliant book (still the best) on Shaw, which, despite Chesterton's avowed dislike of "time snobbery," was an attempt to make Shaw sound dated.

In 1913, D. H. Lawrence wrote that there ought to be a revolt against the generation of Shaw and Wells. In the same year a young English critic, Dixon Scott, who was soon after to be killed at Gallipoli, interpreted Shaw, in one of the best critical essays of that generation, as essentially a child of London in the 'eighties. Shortly after the First World War the leading poet of the new generation, T. S. Eliot, was careful to put Shaw in his place as "an Edwardian," a quaint survivor from before the flood. Several of the clever critics of this clever decade wrote essays to prove Shaw an old fool. Theatrical criticism followed the general trend. The gist of George Jean Nathan's notices in the 'twenties and 'thirties is that Shaw is played out.

When William Archer conferred the title of Grand Old Man, Shaw was not yet seventy. The wheel turned, and lo! an ancient of seventy-five, eighty, eighty-five. Diamond jubilees followed jubilees as the figure rose and rose. This year, when Shaw is ninety, some will laugh with him and some will laugh at him, some will laugh sentimentally and some will laugh superciliously. Few will laugh in the true Shavian fashion—seriously.

I hope some of the main features of Shaw's career are now clear. To gain an audience he invented a pose. The pose gained him his audience but prevented him from having any influence. The mask of clowning in Shaw's career has as its counterpoint the mask of clowning, of farce and melodrama, of *Kitsch* and sheer entertainment, in his plays. Of this second mask a great theatrical critic, Egon Friedell, remarked that it was clever of Shaw so to sugar his pill but that it was even cleverer of the public to lick off the sugar and leave the pill alone. In that battle with his audience which is the main conflict in Shavian drama, in that battle with the public which is the main conflict in everything that Shaw writes or says, the audience, the public, has won. "I have solved practically all the pressing questions of our time," Shaw says, "but . . . they keep on being propounded as insoluble just as if I had never existed."

Up to this point Shaw's secret is an open one. Shaw's famous method, his "Shavianism," by which people mean his pose of arrogance, was a deliberate strategy in an altruistic struggle. As I have suggested, it was precisely because Shaw was so unusually immune from the common frailties of ambition and egoism that he could adopt the manner of the literary exhibitionist without risk to his integrity. His campaign of self-promotion was not the campaign of a clever careerist who decides to secure at once by cunning what he will never secure later by genius. Shaw had artistic genius enough, and knew it, but he was not primarily interested in artistic genius and artistic reputation. He wanted his pen to be his sword in a struggle that was more ethical than aesthetic.

Wishing to change the world, Shaw wished to speak to the public at large, not merely to his literary confreres. So he put his genius at the service of his moral passion. He knew that he risked sacrificing altogether a high literary reputation (like, say, Henry James's); and the fact that his name is so often linked with the publicist Wells indicates that, for a time at least, Shaw has forgone that kind of reputation. The arrogant pose was an act of self-sacrifice. Shaw's modesty was offered up on the altar of a higher purpose. In order to be influential he consented to be notorious.

His failure was double. Willingly he forwent his literary reputation. Unwillingly he had to admit his lack of influence as a thinker. The term Artist-Philosopher which Shaw coined for himself is perhaps a concealed admission that both as artist and as philosopher he had failed to make his mark.

III

If this were the whole story, Shaw would be no more important than a hundred other men who have abandoned art for "action" or propaganda without making any noticeable dent in the world's armor. Shaw's is a more complicated case. If he is today a sad old man it is not himself that he has found disappointing. His unhappiness is not that of a Citizen Kane finding that success does not bring contentment. It is in *us* that he is disappointed. It is modern civilization he grieves over. To the man who now proceeds to ask: but is not Shaw one of us? is he not an integral part of modern civilization? one would have to reply: his ideas are indeed typically modern, a synthesis of all our romanticism and realism, our traditionalism and our revolutionism, yet he himself is not one of us. He is further apart from his contemporaries than any other thinker since Nietzsche.

Shaw was born and bred a Protestant in the most fanatically Catholic city in the world. That indeed is his situation in a nutshell. His home, far from being one of puritanic pressures like Samuel Butler's, was one of abnormally tepid relationships. From the beginning Shaw was encouraged to be independent. Practically the only thing his education taught him was how to stand alone. His keenest pleasures were those which the imagination could feast on without intrusion from people around him; when he speaks of his voluptuous youth he means he read novels, wandered round an art gallery, reveled in opera and melodrama. Since his schooling was as untyrannical as his home, he was largely unaffected by it. The first time he felt the pressure of society was when he became a clerk. It was too much for him. He broke with his whole environment by going to seek his fortune in London. If he lived with his mother there, it was only to save money. Mother and son continued to see little of each other.

Shaw entered British society by the Bohemian gate. He never tried to become an established member of the upper, middle, or lower class. He remained "unassimilated." His first circle of acquaintance consisted largely of musicians, his later circle of writers and actors. Even his journalistic experience did not bring Shaw overmuch into contact with the general run of men. As book reviewer, art, drama, and music critic, he worked at home, at the gallery, the theater, and the concert hall, not at the office. A brief connection with the telephone business convinced Shaw for a second time that he must never try to "earn an honest living."

From 1882 on, Shaw was a socialist, addressed mass audiences, served on committees, was elected borough councillor, stood as candidate for the London County Council. But how far all this work was from any mingling with the working class, the middle class, or any class except that of intellectuals is clear to anyone who studies the life of Shaw in particular or the history of the Fabian Socialists in general. The Fabian Society should be thought of less as one of the several branches of the British Labor movement than as one of the many societies for intellectuals which abounded in Victorian, and especially Late Victorian, England.

One might almost say that the Fabians were nearer to the Aesthetes than to the trade-unions. Theirs was but another form of Bohemianism. "Instead of velvet jackets and a slap-dash joviality," as Dixon Scott put it, the young writers of the 'eighties "took to *saeva indignatio* and sandals," to "Jaeger and Ibsen and Esoteric Buddhism." "They became infidels," he added, "atheists, anarchists, cosmogonists, vegetarians, anti-vivisectionists, anti-vaccinationists." Far from involving Shaw personally in ordinary British society, socialism helped to keep him out of it. And for good. For he married a wealthy Fabian in 1898, and in the twentieth century has barely pretended to be a part of our world at all. At best he descends upon us from his country house at Ayot St. Lawrence like a prophet descending from mountain solitude.

If this version of Shaw's career seems fanciful, turn to the last page of the preface to *Immaturity,* the long essay which is the nearest approach to an autobiography that Shaw will ever write. Calling himself "a sojourner on this planet rather than a native of it," Shaw continues:

Whether it be that I was born mad or a little too sane, my kingdom was not of this world: I was at home only in the realm of my imagination, and at my ease only with the mighty dead. Therefore I had to become an actor, and create for myself a fantastic personality fit and apt for dealing with men, and adaptable to the various parts I had to play as author-journalist, orator, politician, committeeman, man of the world and so forth. In this I succeeded later on only too well. In my boyhood I saw Charles Mathews act in a farce called Cool as a Cucumber. The hero was a young man just returned from a tour of the world, upon which he had been set to cure him of an apparently hopeless bashfulness; and the fun lay in the cure having overshot the mark and transformed him into a monster of outrageous impudence. I am not sure that something of the kind did not happen to me; for when my imposture was at last accomplished, and I daily pulled the threads of the puppet who represented me in the public press, the applause that greeted it was not unlike that which Mathews drew in Cool as a Cucumber. . . . At the time of which I am writing, however, I had not yet learned to act, nor come to understand that my natural character was impossible on the great London stage. When I had to come out of the realm of imagination into that of actuality I was still uncomfortable. I was outside society, outside politics, outside sport, outside the church. If the term had been invented then I should have been called the Complete Outsider.

Shaw was certainly an outsider. And, as we have seen, the ruse by which he sought to get Inside was by no means successful.

IV

At this point Shaw's career is revealed to us as something more than a picturesque misadventure, and Shaw as something more than a frustrated propagandist or a frustrated man of action. Of course he *is* a frustrated propagandist to some extent—all preachers are. But he is not a man of action at all. He is an artist, and therefore, whatever his didactic urge, whatever the naturalistic ardor with which he seeks to portray the outer world, he gives expression to his own nature and tells the story of himself. In the art of persuasion one Hitler or one Hearst is worth a thousand Shaws. The fact that Shaw did not descend to the methods of the politician, let alone of the demagogue, would indicate that—in spite of himself—he was not fundamentally a propagandist.

When remarking that the good advice of the Gospels, Dickens, Plato, has never been heeded, Shaw says in the foreword to his *Prefaces:* "You may well ask me why, with such examples before me, I took the trouble to write them. I can only reply that I do not know. There was no why about it: I had to: that was all." A cryptic solution? To those who know their Shaw it is suggestive of other Shavian tenets. Most basic of them is the statement in *The Sanity of Art:* "We are afraid to look life in the face and see in it, not the fulfilment of a moral law or of the deductions of reason, but the satisfaction of a passion in us of which we can give no account whatever." To satisfy passions we do many things because we "have to"—there is "no why about it." If the passion is a sufficiently high one—according to Shaw, chastity is passion, thought is passion—the action is justified.

Shaw's passions are high. In the preface to *Immaturity,* which I have already cited, Shaw refers to himself as an Insider. "The moment music, painting, literature, or science came into question the positions were reversed: it was I who was the Insider. I had the intellectual habit; and my natural combination of critical faculty with literary resource needed only a clear comprehension of life in the light of an intelligible theory: in short, a religion, to set it in triumphant operation." One of the most interesting portraits of Shaw is his own John Tanner, the man of ideas who in this world of ours is rightly regarded as even more a gasbag than an iconoclast, but who in the realm of the spirit, as Don Juan Tenorio, is a true master.

Whatever his duties to us, Shaw had his duty to himself. Whatever his function as a deliberate preacher, Shaw also knew himself to be a *force* that had to act according to the inscrutable laws of its own nature. He was being used—for an unknown purpose—through the agency of a passion "of which we can give no account whatever." This passion led the man who thought of himself as a propagandist to what looks like the weakest and most unpromising of all propagandist media—the theater. Nor are the plays the most propagandist of plays. As far as the presentation of opinions is concerned, Shaw's forte is for presenting both sides of a question with equal conviction, an art he brought to such a pitch that some thought his *Saint Joan* a defense of the Inquisition, while others thought his later political plays a defense of fascism. From beginning to end Shaw's drama expresses his nature—his apprehension of many-faceted reality—much more than it champions particular doctrines. It even mirrors Shaw's life rather closely in a series of self-portraits.

V

It is not of course true, despite Mr. Wells, that *all* Shaw's characters are Shaw—at least not in any obvious or important way. Nor can one, as Mr. Laski hints, simply look for a character who talks a lot, who believes in socialism, or creative evolution, and stamp him as Shaw. In *Candida,* for example, there is actually more of Shaw's philosophy, more of Shaw's plight too, in the Pre-Raphaelite poet Marchbanks than in the platform-speaking socialist Morell. These two characters might perhaps be taken as two halves of Shaw's nature: his outer, glib, and confident half, at once socialist and social, and his spiritual, lonely, and artistic half, the half that puts him beyond the pale of society. Certainly the secret in the poet's heart is the secret of Shaw the Outsider who is the real Insider, the man who is strong enough to leave the homestead and live with himself and his vision.

In the later plays the two most interesting self-portraits are Captain Shotover in *Heartbreak House* and King Magnus in *The Apple Cart*. Both portray Shaw's role in modern civilization and in England in particular. In *Heartbreak House,* England is represented as a ship, with no captain, heading for the rocks. In a ship within this ship—a house in which the only room we see is got up like a ship's cabin—lives Shotover, half lunatic, half sage, an ex-sailor

who sold himself to the devil at Zanzibar. He is conducting researches with
the aim of discovering a death ray ostensibly "to blow up the human race if it
goes too far."

- Actually Shaw borrowed the death ray from a novel by Bulwer Lytton in
order to repeat a fancy he had aired long before in an essay: either we must
learn to respect justice as such or acquire the power to kill each other instantaneously by merely thinking. *Responsibility* (our supreme desideratum according to Shaw) must be attained by whatever method—if not by a passion
for justice, then by the passion of fear. It is significant that Shaw does not
present Shotover as a noble character but as a senile eccentric. As poignantly
as Nietzsche, Shaw recognized his own limitation. Although Shotover marries
a young woman, in sadly ironic recognition of the Shavian union of Artist
Man and Creator Woman, he does not discover the death ray any more than
England learns to respect justice. The end is chaos and misunderstanding.

The Apple Cart was discussed flat-footedly at the time of its first productions as a play advocating monarchy. This is a misunderstanding. The situation of the play—a king confronting his Labor cabinet—is actually a fantasy
which, like all Shavian fantasies, has very concrete implications. The king is
a philosopher-king. In fact he is Shaw (even to his love life, which includes a
humdrum wife whom he prefers to a romantic mistress). The problem of the
play is not King George versus Ramsay MacDonald but the question: Who
knows better what is going on and who is better fitted to cope with it—
Bernard Shaw the artist-philosopher or Ramsay MacDonald the prime minister? Their common enemy is Breakages Limited—that is, capitalism, the sinister power, thriving on destruction, which the critics took no notice of because
it is not personified on the stage. It lurks in the background. Now just as in
Shotover Shaw does not make himself patriarchal, so in Magnus he does not
make himself majestic. It is not clear that Magnus could really have won if he
had gone to the polls, as he threatened, against the politicians. It is not clear
that the philosopher can replace the prime minister. No basic problems are
cleared up at the end. We are left with the not very encouraging title of
the play.

But perhaps the most complete picture of what I have called "Shaw's role in
modern civilization" was long ago provided in *John Bull's Other Island*. As
in *Man and Superman* Shaw represents himself by two characters and, as in
Candida, the two Shaws are brought up against a more masterful person, one
who really assumes that he—in *Candida*, it is *she*—has inherited the earth. In
Candida the emphasis is chiefly psychological. In *John Bull's Other Island* it
is chiefly philosophic, a matter of rival outlooks. The Antagonist is not a
charming lady but the Shavian Englishman, the Shavian professional man,
the Shavian politician, Broadbent, the two syllables of whose name tell us
nearly all we need to know of him. Shaw himself, I think, is part Larry Doyle,

part Father Keegan; that is, partly the worldly Irishman whose realism drives him to have his revenge on England by "succeeding" as an Englishman, partly the divinely mad priest who believes (Shaw has been quoting the line ever since) that "every jest is an earnest in the womb of time."

There is no passage in Shaw that more clearly shows what he is for and what he is against; there is no passage that more openly reveals his estrangement from our world, than this brief encounter between Keegan and Broadbent:

BROADBENT: I find the world quite good enough for me: rather a jolly place in fact.

KEEGAN: You are satisfied?

BROADBENT: As a reasonable man, yes. I see no evils in the world—except of course, natural evils—that cannot be remedied by freedom, self-government, and English institutions. I think so, not because I am an Englishman, but as a matter of commonsense.

KEEGAN: You feel at home in the world then?

BROADBENT: Of course. Don't you?

KEEGAN (*from the very depths of his nature*):   No.

BROADBENT: Try phosphorus pills. I always take them when my brain is overworked. I'll give you the address in Oxford Street.

At the end of the play, when Larry Doyle again expresses his contempt for dreaming—it is Shaw's own contempt for illusions, for idealism—and Broadbent tells us he has dreamt of heaven as a dreadful place, "a sort of pale blue satin," Keegan gives us *his* dream. It is Shaw's own ideal, which he hopes is no illusion:

In my dreams it is a country where the State is the Church and the Church the people: three in one and one in three. It is a commonwealth in which work is play and play is life: three in one and one in three. It is a temple in which the priest is the worshipper and the worshipper the worshipped: three in one and one in three. It is a godhead in which all life is human and all humanity divine: three in one and one in three.

But Father Keegan is obviously even madder than Captain Shotover. He summarizes his own vision: "It is in short the dream of a madman." To which Shaw's Englishman retorts: "What a regular old Church and State Tory he is! He's a character: he'll be an attraction here. Really almost equal to Ruskin and Carlyle." To which Shaw's other half, Larry Doyle, adds: "Yes: and much good *they* did with all their talk!"

Shaw's dream of a better world, his impatience with dreams of a better world, his idealism and his anti-idealism, his knowledge of the world of "Englishmen" and his alienation from this world—all these are implicit in the last pages of *John Bull's Other Island*. These are not pages of the Bernard Shaw the public knows. They are pages of the man who once wrote haughtily: "My heart knows only its own bitterness." They are pages of one whom the poet A. E. called a "suffering sensitive soul."

VI

We are now in a position to see what Shaw's career means over and above the well-attested fact that he wanted to be taken seriously and was not taken seriously. We can see that Shaw is a clear case of misunderstood genius. But, lest the story sound too much like that of the perennial "clown with a broken heart," we must see also that Shaw never relaxed into self-pity; that his celebrated gayety is precisely a prophylactic against such relaxation; that, alienated as he was, Shaw made a very special and subtle adjustment. He turned his alienation to artistic and moral profit. He is one of the very few great modern artists who have not been dismayed by their own estrangement.

Our times suffer from sick conscience, and our geniuses suffer with the times. Modern artists are mainly of two types. The first, to use Flaubert's figure, wants to vomit at the thought of the horror of our epoch, which it nevertheless looks straight in the eyes. The second looks in the other direction and calls loudly for literary Uplift, Patriotism, and something Wholesome. Shaw belonged to the first group. He vomited, but eventually emerged from the *vomitorium* with an incredibly optimistic smile on his face. Had he decided to join the second group? No, but he had decided that vomiting did no good, that the facts had to be faced but that they had also to be changed, and that if one is alienated from one's environment one can recognize the fact and work out a plan of campaign.

Shaw's older contemporary, Nietzsche, had come to a similar conclusion but had followed up his affirmations of health by losing his reason. Shaw found a happier though in some ways a no less desperate solution: he pretended to have no reason to lose. If modern life was as unreasonable as *King Lear,* Shaw would cast himself as the Fool. Trace the word *mad* through his plays and you will find that the finest characters and the finest actions usually have it applied to them.

Accordingly I do not think Shaw can find a place in the paradise of the middle-brows despite his cheerful and moralistic manner. To be sure, there are subterraneous realms which Shaw never enters, and we cannot find in him what we go to Dostoevsky, Proust, or Kafka for. Yet, like Ibsen, Shaw has had "a strange, fairy-tale fate," strange because in some ways so close to his age and in others so remote from it, strange because it was so hard for him to *communicate.* The problem of communication in the arts is never simple; the artist is one who tries to communicate the incommunicable. For the *modern* artist the problem, I think, is especially acute, and Shaw resorted to some very bizarre shifts. Living in this queer age, he found he had to give the impression that his highest quality—a sort of delicate spirituality, purity, or holiness—was fooling when what he meant was that his fooling was holy. The devil's advocate was a saint. The clown was a superman.

Unlike Nietzsche, who finished few of his major works, Shaw has been able to give his very remarkable mind full expression. Although the ninety-year campaign of his life has not abolished war or even capitalism, it has at least made us the beneficiaries of some of the best pamphlets and plays in the language. And in them is recorded for all time a great spirit.

I have reiterated the fact that, on his own confession, Shaw has been a failure as a propagandist. I would not say he is a failure as a teacher. (The teacher not only *need* not be a propagandist; I would say he *cannot* be a propagandist—defining a teacher as one who helps people to learn, learning being something a man has to do for himself.) *John Bull's Other Island* does not solve the Irish problem. It does not, as Mr. Odets's *Waiting for Lefty* tried to do, send the audience rushing out to take action. Nor does it present a situation with the merely external truth ("objectivity") of naturalists like Galsworthy. When Shaw feels the importance of a human situation, he presents it truthfully—that is to say, in all its many-sidedness—and with a passionate accuracy that betokens commitment without prejudice. This is teaching. Shaw's plays are not, though they seem to be, entertainments with propaganda awkwardly added. Their "propaganda" is itself a high art, their art is itself didactic. When they are faulty it is the "entertainment" that is awkwardly added—added to the art, added to the didacticism, added as a sheer redundancy.

The fact that Shaw really wrote his plays because he "had to" (and not to change the world) was in the end the saving of Shavian drama both as art and as teaching. Writing merely what he *had* to write, Shaw will leave us a rich legacy. He has obeyed the Life Force, lived out his Destiny, worn the mask of the madman "G. B. S." without really knowing why. We may learn in time not to despise even the mask, much less Bernard Shaw, as we have learned (I hope) not to despise the Bohemian mask of Oscar Wilde and the Diabolical mask of Nietzsche, two other lonely, estranged teachers of our times. The influence of a propagandist may be prodigious, as we learned from the case of Josef Goebbels. But that was not all we learned from the case of Josef Goebbels. The influence of teachers is lamentably small—or the world would not be in its present state. Yet to the extent that we believe that influence negligible we are cynics. To the extent that we find in that influence a solace and a hope we are men.

From *The Atlantic Monthly,* Vol. CLXXVIII (July, 1946), pp. 109–115. Reprinted by permission of the author and editor. The material of this essay was adapted by Mr. Bentley in a different form in his book *Bernard Shaw* (New Directions, 1947).

HORACE GREGORY

D. H. Lawrence: The Posthumous Reputation

[1937]

I SHALL live just as blithely, unbought and unsold," wrote D. H. Lawrence in 1925. And in this remark there is a note of warning that describes the curious nature of his survival during the half dozen years following his death. Perhaps none of the earlier objections to his work has been removed since 1930, yet his influence has endured in the kind of fame that Matthew Arnold perceived in Shelley's reputation which was both legend and literature and both "ideal" and "ridiculous." Much of his ardent pamphleteering which gave his latter years the semblance of vivid, inexhaustible energy is now outmoded. And nothing seems to have grown so clearly out of fashion in a few short years as Lawrence's specific lectures on sex and obscenity. Today they seem to have gone to the same place reserved in memory for the events of early postwar Europe and America. Yet even in Lawrence's most perishable writing the character of his influence remains.

However, where Lawrence is reread, whether in scattered posthumous papers, or in the poems, short stories, or in the novels, it is the speaking voice that is heard clearest and remembered. We then recall Lawrence's letters, which seem always to renew at each date line a briefly interrupted conversation and with them we remember Mr. David Garnett's little sketches of how he worked: writing as he cooked his meals or sat in one corner of a room while others talked, writing as he unpacked boxes and suitcases, writing almost as he moved and breathed, as though the traveling of his hand across paper were the very reflex of his being. Surely this prodigality was "art for my sake" and was the visible power of the thing he called his "demon," which is to say that much of it was scarcely art at all. Artfulness was sometimes deftly concealed within the larger rhythm of conversation; and sometimes his "demon" was called upon to gratify an urgently explicit demand of form: these moments are identified with the writing of *Sons and Lovers* as well as the writing of a half dozen poems and three or four short stories, but in the rest of everything he wrote the more flexible rule of "art for my sake" was applied and satisfied.

Lawrence, of course, was by no means unaware of what was happening; he had read his critics and matched his wit with theirs:

D. H. LAWRENCE 371

For me, give me a little splendour, and I'll leave perfection to the small fry . . . Ugh, Mr. Muir, think how horrible for us all, if I were perfect! or even if I had "perfect" gifts! Isn't splendour enough for you, Mr. Muir? Or do you find the peacock more "perfect" when he is moulting and has lost his tail, and therefore isn't so exaggerated, but is more "down to normal"?—For "perfection" is only one of "the normal" and the "average" in modern thought.

How well he knew that the image of the peacock's tail would fill the reader's eye; and there in the image itself, he had uncovered a fragment of the "splendor" he had sought, and with an eloquent gesture, passed it over to the reader. It was as though he had been saying: Mr. Muir has given me bread and I give you cake. My transformation of Mr. Muir's gift, dear reader, is your reward for reading me. This answer was always Lawrence's reply to authority, whether the authority was the Evangelist, preaching from a Nottinghamshire pulpit, or Roman law concealed within the new laws of the Fascisti, whether it was the British censor or Mr. Muir. But he was always least fortunate whenever he attempted to answer that authority directly: his ingenuity lay in the art of improvised distraction. And in distracted argument he was never more successful than in his reply to Mr. Muir.

With Lawrence's rejection of the average man came his distrust of the society around him: "Only the people we don't meet are the 'real' people," he wrote in "Jimmy and the Desperate Woman"—and his "real" people were "the simple, genuine, direct, spontaneous, unspoilt souls," which, of course, were not to be found among the people Lawrence saw on city streets, not in "London, New York, Paris," for "in the bursten cities, the dead tread heavily through the muddy air," and in each face he saw the same stigmata Blake had witnessed, "marks of weakness, marks of woe." These were his average, "normal" people, branded by service in the World War like Captain Herbertson in *Aaron's Rod*, mutilated by war and sanctified by bourgeois wealth like Chatterley, malformed by ignorance and poverty like the Nottinghamshire miner, or tricked and defeated like the American Indian, "Born with a caul, a black membrane over the face." And as Lawrence traveled he saw the same disease spread over half the earth—and he was not to be identified with any of that kind, the meek or humble or the dead. Though the physical resemblance to Lawrence's speaking voice may be traced throughout his novels, through Paul Morel, Lilly of *Aaron's Rod* or Mellors of *Lady Chatterley's Lover*, he was happiest in another kind of personality; the image of the bird was best: the mythical phoenix, the peacock, or the Tuscan nightingale. To defend the nightingale (as well as himself) against the "plaintive anthem" of John Keats' ode, he wrote:

How astonished the nightingale would be if he could be made to realize with what sort of answer the poet was answering his song. He would fall off the bough with amazement.

Because a nightingale, when you answer him back, only shouts and sings louder. Suppose a few other nightingales pipe up in the neighboring bushes—as they always do. Then the blue-white sparks of sound go dazzling up to heaven. And suppose you, mere mortal, happen to be sitting on the shady bank having an altercation with the mistress of your heart, hammer and tongs, then the chief nightingale swells and goes at it like Caruso in the Third Act—simply a brilliant, bursting frenzy of music, singing you down, till you simply can't hear yourself speak to quarrel.

Of course the nightingale was the very thing Lawrence wished himself to be, the thing apart from the quarreling couple on the shady bank and his "art for my sake" had for its model the work of a creature who

. . . sings with a ringing, pinching vividness and a pristine assertiveness that makes a mere man stand still. A kind of brilliant calling and interweaving of glittering exclamation such as must have been heard on the first day of creation.

This was the splendor that was Lawrence's great concern, the "bursting frenzy of music" that emanated from a source within the body, and was itself the body, the physical being of a living creature. The lack of that physical force was his definition of modern tragedy, and it was the same emptiness he had witnessed in the lives of the civilized people who surrounded him. In that self-pitying, sad, silent company he had seen the image of Paul Morel, his early self of *Sons and Lovers*.

. . . left in the end naked of everything, with the drift toward death. . . . It's the tragedy of thousands of young men in England.

But Lawrence's instructions to live the splendid life always had the tendency to oversimplify the cure for complex (and human) silences and fears. They were all too much like telling friends and neighbors to be natural, to go be a *man*. His work had all the skill and all the confident lack of knowledge of a man who had carefully trained himself to conduct an orchestra by ear. Throughout Lawrence's verse and prose a dominant rhythm persists above loose phrasing and verbal monotony; his ear had been trained to catch the idiomatic inflection of English speech, avoiding always the outmoded rhythms of literary usage. In this respect his work shares the vitality of Whitman's verse and Melville's prose, and like them it contains the same self-taught art that controlled its imagery.

Even the most casual reader of Lawrence will soon become aware of how deliberately he avoided the urban image and how through prose and verse there is a literal predominance of "birds, beasts and flowers." And as their number increases, how tropical they seem, and we remember that his need for physical well-being followed the hot course of the sun. But it is characteristic of Lawrence's imagery that its action remains suspended in utter darkness or in the full flood light of noon; and though it is frequently breathing and alive, it seldom extends its force to an actual climax. How many of his images start bravely and end in helplessness, as though they could not carry the burden of their swelling heat and color to move elsewhere. And this same helplessness enters the majority of his many poems, all incomplete, all lacking in the distinction of a verb to give them motion and finality. How many of his novels end with the promise of a life beyond them yet to be fulfilled in the next novel, perhaps, but for the moment still unwritten. Only in *Sons and Lovers,* and in a few of the short stories do we find a definite space of time and action brought to an ultimate conclusion—only in these and in three or four of the *Last Poems.* The rest of his work leans heavily into the future, as though the next page to be written would complete the large design of which his fragments were pencil sketches from the living model.

I suspect that this very characteristic of incompleted action is responsible for the air of expectancy which welcomed the publication of each posthumous volume of letters, stories, poems, essays or incidental papers. Lawrence in death seemed still in flight around the globe and it has been difficult to think of him as a middle-aged writer dying nerveless and exhausted in a sun-lit room in Southern France. The biographies of Lawrence, his self-imposed exile from England, the disorder among camp-followers of the Lawrence household may be used as sources for a facile parallel to Shelley's death and the legends which grew out of it. But how eagerly Lawrence would have hated Shelley and would have cheerfully denied all he had written, and did in fact answer his "Skylark" in the same language in which he replied to Keats' nightingale:

"Hail to thee, blithe Spirit!—bird thou never wert." Why should he insist on the bodilessness of beauty when we cannot know of any save embodied beauty? Who would wish that the skylark were not a bird, but a spirit? If the whistling skylark were a spirit, then we should all wish to be spirits. Which were impious and flippant.

We need not stop to consider the flaws in Lawrence's heavy-footed questioning, but in this reply there is implied an entire century's increased distrust of Platonic reasoning. Between Shelley and Lawrence arose the shadow of Nietzsche's Zarathustra, who said as he descended from the mountain:

To blaspheme the earth is now the dreadfulest sin. . . . Man is a rope stretched between the animal and the Superman. . . . Aye, for the game of creating, my brethren, there is needed a holy Yea unto Life. . . .

Lawrence's great error, of course, was to echo the sound of Zarathustra's warning without clear knowledge of the myth from which Nietzsche's hero sprang, and lacking this knowledge he could not stride into another world that lay beyond good and evil. The literary heritage of the early nineteenth century had come down to him by way of Herman Melville and Walt Whitman. As he entered the latter phases of his career, traces of Whitman's eloquence spread throughout his writing, yet he was always to reject Whitman's democracy with uneasy violence. Whatever was to remain revolutionary in Lawrence's thinking was something that resembled philosophic anarchy. In a recently discovered paper, "Democracy" in the posthumous volume *Phoenix,* written in 1923, he used Whitman as text, in praise and blame, to reiterate his distrust of a bourgeois democracy and its possession of property. His rejection of authority included a consistent denial of Marx as well as Plato, of Aquinas as well as Judaism and all law of church and state.

Yet in this wide negation of authority lies one secret of his influence with a younger generation of post-war writers. To deny bourgeois authority and to leave England was to break down the barriers of class and national prejudice that had seemed impassable before 1918, or rather, had remained unbroken for nearly a hundred years. He had survived many forms of British bourgeois hostility which brought with them the lack of a large reading public, persecution from the War office, and the action of the British censor as well as charges of religious heresy. And there was ample evidence to convict him on any or all of these charges of public disfavor. His reply was that he alone remained alive in a dead world, a world in which the memory of its millions killed in a World War had spread the shadow of mass murder as well as lonely suicide over the furthest reaches of Anglo-Saxon civilization. And when his own death came, he made his own choice in preparation for it, convincing himself and those who read him that he had chosen the path of stilled and dark waters into oblivion.

Almost with his last breath he was to write, "For man the vast marvel is to be alive. For man, as for flower, and beast and bird . . ." and this reassurance in the goodness of physical being from someone whose self-taught and imperfect gifts alone sustained his eloquence, created a hero for a generation that feared the stillness of its own despair. It is not without perception that T. S. Eliot as well as others have read the warning of disease in Lawrence's heresies of behavior and craftsmanship. We know only too well his many failures, and among them we learn his refusal to abide by the truth of his observation in writing a brilliant analysis of Baron Corvo's *Hadrian the Seventh:* "A man must keep his earnestness nimble to escape ridicule." Yet his insight was never more profound or more direct than when he associated Whitman with his own name, for it is through the work of Lawrence that the younger men in the present generation of British writers have learned the actual significance of Whitman's enduring reputation. Like Whitman, Lawrence left behind him no model of technique that would serve to crystallize the style of prose or poetry in those who followed him; like Whitman's, Lawrence's influence as a teacher was irrevocably bad; surely his literal imitators, like Horace Traubel's discipleship of Whitman, illustrate the master's flaws until their burlesque becomes so clear that pity or contempt deflects all criticism. Such imitation is the pathetic attempt to reproduce the absence of form, as though the devoted student had amputated his arm to stimulate the sensation of his master's missing hand. Lawrence's real strength, like his invisible presence living "blithely, unbought and unsold," is explicit only in the combined force of his legend with a small selection from his prolific work of less than twenty years, and from these fragments we learn again how vividly he revived the memory of the maker in English literature, restoring the moment of vision and insight as a mark of genius in English prose and poetry.

First published in the first edition of the present book, *Literary Opinion in America*, in 1937. Later included by the author in his collection of critical essays, *The Shield of Achilles*, published by Harcourt, Brace and Company, Inc., 1944.

AUSTIN WARREN
Franz Kafka
[1941]

KAFKA's novels evoke a world as self-coherent and characteristic as that of Dickens, of Dostoevski, of Proust, of Poe, of Hawthorne. Like Hawthorne's and Poe's, Kafka's is a limited, a lyric, world. Kafka is a metaphysical poet in symbolist narrative.

His is a city world. Like Dickens' London, it flourishes in grotesques. But they have not the vigor, the delight in their own salt being, of Quilp and Miss Mowcher; and they are chiefly unnamed and seen but momentarily. Old women look out of inquisitive windows; in the gutters sit leering irreverent mocking children; a young lad, his nose half eaten away, scrutinizes arrivals; the warden wears a gross body, ill-adjusted to his "dry bony face, with a great nose twisted to one side."

It is an overcrowded, airless world, within which it is difficult to sustain faith in the weight and worth of the individual. In Georg Salter's illustration to *The Trial*, most persons except the hero are but shapes of shadow. Kafka's solipsism is intelligible, is defensible, as necessary to sustaining, in a city of the anonymous, the belief that the soul and its choices matter.

Even Kafka's imagined America is not a land of broad cornfields shining in the sun but a chiefly metropolitan affair, already stratified, weary, and hopeless—a land of hotels and of slums. "Karl thought of the east end of New York which his uncle had promised to show him where it was said that several families lived in one little room and the house of a whole family consisted of one corner where many children clustered around their parents." Kafka read Franklin's *Autobiography*, we are told, and admired Walt Whitman, and liked the Americans because he believed them to be "healthy and optimistic." But his imagination does not so present them. A sort of W. P. A. theater opens hospitably at the end, to be sure; yet the novel follows Dickens, not Alger. Karl is the young Copperfield, the young Oliver Twist, the sensitive boy ejected from home on charges which puzzle him. He finds America gleaming but hard. Before landing, he encounters social injustice in the case of "The Stoker"; his uncle, who suddenly appears and assumes his support, as suddenly and less plausibly renounces responsibility; he is deceived and mal-

376

treated by his chance traveling companions; for no fault of his own, he is discharged from the hotel; he comes near to ending as a slavey in a delirious apartment. America is a world in which elevators whiz up and down, phonographs play incessantly without anyone's listening, political candidates get lost in the crowds which are to elect them. It offers the image of the ascent to Brunelda's apartment: long stairs moving up into squalid darkness; beside the stair-railing, a little girl weeps, then rushes up the steps gasping for breath.

Kafka's is a world known in nightmares—a rational, unnatural world in which unnatural situations are rationally worked out—in which everyone is able, like Lewis Carroll's creatures, to argue long, ingeniously, and convincingly. It is a nightmare world in which the "I," all innocent and eager to submit, all desirous to propitiate, is pushed about, pursued, regimented by potencies veiled of visage—in which one is forever being orally examined by dignitaries who forever flunk one. The self and the world are juxtaposed in opposition. If one is not being pursued by the world or carried off by the world, one is running after it. There is the image of the old father trying to catch the ear of the Castle dignitaries—trying in vain, for the officials go at a gallop, their carriages "race like mad." It is the world of a Mack Sennett comedy—one of chase and pursuit, of intense movement, horizontal and vertical: of running and climbing. It is a world of uncertainty and insecurity, of fear and trembling.

It is a world of hierarchy, created by Kafka in the parodic imitation of the Austrian bureaucracies under which he lived, within which, as underofficial, he worked. In its chief traits it could be a feudal estate or it could be an American department store or a chain of restaurants or a metropolitan public library. Hierarchy provides, negatively, for deferment of responsibility or infinite regress. One's complaint always reaches the wrong office; one is passed on from office to office, in general moving up the scale of delegated authority, only to find that the proper official to handle the complaint is out of town, or the necessary documents are lost, or by delay one's claim is outlawed. Wonderful is the efficiency of an order so complexly gradated that every expert is inexpert at satisfying the simple need for justice.

There are other difficulties. Hierarchic order is necessary in a universe densely populated, whether with atoms or souls; yet, in an order so intricate, instrumentalities must, almost unavoidably, turn into ends: readers exist in order that librarians may make card catalogues, pupils in order that educationalists may publish books on Methods of Teaching, worshipers in order that janitors may sweep and lock churches. Underofficials, those who administer the rules to the public, can scarcely be expected to understand the spirit of the rules or what, as formulated by unseen and doubtless long dead "higher-ups," the rules aimed at. A teeming universe must, of course, be a "planned," even if an ill planned, or a too fussily planned, society. The easy improvization which fits the New England village cannot be transported to the city. Indeed, by one of his most brilliant audacities, Kafka imagines that even the Village cannot really be a village, for if its multiple needs are adequately to be taken care of, there will be business enough to require busy attention from a whole caste of officials.

Kafka's novels can be taken as burlesques of bureaucracy. Satiric of course they are. Yet they lack satiric norm, a contrasting model of elegance and humanity. The hero is too uncertain of himself to sit in judgment on duly constituted authorities and too intent upon learning their ways to have leisure for criticizing them. As for bureaucracy, it is even at its worst a corruption of order; and order is a state so blessed, so indispensable, that even its parodies deserve respect. As for bureaucrats, the common charge against them is that they are too insistent upon the importance of their work, too narrow in their conception of it; but surely it is the duty of officials to be officious, and narrowness and even scrupulosity are marks of their being dedicated to their profession. The work of the world is carried on by experts, not by gentlemen; and if we want to deepen the sense of "work" and "world," we must add, "strait is the gate and narrow the way"; the price of salvation is the forced sale of all that one has.

Hierarchy is pyramidal. Is there, for Kafka, any Reason, any Supreme Will, at the top and the end? Or is hierarchy a staircase which ends not in a dome or a tower but in a fall into darkness? The answer is uncertain. Of a chief justice we never hear or of a head-manager of a hotel. In *The Castle,* we hear for a preliminary moment of the "Count West-West," but soon he and any direct view of the Castle itself are lost or forgotten. Doubtless there is an ultimate authority, but we never reach it except through its intermediaries: there is no direct vision. In "Before the Law," the lowest doorkeeper can see a few doors ahead of him into what he believes to be a vast series of ascents: "From hall to hall keepers stand at every door, one more powerful than the other. Even the third of these has an aspect that even I cannot bear to look at." Of the ascending series we can say that there is no point at which we observe it to stop. Olga explains to K.: "Who is it that Barnabas speaks to there in the Castle I have no idea—perhaps the clerk is lowest in the whole staff; but even if he is lowest he can put one in touch with the next man above him, and if he can't even do that he can refer to somebody who can give the name." They are men set under authority; and "Does not the least degree of authority contain the whole?"

In both *The Trial* and *The Castle,* under-officials, advocates, and villagers spend much time in speculating upon the ways of the "higher-ups." In the latter we hear Amalia ask, "Is it Castle gossip you're at? . . . There are people in the village who live on it; they stick their heads together just like you two and entertain each other by the hour"; to which K. replies that he is just such a person, "and moreover people who don't care for such gossip and leave it all to others don't interest me particularly." So the talk goes on. We "gossip" or speculate about Klamm, attempting to adjust to coherence the glimpses we catch. A man like Klamm "who is so much sought after and rarely seen is apt to take different shapes in people's imaginations"—to give rise to theophanies very diverse each from the other.

Yet Kafka's officials, however otherwise various, have in common a certain obtrusive perversity, their lack of elegance. So, too, the rooms in which the courts sit have none of the grandeur or even decent neatness we might anticipate, and the Castle is unimpressive, disappointing to strangers. Instead of being better balanced and more humanistic than the villagers, the officials are officious, pompous, and pedantic. But the "virtues of the pagans are splendid vices"; "officious, pompous, and pedantic" are dyslogistic terms to be transvaluated as "conscientious, dignified, and properly accurate."

These paper-reading officials are scholars, intellectuals; and their scholarly life bears no discernible relation to their biological and affective lives: they have their mistresses; and they have their papers.

"Papers," we see, both bless and curse. They are not only the records of law and the ledgers of business but the annals of history and the memory of the race, the possibility of preserving and interpreting our past experience. They represent the effort of the intellect to understand by dissection, arrangement, systemization. "Papers" constitute civilization; without them we remain barbarians. Yet they clutter up the world and menace our freedom. They may be "busy work" to amuse old children, to keep scholars from thinking and the timid from knowing themselves afraid. The academic vice is the substitution of "research" for existential thinking; to preserve records without selection, to multiply discriminations until one is incapable of singleness of mind and simplicity of action. Papers assemble, by the most laudable of intentions, into libraries; yet for every man who, like Arnold, fears he may know more than he feels, a great library must be an object of terror—a monument to the futility of past speculation, a deterrent to future action.

There are some rich, fantastic scenes in which Kafka's papers become objects in themselves, figures in a Disney cartoon: in *The Castle* the search through the superintendent's bedroom for a missing document—in the process of which papers half cover the floor and go on mounting—or the description of Sordini's office, every wall of which is covered with columns of documents tied together, piled on top of one another; "Those are only the documents that Sordini is working on at the time, and as bundles of papers are continually being taken away and brought in, and all in great haste, those columns are always falling on the floor, and it's just those perpetual crashes, following fast on one another, that have come to distinguish Sordini's workroom."

The copiousness of the papers has an approximate correspondence in the volubility of official speech. Ready argument characterizes almost all Kafka's people—not merely his lawyers and secretaries. In these novels all are dialecticians: all are conscious of *pro et contra*, fertile in "various lections." Unlike Mann's controversialists, Naphtha and Settembrini, who argue in abstract terms, Kafka's are existential thinkers and deploy their subtlety on the obscure and difficult matter of how to live aright.

The Trial and *The Castle* are composed very largely of dialogues, and dialogues dialectic. Indeed, the characteristic excitement of these later novels, written by a student of Plato and Kierkegaard, lies in the wit and intellectual suspense of the dialogue. No more than the papers in Sordini's office do the thoughts stand still; like the action in a murder mystery, they move by sudden shifts of direction, convincing evasions of the foregone conclusion.

What does Kafka intend us to make of his argumentation? Is it ridiculously specious, or—so far as it goes—true: "Both" would have to be the answer. It is absurd to speculate about the nature of the highest, for of course we cannot know; we cannot even know how near we come to knowing. Yet it is man's true nature and highest function to engage himself upon these speculative questions concerning the nature of reality; and there can be no delegation of this duty to others.

Kafka's world is one of mystery. In stories like "The Country Doctor" and "Metamorphosis," the unnatural thrusts itself into the orderly sequence of nature. The redaction of a young clerk into a bug neither allows of allegorical sterilization, nor is presented as a dream. It is the chief horror of the story, perhaps, that no one within it sees what happens as "impossible"; it is horrible, to be sure, but in various ways these people, obviously sane and simple, adjust themselves to a painful situation. There are occasional bits of near or even sheer magic in Kafka: in *The Castle,* Barnabas disappears with the rapidity of an elf or a thought; the first day passes and it grows night, within an hour or two after morning; after a few days of living with K., Frieda, formerly "unnaturally seductive," is withering in his arms. But it is not Kafka's ordinary or best practice thus to deal in legerdemain. He secures his sense of mystery chiefly through his device of multiple interpretation.

His method offers a superficial analogy with that of Hawthorne. But Hawthorne offers alternatives—usually supernaturalism and some form of naturalism. Thus, at the elaborate ending of *The Scarlet Letter,* we are tendered the preliminary option of supposing that there was, or was not, a scarlet letter imprinted upon the breast of the minister, and then a choice of three methods for the possible production of the stigmata: by the natural means of penance; by means of magic and drugs; or by the outgoing operation of the spirit. "The reader," says Hawthorne, "may choose among these theories."

It is not Kafka's method thus to contrast a supernatural with a natural reading. It is, for him, in and through the natural that the supernatural operates and, with whatever intermittence and illusion, is revealed.

Kafka's world is neither the world of the average sensual man nor yet fantasy. It is the world seen slightly askew, as one looks through his legs or stands on his head, or sees it in a distorting mirror. Nor does his adjustment take, like Swift's in *Gulliver*, the method of segregation. With Swift, the fantastic is safely corralled and tucked away in the initial assumption; with Kafka, realism and fantasy move in more close and sensitive relation. In *The Trial* and *The Castle* the whole sequence is so improbable as to suggest some kind of pervasive allegory, but at no point (or almost no point) does one encounter downright impossibility. It is improbable that any law courts of a wealthy city should be lodged high up in dingy tenement houses or that a village should require the service of a vast staff of busy, hurrying officials, or that, upon looking into a lumber-room in one's own office building, one should discover two court-wardens being flogged. Yet these things "could be"; they are not like centaurs, oceans flowing with lemonade, and trees growing greenbacks. And Kafka's multiple interpretations are all possible options within one world. They represent the same fact or situation read from successive views, as the operations of a mind which keeps correcting itself.

Kafka offers a convincing interpretation; then, with rapidity, substitutes another, yet more convincing. A scene in *Amerika* shows Robinson, his face and arms swathed in manifold bandages. "It was horrible to see him lift his arms to his eyes to wipe away his tears with the bandages—tears of pain or grief or perhaps even of joy at seeing Karl again." Then we see the horror dissolve. "The trivial nature of his wounds could be seen from the old rags of bandages with which the lift-boys, obviously in jest, had swathed him round." *The Castle* abounds in more subtle shifts. A woman sits in a chair in a kitchen. The pale light gives a "gleam of silk" to her dress; she seems to be an aristocrat, "although of course illness and weariness give even peasants a look of refinement." To a question from K., the woman replies disdainfully, but "whether contemptuous of K. or of her own answer was not clear." If one is self-conscious or otherwise fearful, it is necessary and difficult to interpret the looks of others. Thus K. sees the peasants gazing fixedly at him; he thinks it done out of malice—yet perhaps they really wanted something from him but could not express it, or, perhaps, on the other hand, they were simply childish. But if the first view of the peasants and their attitude was mistaken, what about the first view of Barnabas? One doubt, one disillusionment, infects the judge with a general mistrust of his judgment. "Perhaps K. was as mistaken in Barnabas' goodness as in the malice of the peasants." Frieda's hands "were certainly small and delicate, but they could quite as well have been called weak and characterless." After Olga's account of Amalia's defiance of Sordini, K. says, "Amalia's act was remarkable enough, but the more you say about it

the less clearly can it be decided whether it was noble or petty, clever or foolish, heroic or cowardly." Longer, more structural examples are the discussion
between K. and the Superintendent concerning the meaning of Klamm's letter, and K.'s talk with Frieda about the landlady, and Olga's discussion with
K. regarding the nature of Barnabas' relation to the Castle.

Kafka's "mystery" is, then, the apparent sign of how elusive is the truth.
What happens is tolerably easy to ascertain, but what it means is precarious
as well as important.

Such scrupulosity of interpretation recalls a characteristic feature of hierarchy everywhere prominent in Kafka's novels—the connection between promotion, pleasing, and propitiation. Kafka's worlds are patriarchies or theoc-
racies. One's success or failure depends on one's skill in divining the wishes of
the great man; and among underlings there develops a necessary skill in cal-
culating his mood by his complexion, step, tone of voice. Cases there naturally
are in which the signs allow of differing interpretation between experts.

The interpretative complexity recalls also the elaborations of rabbinic and
patristic commentary. John Mason Neale's commentary on the Song of Songs
offers, out of innumerable Fathers, Doctors, and Saints, all manner of conflicting yet severally edifying glosses: on the text, "his left hand is under my
head, and his right hand doth embrace me," for example. What is the distinction between the hands, and why their positions? According to some, the
hands distinguish temporal from spiritual goods; according to another view,
the left hand equates the law, the right hand the gospel; according to another,
the left hand indicates punishment, the right, blessings and rewards. Other
comments differentiate mystical states—the left being the Illuminative as the
right is the Unitive Way. And "the loveliest interpretation of all," says Neale,
is that which sees in the left the Manhood of Christ, and in the right his
Godhead.

Not until late in his life did Kafka begin to study the *Talmud;* but already, in the priest's discourse at the Cathedral (*The Trial*), Kafka shows
his ingenuity and depth as the exegete of a given fable. The priest cites the
studies of innumerable rabbis who had already concerned themselves with
the story. "I am only showing you different opinions about it," he says.
"You mustn't have too much regard for opinions. The text is unchangeable
and opinions are often only an expression of doubt about it." Like Kierkegaard, whose *Fear and Trembling* starts from and repeatedly returns to the
story of Abraham and Isaac, so Kafka, delighting in speculation, yet offers
his story as a mythic fable the meaning of which is anterior to and un-
exhausted by any included commentary.

Myth is not allegory; and Kafka is not an allegorist. An allegory is a series
of concepts provided with a narrative or a narrative accompanied by a conceptual parallel. Strictly, it is a philosophical sequence which systematically

works itself out in images. But allegory is rarely as pure as *Pilgrim's Progress* or *The Romance of the Rose*: it deviates from purity in two directions—by losing its systematic character, becoming a series of intermittent symbolisms; or by keeping its system but abstaining from offering a conceptual key to its parable.

The novels of Kafka are not, in any exact sense, allegorical. From his diaries and aphorisms and his friend Brod's commentaries, we know that he intended the novels to give creative expression to the mysteries of Justice and Grace; that they are "metaphysical" novels we should surely have discerned without aid. But Kafka provided them with no conceptual chart; they require none; and it is their special richness that they have much particularity untranslatable into generality. We need not systematically recall that the Castle is Heaven or that K.'s disappointments show the mysterious ways in which God moves. The ways of men are, for men who seek to understand them, baffling enough.

Kafka's symbols are, indeed, capable of more than the religious interpretation. According to Brod, K. symbolizes the Jew, in his exclusion from society and his eagerness for inclusion, as well as the seeker after the Kingdom of Heaven. But K. is also the bachelor in search of marriage and companionship; and K. is also every man in respect to his final aloneness.

The novels all, significantly, remained unfinished. Of them Kafka wrote: "What sense would there be in reviving such . . . bungled pieces of work? Only if one hoped to create a whole out of such fragments, some complete work to which one could make a final appeal. . . ." We have for each novel, however, a notion of the ending. *Amerika* was to conclude with the young hero's finding, within the Nature Theatre of Oklahoma, his freedom, "even his old house and his parents." *The Trial* is of Brod's assembling, and a chapter like "The Whipper" could only vaguely be placed. Parts of the novels—for example, "The Stoker" and "Before the Law"—were published separately.

With some plausibility, one might call these books novels of the spiritual picaresque. Yet they are not completely episodic: even in the loosest, *Amerika*, the two rascals, Delamarcke and Robinson, reappear after we suppose ourselves to have seen the last of them; and in *The Castle* there is a very considerable integration of the materials: one notes in particular the fashion in which the matter of chapter I (the teacher, the Lasemann family, Hans Brunswick and his mother) is subsequently developed. Each novel begins in substantially the same way: the hero breaks with his past. In two of them he has left his home, and we meet him as he enters a new world; in a third his thirtieth birthday and his summons collaborate to start a new life.

The question of method is: Can there be a logic of composition when one's theme is the irruption of the irrational? There might, of course, be a psychological unwinding; the episodes might grow more complex, deeper, or more wry. In the unfinished state of the novels, no such progress is obvious. If one compares these novels with the mystical documents of SS. Teresa and John of the Cross, he finds no such obvious symmetry and development as that of *The Interior Mansions*. Such systematic structure was too rational for Kafka.

It is Kafka's narrative method (with occasional lapses) to write from within the mind of the hero. The introspective hero, through whose eyes we have glimpses of other persons, static figures, is man alone, man hunted, man confronted with powers which elude him and with women with whom he is never at ease, man prosecuted and persecuted. He is the man eager to do right but perpetually baffled and thwarted and confused as to what it is to do right—the man for whom the sense of duty, of responsibility, the ir-reducibility of "ought," has survived the positive and particular codes of re-ligions and moral systems—the man in search of salvation.

A narrow, moving writer, Kafka is both an artist and a symbol. The appeal of this symbol has been extraordinarily wide to Europeans and Americans in the past decade. One secular hope after another has failed. Kafka can be the symbol for what is left. He is illiberal, unrelenting, unsentimental; as Spender has said, he combines the power of the visionary with the self-criticism of the skeptic, so that he communicates the sense of there being something to be-lieve without the claim of being able to define what it is. It is difficult today to believe in the reality of a world of comfort, good sense, and progress; we doubt that we shall ever see such a world again; we think it wise to prepare ourselves spiritually for worlds more exacting and metaphysical; and of such worlds Kafka is initiate.

From *Rage for Order: Essays in Criticism* by Aus-tin Warren, pp. 104–118. University of Chicago Press, 1948. Reprinted by permission of the au-thor and publishers. First published as "Kosmos Kafka" in *The Southern Review*, Vol. VII (Au-tumn, 1941), pp. 350–365.

MORTON DAUWEN ZABEL

A Literalist of the Imagination

[1935]

MARIANNE MOORE's poetry demands gratitude, but to express it by referring to the qualities for which her work has usually been ignored or disputed may seem more a matter of convenience than of good grace. She is a poet about whom praise and blame are not wholly at odds; her detractors and admirers see fairly eye to eye. What irritates the hostile reader exhilarates the admiring, and in the case of a poet so prominent among "difficult" writers, it is pleasant to have no doubt about what is up for reference. Miss Moore's meanings may be mistaken, but not her character. Compared with her, many of her contemporaries become chameleons of evasive and convenient color. She stays fixed under scrutiny and refuses to pose as an illusionist. From the beginning she has protected herself by working out her poetic problems before allowing her poems to be printed; she has had no need to practice the subterfuges of less vigilant writers—the changes of face, manner, and other sleights of hand demanded by public success or moral insecurity. The external traits of her latest poems are those of her earliest: a dispassionate accuracy of detail, literalness of manner, indifference to the standardized feelings and forms of verse, and an admission that virtually any subject-matter or reference is fully as appropriate to poetry as to prose. It would not require the addition of eccentric titling, typography, and rhyming to give the suspicious their argument or the irritated a voice.

Her *Observations* of 1924 were rightly named. Among modern poets she is exceptional for a detachment that lifts personal enthusiasm above private uses. She observes, but her eye shows neither the innocence nor the wile of showmanship that obstructs the vision of her contemporaries. It is a vision as complex as it is candid, and as easily mistaken. She would not have survived the decade of post-war innovations if her stylistic novelty rested on nothing but the strained intellection, the forced sophistication, for which it is commonly dismissed. She is a complicated poet, but one suspects that her finished poem is far simpler than the experience from which it sprang. The process that complicates it is not one of artificial refraction. It is Miss Moore's way of piercing—with the aid of humor, obliquity, and an instinctive compassion—

through the pretense, erudition, and false emotion that encrust the essential meaning in the life around her.

She may be writing about marriage and poetry with the evasive casuistry of "culture"; or about art and statecraft in the polysyllabic rhetoric of senators and undergraduates; or about animals with the passionless accuracy of a treatise or text-book. Her style combines the frigid objectivity of the laboratory with the zeal of naïve discovery; it mixes the statistics of newspapers with the casual hints and cross-references of a mind constructed like a card catalogue. This is not a perversity of erudition, or of ironic parody. It is a picture of the problem of the modern intelligence. Irony and curiosity are means towards Miss Moore's intense discriminations, but her purpose is essentially plain and carries the pathos of a passionate sincerity. When asked, in a recent questionnaire, what distinguishes her, she answered: "Nothing; unless it is an exaggerated tendency to visualize; and on encountering manifestations of life— insects, lower animals, or human beings—to wonder if they are happy, and what will become of them."

But her problem is not simple, and grants her neither the charm nor the success of conventional poetry. Hers is no book of neat lyric masterpieces. She is not satisfied to search out the law or purpose beneath the swarming phenomena around her; she feels it in the words she uses. Her language reveals, beneath its calculated technicalities and pastiche, the shock of concealed rhymes and harmonies. Her sentences, whether colloquial or rhetorical, move with a rhythm nerved by humor and "elegance." Her care for meaning makes her break a phrase, or even a word, to bring to the surface a suppressed quality—an embedded assonance, cadence, or tone of thought. Hers is a poetry of superimposed meanings, and her object is to lift the layers of convention, habit, prejudice, and jargon that mask the essential and irreducible truth. She is neither facile nor insincere enough to pretend that these impediments do not exist. In facing them she has not only defined, with the minuteness of an exorbitant sensitiveness, the ordeal of the contemporary conscience; she has energized, by the agility of her imagination, the language in which she works.

In the *Selected Poems* Miss Moore has omitted several short poems which a discussion might conveniently use as "beginnings." Simple aphorisms like "To an Intra-mural Rat" and "To a Prize Bird," and examples of imagism like "To a Chameleon" and "A Talisman," are not reprinted, although Mr. Eliot has fitly quoted the last-named in his preface. These slighter works served their purpose in *Observations,* in 1924, but they would not be out of place here also. Even a brief epigram on Shaw like "To a Prize Bird" escaped the risk of cleverness; it contained three metaphors of exact wit; and one is inclined to guess that it has now been omitted as much because Miss Moore has modified her opinion of Shaw during the past fifteen years as because she finds the style of the poem less than wholly her own. Similarly "A Talisman" departed from the conventional symbolism of the Imagists by not allowing its image to act beyond its powers: the figure of the seagull is developed through a severely spare stanzaic form, it is brought to terms with the formal attitude described by such a structure, and it still retains the impersonality required of true imagism. Of her new poems only one shows Miss Moore working in this simplified manner—"No Swan So Fine." The others exhibit a method much more elaborate than in any of the individual items of *Observations* with the possible exception of "An Octopus" and "Marriage," the second of which still remains her one extended venture in the field of human phenomena where obliquity of treatment is offset by the authority and convention of practical judgment. Only "The Hero" re-enters that province, but it does so with a stricter detachment, and with less assistance from the irony and erudition of quoted texts.

Her special world reappears: the world of lesser life—plant, animal, and mineral—which she scrutinizes unsparingly and translates into a major reality through a sympathy that surpasses mere pathos in becoming intellectual; but it is now far more extensive. This comes not merely by selecting from nature objects of a more formidable character—formidable in their complexity like the Plumet Basilisk or the Frigate Pelican, their wiry delicacy like the Jerboa, their massive subtlety like the Buffalo, or in their sumptuous elegance like *Camellia Sabina* and the porcelain nectarines. All these suggest a greater complexity of attention; they have encouraged a corresponding elaboration of form which marks the one notable advance made by the *Selected Poems* over Miss Moore's two previous books. Her idea of the stanza was already established there, but it had not reached such massive effects of verbal interplay and structure as in seven of the later poems. Along with this there has developed a greater luxuriance of detail, austere annotation having given way to a freer imaginative fascination. The cat, fish, and snake have been supplanted by creatures of a subtler and more exotic existence, and from this one may infer a similar elaboration in the mind that has observed and conferred on them, with unfaltering deftness, the form and scale of its ideas. Where Miss Moore once defined the fish's life of fluid and evasive grace, the cat's imperturbable self-sufficiency, and unity made absolute in the snake, she now analyzes the life of miraculous co-ordination ("The Frigate Pelican"), of impenetrable purposes ("The Plumet Basilisk"), of exquisite nervous vitality ("The Jerboa"), of masked and submissive wit ("The Buffalo"). Her animals have grown in meaning as well as in size and mechanism; they may be considered enlargements of the original vision; but they show the same rigor in definition and sympathy, the same scruple in activity and feature. The swan moves with its "gondoliering legs"; the jerboa with its "three-cornered smooth-working Chippendale claws . . . makes fern-seed foot-prints with Kangaroo speed";

388 MORTON DAUWEN ZABEL

the lizard "smites the water, and runs on it—a thing difficult for fingered feet"; the Pelican "rapidly cruising or lying on the air . . . realizes Rasselas' friend's project of wings uniting levity with strength"; the Indian buffalo wields "those two horns which, when a tiger coughs, are lowered fiercely and convert the fur to harmless rubbish."

Attributes like these are found among the animals and human beings of literature only when the physical reality of the creature has become so passionately accepted and comprehended that its external appearance, noted with the laconic felicity of science, is indistinguishable from its spirit, and all the banalities of allegory can be discarded. At that level the imagination seizes attributes and makes them act in place of the false sentimental values upon which man's observation of nature usually thrives. In her poem on "Poetry" Miss Moore improves Yeats' characterization of Blake by insisting that poets must be "literalists of the imagination"; they must see the visible at the focus of intelligence where sight and concept coincide, and where it becomes transformed into the pure and total realism of ideas. By this realism, the imagination permits ideas to claim energy from what is usually denied them—the vital nature that exists and suffers, and which alone can give poetic validity to the abstract or permit the abstract intelligence to enhance experience. Blake had such a notion of poetry in mind when he stated his theory of vision: "I question not my corporeal or vegetative eye any more than I would question a window concerning a sight; I look through it and not with it." And he reminds us especially of Miss Moore's rapt gaze at birds:

> How do you know but every bird that cuts the airy way
> Is an immense world of delight, closed by your senses five?

Miss Moore means this when she holds that poetry stands "above insolence and triviality and can present for inspection, imaginary gardens with real toads in them"; that it combines "the raw material . . . in all its rawness and that which is on the other hand genuine." Her literalness of manner should not remain a source of confusion after one has read the works in which her poetics is made fairly explicit—"Poetry," "When I Buy Pictures," "Critics and Connoisseurs," and "Picking and Choosing." If that manner seems ambiguous, it is because she considers poetic truth in opposite terms from those commonly accepted by lovers of the lyric. For her the spirit gives light, but not until the letter gives it first. If the letter is lifeless until the spirit enters it, without it the spirit is equally wasted: it has no body to animate and no clay in which to breathe. She stands poles removed from the poets of disembodied emotion, of Love, Honor, Hope, Desire, and Passion in capitalized abstraction. She does not write in the large and easy generality of sentiment or sensation. She has written about animals without dramatizing her pity, about wedlock without mentioning love, about America with none of the usages of patriotism, and about death without parading awe or reverence. But it would be difficult to name four poems more poignant in their sense of these emotions, or more accurate in justifying them, than "The Buffalo," "Marriage," "England," and "A Grave."

It is not the intention of any of these poems to free the reader from effort, but it is remarkable that difficulty diminishes statement by statement if the poems are read in that order. It is only when read through the translating medium of the whole poetic attitude and form (as they must be ultimately, since they are poems), or under the inhibition of prejudices and conventions about these, that Miss Moore's meaning itself can be, in the initial stages of one's appreciation, an obstruction. Her poems are complex both in origin and in process, and they will remain so finally, thus resembling all poetry of considerable weight; but their first complexity lies in the way they have avoided using the simplifications of the lyric tradition—its language, form, and rhythms. When they present a thought, they do so in terms of all the accidents, analogies, and inhibitory influences that went into its formulation; thus they preserve, along with the clarifying idea, a critical sense of how these accidents and impurities condition the use of the contemporary intelligence. It is, in fact, her recognition and use of such impediments to direct lyric clairvoyance that enables Miss Moore to combine the functions of critic and poet in one performance, and to preserve, along with the passion and penetration of her emotions, her modernity of appeal. One aspect of this is her use of the erudite style—the tone of wordy decorum and learnedness which probably wins her the harshest reproach. This has become her natural manner, but one is never left without hints of its sources; the rhetorical decorum of the past (Bacon, Burke, Richard Baxter) and the literary casuistry of the present (James, Yeats, Pound) combine with ironic overtones derived from the naïveté, pretentiousness, or candor of scientific treatises, orations, "business documents and school books," and intimate conversation. The interpenetration of these tones is not left entirely to the reader's guess-work. Miss Moore's "Notes" at the back of her volumes are a consolation and a stimulus. It is because they give just enough hint of the clues she has used in tracing out a conception or a truth that they spur the reader to analysis, without drugging him by explanation. In this they exceed the notes to *The Waste Land*. It is both amusing and provoking to know that the poem "New York" was given substance through an article on albino deer in *Field and Stream*, that "Novices" drew hints from Gordon's *Poets of the Old Testament*, Forsyth's *Christ on Parnassus*, Landor, and the *Illustrated London News*, that the biological subjects are reinforced by the treatises of R. L. Ditmars, W. P. Pycraft, and Alphonse de Candolle, that "No Swan So Fine" combines a remark from the *New York Times* with "a pair of Louis XV candelabra" with

Dresden figures of swans belonging to Lord Balfour," and that Peter is a
"cat owned by Miss Magdalen Hueber and Miss Maria Weniger." Beyond
or below this information and the tentacular curiosity it sets growing, lies a
basis of moral and intellectual absolutes—the truth; but Miss Moore has no intention of reducing her sense of this truth to impotence by abstracting it from
the details and confusion with which experience happened to surround it.
To do so would not only be an act of unscrupulous evasion; it would not be
poetry.

It is profitable to make an attempt at separating in such verse the simpler
components that make it up—its basic information, the inference made from
it, and the conviction or judgment finally established; and to see in these a
possible correspondence with the three stylistic elements that immediately arrest the reader—imagery, syntax (with its diction and rhetorical tone), and
the final form (stanzaic or otherwise) of the complete poem. These pages are
particularly safe against studious demolition of this kind. "The Fish" is one
of Miss Moore's most brilliant and condensed achievements. The poem is first
a matter of acute observation: "the crow-blue mussel-shells," one of which
"keeps opening and shutting itself like an injured fan," "ink-bespattered jelly-
fish," "crabs like green lilies." These reach a second existence—become mobile
without ceasing to be objects of exact and literal statement—when arranged
into sentences; and anyone who finds the poem obscure as a whole will be
shocked to find how straightforward it becomes (at least through its first five
stanzas) when considered in its normal syntax:

The fish wade through black jade. Of the crow-blue mussel-shells, one keeps adjusting the ash-heaps; opening and shutting itself like an injured fan. . . . The
water drives a wedge of iron through the iron edge of the cliff; whereupon the stars,
pink rice-grains, ink-bespattered jelly-fish, crabs like green lilies, and submarine
toadstools, slide each on the other. . . .

But one immediately sees what this sequence of statements has produced
in the details: a sense of impersonal scrutiny that minimizes the exotic character of the original images, and at the same time an austere alignment that
heightens and perfects it. Then, imposed on these statements, comes the shaping poetic form of the stanzas, with their regularly varying line-lengths and
suddenly discovered rhymes; the physical and emotional impact of the whole
experience is confessed; observation and statement have abruptly advanced
into the brilliance and intensity of a poetic vision.

THE FISH

wade
through black jade
    Of the crow-blue mussel-shells, one keeps

adjusting the ash-heaps;
    opening and shutting itself like

an
injured fan.
    The barnacles which encrust the side
    of the wave, cannot hide
        there for the submerged shafts of the

sun
split like spun
    glass, move themselves with spotlight swiftness
    into the crevices
        in and out, illuminating

the
turquoise sea
    of bodies. . . .

Whether this process was gradual in the poet, or immediate and involuntary, is beside the point; the reader has, if he is serious, a reverence in his
destruction, and a duty in his analysis. He sees the three simplest elements in
the work; he notices its double structure, syntactical and stanzaic; and by
realizing the interdependence of the two he approaches Miss Moore's method.
He begins to see that ambiguity has not only advanced from imagery and
syntax to the form of the stanzas themselves, but that it is deliberate and
functional. It continues to be so in other poems. In "England" there is an intended duplicity of meaning both in the formal organization of the thought
and in the contrasts by which it is developed. In "Those Various Scalpels" a
criticism of feminine vanity is made by means of romantic comparisons, and
by exaggerating the intended effect of jewels, clothes, and cosmetics until
they react upon themselves and become their own criticism. In "A Grave"
"the disturbing vastness of ocean" is made fatal and sublime by the calm and
contradictory lucidity with which its casual incidents are observed:

men lower nets, unconscious of the fact that they are desecrating a grave,
and row quickly away—the blades of the oars
moving together like the feet of water-spiders as if there were no such thing as
    death.
The wrinkles progress upon themselves in a phalanx—beautiful under networks of
    foam,
and fade breathlessly while the sea rustles in and out of the seaweed. . . .

Confronting Miss Moore's poems, in other words, calls for a renovation not
only of the attention, but of one's habits, definitions, and prejudices; and of
what these have done to one's understanding of the words, rhythms, and
sentences of poetry. Here, as Mr. Eliot says, "an original sensibility and alert

intelligence and deep feeling have been engaged in maintaining the life of the English language," but to any self-improving reader it is also valuable to discover that such external discouragements as novelty, eccentricity, and intellectual irony can be justified by a scrupulous poetic purpose; they cease to appear as irritants or as abuses of originality, and become agents of a new vitality in the reader himself. If there is presumption in these poems, it is the presumption of a sincere and ruthless insight; if there are limitations—and there obviously and deliberately are—they are those of a contented but passionate humility. I think these virtues must be admitted by anyone; only then will qualifying criticisms be in order. When Miss Moore instructs herself on art she also instructs her reader:

Too stern an intellectual emphasis upon this quality or that detracts from one's enjoyment.
It must not wish to disarm anything; nor may the approved triumph easily be honored—
that which is great because something else is small.
It comes to this: of whatever sort it is,
it must be "lit with piercing glances into the life of things";
it must acknowledge the spiritual forces which have made it.

From *The New Republic*, Vol. LXXXIII (August 7, 1935), p. 370; and *Poetry: A Magazine of Verse*, Vol. XLVII (March, 1936), pp. 326–336. Reprinted by permission.,

Addendum

ARTHUR MIZENER

Scott Fitzgerald and the Imaginative Possession
of American Life

[1946]

I

THE commonplace about Scott Fitzgerald is that he was "the laureate of the Jazz Age." If this means anything, it means that he was a kind of eulogistic fictional historian of the half dozen years following the first World War when there was such a marked change in American manners. In fact, however, Fitzgerald never simply reported experience; every one of his books is an attempt to recreate experience imaginatively. It is true that the objects, the people, the events, and the convictions in terms of which his imagination functioned were profoundly American and of his time. Even in his worst book, as John O'Hara once remarked, "the people were right, the talk was right, the clothes, the cars were real." The substance out of which Fitzgerald constructed his stories, that is to say, was American, perhaps more completely American than that of any other writer of his time. It is possible, therefore, to read his books simply for their sensitive record of his time; but there is a great deal more to them than this.

Fitzgerald's great accomplishment is to have realized in completely American terms the developed romantic attitude, in the end at least in that most responsible form in which all the romantic's sensuous and emotional responses are disciplined by his awareness of the goodness and evilness of human experience. He had a kind of instinct for the tragic view of life and remarked himself how even at the very beginning of his career, "all the stories that came into my head had a touch of disaster in them—the lovely young creatures in my novels went to ruin, the diamond mountains of my short stories blew up, my millionaires were as beautiful and damned as Thomas Hardy's peasants." He had, moreover, with all its weakness and strength and in a time when the undivided understanding was very rare, an almost exclusively creative kind of intelligence, the kind that understands things, not abstractly, but only concretely, in terms of people and situations and events.

From the very beginning he showed facility and that minute awareness of the qualities of times and places and persons which is sharpened to a fine point in the romantic writer by his acute consciousness of the irrevocable passage of everything into the past. "He was haunted," as Malcolm Cowley has said, "by time, as if he wrote in a room full of clocks and calendars." A romantic writer of this kind is bound to take as his characteristic subject his own past, building out of the people and places of his time fables of his own inner experience, working his way into his material by identifying himself with others as Fitzgerald, in a characteristic case, made the doctor in "Family in the Wind" an image of what he saw in himself, a talented man who had achieved great early success and then gone to pieces. As a young man he identified himself imaginatively with his beautiful but less clever sister and practically lived her early social career; in middle age he entered so completely into his daughter's career that, as one of his friends remarked, "Scott, not Scottie, went through Vassar." Thus, always, Fitzgerald lived imaginatively the lives of those with whom, through family affection or some obscure similarity of attitude or experience, he was able to identify himself.

At its best the attitude Fitzgerald possessed produces an effect which is compounded of three clearly definable elements. There is in his mature work an almost historical objectivity, produced by his acute sense of the pastness of the past; there is also a Proustian minuteness of recollection of the feelings and attitudes which made up the experience as it was lived; and there is, finally, cast over both the historically apprehended event and the personal recollection embedded in it, a glow of pathos, the pathos of the irretrievableness of a part of oneself. "Taking things hard—" he wrote in his notebooks, "from ——— to ———: that's [the] stamp that goes into my books so that people can read it blind like braill[e]." The first of these references is to the first girl Fitzgerald was ever deeply in love with; he used his recollection of her over and over again (out of that recollection, for example, he made Josephine, who dominates a whole series of stories in *Taps at Reveille*). The second reference is to the producer who hacked to pieces his finest script. The remark thus covers the whole of Fitzgerald's career.

What develops slowly in a writer of this kind is maturity of judgment, for it is not easy to control what is so powerfully felt initially and is never, even in recollection, tranquil. Fitzgerald was three-fifths of the way through his career as novelist, though only five years from its start, before he produced a book in which the purpose and the form it imposes are adequate to the evoked life. With *The Great Gatsby* the "smoldering hatred" of the imaginative obtuseness, the moral vulgarity, and the sheer brutality of the rich—

with its tangled roots in Fitzgerald's puritanical Catholic background, in his middle-class, middle-western upbringing, and in his early poverty—had emerged enough to serve as a dramatic balance for the wonderful freedom and beauty which the life of the rich had for him. "Let me tell you about the very rich" he began in one of his finest stories; and with the establishment of this dramatically balanced view of the rich in *The Great Gatsby* he had found his theme and its fable, for wealth was Fitzgerald's central symbol; around it he eventually built a mythology which enabled him to take imaginative possession of American life.

With this view of his material he could at last give expression to his essentially tragic sense of human experience without forcing that feeling on the material so that it ceased to be probable, as it does in *The Beautiful and Damned* where the characters drift without understanding into disaster and our conviction of their suffering is undermined by the inadequacy of its causes. Until he wrote *The Great Gatsby* Fitzgerald's ability to evoke the nightmare terror of disaster was greater than his ability to motivate the disaster. It is different at the moment in *The Great Gatsby* when we are confronted with Daisy's completely prepared betrayal, seeing her sitting with Tom at the kitchen table over a late supper with "an unmistakable air of natural intimacy," and then find Gatsby watching the house from the driveway, imagining that he is guarding Daisy from Tom. "I walked away," says Nick, "and left him standing there in the moonlight—watching over nothing." Here Fitzgerald's view of his material is completely adequate to his feeling about human experience in general, the life of the people he knows has become the fully rounded particular case for the expression of his whole understanding.

Both his admiration for the wonderful possibilities of the life of the rich and his distrust of it probably go back to Fitzgerald's childhood. He was born in St. Paul on September 24, 1896. Very early in his life he began to weave fantasies around the Hill Mansion, only two blocks but a good many million dollars away from his home on Summit Avenue; and it was certainly Fitzgerald at Newman as well as Basil Lee at St. Regis who "writhed with shame . . . that . . . he was one of the poorest boys in a rich boys' school." But he was proud, too, of his family, which was not rich, particularly of the Francis Scott Key connection, and included his family among what he once called "the few remnants of the old American aristocracy that's managed to survive in communicable form." The Basil Lee stories, with their wonderful recreation of the emotional tensions and social conflicts of middle-class American childhood and youth, give a reasonably accurate impression of the life he lived as a boy and for two years at Newman.

In the fall of 1913 he went to Princeton, full of an intensified but otherwise normal American boy's ambition to succeed. There he plunged with characteristic energy and passion into the race for social prominence. But for all that he wore the right clothes, had the right manners, belonged to one of the best clubs, and was an important figure in the politically powerful Triangle Club, he neither was nor appeared to be a typical Princeton man. Of the highly competitive, socially subtle, ingrown life of Princeton he made for himself, with his gift for romance, an enormously significant world. The very imaginative intensity with which he took the normal preoccupations of a Princeton undergraduate distinguished him radically from his fellows. There was something unusual, almost flamboyant, even about his looks, which set him apart. Twenty-five years later that oddness of appearance was still before Edmund Wilson's eyes when he remembered their first meeting:

> I climbed, a quarter-century and more
> Played out, the college steps, unlatched my door,
> And, creature strange to college, found you there!
> The pale skin, hard green eyes, and yellow hair.

You can still see something of "the glitter of the hard and emerald eyes" in his pictures and, perhaps too, feel in Fitzgerald's personal history something of what Wilson meant by this figure.

Fitzgerald quickly discovered that Cottage Club was not quite the brilliant society he had dreamed of and presently turned to literature. "I want," he said to Wilson at this time, "to be one of the greatest writers who have ever lived, don't you?" But all this extracurricular activity—in addition to his social career and his writing there were the Triangle Club and a debutante in Chicago—was too much for his health and his academic standing. In November of his junior year he was forced to retire to St. Paul. He returned in 1916 to repeat this year, but his senior year lasted only a couple of months, for he left Princeton in November to join the army.

Before he left he completed the first of three versions of *This Side of Paradise*. This version appears to have contained almost nothing of what is in the final version except the early scenes of Amory's arrival at Princeton, and one of the few people who saw it has remarked that "it was actually flat, something Scott's work almost never was." One of the worst disappointments of his life was that he never got overseas but ended his military career as what he once called "the worst aide-de-camp in the army" to General A. J. Ryan at Camp Sheridan, near Montgomery, Alabama. Here he met and fell in love with Zelda Sayre, and here too, in the officers' club in the evenings, he rewrote his novel and submitted it to a publisher under the title *The Romantic Egotist*. This is the subtitle of Book I of *This Side of Paradise*, which presumably covers about the same ground. *The Romantic Egotist* was rejected.

When he was discharged in February 1919, Fitzgerald came to New York to make his fortune so that he could marry Zelda. He sold a story to *The Smart Set* for $30 and bought Zelda a stylish feather fan; for the rest he collected rejection slips and began to realize that he was not going to make a fortune as a copy-writer at $90 a month. So did Zelda, and sometime late in the spring she decided that the whole thing had been a mistake. At this Fitzgerald threw up his job, got drunk, and went back to St. Paul to write his book once more. By the end of the summer it had become *This Side of Paradise* and in the fall Scribner's accepted it. Fitzgerald hurried off to Montgomery and Zelda. The nightmare of unhappiness was over, but he never forgot it: "The man with the jingle of money in his pocket who married the girl a year later would always cherish an abiding distrust, an animosity, toward the leisure class—not the conviction of a revolutionary but the smoldering hatred of a peasant. In the years since then I have never been able to stop wondering where my friends' money came from, nor to stop thinking that at one time a sort of *droit de seigneur* might have been exercised to give one of them my girl."

II

This Side of Paradise is in many ways a very bad book. Edmund Wilson's judgment of it, made at the height of its fame, is perfectly just: "Amory Blaine is an uncertain quantity in a phantasmagoria of incident which has no dominating intention to endow it with unity and force. . . . For another thing, it is very immaturely imagined: it is always just verging on the ludicrous. And, finally, it is one of the most illiterate books of any merit ever published. . . . It is not only ornamented with bogus ideas and faked references but it is full of English words misused with the most reckless abandon."

These charges could be documented at length, and some of them were; F.P.A. devoted a number of columns to the misspellings, and the energy with which Francis Newman supported the further charge that the book was imitated in detail from Mackenzie's *Sinister Street* stung Fitzgerald to reply. Nevertheless it is obviously true that the general idea and structure of *This Side of Paradise* were suggested by *Sinister Street* and that Fitzgerald had little realization of the importance for this episodic kind of book of unity of tone. The lack of unity of tone in the book is partly due to its being made up of stories written, over a considerable period of time, before the novel was contemplated. One of the reviewers called the novel "the collected works of Mr. Scott Fitzgerald" and Fitzgerald himself once remarked, speaking of his editorship of the *Nassau Lit:* "I wrote stories about current prom girls, stories that were later incorporated into a novel."

The quality which Mr. Wilson ascribes to the book's being immaturely

imagined displays itself most in the latter part and especially in the accounts
of Amory's love affairs. Fitzgerald's lovers conduct their affairs by making
speeches at each other, full of sentiment from Swinburne and of sweeping
generalizations about "Life"; as lovers they show all the hypnotized egocen-
tricity and intellectual immaturity of college freshmen. There is a sentence in
The Beautiful and Damned, where Fitzgerald is describing the novels of
Richard Carmel, which is an unintentionally eloquent comment on his own
resources at this time. "There was," he says of Richard's novels, "a measure of
vitality and a sort of instinctive technic [*sic*] in all of them."

Yet for all these faults the book is not essentially a bad one. There is in the
writing something of the intensity of felt experience which is in the language
of Fitzgerald's mature books. This is especially true of the first part, for the
experience of Princeton life on which this part of the book was based was far
enough behind Fitzgerald to have been to some extent emotionally distanced
and evaluated. But even in the latter part of the book, beneath all the author's naïve earnestness about the romantic cynicism and "philosophizing" of
Amory and Rosalind and Eleanor, you feel something of the real suffering of
unhappiness. Fitzgerald's judgment and technique are inadequate almost
everywhere in the book, but the fundamental, almost instinctive attitude toward experience which emerges, even at times through the worst of the book's
surface, is serious and moving. Sixteen years later Fitzgerald himself, still
remembering Edmund Wilson's remark, said of it: "A lot of people thought
it was a fake, and perhaps it was, and a lot of others thought it was a lie,
which it was not."

This Side of Paradise was an enormous success, and Fitzgerald, in a way
very characteristic of him, responded to success with a naïve, pompous, and
fundamentally good-humored vanity. He gave interviews in which he told
what a great writer he was; he condoled with Heywood Broun over the latter's lost youth (Broun was thirty); he condescended to his elders and betters.
He and Zelda were married in April and plunged happily into the gay and
strenuous life of New York. Fitzgerald rode down Fifth Avenue on top of a
taxi, dove into the Plaza fountain, and in general displayed his exuberance
in the ways which were fashionable in 1920. He also worked all night again
and again to pay for the fun and "riding in a taxi one afternoon between very
tall buildings under a mauve and rosy sky . . . I began to bawl because I
had everything I wanted and knew I would never be so happy again."

For a brief period of three years following the publication of *This Side of
Paradise* the Fitzgeralds were figures around New York and their house
parties at Westport and Great Neck were famous. It was all very gay and
light-hearted; the house guests at Great Neck were advised in a set of Rules
for Guests at the Fitzgerald House that "Visitors are requested not to break
down doors in search of liquor, even when authorized to do so by the host

and hostess" and that "invitations to stay over Monday, issued by the host and hostess during the small hours of Sunday morning, must not be taken seriously." There was a trip to Europe in the summer of 1921 and that winter they went to St. Paul for the birth of their only child. ("It was typical of our precarious position in New York," Fitzgerald wrote later, "that when our child was to be born we played safe and went home to St. Paul.") In 1922 there was another novel, *The Beautiful and Damned,* and a second volume of stories, and in 1923 a play, *The Vegetable,* written with the rosiest expectations of profits, for they were, as usual, out of money. But the play flopped dismally in Atlantic City, and there was no attempt to bring it to New York. In 1924, in order to live more cheaply, they went abroad.

The Beautiful and Damned is an enormous improvement on *This Side of Paradise,* more than anything else because Fitzgerald, though he has not yet found out how to motivate disaster, has a much clearer sense of the precise feel of the disaster he senses in the life he knows. The book is also a great advance on its predecessor technically, much more unified, much less mixed in tone. The tendency to substitute lectures for dialogue is subdued, though as if to compensate for this restraint Fitzgerald lets himself go in a scene where Maury Noble produces an harangue which, as *The Dial's* reviewer remarked, sounds "like a *résumé* of *The Education of Henry Adams* filtered through a particularly thick page of *The Smart Set.*" The tone, too, is more evenly sustained, though Fitzgerald is still tempted by scenes in play form and once allows himself an embarrassing Shavian scene between Beauty and The Voice. There is still the curious shocked immaturity about sex. Fitzgerald obviously feels that Anthony's prep-school philandering with Geraldine is daring, and his lovers, pushing about menus on which they have written "you know I do" and describing each other as "sort of blowy clean," are childish.

Nevertheless, *The Beautiful and Damned* is much more successfully focused on a central purpose than *This Side of Paradise,* and much less often bathetic in its means. Of this central purpose Edmund Wilson wrote rather unsympathetically: "since his advent into the literary world [Fitzgerald] has discovered that there is another genre in favor: the kind which makes much of the tragedy and 'meaninglessness of life.' Hitherto, he had supposed that the thing to do was to discover a meaning in life; but he now set bravely about to produce a sufficiently desolating tragedy which should be, also, 100 percent meaningless." But the sense of tragedy is very real with Fitzgerald and his ability to realize the minutiae of humiliation and suffering seldom fails him. His difficulty is in finding a cause for this suffering sufficient to justify the importance he asks us to give it and characters of sufficient dignity to make their suffering and defeat tragic rather than merely pathetic.

Nor is it quite true that Fitzgerald did not try to give the disaster a motive and meaning. There is a fairly consistent effort to make Anthony the sensitive and intelligent man who, driven into a difficult place by his refusal to compromise with a brutal and stupid world, finds his weaknesses too strong for him. He is tempted to cowardice and drifting by his own imagination and sensitiveness; he cannot blame and fight others because of "that old quality of understanding too well to blame—that quality which was the best of him and had worked swiftly and ceaselessly toward his ruin." Over against him Fitzgerald sets Richard Carmel, too stupid to know he is compromising or that the success he has won by compromising is not worth having, and Maury Noble, cynical enough to surrender to compromise even though he knows the worthlessness of what he gets.

The trouble is that Anthony is not real as the sensitive and intelligent man; what is real is the Anthony who is weak, drifting, and full of self-pity. The Anthony who drifts into the affair with Dot under the momentary stimulus of his romantic imagination, knowing perfectly well that he does not believe in the thing; the Anthony who is continually drunk because only thus can he sustain "the old illusion that truth and beauty [are] in some way intertwined"; the partly intolerable, partly absurd, partly pathetic Anthony who seeks again and again to sustain his now fantastic vision of his own dignity and honor; this Anthony is marvelously realized. But the thing that would justify this pathos, the conviction that here is a man more sinned against than sinning, is wholly lacking. *The Beautiful and Damned* is full of precisely observed life and Fitzgerald is often able to make us feel the poignancy of his characters' suffering, but he is able to provide neither an adequate cause for their suffering nor an adequate reason within their characters for their surrender. In the end you do not believe they ever were people who wanted the opportunities for fineness that the freedom of wealth provides; you believe them only people who wanted luxury. They are pitiful, and their pathos is often brilliantly realized; but they are not tragic.

With occasional interruptions, the Fitzgeralds remained abroad from 1924 until the autumn of 1931, traveling a good deal and living in a great many hotels but usually returning for the summer to the Cap d'Antibes. They came back to America in 1927, went to California for a while, and then rented a big old house on the Delaware "to bring us a judicious tranquility." But they were soon back in Europe where they remained, except for a short trip in 1929, until their final return. Fitzgerald later described the period quite simply as "seven years of waste and tragedy," but at the time their life, particularly the summers on the Riviera, seemed the life of freedom and culture and charm. The little group which made the summer Riviera its private style for a few years before everyone else began to come there was brilliant and varied. There were the rich and cultivated like the Gerald Murpheys, the writers like Charles MacArthur and Alexander Woollcott, and the musicians like Grace Moore. They led a busy, unconventional, and, as it seemed to them, somehow significant life; "whatever happened," Fitzgerald wrote later, "seemed to have something to do with art." They made private movies about such characters as "Princess Alluria, the wickedest woman in Europe," writing the unprintable subtitles on the pink walls of Grace Moore's villa and deliberately forgetting to erase them after they had been photographed; they kidnaped orchestras to play for them all night; they gave high-comedy dinners; and they drank a great deal.

But all the time Fitzgerald's almost animal sensitivity to potential disaster was at work: "By 1927 a wide-spread neurosis began to be evident, faintly signalled like a nervous beating of the feet, by the popularity of cross-word puzzles. I remember a fellow expatriate opening a letter from a mutual friend of ours, urging him to come home and be revitalized by the hardy, bracing qualities of the native soil. It was a strong letter and it affected us both deeply, until we noticed that it was headed from a nerve sanatorium in Pennsylvania." Looking back at the period afterwards he could see its weaknesses clearly without forgetting its charm. "It was borrowed time anyhow—the whole upper tenth of a nation living with the insouciance of grand ducs and the casualness of chorus girls. But moralizing is easy now and it was pleasant to be in one's twenties in such a certain and unworried time."

It was a period during which Fitzgerald produced very little serious work. *The Great Gatsby* was written during the fall and winter of 1924 and he published no other novel until *Tender Is the Night,* ten years later. This was not, however, wholly the fault of the kind of life he and Zelda were living, even indirectly; it was partly the result of the extremely ambitious plans Fitzgerald laid for himself after *The Great Gatsby's* critical success.

III

The Great Gatsby was another leap forward for Fitzgerald. He had found a situation which would allow him to exploit without loss of probability much more of his feeling about his material, and he had arrived at the point where he understood the advantage of realizing his subject dramatically. He had been reading Conrad and as a result adopted the modified first-person form which suited his purpose so well. For Fitzgerald needed a form which would at once allow him to color the scene with the feelings of an observer and yet hold the feelings within some determined limits. In earlier stories he had splashed whatever colors he wished over the scene without much regard for the structure as a whole or for the disruptive effect on the dramatic representation of the constant interference of the author's own person. But here, as later in *The Last Tycoon,* he selected a narrator sufficiently near the center of things to know all he needed to know, tied into the action by the affair with Jordan Baker which is, though muted, carefully made parallel to the affair between Gatsby and Daisy. By means of this narrator he was able to focus his story, the story of a poor boy from the Middle West who, in the social confusion of the first World War, met and fell in love with a rich girl. Daisy marries while he is in France, but he never ceases to dream of making enough money to be "worthy" of her, taking her from her husband, Tom Buchanan, and starting their life again exactly where it had stopped when he had gone to France. He therefore devotes himself to making money in whatever way he can, not because he wants money, but because he wants his dream of a life with Daisy.

Nick Carraway, the narrator, is equally carefully placed so far as his attitude is concerned. He has come East to be an Easterner and rich, but his moral roots remain in the West. In the most delicate way Fitzgerald builds up these grounds for his final judgment of the story and its people. In the book's first scene, Nick's humorous awareness of the greater sophistication of these people is marked: " 'You make me feel uncivilized, Daisy,' I confessed. . . . 'Can't you talk about crops or something?' " But only a moment later, when Daisy has confessed her unhappiness with Tom, he has an uneasy sense of what is really involved: "The instant her voice broke off, ceasing to compel my attention, my belief, I felt the basic insincerity of what she had said. . . . I waited, and sure enough, in a moment she looked at me with an absolute smirk on her lovely face, as if she had asserted her membership in a rather distinguished secret society to which she and Tom belonged."

Nick's father has told him that "Whenever you feel like criticizing anyone just remember that all the people in this world haven't had the advantages you've had." Nick does not forget; when, at the end of the book, he meets Tom, "I couldn't forgive him or like him, but I saw that what he had done was, to him, entirely justified. . . . I shook hands with him; it seemed silly not to, for I felt suddenly as though I were talking to a child. Then he went into the jewelry store to buy a pearl necklace—or perhaps only a pair of cuff buttons—rid of my provincial squeamishness forever."

Nick goes back to the West, to the country he remembered from the Christmas vacations of his childhood, to "the thrilling returning trains of my youth, and the street lamps and sleigh bells in the frosty dark and the shadows of holly wreaths thrown by lighted windows on the snow. I am part of that, a little solemn with the feeling of those long winters, a little complacent from growing up in the Carraway house in a city where dwellings are still called through decades by a family name." The East remains for him "a night scene from El Greco" in which "in the foreground four solemn men in dress suits are walking along the sidewalk with a stretcher on which lies a drunken woman in a white evening dress. Her hand, which dangles over the side, sparkles cold with jewels. Gravely the men turn in at a house—the wrong house. But no one knows the woman's name, and no one cares."

Thus, though Fitzgerald would be the last to have reasoned it out in such terms, *The Great Gatsby* becomes a kind of tragic pastoral, with the East the exemplar of urban sophistication and culture and corruption, and the West, "the bored, sprawling, swollen towns beyond the Ohio," the exemplar of simple virtue. This contrast is summed up in the book's title. In so far as Gatsby represents the simple virtue which Fitzgerald associates with the West, he is really a great man; in so far as he achieves the kind of notoriety which the East accords success of his kind, he is great about as Barnum was. Out of Gatsby's ignorance of his real greatness and his misunderstanding of his notoriety, Fitzgerald gets much of the book's irony. These terms, then, provided the occasions for all Fitzgerald's feelings, so that he was able to say everything he had to say within the terms of a single figure and to give his book the kind of focus and freedom which comes only from successful formal order.

His hero, Gatsby, is frankly romantic, a romantic, like Fitzgerald, from the West, who has missed the girl on whom he has focused all his "heightened sensitivity to the promises of life" because he had no money. He gets it, by all sorts of corrupt means, and comes back five years later to find Daisy and to fulfill "his incorruptible dream." "I wouldn't ask too much of her," Nick says to him once, "you can't repeat the past." " 'Can't repeat the past?' he cried incredulously. 'Why of course you can!' " But he could not repeat the past with Daisy, changed by her momentary passion for Tom at the time of their marriage and corrupted all her life by her dependence on the protection of wealth and the conventions of the wealthy life which have preserved and heightened her beauty, until in the end she lets Gatsby die for the murder she has committed. He dies waiting for a telephone message from Daisy, and Nick observes: "I have an idea that Gatsby himself didn't believe it would come, and perhaps he no longer cared. If that was true he must have felt that he had lost the old warm world, paid a high price for living too long with a single dream. He must have looked up at . . . a new world, material without being real, where poor ghosts, breathing dreams like air, drifted fortuitously about."

Against Nick's gradual understanding of the incorruptibility at the heart of Gatsby's corruption, Fitzgerald sets his gradual penetration of the charm and grace of Tom and Daisy's world. What he penetrates to is corruption, grossness, and cowardice. In contrast to the charm and grace of this world, Gatsby's fantastic mansion, his absurd pink suits, "his elaborate formality of speech [which] just missed being absurd" appear ludicrous; against the corruption which underlies this grace, Gatsby's essential moral incorruptibility is heroic. To the representation of this double contrast Fitzgerald brings all his now mature powers of observation, of invention, of creating for the scenes and persons the quality and tone of the story requires. Because of the formal perfection of *The Great Gatsby*, this eloquence is given a concentration and intensity Fitzgerald never achieved again. The art of the book, in the narrow sense, is nearly perfect. Its limitation is the limitation of Fitzgerald's nearly complete commitment to Gatsby's romanticism. This commitment is partly concealed by Gatsby's superficial social insufficiency, and our awareness of this insufficiency is strengthened as much as Fitzgerald dares strengthen it by Nick's constant, ironic observation of it: Gatsby is, as a cultured "Oggsford man," after all a fake. But this is a romantic irony which touches only the surface; it does not cut to the heart of the matter, to the possibility that there may be some fundamental moral inadequacy in Gatsby's attitude. The world of Daisy and Tom which is set over against Gatsby's dream of a world is beautiful and appealing but in no sense justified: Tom's muddled attempts to offer a reasoned defense for it are only a proof that it is indefensible. Fitzgerald's book is a *Troilus and Cressida* with an Ajax but no Ulysses.

IV

After *The Great Gatsby* Fitzgerald set himself a task which, as Edmund Wilson once remarked, would have given Dostoevski pause. It was to be a story of matricide, and though an immense amount of work was done on it, all that appears to remain is the short story "Absolution," which was originally written as its first chapter. As if to mock his failure, and perhaps too his deep concern for the subject, Fitzgerald wrote a comic ballad about matricide which he used to perform with great effect as a parlor trick.

In 1930 Zelda, who had been working for several years with all her energy to become a ballet dancer, broke down, and late in 1931 the Fitzgeralds returned to America and settled in a rambling old brown house at Rodgers Forge, between Baltimore and Towson. Here they remained until Fitzgerald went to Hollywood in 1937. Meanwhile Fitzgerald had been struggling with *Tender Is the Night*; he managed, by a furious effort in the latter part of 1933, to get it into shape for publication in *Scribner's* in 1934; he revised it considerably again before book publication, and there is in existence a copy of the book with further revisions in which Fitzgerald has written: "This is the *final version* of the book as I would like it."

Much of this revision appears to have been the result of his having felt his theme everywhere in his material without always seeing a way to draw these various aspects of it together in a single whole. The war, the ducal perversion and ingrown virginity of the Chicago aristocracy which the Warrens represent—stronger and so more terrible than the corruption of the English Campions and Lady Sibley-Bierses; the hardness and lack of moral imagination of the rich in general, the anarchic nihilism represented by

Tommy Barbran, the self-indulgence of Abe North, destroyed, beyond even an awareness of his own destruction, as Dick will be destroyed; all these forces are beautifully realized. But, though their general bearing on the situation is clear enough, their exact incidence and precise relation to each other sometimes is not.

The result is that *Tender Is the Night*, though the most profoundly moving of all Fitzgerald's novels, is a structurally imperfect book. To this difficulty must be added the fact that its central theme is not an easy one. We believe overwhelmingly in the collapse of Dick Diver's morale because we are made to see and hear, in the most minute and subtly shaded detail, the process of that collapse. It is very like the collapse of Fitzgerald's own morale as he describes it in "The Crack-Up." But it is not easy to say in either case what, in the immediate and practical sense, happens to cause the collapse. As do many romantics with their horror of time and age, Fitzgerald tended to think of spiritual resources—of courage and generosity and kindness—as he thought of physical resources, as a sum in the bank against which a man draws. When, in his own life, he realized "with finality that in some regard [he would] never be as good a man again"; when he began to feel that "every act of life from the morning tooth-brush to the friend at dinner had become an effort . . . that my casual relations—with an editor, a tobacco seller, the child of a friend, were only what I remembered I *should* do, from other days"; then he knew the sum in the bank was nearly exhausted and that there was nothing to do but to reduce his scale of living accordingly. "In a really dark night of the soul," he wrote in "The Crack-Up," "it is always three o'clock in the morning, day after day"; and though the dazzling Mediterranean sun blazes everywhere in *Tender Is the Night,* the passage Fitzgerald chose to quote along with the title line from Keats' poem is:

> But here there is no light,
> Save what from heaven is with the breezes blown
> Through verdurous glooms and winding mossy ways.

As always, however, Fitzgerald began not with a theme but with a body of material. Describing the life portrayed in *Tender Is the Night* in an earlier essay, he had written: "Charm, notoriety, good manners, weighed more than money as a social asset. This was rather splendid, but things were getting thinner and thinner as the eternal necessary human values tried to spread over all that expanse." With this world in all its variety of corruption, hardness, sterility, and despair Fitzgerald confronts his hero and the fundamentally simple "necessary human values" which his father had given him— " 'good instincts,' honor, courtesy, and courage." At the very beginning Dick Diver has to choose between becoming a great psychologist and a fully human being when Nicole, beautiful and schizophrenic, falls in love with him.

"As you think best, Professor Dohmler," Dick conceded. "It's certainly a situation."

Professor Dohmler raised himself like a legless man mounting a pair of crutches.

"But it is a professional situation," he cried quietly.

But for Dick it is a human situation; "wanting above all to be brave and kind, he . . . wanted, even more, to be loved." So he accepted the responsibility of being loved by Nicole and, gradually, of being loved by all the others whom his life drew around him. To them he gave lavishly of his strength, of his ability to translate into their terms the necessary human values and so remind them of their best selves. "My politeness," as he says, "is a trick of the heart." But the people he worked this trick for had no energy of their own, and gradually he exhausted his supply, spun out all his strength for other people until he had none left: "If you spend your life sparing other people's feelings and feeding their vanity, you get so you can't distinguish what *should* be respected in them."

Because he is proud and sensitive, Dick deliberately breaks Nicole's psychological dependence on him, aware that Nicole's love for him is bound up with her dependence and will cease with it, has already declined with the decline of her need for him; knowing that he has exhausted even his own power to love her in the process of making her psychologically whole again. By a terrible irony it comes about that what he had refused to treat as a merely professional situation is just that. "Dick waited until she was out of sight. Then he leaned his head forward on the parapet. The case was finished. Doctor Diver was at liberty again."

"That," says Baby Warren, speaking for them all, even for Nicole, "is what he was educated for."

Whether one accepts Fitzgerald's conception of the cause of this spiritual death or not, *Tender Is the Night* remains his most brilliant book. All his powers, the microscopic observation of the life he describes, the sense of the significance and relations of every detail of it, the infallible ear, and the gift of expression, all these things are here in greater abundance than ever before. And as never before they are used for the concrete, dramatic presentation of the inner significance of human experience, so that all the people of his book lead lives of "continual allegory" and its world is a microcosm of the great world. Its scope is such as to make *The Great Gatsby* seem small and simple, for all its neatness and perfection, and its dramatic realization so complete that Fitzgerald need not ever say what is happening: we always see.

In 1935 Fitzgerald had a recurrence of the tuberculosis which had first attacked him when he was an undergraduate and he was never entirely free from it again (he had a bad four months in 1939). In August 1937 he signed a contract with Metro-Goldwyn-Mayer and settled down in Hollywood to write for them. He worked on a number of important scripts, including *Three Comrades, Gone with the Wind,* and *Madame Curie;* he produced a large number of short stories, mostly for *Esquire;* and he began to work on a novel, *The Last Tycoon.* He said himself that he had been thinking about the subject almost from the time of his arrival in Hollywood; he certainly had a great deal of work done on it by late 1939 when he apparently began the actual writing. About half the story was written when he died, though none of it in the final form he had visualized for it.

Thanks to Edmund Wilson's brilliant unraveling of Fitzgerald's notes, it is possible to see pretty clearly what his plans for *The Last Tycoon* were, how rich its theme was to be, and how tight its structure. Of what he planned to make of the book he said: "Unlike *Tender Is the Night,* it is not a story of deterioration. . . . If one book could ever be 'like' another, I should say it is more 'like' *The Great Gatsby.* But I hope it will be entirely different—I hope it will be something new, arouse new emotions, perhaps even a new way of looking at certain phenomena."

On the evidence of what he had actually written there is every reason for supposing that, had he lived, he would have fulfilled these hopes. The material and the people he is dealing with are entirely new, yet his command of the tangled social, industrial, and creative life of Hollywood is so complete that there is no moment in what he has written which is not utterly convincing, at the same time that it exists, not for itself alone, but for what Fitzgerald wanted to say, about Hollywood, about American life, about human experience as a whole. The writing, even though none of it is final, is as subtle and flexible as anything he ever did, and so unremittingly disciplined by the book's central intention that it takes on a kind of lyric intensity, glowing with the life of Fitzgerald's feelings for everything he was trying to say. This intensity is a remarkable achievement for a man who thought—and at least on physical grounds had some reason for thinking—a year before he started to write *The Last Tycoon* that he had only enough talent left "to stretch out over two more novels" (and "I may have to stretch it a little thin"). Most remarkable of all, though less final, is the evidence that he was succeeding, as he never had before with so much to say, in holding everything within the focusing form to which he had committed his story in the beginning.

Around December 1, 1940, Fitzgerald had a serious heart attack. He went on working on his novel, however, with such persistence that on December 20 he put off a visit from his doctor in order to finish a draft of the first episode of Chapter VI. The next day he had another, fatal, heart attack. In some sense Fitzgerald's wonderful natural talent was always haunted by the exigencies of his life. This final exigency aborted what promised to be his best novel, so that it is possible to say of it only what can be said of his work as a whole, that it is very fine and that, with a little more—or a little less—help from circumstances, it might, such was his talent, have been far finer. As John Peale Bishop said in his elegy for Fitzgerald, when we think of his death we

> think of all you did
> And all you might have done, before undone
> By death, but for the undoing of despair.

V

Mr. T. S. Eliot once remarked that "art never improves, but the material of art is never quite the same." But this is a dangerous way for a writer to look at the matter, however useful it may be to the critic, because it tends to separate in his mind the material from the form and meaning; and whenever the meaning is not something that grows out of the particular circumstances which are the occasion for writing, meaning tends to become abstract, to develop independently of the circumstances, and in some sense to violate their integrity. The safest attitude for the writer seems to be a single-minded desire to realize his material, so that the meaning of the circumstances, the permanent values which emerge for the critic from the representation, are for the writer merely such a further penetration of the particular circumstances as will allow him to realize them more completely. Fitzgerald's difficulty was always of course that his characters and their circumstances were likely to be too much individuals and local habitations, too little what Dr. Johnson approvingly referred to as "general nature." But what general nature there is in Fitzgerald's books—and there is always some and sometimes a great deal—is there because he had found it a part of his knowledge of his world. Such an undistorted imaginative penetration of the particular American world Fitzgerald knew had hardly been made before. Like James, Fitzgerald saw that one of the central moral problems of American life was raised in an acute form among the rich, in the conflict between the possibilities of their life and—to give it no worse name—their insensitivity. So long, therefore, as one realizes that Mr. Eliot is not comparing the two men in stature, it is not too much to say of Fitzgerald's best work what Mr. Eliot wrote him about *The Great Gatsby:* "In fact it seems to me to be the first step that American fiction has taken since Henry James."

After *The Great Gatsby* Fitzgerald produced only two books in fifteen years, one technically less perfect than *The Great Gatsby* and one unfinished. He did, of course, produce a large number of short stories, some of them as good as anything he ever wrote, but a considerable number of them only more or less skillful hackwork. All his life he worried about the hackwork and repeated over and over again a remark he made in 1924: "I now get $2,000 a story and they grow worse and worse and my ambition is to get where I need write no more but only novels." It is easy to condemn him for not having realized this ambition; there was much extravagance in his life and, at the end, debts and unavoidable expenses. But the ambition was there to the end and, in 1939, sick, tired, and under the ceaseless pressure of tragedy, he was writing an editor to whom he proposed to sell *The Last Tycoon:* "I would infinitely rather do it, now that I am well again, than take hack jobs out here." The wonder really is, given his temperament and up-bringing, the social pressures of his times and the tragic elements in his personal life, that Fitzgerald did not give in entirely to hackwork, as so many of his contemporaries did, but returned again and again, to the end of his life, to the self-imposed task of writing seriously. For all its manifest faults and mistakes, it was in some ways an heroic life. But it was a life of which Fitzgerald himself, writing to an old friend, a lawyer, could only say rather sadly: "I hope you'll be a better judge than I've been a man of letters."

It is not easy at this close range to separate our opinion of the man from our opinion of the writer, particularly since circumstances combined to make the man a legendary, eponymous figure. But as the accidents of the man's life—and the lies about it—gradually fade, we may well come to feel about the writer, with his purity of imagination and his imperviousness to the abstract theories and intellectual fads which have hag-ridden our times, as Stephen Vincent Benét did when he remarked after Fitzgerald's death: "You can take off your hats, now, gentlemen, and I think perhaps you had better. This is not a legend, this is a reputation—and, seen in perspective, it may well be one of the most secure reputations of our time."

From *The Sewanee Review,* Volume LIV (Winter, 1946), pp. 66–86. Reprinted by permission of the author and *The Sewanee Review.* The essay was included in *The Lives of Eighteen from Princeton,* edited by Willard Thorp (Princeton University Press, 1946). Mr. Mizener's full-scale account of Scott Fitzgerald appeared in his volume *The Far Side of Paradise: A Biography of F. Scott Fitzgerald* (Boston: Houghton Mifflin Co., 1951; reissued New York: Vintage Books, 1959).